Genocide in Cambodia

Pennsylvania Studies in Human Rights
Bert B. Lockwood, Jr., Series Editor

A complete list of books in the series
is available from the publisher.

Genocide in Cambodia

Documents from the Trial of Pol Pot and Ieng Sary

Edited by
HOWARD J. DE NIKE, JOHN QUIGLEY, and KENNETH J. ROBINSON
with the assistance of
HELEN JARVIS and NEREIDA CROSS

PENN

University of Pennsylvania Press

Philadelphia

Printed in the United States of America on acid-free paper

10 9 8 7 6 5 4 3 2 1

Published by
University of Pennsylvania Press
Philadelphia, Pennsylvania 19104-4011

Library of Congress Cataloging-in-Publication Data
Pol Pot.
Genocide in Cambodia : documents from the trial of Pol Pot and Ieng Sary / edited by Howard J. De Nike, John Quigley, and Kenneth J. Robinson, with the assistance of Helen Jarvis and Nereida Cross.
p. cm. — (Pennsylvania studies in human rights)
Includes bibliographical references and index.
ISBN 0-8122-3539-8 (alk. paper)
1. Pol Pot—Trials, litigation, etc. 2. Ieng Sary—Trials, litigation, etc. 3. Trials (Genocide)—Cambodia. I. Ieng Sary. II. De Nike, Howard J. III. Quigley, John B. IV Robinson, Kenneth J. (Kenneth Jay). V. Cambodia. Tribunal populaire révolutionnaire. VI. Title. VII. Series.
KNM41.P65 P65 2000
345.596'0251—dc21 99-055971

Contents

*Missing Documents

Editors' Note: The Documents of the People's Revolutionary Tribunal

The documents in this volume are those of the People's Revolutionary Tribunal, which was constituted in Cambodia in 1979, in connection with the trial for genocide in August of that year of Pol Pot and Ieng Sary. The documents, which are of three types, are divided into three parts. Part I consists of documents relating to the establishment of the tribunal. These include governmental decrees setting the tribunal's jurisdiction and appointing the presiding judge and the jury. They also include decrees of the presiding judge and the prosecuting attorney involved in bringing the case to trial. Finally, they include lists of participants: witnesses, invited foreign lawyers, and invited foreign journalists.

Part II, the bulk of the volume, consists of the documents produced during the investigation into the alleged offenses. These documents formed the basis for conducting a trial. They are the evidence gathered by investigators, which falls into five categories:

Statements of witnesses, relating their knowledge of acts that might show genocide by Pol Pot and Ieng Sary. The acts described are principally killings, and the creation of conditions that led to deaths, such as the forced evacuation of cities and forced residence in rural communes with minimal rations and health care.

Reports by government investigators of field investigations they carried out at alleged mass grave sites.

Reports commissioned by government investigators and written by experts in particular fields of endeavor, with regard to the impact of the actions of Pol Pot and Ieng Sary on various aspects of life in Cambodia. The point of these reports was to generalize from the evidence of particular acts to give an overall view of the killings, to show how many people perished overall in certain locations, and to show the adverse impact of Khmer Rouge practices on social relations.

Excerpts from Khmer Rouge documents tending to show that the practices that resulted in deaths were centrally directed.

Accounts from the foreign press, and several locally written, describing atrocities of the Khmer Rouge.

Part III consists of documents relating to the trial stage. First is the prosecutor's indictment, which sums up the evidence contained in Part II. Next are the speeches at the conclusion of trial by the prosecutor and defense attorneys, as well as by the invited foreign lawyers. Then comes the court's written decision, finding Pol Pot and Ieng Sary guilty and sentencing them to death.

The documents are presented in an order devised by the People's Revolutionary Tribunal, which assigned a number to each document. The numbering system groups documents of a particular category. The headings that appear for the categories are taken from a table of contents produced at the time of the trial, but not given a document number.

Some obvious errors were made by tribunal staff in assigning numbers to documents. Some documents had no number. In a few instances the same number appeared on more than one document. In other instances, the document number was not consistent among the three languages in which the document was issued. Some documents bore numbers that would have assigned the document to what was obviously an incorrect category. In instances of apparent error, the editors have used a number that they surmise was intended for the particular document.

The documentation as reflected in this volume bespeaks a proceeding that differs from the style of criminal proceedings in common law countries. It is rather in the civil law tradition as found on the European continent, a fact that is not surprising since the legal system in Cambodia is based on that of France, which ruled Cambodia as a colony until World War II. In the civil law system, the investigation is documented meticulously in writing. These documents provide a basis for a decision either to drop the case or to take it to trial. These documents are also presented to the court prior to the trial. The court hears evidence at the trial and bases its decision on that evidence. However, the pretrial documents provide the court an indication of the evidence and thereby serve as a base of evidence that the trial court may either confirm or reject after hearing the evidence presented at trial. In the civil law system of procedure, the pretrial phase is more significant in the overall fact-finding in relation to the trial phase, as compared with the common law system.

Another feature of the documents that reflects the civil law tradition is the detailed nature of the indictment and the judgment (Document 3.01). Whereas in common law countries an indictment is typically sparse, an indictment in civil law countries typically recites the evidence gathered during the pretrial investigation. Whereas in common law countries a verdict is typically a statement of "guilty" or "not guilty" from the judge or jury, in civil law countries the judgment, which includes both a verdict, and, in case of guilt, a sentence, is a detailed document reciting the evidence that led the court to its conclusion.

Still another feature that is typical of Civil Law proceedings is the inclusion of a claim by victims for compensation (Document 3.03d). In civil law jurisdictions, a crime victim may make a claim, typically for monetary compensation, that is heard as part of the criminal case, and the court, if it finds the defendant guilty, also decides if the victim should be compensated by the defendant. The victims are called "civil plaintiffs," meaning that they are plaintiffs in a civil action against the accused.

One other feature typical of civil law jurisdictions is a mixed decision-making panel, that is, one made up of both professionals and nonprofessionals. The panel that tried Pol Pot and Ieng Sary consisted of one individual characterized as "judge," and ten others, characterized as "assessors" (Document 1.08). This reflects a way of bringing lay persons into judicial decision making in criminal cases different from that found in common law jurisdictions, where the lay persons, composed as a jury, serve as sole finders of fact, while a judge determines the penalty. In the civil law procedure, a mixed panel is used in some, typically more serious, cases, and the mixed panel both decides on guilt or innocence and sets the penalty.

In preparing this volume for publication, the editors worked from materials provided to John Quigley as a participant in the trial of Pol Pot and Ieng Sary. This included photographs taken by SPK, the Cambodian government press agency, as well as typescript People's Revolutionary Tribunal documents. The editors gained access to additional tribunal documents from a set collected in Phnom Penh in the 1990s by Helen Jarvis, Head of the School of Information, Library and Archive Studies, University of New South Wales. Jarvis describes how she came upon these documents in "A Personal View of the Documents of the People's Revolutionary Tribunal," in this volume. Both Jarvis and Nereida Cross, research assistant in Information, Library and Archive Studies, University of New South Wales, collaborated with the editors in locating documents that were not found in any of the existing collections.

The editors referred as well to a selection of documents of the trial as published in 1988 in Phnom Penh by a group of Cambodian lawyers in English under the title *People's Revolutionary Tribunal Held in Phnom Penh for the Trial of the Genocide Crime of the Pol Pot–Ieng Sary Clique (August 1979): Documents*, and in French under the title *Tribunal populaire révolutionnaire siégeant à Phnom Penh pour le jugement du crime de génocide commis par la clique génocidaire de Pol Pot–Ieng Sary (Août 1979): Documents.*

People's Revolutionary Tribunal Documents 2.1.1.19, 2.1.1.20, and 2.1.1.22 are pretrial statements of witnesses that the editors were unable to locate. These three witnesses testified orally at the trial of Pol Pot and Ieng Sary, and summaries of their oral statements were published by the Ministry of Information and Culture in 1981 in a Khmer-language collection of materials about the tribunal titled *Documents of the Court Trial for Genocide of Pol Pot and Ieng Sary (August 1979)*. The editors used these summaries in place of the pretrial statements of the three witnesses as Documents 2.1.1.19, 2.1.1.20, and 2.1.1.22.

The editors were unable to locate Documents 2.6.02 and 2.6.06 but used the published accounts on which they were based and translated from Serbo-Croatian and French, respectively. With three other documents containing published sources, Documents 2.6.07, 2.6.10, and 2.6.15, the editors used the tribunal document but consulted the published accounts in Russian, French, and German, respectively, to clarify ambiguities.

The editors have been unable to locate a small number of documents that they have reason to believe were printed by the tribunal. Several witness statements and several procedural documents that are mentioned in other tribunal documents are not to be found in any of the extant collections of tribunal documents. In these instances, the editors have included the document in the List of Documents but have marked it with an asterisk to indicate that it is not contained in this volume. The editors' purpose in including these documents in the List of Documents is to give as complete a list as possible of tribunal documents.

With a few documents, certain pages are missing from the texts available to the editors. In these instances, the editors have included as much of the document as was available, with a notation at the point of the missing pages.

The People's Revolutionary Tribunal issued its documents in three languages: Khmer, French, and English. The editors have endeavored to provide a readable text in English using the documents that were available to them. Since in many instances, the English-language text issued by the tribunal fell short of being in proper English, the editors frequently translated from the Khmer or French-language texts.

At the top of the first page of each tribunal document appeared the following heading:

People's Republic of Kampuchea
Independence — Peace — Happiness
Revolutionary People's Tribunal at Phnom Penh
to try the Pol Pot–Ieng Sary Clique
for the Crime of Genocide

The editors have omitted this heading for space considerations.

The editors have composed titles for most of the documents. The witness statements in the original are variously titled "Witness statement" or "Witness declaration." The editors considered these titles inappropriate for use since many documents would have identical titles. The editors omitted these titles and instead used the name of the witness as the title.

Since the Khmer language does not use the Latin alphabet, the editors have transliterated proper names and place-names. There is no universally recognized system for transliterating the Khmer script, and the matter is one of some complexity, because the earliest attempt to transliterate Khmer was done in French, and the effort was to make them sound correct to French speakers. Thus, in French-language sources, one finds spellings of Khmer names that differ from those found in English-language sources. The editors have attempted to transliterate in a way that presents proper names and place-names in the way in which they are customarily rendered in English-language sources. Because there is no standard system of transliteration, however, a particular Khmer proper name or place-name may appear in other English-language sources with a spelling different from what the editors have used. The editors have, in general, followed a system of spelling Cambodian place-names developed at Yale University and the University of New South Wales for the Cambodian Genocide Program.

Many of the documents, in particular the witness statements, are signed by the declarant and other parties involved in composing the document. On many of the documents, the word "(signed)," in parentheses, appears with the name. The editors have omitted this word when it appears, since when a name appears at the end of a document, it is to be understood that the named individuals were signing.

In the documents, the editors have spelled the name of the country as Kampuchea, rather than the more familiar Cambodia. Cambodia is an Anglicization of "Cambodge," the name of the country as pronounced by the French during the colonial period. "Cambodia" was thus regarded as having a colonial tinge, whereas "Kampuchea" was regarded as closer to the pronunciation in Khmer, hence more authentic. "Kampuchea" was the spelling used by the government at the time of the trial when rendering the name of the country in English.

A Personal View of the Documents of the People's Revolutionary Tribunal

Helen Jarvis

One night in December 1990, I was on my second visit to post-Pol Pot Cambodia working to assist the reestablishment of the National Library of Cambodia. As dinner time approached I walked as usual from my rundown hotel out into the darkened streets, using a small flashlight to illuminate the potholes and open monsoon drains along the road to the grandly named Medical Faculty Restaurant, in truth nothing but a bare earth area with a battered roof and open sides, but cheerfully lit and serving a limited range of quite delicious fare.

As usual, before long a young barefoot boy approached my table with a motley collection of half a dozen books and a few maps. As usual, I spent a few minutes chatting with him and looking through his wares, saying I had already bought this and thus, for the titles were generally the same each night. But this night he proudly proffered something new, a larger format book with a bright green-and-white cover. It was the English edition of selected documents submitted to the 1979 People's Revolutionary Tribunal, with a set of intriguing bibliographic indicators. The statement of responsibility is ascribed to "A group of Cambodian jurists"; the imprint and "Editor's note" give the date 1988; but the foreword is dated June 1990 and states that the work was being published by the Commission for Propaganda and Education of the Foreign Languages Publishing House from documents given to it by the Press Department of the Ministry for Foreign Affairs.

I bought a copy and immediately started to read it, astonished that I had heard so little of the depth and range of testimony that had been made ten years previously at a court proceeding that had been dismissed by most foreigners as a "show trial." I am no lawyer, and elsewhere in this volume Howard J. De Nike discusses what the phrase "show trial" entails and signifies, and the extent to which the 1979 People's Revolutionary Tribunal falls into that category. But as a documentalist, and as a person passionately involved with the political situation in Cambodia, I knew that what I held in my hand was an important, though limited, record of an important, though limited, political and legal proceeding.

Some time later I saw a number of copies of a Khmer-language collection of documents relating to the trial at the National Library of Cambodia, and Um Neang, the director, gave one to me. This edition, which is printed on poor quality paper and has a black-and-white cover photograph of exhumed human remains, states that it is the first edition, and bears the imprint Phnom Penh: compiled and published by the Ministry of Information, Culture and Press, 1981. It was only in 1994 that I gained a copy of a French edition of selected documents, which appears to be identical in content to the English edition (except that my copy has an *errata* sheet inserted). This French copy was given to me by the Secretary of State for Information, Khieu Kanharith.

In January 1992 I was conducting a short course on library services in the National Library of Cambodia, with participants from a number of libraries and documentation centers. Among the participants were several staff members of the National Archives of Cambodia, which is housed in a building right behind the National Library. From the time of their establishment by the colonial French administration in the 1920s, the National Archives and National Library were administered as part of the same department, until they were separated in 1984. The National Library remained under the Ministry of Culture, while the National Archives was now administered directly by the Council of Ministers. As such, it was considerably harder to visit and definitely not covered by my permits from the Ministry of Culture. It was my lucky break that Lim Ky from the archives staff arranged for the participants in the short course and their teachers to visit the archives.

So, quite unexpectedly, on the last afternoon of the course, someone from the archives ran across to the library and said we had permission to come and have a look. Mindful of the fact that this was indeed a rare opportunity, I took my notebook and my camera with me. Lim Ky showed us around the beautiful but decrepit building. While the reading room held elegantly carved wooden catalogue cabinets, of the same style as the library's, and while the first few rows of shelves held bound volumes arranged in some sort of regular order, the two upstairs floors held many piles of documents in complete disarray, alongside the boxes organized in previous regimes.

Two special collections on the ground floor caught my eye. First, in steel stationery cabinets were a rare set of official documents from Democratic Kampuchea. These were records from the Ministry of Commerce. Then I turned around and noticed a whole bookshelf filled with parcels wrapped in brown paper, and somewhere I saw the letters "PRT" written on the outside. I was elated, and knew I had come across another, even more valuable piece of the documentary puzzle surrounding the trial.

I sought a meeting with Sin Khin, director of the National Archives, and asked if I might have permission to study this collection at close hand. After some months I was given a permit to access the archives. I was told I was only the second foreigner to be given this privilege since the archives had been administered by the Council of Ministers. (Several foreign researchers had been able to visit the archives in 1979 and the early 1980s.)

So it was that I spent two weeks working with Lim Ky on the collection, which had been donated to the National Library by Thun Saray, who had been one of the witnesses at the PRT, and is now a well-known Cambodian human rights activist. We opened each package and assessed what was inside. When it became clear that the collection was in a very precarious physical state, and that most of the documents were present in more than one copy, I sought permission to take a copy of each back with me to be lodged in the National Library of Australia. I should add that I also had broader concerns to ensure the survival of this collection outside Cambodia, since in mid-1993 Cambodia was in a fragile political situation, with the results of the May elections being contested. The threat of secession loomed prior to the formation of a coalition government of parties formerly in conflict. The Khmer Rouge had refused to participate in the elections, despite having signed the Paris Peace Agreements in October 1991, and still represented a clear and present danger. It would be in its interests to destroy evidence of its crimes.

Permission was granted, and so Lim Ky and I tied *krama* (traditional scarves) around our faces to form dust masks, and set to work opening each package. The collection was divided into three sets corresponding to the languages in which each document had been presented at the tribunal—Khmer, English, and French. Unfortunately, despite the fact that each document had been assigned a number, each language set had been arranged in a different sequence, so there was no way to see which document was present in which language—I knew that would need to be done on a database after I returned home to Australia. In the time available all we could do was see how many copies of each was held, and extract one.

Where there were more than three copies, I set one aside for me to take away. I felt it was important for the National Archives to retain at least three full sets, so where there were three or fewer copies, I decided I would only take a photocopy. But the problem was that at that time the National Archives was entirely without electricity. I therefore had to gain permission to go with a member of staff to a small shop on the main street where a copy could be made. I was acutely aware of the trust that had been extended to me, and the responsibility I held literally in my hand, as I climbed into my pedicab, or perched precariously on the back of a motorbike dodging the traffic and even the occasional downpour, sometimes with what may have been the sole surviving copy of one of these documents.

Once back in Sydney we photocopied another complete set of the documents as a working set, and then lodged the set brought from Phnom Penh with the National Library of Australia manuscripts collection.

In 1995 I was awarded a Small Grant from the Australian Research Council, supplemented by a Special Research Grant from the Faculty of Professional Studies of the University of New South Wales, to analyze the People's Revolutionary Tribunal documents via the design and development of a database. In my application I argued that "these documents form a key primary source on the largely unrecorded history" of the Tribunal.

My colleague and database expert Nereida Cross and I decided to utilize CDS/ISIS—the UNESCO database management package. We constructed a record for each document, beginning with the English set (178 documents). Then the French set (161 documents) was analyzed, and added to the corresponding record, if it was already held in English, or otherwise a new record was created. The process was repeated for the Khmer collection (206 records). We were fortunate in the fact that the Windows version of CDS/ISIS has since become available, allowing the input and display of Khmer script.

The process of matching the different language versions of the same document was quite problematic. A preliminary listing had been made by Lim Ky for the National Archives of Cambodia. Unfortunately, however, the "brief title" given was generally the first few words of the document, most often being the heading for the tribunal itself, and rarely bearing any distinctive word or phrase. As mentioned above, each language set had been arranged in its own sequence, but almost all documents did have what we concluded must have been the People's Revolutionary Tribunal document number in the top left-hand corner of the first page. This number clearly showed that the documents had been classified into several groups, and this was later verified when we came to a French-language list of the documents of the tribunal. Unfortunately, this document is itself without a title or document number, but its typography, structure, and layout suggest strongly that it was compiled for the tribunal.

1 Procedural documents
2 Documents of the investigation
  2.0 Identity of the accused
  2.1.1 Witness statements
  2.1.2 Religious issues
  2.1.3 Issues of the workers of Tuol Kauk
  2.1.4 Military issues
  2.1.5 Issues of ordinary citizens
  2.2 Statements of former agents of Pol Pot and Ieng Sary
  2.3 Reports of field investigations
  2.4 Reports on various aspects of social life

The document concludes here, but it is clear from the numbers on the documents themselves that there were three other categories:

2.5 Excerpts from captured documents
2.6 Excerpts from published accounts
3 Indictment and Judgment

Some documents did not carry the People's Revolutionary Tribunal document number, however, and some had it printed so faintly as to be indecipherable. Furthermore, once the PRT document number had been determined, matching the different language versions still sometimes was tricky, due to the fact that typographical errors had been made. It was necessary to verify every tentative document number match by checking the title, date, and signing officer, a task made more complicated by the fact that different transliterations of the Khmer names were frequently used in the English and French versions, and sometimes even within a single document several versions of the name occur.

We were fortunate that during 1995 several members of staff from the National Library of Cambodia came to study at the School of Information, Library, and Archive Studies (SILAS) of the University of New South Wales, and were able to spend time on this project. Ros Sarou was responsible for the bulk of the data entry and scanning of the Khmer set, and Im Sothearith worked on matching the Khmer set to the English and French, sometimes involving a good deal of sleuthing as noted above.

We knew we wanted to be able to link the bibliographic record with its full-text original. Unfortunately, the print quality of the originals was not good enough for optical character recognition, as we had hoped, but it did suffice for creation of scanned images. CDS/ISIS has provision for invoking Pascal programs from within a database record, and UNESCO had provided a routine known as SHOWP to "show" or display a picture or image. Another student, Vivian del Castillo from the Philippines, wrote an enhancement of SHOWP to allow for the complexity of the People's Revolutionary Tribunal database with multiple language versions (and sometimes even several versions of one language). This new routine (SHOWB) allows the user to see and choose for screen display or printing any page of any version of each document. A number of students from SILAS have carried on with the scanning process as volunteers.

After John Quigley began work on this book, he reconciled the documents in our database with various other lists he had compiled, and he identified a number of missing documents. We assisted searching for them, first from the three printed volumes of selected documents, second from personal sets held by John Quigley, Ben Kiernan, and Helen Ester (whose set was brought to Australia and was also given to the National Library of

Australia), and third by asking Lim Ky to check again in the National Archives, and to ask other government officials in Cambodia whether they might have some additional documents. This work has proved slow and difficult, but it has narrowed down the number of missing documents to a very few. So it is that the volume consists of 196 documents.

The PRT documents database is also available for interrogation and access as part of the Cambodian Genocide Data Bases (CGDB) when they were developed in early 1995, following the establishment of the Cambodian Genocide Program (CGP) at Yale University, directed until May 1999 by Ben Kiernan. As the Consultant on Documentation for the CGP, I was pleased to be able to contribute the People's Revolutionary Tribunal documents to form, quite appropriately, the first component of the CGDB. The documents can be found in the Cambodian Bibliographic Database (CBIB) section on the CGP web site *http://www.yale.edu/cgp* and also at *http://www-cgp.silas.unsw.edu.au.* To limit one's search to the PRT set, one may simply type in "PRT" as one of the search terms. Individual documents are best located by searching for the PRT document number (e.g., 2.1.1.01), and the record reveals the variant versions and languages in which the document is held.

Introduction

John Quigley

The trial of Pol Pot and Ieng Sary was held in August 1979 in Phnom Penh, Cambodia. In the government that ruled Cambodia from 1975 to early 1979, Pol Pot was prime minister, and Ieng Sary was deputy prime minister for foreign affairs. This government was generally referred to as the Khmer Rouge, "Khmer" for the majority ethnic group in Cambodia, and "Rouge," the French word for "red," because of the government's leftist character. The Khmer Rouge was widely accused of atrocities against the population of Cambodia, in connection with its pursuit of a policy of radical communalization. The Khmer Rouge was replaced in January 1979 by a new government composed largely of Khmer Rouge functionaries who broke away from the Khmer Rouge and overthrew it, with substantial military backing from the army of Vietnam.

The trial of Pol Pot and Ieng Sary was conducted under the auspices of this new government. A number of foreign lawyers, of whom I was one, were invited to participate in the trial in various capacities. At the time of the trial, Phnom Penh was a ghost town, having been emptied by the Khmer Rouge when they captured the city in 1975. Attractive urban villas still stood empty, many with rusting Renaults parked in the driveways where their owners had abandoned them during the 1975 evacuation. There was no industry in the city, and shops were closed. My initial reaction upon arriving in Phnom Penh was to wonder why anyone was bothering to hold a criminal trial, when so much needed to be done to restore normal life. Around the auditorium where the trial was held, an overflow audience milled, anxious to talk with anyone who would listen about what they and their families had suffered under the Khmer Rouge. Security in Phnom Penh was uncertain, as the Khmer Rouge still operated in many parts of the country. Along with other foreign participants, I traveled each day to Chakdomuk Hall, the venue of the trial, in a military-style convoy, with armed vehicles at the head and rear.

Genocide

The tribunal to which I had been invited was not a regularly functioning court, but rather one that had been constituted to try Khmer Rouge leaders, as well as others suspected of committing atrocities under Khmer Rouge auspices. Foreign lawyers were invited to participate for the evident reason of reflecting international standards of justice and thereby enhancing the legitimacy of the proceedings. I was the only invited foreign lawyer who was a specialist in international law, and I was asked for a legal opinion on whether the acts of the two defendants qualified as genocide. I was asked to prepare a statement in writing for inclusion in the trial documents, and to present that statement orally at the trial as part of the closing statements.

I approached the task with care, because I understood the use to which my conclusion would be put. I was anxious to give an accurate reflection of the law regarding genocide. Genocide is defined by the Convention on the Prevention and Punishment of the Crime of Genocide of December 9, 1948, a treaty that was drafted at the United Nations. The impetus for the drafting of the convention was the mass killings committed by Nazi Germany during World War II, but the convention's definition required nothing on that scale. Killing, or even acts short of killing aimed against a particular group, may qualify as genocide under the convention's definition, even if there are only a modest number of victims. Thus, a conclusion that a particular situation involves genocide is not tantamount to equating it with the Holocaust of World War II.

On a legal pad, I wrote out a statement in English that was then translated into Khmer and French, and was typed on one of the few functioning typewriters in the city (see Document 303e). In my statement, I said that genocide had been committed. That conclusion involved both a factual and a legal aspect. The factual aspect concerned the question of whether the two accused were responsible for killings under circumstances that might constitute genocide. I had only a modest opportunity to do fact-finding during my short time in Cambodia before and during the trial. I visited mass grave sites. I visited Tuol Sleng prison and saw the detailed lists of persons executed, lists that had by then been put on display (see Document 2.4.10). I visited a crocodile farm where, it was alleged, persons had been thrown to the crocodiles (see Documents 2.3.1.01 through 2.3.1.03). I had an opportunity for extensive discussion with one of the tribunal witnesses, Denise Alfonso. As indicated by her statement (see Document 2.6.21), she was a fluent speaker of French, and I had an opportunity to speak with her at length in French and to question her about particulars.

I was, of course, already aware of the considerable international attention on the conduct of the Khmer Rouge government. There had been investigations in the U.S. Congress, and questions had been raised at the

Opening session of people's Revolutionary Tribunal, August 15, 1979. Keo Chanda, presiding judge, is flanked by the ten people's assessors. Two prosecutors are seated left, and two defense lawyers right. Photo: SPK.

United Nations. A body of information existed about atrocities under the Khmer Rouge.

The Khmer Rouge had sought to create an agriculturally based society, without cities, to combat the Westernization that had accompanied France's colonization of Cambodia. The extreme methods the Khmer Rouge used to obtain this objective caused many deaths. The evacuation of Cambodia's cities had been carried out with extreme indifference to human life. The conditions of life enforced upon the population in the newly established rural communes were also calculated to result in many deaths. The elimination of scientifically based medical care was a measure that would obviously result in many preventable deaths.

Execution-style killings initially targeted the military personnel of the former government and then were expanded to include other groups: clergy; persons with education, often identified by the fact that they may have worn eyeglasses; and ethnic minorities, prominently the Cham, Vietnamese, and Chinese. The elimination of all these groups was apparently calculated to reduce opposition to the establishment of the agriculturally based society the Khmer Rouge was pursuing. Later on, when opposition to the extremist

Audience at the opening session of the People's Revolutionary Tribunal, August 15, 1979. Photo: SPK.

policies emerged within Khmer Rouge ranks, the killing extended to Khmer Rouge personnel.

The larger number of deaths resulted not from execution but from the conditions of life and lack of medical care. Still, hundreds of thousands at the very least had been executed, and responsibility for the other deaths seemed clear because they resulted, for the most part, from centrally directed policies whose effects had to be apparent to the leadership.

During the 1980s and 1990s, additional evidence has emerged of Khmer Rouge atrocities. Much of that evidence is the work of the Cambodian Genocide Program at Yale University, which found mass graves that had not been discovered by the summer of 1979. Even on the basis of the evidence available in 1979, however, the atrocities were considerable.

A conclusion that genocide had been committed turned not only on the facts but as well on the legal definition of genocide. Pol Pot and Ieng Sary had apparently not killed with their own hands, but under the Genocide Convention responsibility is provided not only for the actual act, but for conspiracy to commit genocide, direct and public incitement to commit genocide, attempts to commit genocide, and complicity in genocide. There was thus, I felt, reason to include as genocide the acts of governmental

Tuol Sleng prison. Evidence was presented to the People's Revolutionary Tribunal of torture and executions there (see Document 2.4.10). Photo: SPK.

leaders who themselves may not have killed but who promoted killing carried out by subordinates.

Killing, moreover, is not the only way in which genocide can be committed under the convention. Article 2 of the Genocide Convention defines genocide as

any of the following acts committed with intent to destroy, in whole or in part, a national, ethnical, racial or religious group, as such:

(a) Killing members of the group;
(b) Causing serious bodily or mental harm to members of the group;
(c) Deliberately inflicting on the group conditions of life calculated to bring about its physical destruction in whole or in part;
(d) Imposing measures intended to prevent births within the group;
(e) Forcibly transferring children of the group to another group.

Under paragraphs (b) through (e), the onerous conditions of life imposed by the Khmer Rouge leadership could constitute genocide, I thought, even apart from outright killings.

The quoted definition, to be sure, limits genocide to acts directed against

Inspection of a mass grave site in Siem Reap province by a group of invited foreign lawyers, including two who participated in the trial: Judge Francisco Varona Duque de Estrada (center, facing camera with wristwatch on left arm), and John Quigley (extreme right, holding camera) (see Document 3.03g). Photo: SPK.

the enumerated groups. This limitation has led to controversy over the nature of the group targeted. Some had suggested that genocide was not committed in Cambodia because most of the victims, like the perpetrators, were Khmer, and thus there was not a racial animus behind the actions. Evidence suggested, however, that a number of ethnic minority groups had been targeted. Evidence also suggested that religious figures, including in particular Buddhist monks, had been targeted.

As for members of the predominant ethnicity, Khmer, who were not targeted on the basis of religion, there was a possible rationale on which the acts against them might be characterized as genocide. The Genocide Convention does not exclude targeting members of one's own national, ethnic, racial, or religious group. Moreover, under Article 2 of the Genocide Convention, genocide is committed if the intent is to destroy a designated group either in whole or in part. Thus, it may be that genocide is present when there is an intent to destroy only a part of an ethnic group, even if the effort is not directed against the entire group. One allegation was that intellectuals or urban residents were targeted. Since they were "part" of the Khmer people, the targeting of them might constitute genocide.

The Genocide Convention had not been the subject of substantial interpretation since its adoption, which meant that there was little on which to rely beyond the wording of the text. Given what I knew at the time about the facts, and given the various ways in which the atrocities might qualify as genocide under the convention, I was comfortable in giving my opinion to the tribunal that genocide had been committed by the two defendants.

China and the United States

Many of the participants in the tribunal adverted to China's role in promoting the genocide of which the two defendants stood accused. I did not feel that I had enough information about China's role to do that, and therefore I did not mention China in my statement to the tribunal. I did, however, make reference in my statement to the United States.

It appeared to me that the stage had been set for the Khmer Rouge to evacuate Cambodia's cities by the United States when it intensively bombed Cambodia's countryside, as it did in support of the government of Lon Nol that ruled Cambodia from 1971 to 1975. The bombing forced an influx of rural residents into the cities. The bombing was done by B-52s, and it was so heavy that when I flew in to Phnom Penh for the trial I could see from the air many of the huge craters left in the ground. By April 1975 the cities were swollen well beyond their normal levels of population and were not able to support those who had flocked in.

A return of the new migrants to the countryside would have been an imperative even if the Khmer Rouge had not planned to empty the cities. Vietnam faced a similar problem after the war and had taken measures to encourage villagers to leave cities to which they had migrated. Thus, when the Khmer Rouge in April 1975 told city residents to depart, they were able to gain compliance in part because city residents understood that public services could not cope with their war-swollen populations. Moreover, the Khmer Rouge told city residents that the United States was about to bomb, and that this was a reason why they needed to depart. This was a believable proposition, since the United States had bombed Khmer Rouge-held rural areas.

Context of the Proceedings

Beyond the issue of whether Pol Pot and Ieng Sary were guilty of genocide lay that of the fairness of the proceedings that were about to be conducted. Except for Vietnam, no support had come from other governments or from international organizations in preparing the proceedings, because they opposed the government in light of its having come to power with the help of the Vietnamese army. The government had just come to power, and institutionalization that would ensure a strict separation of the judicial function from the executive function had not taken place.

Personnel and facilities were lacking. People trained in law suffered the fate of other intellectuals in Cambodia under the Khmer Rouge. As of August 1979, no one practiced law in the country, and there were no regular courts. There were few police personnel with knowledge of scientific methods of evidence gathering.

Moreover, bias against the accused was inevitable in the situation. Few persons in Cambodia had not been adversely affected by the Khmer Rouge government. In 1979 it was not possible to find in Cambodia persons who had not formed a strong opinion about the guilt of Pol Pot and Ieng Sary. Some of the participants in the trial had provided incriminating information at the pretrial stage. One of the assessors, a member of the panel of ten that would decide the case, had filed a statement as a victim (see Document 2.1.1.06). Another assessor, a medical doctor, had written a report about the effects of Khmer Rouge policy on the health of children (see Document 2.4.03c).

The new government of Cambodia was being denied recognition because of the key role that Vietnam's army had played in bringing it to power. The international community still dealt with the Khmer Rouge as the official government of the country. As of August 1979, the U.N. General Assembly accepted the Khmer Rouge as the government of Cambodia, despite its record of rights violations, and despite the fact that it was no longer in power.

In holding the trial, the new government of Cambodia sought to discredit the Khmer Rouge and to challenge the international community over its recognition policy on Cambodia. After the trial ended, Vietnam's representative at the United Nations asked the U.N. secretary-general to circulate a copy of the tribunal's judgment as a U.N. document, and this was done.[1] But the trial got little international press coverage or attention from foreign governments, being widely viewed as an event staged by Vietnam to justify its military intervention.

The government hoped that the trial would aid in its battle for international recognition. At a reception I attended, held to welcome foreign participants, Ros Samy, a government official, denounced China and the United States for "trying by all means to shield and aid the remnants of the Pol Pot-Ieng Sary clique, with a view to restoring the barbarous regime of genocide in Kampuchea." Ros Samy said that the establishment of the tribunal "places before the Kampuchean people and the peace-loving and progressive forces in the world, a burning issue that is to do away with the aftereffects of the Pol Pot-Ieng Sary clique, and at the same time, to prevent the crimes of the Peking expansionists and their like" (see Document 1.19).

The tribunal's presiding judge, Keo Chanda, himself a member of the

1. *Letter dated 17 September 1979 from the Permanent Representative of Viet Nam to the United Nations addressed to the Secretary-General*, U.N. Document A/34/491, September 20, 1979.

government, described the aim of the trial as follows: "Trying the Pol Pot-Ieng Sary clique for the crime of genocide will on the one hand expose all the criminal acts that they have committed and mobilize the Kampuchean people more actively to defend and build up the people's power, and on the other hand show the peoples of the whole world the true face of the criminals who are posing as the representatives of the people of Kampuchea" (Document 1.01bis).

Cambodia's ambassador to Vietnam, Chea Soth, held a press conference to explain the need for the trial. He said, "the imperialists and international reactionaries are attempting to restore such a genocidal and criminal regime in order to obstruct the Kampuchean people's national reconstruction and undermine peace and stability in Southeast Asia."[2]

The Khmer Rouge, denouncing the trial just prior to its opening, sought to discredit it on this same ground. Condemning Vietnam for intervening in Cambodia, the Khmer Rouge said that the trial was "part of their [Vietnam's] trick to shift the responsibility for their widely known and glaringly monumental crimes onto the shoulders of Democratic Kampuchea."[3] Democratic Kampuchea was the name used for the country by the Khmer Rouge.

The Khmer Rouge radio, commenting on the trial, said that it was staged by "the Vietnamese Le Duan-Pham Van Dong clique," whose "dark design was laid bare immediately after this abject farce was staged. The clique aims at attacking the Democratic Kampuchean government's influence in the international arena, particularly attempting to oust the government of Democratic Kampuchea from the nonaligned movement and United Nations organizations and to replace it with the Vietnamese henchmen that it installed in Phnom Penh to be used in the immediate and long-term strategy of Vietnam, the Soviet Union and their associates, in the strategy to control the nonaligned movement and in the strategy of aggression, expansion, occupation, interference and domination against all people the world over."[4]

The political context doubtless provided the reason to hold the trial at a time when all resources were needed to restore normal life in the country. Given the continuing threat that the Khmer Rouge posed, a trial of Khmer Rouge leaders that would highlight their dangerousness held the promise of ending the civil war in which the country still found itself.

An aim of self-justification may not delegitimize a trial that in other

2. *Kampuchean Envoy Holds Press Conference on PRK Tribunal,* Hanoi VNA in English 1635 GMT 30 July 1979, Foreign Broadcast Information Service, Asia & Pacific, July 31, 1979, p. K4.

3. *What Kind of a Tribunal Are the Vietnamese Le Duan—Pham Van Dong Criminals Trying to Set Up?* Voice of Democratic Kampuchea radio, August 2, 1979, FBIS Asia & Pacific, *SRV has no right to set up tribunal in Phnom Penh,* August 13, 1979, p. H4.

4. *Statement by the Press and Information Section of the Foreign Ministry of Democratic Kampuchea on the Vietnamese Le Duan-Pham Van Dong Clique Setting Up a Farcical Vietnamese Tribunal in Phnom Penh,* Voice of Democratic Kampuchea radio, August 22, 1979, FBIS Asia & Pacific, *Democratic Kampuchea Statement Calls Phnom Penh Tribunal "Farce,"* August 24, 1979, p. H1.

Chakdomuk Hall, Phnom Penh, during a session of the People's Revolutionary Tribunal. Photo: SPK.

respects is conducted properly. The Nuremberg proceedings after World War II were held, in some measure, to justify the Allies. The World War II Allies had required great sacrifice from their populations to defeat Germany. The Allies sought to show their populations that the effort had been worthwhile. The Nuremberg trials, as well as those held at the same time in Tokyo against Japanese defendants, have been criticized as reflecting victor's justice. Whereas after World War II, Germany and Japan lay defeated, the Khmer Rouge was very much alive. The need to prove the victorious government's correctness was stronger than it had been for the World War II Allies.

Proceedings in Absentia

From the standpoint of procedures followed in the trial, the factor that stood out most starkly as I sat in Chakdomuk Hall was the absence of the two defendants. A program was distributed by the tribunal in advance, showing a schedule of witnesses and setting the fifth day as the end date, when the judgment would be read aloud (Document 1.18). The absence of the defendants allowed the trial to be scheduled in advance.

I had never before observed an in absentia trial, although they are used in many countries, notably in France, the former colonial power in Cambodia, and the country from which Cambodia derives its legal system. France permits a person tried in absentia to be retried upon appearing subsequently, rather than being incarcerated on the basis of the in absentia judgment.

Some years after the Pol Pot-Ieng Sary trial, I had occasion to consult, on behalf of the U.S. government, with judges in Ethiopia as they were preparing to try leaders of a recently overthrown government on charges of major atrocities. Many were in custody, but some were abroad and were to be tried in absentia. I asked a leading judge in Ethiopia if he thought that a trial in absentia was consistent with the right to defend oneself. His answer was that the absent defendants had a right to defend themselves, but they were choosing not to take advantage of that right. I asked how the absent defendants had been notified that they stood accused. He said that the charges had been broadcast by radio into neighboring countries, where the absent defendants were thought to be.

In absentia proceedings are not violative of accepted international standards. The International Covenant on Civil and Political Rights (Article 14) guarantees an accused person the right to be tried in his presence and to defend himself. However, this provision is not construed to prohibit in absentia trials, on the rationale given me by the Ethiopian judge, namely, that a nonappearing accused has chosen not to take advantage of the right to defend. In a case involving a Zairian official who was tried in absentia in Zaire, the Human Rights Committee that hears complaints under the International Covenant on Civil and Political Rights said that if the accused is properly informed of the proceedings and chooses to absent himself, then the right to be tried in one's presence has not been violated.[5] Like the Ethiopian defendants, Pol Pot and Ieng Sary were notified by the public media of the pendency of the proceedings (see Documents 1.16, 1.16bis, 1.17, 1.17bis).

The Defense

The court appointed two Cambodian attorneys and one attorney from the United States to represent Pol Pot and Ieng Sary. These attorneys, of course, were not in communication with the two defendants and thus made arguments of their own devising. One may speculate what Pol Pot and Ieng Sary might have argued had they been present. Pol Pot's statements, which are in part exculpatory, made in 1997 after he surfaced, suggest that he felt himself under serious threat from Vietnam, and that the killings of suspected opponents were necessary to ensure that Cambodia remain free of Vietnamese control. He did deny one specific allegation, the large number of killings of opponents in the Tuol Sleng prison, by saying that the Tuol Sleng

5. *Mbenge v. Zaire*, communication no. 16/1977, Report of the Human Rights Committee, p. 134, U.N. Document A/38/40.

Mrs. Khem Maly Chan testifying before the People's Revolutionary Tribunal (see Document 2.1.1.22). Photo: SPK.

prison did not exist. He did not, however, elaborate, to indicate whether he meant that prisoners were held there but that torture and killing did not occur, or whether Tuol Sleng was not used as a prison at all.

Defensive assertions along these lines would have fallen on deaf ears at the 1979 trial. There were simply too many people who had had experience with killings and with deaths resulting from living conditions for Pol Pot's exculpatory stance to carry credibility. The appointed attorneys did not seriously contest that Pol Pot and Ieng Sary were responsible for mass killings but argued that China was the real culprit behind the scenes, and that that fact, while not totally exonerating Pol Pot and Ieng Sary, mitigated their responsibility.

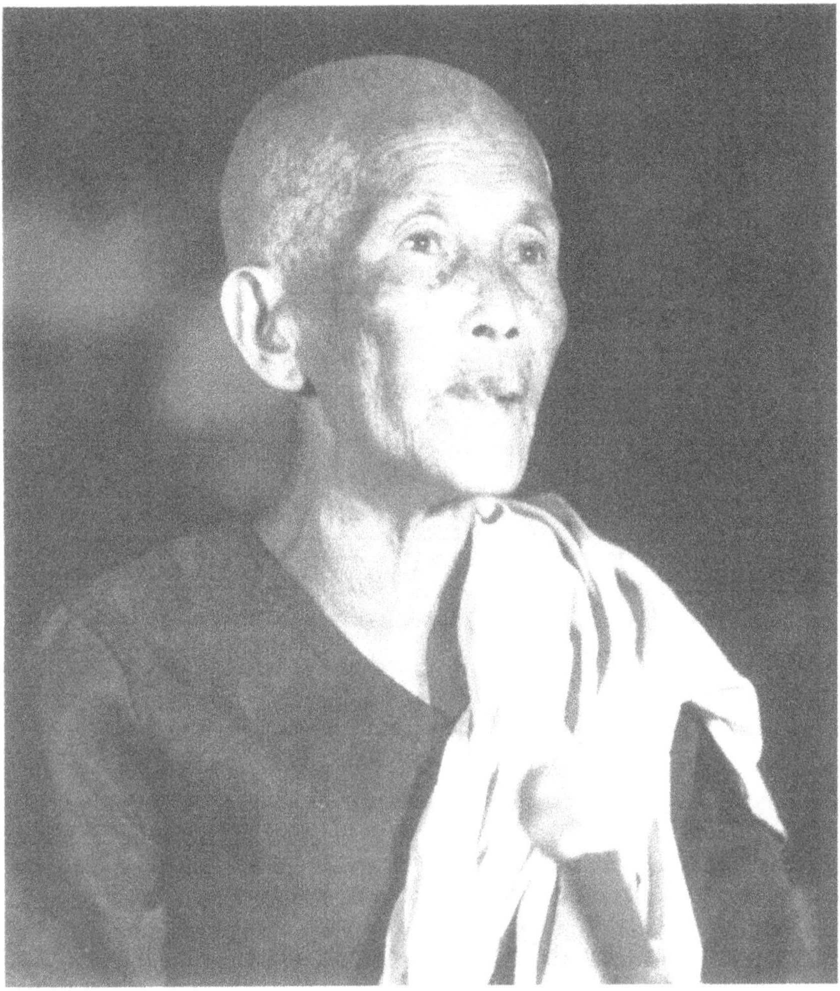

Mrs. Khang Chiem testifying before the People's Revolutionary Tribunal (see Document 2.1.5.21). Photo: SPK.

Another potential line of defense would have been that mass killing occurred, but that Pol Pot and Ieng Sary did not personally order it or condone it. In an interview, Ieng Sary admitted the truth of some of the allegations of atrocities but denied that they were centrally ordered. Ieng Sary said, "We acknowledge the excesses. They do not emanate from the leadership. They are excesses at the local level, and caused by Vietnamese infiltration. We do not disclaim our responsibilities in the killings, but our role has been minimal. It is true that our revolution is radical, but we have weighed

Audience members at the People's Revolutionary Tribunal in tears in reaction to testimony about atrocities. Photo: SPK.

the pros and cons about the population transfers, about the elimination of currency, etc. The need (in 1975) was to stabilize the country. Even then we foresaw war with Vietnam. The Vietnamese are using this propaganda to conceal their own crimes at home and in our country."[6]

Questioned about conditions in the agricultural communes, Ieng Sary said in the same interview: "This was hard work, but it was not forced labor." By so stating the matter, Ieng Sary would seem not to be denying that there was central direction involved in the conditions of life and labor in the cooperatives; rather, he denied that deaths resulted from overwork and/or malnutrition.

In 1998, Khieu Samphan and Nuon Chea, two leading Khmer Rouge figures, turned themselves in. After Prime Minister Hun Sen indicated they might be tried, a Khmer Rouge spokesperson said that if such trials were held, Khmer Rouge defendants would cast blame on the United States, for its extensive bombing campaign of the early 1970s.[7]

One striking feature of the approach of the appointed defense counsel, as

6. *Le Monde*, June 2, 1979, p. 3.

7. Seth Mydans, "Cambodian Denies He Opposed Trial for Khmer Rouge," *New York Times*, Jan. 2, 1999, p. A1.

I watched the proceedings, was the absence of cross-examination of witnesses who inculpated the accused. The procedures adopted for the trial specifically ensured the right to cross-examine witnesses (see Document 1.07), but the defense lawyers made little use of this right.

As the presiding judge and the prosecutors conducted the trial, each witness was permitted to give a lengthy statement without being interrupted by questions. Most of the witnesses were extremely emotional. Many were in tears early in their testimony. The stories the witnesses told were sufficiently compelling that cross-examination might only have served to reinforce the impact of the witnesses' statements.

Credibility of Witness Statements

Another issue relevant to the fairness of the proceedings is the character of the pretrial witness statements that formed the basis for the trial. One feature of these statements, at least of quite a few, is that they conclude with passages in which the declarant expresses gratitude to the new government that replaced the Khmer Rouge, and affirms loyalty to the new government. In mid-1979, the Khmer Rouge still held substantial territory and showed no prospect of ending its armed opposition. Thus, loyalty to one side or the other was a matter of considerable significance.

While these sentiments on the part of the declarants may well have been genuine, given the horror that reigned in the country under the Khmer Rouge, these passages may create an impression that the declarant was motivated in giving the statement by a desire to distance him- or herself from the Khmer Rouge or to put himself or herself in good standing with the new government. This impression is reinforced by the fact that many of the declarants used the jargon in vogue for the new government, for example, in referring to the prior leadership as "the Pol Pot-Ieng Sary clique," or in referring to the new government's forces as the troops of liberation.

Part of the explanation for this aspect of the witness statements may be that the statements were typically written by a person identified in the document as a secretary, rather than by the declarant personally. Moreover, the same individuals appear as secretary in many different witness statements. It may be that the secretaries used standard phrasing. While the possibility cannot be discounted that particular declarants may have embellished facts to strengthen their denunciations, the content of the statements overall is consistent with what is otherwise known about the Khmer Rouge period.

New Khmer Rouge Trials

Recent years have seen repeated calls that the Khmer Rouge leadership be prosecuted for atrocities that took place during the four years that the Khmer Rouge held power. When Pol Pot surfaced in 1997, U.S. Secretary of

State Madeleine Albright said the United States would press for an international war crimes trial of him.[8] A spokesperson for the U.N. secretary-general reported the view of the U.N. legal counsel that either the U.N. Security Council or the U.N. General Assembly had the power to create a war crimes tribunal for Cambodia, since, under the U.N. Charter, these two bodies are empowered to create subsidiary bodies.[9]

No implementation followed these statements, and in 1998 Pol Pot died. Commenting on his death, U.N. Secretary-General Kofi Annan "regret[ted] that Pol Pot's death rules out the possibility of his trial under international law for crimes against humanity." The Secretary-General said that he "shares the continuing anguish of the Cambodian people who suffered terribly under Pol Pot's rule, as well as their wish that justice ultimately be served on those who share his guilt for one of history's most notorious reigns of terror."[10]

Special Representative of the Secretary-General for Human Rights in Cambodia Thomas Hammarberg said that the death of Pol Pot did not remove the need to assist the Cambodian people in establishing justice for what happened when the Khmer Rouge ruled the country.[11] Hammarberg organized a three-member group of legal experts which, in accordance with a 1997 General Assembly resolution, would "evaluate the existing evidence and propose further measures, as a means of bringing about national reconciliation, strengthening democracy and addressing the issue of individual accountability." The former chief justice of Mauritius, Rajsoomer Lallah, was named leader of the team.

Again in 1998, U.S. Ambassador Nancy Soderberg told the U.N. Security Council that an international tribunal should be created to try Khmer Rouge leaders.[12] Soderberg said that the United States "hopes the council will . . . work constructively on the important issue of establishing a tribunal to bring to justice senior Cambodia Khmer Rouge leaders during the period 1975 through 1979."[13]

In 1999, the U.N. legal team reported back to the secretary-general, and it recommended the creation of an international tribunal. However, the government of Cambodia said that it preferred domestic trials. Proceedings

8. U.N. Law Reports, vol. 31, no. 12, p. 108, August 1, 1997.

9. U.N. Law Reports, vol. 31, no. 12, p. 108, August 1, 1997 (statement of July 15, 1997).

10. U.N. Law Reports, vol. 32, no. 9, p. 109, May 1, 1998, UN Doc. SG/SM/6526.

11. U.N. Law Reports, vol. 32, no. 9, p. 109, May 1, 1998, U.N. Doc. SG/SM/6526 (statement of April 16, 1998).

12. USUN press release #84-(98). U.N. Law Reports, vol. 32, no. 9, p. 109, May 1, 1998 (Security Council 30 April 1998, statement by Amb. Nancy Soderberg, USA., in explanation of U.S. vote on Resolution 1165 to establish a third chamber for the International Criminal Tribunal for Rwanda).

13. U.N. Law Reports, vol. 32, no. 9, p. 109, June 1, 1998, citing U.N. Doc. S/PV.3878, at p. 6 (statement 13 May 1998 during Security Council debate on a resolution to establish a third chamber for the International Criminal Tribunal for Yugoslavia).

were initiated against one Khmer Rouge leader, Ta Mok. The government left open the possibility that other Khmer Rouge leaders might also be tried but appeared to distinguish between those like Ta Mok who had not given themselves up, and others who had done so.

In 1996, King Sihanouk granted amnesty to Ieng Sary, when he defected from the Khmer Rouge with a large number of troops. In granting that amnesty, the king referred to the 1979 verdict and freed Ieng Sary from punishment under it. Later, the government suggested that the amnesty given to Ieng Sary was not unlimited.

At the same time, Prime Minister Hun Sen reflected the view that the 1979 trial served as an adequate judicial response to the Khmer Rouge atrocities. In an interview, Hun Sen said, "You can review all the documents form the trial in 1979. We had international lawyers join the trial in 1979. You cannot do better than that." Hun Sen said that if those who supported the Khmer Rouge in 1979 now thought their leadership to be guilty, "then the 1979 trial is recognised as legal, and the trial of the Khmer Rouge leaders has already been done, legitimising the sentence imposed on them in 1979." As for possible new cases, Hun Sen said, "We cannot hold a trial to try one or two cases without connecting these to the earlier cases. I said this to the UN committee of experts when they came to meet me [in November 1998]."[14]

Significance of the Trial of Pol Pot and Ieng Sary

Beyond its significance for events in Cambodia, the trial of Pol Pot and Ieng Sary was important in several other respects. It was the first trial of a government leader, or of anyone else, under the Genocide Convention. The trial, moreover, was held at a time when the perpetrators of genocide still controlled territory. Thus, the trial might serve to deter future atrocities by the defendants. The Nuremberg and Tokyo trials were held only after the forces represented by the defendants were no longer active.

In this respect, the trial of Pol Pot and Ieng Sary was the precursor of the judicial proceedings that would be instituted in 1993 regarding atrocities in Bosnia. Bosnia sued Yugoslavia in the International Court of Justice to stop atrocities then being committed in Bosnia with, as Bosnia alleged, the assistance of Yugoslavia. Bosnia's suit charged genocide under the Genocide Convention. The suit was filed at a time when Bosnia, deprived of armaments by a U.N. Security Council embargo, was unable adequately to defend segments of its population against genocide. A judicial remedy was sought in order to highlight the atrocities, in the hope that a determination by the court that genocide was occurring might spur the world community to bring it to an end. I was privileged to be advocate and counsel for Bosnia, as

14. Helen Jarvis, "Who Helped the Khmer Rouge to Survive?" *Green Left Weekly*, Feb. 17, 1999.

a member of the legal team that represented it in that proceeding. I can attest to the sense of urgency that surrounded the Bosnia case. The same had been true of the 1979 trial in Phnom Penh. Participants in both proceedings were keenly aware that the attention drawn to the atrocities in court might save lives.

Whether either proceeding achieved that purpose can be a topic for speculation, but what cannot be gainsaid is the historical precedent that was established. Only in 1998 was a statute finally drawn up to establish a permanent International Criminal Court that could bring such proceedings while atrocities occurred. Although the prospects for implementation of that statute are unclear, the very adoption of the statute bespeaks the importance attached by the international community to promoting judicial remedies as one avenue for preventing atrocities. The trial of Pol Pot and Ieng Sary was a step in that direction.

Reflections of a Legal Anthropologist on the Trial of Pol Pot and Ieng Sary

Howard J. De Nike

Anthropologically speaking, Cambodia was long a sort of ethnographic black hole. While directing a legal education program in Phnom Penh from April 1996 through July 1997, I seemed to meet more anthropologists whose Cambodian investigations in the late 1960s and early 1970s had been cut off by hostilities than those who had completed fieldwork then or later. French colonial archaeology and the investigations of May Ebihara were exceptional; and only recently, Judy Ledgerwood and Alex Hinton have entered the ethnographic terrain once again.[1] Accordingly, I readily accepted the opportunity to examine the record of the 1979 proceedings held in Phnom Penh, and the chance presented to apply both my legal and cultural knowledge.

Prior to 1996, my contact with Cambodia was limited to membership in a 1978 delegation of U.S. lawyers to Vietnam. In the province of Tay Ninh we met refugees fleeing Democratic Kampuchea, and heard some of the first personal descriptions given to outsiders of Khmer Rouge killing. But also, from my examination of the post-1990 legal processes accompanying the unification of Germany, I was familiar with the utilization of trial proceedings in the changeover of regimes.[2] With these initial interests and backgrounding, I commenced reading the roughly six hundred pages of the trial record, about which a great many things may be noted legally and anthropologically. For purposes of this essay, I confine myself to two subjects: what can be said about the role of the trial in the installation of the new Cambodian government, and how to evaluate the witness reports of Khmer Rouge consuming the livers of murdered persons.

1. May Ebihara, "A Khmer Village in Cambodia," Ph.D. diss., Columbia University (Ann Arbor, Mich.: University Microfilms, 1968); Judy Ledgerwood, "Changing Conceptions of Gender: Woman, Stories, and the Social Order," Ph.D. diss., Cornell University, 1990; Alexander Laban Hinton, "Cambodia's Shadow: An Examination of the Cultural Origins of Genocide," Ph.D. diss., Emory University, 1997.

2. Howard J. De Nike, *German Unification and the Judges of East Germany: An Anthropology of Law, Nation, and History* (Moenchengladbach, Germany: Godesberg Forum Verlag, 1997).

The Trial

The well-worn shibboleth "show trial" is a negative phrase sometimes used to characterize criminal proceedings in a political context. The outcome is known beforehand; absent are the fundamentals of due process: an impartial magistrate, an opportunity to confront the evidence and defend against the charges, and a verdict based upon the evidence. The phrase has been applied to the trial of Pol Pot and Ieng Sary held in Phnom Penh in 1979.[3] Mentioned in the same breath is the absence of the principals, that is, the two defendants were tried in absentia. The suggestion is the proceedings were held not to attain justice, but to create guilt for "show." By convening what had the appearance of a trial, the public, domestic and international, would be suitably edified.

At times the ascription "show trial" seems to connote a defendant wrongly accused, that a conviction was manufactured despite innocence. The so-called Doctors' Trials in Moscow of the early 1950s or Stalin's trials purging the Old Bolsheviks in the 1930s are examples. If applied to the 1979 trial of Pol Pot and Ieng Sary, however, "show trial" is hardly meant to convey anyone's belief in the innocence of these men. Yet it is not always evident what is intended: perhaps a suggestion that authority to try Pol Pot and Ieng Sary by the government of the People's Republic of Kampuchea was lacking. What may be missing in the multiple uses of the phrase is an appreciation of the manner in which all trials, especially those involving political figures, are inevitably "show trials," conducted in large measure in order to instruct the public.

This blind spot is surprising when we realize authorities from Durkheim to Foucault agree that a chief rationale for any criminal proceeding is its deterrent effect. In simplest terms, others must be shown the effects of transgressing the criminal law's requirements, and be deterred from engaging in like behavior. It goes without saying therefore that a public audience is an essential element in any prosecution expected to have a deterrent effect. Indeed, holding trials in secrecy would frustrate such intended purpose. That the citizenry must be shown how the state regards persons such as Pol Pot and Ieng Sary cannot be distinguished from the ordinary didacticism of any criminal proceeding.

If Stalin's proceedings constitute the prototypically political "show trial," the popular antithesis is the International Military Tribunal conducted at Nuremberg following World War II. Due process was scrupulously followed. Each defendant was ably defended, the evidence was massive to the point of being overwhelming, and the panel of magistrates was composed of well-

3. Kathryn Railsback, "A Genocide Convention Action Against the Khmer Rouge: Preventing a Resurgence of the Killing Fields," *Connecticut Journal of International Law*, 5 (1990): 457, at p. 460 note 15.

regarded jurists who, if they were not absolutely untainted by prior expressions of bias against the defendants, were of such stature they could credibly maintain their ability to judge the matters before them exclusively upon the evidence presented. Although for some of the defendants, for example, Field Marshall Hermann Goering, or anti-Semitic hate-monger Alfred Rosenberg, the outcome—conviction and sentence to hanging—could have been readily predicted, the proceedings produced varied results for other accused, including outright acquittal.

Out of this contrast of "standards of performance" for notorious political trials—the Allies on one hand, Stalin's on the other—the former becomes the gauge with which to measure cases of this nature, at least among Western analysts. What is ultimately at stake, as observed by Richard Posner, is whether it is law that is applied in such a proceeding, and whether, because it calls itself a court, the judgment of the tribunal is law. The first problem for Posner is: by whose authority such a tribunal acts. In the case of the court at Nuremberg the answer stems from its status as a supranational body. In contrast, the proceedings in Phnom Penh in 1979 operated under a national "license"—from a government lacking universal recognition. As Posner hastens to point out, however, law should be seen less as a "set of concepts" and more as an "activity." Referring to Nuremberg, he declares: "We should consider the pragmatic question whether punishing the Nazi leaders using the *forms* of law was a sensible way to proceed" (emphasis in original). Posner concludes it was: "It was unthinkable to let those monsters go free, so the question can be recast as whether they should have been killed summarily or after a trial." For practical reasons, namely, Pol Pot, Ieng Sary, and the other known leaders of the Khmer Rouge remained "at large," the option of summary execution was unavailable. The question, nonetheless, persists: Was a trial of these figures a "sensible way to proceed"? Conceding some "deficiencies" of due process at Nuremberg ("adequate warning of criminal liability, an unbiased tribunal"), Posner nonetheless concludes: "The value of the trial . . . was that it enabled a public record to be compiled . . . as a result their moral guilt was established more convincingly in the eyes of the world than if they had been eliminated hugger-mugger."[4]

Posner adds that an advantage of Nuremberg was that it "gave the defendants a chance to say what they could in their behalf, which for most of them was very little."[5] Since Pol Pot and Ieng Sary were not present in Phnom Penh in 1979, this aspect was lacking—whatever might be said for the arguments advanced on their behalf by designated counsel. On the other hand, as exemplified even by the proceedings held at Nuremberg (as well as in other postwar trials conducted in Western Europe)[6] where a major defen-

4. Richard A. Posner, *The Problems of Jurisprudence* (Cambridge: Harvard University Press, 1990), pp. 228–29.

5. Ibid., p. 229.

6. See Telford Taylor, *Anatomy of the Nuremberg Trials* (New York: Alfred A. Knopf, 1992).

dant, for example, Hitler's adjutant, Martin Boremann, was tried in absentia, lack of personal jurisdiction over a defendant was not considered fatal to going forward to judgment.

Should the People's Republic of Kampuchea have forestalled convocation of a tribunal in anticipation of the moment when a Cambodian state enjoyed greater international acceptance? This is a difficult, if not impossible, question to answer. Surely the rapid initiation of the trial in 1979, no more than nine months after the ouster of the Khmer Rouge, lends credence to the notion that the proceedings were precipitate. Nevertheless, in hindsight, since to this date no other body with ostensible authority has undertaken to prosecute the Khmer Rouge leadership,[7] the international community should perhaps allow itself a measure of gratitude to the Cambodians who in 1979 established the People's Revolutionary Tribunal. As with any activity possessing a temporal factor, that is, where memories grow dim, and where over time the earth consumes the flesh and bones of victims, the earlier an effort is made to gather and preserve evidence, the better one is able later to reconstruct what in fact happened. How well this was accomplished in 1979, the reader can begin to judge from the declarations and accounts presented in this volume.

Whatever conclusion is reached, for instance, concerning the objectivity and scope of the evidence assembled, one should be suitably impressed with certain aspects of the process. Here a reader, especially one unfamiliar with civil law criminal procedure, should bear in mind that it is primarily through affidavits and declarations that courtroom presentation takes place in non-common-law fora. The documents in this book were therefore the chief evidentiary materials before the tribunal and upon which it was called to render its judgment. As Posner notes, the value of a proceeding can rest in its opportunity for establishing a public record. At least preliminarily, one may ask how well this goal was accomplished.

The celerity with which the proceedings were mounted in Cambodia following the dethronement of the Khmer Rouge was hardly uncalculated. It has been remarked that East Germany played a role in the design of the exhibition of torture and execution found at the infamous Khmer Rouge interrogation site preserved at Tuol Sleng.[8] It may well be surmised that guidance was also summoned from the East Bloc in the prosecution of Pol Pot and Ieng Sary.

Following the end of World War II, the two German states vied for primacy

7. Not only has no other body initiated a prosecution of the Khmer Rouge principals, in 1996 Ieng Sary was granted a royal pardon by King Norodom Sihanouk, and at the time of his overthrow in July 1997, First Prime Minister Norodom Ranariddh was negotiating with other Khmer Rouge leaders for additional grants of amnesty.

8. Joshua Eliot, Jane Bickersteth, and John Colet, eds., *Vietnam, Laos, and Cambodia Handbook* (Chicago: Passport Books, 1995), p. 475.

as the authentic antifascist German nation.[9] East Germany chose a radical break with the past and pursued a policy of rigorous prosecution of Nazis. (West Germany, opting for legal continuity, sought to rediscover democratic roots from the Weimar Era and earlier, while simultaneously reintegrating most of the jurists who had willingly served during the Nazi period.)[10] The People's Republic of Kampuchea, like East Germany, embarked upon a project of state-building in 1979, in which it was critical to distinguish the new regime from that of the immediate past, including Democratic Kampuchea's incriminating association with the People's Republic of China.

As was so successfully demonstrated at Nuremberg, a public trial usefully dramatizes the horrifying record of the previous regime. It is perhaps little recognized today that the "newsreels" of the Nazi concentration camps that come so easily to mind, and that are still frequently seen in network file footage, were actually first assembled by the Allied prosecutors as evidence for presentation before the International Military Tribunal.[11] The gaunt faces and emaciated bodies witnessed in latter-day Bosnian prison camps attest to the enduring resonance of such imagery.

In displaying the horrors of massive population dislocation, widespread political purges, virulent (anti-Vietnamese) xenophobia, deliberate starvation, destruction of families, and other crimes against humanity for the world to see (mostly for the first time), but especially for their Cambodian audience, the leadership of the new state hoped to sever ties with the recent past and to launch a government free of the criminal taint laid upon the erstwhile power wielders. Moreover, in utilizing, however falteringly, a language of prosecution and precedents drawn from Nuremberg, the 1948 U.N. Convention on the Prevention and Punishment of the Crime of Genocide, and seminal human rights documents, the new Cambodian government signaled its willingness to do what Democratic Kampuchea fought so stridently, namely, to be embraced among the "community of nations."

It was, accordingly, important for the architects of the case against Pol Pot and Ieng Sary to assemble rapidly the data seen in these pages. The extent to which the goals of thoroughness and clarity of legal articulation were compromised under this imperative is something to be kept in mind. If the form and content are less than perfect, the urgency of the proceedings may help explain the state of the record. Nor should one fail to note the dearth of precedent for this prosecution. One would, perhaps, be venturing too far to permit that the case against the two Khmer Rouge leaders stands as a model for subsequent prosecutions. It cannot, however, be gainsaid that

9. Christian Joppke, "Intellectuals, Nationalism, and the Exit from Communism: The Case of East Germany," *Comparative Studies in Society and History*, 37 (April 1995).

10. Ingo Mueller, *Hitler's Justice: The Courts of the Third Reich*, Deborah Lucas Schneider, trans. (Cambridge: Harvard University Press, 1991).

11. Taylor, *The Anatomy of the Nuremberg Trials*, pp. 186–87.

the 1979 Phnom Penh proceeding was the first of its kind since postwar Germany.

Whatever shortcomings are presented legally, from a cultural-legal perspective, the trial does offer a unique theory, one deserving future scholarly examination. As John Quigley explains above in his introduction, genocide is found in acts intended to destroy a national group in whole or in part. Throughout the testimony placed before the People's Revolutionary Tribunal, one cannot avoid confronting the charge that genocide was attempted by the defendants in their efforts to "destroy the Cambodian people" as they were constituted by culture and tradition. Dith Munty declares, "The Khmer Rouge despised all the traditions, the manners, and customs of our people. They destroyed or made prisons out of the pagodas and temples, and they made the monks abandon their robes" (Document 2.1.1.18). Khem Nary is quite explicit: The Pol Pot-Ieng Sary clique "undertook genocide against the entire Kampuchean people" (Document 2.1.5.05). Over and over, the declarants insist Pol Pot and Ieng Sary's ultimate goal was the very destruction of the Cambodian, that is, their own, people—certainly an ironic proposition, perhaps one unforeseen by the drafters of the 1948 Convention.

In this light, the prosecution takes on added symbolic weight in the effort of the new government's leadership, some of whom were themselves former Khmer Rouge members, to separate the emergent, "authentically Khmer," People's Republic of Kampuchea from the prior regime. It is renegade Pol Pot and Ieng Sary who have bartered Cambodian patrimony for Maoist cultural revolution. Document 2.4.08 sums up this "cultural case":

> The list of crimes committed by the Pol Pot-Ieng Sary clique against Khmer culture is a very long one. This clique carried out an obscurantist policy advocated by Peking in its "great cultural revolution." Their masters taught them how to suppress all human feelings, all human relations. All inhabitants had to become robots who would automatically execute all orders. A Kampuchean had to cease being human: death would befall him immediately if he only tried to become a human being again. The notions of freedom of the human being, of personal rights and liberties were old fashioned in Kampuchea as well as in China because they belonged to the bourgeoisie. They had to be banned if a new society was to be built on an entirely new basis, without any links to Kampuchea's glorious past. This social breakup went together with the breakup in family relations. School "masters" taught children how to spy on their parents to loosen ties with them and even to kill them if they are suspected of rebelling against the policy of Pol Pot and Ieng Sary.
>
> Under such conditions, all culture had to be abolished and was in fact abolished during the Pol Pot-Ieng Sary years. The consequences were numerous. Besides the great loss in artists, men of science, and a considerable loss in material, it should be stressed that the losses in human terms are incalculable. The children and young people who have been seriously intoxicated by Pol Pot-Ieng Sary's cultural revolution must become again Kampucheans with genuine Khmer culture.

Taking a fresh look at these now twenty-year-old documents allows a better assessment of contemporary Cambodian events. The August 1997 one-day jungle "trial" of Pol Pot by his own comrades-in-arms underscored the centrality of the Pol Pot regime to the situation in Cambodia, both domestically and internationally. While his "surfacing" produced renewed calls from various states and human rights organizations for an international tribunal (for the most part taking no heed of the 1979 trial), the trial in 1997 was noteworthy for the absence of charges premised on anything other than an accusation that Pol Pot "betrayed the revolution" with misguided strategies and tactics.[12] Pol Pot may have stumbled along the path leading from Year Zero,[13] but as to genocide, the world remains limited at this writing to the case presented at Phnom Penh in August 1979.

Reflections on Reports of Khmer Rouge Consuming Their Victims' Livers

In as many as ten separate instances, the trial documents describe Khmer Rouge not only killing their victims, but also extracting their livers, often consuming the organ, usually on the spot. These reports provoke such an immediate revulsion in most readers as to warrant special attention. Arens urges caution, warning that anthropological accounts of cannibalism commonly lack academic rigor, leading to the confusion and conflation of the idea or ideology of cannibalism with its actual practice.[14] Of course, the trial documents are not "anthropological accounts." And, attribution of cannibalism is made by Khmers against Khmers, not by Eurocentric outsiders against "exotic" others. Nonetheless, as noted above, witness declarations were prepared in part with a foreign audience in mind, in the context of what was, for the witnesses and evidence-gatherers alike, an exotic proceeding.

One must begin with the references to cannibalism as they appear in the pages of the trial. In only four instances are the reports clearly those of eyewitnesses. In each of the others the account is explicitly secondhand, or vague about its source. Moreover, even in the cases of purported eyewitness testimony, there is often an unsettling lack of confirmatory detail. Only in the testimony of the witness Denise Alfonso, a Cambodian with a Vietnamese mother and a French father, does the reader find palpable descriptive terminology indicating personal observation:

> When I got to the spot, I hid in a thicket from which I could watch the "ceremony" without being seen. But I was so horrified by what I saw that I nearly fainted. The condemned man was tied to a tree, his chest bare and a blindfold over his eyes. Ta Sok, the executioner, using a large knife made a cut in the stomach of the poor man.
>
> In pain, the man screamed like a wild beast. Even today his cries still ring in my ears. Blood rushed out everywhere, his insides were all laid bare, and Ta Sok cut out

12. Nate Thayer, "Brother Number Zero," *Far Eastern Economic Review*, 160, no. 32 (August 7, 1997).

13. François Ponchaud, *Cambodia Year Zero* (London: Allen Lane, 1978).

14. W. Arens, *The Man-Eating Myth* (Oxford: Oxford University Press, 1979).

> the liver and cooked it on a little stove that Ta Chea had just heated up. A strange fact to mention is that the human liver, cooking on the stove, made little jerks like frying pancakes. They divided up the liver among them and ate it hungrily. (Document 2.6.21)

Compare the vivid tangibility of Alfonso's statement with the arid spareness of the account of Nhem Heng, a forty-five-year-old farmer:

> One day, while I was working I saw Khum, 75 years of age, and Rat, about 25 years of age, the two guards of the cooperative's prison, eating human liver. They often caught people trying to escape, tied their feet and hands, and then they cut open their backs to take out the liver. Then they roasted the liver and ate it. They have eaten many human livers this way. That time they said that it was the liver of a man who had fled that morning into the forest, and whom they managed to stop. (Document 2.1.5.10)

Not only is the "sound" and visual imagery that one might expect from such a profoundly disturbing episode absent, there is the possibility, since the witness does not claim to have seen the actual killing nor the extraction of the liver, that Khum and Rat have merely told a tale intended to intimidate Nhem, and thus ease their jobs as prison guards. Even accommodating the untrained character of witnesses and evidence-gatherers, which may account for the discrepant physiology of the liver's location, one must be cautious in accepting such testimony at face value. A jurist would also be constrained to recall that it is these very pitfalls that undermine proceedings conducted in absentia, free of the challenges offered by a fully adversarial process.

Claiming liver consumption in order to terrorize, of course, does not necessarily mean that the practice did not in fact occur. There is no gainsaying open assertions by the Khmer Rouge themselves of eating human livers. We find, for instance, the statement of Yeng Mara, who identifies one of his tormentors as someone "nicknamed Mr. 'One Hundred' because he had eaten 100 human livers" (Document 2.1.5.09). Presumably, the name was either self-ascribed to induce terror, or Mr. One Hundred simply made no secret of his grim predilection. Similarly, Saleh Sen recounts how "a man named Mit bragged to several persons of having killed many people by disemboweling them to get livers or gallbladders" (Document 2.1.5.17). What is troubling about such avowals is that in ordinary legal terminology they ought to be considered "admissions against interest." Because they bring the individuals who make the statements into disrepute, admissions against interest are accepted as trustworthy. In the circumstances described by the witnesses, however, Khmer Rouge stories of liver-eating are characterized as boastful, not shameful, and thus the usual assumption may not apply.

A factor that lends credence to Khmer Rouge cannibalism is its appearance in the accounts of several witnesses together with sexual subject matter. Anthropological literature reveals a common thematic association of man-eating and sexuality, particularly in settings of war and vengeance raids.[15] In the proceedings, Rous Rin, a cement worker from Battambang, describes witnessing the torture of a woman named Khen, accused by the Khmer Rouge of improper sexual relations: "They tied her to a tree and let yellow ants bite her. Then they stuck a stick into her vagina and disemboweled her, taking out her liver" (Document 2.1.5.16). Similarly, the troops of Khmer Rouge leader Vann are reported by Kry Beng Hong to have been "raping the girls and disemboweling them to see their livers" (Document 2.1.1.09). Just as the ritual consumption of human body parts is thought by its practitioners to enable the devourer to acquire the body's vital energy, so also it is believed to communicate the fertility of the victim.

As Lewis observes, cannibalism provides a ground for a double-edged imagery: "The appellation 'cannibal' is not merely an appropriate term of contempt for uncouth subjects at the bottom of the political hierarchy or on the edge of the civilized world. . . . It may be applied equally appropriately by the victims of oppression to designate their superiors. The designation 'cannibal' can thus convey a sense of impotence and desperation."[16] During the reign of the Khmer Rouge, this "sense of impotence" would surely have belonged to those oppressed, and would have been, moreover, a consequence intended by the perpetrators of such pitiless acts.

The body symbolism inherent in these reported episodes, however common or uncommon they were in reality, is unmistakable. Sahlins expresses it most confidently: "Cannibalism is always 'symbolic' even when it is real."[17] What is unclear at this juncture, and thus deserving of future scholarly inquiry, is the degree to which cannibalism in Cambodia between 1975 and 1979, actual and hyperbolic, reflected a dystonic society, one stripped of its usual ordering hierarchies and thereby sent cascading into a vortex of brutality and sexual aggression.

What is perhaps most salient about Khmer Rouge consumption of human livers is its association with episodes of torture. As such, it should be seen within the entire context of violence that accompanied the Khmer Rouge's initial rise and subsequent retention of power. This period embraced not only the widespread executions documented in the trial, but the preceding years of warfare and U.S. aerial bombing, the ravages of disease and hunger, stillbirths and infant deaths, and the traumatic elaboration of social rankings predicated upon Khmer Rouge notions of political reliability, which effectively turned the former society on its head. Instead of a system that respected traditional stratifications of classical learning and public virtue,

15. I. M. Lewis, *Religion in Context: Cults and Charisma* (New York: Cambridge University Press, 1986), p. 75.

16. Ibid., p. 64.

17. M. Sahlins, "Raw Women, Cooked Men and Other 'Great Things' of the Fiji Islands," in *The Ethnography of Cannibalism*, P. Brown and D. Tuzin, eds. (Washington D.C.: Society for Psychological Anthropology, 1983), p. 88.

the new society espoused an ideology denigrating education and the Buddhist priesthood, while simultaneously elevating the peasantry and the increasingly constricted inner circles of the Khmer Rouge leadership.

In another setting noted for torture, among seventeenth-century Iroquois, the ironic quality of the practice is unmistakable. In the face of imminent social collapse upon the arrival of White settlers, the Iroquois engaged in notorious rituals of torture and cannibalism, primarily, according to contemporaneous Jesuit accounts, against the Iroquoian-speaking Hurons. Thus, for every torturer there was a victim whose courage bespoke the power of the nation.[18] In a similar vein, the liver according to Khmer and Chinese medical lore is regarded as a locus and source of personal strength. Hinton, in an article examining the phenomenon of Khmer Rouge liver-eating, suggests that the practice serves both to deprive the victim of vitality and empower the consumer with daring.[19]

Contemplating each of these factors, one is left concerning the Khmer Rouge with the abiding view also reached by Christy Turner II in his investigations on the Anasazi of the American Southwest: the effectiveness of cannibalism as a fulcrum of terror. Building upon the archaeological record, Turner theorizes in *Corn Man* that cannibalism was used by a powerful elite at Chaco Canyon to enforce social control: "What better way to amplify opponents' fear than to reduce victims to the subhuman level of cooked meat, especially when they include infants and children from whom no power or prestige could be derived but whose consumption would surely further terrorize, demean, and insult their helpless parents or community."[20]

Indeed, the ultimate legacy of the 1979 proceedings in Phnom Penh, so diligently and courageously undertaken by its conveners, will be its enduring record of one of history's most ruthless attempts at social transformation, one marked by a will at the top to change Cambodia at whatever cost, communicated through the ranks of the peasantry, and expressed indelibly in seemingly endless brutality.

18. Peggy R. Sanday, *Divine Hunger* (Cambridge: Cambridge University Press, 1986).

19. Alexander Laban Hinton, *Anthropologies of the Khmer Rouge: Genocidal Bricolage*, Working Paper Series (Working Paper GS 06) (New Haven, Conn.: Yale Center for International and Area Studies, 1998), pp. 23–25.

20. Christy Turner II, *Corn Man* (Salt Lake City: University of Utah Press, 1999).

Documents

Documents

Missing documents are not followed by a page number (see Editors' Note).

Part I
Procedural Documents

1.01

Decree Law No. 1: Establishment of People's Revolutionary Tribunal at Phnom Penh to Try the Pol Pot–Ieng Sary Clique for the Crime of Genocide

The People's Revolutionary Council of Kampuchea,

In light of the tasks of the People's Revolutionary Council of Kampuchea as stated in the Declaration of January 8, 1979;

Considering that the Pol Pot–Ieng Sary clique have massacred millions of persons, forced the entire Kampuchean people to live in genocidal conditions, physically and morally, destroyed all economic, cultural, and social structures, thus bringing them the danger of extermination;

Considering that point 8 of the Declaration of December 2, 1978, of the National United Front for the Salvation of Kampuchea expressed the people's wish that "all reactionary ringleaders, who stubbornly oppose the people and owe a heavy blood debt to them, should be sternly punished"; and

Considering that genocide is also defined in international law;

Has taken the following decisions:

Article 1

To set up a People's Revolutionary Tribunal at Phnom Penh to try the acts of genocide committed by the Pol Pot–Ieng Sary clique, namely, planned massacres of groups of innocent people; expulsion of inhabitants of cities and villages in order to concentrate them and force them to do hard labor in conditions leading to their physical and mental destruction; wiping out religion; destroying political, cultural and social structures and family and social relations.

Article 2

1. The instigators and planners of genocidal crimes shall be condemned to 15 to 20 years' imprisonment, life imprisonment or to death.

Persons who committed multiple acts of cruelty and barbarity shall be punished by 5 to 15 years' imprisonment, but in case of particularly mitigating circumstances the sentence may be less than 5 years of imprisonment.

Besides this main form of punishment, the criminals may have their property partially or completely confiscated.

2. The people's power continues to apply the policy of leniency towards those people who participated in the armed forces or administration of the Pol Pot–Ieng Sary clique but are sincerely repentant, and the policy of giving appropriate reward to those who have contributed to the revolution, as stipulated in the Declaration of December 2, 1978, of the National United Front for the Salvation of Kampuchea.

Article 3

The People's Revolutionary Tribunal for the trials consists of a presiding judge and 10 people's assessors. Any of these members, when absent, shall be replaced by an alternate member.

The presiding judge and the alternate judge of the People's Revolutionary Tribunal are appointed by the People's Revolutionary Council of Kampuchea.

The people's assessors of the People's Revolutionary Tribunal and four alternate people's assessors are appointed by the People's Revolutionary Council of Kampuchea on the basis of a list of people's assessors proposed by the Central Committee of the National United Front for the Salvation of Kampuchea.

In the trials, the people's assessors have powers equal to those of the presiding judge, and any decision of the People's Revolutionary Tribunal is to be made by a majority.

Article 4

The Prosecutor of the People's Revolutionary Tribunal is appointed by the People's Revolutionary Council of Kampuchea.

It is the duty of the prosecutor to gather and verify evidence, institute prosecution in court, draw up the indictment and present the state's case in court.

Article 5

The indictment and the decision to put a person on trial should be sent to him at least seven days before the date scheduled for trial.

The defendant is entitled to represent himself or to be represented by a lawyer or by a Kampuchean citizen. If necessary, the presiding judge of the People's Revolutionary Tribunal may appoint an advocate for the accused.

The choice of a lawyer of foreign nationality, or of a defender who is not a lawyer, must be approved by the presiding judge of the People's Revolutionary Tribunal.

Article 6

If a defendant has fled, the People's Revolutionary Tribunal may try him in absentia and appoint a lawyer for his defense.

The summons to appear in court and the judgment pronounced in absentia shall be published by appropriate means.

Article 7

The People's Revolutionary Tribunal acts as a court of last resort. A person sentenced to death has the right to ask for mercy from the People's Revolutionary Council of Kampuchea within 7 days from the date the sentence is pronounced.

If the defendant is convicted in absentia, that time limit is calculated from the day when the text of the sentence is posted at the office of the Municipal People's Committee in Phnom Penh.

Article 8

In accordance with the Convention on the Prevention and Punishment of the Crime of Genocide adopted by the U.N. General Assembly on December 9, 1948, this decree applies to the criminal acts of the Pol Pot–Ieng Sary clique committed prior to its signing.

Phnom Penh, July 15, 1979
Heng Samrin, President
People's Revolutionary Council of Kampuchea

1.01bis
Press Conference of Keo Chanda, Minister of Information, Press, and Culture, Chair of Legal Affairs Committee, July 28, 1979

Dear comrades and dear friends, on July 15 of this year, the Chairman of the People's Revolutionary Council of Kampuchea signed a Decree Law to establish a People's Revolutionary Tribunal at Phnom Penh to try the Pol Pot–Ieng Sary clique for the crime of genocide.

The People's Revolutionary Council of Kampuchea also appointed the members of the tribunal and the members of the prosecution. Here, dear comrades and friends, you are receiving copies of the Decree Law that I have the honor to give you at this press conference.

As you know, after the National United Front for the Salvation of Kampuchea was set up, it denounced, in its statement of December 2, 1978, the crime of genocide committed by the Pol Pot–Ieng Sary clique. The peoples of the whole world have also condemned that crime. However, it was only after the fall of the Pol Pot–Ieng Sary clique that power passed into the hands of the people. At that time we were able to gain better knowledge of these crimes, specifically, that more than three million innocent people were savagely killed, and many communal graves were discovered all over, in fields, in forests, and in urban locations, even in pagodas and schools.

Everywhere, the entire population was persecuted, subjected to such forces that its overall health suffered and it became susceptible to all sorts of diseases. Freedom of thought was totally absent. The people had no right to discuss anything, the people were only to follow and carry out meekly the orders issued by the Pol Pot–Ieng Sary clique. The clergy and believers were persecuted, and pagodas were turned into fertilizer warehouses or simply destroyed.

The intellectuals were almost completely wiped out.

It is clear that the Pol Pot–Ieng Sary clique committed the crime of genocide not only against a particular ethnic group or against a particular social stratum of the population, but against the Kampuchean people as a whole. In its flight, the Pol Pot–Ieng Sary clique is still killing tens of thousands of innocent people. Right now, thanks to the support given it by the Peking expansionists, the Pol Pot–Ieng Sary clique is continuing its policy of treason and devastation against the Kampuchean people.

It is obvious that the damage caused by the Pol Pot–Ieng Sary clique is incalculable. It will take several dozen years for the Kampuchean people to recover.

To respond to the wishes expressed by the people that the criminals must answer for their crimes, the National United Front for the Salvation of Kampuchea, in its statement of December 2, 1978, adopted the following policy: to punish severely the reactionary, recalcitrant leaders, who must pay their many blood debts to the people. Pol Pot and Ieng Sary were the leaders and committed many criminal acts. Therefore, they must be tried. As for those who served in the repressive machinery of the Pol Pot–Ieng Sary clique, they too will be tried if the two savage leaders are convicted of committing many criminal acts, and they too will have to pay many blood debts to the people. However, we will judge them less severely than their leaders, to give them a chance to reform.

At the same time, as indicated as well in the Decree Law, the people's power continues its policy of leniency towards all those who are sincerely repentant and gives appropriate rewards to those who have contributed to the revolution. This is why the trial of the Pol Pot–Ieng Sary clique as contemplated in the Decree Law is not an act of vengeance against all those who served in the armed forces or in the administration of Pol Pot and Ieng Sary.

The trial for the crime of genocide of the Pol Pot–Ieng Sary clique falls within the prerogatives of the people and of the people's state of Kampuchea, as an independent and sovereign state. This is in keeping with the domestic penal law of all states. It is at the same time an application of international law, because the peoples of the whole world have long considered the crime of genocide to be a crime against humanity, whose prevention and punishment have been approved by the United Nations in the convention of December 9, 1948.

Trying the Pol Pot–Ieng Sary clique for the crime of genocide will on the one hand expose all the criminal acts that they have committed and mobilize the Kampuchean people more actively to defend and build up the people's power, and on the other hand show the peoples of the whole world the true face of the criminals who are posing as the representatives of the people of Kampuchea.

The Pol Pot–Ieng Sary clique has committed the crime of genocide against our whole people. That is why representatives of all strata of the Kampuchean people will sit in judgment of their crimes. The list of people's assessors was presented by the Central Committee of the National United Front for the Salvation of Kampuchea to the People's Revolutionary Council, which then appointed them.

The investigation and the collection of evidence have begun. During the time of this process, we hope that various mass organizations will send their denunciations or furnish information about the crimes of the Pol Pot–Ieng Sary clique to the various people's committees, or directly to members of the prosecution or the People's Revolutionary Tribunal. To ensure that the tribunal's judgment is fair, the People's Revolutionary tribunal will apply fundamental norms on criminal procedure, in particular as regards the right of the accused to a defense. The accused have the right to defend themselves in person, or to defend through a lawyer, or through some other person of Kampuchean nationality. If the trial turns out to be difficult to conduct, or if the accused are tried in their absence, the People's Revolutionary Tribunal can appoint lawyers to defend them.

I have completed my statement. Comrades and friends, we hope that as journalists responsible for defending truth and justice you will let the people of Kampuchea and of the whole world know the complete truth about the crime of genocide committed by the Pol Pot–Ieng Sary clique, and that, by your action, you will lend your support to the revolutionary cause of the people of Kampuchea.

If you have questions to ask, I am ready to answer.

1.02
Decree Law No. 4: Appointment of Presiding Judge and Alternate

The President of the People's Revolutionary Council of Kampuchea,

In light of the tasks of the People's Revolutionary Council of Kampuchea as set forth in its statement of January 8, 1979;

In light of Decree Law No. 1 of July 15, 1979, to establish a People's Revolutionary tribunal at Phnom Penh to try the Pol Pot–Ieng Sary clique for the crime of genocide;

After consultation with the People's Revolutionary Council of Kampuchea;

decrees:

Article 1: In implementation of Article 3 of Decree Law No. 1 of July 15, 1979, the following comrades are appointed presiding judge and alternate presiding judge of the People's Revolutionary Tribunal at Phnom Penh to try the Pol Pot–Ieng Sary clique for the crime of genocide:

(1) Keo Chanda, Presiding Judge of the People's Revolutionary Tribunal;

(2) Chim Chandara, Alternate Presiding Judge of the People's Revolutionary Tribunal.

Article 2: Comrades Keo Chanda and Chim Chandara are responsible for implementing this Decree.

Phnom Penh, July 20, 1979
Heng Samrin, President
People's Revolutionary Council of Kampuchea

1.03

Decree Law No. 25: Appointment of Members of the Tribunal

The President of the People's Revolutionary Council of Kampuchea,

In light of the tasks of the People's Revolutionary Council of Kampuchea as set forth in its statement of January 8, 1979;

In light of Decree Law No. 1 of July 15, 1979, to establish a People's Revolutionary Tribunal at Phnom Penh to try the Pol Pot–Ieng Sary clique for the crime of genocide;

On the basis of the list of people's assessors presented by the Central Committee of the National United Front for the Salvation of Kampuchea;

After consultation with the People's Revolutionary Council of Kampuchea;

decrees:

Article 1: In implementation of Article 3 of Decree Law No. 1 of July 15, 1979, the following comrades are appointed people's assessors and alternate people's assessors of the People's Revolutionary Tribunal at Phnom Penh to try the Pol Pot–Ieng Sary clique for the crime of genocide:

People's Assessors:

1. Mr. Chhuor Leang Huot, Bachelor of Law
2. Mr. Pen Navuth, former head of the Adult Education Section, Ministry of Education and Training
3. Mrs. Chea Samy, former teacher of traditional dance
4. Mr. Meas Savatha, Acting Battalion Chief, First Brigade
5. Mr. Nouth Savoeun, Doctor of Pediatrics
6. Mr. Nouth Thon, Secretary, Central Committee, Kampuchean Youth Organization

7. Miss Chhouk Chhim, Vice-President, Association of Kampuchean Women
8. Mr. Kim Kun, worker at the power plant of Phnom Penh
9. Mr. Kim Kaneth, worker at the power plant of Phnom Penh
10. Mrs. Lek Sarat, Official in the Department of Propaganda and Education of the Central Committee

Alternate People's Assessors:

1. Mr. Yuon Mala, Official of the Department of Propaganda and Education of the Central Committee
2. Mr. Kol Touch, Engineer, Tire Plant
3. Mr. Aun Sam Ol, Doctor in Pharmacology
4. Mr. Moeun Say, accountant at the power plant of Phnom Penh

Article 2: The agencies in which the above-named comrades presently work are charged with implementing this Decree.

Phnom Penh, July 20, 1979
Heng Samrin, President
People's Revolutionary Council of Kampuchea

1.04

Decision No. 2: Prosecutor of the People's Revolutionary Tribunal at Phnom Penh, Decision to Open an Investigation

The Prosecutor of the People's Revolutionary Tribunal at Phnom Penh,

In light of Decree Law No. 1 of July 15, 1979, to establish a Revolutionary Tribunal in the city of Phnom Penh to try the Pol Pot–Ieng Sary clique for the crime of genocide;

In light of Article 4 of that Decree Law, referring to the tasks of the Prosecutor;

Considering that Pol Pot and Ieng Sary are the leaders of the former state administration that led the people of Kampuchea into the danger of genocide;

decides:

1. An investigation into the crime of genocide is hereby opened against the following two suspects:

- Pol Pot, alias Saloth Sar, born in 1925, former prime minister of the former government of Kampuchea that was overthrown by the people, husband of Khieu Ponnary,
- Ieng Sary, born in 1925, former deputy prime minister in charge of

foreign affairs in the former government of Kampuchea that was overthrown by the people, husband of Khieu Thirith.

2. Since Pol Pot and Ieng Sary are presently in hiding, this Decision shall be posted at the office of the People's Revolutionary Committee of the city of Phnom Penh and shall be broadcast by National Radio of Kampuchea to bring it to their notice.

Mat Ly, Prosecutor
Phnom Penh, July 25, 1979

1.06
Decision No. 3: Prosecutor of the People's Revolutionary Tribunal at Phnom Penh, Arrest Warrant

In light of Decree Law No. 1 of July 15, 1979, to establish a People's Revolutionary Tribunal in the city of Phnom Penh to try the clique of Pol Pot and Ieng Sary for the crime of genocide, the Prosecutor, by his Decision No. 2 of July 25, 1979, decided to open an investigation against Pol Pot and Ieng Sary for the crime of genocide that was defined in Articles 1 and 2 of the said Decree Law;

The two suspects:

1. Pol Pot, alias Saloth Sar, born in 1925 in the village of Prek Lean, former prime minister of the former government of Kampuchea that was overthrown by the people, husband of Khieu Ponnary;

2. Ieng Sary, born in 1925 in Hoa Lac village, Nhan Hoa subdistrict, Chau Thanh district, former province of Tra Vinh, presently the province of Cuu Long (Vietnam), former deputy prime minister in charge of foreign affairs in the former government of Kampuchea that was overthrown by the people, husband of Khieu Thirith;

are presently in hiding.

As a result, the Prosecutor of the People's Revolutionary Tribunal at Phnom Penh orders the two suspects to turn themselves in to the authorities, and orders all police agencies to search for them and arrest them.

Any citizen shall have the right to arrest Pol Pot or Ieng Sary and to bring them to the nearest security agencies or people's power agencies. Anyone who arrests them shall be rewarded in an adequate amount. Anyone who conceals them must bear responsibility under the law.

This search order shall be posted at the office of the People's Revolutionary Committee of the city of Phnom Penh and broadcast by the National Radio of Kampuchea.

Phnom Penh, July 26, 1979
Mat Ly
Prosecutor of the People's Revolutionary Tribunal at Phnom Penh

1.07

Presiding Judge, Decision on Trial Procedure at the Session on the Crime of Genocide of the Pol Pot–Ieng Sary Clique

The presiding judge of the People's Revolutionary Tribunal at Phnom Penh,

Acting under Decree Law No. 1 of July 15, 1979, of the Revolutionary People's Council of Kampuchea on the establishment of the People's Revolutionary Tribunal to try the Pol Pot–Ieng Sary clique for the crime of genocide,

Deems it necessary to determine the legal procedure of the People's Revolutionary Tribunal in order to ensure the correctness of its judgment,

Decides the following:

I. Composition of the People's Revolutionary Tribunal

1. The People's Revolutionary Tribunal is composed of a presiding judge and 10 people's assessors.

In case a people's assessor is absent or is attending the session but cannot carry on his (or her) tasks, the presiding judge of the People's Revolutionary Tribunal shall replace him (or her) with an alternate people's assessor.

2. The alternate people's assessors must be present at the session and follow the prosecution so that they can replace official people's assessors, if need be.

The People's Revolutionary Tribunal in any event continues the prosecution in case of the replacement of people assessor(s).

3. The prosecutor, the accused, and the counsel have no right to ask for a change in the composition of the People's Revolutionary Tribunal.

II. The Right of Defense of the Accused

1. The accused has the right to represent himself or to ask a lawyer or a Kampuchean citizen to represent him. In case the accused uses someone to plead his case, he must inform the People's Revolutionary Tribunal of that person's name and domicile at least three days before the opening of the trial.

If the accused is absent, the Tribunal may appoint someone to represent the accused.

2. At least seven days before the session, the accused and his representative must be given a copy, by hand delivery, of the indictment and of the decision to put the person on trial.

If the said delivery cannot be effected because the accused is hiding, then seven days before the opening of the trial, the presiding judge of the People's Revolutionary Tribunal will post the subpoena at the office of the

Phnom Penh city People's Committee or, if deemed necessary, broadcast it on the radio.

3. The accused and his representative have the right to:

(a) advance exonerating evidence,
(b) pose questions to the victims and witnesses in court,
(c) present a defense.

4. The representative is entitled to study the file of the case and to see the accused in detention.

III. The Participation of Representatives of Mass Organizations in the Session

1. In the course of the proceedings, all citizens and citizen organizations may send denunciations of the Pol Pot–Ieng Sary clique's genocidal acts to the prosecutor or the People's Revolutionary Tribunal.

2. Representatives of Kampuchean citizen organizations may be invited to attend the session to produce evidence on the Pol Pot–Ieng Sary clique's genocidal acts and express the people's will regarding the punishment to be inflicted on them.

The presiding judge of the People's Revolutionary Tribunal may also decide to authorize representatives of foreign social organizations or foreign social activists to attend the session to express their views on the Pol Pot–Ieng Sary clique's crime of genocide.

IV. Interpreters

Foreign participants may use French or English at the session. Interpreters are to be appointed by the presiding judge of the People's Revolutionary Tribunal.

V. Evidence

1. Following are the different kinds of evidence which can be produced:

(a) statements, orders, minutes of meetings, reports, notebooks of the Pol Pot–Ieng Sary clique,
(b) statements of those who carried out their lines and policies,
(c) testimony of the victims or of members of their families,
(d) reports of administrative agencies, local authorities and citizen organizations on genocidal acts perpetrated by the Pol Pot–Ieng Sary clique,

(e) records of inspection of crime scenes,
(f) motion and still pictures, and documents in publications at home and abroad on the crimes of the Pol Pot–Ieng Sary clique.

2. The People's Revolutionary Tribunal has the full right to decide on the validity of the evidence produced and may omit to demand further confirmation of events known to the entire people, of reports of administrative agencies, local authorities and citizen organizations, and of documents seized from the Pol Pot–Ieng Sary clique.

VI. Discipline at the Session

1. All the participants must respect the People's Revolutionary Tribunal's strict order and comply with the injunctions of the presiding judge.

2. The accused, in case of violation of discipline of the session, may be expelled by the presiding judge from the courtroom for a time or for the whole remaining time of the session.

In the latter case, the People's Revolutionary Tribunal shall continue prosecuting, and the judgment will be considered to be passed in the presence of the accused.

VII. Prosecuting Procedure at the Session

1. All the cases are tried in public.

2. The presiding judge of the People's Revolutionary Tribunal presides over the session.

On behalf of the members of the Tribunal, the presiding judge decides the order and course of examination and settles questions of legal procedure arising at the session.

3. During examination by the presiding judge, the people's assessors may ask additional questions.

The prosecutor and the representative of the accused are also entitled to examine and cross-examine.

The accused may also request the presiding judge to ask the victims and witnesses necessary questions.

4. The order of prosecution of the session is the following:

(a) The clerk reads the indictment of the prosecutor, who can then give further necessary explanations.
(b) The People's Revolutionary Tribunal begins prosecution and, if needed, may go to the sites of crimes to examine evidence.
(c) The prosecutor makes his final statement.
(d) The victims and their counsel present their complaints.

(e) The accused and their representatives present their final statements.
(f) The accused give their final statement.
(g) The People's Revolutionary Tribunal deliberates and passes judgment.

5. If the defendants are absent, the People's Revolutionary Tribunal reads any depositions they may have made to the investigator, or, if no depositions have been obtained, the Tribunal examines necessary evidence to try the case all the same.

6. A judgment passed in the absence of the defendants shall be posted at the office of the Phnom Penh city People's Committee and, if deemed necessary, broadcast on the radio.

VIII. Proceedings of the Session

Every development of the session must be recorded by the clerk of the proceedings.

The proceedings must bear the signatures of the presiding judge of the People's Revolutionary Tribunal and the clerk of the court.

IX. Execution of the Judgment

In general the judgments passed by the People's Revolutionary Tribunal are to be executed without delay. In case of the death penalty, if the condemned asks for no mitigation, the judgments will be executed after the time limit for requesting mitigation. If the condemned asks for a remission, the judgments will be executed only after the Revolutionary People's Council of Kampuchea decides on the matter.

Phnom Penh, August 4, 1979
Keo Chanda, Presiding Judge
People's Revolutionary Tribunal

1.08

Composition of the People's Revolutionary Tribunal at Phnom Penh to Try the Pol Pot–Ieng Sary Clique for the Crime of Genocide, Instituted by Decree Law No. 1 of July 15, 1979, of the People's Revolutionary Council of Kampuchea

The composition of the People's Revolutionary Tribunal at Phnom Penh to try the Pol Pot–Ieng Sary clique for the crime of genocide, instituted by the Decree Law No. 1 of July 15, 1979, of the People's Revolutionary Council of Kampuchea,

I. Presidency

1. Mr. Keo Chanda, Minister of Information, Press and Culture, Presiding Judge
2. Mr. Chim Chandara, Alternate

II. People's Jury

A. People's assessors

1. Mr. Chhuor Leang Huot, Ex-Judge, Bachelor of Law
2. Mr. Pen Navuth, Head of the Adult Education Section, Ministry of Education and Training
3. Mrs. Chea Samy, teacher of traditional dance
4. Mr. Meas Savatha, Acting Battalion Chief, First Brigade
5. Mr. Nouth Savoeun, Doctor of Pediatrics
6. Mr. Nouth Thon, Secretary, Central Committee, Kampuchean Youth Organization
7. Miss Chhouk Chhim, Vice-President, Association of Kampuchean Women
8. Mr. Kim Kun, worker at the power plant of Phnom Penh
9. Mr. Kim Kaneth, worker at the power plant of Phnom Penh
10. Mrs. Lek Sarat, Official in the Department of Propaganda and Education of the Central Committee

B. Alternate people's assessors

1. Mr. Yuon Mala, Official of the Department of Propaganda and Education of the Central Committee
2. Mr. Kol Touch, Engineer, Tire Plant
3. Mr. Aun Sam Ol, Doctor in Pharmacology
4. Mr. Moeun Say, accountant at the power plant of Phnom Penh

III. Secretary

1. Mr. Hul Sam Ol
2. Mr. Ouk Chandara

IV. Public Ministry

1. Mr. Mat Ly, Chief Prosecutor
2. Mr. Lim Nay, Assistant Prosecutor

V. Appointed Defense Lawyers

1. Mr. Dith Munty, former judge, LL.B.
2. Mr. Yuos Por

1.09
Decision No. 61: Prosecutor of the People's Revolutionary Tribunal at Phnom Penh, Request for Reports

To the Minister of the Interior, the Minister of Information, Press, and Culture, the Minister of Education, the Minister of Health and Social Issues, the Minister of the Economy and Welfare; To the Central Committee of the National United Front for the Salvation of Kampuchea; To the People's Committee of the city of Phnom Penh.

In implementation of Decree Law No. 1 of July 15, 1979 to establish a People's Revolutionary Tribunal at Phnom Penh to try the Pol Pot–Ieng Sary clique for the crime of genocide, the prosecutor is collecting evidence pertaining to the crimes of that group.

As a result, we ask you to furnish us and to turn over to us the following documents:

- Ministry of the Interior: the statements of victims and witnesses, and records of visits to locations where common graves have been found, which documents have been prepared by agencies of your ministry.
- Ministry of Information, Press, and Culture: document summarizing the crimes of the Pol Pot–Ieng Sary clique in relation to the destruction of culture.
- Ministry of Health and Social Issues: documents summarizing their crimes against public health and in respect of social issues.
- Ministry of Economy and Welfare: document summarizing their crimes in relation to the destruction of the economy.
- Ministry of Education: document summarizing their crimes in relation to the destruction of education.
- Central Committee of the National United Front for the Salvation of Kampuchea: documents summarizing their crimes in relation to the destruction of religion and nationality groups.
- People's Committee of the city of Phnom Penh: document summarizing their crimes in relation to the expulsion of the inhabitants of the city.

We hope that these documents can be sent to us immediately.

Mat Ly
Prosecutor of the People's Revolutionary Tribunal at Phnom Penh
July 25, 1979

1.10
Order No. 1: Presiding Judge, Order to Hold a Trial

The Presiding Judge of the People's Revolutionary Tribunal at Phnom Penh,

After examining the case file of the matter concerning the accused Pol Pot and Ieng Sary,

Considering:

That by Decision No. 2 of July 25, 1979, the Prosecutor of the People's Revolutionary Tribunal, acting under Article 4 of the Decree of July 15, 1979 of the Revolutionary People's Council establishing a People's Revolutionary Tribunal, has investigated Pol Pot and Ieng Sary for genocide, a crime defined and punished by Articles 1 and 2 of the said Decree,

That an examination of the items in the case file shows that the matter is at a stage appropriate for being referred to a public session for judgment,

Orders:

That the accused:

(1) Pol Pot, alias Saloth Sar, born in 1925 in the village of Prek Lean, former prime minister of the former government of Kampuchea who has been overthrown by the people, husband of Khieu Ponnary, and who is now at large;

(2) Ieng Sary, born in 1925 in Hoa Lac village, Nhan Hoa subdistrict, Chau Thanh district, former province of Tra Vinh, presently the province of Cuu Long (Vietnam), former deputy prime minister for foreign affairs of the former government of Kampuchea, husband of Khieu Thirith, and who is now at large;

are referred to a public session of the People's Revolutionary Tribunal, to be held at Phnom Penh August 15, 1979, at 8:00 a.m., to be tried for genocide, a crime defined and punished by Articles 1 and 2 of the Decree No. 1 of July 15, 1979, of the Revolutionary People's Council of Kampuchea.

Mr. Yuos Por and Mr. Dith Munty are appointed by the Tribunal to present a defense for the two accused.

Attached are:

- A list of witnesses, and of experts called to the session.
- An inventory of items of material evidence to be presented at the session.

Done at Phnom Penh, August 5, 1979
Presiding Judge
People's Revolutionary Tribunal

1.11
Decision No. 25: Presiding Judge, Appointment of Defense Lawyers

The Presiding Judge of the People's Revolutionary Tribunal at Phnom Penh,

In light of the proceedings being taken against Pol Pot and Ieng Sary, who are accused of the crime of genocide as defined and punished by Articles 1 and 2 of Decree Law No. 1 of July 15, 1979, of the People's Revolutionary Council of Kampuchea;

On the basis of Articles 5 and 6 of the said Decree Law concerning the right of the accused to a defense;

appoints

1. Mr. Dith Munty
2. Mr. Yuos Por

as defense lawyers for Pol Pot and Ieng Sary.

As soon as notification is made of this appointment, these lawyers shall have the right to examine the case file.

Phnom Penh, August 6, 1979
Presiding Judge
People's Revolutionary Tribunal at Phnom Penh

1.11a
List of Invitees[1]

1. Francisco Varona Duque de Estrada, Vice-President of the Supreme Court of the Republic of Cuba
2. Jitendra Sharma, Secretary-General of the Association of Democratic Lawyers of India
3. Omar Bentoumi, Algerian lawyer
4. Mohammed Hikmet Turkmanee, Syrian lawyer
5. Susumi Ozaki, President of the Committee for Japan-Kampuchea Solidarity
6. Tarakusagi, American lawyer[2]
7. John Bernard Quigley, American lawyer
8. Valentin Vasilievich Shubin, Vice-President of the Supreme Court of the Russian Soviet Federated Socialist Republic
9. Vladimir Kuznetsov, Secretary-General, Association of Lawyers of the USSR
10. Bhagat Vats, member of the World Peace Council
11. Hope R. Stevens, American lawyer
12. Facine Bangoura, Secretary-General of the Afro-Asian People's Solidarity Organization
13. Miss Eva Rannaer, Secretary of the Organization for Solidarity of Afro-Asian Countries

1. Not all invitees actually attended the trial. For example, John Pilger (no. 17 under correspondents and journalists) and a film and sound crew accompanying him in Kampuchea (nos. 18–21 in that list) did not attend. — Eds.

2. Tarakusagi was Japanese, not American. — Eds.

14. Tap Kim Rao, Organization of the Asiatic Church
15. Tuniwa, Organization of the Asiatic Church
16. Robert Longid, Organization of the Asiatic Church
17. Val Lelyveld, Organization of the Asiatic Church
18. Gabriel Luis Calaforra Sales, Delegate of the Organization for Solidarity of the Countries of Asia, Africa, and Latin America
19. Colette Pham Ngoc Thach
20. Laotian delegate: Oulom Souvannavong, lawyer
21. Laotian delegate: Heuang Chantho, lawyer
22. Phan Anh, President of the Vietnam Lawyers Association
23. Mrs. Ngo Ba Thanh, Vietnam Lawyers Association
24. Hoang Nguyen, Vietnam Lawyers Association

Correspondents and journalists:

1. Andrei Mineev, TASS
2. L. Erishevski, Moscow Radio-Television
3. E. Boikovskii, Soviet correspondent
4. Ganash Shukla, Delegate of the Journal *New Wave*
5. Kitahara Toshifumi, Correspondent of Akihata
6. Kazuo Yoshinaga, Nihon Denpa News
7. Alain Ruscio, Humanité
8. Francis Cremieux, Journal *France Culture*
9. Jean Pierre Gallois, Agence France Presse
10. Miss Letecia Singer, Journal *Siempre*, Mexico
11. Bohumil Lodja, Czech News Agency CTK, Czechoslovakia
12. Jerzy Chocizowski, Polish correspondent
13. Wilfred Burchett, Magazine *Afrique-Asie*
14. Souami Hachemi, Algerian correspondent
15. Charan Yobanyonka, Thailand correspondent of Federal Republic of Germany
16. Alexander Goeb, German correspondent (Federal Republic of Germany)
17. John Pilger, English correspondent
18. Eric Piper, English correspondent
19. Gerald Pinches, English correspondent
20. Philips Stephens, English correspondent
21. David Munro, English correspondent
22. Klaus-Dieter Pflaum, Hanoi, News Agency ADN (German Democratic Republic)
23. Hutz Herden, German TV (German Democratic Republic)
24. Helmut Kessmer, German correspondent (German Democratic Republic)
25. Luu Quy Ky, Secretary-General of the Vietnam Journalists Association

26. Bui Tinh, Vietnamese correspondent
27. Tran Thanh Xuan, Vietnam Radio and Television
28. Khamsi Chanthvi, Lao journalist
29. Professor Henri Van Regemorter

1.11b List of Foreign Lawyers

1. Algeria: Omar Bentoumi (Algeria), Attorney in the Supreme Court of Algeria, Former Minister of Justice. Secretary of the International Association of Democratic Lawyers. Observer representing the International Association of Democratic Lawyers.

2. Cuba: Francisco Varona Duque de Estrada (Havana), Deputy Presiding Judge of the Supreme People's Court of Cuba, Professor of Criminal Law, University of Havana. Representing the Lawyers Association of Cuba. Oral presentation to the court in Spanish.

3. India: Vitendra Sharma (New Delhi), Attorney in the Supreme Court of India, Secretary of the Association of Indian Lawyers. Observer, written statements sent to the court.

4. Japan: Susumi Ozaki (Tokyo), Attorney. Oral presentation to the court in Japanese.

5. Laos: Oulom Souvannavong (Vientiane), Graduate in Law. Director of the Complaint Section of the Ministry of Justice; Heuang Chantho, official of the Ministry of Foreign Affairs. Observers.

6. Syria: Mohammed Hikmet Turkmanee (Damascus), Attorney. Attorney for the civil plaintiffs, speaking in Arabic.

7. USSR: Valentin Vasilievich Shubin, Council member of the Association of Soviet Lawyers, Deputy Presiding Judge of the Supreme Court of the Russian Soviet Federated Socialist Republic; Vladmir Kuznetsov, Secretary-General, Association of Lawyers of the USSR Observers.

8. USA: Hope R. Stevens, LL.B., LL.M. O.B.E. (New York), Attorney, Member of the Bar of the Supreme Court of the United States. Co-President, National Conference of Black Lawyers of the United States and Canada, defense of the accused, speaking English; John Quigley (Ohio), Professor of Law at the Ohio State University (international law and criminal law). Oral presentation to the court in English.

9. Vietnam: Phan Anh (Hanoi), President of the Vietnam Lawyers Association; Madame Ngo Ba Thanh (Ho Chi Minh City), Doctor in Law, Member

of the Vietnam Lawyers Association; Hoang Nguyen (Hanoi), Bachelor in Law, Member of the Vietnam Lawyers Association. Observers.

10. International Association of Democratic Lawyers (IADL): Omar Bentoumi, Attorney in the Supreme Court of Algeria, Former Minister of Justice, Secretary of the International Association of Democratic Lawyers. Observer.

1.13
Names of Witnesses Who Are to Testify at the People's Revolutionary Tribunal at Phnom Penh

No. Name	*Province or Ministry*	*Remarks*
1. Nuon Thok	Siem Reap province	
2. Chum Rithy	ditto	
3. Sim Phia	ditto	
4. Mach Sarin	ditto	
5. Sok Ros	ditto	
6. Aun Chua	ditto	
7. Kung Sary	ditto	
8. Mun Ny	ditto	
9. Khang Chiem	ditto	
10. Leung Lada	ditto	
11. Tik How	ditto	
12. Tim Moeun	ditto	
13. Mok Moeun	ditto	
14. Min Ban	Kompong Cham province	
15. Sieu Sien	ditto	
16. Long Lai	ditto	
17. Touch Sakun	ditto	
18. Pham Van Ngoc	ditto	
19. Pham Thy Nga	ditto	
20. Ming Noi	ditto	
21. Nhim Sokha	Kompong Speu province	
22. Sa Vin	ditto	
23. Bui Bun	ditto	
24. Cao Lui	ditto	
25. Khieu Kola	ditto	
26. Denise Alfonso	ditto	
27. Tep Vung	ditto	
28. Chum Sary	ditto	
29. Abdul Koyum	ditto	

30. Sit Sakarya	Sang Khat	(7th ward, Phnom Penh)
31. Chhay Ny	ditto	
32. Nhek Houn	ditto	
33. Vang Pheap	ditto	
34. Men Khoeun	ditto	
35. Siv Samon	ditto	
36. Sao Soeun	ditto	
37. Khem Maly Chan	ditto	
38. Khem Nary	ditto	
39. Bun Chantini	ditto	
40. Rous Rin	ditto	
41. Chan Sary	ditto	
42. Ay Nasoeun	ditto	
43. Sok Chhoy	ditto	
44. Nhem Heng	ditto	
45. Sok Li Mut	ditto	
46. My Sambath	ditto	
47. Yeng Tinh	ditto	
48. Eum Ra	ditto	
49. Thaong Chin	ditto	
50. Saleh Sen	ditto	
51. Yen Sina	ditto	
52. Khun Yan	ditto	
53. In Pech	ditto	
54. Preum Them	ditto	August 7, 1979

1.16
Order No. 2: Presiding Judge, Order to Appear at Trial (to Pol Pot)

The People's Revolutionary Tribunal at Phnom Penh notifies the accused Pol Pot, 54 years of age, former prime minister of the former government overthrown by the people that by Indictment No. 2 of July 25, 1979, the prosecutor has charged him along with Ieng Sary, former deputy prime minister of the said government in charge of foreign affairs with the crime of genocide, a crime defined and punished by Articles 1 and 2 of the Decree Law No. 1 of July 15, 1979, of the People's Revolutionary Council of Kampuchea.

By Order No. 1 to Hold a Trial of August 5, 1979, the People's Revolutionary Tribunal decided to begin the session to try the case on August 15, 1979, at 8:00 a.m.

Since the accused Pol Pot is in hiding and is the object of a search order, we order him to appear at the trial to respond to the allegations against him. In the event of his absence, the People's Tribunal will try him in absentia.

In implementation of Article 6 of Decree Law No. 1 of July 15, 1979, this order shall be posted at the office of the People's Revolutionary Committee of the city of Phnom Penh and broadcast by the National Radio of Kampuchea.

Phnom Penh, August 6, 1979
Keo Chanda, Presiding Judge
People's Revolutionary Tribunal at Phnom Penh

1.16bis

Order No. 3: Presiding Judge, Order to Appear at Trial (to Ieng Sary)

The People's Revolutionary Tribunal at Phnom Penh notifies the accused Ieng Sary, 54 years of age, former deputy prime minister in charge of foreign affairs of the former government overthrown by the people that by Indictment No. 2 of July 25, 1979, the prosecutor has charged him along with Pol Pot, former prime minister of the said government with the crime of genocide, a crime defined and punished by Articles 1 and 2 of the Decree Law No. 1 of July 15, 1979, of the People's Revolutionary Council of Kampuchea.

By Order No. 1 to Hold a Trial of August 5, 1979, the People's Revolutionary Tribunal decided to begin the session to try the case on August 15, 1979, at 8:00 a.m.

Because the accused Ieng Sary is in hiding and is the object of a search order, we order him to appear at the trial to respond to the allegations against him. In the event of his absence, the People's Tribunal will try him in absentia.

In implementation of Article 6 of Decree Law No. 1 of July 15, 1979, this order shall be posted at the office of the People's Revolutionary Committee of the city of Phnom Penh and broadcast by the National Radio of Kampuchea.

Phnom Penh, August 6, 1979
Keo Chanda, Presiding Judge
People's Revolutionary Tribunal at Phnom Penh

1.17

Bailiff, Record of Notification of Summons to the Fugitive Suspect Pol Pot

We, Hul Sam Ol, bailiff of the People's Revolutionary Tribunal, are charged with notifying the suspect:

Pol Pot, 54 years of age, former prime minister of the former government that was overthrown by the people, domiciled at Phnom Penh, of a summons of the People's Revolutionary Tribunal ordering him to a session on August 15, 1979, of the People's Revolutionary Tribunal to be tried for genocide, a crime defined and punished by Articles 1 and 2 of Decree Law No. 1 of July 15, 1979 of the People's Revolutionary Council of Kampuchea.

The suspect is in hiding and has been the object of an arrest warrant. Being unable to hand him his summons, we have:

1. Posted a copy of the said summons at the office of the People's Revolutionary Council of the city of Phnom Penh;

2. Arranged for the gist of the said summons to be broadcast on the National Radio of Kampuchea on news frequencies for seven consecutive days, beginning August 8, 1979.

In keeping with Article 6 of Decree Law No. 1 of July 15, 1979, of the People's Revolutionary Council of Kampuchea, if the suspect does not appear at the session, he will be tried in absentia.

This Record was made at Phnom Penh, August 6, 1979.

Hul Sam Ol

1.17bis

Bailiff, Record of Notification of Summons to the Fugitive Suspect Ieng Sary

We, Hul Sam Ol, bailiff of the People's Revolutionary Tribunal, are charged with notifying the suspect:

Ieng Sary, 54 years of age, former deputy prime minister in charge of foreign affairs of the former government that was overthrown by the people, domiciled at Phnom Penh, of a summons of the People's Revolutionary Tribunal ordering him to a session on August 15, 1979, of the People's Revolutionary Tribunal to be tried for genocide, a crime defined and punished by Articles 1 and 2 of Decree Law No. 1 of July 15, 1979 of the People's Revolutionary Council of Kampuchea.

The suspect is in hiding and has been the object of an arrest warrant. Being unable to hand him his summons, we have:

1. Posted a copy of the said summons at the office of the People's Revolutionary Council of the city of Phnom Penh;

2. Arranged for the gist of the said summons to be broadcast on the National Radio of Kampuchea on news frequencies for seven consecutive days, beginning August 8, 1979.

In keeping with Article 6 of Decree Law No. 1 of July 15, 1979, of the People's Revolutionary Council of Kampuchea, if the suspect does not appear at the session, he will be tried in absentia.

This Record was made at Phnom Penh, August 6, 1979.

Hul Sam Ol

1.18
Working Schedule for the People's Revolutionary Tribunal During Its Present Session

Morning: 7:30 to 11:30 a.m.
Afternoon: 2:00 to 5:30 p.m.

August 15, 1979
Morning 8:00 a.m.
Opening
Procedures
Reading of the indictment by the Secretariat
Afternoon
Statements of witnesses concerning "The expulsion of the population" and "Forced labor in the so-called communes" (Statements of 8 witnesses anticipated.)
Evening 7:00 p.m.
Reception for invited foreign guests

August 16, 1979
Morning
Reading of investigation reports

- concerning Phnom Penh
- concerning religions
- concerning national minorities

Statements of witnesses. There will be called to testify:

- a religious figure
- an official of Cham nationality
- a young Vietnamese resident

Afternoon
Statements of witnesses concerning mass killings, and reading of reports of field investigations:

- Two survivors of massacres will testify
- Mass killings in the Army (one witness)
- Massacres at Kompong Cham (reading of a report of a field investigation; three witnesses)
- Massacres at Siem Reap (reading of a report of a field investigation; one witness)

Evening
Cultural evening at the National Theater

August 17, 1979
Morning
Statements of witnesses (continued) concerning mass killings:

- cremation pits (reading of a report of witness interrogations)
- human beings thrown into crocodile pits (one witness)

Reading of a report on health
Reading of an investigation report on the Tuol Sleng prison

- interrogation of physicians, legal specialists
- interrogation of witnesses

Presentation of items of material evidence

- Visit of invited persons to Siem Reap

Afternoon
Statements of criminal figures (three criminal figures)
Reading of a report on the national economy
Reading of a report on education (one witness)
Reading of a report on culture (one witness)
Evening 7:00 p.m.
Meeting of foreign journalists with Kampuchean journalists

August 18, 1979
Morning
Showing of films (films will be shown during statements and readings; one session of film showing is anticipated)
Massacres perpetrated during the rout after January 7, 1979 (reading of a field investigation report and statements of four witnesses)
Several international jurists express their opinion as witnesses (if there are any)
Prosecutor reads indictment
Visit to Siem Reap of invited persons
Afternoon
Defense of victims by foreign jurists (if there are any)
Defense of the accused by the lawyers
Evening 7:00 p.m.
Showing of films at guest house of the National Ministry of Defense

August 19, 1979
Morning
Statements in defense of the accused by foreign jurists (if any)
Closing arguments by the prosecutor and the lawyers
The Tribunal deliberates
Afternoon
Reading of the judgment
Evening 7:00 p.m.
Cocktail party in honor of foreign guests

Note:

- August 14, 1979, 2:00 p.m.: Legal commission visits crime scenes at Tuol Sleng
- August 16–17, 1979, 2:00 p.m.: Foreign guests visit crime scenes at Tuol Sleng

1.19
Speech Delivered by Mr. Ros Samy, Secretary General of the Central Committee of the National United Front for the Salvation of Kampuchea, Member of the People's Revolutionary Council in Charge of the Ministry of Economy and Social Welfare, at a Reception in Honor of Foreign Guests to the People's Revolutionary Tribunal at Phnom Penh to Try the Pol Pot–Ieng Sary Clique for the Crime of Genocide, August 15, 1979

Esteemed President Heng Samrin, esteemed Vice-President Pen Sovan, foreign guests, comrades and friends, allow me, on behalf of the Central Committee of the National United Front for the Salvation of Kampuchea, the People's Revolutionary Council and the people of Kampuchea, to extend our warm greetings and most profound gratitude to you who have come from different continents to the capital city of Phnom Penh for the People's Revolutionary Tribunal to try the Pol Pot–Ieng Sary clique for the crime of genocide.

Ladies and gentlemen, comrades and friends, during the past three years or more, under their rule, the Pol Pot–Ieng Sary clique have turned once prosperous Kampuchea into a land of suffering, devastation and ruins. They have massacred more than three million people by extremely barbarous methods, forced the population to leave their cities and villages, concentrated them and forced them to do hard labor so as to exterminate them physically and mentally, abolished religions, and destroyed economic and cultural institutions, and family and social relations.

It is impossible to record fully the genocidal crime committed by the Pol Pot–Ieng Sary clique, a heinous regime, a bunch of henchmen of the Peking reactionary ruling circles, which has defiled the Angkor civilization and has challenged the conscience of progressive mankind. The people of Kampuchea resolutely demand retribution for their crimes.

In their revolutionary struggle, the people of Kampuchea have won a glorious victory, destroying the extremely barbarous rule of the Pol Pot–Ieng Sary clique, and founding the People's Republic of Kampuchea. At present our people are actively and enthusiastically striving to build up and defend our beloved Fatherland, gradually overcome the serious aftereffects of the Pol Pot–Ieng Sary genocidal regime, and have achieved encouraging initial successes. However, the Peking reactionary ruling circles in collusion with the U.S imperialists and other reactionary forces have frantically sabotaged the revolutionary cause of the Kampuchean people, trying by all means to shield and aid the remnants of the Pol Pot–Ieng Sary clique, with a view to restoring the barbarous regime of genocide in Kampuchea. Recently they resorted to the trick of calling for an international conference on the so-called "Kampuchea question" in an attempt to set up "a new administration," negate the unique, genuine and legitimate role of representation of the People's Revolutionary Council of Kampuchea, distort the assistance of the Socialist Republic of Vietnam for the people of Kampuchea, and sow discord between the Kampuchean people and the Vietnamese people.

The unsavory alliance between Peking and other reactionary forces aims at blocking the advance of the Kampuchean revolution, realizing their hegemonistic expansionist design, thus sabotaging peace and stability in South-East Asia.

Accordingly, the setting up of the Tribunal to try the Pol Pot–Ieng Sary clique for genocide is an urgent task, and it meets the aspirations of the Kampuchean people and mankind's conscience. This places before the Kampuchean people and the peace-loving and progressive forces in the world, a burning issue that is to do away with the aftereffects of the Pol Pot–Ieng Sary clique, and at the same time, to prevent the crimes of the Peking expansionists and their like.

The setting up of the People's Revolutionary Tribunal at Phnom Penh to try the Pol Pot–Ieng Sary clique for the crime of genocide, with undeniable conclusions from the findings and irrefutable evidence in the documents of the Tribunal, conforms to national and international laws, and eloquently testifies to the uprightness and justice of the policy of the National United Front for the Salvation of Kampuchea and the People's Revolutionary Council.

Ladies and gentlemen, comrades and friends, at present, the People's Revolutionary Council of Kampuchea, which has taken control of the country in all aspects, in internal and foreign affairs, is doing its best to restore production, stabilize and improve the welfare of the people, thus manifesting the true nature of a people's government, proving itself to be the only genuine and legitimate representative of the Kampuchean people. This can in no way be reversed. In their history of struggle for national liberation, the militant solidarity between the peoples of Kampuchea, Vietnam and Laos is a historical necessity. Now Vietnam is doing its utmost to help our people restore a normal life. This is a problem concerning the relations between the two independent and sovereign states based on ethics and laws. This relationship threatens nobody and nobody has the right to carry out intervention. There is no such thing as the "Kampuchea question," but the intervention and aggression by the Peking reactionary ruling circles, which are continuously helping the remnants of the Pol Pot–Ieng Sary clique to oppose the Kampuchea revolution. Any international conference held on the Kampuchea question not at the request of the People's Revolutionary Council will surely be doomed to ignominious failure.

There are still many difficulties and obstacles ahead for the revolutionary struggle of the Kampuchean people. The enemy has not resigned to defeat. However, we are firmly confident that with the strong sympathy, support and assistance from the brotherly countries and friends the world over, the Kampuchean people will win victory in national construction and defense. I would like to avail myself of this opportunity to express our sincere thanks for their valuable assistance.

The People's Revolutionary Tribunal to try the Pol Pot–Ieng Sary clique for the crime of genocide, a tribunal which enjoys the approval and support of broad public opinion and friends the world over, will certainly be successful.

I am sure that your active contributions will make up part of the success of the People's Revolutionary Tribunal at Phnom Penh.

May I propose a toast for your health, and for our successes.

Part II
Documents of the Investigation

Witness Statements

2.1.1.01
Mr. Ung Pech

The bitterest period in my life came after the Pol Pot–Ieng Sary clique of traitors seized power in Kampuchea.

I am Ung Pech, formerly a heavy construction machine engineer at the Building Service of the Ministry of Public Works in Phnom Penh and a specialist in the use of a machine to prepare a new type of asphalt called "bituminous asphalt," the product of which can be seen on the Phnom Penh—Kompong Som highway. In 1973, I decided to give up the job at the Ministry of Public Works and began to work for a private company which needed me and paid much better.

In 1975, the Pol Pot–Ieng Sary clique seized power in Phnom Penh and other provinces. On April 13, 1975, the reactionaries entered the city of Kompong Som. At first, the people were enthusiastic because they believed that a happy and peaceful life had begun. Contrary to our expectation, from the time of their entry into the city they deceived the population, telling them to abandon their houses temporarily, for 3 days, to avoid enemy aerial bombardment and to go to the countryside.

Our group of 24 heavy construction machine engineers were taken to Prey Nop district to do farming. Each of us was given 300 grams of rice a day. We had to make rice soup of it to calm the stomach. I stayed there for 4 months. One day they ordered me to help them in the city of Kompong Som. There I saw many Chinese ships full of trucks, tanks, artillery pieces, anti-aircraft guns and other kinds of military equipment. I saw many Chinese advisors there ordering Pol Pot–Ieng Sary agents about as puppets.

In November 1975, I arrived in Kompong Som, where their chief gave me a job that others had been unable to do, because they could not use the equipment as a result of their lack of technical knowledge. I was forced to work hard day and night, from 6:00 a.m. to 11:00 p.m., without rest, except a short break for soup. Whoever did not work hard was insulted, punished or sent to unknown places. They often said at the meetings that to leave such persons here brings us no benefit, so that in sending them away we lose nothing.

I lived with them for more than a year without any freedom, without going out or talking with other people. I had to be at the workshop all the time. One day, I was sent to repair machines at a canned-fish factory near the seashore. I saw many Chinese ships waiting to load goods from Kampuchea. Hundreds of trucks full of Kampuchean goods drove towards the ships to be sent to China. All the trucks were entirely covered, and the unlabelled packages were so heavy that they could be carried only by 5 or 6 men. I think that these were Kampuchean products of some value. I tried to see, to find out what kinds of goods they were, but I could not, because no one was allowed to go near. Only the Chinese and high ranking officials could look closely.

In July 1977, I was designated to lead a technical group in charge of making machines for unloading products from abroad, and they ordered me to teach the technique to new workers. The new workers were children, from 10 to 16 years old, learning to be welders, turners, blacksmiths, mechanics, and electricians. It was very difficult to teach technical matters to these children because they were illiterate, did not know numbers and, because of their age, did not have minds sufficiently developed. At each meeting they ordered me to teach them so that they could work by the end of 3 months. I replied that I could not do this in so short a time, that I needed at least a year. My reply did not satisfy them. They forced me to teach the children the practical use of the machines and they called me an imperialist wanting to hide my technical knowledge.

The workers' rations were meager. We never saw a large fish or meat soup. Every day we ate banana trunks cooked with a Kampuchean sauce, and lacking nutritional value. For their part, the Chinese came simply to watch the Khmers. The Chinese could not eat these foods and threw them to the dogs. The officials did not worry about the suffering of the workers or the Khmer inhabitants. The officials only served their Chinese patrons, who went walking after eating their fill.

On April 28, 1977, the traitors arrested me at the Kompong Som Hospital. I was charged with being an enemy. I was maltreated for a time, then taken to Phnom Penh. After arriving at Phnom Penh, the car stopped for 2 hours north of the imperial palace. Then a Peugeot 404 tightly closed arrived. They blindfolded me and tied my hands behind my back. The Peugeot headed south, and I tried to see between the folds of the cloth. Shortly thereafter, the automobile stopped on the road, guards checked it, and it took off. At another location, the automobile stopped again, and 4 or 5 guards came and asked loudly how many persons were in the automobile. They made 2 persons get out of the car. Another person and I got out. They asked us, "Where do you come from, traitor?" They made me tell my identity. They despised us more than beasts. They mistreated us savagely and said again, "One must treat them this way." I wondered what I had done so bad to be treated as a traitor. I was ordered to go to be photographed, and they put us in cell No. 4, on the third floor of house No. 4. In escorting us, they acted as if they were irritated. They threatened to kill us to hurry us along. At that moment I did not know anything at all. When we got to the house, they opened the door and pushed us into the room. Then they took all my clothes, leaving me in only my undershorts. They shackled my foot and removed my blindfold. They then asked if I knew anyone there. They looked at me, but I did not know any of them.

At noon they gave us lunch: 2 bowls of rice and 2 spoons of salt. I could not swallow it. Other prisoners asked me for the rice I was unable to eat, but the guards came in. The guards asked the others where they got their rice. They responded that it was my uneaten rice. The guards then beat and whipped the prisoners with electric wires. It was really awful. The guards then turned to me and ordered me never to give away my ration again. They said, "if you give them your rice a second time you will be beaten as they were."

The guards then showed me the rules which were written on a large chalkboard:

- No talking with anyone or asking questions of anyone!
- Absolute respect for discipline!
- Ask permission from the guard before doing anything!

From that day on, I tried to take care to avoid any possible trouble.

All the prisoners living in my room had to get permission to relieve themselves, to sit down or change positions. If they did these things without permission, they were brutally beaten with electric wire until their bodies were bloody. Before we were given meals, the guards counted the bowls and spoons, and if any were missing after the meal, when they counted again, the prisoners were savagely beaten like animals. One day a new prisoner used two spoons. The guards noticed that a spoon was missing so they searched the room. The new prisoner with two spoons was accused of stealing the spoon. The guards reported him to the head guard. Half an hour later, the head guard, his name was Peng, came with a whip. He threatened the prisoner, asking, "What were you going to do with the spoon?" The prisoner responded that he thought he was allowed to use two spoons, and he apologized. Despite his pleading, the head guard brutally beat him, kicking him in the head. He beat him for an hour, and then another guard replaced him, and then a third guard. The prisoner's blood was running everywhere. The other prisoners were frozen with fear. They were unable to move because their legs were shackled.

The Searches

Every morning at 4:00 a.m., the guards ordered the prisoners to strip, the guards then searched everywhere. Anyone who had a stitch of clothing left on or who seemed at all suspicious could be beaten. They searched the rooms three times a day: morning, afternoon, and at night. Sometimes the head guards searched once or twice more during the day.

The Food in Prison

I was in prison for 3 months and 28 days. During the first month, in the mornings, I was given a plate of rice, in the afternoons, rice soup. This was satisfactory, but later on, it was just the soup for the whole day. Four of us shared a bowl of watered-down soup. Each of us was given 5 to 10 grains of salt, which is nearly none nothing at all. Mealtime was not fixed. Sometimes we had soup at 4:00 p.m. and the following lunch at 1:00 or 2:00 a.m. One bowl of watered-down soup.

The Prisoners' Living Conditions

The prisoners were deprived of all their clothes except their undershorts, year round. Each time it rained the water leaked in everywhere in the cell and the prisoners were forbidden to sit up, forcing them to lie down on the wet floor. Once a month, prisoners had the opportunity to wash their undershorts. There was a rule that prisoners should get to take a bath every 3 to 5 days, but in reality they got to bathe once a month, and only in the summer. The prisoners' bodies were covered with blisters and scabs. Many of them died in prison from disease. The dead were left where they were for 24 hours, and the living prisoners had to sleep together with the dead. At times a prisoner would be sleeping with two or three corpses beside him, but what can one do in prison?

Where Were the Prisoners Taken When They Were Taken Away?

I was thrown in prison in April, 1977. Each cell had 40 to 60 prisoners, and there were about 7,000 to 8,000 prisoners in the prison including a number of revolutionaries, workers, and anyone who opposed their regime. My cell had 35 prisoners. Among them were Pol Pot officials, teachers, factory workers, electricians, as well as innocent people accused of being agents of the CIA or KGB or some such organization.

In the mornings of the 10th, 20th, and 30th day of every month, guards came into the cell with a list of names to identify the prisoners. At 4:00 p.m. a guy who used the alias Hau Thi came with some other guards and began calling out names one by one. A prisoner hearing his name called would raise his hand, and he would have his arms tied and would be blindfolded. Then the leg shackles were removed, and the prisoner was ordered out. They were pushed outside like animals. Each had a noose tied around his neck and each one was tied to the other prisoners by this noose. They were beaten to the ground and some could not walk following their long detention and were brutally beaten, tripping as they walked, and in falling to the ground some broke their arms and legs.

They were thrown into the back of a covered car, like animals, and they were taken away. I tried to find out where they were taken. No one knew. Some said that they were taken to Prey Sar to farm land. Afterwards, however, we met some prisoners from Prey Sar. They informed us that they had not seen anyone sent there to work. This information made it clear that these prisoners were killed. I finally understood that prisoners were brought here, interrogated, and then killed.

Why Am I Still Alive?

After four months and 28 days in prison I was ordered, by the guard named Thi, to go to fix the generator. At 10:00 a.m. he untied my hands and I followed him. I had trouble walking because I had grown very weak in prison. I examined the generator and said that it did not work because it had been exposed to the rain and had rusted. The head of the prison, Ho, told me that I would be killed if I failed to fix the machine. I asked for permission to take the generator apart so I could repair it. He consented. There I happened to meet a friend named Peng Kik, a radio specialist. We pretended not to recognize each other for fear of endangering each other's lives. Peng and I were told to repair the generator that day. I worked hard until 3:00 a.m., I was returned to my cell and given four cigarettes as a reward. I shared them with my cell mates. We passed the cigarettes from mouth to mouth, alternating smokes and swallowing the smoke.

The next morning I continued my work and succeeded after 2 days and nights with the help of my friend, Mr. Peng. After that, I was supposed to operate the machine whenever the city electrical current was disrupted.

I was transferred to a cell on the lower floor where I lived with 15 others, including 2 teachers, 2 engineers and one Pol Pot–Ieng Sary official. The others were young soldiers. I recognized a man named Seng Po Se, an ex-member of the resistance forces against the Sihanouk regime who fled into the forests in 1972. I learned that many of my friends who had taken part in the revolution were arrested. I was astounded to learn that around 600 students and civil servants returned from abroad, tricked by the propaganda, and were killed. Among them were Hou Yuon, Hu Nim, Toch Phoeun, Toch Kham Doeun, Chau Seng, Sok Challa, Pok Chhai, Pok Ki, and others whose names I cannot remember because it was difficult to talk in prison.

After three days in this cell, I was ordered to go to work in a prison workshop with other mechanics, radio repairmen, and carpenters. From that day, I was no longer imprisoned. It was only then that I learned that the prison was the old Tuol Sleng High School located south of the hospital for Chinese residents.

The high school had 4 rows of brick buildings. Buildings A and D faced each other, and the two others faced east. In the back there was a house which had previously been classrooms and had been converted into living quarters for the workers. The kitchen and the pigsty in front of Buildings B and C were brick and were used for storing documents and for photographing the prisoners. Each of these 4 buildings had three floors and each floor had 4 rooms. On the ground floor, they had interrogation cells and torture chambers for their more senior officials. The prison was surrounded by 2 or 3 rows of barbed wire that were hidden behind sheets of corrugated metal.

As for my work there, I made all sorts of machines (paper-cutting machines, noodle presses, for repairing cars, etc.). Each day they brought out prisoners for interrogation. Everyday I heard screams and the crack of whips (rattans). These interrogations lasted from 6:00 to 11:00 a.m., and then from 1:00 to 5:00 p.m., and again from 7:00 to 11:00 p.m.

How Were the Interrogations Conducted?

A prisoner would be seated on the floor, his hands and feet chained to a table. One guard did the questioning, another had a stick that he would use to hit the prisoner. The victims were accused of being either a CIA or KGB agent, or of having connections with the Vietnamese. Often innocent people were accused and tortured who had nothing to which they could confess. Some endured interrogation for two or three months. Others, who could no longer stand the torture, admitted to being agents of the CIA or KGB; they were forced to write on paper that they admitted to infiltrating the ranks of Pol Pot. Ten days later they would be killed.

Women who were interrogated had to take off their clothes, and they would be tortured, and the pretty ones would be raped. Next to Building B, I could hear their cries day and night. In torturing the prisoners, they used electric shock and poured water brine into their nostrils. Guards would pull off the prisoners' fingernails and pour alcohol on their exposed finger tips. They hung prisoners upside down by their feet and poured water into their nostrils, or wrapped water soaked towels onto the prisoner's head to suffocate, or bashed a prisoner's head against a piece of furniture, or a table, or the cement floor. Many of the ex-resistance fighters killed themselves, including Hou Yuon, who committed suicide by cutting his wrists with a broken spoon in early 1977. That is why the guards hunted for extra spoons.

Their Plans for the Prison

In the beginning of 1978, they summoned all the prisoners who were engravers and molders to draw Pol Pot's likeness and make a bust of Pol Pot in cement and another smaller bust in plaster. They found two artists and three engravers. The artist, named Khu, was a student who had returned from France and, upon his return, he was imprisoned. Another artist, named Meng, had worked in the Phnom Penh theater, enlisted in their army in 1975 and was accused of treason and thrown into prison. The three engravers were Tuch, Nath, and a third who had worked in the Angkor Wat museum in Siem Reap. They painted Pol Pot's picture in all sizes. The engravers were ordered to make a gold statue of Pol Pot, weighing 80 to 100 kilograms, three statues in silver, and ten in bronze. They brought gold and silver to the prison for this purpose. Leng tried an experimental one but he failed and they stopped work on it.

In late 1978, a second attempt also failed. They built a number of statues of workers and peasants and soldiers with Pol Pot in the center. The figure of Pol Pot was to be seven meters tall while the other figures were to be two meters tall. The Wat Phnom temples were to be destroyed and replaced by this statue, which would resemble the statue of Mao Tse Tung in China.

Pol Pot and Ieng Sary's Plans

They had planned to kill nearly all of the Kampuchean people. They then planned to claim that they lacked manpower in Kampuchea and they would bring Chinese people into Kampuchea, which would become a Chinese colony. China would use Kampucheans to kill Kampucheans, and no one could criticize China.

After April 17, 1975, I saw Chinese advisors everywhere. Many of these advisors had no expertise. At Kompong Som, I saw the Chinese teaching Pol Pot's men how to repair machinery, and how to drive cars. It was ridiculous. These Chinese experts did not know how to fix machinery, or to drive cars. They said that in China, if repairs needed to be done they did not repair the machines, rather they used new parts.

Without the National United Front for the Salvation of Kampuchea our country would be a part of China. It is a shame that we have not yet captured these two traitors Pol Pot and Ieng Sary to find out whether they are Chinese or Kampuchean.

As a Kampuchean victim of the Pol Pot–Ieng Sary's genocidal policies, I vehemently denounce their savage acts. I ask that world public opinion condemn their crimes.

My Entire Family Was Killed

After April 17, 1975, they made my family go to the village of Cham Roa, in Mong Russey district, Battambang province. There were 48 members in my family, and only my son survived. All the others died from disease or starvation. This was a crime of genocide.

Here are the aliases of the security agents at the Tuol Sleng Prison (I did not know their real names):

(1) Duch, head of the prison. He had the authority to kill anyone without an order from a superior officer.
(2) He, prison camp commander. He had one eye and he kept the files on each prisoner.
(3) Chan, an ex-teacher from Kompong Thom. He was in charge of the law department and decided on sentencing of prisoners.
(4) Thi, 25 to 30 years old. He kept the list of prisoners.
(5) Peng, 25 years old. He was a security agent in the prison; he was cruel and was brutal to the prisoners.
(6) Bu, 25 to 28 years old. He was an interrogator.
(7) Srieng, a radio operator.
(8) Sri, 25 years old. He was a photographer and a security agent.

Four survivors of the Tuol Sleng Prison are (1) Ung Pech; (2) Lep Chan, an engraver; (3) Nath, an artist (engraver); and (4) Rui Na Kong, a carpenter. We four presently work together in the First Brigade, Phnom Penh.

My son who survived is named Ung Veng Ieng and is a law student at the Faculty of Law in Phnom Penh.

Ung Pech, done at Phnom Penh, June 25, 1979

2.1.1.03
Mr. Proum Doch Boranann

April 17 was a day of triumph for the revolutionary forces and a day on which the American capitalists and their troops were defeated. It was supposed to be a day of happiness for our people, but the clique of the traitors Pol Pot and Ieng Sary brutally shot, killed, and expelled the people.

We were expelled by the traitors Pol Pot and Ieng Sary under threat of being shot. They tricked us by saying that it would be for only three days. My family and I left Phnom Penh on April 17 at 2:00 p.m.

Under this brutal threat, with weapons and vulgar language that made us afraid, we hurried to gather up what we could and left our house. Anyone who got lost had to look for their relatives among the people who were moving slowly. But the clique of Pol Pot and Ieng Sary traitors shot over the people's heads to force them along faster. They took motorbikes and bicycles from the people without worrying that anyone would stop them. They did not hesitate to take even watches, radios, and other such items. During my trip to my native village I was repeatedly threatened. They took my property as they pleased. It was piracy. We got this kind of treatment all the way to the native village of my parents in Prek Ta Nong subdistrict, Chamkar Leu district, Kompong Cham province.

After we got to the village, the Pol Pot–Ieng Sary clique confiscated still more of my property, accusing us of being traitors or enemies. Under the Pol Pot–Ieng Sary regime I knew only suffering, misery, and a tragic life. Under the yoke of the traitors, they made us work, they exhausted us, they mistreated the people to the point that the people became ill. But we got no care, no medication, no suitable hospital. From one month to the next our health deteriorated rapidly. Forced labor day and night left us very weak. Our life began to lose all balance. My family and I began to get sick one after the other.

In September 1975, since we had nothing to eat, my younger sister, who was called Sokun, seven years of age, died of a fever. But the clique of Pol Pot–Ieng Sary traitors did not let us practice our traditional customs. They destroyed our customs and would not let us follow our religious beliefs. There were only two persons at the burial of my younger sister. The morning after my younger sister died, my mother, my brothers, and my sisters had to work, even in their grief. Only my father and I were allowed to bury her. My younger sister's body was wrapped in palm leaves, and we buried her, shedding many tears on her grave.

On December 12, 1975, we were ordered by Pol Pot agents to leave the Prek Ta Nong subdistrict, Chamkar Leu district, Kompong Cham province, and to go live in the Bos Khnor subdistrict, Chamkar Leu district, Kompong Cham province. In this new place my misery grew and grew. They mistreated us brutally. They accused me of being a Lon Nol soldier or of having been a police officer. That made me shudder every day.

This style of making unjust accusations was not only for me, but they accused everyone, especially the city people. That is why many people died unjustly every month.

Every night the clique of Pol Pot–Ieng Sary traitors had their spies walking around my house and around the houses of the other city people. This was out of fear that we might speak against their policies, their dictatorship. If anyone spoke on this topic, they killed him immediately.

On January 20, 1976, the Pol Pot clique sent me to a work site 27 kilometers away. In the dry season they made us work so hard that we could not keep it up. We worked day and night, twelve hours a day, with no day off. They never gave any thought to housing, or to time off, or to the living conditions of the people. At the work site I fell seriously ill. For taking care of us and for medication there were only roots and other traditional medications. For injections, there was only vitamin C or vitamin B12 that they put in a bottle of orange soda. And the Pol Pot people misdiagnosed diseases.

The Pol Pot–Ieng Sary medical people were poorly trained, meaning that they had no medical training, not even first aid. They used people as guinea pigs. That is why people died every month, one after another, because of this stupid experimentation. Any shot led to serious infection because they used medications produced locally. I got an infection. People who were sick had to work like everyone else. They said that no one eats who does not work. That shows that the Pol Pot people are cruel people who have no care for the misfortune of the population. For their clique, there is only rebuke, ordering about, repression, killing, and suppression of any liberty.

In June 1976, the Pol Pot people killed Mr. Thong and his family (five children) as a result of bad health.

In July 1976, they killed Mr. Yen because he dug up some potatoes. In October 1976, they sent me from Chamkar Leu district to Lvea district, where I was forced to work very hard with other young comrades. To eat, they gave us only broth mixed with corn and banana. The Pol Pot lackeys on the other hand ate well, which shows inequality and injustice, contrary to their statement that in this new society we are equal, with no rich or poor, no ruling classes or subordinate classes.

Seeing that, I was very sad. For lack of shelter, they put us up in the Lvea pagoda, about 4 kilometers from Chamkar Leu. I was quite affected when I saw that the Pol Pot nonbelievers had destroyed the statues of Buddha.

On January 3, 1977, they sent me to Sre Krom, about 90 kilometers from my village where my friends and I were subjected to forced labor as before. All the members of my family were now separated. I was sent to work far from home. I saw my family only after 20 or 30 days of work in distant regions. Other families underwent the same separation. My brothers and sister, who ranged in age from five to fifteen years, were separated from their parents because they were put into mobile teams. In addition, these little children were forced to work like adults and got no education or instruction. The fact that they made school-age children work shows their lack of concern for the future of these children. The Pol Pot people sent my brothers, from five to fifteen years of age, to a work site for digging irrigation canals where they were frequently tortured.

On July 14, 1977, the Pol Pot people killed two families of my relatives in a savage way. These two families had a total of thirteen members. On July 15, 1977, the Pol Pot–Ieng Sary people killed my parents and my six brothers and sister. This savage act made me terribly sad. The executioners carried out this mass killing in the Svay Mea rubber plantation that is located between Bos Khnor and Ta Ang.

The Pol Pot people had dug pits, and they led my parents and the other villagers and beat them with iron bars or stabbed them with knives. What had my parents and brothers and sisters done to them? How sad my parents must have been at the moment they were being killed by the Pol Pot people. Every day,

[There is a hiatus here because two pages of this document are not available. The document continues after the hiatus as follows. — Eds.]

take care of the people, and there was a scarcity of effective medicines. Finally, he used our people for experimenting with his medicines, and many sick people regrettably died as a result.

In addition, the Pol Pot–Ieng Sary clique defrocked our monks and made them do forced labor. They suppressed religions and believers, destroying temples and pagodas.

As for culture, the Pol Pot–Ieng Sary clique eliminated all students, intellectuals, teachers, engineers, and medical doctors without a second thought.

To suppress national literatures, they killed all the intellectuals.

During the four years of the fascist Pol Pot–Ieng Sary regime, our children were unfortunately condemned to illiteracy. Schools were destroyed by the Pol Pot troops and they became warehouses for fertilizer. Rare books were all burned. University faculties and schools were closed.

January 7, 1979, was the end of the fascist Pol Pot–Ieng Sary regime, and also of the elimination of races having the same blood as they. The troops of the National United Front for the Salvation of Kampuchea freed entire populations. That is why we render thanks to the National United Front for the Salvation of Kampuchea, which liberated us from the criminals Pol Pot and Ieng Sary. Along with our joy, we Kampucheans are enthusiastic to live under the new regime.

After two weeks of liberation, we returned to Phnom Penh, and I worked in the Ministry of Urban Affairs. I am taking this opportunity hopefully to reinforce the solidarity among us to eliminate the Pol Pot–Ieng Sary clique completely. We are beginning to rebuild our lovely homeland so that Kampuchea can be a developed and civilized country.

Done at Phnom Penh, May 28, 1979
Proum Duch Boranann

Additional Statement

Under the Pol Pot regime, I lived in North Trapeang Sary village, Bos Khnor subdistrict, Kompong Cham province. This village was inhabited by 217 families. During the period from April 17, 1975, to January 7, 1979, the Pol Pot–Ieng Sary people killed families of the "April 17" people as well as 33 people of local origin and one youth.

As for killing at North Trapeang Sary village, Bos Khnor subdistrict, in 1976, the killings of Mr. Yeng and of the family of Mr. Thong should be mentioned. On July 14, 1977, the Pol Pot people killed eight families. We should mention those of Mr. Khun, Mr. Phalla, Mr. Yan, Mr. Sum Nay Peou, Mr. Chheng, and Mr. Tara, plus one other family whose name I have forgotten. These families were gotten together by Thoeun and Lonn.

On August 29 and 30, 1978, they killed 32 people. On August 29, at 5:00 p.m., 17 were killed: (1) Pho, (2) Him, (3) Nhim, (4) Hour, (5) Chhon, (6) Hegang, (7) Tong, (8) Kheang, (9) The, (10) Smas, (11) Kong, (12) Kim,

(13) Sim, (14) Hong, plus three others I don't know but who were named Chonne.

On August 30, 1978, they killed 15: (1) Puy, (2), Chhoeunry, (3) Thoeun, (4) Srun, (5) Tara, (6) Leng, (7) Chhean, (8) Yem, (9) Nha, (10) Koy, (11), Sa, (12) Him, (13) Var, (14) Yan, (15) Heng. These men were taken by the deputy chief of the village at 1:00 p.m.

Others whom I knew that were killed by the Pol Pot people are: (1) Phalla, (2) Nhoeun (North Trapeang Sary village), (3) Mao (Tuol Prasoeu village), (4) Van (Tuol Prasoeu village), (5) Bo, (6) Ham, (7) Sem (at Thlok Kravann), (8) Sao (at Chranom), (9) San (chief of Chranom village), (10) Sun Heng, (a village chief in Bos Khnor subdistrict), (11) Yet (police chief in Bos Khnor subdistrict). These men had been Pol Pot people.

As for the sites of killings, there were two of which I knew. One is near the "April 1" village near the Conga field, and the other is west of the Caouta rubber plantation about two kilometers from the "April 1" village.

After the victory of January 17, 1979, at Bos Khnor subdistrict, a self-defense group was set up to ensure security in the subdistrict. Many young people voluntarily joined. But among the recruits one finds as well the former Pol Pot executioners named Phalla, Nhoeur, and Tha. The presence of these three executioners frightens everyone in the village, and the "April 17" people had to leave Bos Khnor village as fast as they could.

Phnom Penh, June 18, 1979
Signature illegible

2.1.1.04

Mrs. Pen En, *My Story Under the Pol Pot Regime*

It was April 17, 1975, and the situation of our country was not good. In fact, my family stayed indoors, not daring to go outside. Pol Pot had taken Phnom Penh. All the ministries and all the houses hoisted white flags. Since I had only one meter of white cloth, I had to tear up a quilt to make a flag, and I put it out on the front of my house. Despite our good feelings for them, the Pol Pot clique did not spare us but made us take off right away. The entire population was expelled by the armed forces of Pol Pot. They made us go ten kilometers from the city, supposedly for three days.

The departure began April 18 at 3:00 p.m. Anyone who refused would have been killed. Having no way out and in despair, since I have a weak heart, I shook all over and got a headache. Everyone had a somber face. I did not know which of my belongings to take or which to leave behind, as I was really upset at having to leave my things. My neighbors set out one by one. My heart beat faster than usual. I did not know what to think or what to do, because I had only ten tins of milk for my child. Finally I decided to take the mosquito net, three bags of rice, some clothes and a few other necessities. I put my things in the car and left crying, because we were leaving our home with such sadness that I could not find words.

The people who lived in Roul Kork had to go south, following National Route 7. There were so many people on the road that we could not drive the car. We had to push it.

I thought about things so much and cried so much that my eyes became swollen and I could no longer see. All the while a Pol Pot propaganda car shouted to make us walk faster. We walked 5, 10, 20, 30 kilometers, but no one said we could stop. In despair, we began to understand that we had been tricked by the traitors. My husband was not at all happy as we left. We had had some arguments between us and a few days later he fell ill. I cried again because I had little medication on me, and if one day someone fell ill, what would I do? At Ba Batheay at the Rakakaong crossroads, we were told that anyone whose native village was in Svay Rieng or Prey Veng provinces should take the Rakakaong road.

I decided to go toward Svay Rieng to see my parents and friends. The Pol Pot clique's armed forces told me that it was only one kilometer to the ferry boat and that they would not let me stay where we were because the organization would not allow it. One kilometer, but in reality it was 30 kilometers. I did not understand what was going on, but I did not say anything.

At the ferry, I had to leave my car. I begged the Pol Pot people to let me keep it, but they absolutely refused. Then we had to carry all our luggage. At that point I had two orphan nephews with me, my sister, and my four children, in all nine persons. I carried my son in my arms. He was only two years old.

Many people who got on the ferry died of cholera. My niece too fell victim to this disease. I was so worried because it was contagious. We put our children in a separate house to avoid this contagious disease. I traded my gold to get medicine to treat it.

A week later, I traded my gold for an old bicycle. But we had to use this bicycle for my niece, who had just gotten over being sick and could not walk. We had to walk day and night, and at night it was cold. During the day my three children walked with difficulty, and they cried a lot. We looked for shelter but there was no house to stay in. We came upon Pol Pot armed forces. They told me that there was a village one kilometer from there. But we walked eight kilometers and found no village.

There were no houses because everything had burned. It was raining. We had only one quilt that my husband had brought. We ran to get to shelter. My children shook from the cold. We found shelter under a tree to change my children's clothes. We set out again because under that tree we got colder and colder. It was getting dark, and we walked as if with our eyes shut, shaking and crying. At times flashes of lightning helped us to see.

Twenty minutes later we arrived at the village. The only houses there had no roofs. We looked for the house that had the fewest people in it. We looked for wood to make a fire. We changed clothes and sat down around the fire to get warm. That night we had no supper because we had no appetite. But my husband fixed quite a bit of rice out of fear that later on it might be hard to find water and wood. Since the children slept well, I was a bit relieved. I wished that it would be daylight as soon as possible so that I could look for wood for our trip. Our difficult trip lasted 32 days.

To get to Svay Rieng, we had to cross Prek Chrouk, Prek Krouch, Prek Touch, Vihea Sour, and Prek Tramak. We had to go back to Dei Ek. There were few people at Dei Ek.

As we were leaving Dei Ek, we met someone we had known before. He had three bicycles. Taking pity on my husband, he gave him a bicycle. Now we had two bicycles, and that gave me some comfort, but we could not stop as we would have liked. At night we would stop and fix supper. The Pol Pot forces did not let us stop. Only persons who were sick or could no longer walk were allowed to stop. They made us go right away. That upset us so much that we no longer wanted to speak with them.

When we got to my native village, the Pol Pot clique stopped us. They did not let the refugees have any relationship with the people who were from those places. Seeing that, my husband scolded me because he had begged me to go to his native village in Takeo province, but I did not agree. He asked me if we would be allowed to see our parents, and what I had to give our children to eat.

But after we waited two days, the new guards let us go to my sister's house. She ran to embrace us, and we all cried, because even my parents had gone to Phnom Penh. Only my sister was left living in the countryside. We all cried because it made us feel better. There was a nice neighbor woman who told us we should stop crying. My sister was saving four families, that is, my family and that of my parents, that of my sister, and that of my younger sister. But my sister almost went mad. We ate all the rice she had in her granary. And worse, she had traded her gold to get rice to feed us. In spite of everything, she didn't say anything for fear of causing us pain.

Two days after we got to my native village, they asked my husband and brothers-in-law to study politics. We didn't say anything because we thought that it would be simple political study. My husband might have realized what would happen to him but didn't talk about it. Perhaps he wanted to keep me from worrying, because he asked my sister to watch out for his children.

A month after he left, my two children fell ill. They ate very little. They always looked sad and rarely spoke. My younger son was sick and could not walk or speak. I left him with his sister, who was 11 years old and who had also taken ill. My smallest son was very hungry. He would find things on the ground to eat, and when he saw me he would hide whatever it was behind his back. If anyone ate something, he would stop and watch him eat. That made me ashamed and caused me great pain.

To die or to live? I took my gold and traded it for chickens and ducks. I cooked them for my children, but it was too late because my child died before getting to eat. He died in my arms, while I was asleep, not knowing that he had died, because I was so tired. I was not unhappy about it, it was good that he should die because I could no longer feed them. But I cried because my husband did not know that his beloved son had died.

Fifteen days later, my eldest daughter fell very ill. I did not go out to work because she was so weak. She was so thin that she was only skin and bones. Even the Pol Pot soldiers said that there was no hope of saving her. Hearing that, I was so upset, my eyes filled with tears. I caressed my daughter's hair and tried to console her sweetly. Since I had never lied to her, she believed me and slept quietly. When I went out to wash her clothes, she fell from the bed. Her stomach hurt her. I held her in my arms. After saying five or six words, she closed her eyes forever. I went mad. I wanted to kill myself, because she was the daughter that I loved more than the others. At that moment, I thought that I could not live without her.

A woman like me, who was the wife of a man who was well known, a woman who did not support herself by work outside the home, was not excused from work in the cooperative. When I felt that I was going to be the object of repression, I wanted to flee to Vietnam. When my husband left, I was two months pregnant, and they were ordering me to husk 75 kilograms a day. That is why my child did not survive, and I had to go to the hospital. They did some diagnosis. I stayed in the hospital for two months. They gave me shots of vitamin C that they extracted from a bottle of orange soda. I lost a great deal of blood. I could not walk for three months. We worked day and night. Even when it was getting dark they made us do the replanting. Anyone who missed work three times was taken away to prison. In my village they took Miss Yut, a singer, two natives of the village named Soy and Sao, Professor Meak Seam, my husband, a navy lieutenant, Mister My Sa Pom, and many students and officials who had been expelled from Phnom Penh, many persons whose names I did not know.

Up to that time, villagers whispered to me that my husband had died. My tragic life continued until the time when there were incidents along the Khmer-Vietnam border. I decided to escape. I did not want to die like my husband. I had to try, because the traitors were about to repress me. I still remembered that my husband had escaped but came back the same evening saying that the situation did not allow it. My situation to be sure was not clear either, because I was not sure that Vietnam would admit me. And if the Pol Pot clique caught me, they would have no mercy on me. They would not shoot us, but they would gouge our eyes out. Or they would burn us alive like the corpses we had seen. For three days we were under flying shells. Three days that we were between life and death. I was so sorry for my child; he was still quite small and did not understand. We had only the clothes we were wearing. But fortunately we got to Vietnam as we had wanted.

Finally my tragic story is over. Only one unforgettable thing stays with me, the death of my daughter.

Please send my statement to the tribunal that is trying the crimes of the Pol Pot–Ieng Sary clique that killed my husband and my children, all of them innocent. But why did they kill them? My good life was destroyed. Is it my fault? Why did it happen?

Phnom Penh, June 2, 1979
Pen En

2.1.1.05
Mr. Tik How

On June 21, 1979, at 9:00 a.m., we, Saes Chhon, official of the Ministry of the Interior, and San Kiri, secretary, took notes of the following:

Question: Your name, age, and where you are from?

Answer: My name is Tik How, age 29, formerly a resident of Phnom Penh. I lived at Lane 39, no. 15, near the Olympic Market, District 5. Since the liberation, I have been living in Wat Svay village, Siem Reap 3 subdistrict.

Question: Can you give any information about yourself and your family in connection with the years you lived in Phnom Penh?

Answer: Under the Lon Nol regime, nearly all of my family lived in Phnom Penh. My father's name was Du Y, of Chinese descent. At the age of 55, my father entered into a partnership with a Chinese resident involving textile trading in Phnom Penh. My mother is Kampuchean, but she spoke Chinese and Vietnamese as well. She sold fabrics with my father. I had four sisters, and still have my grandfather and an uncle.

I completed my studies at the Phnom Penh University Faculty of Arts in 1973. In 1974, I was not yet looking for a job, as it was my intention to pursue further studies abroad. In April 1975, Pol Pot seized power and forced everyone, including my family, to leave Phnom Penh.

Question: Under the Pol Pot regime, to which region was your family exiled?

Answer: On April 17, 1975, 13 members of my family, including my grandmother, my uncle, my brother-in-law and my nephews were driven out of Phnom Penh and forced to settle in Saang district, Kandal province. My entire family was assigned there for five months to do forced labor, but they were later forced to move to another region.

My family was divided in two groups: eight in my family were sent to Pong Ro village, Pau Chal subdistrict, Phnom Sarok district, Battambang province. They consisted of my grandmother, my parents, my younger brother and my younger sister, two of my elder sister's children and me.

Question: How was the displacement done?

Answer: I do not know exactly how people were sorted in Saang district, but 8 people from my family were ordered to go to Battambang and 5 others to Kompong Thom.

As the journey to Battambang was a long one, we had to travel by truck. From Saang, we went by boat to Kompong Chhnang; from Kompong Chhnang, by truck, to Pursat. Then we were packed into a train and taken to Svay Sisophon, Battambang province; from Sisophon, we went by truck to Pong Ro village.

When we left Phnom Penh, we could not take any luggage with us.

Question: How many people are in your family?

Answer: In our family, 9 people were killed or died, en route; as of the day of liberation, only four people in my family were left.

Two days after our arrival in Battambang, Pol Pot soldiers declared that my father had been an officer under Lon Nol, perhaps because he was Chinese. He was big and had a fair complexion. Despite my father's objections, he was sent to Pong Ro village, Pau Chal subdistrict, where he was killed. He died on September 29, 1975.

My grandmother, my mother and my nephews were unable to bear the hardships; they died from illness in Pong Ro village.

Therefore, out of the 8 members of my family forcibly moved to Battambang, only 3 remain: my two younger brothers and I.

In Kompong Thom, of the 5 family members forcibly evacuated, only one has survived; my sister's oldest son, whom I brought here (Wat Svay village) three days ago. My nephew and some other people arriving from Kompong Thom have informed me that my uncle, my sister, her husband and their two sons were taken to Sres village, Sra Yuav subdistrict, Kompong Thom district, Kompong Thom province. Here, the eldest boy went to work for another family, the second died of an illness.

The Pol Pot officials viewed my uncle, my sister and her husband as foreign residents and treated them as such. When asked if there were any other people in my family, my sister said that there were no more than four people. So, they killed all four family members present, my nephew survived. Now we are a family of four; we live together in Wat Svay village.

Question: What did you do during those years?

Answer: In Battambang, I had to dig ditches, reclaim land, and watch over ducks in the rice paddies.

Question: You are nearsighted. Did they ask you about your eyeglasses?

Answer: I am nearsighted. Yes, they asked me why I was wearing eyeglasses. I dared not say that I had graduated from the university, rather, I only said that I had attended secondary school for six years. I spent all day in the rice paddies with the ducks, so I went unnoticed most of the time.

This statement was done at 12 noon, the same day. The minutes were reread to Tik How, who acknowledged them as conforming to his statements and signed here below.

Witness	*Official present*	*Secretary*
Tik How	Saes Chhon	San Kiri

2.1.1.05a
Denunciation Letter by Mr. Tik How

I, the undersigned Tik How, age 29, of Khmer nationality, native of the Wat Svay village, Siem Reap 3 subdistrict, Siem Reap district, Siem Reap province, have the privilege to make the following statement:

I have recently managed to escape from the clutches of the Pol Pot–Ieng Sary gang, thanks to the great efforts of the National United Front for the Salvation of Kampuchea. That is why I am writing this letter of denunciation of the crimes perpetrated by those traitors and ask the competent Kampuchean authorities to bring to the attention of world public opinion the barbarous crimes committed by the Pol Pot–Ieng Sary gang and the painful history of the Kampuchean people in general and my family in particular under the perfidious regime of these traitors.

After April 17, 1975, my family, composed of 14 people, was driven out of Phnom Penh and forced to settle in Prek Youn village, Troeui Sla subdistrict, district no. 20 (Sean Thom), Kandal province. My family was separated into two groups:

The first group included my uncle, my elder sister, my brother-in-law, and my two nieces. Those five people were ordered to return to their native province of Siem Reap, but halfway had to stop in Kompong Thom.

The second group included my grandmother, my father, my mother, my younger brother, my younger sister, my nephew, my niece and myself: eight people in all. This group had to go to Youhan village to take part in production work, together with other people. We did forest exploitation, water conservation work, cultivation, working hard all day without any rest. My grandmother, my parent, my nephew and my niece could not work, the former ones because of their physical weakness, the latter because of their young age. The people in the Pol Pot–Ieng Sary clique only gave them a half bowl of rice and a half bowl of corn a day. Those who could not work (the sick, the old, the small children) received only half of the ration or nothing at all when food got scarce.

After five months of this ordeal, hunger and thirst, my family was once again driven out of Youhan village to be settled in sector no. 5, Phnom Sarok district. How hard this displacement was! My family was packed in the hold of a small fishing boat, full of human excrement, to be taken to the province of Kompong Chhnang. As soon as we arrived there, we were pushed onto a GMC truck, together with other families, totaling around 120 people, crammed into a box. Night fell, suddenly rain and wind forced the entire convoy to stop at Pursat. From there, we were taken to Sisophon by rail. The trip caused us endless misery. Two hundred people were packed into a wagon normally used for transporting cattle. We were pressed so close together that we could hardly budge. Some of us had diarrhea and relieved themselves on the spot, others caught cold and vomited, we quarreled and the children screamed and cried.

At Sisophon, we left the train to be taken by car to Phnom Sarok district and then taken, on foot, to Pong Ro village, Pau Chal village, Phnom Sarok district, Battambang province. This was October 1975. In this village, my father was taken away to be killed. Later, we came to learn that he was taken to a forest east of the village and murdered there. He was accused of being a former rebel-officer despite the fact that he was a well-known businessman.

In Pong Ro village, the lack of food and everything caused the death of many people. Other than being killed, people in Pong Ro died of malaria, dysentery, beri-beri, or of starvation on the very spot where they worked hard digging irrigation canals night and day without food, drink, or even water for washing. My family suffered the same fate. My grandmother, my mother, my nephew and my niece, cursed with paralysis and dysentery, died one after the other, due to the lack of medicines and food.

I was particularly affected by the circumstances accompanying the deaths of my nephew and my niece: no one was there to help me incinerate or bury them. I had to bury them while I was so weakened by beri-beri that I could hardly walk. Then, with all of my strength, I pressed the dead bodies against me and I made my way, with tears in my eyes, to the forest east of the village to bury them. Thus, of my family, only three people remained: my younger brother, my little sister, and I. We worked hard day and night, in the rain, under the burning sun, sharing a daily ration of one bowl of rice for every 40 to 50 people, every 24 hours.

The people in Pong Ro village lived in constant fear of being spied upon, of being beaten by the brutes, while at work. Even worse, the elderly and children, men and women, were afraid of being executed at any moment. Fortunately, in late January 1979, we were liberated, in time, by the forces of the National United Front for the Salvation of Kampuchea, otherwise, we would have been turned into manure or hit on the skull to be thrown into ditches at the foot of the Kon Khleng Mountain (Phnom Sarok district).

We are immensely grateful to the National United Front for the Salvation of Kampuchea for their efforts, but never shall we forget our hatred for the Pol Pot–Ieng Sary clique.

Later I learned that the 4 family members in Kompong Thom were killed by these brutes. Only my niece, who was fed and protected by my fellow countrymen from these savage brutes, survived. I returned to Sare village, Sivilag subdistrict, Kompong Thom district, Kompong Thom province, to find her and, at present, I am raising her in Wat Svay village, Siem Reap 3 subdistrict, Siem Reap district, Siem Reap province.

The painful story of my family is an unforgettable, bitter story like that of so many others of my Khmer compatriots. The image of the Kampuchean people's blood mixed with their tears under the Pol Pot–Ieng Sary regime is an indelible image. The bright red blood covering the piles of human bones in the bulging graves is permanently etched in the memory of the Kampuchean people: unforgettable atrocities caused to our country by the barbaric and perfidious hands of the faithless and lawless Pol Pot–Ieng Sary clique. The bright red blood calls us all to demand blood for blood, to forever erase the existence of the clique from our territory.

The painful story of my family related above in my letter of denunciation is a truthful account laying bare, before the whole world, the crimes perpetrated by the Pol Pot–Ieng Sary clique against innocent people.

I am a victim, a Khmer student who has escaped from the clutches of traitors determined to drown Kampuchea in blood and who pursued the outrageous policy of genocide against Khmer intellectuals. I hope that the patriotic Khmer intellectuals who have survived and are staying abroad or are in this country will do whatever they can to help me make the Pol Pot–Ieng Sary clique pay for their debt of blood and tears.

Done at Wat Svay village, Siem Reap 3 subdistrict, Siem Reap district,
Siem Reap province, June 29, 1979.

Tik How, victim

2.1.1.06
Mr. Pen Navuth

I am Pen Navuth, 44 years of age, a former professor of history at the Faculty of Dramatic Arts and the Faculty of Letters and Human Sciences in Phnom Penh. My wife is Ros Man. We have four sons. We are now working at the Ministry of Education.

Before April 17, 1975, we lived in a building near the Bassac River (apartment C-17). At that time there were seven in my family: my wife, my three sons, my two brothers, and I.

On the morning of April 17, 1975, at 10:00 a.m., we saw small boats of the armed forces of the National United Front of Kampuchea tie up near our home. We raised a white flag on our house to welcome them.

Two hours later, soldiers came to drive us out of our house and outside the city for three days, they said. But we could not come back. We left the city in an easterly direction along National Route 1. Then we stayed for more than a month in Prek Eng village because we could not find a place to live. Besides, we wanted to return to Phnom Penh on hearing the appeal the new rulers made to professors, pharmacists, doctors, artists, technicians, and military personnel to take part in the reconstruction of the country.

In that village many people died every day, especially children and the elderly. The people there were constantly frightened by the Pol Pot–Ieng Sary troops who pillaged valuable things such as watches and radio sets, and arrested people to kill them.

On May 15, 1975, I met members of two other families: Pen Fanny, the wife of Ly Den, and Pen Phy, the wife of Tep Hen. Our three families decided to go to our native village, located in Battambang province, by going through Kompong Thom and Siem Reap provinces.

Unfortunately, on June 7, 1975, Pol Pot–Ieng Sary troops stopped us and made us stay in Ngan subdistrict, San Dann district, Preah Vihear province.

At that time the inhabitants were scattered in the villages of Prey Srong, which was said to be a malaria-infested area.

Under the Pol Pot–Ieng Sary regime, which was the most fascist and cruel we have known, we suffered all kinds of misery. We were compelled to do hard labor but received little food. We had no medications to treat ourselves when sick. We could be denounced at any time by the traitors and killed without being taken to any court. We lived constantly in fear.

On December 25, 1975, my brother-in-law, Ros Saman, who was 40 years old, died of malaria and bloating caused by lack of food and medication.

On December 20, 1975, my friend Thai Si Chin, who used to be a physician, died of bloating. Five days after the death of my brother-in-law, that is, on December 30, 1975, Lanh, the head of the commune, sent me to the town of Kompong Thom with thousands of others to build irrigation work and dikes.

As a result of forced labor and insufficient and irregular meals, and constantly tormented by fear, I became weaker and weaker. When this work ended, in April 1976, I went back to my house, 80 kilometers from the work site.

I suffered from bloating. At that time Pen Phy, my sister, a physician, and my wife decided to go to San Dann village to exchange gold and diamonds for food and fruit. Unfortunately, on May 8, 1976, my wife was arrested upon her return from San Dann by Lanh, the head of the commune, who detained her in a barn all night and then made her work in a potato field for the next week.

Soon after, I was evacuated again, to Svay village, where I stayed at the house of Mak Preng, who was the widow of a former official at the ministry of post and telecommunications in Phnom Penh. She had four children to care for: a daughter named Sarin, and three boys, named Reth, Khna, and Pau.

Late in May 1976, that family was said to have been transferred by the village head to Svay Lan village. In fact, its members were killed, as I was told by my friend Sa Oum. He told me that he was trapping animals at Veal Prinh village. While he was between Ngorn village and Veal Prinh village he heard cries, tears, and moans of grief mixed together with laughter and joking.

As he went through bushes and clearings, he arrived at the site of the noises. From a hiding place, Sa Oum saw Kim Chea, the commune head, and his men Vuon Lot Chham and Loy Lay, who were quite animated. In front of them was a group of victims, their hands tied behind their backs.

The killers raped the widow Mak Preng and her young daughter. Then they disemboweled them without any mercy and threw their bodies into a deep pit. Then they struck the two boys with pickaxes and threw them into the same pit. The last son, Khna, was disemboweled. The killer took out his liver and ate it.

How we trembled in fear upon hearing Sa Oum's account, both for ourselves and for our children!

We thought a great deal about the future of the children. How heart rending were the scenes we saw of them doing hard work as they were forced to do by the soldiers.

One day in April 1977, the woman who was head of Rong village abused my wife because she helped my six-year-old daughter carry a bucket of water that was 0.4 meters high and 0.35 meters in diameter. My wife could only weep.

Think about the deeds of the Pol Pot–Ieng Sary clique!

What a sea of suffering was caused by these criminal acts of genocide?

Done at Phnom Penh, June 25, 1979
Pen Navuth

2.1.1.07
Mrs. Yasuko Naito

Name: Yasuko Naito
Age: 47
Birth date: 1932
Origin: Tokyo, Japan
Present domicile: Phnom Penh
Family: Father: Toque Naito (deceased)
Mother: Umiko Naito (deceased)
Husband: Sar Teung Leung (deceased)
Children: Sar Thomory, born 1958 (deceased)
Sar Thonory, born 1960 (deceased)

My name is Naito Yasuko, age 47. I am of Japanese nationality and was born in Tokyo. My husband's name was Sar Teung Leung. He worked at the Ministry of Foreign Affairs under the Lon Nol regime.

On the night of April 16, 1975, enemy rocket launchers shelled the capital. No one could sleep. At 5:00 a.m. there was a lull in the shelling, and we took breakfast. The radio was off the air. This made us think that the radio station had been hit during the night. Just at that moment there was a great deal of noise in the city. Pol Pot's armored cars, filled with soldiers flying white flags, rolled down the streets. A crowd that had gathered on the sidewalk applauded wildly. We said to each other that at last the war was over. Our maid asked me: "A loaf of bread that used to sell for 100 riels is selling now at 500 riels, and the shops are closing. Should we buy some to have a few extra?" I told her to buy eight loaves.

Through the window I could see Pol Pot's soldiers carrying loaves of bread, and they looked hungry. The radio announced: "The government has been overthrown. The Khmer Rouge of Kampuchea has occupied the city." The announcement was made by the superior priest and by Mr. Khieu Samphan. We could not hold back our tears at this historic moment. By 11:00 a.m., we had had our lunch. In the afternoon, a bus arrived with armed soldiers wearing helmets. They said that anyone who tried to flee would be arrested and punished. My husband's brothers obeyed and went out. Cars came up and took them away. Pol Pot's soldiers used megaphones to tell everyone to go outside. They fired at any doors that were closed. For the next two to three days, the inhabitants of the capital had to register their names at Prek Pnauv and were ordered to evacuate immediately, taking only a few items of clothing because, they were told, they would return home soon.

My husband told me to hide my rings, bracelets, and earrings to reduce the risks of the trip. I obeyed him right away and stuffed all my jewelry into a briefcase of my husband's and then put the briefcase into a wardrobe. We carried with us only our identity cards and a few personal belongings. They urged us to evacuate quickly because enemy aircraft would supposedly bomb the city. At that moment in front of the goldsmith's shop across the street, we saw a man with both hands tied to a large carriage gate, screaming desperately. In reply to my questions, he indicated that he did not want to evacuate right away because his wife was away at the moment. That is why he was arrested and tied up, "to stay there, since he couldn't go to the trouble of going elsewhere."

The same day, at my husband's brother's house, they were not urged to evacuate. On the morning of April 18, Radio Phnom Penh broadcast an order to foreigners to go to the Phnom Penh Hotel, which had become at the time an international center. We went that way, but half way there, in front of the Air France office, we ran into a barricade thrown up by Pol Pot troops. They did not let us pass, even though my husband showed them our passport. At the house of a friend who lived nearby, we were urged by soldiers to evacuate. If we did not obey, they said, we would be tied up and thrown into one of four trucks that they had. As we approached our house, our younger son Thonory arrived back there to see what had happened. On April 15, the son of my husband's brother had advised us to take shelter at his father's house because it would be dangerous to stay at our house. That is why we had carried with us only a few belongings.

Thonory let us know that our house had not been touched, and that some of our neighbors were staying on. That night we stayed put, to see how things would turn out. My husband's brother became frightened, however, out of concern that he might be forced out of the city in the middle of the night with his young children. That is why we took our supper before nightfall and drove in our car to Prek Pnauv. Our two faithful dogs followed us, but we were forced to leave them behind. We took with us some salt, rice, kitchen utensils, and dishes. When we got to the fish-breeding center at Prek Pnauv, it was still early, but the personnel had left, and the center was abandoned.

The next day we caught some fish and salted and dried them to eat during our trip. Mosquitoes were everywhere, and we had only one mosquito net. I bought three more at a price of 3000 riels each, a container of cooking oil at a price of 2500 riels, and six mats at a price of 300 riels each. We left the fish-breeding center and travelled along Route 7. Along the way, we met patients who had been forced out of the Calmette Hospital and other hospitals. Some who were weak walked with the help of nurses, having been operated upon only a few hours before. The places where the operation had been performed were still bleeding, with flies swarming around. They all wore hospital clothing. It made me think of a painting I had seen somewhere depicting scenes of hell.

Farther along, I saw the naked body of a man, nailed to a door. On his chest was written in large letters: "enemy." Soldiers of Pol Pot standing by the body watched the people passing by. They broke out laughing and told everyone to open their eyes and look at it. We all worried about the future.

That night, we slept under the stars. In the morning, we were encouraged to press on. We walked without resting. We came to a brick kiln, from which we smelled a nauseating odor. That morning, bodies of soldiers had been found in the furnace. It was whispered that the families of anyone who wore the uniform of a Lon Nol soldier was killed, because they were considered to be soldiers. Hearing this, our older son immediately burned up his new khaki trousers. My husband's brother wrapped up a nylon tent, a wool blanket, and some American canned goods and threw it all in the river.

We were told that we would be shot if Pol Pot's soldiers found our passport. I quickly made a little bag out of a handkerchief, and I put my passport inside and slipped it behind my back. The road was full of people. All day long I had to drag a small cart carrying my husband and my child, who had taken ill. We ate near the river, then climbed down the river bank to get a drink. But at that moment everyone screamed and pointed at something. Corpses of soldiers were floating adrift. People said they had seen dozens of corpses since morning.

We continued along. We saw women in labor along the road. An elderly man who had been abandoned by his son held his hands together and begged passers-by to take him with them. We wanted to help him but did not know what to do.

I needed to go down to the riverbank to urinate, but people shouted at me to stop, warning me that there were land mines all around. Just then I spotted mines hidden all around in the grass. One step forward and I would have been ripped to pieces. The thought of it made me break out in a sweat.

Near the Prek Kdam bridge, we were ordered to leave our automobile. We turned over our keys to them. Here my husband had a discussion with his brother. His brother wanted to drive as far as Kratie, but my husband replied that there was not enough gas, and that all the gas stations were closed. My husband said that we should continue on foot. So we split up, our eyes full of tears. We switched our luggage onto the bicycles. Our elder son rode a bicycle because he could no longer walk. By the Prek Kdam ferry boat, it rained hard, and we got soaked to the skin. Since we could not change our clothes or dry them, we spent the whole night shivering, and none of us could sleep. Our elder son was completely exhausted.

A truck came along, and the driver let us climb in, but we had to leave our bicycles. We were taken to the back yard of the Oudong pagoda. Our younger son ran to say that he had seen my husband's brother's car. He recognized it by the registration number on the license plate. When some Pol Pot soldiers and a monk got into the car, he asked them about its owner. They told him that the owner was two kilometers west of there. He went there and asked everyone he saw, but he could not find his uncle.

Several Pol Pot soldiers called to us and gathered us together and wrote down our names. When it was my turn, they were surprised to hear me say that I was Japanese. They looked at me intently and then reported to another soldier, probably a superior. We asked whether Umiko and I might return to Japan. They told us to wait. Then they took us to Phnom Oudong, supposedly to give us some rice paddy land. There it was cold. Among our acquaintances was a physician there who gave my son an injection with a syringe he had hidden in his things when he left Phnom Penh. He whispered in my ear: "Your son will not last long." At 3:00 p.m. on December 5, Thomory died of enteritis. I buried him and carved his name on a tree nearby.

We stayed ten days at Phnom Oudong. Then a meeting was called and we were ordered to leave Phnom Oudong within twenty-four hours to go to Phnom Praseth, Preah Reach Trop, at Pepour village, which is near Phnom Penh, to wait to return to Phnom Penh. We left Phnom Oudong and reached a village near Pepour. The food we brought from Phnom Penh had run out. For lack of anything to eat, we went in search of food. I bartered a sarong for twenty-five containers of rice. Finally we had nothing left to trade, and our worries increased day by day. Each family got three containers of rice a day. A family of twelve persons got three containers, the same as a couple without children. Each family also got one spoonful of salt.

We had to get up at 4:00 a.m. to weed, work the rice paddies, and replant rice. On July 31, 1975, Thonory, our younger son, fell to the ground while climbing a palm tree to gather leaves to make a roof for our hut. I asked the president of the administrative committee of the village to have my son taken to a hospital, but he refused. I gathered medicinal herbs and made a concoction for my son to drink, but it did not work. In two weeks, my son died.

In September 1975 we were taken by buffalo cart to a place twenty-one kilometers away. Umiko had so many boils all over her body that she was unable to sit. She was tossed around while riding in the cart, and her condition got worse. She needed to be hospitalized, and this brought another separation.

We continued along in a truck. At Pursat, we boarded a train going to Sisophon. There we switched again to a truck. At that time, my husband's health took a turn for the worse because of continuing diarrhea. Once again we got into a buffalo cart and went to Tapaing Tamau. There we got a piece of land and put up a hut. We managed to finish it. This was the second hut we had built. We could have lived in the first hut built with Thonory's help.

The grass grew waist high at that place. To deal with the larger trees, we asked others to help. For the smaller trees, we borrowed axes and cut them down ourselves. We cleared a piece of land big enough to put up a tent. We spread out our mats on the dry grass to make a temporary dwelling.

My husband was required to carry firewood. Three days later he came back, pitifully fatigued. I asked permission to replace my husband in carrying wood, and after four days of this work a tumor on my ankle burst and caused me serious pain. I forced myself to work. After this difficult work, pus began to ooze from my instep, and I got permission from the group chief to rest for four days. I was tortured by my wound, and it was painful to walk. I tried herbal concoctions, but they did not help.

My husband took sick with malaria and diarrhea. He was seriously malnourished, and his body became swollen. A yellowish liquid oozed from his feet. He died December 19, 1975.

I was left alone. Six months later, again I was transferred. I had to leave my husband's grave to go to another village called Mara. The villagers there were kindhearted. They were afraid that the Pol Pot soldiers might find out that I was Japanese and kill me. They hid me with a Kampuchean family. There I turned the wheel to spin silk, did cooking, and weaved wattles for the roofs of houses.

The most difficult work was collecting animal dung. In the morning, I had to get up early to collect buffalo and cattle dung and pile it up. Each day ten adult women had to collect two tons of dung. This was very difficult work. At the beginning of 1977, because of a shortage of rice, for one hundred sixty persons we got only fifteen containers of rice per meal. Hunger forced us to eat green papayas, and even papaya stems, banana stems, rotten plants, and all kinds of edible grasses.

On June 12, 1977, about one hundred Pol Pot soldiers surrounded the village and kept the residents from going more than fifty meters from their houses and ordered them to stop all work. Five families who had had some family members working in Vietnam for a month or so were called out. Another family was also picked out. These families were ordered to go with their luggage to Tomop. They said goodbye to everyone and left on six buffalo carts that came back a half hour later. Their friends found out what had happened to them. At three hundred meters from the village, the six families were ordered to leave their luggage and get into trucks that had arrived to take them. The six buffalo carts came back to the village.

That day black-clad men came to the village and followed us everywhere, even when we were bathing. Everyone listened to hear the humming of truck engines. The village was in total silence. That night there was a downpour, and no one could sleep. The next day, Pol Pot soldiers gave back to the villagers spades, hoes, and baskets they had borrowed the day before. On these tools we could see traces of blood and hair, which frightened us very much. After the Pol Pot soldiers left, villagers who had had family members killed went out to see and found little hills of freshly piled dirt near bamboo bushes. They also found pieces of clothing, like sarongs.

Over a period of two months, there were three similar collective killings. The number killed was one hundred fifty-seven persons, which included women eight months pregnant, and women who had given birth only two days earlier. There were three graves. One was for children, one for women, and one for men. Those who were called out the second time were persons who had connections with the previous government, as well as professors and doctors. Those called out the third time were persons over thirty years of age. I could have been among this group. Every day I lived in anguish, awaiting the time I would be called.

On January 8, 1979, the radio announced the liberation of Phnom Penh. This was a great joy for the entire village. This meant the return of the country. It was the greatest joy of our lives. Liberated from a life worse than that of animals, everyone was happy. Again we could see loved ones after several years of separation. Religion would be restored, and we could again see monks. Women could again wear clothes of the colors they preferred. We could again see children going merrily to school. We could see weddings with traditional singing and dancing. Again we could exchange wishes for a happy life. All that had disappeared under the Pol Pot–Ieng Sary regime. Under their yoke, if you tried to rest, you would not get your ration of rice, you could not even go to the next village. Now we are free to go to look for our relatives. It was a change for me to stay alive and to hold a pen to write these lines. I am immensely happy.

June 25, 1979
Yasuko Naito

2.1.1.08
Mr. Pech Tum Kravel

Name: Pech Tum Kravel
Nationality: Khmer
Age: 36 years

I was a National Artist, I worked in the supervision section of the national service for the performing arts. I was a writer, an impresario, and I was a performer in traditional performances.

April 17 was a day of despair. I assure you that in all my work as a writer, and as an impresario I was always in opposition to the Lon Nol regime and criticized it as a bad regime. They were imbeciles, and bloodthirsty. And I hoped that the revolution would win, and that I could come to know a pure society, a true society.

To the contrary, however, April 17, 1975, was the day the Pol Pot–Ieng Sary clique, who were the dogs, the lackeys, the slaves of the Peking hegemonists, kicked out the whole population to live in the countryside. They separated me from my wife and my children. They sent me to live in the forest of Batt Baeng, in Koh Chen subdistrict, Ponhea Leu district, Kandal province. It was then that I saw crimes, genocide, of the Pol Pot clique with my own eyes. They were cruel, barbaric, fascist. They killed men with sticks, tied them up by the neck, and burned them alive. I saw corpses while I was out clearing the forest, when I was looking for weeds to make nets. They killed them and pushed them into rivers. I assure you that in a river 100 meters wide and 3 kilometers long, one could no longer drink the water because there were so many corpses floating on the surface. Even the fish in these rivers could no longer be eaten. In 1976 I was accused by the Pol Pot clique of having been a Lon Nol colonel, but since I was supported by the people, I was saved from this accusation.

In late 1976, after finding out that I was alive, my wife and my children rejoined me in Sector 32.

At that time the Pol Pot clique accused our village of sympathizing with the white Khmers, that is, they considered us as their No. 1 enemies. Most of the people in our village were killed. The rest were forced to leave for Ang Serey-Phnom and Rus, in northern Kompong Speu province.

In 1977, I was closely watched and they accused me again that I had been a Lon Nol soldier. But since I enjoyed a good reputation, the people supported me and said that I was only a milk vendor. Again I was saved.

Living for three years under the Pol Pot regime, my family and I lost all human rights. We lived like animals. Every day we lived in fear, in poverty, in grief, in a tragedy that we had never before known. We had no right to speak, to listen, even to read a book, that is, we had to live like a deaf and dumb person, or a blind person.

The traitors made us work hard. I had to wash toilets and carry the excrement of the entire village from morning to night to make fertilizer. All night long they made us look for termite hills and dig ditches. To eat they gave us only soup, every month, all year long. Since the work was excruciating and the meals were inadequate, I fell seriously ill and almost died three times.

Speaking as a former National Artist and as a nationalist, I lived in incomparable grief, sorrow, and sadness. I could not forget what I did for my country and what I have endured in my life. Many times in silence I have not been able to hold back my tears thinking about the future of the Khmer peoples, and about my dear country. I thought of the arts and culture that were the Khmer soul that the Pol Pot–Ieng Sary traitors destroyed. I thought of my dear country that was ruined by the savage Pol Pot–Ieng Sary clique who were the lackeys of Peking.

At that time I had no greater hope than to be reunited with my family, and I could do nothing against the traitors.

But January 7 arrives . . .

How it was that the National United Front for the Salvation of Kampuchea with our dear friend Vietnam sacrificed everything, and the other socialist allies supported us, so now I, my family, the Khmer people, the arts, the soul of my country were all saved.

We are so happy, and we will never forget the good deeds of the National United Front for the Salvation of Kampuchea and our dear friend Vietnam that have saved us from death.

To respond rightfully to these good deeds, I swear:

- to respect and follow the path set out by the National Front for the Salvation of Kampuchea!
- to solidify and strengthen forever the friendship between Khmer and Vietnam!
- to serve the nation and the people completely.

Phnom Penh, July 1, 1979
Pech Tum Kravel

2.1.1.09
Mr. Kry Beng Hong

On April 17, 1975, while waiting for news about the negotiation of a cease fire between Pol Pot and Lon Nol, my brothers, uncles, aunts, and my family all stayed inside my house to avoid the bombardment in the city of Phnom Penh. A short time later I noted the despair felt by the city's inhabitants, who were forced out of all the houses under the military rule of the Pol Pot clique. At that time we hid quietly in our house.

At 7:00 a.m. on April 18, the Pol Pot forces quickly evacuated the entire population of the city. I hastily grabbed a few old clothes and mosquito nets and fifteen kilograms of rice. My wife did not have time to get her clothes and valuables because of the insistence of the Pol Pot armed units that we leave.

For lack of other means of transport, I took my bicycle, even though it had no tires, to carry sacks of clothing. We attached my children to each other with a long rope, and they walked. My wife carried her six-month-old baby. Forced out by the Pol Pot troops, I left my house with great regret.

Monivong Boulevard, even though quite broad, was full of people. They walked slowly and with difficulty. On the Monivong wharf, in the heat of the sun, I saw hundreds of corpses. I also saw old people who looked as if they would not survive. Even though we started at 7:00 a.m., by noon we got only as far as the Law Faculty, which is about two kilometers from our house.

On April 21, I crossed the Mekong River on a boat to Wat Svay village and Peam Oknhar Ong subdistrict. Corpses were floating in the river, and the stench from them was horrible. When we got to the other side of the river, my wife took our children off, and my nephew Alo stayed to guard the boat. I carried our household articles onto shore. A short time later, I heard wrenching cries. It was my nephew Alo, who had drowned. I could not save him, because the current was so strong. Thirty-six hours later I found my nephew's body floating in the river.

We stayed for more than twenty days in Wat Svay subdistrict. On May 15, 1975, the Pol Pot clique forced my family out of this subdistrict, and at that time I was separated from my aunt, my brothers, and my grandmother, who was blind and eighty years old. Because of the bad hygienic conditions, my small son got very bad diarrhea. On May 17, 1975, I crossed the Mekong River by canoe to the village of Thlok Chrau, which Pol Pot troops had stripped of anything of value. I had only two suits left that I could wear.

The health of my young son had gotten even worse, so I borrowed a cart from a farmer to go to join him at my own village, Roka Koy, twenty kilometers from Phnom Penh. It took two days to get there, and I arrived at about 5:00 p.m. on May 19. My aunt and brothers were in despair. On May 22, my son died.

On the day I arrived at my own village, some boys fifteen to seventeen years old came and asked questions about my personal history. Each of them tried to say that I was a lieutenant or a commander who should therefore be eliminated right away. I am a straightforward man, and from the time I left Phnom Penh I had said that I was a construction engineer, because I thought that such work was not antagonistic to the revolution.

On May 25, 1975, the village committee gathered the villagers together, including me of course, to hold a meeting to classify the population into three categories: (1) the original population, or the population of the year 1970; (2) the people who had become refugees in 1973, who were referred to as the population of the year 1973; (3) the city dwellers, refugees of 1975, who were called prisoners of war, and who could be eliminated at any time. From that time, we had to perform very hard work, under penalty of death if we complained.

On May 26, 1975, under the auspices of the village, I went to clear some land near a lake, because this land was supposed to be good for cultivation. On June 1, the Pol Pot clique set new quotas to make us work harder. The new population (meaning the 1975 people) had to dig and carry three cubic meters of dirt per day per person. After we started working at that level, one or two persons began to disappear every day. At that time I was very sad.

On June 24, 1975, about 700 persons (all 1975 people) were forced out by the village committees and put into a concentration camp at Roka Koy pagoda, a small and miserable place. Conditions there were quite deplorable: no hygiene facilities, no food, and forced labor. Contact between the 1975 people and the 1970 people was forbidden.

On June 30, 1975, Pol Pot troops (more than a dozen) with guns drawn called meetings to interrogate the new population about the murder of some high ranking officials or military officers. At that time, they said in front of the whole group that I was Construction Engineer "Hong." I thought they would shoot me then and there. A short time later, seven military personnel of the Pol Pot clique were posted outside my house. My family was in a state of despair as a result, and I could do nothing but pray. Fifteen minutes later, these traitors moved on to the house of Sun Oeur, the former subdistrict head. They led him to Otakuon pagoda, three kilometers from the Peam Chikang market and killed him there.

Regarding the famine, these traitors made the local population do forced labor without trying to solve the food question. On February 2, 1976, I was sent to a work site forty-five kilometers from my house. I stayed there ten days, when I got a new order to return right away to the village, even if it meant going in the middle of the night. I was petrified, because I did not know exactly what they planned to do. Typically, a person ordered to go back to the village would either be killed or sent for a very difficult reeducation. In any case, I did not know how to react. Accompanied by the village chief, I set out at 3:00 a.m. and got back to the village the next day in the evening. Once I was there, the village official told me that I was supposed to go to the site of construction of irrigation canals at Roka Koy. There, men had to dig four cubic meters of dirt a day, and women three cubic meters.

On April 3, 1976, I was sent to a work site at the village of Svay Po and Prek Live, located about forty kilometers from my home. On April 20, 1976, more than 400 new people (1975 people) were poisoned due to the negligence of the cook, who prepared a meal with water hyacinth[1] that had been picked near rice paddies that were full of endrin powder (an insecticide). We all got diarrhea and were sick the whole night. In the morning, a village official named Ly made us go to our work site. The more elderly became exhausted, and many collapsed in the rice paddies. At noon, the official got us together and warned us, "You are very lazy. If you act this way, you will never make it back home to see your wife or children."

On May 12, 1976, I was ordered to return home. But on May 14, 1976, I

1. The text gives the name of this plant in Khmer as *trakeat* and identifies it as "an aquatic plant." The plant is *Echarnia crassipes*. — Eds.

was sent to a dam-building site at Phum Thmey, three kilometers from the village. There the traitors made us work very hard. They put us in a camp five kilometers from the work site. Every morning, they woke us at 3:00 a.m. to go to the work site. We came back at 10:30 a.m. to eat. I would go to carry dirt from 12:30 until 5:00 p.m. After supper I would carry dirt from 6:30 until 9:30 p.m. The distance between the camp and the work site was about five kilometers. During work, talk was forbidden, because they treated the new populations as prisoners of war. All this was directed by a security chief named Ly. I was told that the soldiers of this traitor followed me all the time because he said that I had been a lieutenant.

On May 20, 1976, four Pol Pot military men came to watch me while I was at work. But a short time later, Ly, the security chief, ordered the four military men to take away a man who had been a lieutenant, to kill him. This victim, Sam Nang, fell to the ground after being kicked many times. I was afraid after seeing such a harsh sanction. I worked hard after seeing that the killer threatened my friend Ham Hang. My group carried 85,000 cubic meters of dirt.

On June 16, 1976, I went to work in the middle of the forest to construct irrigation canals, eighty kilometers from Roka Koy. During the trip, I saw men drawing plows like water buffaloes.

One day I visited my aunt, Suon, whose husband had died in 1973. She told me that on the other side of the river was a prison camp called Ansoeum Duoch, where thousands of men and women had been condemned to forced labor and to death by the traitors of Pol Pot. On the night of July 30, 1976, I heard very loud cries not far from my house. I followed them and took up a position under a tree. The Pol Pot traitors counted up to 185 corpses that were piled like fish.

On August 4, 1976, I returned home to Roka Koy. Once there, I worked collecting 300 kilograms of fertilizer. I worked hard because the Pol Pot people wanted to kill me. On September 4, 1976, I saw security troops arrive at the mess hall in jeeps. I was very frightened and made myself work hard and quietly.

On September 16, 1976, the general committee of the village gave me a pair of buffalo with a cart to transport fertilizer. The chief of the fertilizer group told me to cross a two meter high dike, which I unfortunately did. The cart turned over in a ditch. Suddenly I fell from the cart and rolled to the ground. The wheel of the cart crushed my chest and broke several of my ribs. I was unconscious from 7:00 a.m. until 11:00 a.m. Because of the lack of medications, they were not able to do much for me at the hospital.

On December 28, 1976, the Pol Pot troops brutally killed about 463 persons in the pagoda of Peam Chikang and Ni Rot in Kompong Cham province. At that time three young militia members arrived in this murder camp and the traitors killed them after killing the 463 persons. These Pol Pot soldiers kept on killing pupils, teachers, and other civilians.

On January 2, 1977, I went to guard corn fields one kilometer from the village, carrying a stick in my hand, even though my wounds had not yet healed.

On March 11, 1977, a pair of buffalo belonging to the original population ate some tufts of corn. I was quite frightened but tied the buffalo to a big tree with a short rope. In a few minutes I was criticized and insulted over what had happened, but I managed to keep calm.

On April 11, 1977, before the Khmer new year, I was summoned to a guerrilla camp where the chief, a man called Ieng, but nicknamed "Great Killer," had threatened and killed many people. He accused me of being a military man, then he started to take me to the Roka Koy security office, at the village of Svay Ta Hen, six kilometers from my house. I was to carry salt, and my family was left in tears. When we arrived at this incarceration center, I saw a large, dark prison, where the prisoners were in chains. The "great killer," accompanied by a young man named Bang, who was armed with a gun and a bayonet, came to meet me. Just outside this prison, which gave off a horrible smell, I was guarded by four or five men with guns, and I waited until 5:00 p.m. Then, on Eang's order, I went back home.

On June 10, 1977, I did land clearing with some others at Roka. New troops arriving from the southwest had carried out massacres of innocent persons at the Otakuon pagoda, west of Peam Chikang.

On August 2, 1977, I went to the rice paddies with other "1975" people and some militia groups to work cleared lands in the Roul Roka forest. For lunch, I was given only corn broth, even though I had to work until nighttime. I got up at 3:00 a.m. every morning to work in the rice paddies. Weak, emaciated, and undernourished, I had to gather tree leaves to mix with the broth. In December 1977, the new heads of work teams arriving from the southwestern zone, who were quite vicious, killed all the militia youth (about 400 persons). The worst of these killers were a district committee member named Kan, a village committee member named Lan, and a girl named Thy. On November 20, 1977, a number of people were killed at Phnom Thmey, in an operation run by Lan, by the intelligence chief, and the guerrilla commander.

They put more than one hundred men and women to work with buffalo, giving these people food that was far from sufficient. A large kettle holds one kilogram of grains of rice for 300 persons. These groups ate nothing but rice.

They kept killing people in the villages and also at the work sites. They also suppressed religion, defrocking all the monks and destroying temples and other places of worship. Temples were turned into poultry houses and manure silos.

On July 3, 1977, the village mess hall was divided into two sections, one for the 1975 people, and the other for the 1970 people. At every meal the food rations for the two groups were different. The 1975 people got only broth containing two spoonsful of rice and three liters of boiling water.

Quite a few people were killed during this period: on July 12, 1977, Mr. Iem, former superintendent of agriculture; on July 16, 1977, Mr. Him and his family; on July 18, 1977, Mr. Meng and his family; on July 19, 1977, Mr. Han, Mr. Phalla, and Mr. Pong and their families; on July 30, 1977, Mr. Ngourn, Mr. Khim and his family; on August 5, 1977, Mr. Touch Mech and his family; on August 13, 1977, Mr. Mean and Mr. Try Heap and their families; on August 19, 1977, Mr. Sek and Mr. El and their families; on August 22, 1977, Mr. Lep and his family; on August 30, 1977, Mr. Sun and Mr. Nay Srim and their families; on September 5, 1977, Mr. Bo, the school teacher, and his family; on September 13, 1977, Professor Por Leng and his family; on September 19, 1977, Mr. Ngourn Chheang and his family; on October 15, 1977, Mr. Kao and his family; on November 24, 1977, Thy, my nephew; on October 9, 1977, Mr. Soeun and Mr. Kheng and their families; on October 16, 1977, Mr. Seang Bun Yon and his family.

I was afraid that my turn would come soon. I told my wife that before dying, I would climb a palm tree and denounce the crime of extermination being committed by the Pol Pot clique. I made up a poison to use to commit suicide, out of toad eggs mixed with poisonous nuts and a strychnine base. I told my wife that we would surely be killed after the killing of Professor Por Leng.

On September 13, 1977, at 4:00 p.m., Professor Por Leng and his family were killed at the Otakuon pagoda. After supper, I decided to take the poison, but my wife asked me to wait a few days. During work time, I would think that one fine day, my life would be ended by the Pol Pot troops. They were worse than Hitler's. I was truly in despair as a result of all the killings. Kampuchea was a civilized and well-developed country, but with the Pol Pot regime it became a prison camp.

I decided that September 14, 1977, would be the end of my life. In the evening of that date I planned to commit suicide together with my family. After returning from the dining hall, my family put on clean clothes. At 11:30 p.m. we woke up together, and I passed around poison pills, forty for myself, and thirty for each of my children.

When I gave pills to my wife, she cried bitterly. As I was about to swallow the pills, my wife managed to stop me. A short time later my mother-in-law woke up. By this time my wife had stopped crying, and she begged me once again not to swallow the poison. In the morning I went to work in the rice paddy. At that time the food shortage had gotten especially bad, even though several hundred tons of rice were kept in storage, and corn was taken by boat to the cliques in Phnom Penh.

On December 1, 1977, one of eight workers was killed by the traitors at the Otakuon pagoda. On December 8, 1977, Kan, an illiterate man of the Kang Meas district committee, called a big meeting in Bos Por village, getting the entire population to attend. At the meeting, I looked around to try to find my brother-in-law Phoeung, but he was not there. I feared for his life.

After the meeting I went to work in the rice paddy with five others, under orders of Sreng, the group chief, and I thought we would be killed. But that night my mother told me that my group had replaced others who had been killed. Since December 7, 1977, Phoeung Var, Sok Kheang, and Yap Rith Se had been killed. At that time I was terribly concerned about my younger sister, who after giving birth had an infant to care for in addition to her five other children, and her husband had been killed. And now they wanted to kill me as they had killed Phoeung, my brother-in-law. What kind of revolution was this?

Then Sreng, the group chief, came on his bicycle and said I should leave right away to go to work. We reached the work site at about 8:00 p.m., and there I saw one of the leaders wearing my brother-in-law Phoeung's shirt. I worked hard at this work site, and in return I got little to eat.

On December 17, 1977, with permission of the group chief, I went to get my mat from my house. At the entrance to the Phum Thmey pagoda, I saw some guerrilla fighters with their bicycles. They stopped about five meters in front of me, including a man named Sem. They said that they were going to kill Hong. I thought they meant me and was grief stricken. But, it turned out, they were looking for another man named Hong from population group 73, who had been the secretary of the Peam Chikang district. He was on a list of persons to be killed. On December 3, 1978, the guerrilla chief Eang was killed, and then on December 8, 1977, Mr. Lim, of the village committee.

According to its plan to kill off the Khmer race, the Pol Pot clique had progressively reduced the food ration, meaning that on one day they would give one milk container full of rice for two or five persons, and the next day only half a milk container.

By good fortune, Kratie province was occupied on December 31, 1978, by the National United Front for the Salvation of Kampuchea. On January 1, 1979, I fled into the forest in the middle of the night and stayed there four days before going to Roka Koy. On the night of January 5, 1979, the city of Kompong Cham was occupied by the National Salvation Front, but on that day the Pol Pot troops chased us out of the Reay Pay commune, trying to kill us.

On January 7, 1979, I arrived back to Phnom Penh at 1:00 a.m. Two days later, I realized that the city of Phnom Penh had been liberated from the Pol Pot–Ieng Sary clique by the National Salvation Front, with the help of our Vietnamese friends.

We Kampucheans are deeply grateful to the revolutionary forces of the National Salvation Front, and to the Vietnamese people, who helped liberate Kampuchea.

As a person with technical skills, I promise to put my knowledge to the service of the people and the nation, and to work to rebuild the country.

Done at Phnom Penh, May 27, 1979

Kry Beng Hong

Additional Statement

While their men were killing the three militia youth, Ly, the security chief of the village, gave a signal to flee to his brother, who lived in Roka Koy village. The brother was my friend Pol Khim, formerly head of public works, and he has survived until now. He was a relative of Sreng, the great killer. Thus Pol Khim was aware of the plans of massacres set by the Pol Pot–Ieng Sary agents, and of their inside information.

As for the killing of the four hundred militia youth, the Pol Pot troops had gathered intellectuals, and students down to the seventh grade. The daughter of Pol Khim, a seventh grade student, was killed by these troops because she was a witness. As for the adults, the troops killed them in the Otakuon pagoda, which is in Peam Chikang subdistrict, Kang Meas district. The bachelors were killed in the So Korng subdistrict, Kang Meas district, and especially in Reay Pay subdistrict.

After raping the girls and disemboweling them to see their livers, the subdistrict chief, whose name was Vann, and thirty or so of his troops got together in the Roka Koy dining hall. His idea was to kill the new people, in order to take over their belongings. These killings were carried out at Roka Koy pagoda, where today one finds large ditches filled with hundreds of corpses. These troops not only raped the pretty young girls but then killed them with their bayonets.

In 1977, the clique people coming from the southwest, gathered together and killed all the groups of Hou Yuon and Hu Nim in Prey Chhor village.[2]

The major killer Thy, who was quite beautiful and very violent, changed her name from one region to the next, in order to keep the people from learning her identity. One day, after gathering some residents together, including Vat, Kam, San, Sour, Hong, Ve, Chhan, Kru and Kueng, Thy tied Ve up and kicked him quite ferociously in front of his wife, who was carrying her baby while husking rice at the work site. Ve fell to his knees and begged for mercy. In another incident, Thy killed an entire family of Malaysian meat sellers whose family name was Sok; she struck them with an axe in Otakuon village.

Done at Phnom Penh, June 20, 1979
Kry Beng Hong

Additional Statement about the Young Woman Criminal Thy

Under the Pol Pot clique's regime, Kan, the brother-in-law of Ng. Thy, who was head of the Kang Meas district committee, in the southwestern zone, and his accomplice Ngourn. Thy imposed forced labor on the people,

2. Hou Yuon and Hu Nim were former Khmer Rouge cabinet ministers who by this time had been killed; their adherents were deemed opposition elements. —Eds.

and as a result many girls suffered uterine diseases, and heavyset women hemorrhaged.

Under Thy's rule, most of the residents of the village were killed over a period of only a few months. In particular, on August 7, 1978, from the cruel work of the killer Thy, one saw hundreds of corpses floating in the river, tied together with chains and wires, some killed in Koh Sotin, in Kompong Cham province, others at the Roka Koy and Otakuon pagodas.

If you want to know the place in which she killed the residents, I could take you and show you exactly the burial sites.

Done at Phnom Penh, June 20, 1979
Kry Beng Hong

2.1.1.10
Mr. Chea Ponlok

On April 17, 1975, at 9:15 a.m., I walked out of my house to watch the arrival of the revolutionary army when Pol Pot's soldiers, dressed in black, ordered me to leave the building as quickly as possible, directing me towards the national highway. My family, many of my cousins, uncles, and aunts mingled in the crowd of hundreds of thousands of other innocent victims of the war. They marched sadly on the road, threatened by guns and under April's oppressive sun.

Late in the evening, I arrived at my father's cousin's house about twenty kilometers from Phnom Penh. I stayed there for three weeks, living under the shade of a mango tree. While there, I studied and learned about the political situation of the country. Meanwhile, I busied myself looking for means to live. I was given an old mat, a torn mosquito net, a cooking pot, two rice bowls and two spoons which were shared among three people. Having no rice, as I left the capital empty-handed, I was compelled to go up the Mekong, towards the liberated zone. There I joined a cooperative where I was asked to work in the field, cultivating the maize with a hoe and pedal windmill used for irrigation. Each day they gave us 200 grams of rice or green beans sometimes with a spoonful of salt; sometimes without salt. However, there were days when we went without food. It was during these times that I was forced to forage for grass to eat.

In December 1975, I was forced to move a second time. I was asked to pack the rucksacks. I was unable to sleep that night because I was afraid that this next trip would be to my death. At dawn, we were taken by trucks toward Kompong Thom, to a village at the foot of Phnom Santuk, where three months later they forcibly walked off with all of our possessions in order to establish, they claimed, a sanitary cooperative that was truly a genuine form of socialism with a big collectivist kitchen.

I was asked to fetch rattan and to cut wood for building the huts. This was the first time I ventured into the jungle and I was panic-stricken when I came across snakes, tracks of a wild boar, and the like. Later on, I was transferred to a plowing team. Meanwhile, our rations were lowered to 2.5 kilograms of rice for about sixty people. The soup was little more than water. I was no longer eating, but I was drinking some. One day, I felt sick but I was not allowed to rest and I was given no care for my sickness because they felt that my illness was imaginary. I forced myself to work but I was so short of breath that I could not steer my buffalo on the right furrow, so I was whipped on my back while the buffalo of the guy behind me trampled on my right foot. The scars are still visible. As for my wife, she had to work about twenty kilometers from the village, leaving our six-year-old daughter alone in the hut.

Next, I was made to work on building a dike. From 3:00 to 10:30 a.m., 2:30 to 5:00 p.m., and from 6:30 to 9:30 p.m., I dug or carried baskets of earth. Despite the forced hard labor, I strove to survive because of my daughter, so little and so innocent. Later on, I was transferred to the mountain to break stones. The work was very, very hard and as grueling as any work that we did as prisoners of war. While I was in the concentration camp in the mountains, my daughter was often ill. One day, after learning of her worsening condition, I asked the guards for permission to go see her but I was insulted by the guards of Pol Pot's regime. They said: "Your seeing her is not worthwhile. You are not a physician and your daughter does not work." I cried because of a father's love for his daughter and I could not stop my tears. I missed family life and conjugal love, because my wife was away from home for two or three months at a time. . . .

On January 9, 1979, after the arrival of the liberation troops, together with my friends, we escaped from the camp to join my family. Then we continued towards the capital because announcements on the radio and on circulating pamphlets asked us to return to our homes. On February 7, 1979, our caravan arrived in Phnom Penh, ending our long voyage. We set up a civil defense plan for our village to protect us against Pol Pot's remaining soldiers. I was elected head of the village and then head of the precinct. I served our compatriots in a spirit of brotherhood and supported our liberator, the Revolutionary People's Council of Kampuchea, against the Pol Pot regime.

Having seen the tortures visited upon the villagers, ex-soldiers, and employees of the former government, among others; having seen the killing of innocent Khmers, men, women, and children, and Muslims; having seen the flagrant violations of human rights. I was filled with hatred against the inhumane regime of Pol Pot and Ieng Sary that is guilty of these bloodthirsty crimes and they were subservient to Peking's expansionism, I joined and served those who liberated us.

Long live the liberation of January 7, 1979, which gave us a new life under a new sun!

Long live the People's Revolutionary Council of Kampuchea!
Long live the People's Republic Of Kampuchea!

Chea Ponlok, Phnom Penh, May 16, 1979

2.1.1.11
Mrs. Oum Parany

On April 17, 1975, at 9:00 a.m., the Pol Pot troops came to my house, firing in the air. They forced me to leave the capital right away under the pretext that the Americans would bomb the city. I left the city on National Route 1. I rested with my mother and daughter at Koki in Kandal province. My husband went to see his mother on April 16, 1975, and since then I have heard nothing from him.

I stayed seven hours at Koki and then left for Peam Chileang in Kompong Cham province. After that I was pushed to Kompong Thom province, where I was put in Chey commune, Kompong Svay district, Kompong Thom province. I was to have only eight days in this concentration camp with my daughter and mother. Then I was sent to work as part of a mobile fishing team in a village called Peam Bang, on the shore of Tonle Sap lake.

As apprentice work, the Pol Pot leaders ordered me to mend fishing nets. Then it was drawing fishing nets with other victims. I was one of eight persons sent from the commune to work in a team of thirty persons. Among the thirty persons was a chief, a man trusted by the Pol Pot clique, and twenty-nine other members, of whom eighteen were women victims. This team of thirty persons was supposed to fish ten tons every day. Fortunately Tonle Sap is full of fish, so that we could get ten tons, or nearly ten tons, every day. But sometimes we got only two or three tons, and then we would be punished or criticized.

Because of the work regime, I had no rest. I worked fourteen hours a day. One saw only water and sky. We took our rest on the boat, we ate on the boat wearing our wet clothes. Since we were soaked with water every day, our clothes wore out and were mended with odd patches. Our team had three long nets and five boats, one for the team leader, one to carry nets, and three others to carry the fish we caught. Even though Tonle Sap was full of fish, we had to work hard. Chest-deep in the water, and thigh-deep in the mud, I was frozen to the marrow in the December wind. Usually we did one or two hauls of the net to get ten tons of fish, but sometimes we did six or seven, and even that might not be enough.

As a rule fishing was done in the dry season. During the rainy season I grew corn, wove new nets, or mended old ones, or changed buoys or plaited bamboo fences. That is how I worked until I was liberated by the revolutionary forces.

As for our food allotment, one bowl of soup was given out twice a day.

During times I was sick, the ration was cut in half, in order to give more to those who were working. As for medical treatment, I got only a concoction made of roots, and leaves of ordinary plants.

I could visit my daughter only twice a year. Tragically, my daughter died on the day I visited my family in 1976. She died of hunger. My two other children died in Phnom Penh in 1975. Just before the arrival of the revolutionary forces, I had to work harder and harder. As a result my health got worse from day to day.

One day in January 1979, the team leader disbanded the team and said we could go back to our villages. But two of our group who were visibly happy that Kampuchea was about to be liberated were arrested and taken away. Perhaps they were killed. After the liberation of the fishing teams, I headed for my house. When I arrived at home, the people in the village told me that Phnom Penh had been liberated on January 7, 1979. What joyous good news!

I stayed ten days with my mother but then we were forced again to go into the bush with the other people of the village. I thought that this time I would be killed. Eight days later the Pol Pot people decided to kill all the villagers who had gone into the forest. Under the guise of calling a meeting, they planned to kill us the next day at dawn. But one of the villagers figured it out and he told me. With this warning, I decided to flee, along with two other victims, who were former teachers. That same night we ran to the Kompong Thom chief to alert the revolutionary forces. At this news, the revolutionary forces went to the village and freed all the villagers, just at dawn.

After my second liberation, I went to the city of Kompong Thom. I arrived on the day of a meeting, organized by the committee of the National United Front for the Salvation of Kampuchea and representatives of the revolutionary forces. That day I met my cousin who worked in the economic service of the province of Kompong Thom. Now he lives in Phnom Penh. My cousin brought me to the capital. Arriving in Phnom Penh, I applied for work with Minister Keo Chanda, who gave me a job as seamstress, a job I still hold.

At present, a Tonle Sap fisherwoman whose heart is happy for being able to live in a new surrounding, and who is full of hope, is working hard for her dear fatherland and paying tribute to the revolutionary forces of a friendly country, Vietnam.

But as for Pol Pot, Ieng Sary and their master, they must be denounced and brought before the People's Tribunal so that they stop their efforts to revive their monstrous regime.

Down with the cowardly assassins Pol Pot and Ieng Sary!

Long live the revolutionary forces!

Long live the People's Republic of Kampuchea!

Done at Phnom Penh, June 19, 1979
Mrs. Oum Parany

Additional Statement

Questions:

1. Did you get your ration of fish every day?

2. You have said that the team leader disbanded the team and that everybody could return to his village. Two of your number who were overjoyed were arrested and abducted. Who are they? What are their names and professions? Where are they? Do you hear from them?

Answers:

1. Yes. They gave us one hundred grams per meal, which means two hundred grams per day.

2. The two fishermen who were arrested by the Pol Pot clique were April 17 people like me, but they lived in villages different from mine. One of them is named Na, and the other Mom. But I do not know if these are their original names or their new names. I don't know their professions. I have not heard from them.

My group was a regional group of three hundred seventy persons. The food ration was one hundred grams of rice and one hundred grams of fish per meal and per day. Although daily production sometimes reached several tons a day, and we caught up to thirty tons of fish a day, we did not get enough to keep from being hungry. According to the leading officials who sometimes came to brief us, all the fish was intended for export abroad.

In 1977, one day in November at 5:30 p.m., I saw a motor boat carrying ten persons. Surprised, I asked a Khmer Rouge soldier about it. He replied that these poor people were being transported to Bac Dao. Bac Dao is a forest surrounded by water where few people dared to venture. It is a place used by the Khmer Rouge to kill people. Ten days later I was sent to work near this place, and the slightest wind brought a foul odor. I was told that a few days before I arrived, the Khmer Rouge killed many people at a place where there was an "altar to the spirit."

Done at Phnom Penh, June 26, 1979
Mrs. Oum Parany

2.1.1.12
Mr. Chean Phanna

April 17 was the day of the glorious victory of the revolutionary forces of Kampuchea. During this period of the re-establishment of peace in Kampuchea, the people were very happy. The people hoped for peace in order to be able to rebuild the country with all the political parties, because under the regime of Lon Nol, the following had occurred:

- pupils, students, and intellectuals had held demonstrations demanding freedom of expression,
- officials demanded salary increases,
- anarchy throughout the country,
- pillage and theft all over the country,
- rockets fell all over the city, holding up traffic,

Our hopes for peace were, however, frustrated.

At 9:00 a.m. on April 17, the Pol Pot–Ieng Sary traitors invaded the capital and deceived the inhabitants by ordering the evacuation of the city for a short period of three days so that they could mop up enemy soldiers in the capital. Being quite happy over the victory, the inhabitants left Phnom Penh without taking clothing or provisions.

On April 18, they forced my family to leave our house right away, threatening us with their guns. Frightened to death, we left our house at 6:00 a.m. on April 18. The road was jammed with vehicles hurrying out of the capital.

Order was maintained by the troops of the traitors firing shots and using rough talk, like "Do you want to die?" By the time we had gone eight kilometers, we realized we had been tricked. At that point, we had used up our provisions, and I decided to go back to our house to find food. But the Pol Pot troops would not let me get into Phnom Penh. That is why we were beset by the problem of food during our trip. During this long trip, I slept with no mat or carpet, but right on the path. All along the way, I saw corpses of innocent inhabitants and of soldiers. On April 21, we stopped at Chruy Ampil to wait for word about returning to Phnom Penh.

But this expectation was fruitless, and since our food was running out, I decided to go to my native village. Our family arrived at Prek Po (District 22 of the province) in June 1975. We now had to find work in order to have anything to eat. We had to work all day, and at night as well. For housing, all the April 17 people were put together on a piece of high ground, where they had built a straw shed. During the night, the police watched our activities. So during the night we could not talk to each other, because the police watched our house. That is how they deprived us of all liberty. Besides, the Pol Pot clique warned us not to think about the former regime, because that was a thing of the past. They told us that the former regime would not come back, and that we would be workers and farmers for the Party.

In December 1975, they called us to a meeting and said that the April 17 people would have to go to Kompong Thom to live, because there was rice and housing there. Our family was then moved to the West Chamnar commune in Stung district of Kompong Thom province. When we got there, I saw that what they had said was a lie, because it was a concentration camp where we had to do forced labor. The daily food ration was very small: two spoonfuls of rice (spoonfuls of rice uncooked) per meal. For lack of food, I had to eat cassava leaves, potatoes, and other edible roots to stay alive. The soup broth was cooked with almost no salt, with no fish or meat, or even any vegetable. They only put in greens and water. We were to be given only one bowl of broth each. But the cooks cheated us by giving more to the local people. We could not say that we were getting too little food, or that it was bad, or we would be killed. Because of this meager ration, I got horribly thin and weak. I got bloated.

The Pol Pot clique asked us to tell what work we had done before, and soon those who had been in the military or officials disappeared.

We were considered prisoners of war or capitalist reactionaries, and that is why we were put into forced, punitive labor. Forced labor was set according to age, but children and the elderly had to do as much as everyone else. Every evening, they held meetings to criticize us and to make us criticize ourselves.

In the rainy season we were forced to work from 4:00 a.m. to 11:00 a.m. without a break. The meal was eaten quickly so as not to lose time from work. Those doing plowing had to start at 4:00 a.m., and each group of four persons had to finish plowing one hectare before 9:00 a.m. They warned us that if we did not work hard we would be accused of having a hostile attitude and we would be arrested. The replanting had to be done very close together, by fifteen persons per hectare.

The oxen and buffalo became thinner and thinner, because they were undernourished, and they, like us, worked without a break. The traitors made me work even when my whole body was swollen from malnutrition. I made myself work until I lost consciousness on the dike. When they saw that I was so sick, they sent me to the infirmary to be hospitalized. At the infirmary the traitors gave me no medication but rather plant roots and pills that did no good.

After a month's rest in the infirmary, I regained my strength a bit, and they sent me back out to the work site. After two weeks, they said that I would have to leave the work site to take up different work. In fact, however, they arrested me on a charge of planning to escape to Thailand. They tied my arms behind my back and took me to a prison that was about ten kilometers from the work site.

Life in the prison was terrible. My feet were tied tight with chains that made it almost impossible to walk.

The prison was a former school, and the classrooms had been turned into cells. In the cells there was a foul odor, and the floor was infested with bugs. As a food ration, they gave me only a ladle full of thin soup broth. Because of undernourishment, all the accused persons turned a yellowish color. At every meal we licked the bowl to the last drop of soup broth.

My body smelled, because I wasn't able to wash myself, and my body was filthy and infested with lice. At night I heard sorrowful shouting from my fellow inmates who were being tortured to get them to confess.

When the interrogation ended, you would hear a piercing cry like "oy," and then silence. The accused person would not come back to his cell. I was very concerned to see that all the accused persons who underwent interrogation then disappeared. All the accused persons were led away with their hands cuffed behind their backs. Guards followed them with guns and threatened to shoot them if they tried to get away. I was let go after a month of imprisonment, because there was no evidence against me.

But before setting me free, the Pol Pot police made me pull a cart full of human manure. As they let me out, they threatened to kill me if I told anyone that I had been imprisoned, that I would have to keep this story to myself. All the accused persons got their heads shaved. When I got home, my mother, who had thought I had been killed, hugged me crying, because it was rare to see an accused person come back after being arrested by Pol Pot. My neighbors felt sorry for me and asked me why I was so thin. I remembered the warning from the Pol Pot police, so I told them that I had taken sick and that I had been hospitalized. I was too weak to work then, and I asked the village chief to let me rest in the infirmary.

After the hospitalization, I was put to work in a mobile team, as was the practice in other villages. At that time the mobile teams had to work on the Stung Chinit dam, which they called the January 1 Dam. To get to the work site, the mobile teams had to walk 70 kilometers.

The work began. On February 18, 1979, at 9:00 p.m., I asked the team chief to let me rest because I was so tired. But he refused, so I made myself work on. At 9:00 p.m., my hoe struck a grenade, and there was an explosion. I was seriously injured and lost consciousness. When I came to, I realized that I was in a hospital. My nose was injured, as well as my upper extremities, and my chest. Grenade fragments were still embedded in my body. My body was all bloody, but the so-called doctors did little for injured persons.

In the hospital, the April 17 people were kept separately. The Pol Pot medical people were very arrogant toward the April 17 people. I stayed in the hospital three months. When my wounds were barely healed, they let me go back to my village.

In all the villages, they searched the personal belongings of the people, and they confiscated gold or silver. When I got back to my village, I saw that the former head teacher and the students had been called away for a short period. Learning this bad news, I was terrified, because the Pol Pot people killed people every night.

My brother, who had been a teacher, was also led away and called up to spread sheaves of rice for the mobile teams of girls. My brother was innocent, but he packed his haversack gladly. However, the Pol Pot people killed him that very night. Soon thereafter, they led away my sister-in-law and her two children, telling her that she was being called up to plant potatoes in the Popok area to help solve the food problem.

At that period they were spreading their terror more and more, killing innocent people family by family. Before being killed, the people had their clothes taken off them, except for their pants, and they were forced to dig their graves themselves. After the killing, the victims' clothes would be distributed to the local original people, because, according to the Pol Pot people, the clothes were goods confiscated from the enemy.

Under their regime, the Pol Pot people closed all the schools and turned them into prisons. As for the cultural domain, the children were not allowed any studies but were forced to do work like spreading manure on the rice, or building up small banks of earth between the rows of rice. The Pol Pot people said that there was no distinction between young and old. They killed all the educated people because they thought that academic degrees were of no value.

As for public health, there were no real hospitals or medications. Nor was there any effort at cleanliness. The doctors were children 12 or 13 years old. As a result of poor hygiene, abscesses were common. The midwives did not observe proper hygiene. They would cut the umbilical cord with unsterilized scissors. The newborn often suffered from tetanus.

The Pol Pot clique destroyed all the pagodas and forbade the practice of Buddhism.

As for manners and customs, they suppressed Khmer tradition, for example as regards marriage. A person had no right to choose a spouse. The Pol Pot clique organized makeshift collective marriage ceremonies for thirty or forty couples at a time. Under the Pol Pot regime, people who got married had no time to live together, as they were kept apart by having to work in different places. The traitors made the people work all the time, but the people were undernourished because the traitors sent the harvest to their masters in Peking.

In 1978, I was put on a list of people to be killed. They asked us to dig a large ditch ten meters on a side and five meters deep. The traitors told us that we must dig this ditch quickly in order to use it to store manure. Their plan was to kill our fellow countrymen and to bury them in this ditch. The Pol Pot clique planned to eradicate the Khmer race in Kampuchean territory, on orders from their masters in Peking.

However, fortunately, on January 7, 1979, the forces of the National United Front for the Salvation of Kampuchea, with help from friendly forces from Viet Nam, overthrew the Pol Pot–Ieng Sary clique.

All the people were happy, because they thereby avoided the apocalypse and could go back to their native villages.

I congratulate sincerely and with all my heart the Front's forces, and I thank with a loud voice the Vietnamese forces for their effective assistance in the liberation of Kampuchea.

I would like to send them my wishes of good health and greater victory.

On behalf of the students of Kampuchea and for myself, I vow loyalty to the cause of the fatherland that has just been freed to build real socialism.

Long live new Kampuchea!

Long live the People's Republic of Kampuchea!
Down with the Pol Pot–Ieng Sary clique!

Chean Phanna
Former fourth-year student of the Pharmacy Faculty

2.1.1.13
Mr. Ung Sam On

I must say quite sincerely that I am truly very moved to be able to relate here the crimes of genocide committed by the fascist Pol Pot–Ieng Sary clique against our nation and against our beloved country.

Our Suffering During Our Trip

On April 18, 1975, like everyone else, my family was forced by the traitors of the Pol Pot–Ieng Sary clique to leave Phnom Penh to go live in the countryside in conformity with the plan of treason. We had to walk in the burning heat of the sun, and at times in the rain. Our health got worse and worse. The mortal remains of children and of elderly people who succumbed dotted our path. We were very moved by this. Skeletons and corpses partially eaten by wolves filled pits carved out by B-52 bombs. Other victims, their hands tied behind their backs, sadly awaited death, with no hope of having a trial. These executioners confiscated the goods of these unfortunate Phnom Penh residents and did everything they could to take them to remote locations. My family decided to go live at Prek Sieng, our native village. But the fear of certain confiscation of rice forced us to go farther. At that point occurred the regrettable separation of our grandmother, my aunts, and my uncles. We went back to Kandal village, where a little hut built by our own hands sheltered us against the heat and the rain. We stayed there fifteen days. Then we were forced to leave for Kok Euv Lek, a poor, remote little village in Kandal Stung district. The conditions were unfavorable for us: on the one hand the stream was far away and the wells were not usable, and on the other hand we were forbidden to go far from our shelter. Thus, the only water we had was in bomb craters filled with moss and rotting debris.

Under the power of the authorities in Kok Euv Lek, even though our hut was not yet completely built, we were required to go with the other victims to clear the fields, to dig up weeds in the rice paddies, to dig and build embankments, etc. They considered us to be prisoners of war or slaves, because we worked hard under the threat of bayonets and at their mercy. They set the work hours and the hours for rest. Having deprived us of any right to make suggestions about work methods, they only needed our physical force. Any work in any field of activity was permitted only under their orders. Secret agents followed us in all our activities and in our work. The less energetic people were reprimanded. The sick were either deprived of their daily rations or sent to the infirmary. Here the quite low daily ration served as a "remedy" to force people to return to work. Those who were chronically ill were the object of special attention. Their activities under the Lon Nol regime were investigated. A good number of them were killed unbeknownst to their families, out of fear that these crimes would evoke hatred and reaction.

On September 17, 1975, came the killing of my father, who was already seriously ill and unable to work. After the death of my poor father the fascist authorities of the village watched the members of my family; they were afraid that we would carry out acts against them. Despite the very great effort exerted by the victims in fulfilling their assigned tasks, they got them all together by units and reprimanded them, scolding the weakest and forcing them to work harder. All the families that did not work so hard were sent to malarial areas where they got a very low food ration. Work brought the benefit of avoiding reprimand and of receiving the daily food ration. All those who were sick got only contempt and little care.

For the living conditions of the victims, the directives could be expressed as follows: Work a great deal but eat little. That is how to become a revolutionary and to discover enemies. Any complaining that you are exhausted or do not get enough to eat would lead to a reprimand or to death. In the distribution of the daily food ration, no one dared utter a word. Nearly all the agricultural production was consumed by the Pol Pot–Ieng Sary clique, and the rest was given to the victims. These fascist traitors said that most of the harvest was stolen, but it is they who were the thieves. At times children got no food ration beyond that of working members of the family.

The difficulties of recruiting workers and of a lack of transport for rice were invoked. Because they were hungry, the people ate rice mixed with stems of papaya or banana, or with edible leaves. This diet caused all kinds of fatal diseases. My six-year-old daughter died horribly from hunger. My four-month-old niece also died for lack of milk from her mother. Some families were wiped out altogether. Others were sent to the top of a hill in Salong village.

My two brothers, two sisters, and I were put into a mobile unit of the district, and my two younger brothers were put into a children's work unit, and another of my sisters was put into the cooperative. From the time the members of my family were separated, we were forbidden to maintain any contact with each other. In keeping with their policy of genocide, in mid-1976 these fascist traitors killed their own colleagues. At that time my uncle was killed, accused of being a military pilot.

My mother suddenly took ill after the tragic death of my brother. Our camp was about three kilometers from the village. Knowing that my mother was seriously ill, I asked the unit chief for permission to go see her. He refused, however. Then I decided to leave the unit to rejoin my mother.

Unfortunately, when I was half way to the village, I came upon another chief, who tied my hands behind my back and made me go back to my unit. Here, he left me to the mercy of the mosquitoes all night, outside the camp. In the morning he reprimanded me and made me work longer than usual. I became depressed and suffered a great deal from the low food ration, the hard work and lack of rest, and the strict regimentation. I truly had become a slave. For lack of food, I was quite exhausted.

However, the chiefs made me crush rocks, work on building the Stung Kantuot dam, and dig in the Tok Thla river to build a bridge. Nearly every day I received some sort of physical or moral punishment. In 1977, the young people, boys and girls, were taken away to a reeducation camp where the fascist Pol Pot–Ieng Sary clique killed one after another. I imagined that my highly intelligent beloved daughter was killed too, accused of being well educated and the daughter of a capitalist. That caused me great pain. These local authorities always asked me about my activities. Several times they made me write up my biography to let them know about my prior work. They kept after me nearly every day making accusations. I was frequently in tears. I was in bad shape. Since my life was always threatened, I thought I would not be able to avoid a cruel death.

January 7, 1979, is the day the Pol Pot–Ieng Sary clique was completely defeated and destroyed by the National United Front for the Salvation of Kampuchea. The soul of the nation began to live again. The people gained their liberty. Happily and in freedom we went back to our native village and saw our house again, our uncles, our aunts, our parents and learned which ones were dead and which were alive. I have been able to return to Phnom Penh to live. Phnom Penh is a dead city. All state property of any great value was destroyed. After four years under the regime of this fascist clique, does Khmer society have any civilization? It is zero, because I knew well and saw with my own eyes everything that happened, as I will now describe.

1. Culture

Arts: Dance, songs, and sculpting were eliminated. They destroyed statues and engravings of great value that were world renowned as the works of our ancestors. Characteristically Khmer dances, songs, and music were replaced by those of their expansionist master in Peking.

National literature: These traitors were never interested in the national literature. They kept the population ignorant to better dominate it and to direct it according to their designs. At any meeting the village authorities always said, "We have no need of intellectuals or any kind of diploma. We need only people who carry out the orders of Angkar to the letter." Most of the students and intellectuals were eliminated one after another and were required to do forced labor under the instructions of their master in Peking. What will be the future of our beloved country if these traitors teach even some of our children by their doctrine "Study little, but do a great deal of practical work." Our ancestors used to say, "The death of literature is the death of the country."

Science: Unlike the developed countries of the world, the Pol Pot–Ieng Sary clique was not interested in science. It took our country backwards. It did not use agricultural machinery but let it stand idle. Medication became a matter distant from medical science.

Tradition: Marriage is forced and is performed without the consent of the parties and without the knowledge of their parents. Traditional festivals were completely suppressed.

Physical education: The clique organizes no physical education for children but makes them do hard labor instead. Because of excessive labor, the children are overworked. They get very thin and exhausted because of inadequate nutrition.

Morals: Children indoctrinated by the clique's education do not obey their elders or their parents and are very insolent. Well indoctrinated in this way, they do not hesitate to kill their own parents or their own brothers or sisters, accusing them of being enemies of Angkar (the party).

Belief: These traitors require the population to have only one belief, a belief in them.

2. Society

In these four years we note that the clique of traitors has done nothing for progress in any field.

With regard to the economy, the people lack rice. Some die of hunger, because the harvest has been exported by these fascist traitors to their chiefs. As a result of their work, the inhabitants of Kampuchea have become slaves of Peking. Industrial production, such as cloth or silk, does not make it into the hands of the people. Agriculture is underdeveloped. The people work with only the force of their arms, without the help of machinery. Even though harvests are plentiful, the people do not get enough to assuage their hunger. Where has this clique exported the harvest? If the harvest has been traded for other products, where are these products? Perhaps they are military equipment.

As for social action, most of the people are illiterate. They have no need for intellectuals. Intellectuals are forced to do hard labor without getting rest. They do not keep track of output. For example, they make the people plant banana and coconut in the dry season and then water them. The hard labor given to the people is a moral and physical punishment. They value materials more highly than the lives of the workers. At work sites where there were unexploded bombs, they made the people go there to work anyway, and that resulted in many people being injured and in tragic deaths from the explosion of bombs that people touched.

Despite all the efforts made by the people to do hard work night and day without complaining, the people were not properly fed. If they fell ill, they did not get properly diagnosed or treated. To the contrary, they were only threatened by their chiefs, who would say, "You only imagine that you are sick; you are lazy." No consolation. As for medicines, they are not scientifically valid and do little good. They closed and destroyed all the pharmacies. Clinics are not kept clean; medical workers have little training or are illiterate. Because of their incompetence, minor diseases become more serious and even fatal in many cases.

As for security, the people lived in a state of perpetual fear, with no happiness, and seeing only death ahead of them, because these traitors killed the people they didn't like. The people knew no glimmer of justice. They killed as they pleased the husband, then the children, the brothers, the sisters, and the mother without saying who had done anything wrong.

They are corrupt and engage in extra-marital love acts. They allow nothing to the "April 17" people. All authority is in the hands of the "old people." The "April 17" people are not allowed to marry the "old people." If the chiefs of the youth organization are sick, they are well cared for, and treated well with good medicines. The "April 17 people," however, have gotten only traditional, ineffective medicines. That shows us clearly that they are very one-sided and unjust.

As a victim, I solemnly declare these savage acts as I have related them here. I state that I will no longer regard these fascist traitors as Khmers, because their hands are soiled with the blood of Khmers. They sold the people, the nation, the country to Peking as living slaves. During four years, Pol Pot and Ieng Sary have been executioners under the control of the Peking imperialist expansionists.

Phnom Penh, May 23, 1979
Ung Sam On

2.1.1.14
Mr. So Sam Ol

Deportation and Some Facts About Our Forced Departure from the City

April 17, 1975, was the day of the great victory of Pol Pot and Ieng Sary. I was very happy, hoping that Kampuchea would stop killing itself. I went out of my house to greet and welcome the Pol Pot army which was arriving in vehicles and tanks. At 7:00 a.m. I left my house and asked my sister-in-law to stay there. I was going to see my mother at her place in Tuol Tompoung, because for several days it had been forbidden to go about. At 8:00 a.m. we had a family meeting to talk about our hopes for the future, that is to say, after this war.

But our hope soon vanished with the arrival of four young Pol Pot soldiers armed with guns and grenades pointed at us. We were quite shocked at these gestures and this visit. A young man dressed in black, about 20 years old, ordered us to get things in order and to leave our houses right away and to head for Takhmau. He explained to us that American planes were going to bomb at any moment. We were astonished. Why ask us to go in the direction of Takhmau since we had bunkers at our houses, but at Takhmau we would have no shelter. A half hour later, they came back and this time pointed their guns at us and made us leave our houses right away, saying that it was for three or four days and that we should not take much with us.

In light of this situation, my mother asked me to go back to my house. On the way back I saw a truck filled with soldiers, thirty or so. They jumped out of the truck and three of them ran toward my house and kicked the door open. The barrels of their guns were pointed at us menacingly. Shaking, I hurriedly arranged things in the house. I was able to take only a few kilograms of rice and some clothing for my kid, and we left our house feeling very forlorn. I wanted to rejoin my parents, but the soldiers did not let us. They pointed with their guns in a different direction, to National Route 5. On our way, for the first time, I saw the body of an old man on the ground in front of the Phsar Tauch "Catholic quarter" market. I was told that this old man had not obeyed the orders of the soldiers because he wanted to go back to the city to find his child.

National Route 5 was filled with thousands of people deported under threat of being shot. We walked twenty days to get to Speu district in Kompong Cham province. We had made ten kilometers a day. Once there, we were forced to relate the personal histories of the members of both our families, the family of my father-in-law and my own four-member family.

May 14, 1975, they separated our two families. They ordered me to organize my affairs and to leave this village to go to a different one. My father-in-law begged them to leave the two families together, but the soldiers armed with clubs who watched us leave did not agree. We separated saddened, our eyes full of tears.

My trip took two days and two nights by cart to get to Cham Bok village, Prek Prasap district, Kratie province, where they left us to live for three years.

In the countryside, all the people who had been expelled from the city on April 17, 1975, were morally and physically oppressed, especially by the people who were from the village, who ruled by the law of the jungle. These people, who previously had been pirates and brigands, were chosen as chiefs of a group, or of a work center, or of a village, to keep close watch on us. From day to day, they accused us of one thing or another, and reprimanded us, even if we had worked hard and followed discipline.

The division of labor was quite unfair. The hardest work, namely, work in the most distant locations for clearing land, and the most malarial areas, were reserved for people who had been expelled from the cities on April 17. Because the new people did not dare to complain. It was as if we had not participated in the liberation and we wanted to contribute our modest part to rebuild the economy.

One day I was sick, because I had worked too hard despite not getting enough to eat. I had malaria, and my wife had to miss work to take care of me at home. She was reprimanded for doing this. No one gave me any pills, even in exchange for gold or diamonds. I had to look for tree roots to make a concoction to drink. My condition got worse, and I could not get up out of bed. I had a high temperature. I asked my wife to peel off some "Kantuot" bark, which is poisonous, to poison me. My wife could only cry. But by a stroke of luck a man named Sokham who used to be a nurse came to see me after coming back from the work site and gave me some medication he still had, and this saved me.

In the area of Prek Prasap, east of the Mekong River, the year 1977 was the year in which the April 17 peasants would lose their lives, because mortar shells could be heard from over by the eastern border of the country. In early February 1977, I was chosen to work at the ANANE agricultural work site, seven kilometers from our village. Every day I made myself work the foot pedal in the sweltering heat to fill the rice paddies with water. On the evening of February 23, I saw the orderly of the village chief deliver a note to our work site chief. This note ordered me to go see him that night.

At 7:30 p.m., two soldiers from the village took me to the village chief, about one kilometer from my house. There I found the chief of the village cooperative, the deputy chief of the cooperative, and the military chief of the village, who were waiting to inform me of accusations against me. I was accused:

(1) of twice having disobeyed the political directives of the village administration,
(2) of having been a police inspector and a battalion chief in the army of the previous government,
(3) of having spoken a lot during work and of having bothered the women who worked with me.

These were pretexts to kill me.

I objected that these charges were baseless. This time they let me go back to my house about 1:00 a.m. From then, they kept me at my house for two weeks to watch me closely. Meanwhile these spies watched all the April 17 families.

On June 20, 1977, an order was received that all the April 17 people of Prek Prasap district should go work at a rubber plantation. At that time I was working in a field planting rice. All those who were picked to go to the rubber plantation were very happy. Then one night they got more than one hundred families in a Chinese school with a large contingent of soldiers guarding them, and they said no one could go anywhere in the area for the next seventeen days. The second night they killed them in the Chambak pagoda and the Chruy Ampil pagoda. I was told about this by villagers who saw it.

Two months later, there was a plan to kill the people originally from the village, including those who were members of the village committee and the subdistrict committee, and those who had been in the military under the French colonialists. Ten people were killed.

From that time the situation got better. The original population of the village and the April 17 people got along better with each other.

In October 1978 in the area east of the Mekong river, as the war raged on the border, another plan by Angkar to kill people was afoot, whereby the future victims were put into three categories: (1) first category for the higher authorities, (2) second category for the lower-ranking authorities, (3) third category for the people in general, especially the April 17 people, and the people originally from the villages.

Those in the third category were to be killed in late 1978. Fortunately, the army of the National United Front for Salvation arrived in time in Kratie province, on January 1, 1979, and their plan was thwarted. So we survived thanks to the army of the National United Front for the Salvation of Kampuchea.

I should also say that my brother-in-law and his family, mentioned above, as to how we got separated in Speu district, Kompong Cham province, were killed by Pol Pot soldiers in Prek Sangke district, Kompong Cham province, in 1977.

I would like to lodge a complaint with the tribunal, and before world opinion against the genocidal acts committed by the Pol Pot–Ieng Sary clique, who are the faithful lackeys of Peking, for acts never before known in the history of humanity.

Phnom Penh, May 25, 1979
So Sam Ol

2.1.1.15
Mr. Kim Sokha

On the day after liberation, that is, April 18, 1975, my family, consisting of my father, my mother, my grandmother, my elder sister, my three younger sisters, my two younger brothers and I, along with my aunt's family, were forced to leave the capital city to go live in the countryside.

It took us six days to get to my native village, which is Damnak Tasek village, Popel subdistrict, Tram Kak district, Takeo province. We arrived on April 23, 1975. Upon our arrival, my grandparents, my uncles, my aunts, all of whom were originally from that place, along with my other relatives, went to hide in their houses and cried for us.

Among my relatives was my uncle, whose name is Hoeung. He had loved me a lot in the past, and he hugged me in tears and said, "My dear nephew, why are you coming back here? You will die here, or at least live very badly. Don't you see that our relatives do not dare greet you because they are afraid of the Angkar organization? Here it is forbidden to shelter refugees. Under the regime that is here now, any communication, any contact between refugees and the original inhabitants is forbidden. Even brothers and sister kill one another."

I could only cry, and said, "How awful, that our relatives cannot even greet each other." Two days later, on April 26, 1975, the Angkar organization, of which we knew little, divided us into groups for work purposes. I was told to build a small dike. One day, as I was working, a soldier of the new regime came and asked me what I used to do in Phnom Penh. I told him truthfully that I had been a student at the Law Faculty (final year).

The soldier said ironically, "So you are an important man! But I ask you, what good did you ever do? You trick others, and the peasants hate you." Others who heard this were afraid for me.

On the night of June 2, 1975, at midnight, in the moonlight, my younger brother, my father, and I were sleeping in the same bed, in front of our cottage. I heard a man call to me, "Brother, brother." I got up quickly and saw a man named Sok, the head of our village, and a soldier carrying a rifle on his shoulder.

I asked him, "Whom are you looking for?" Sok replied, "Angkar is looking for your father." I awoke my father by shaking his legs. He got up quickly, quite frightened. The soldier told my father, "Brother, get your luggage ready and come with me. The organization orders you to go to the political school for two weeks. Don't bring much with you because you will be back soon."

Thinking back on my conversation the other day with the soldier, I asked, "Are you asking for my father or for me?" My father interrupted, "He is calling me, not you." Then my father went into the cottage to say goodbye to my mother, who was shaking in fear. He came out and joined the two men with his luggage and left. They headed south. But at a distance of about fifty meters, I saw seven or eight men, all armed, coming out of the bamboo woods to take my father south of the woods. My mother, my grandmother, and I watched until they were out of sight.

I could not keep my composure. I shouted and cried. I felt as if I were suffocating. I fell to the ground and fainted. My grandmother ran to find neighbors to ask for help. Some neighbors who knew our past came but did not dare to stay long. They went back to their houses and quickly closed the door. That night no one in my family could sleep. They wished that daylight would come as soon as possible.

The next day we wanted to do everything we could to find out where they had taken my father. I went to make inquiries, but that morning there was a meeting. The following day, at noon, I asked my uncle to go with me south of the woods that was about five hundred meters from my village, under the pretext that we were looking for wood to build our shelter.

When we got to the middle of the woods, near a kdol tree I saw an old scarf stuck on a thorny plant. It was my father's scarf. I jumped back. Five meters to the south I saw a new grave. There was blood on the ground and on the plants near the grave. There was also a bamboo stick all bloody near the grave. That is how my father was killed!

After the death of my father came that of my brother, the same year in Kompong Chhnang province. Then my sister and her husband were killed with his relatives in 1976 in Batheay subdistrict, Kompong Cham province. My aunt and her two sons were killed in 1977 in Prey Phav subdistrict, Treang district, Takeo province.

Phnom Penh, June 18, 1979
Kim Sokha

2.1.1.16
Mr. Em Darakun

My name is Em Darakun. I am 31 years old. I was born at Baray in Kompong Thom province, April 16, 1948, the son of a peasant family. My parents have four children. My father is Em Koch Moeun, 73 years old. My mother is Ouk Saem, 73 years old. My elder sister is Em Maren, 45 years old. My second oldest sister is Em Mak Prang, 40 years old. The third child is my brother, Em Mavy, 35 years old. I, Em Darakun, 31 years old, am the fourth child.

I attended the Baray primary school and then secondary school in Phnom Penh, finishing in 1967. I went to the teacher training school and got certified as a teacher in 1968. Three years later, to expand my knowledge, I left my job and took up studies again, at the Faculty of Letters, specializing in English and French. In 1975, after my second year in the Faculty of Letters, I passed the English teacher examination.

I married Miss Ek Praney, who is 25 years old, and who was a teacher during the Lon Nol regime. She is the daughter of a peasant family. Her father is Ek Em. Her mother is Som Chheng (deceased).

We had a happy life. Several months after our wedding, April 17, 1975, came, and the country passed into the hands of Pol Pot and Ieng Sary and their gang of traitors. My family was forced to leave Phnom Penh April 18, 1975, at 10:00 a.m., at the point of guns of the Pol Pot army. We were forced to leave our house without even the time to arrange our affairs, other than to get a small bag of rice. The traitors told us that we would be able to return home after three days. I left brokenhearted, in the heat of the noonday sun.

Along the way, I saw many people with their luggage. Boys and girls shouted because they had gotten lost from their families. When I passed by a theater, I saw several corpses. These poor people were innocent victims. At night I slept outdoors with no covers to put over me. Because of these awful conditions I got separated from my father, who was blind, my beloved mother, and from my brother, sisters and nieces. I ran everywhere looking for them, but to no avail.

On May 25, 1975, after a month at Chruy Ampil, I was displaced to Prek Po village, in Kompong Cham province, taken there by boat. Within two hours of arriving at this village, my family along with others were required to go on foot to Tonle Pet, where Pol Pot soldiers, weapons in hand, ransacked our belongings to find gold, watches, bracelets, or medicines that we had with us for personal use. They threatened us to give them all medicines that we had with us for personal use. A bit later, in the morning hours, I was sent by truck to Suong, where for a meal I was given a small (200 gram) tin of rice and a little salt.

Three days later, my nephew Youran, who was 18 years old, came down with diarrhea. In view of his condition, I went to the clinic to ask for some medicine. When I got there the nurse, dressed in black, looked me up and down and accused me of being an officer in the Lon Nol army. I tried to make her understand that I was not a soldier or an officer. With a dour face, she gave me four pills made with locally derived medicines. I gave the pills to my nephew, hoping to help him get better,

[There is a hiatus here because two pages of this document are not available. The document continues after the hiatus as follows. — Eds.]

In December 1978, Pol Pot and Ieng Sary and their gangs of killers had become weak. They expelled the people living east of the Mekong River to the west, at first to heavy forests, and then to cooperatives. We lived like animals, starving, and without any liberty.

Under the Pol Pot–Ieng Sary regime, the traitors tried fiercely to dominate, to control every step, to spy and exert great pressure on all aspects of daily life. At that time, genocide was carried out against the Khmer people by the Pol Pot people. They wanted at any cost to facilitate Chinese expansionism and Chinese interests.

What happened in Kampuchea during the time of this criminal government could not be hidden because everyone knew it, saw it, and heard it. This crime is more savage, more atrocious than that of the fascists. Around the world one senses a bad odor from this criminal government. The Pol Pot–Ieng Sary slaughterhouse has brought the Khmers so much grief. We will never forget this grief, but the infamous crime could not go on longer. The lives of millions of innocent citizens has been saved from horrible extermination. And who is our savior? It is the army under the direction of the National United Front for the Salvation of Kampuchea, which is fighting with the assistance of the army of our Vietnamese friends. We are deeply grateful for this.

One month after liberation, I decided to go back to my house to find my blind father, my mother, and my brothers and sisters. But so far none of them have come back to our old and dear house.

I think that I am the only one who has a chance of seeing the reality of the light of peace. I dare to say that all the members of my family are dead. I will feel these losses for the rest of my life. I hate and strongly condemn the crimes of Pol Pot and Ieng Sary and their clique.

Finally I am full of anxiety, deeply sad. My broken heart showed its indignation towards the regime of the executioners and producers of forced labor of Pol Pot and Ieng Sary and their cliques.

For the three years eight months and twenty days of the awful extermination, these executioners reduced us to slaves, imprisoned, exploited, oppressed, and killed some millions of innocent people in the country.

Although I am young and without experience in international politics, from today I will serve my country. I must make my contribution to the work of building up my country into a strong modern socialist country.

Done at Phnom Pen, June 20, 1979
Em Darakun

2.1.1.17
Mr. Yi Thon

On April 13, 1975, the inhabitants of Phnom Penh were celebrating the New Year.[1] I was looking forward to the arrival of the revolutionary army. Since 1960 I had taken part in every anti-imperialist demonstration. The Lon Nol regime had carried out some dictatorial repression against the revolutionary youth groups, and so the demise of the Lon Nol regime made me happy. It was the joy of living in a revolutionary time, the joy of seeing another horizon, a different society full of happiness and hope.

But what happened on April 17, 1975? First, at 9:30 a.m., I saw Pol Pot troops with a cold look about them, and with their bayonets fixed. Then I heard bomb blasts and machine gun fire. I came out of my house to welcome the newcomers, but in reply they made me leave the capital city immediately. We were not allowed to take any provisions or clothing with us, under the pretext that we would be going for only two or three days so that they could mop up the Lon Nol troops.

I had to walk with my family from Phnom Penh to Sre Leap subdistrict in Tbong Khmum district, Kompong Cham province. I was jailed there until

1. A reference to the Khmer new year. — Eds.

December 30, 1978. It is true that January 7, 1979, was the day of the glorious victory of the revolutionary forces over Pol Pot's traitorous forces. But in the eastern zone the traitors were put out of action on December 30, 1978.

Under the militarist, fascist, totalitarian, and despotic regime of the Pol Pot–Ieng Sary clique from April 17, 1975, to December 31, 1978, I was forced at gunpoint to do heavy forced labor. Every day I worked from 3:00 a.m. to 10:00 p.m., or even midnight. In addition to forced labor in the rice paddies and the fields during the rainy season, I was put at forced labor during the dry season cutting down trees in the dense woods to clear new fields and digging big irrigation canals. Forced labor went on all year round, with physical labor and outmoded tools. I worked 365 days a year. For me as for the others there were no days off, no holidays, no rest, no Sundays. We worked whether the sun was shining or it was raining. They gave me only a ladle full of clear broth with a few grains of salt. And this despite the fact that the harvest was good every year. Broth was the standard food for everyone. Once or twice a year they gave us meat, but only one kilogram for one or two hundred persons.

In the four years I lived with them, I wore only clothes in tatters pieced together. I got only four meters of poor quality black cloth.

How could we work hard without food? I got sick because of physical and mental stress due to the poor nutrition and forced labor. What medications did they give us? Not even an aspirin tablet, no shots, no pills, only a concoction of leaves, roots, and bark of ordinary trees, or sometimes a compress of cassava powder made locally. It was from this ridiculous treatment that my mother, my sister, and my brother died of malaria.

In addition, they broke any real relations between my family and me, and between my relatives and me. As for education, I did not have the right to educate my children or teach them. They forced little children to prepare manure and tend cattle. There was really no school in the concentration camp. Under pretext of going to school the children were forced to work like the adults. My children left the house at 4:00 a.m. and came back only after dusk. The older children were sent to mobile groups. The younger children, their clothes in tatters, tended cattle. My children and my wife became emaciated and weak.

After the evening meal we went to bed without talking. We lived in an unhealthy hut. When the moon was full, the soft light came into the room from all sides. In this worst of all prisons we were deprived of any liberty: freedom of speech, freedom of correspondence, freedom to read and to listen.

In April 1978 I was arrested because of something I did not intend. At the work site they sometimes gave us rice to eat. One day, in order to keep the rice from burning, I pulled out too much wood from the fireplace, and the rice wound up being undercooked. I was freed after seven days of imprisonment and savage torture.

1978 was the worst year. The slightest mistake would lead to capital punishment. One was always at risk of being killed. In October 1978 all the villagers decided to rebel against the Pol Pot regime. But since they had no arms or ammunition, they secretly awaited the arrival of the revolutionary forces. On December 30, 1978, Pol Pot's first defense line was overrun. At the same time as this victory, the population of Tbong Khmum rose up and destroyed all the organizations at the subdistrict, district, and province level. The whole population was freed from the clutches of the devils. In the days that followed, the population of Sre Leap village got together along National Route 7 to welcome the revolutionary troops. Faces once again were bright. One heard only cries of well wishing, songs, and laughter. Everyone was happy to be free, happy to have liberty, especially freedom to eat at home and freedom to go live in their own villages.

It was thanks to the clearsightedness of the National United Front for the Salvation of Kampuchea that we could see new horizons. I wanted to go back to my native village, but my wife wanted to return to hers. Since I had lived in Phnom Penh before 1975, my family and I decided to return to Phnom Penh. I arrived to the outskirts of the capital city February 2, 1979, but I could not enter. So I went to Prek Leap where I was appointed as a counsellor on teaching methods to the committee on primary instruction of the Muk Kampoul district.

On May 1, my brother, who was in the people's army, came to find me in Prek Leap and took me to the Minister of Information and Culture. The minister agreed to find me a post in his ministry. Since that time I have felt great joy, and joy of becoming a citizen sharing responsibility for the destiny of his country. I am trying to use all my physical and moral strength to serve my dear People's Republic of Kampuchea.

What I Have Known and Seen

In Kompong Cham province, Tbong Khmum district, a victim named Mau, a resident of Khlong village, Sre Leap subdistrict, Tbong Khmum district, who escaped death, told me his heroic story. It was a dark night at the Chup rubber plantation. My executioner tied my hands behind my back. My eyes were blindfolded. There were about fifty of us. Among us was my cousin Saren, who marched at the head of the line. The time arrived for the killing to start. The executioner led my cousin away. Fifteen minutes later I heard a sorrowful cry that ripped through the dark sky. It was the voice of my cousin. I recognized his voice quite readily. Perhaps he was hit with an axe on the neck. I decided to save myself, if I were to have a chance to escape. I asked the man next to me to untie my hands, and I untied his.

The time came for me to go to the place where I would be killed. I saw, because my eyes were not tightly blindfolded, a boy armed with a Chinese-made gun. He kicked me, which was a way of telling me to walk. I walked quietly about five meters in front of him. In the dark I ran into a rubber tree, and I decided that this would be a good opportunity to save myself. My executioner came quite close and pushed me with the end of his gun. Taking advantage of the opportunity, I kicked him sharply in the chest. The executioner fell hard, and I took off at top speed. Since I knew the place as well as the back of my hand, I could run without risk. I heard a gunshot thirty meters behind me, and bullets whizzed over my head. Luckily I got away. I left my native village with my family that night, and no one knew where we went to hide.

I was told another dreadful story. In Anh Chanh subdistrict in the same district, an eighteen-year-old girl whose name I don't know was forced to marry a young man. In the afternoon of the same day, her intended husband was arrested and taken away by an agent of the Pol Pot police. The next day the same police agent came back to take the young newlywed woman, under the pretext that she was an accomplice of her husband. Trembling with fear, she asked the agent to have mercy on her, telling him that even though she was married to the young man, she could not be an accomplice in his affairs because she hadn't even passed the wedding night with him. The monster turned a deaf ear to the poor girl and took her away.

She returned home the next day at dawn, stark naked and her throat cut and bleeding. In a barely audible voice, she told her relatives, "I was stabbed in the throat after being savagely raped by ten monstrous agents of the Pol Pot police. But by chance the point of the knife did not hit a vein or artery, only my throat was cut. I lost consciousness and fell into a ditch full of corpses. The police thought I had been killed and went back to their headquarters. At midnight a breeze and the mist revived me. Little by little I regained my strength and came here."

Two days later the police agents learned that the girl had not died. They came back to take her again. She has never returned.

In Ponhea Krek district, Kra Nhoung village, three large bomb craters made by the American B-52 bombers were full of the mortal remains of men, women, old people, pregnant women, girls, boys, and newborns.

At Suong, the district center of Tbong Khmum district, and at Chup, in the enclosure of the Prek Dambok pagoda and at Prek Po in Prek Po district, I saw wells full of corpses and blood stains that killed the grass nearby.

Done at Phnom Penh, May 16, 1979
Yi Thon

2.1.1.18
Mr. Dith Munty

On April 17, 1975, when the Khmer Rouge entered Phnom Penh, early in the morning, I was with my parents and my three (female) cousins. We were quite happy because we were convinced that after five years of war, we had regained peace.

People lowered white flags from the windows of their houses, people smiled, and people went out on the street to welcome the Khmer Rouge. On each face one could read the same expression of rediscovered hope. But this appearance of the first hours of the victory of the Khmer Rouge was not to last. A few hours later, a Khmer Rouge, probably the chief, announced in a menacing voice by radio that government ministers and other leading figures were required to go to the Ministry of Information. He said that the Khmer Rouge had come "as victors and not to negotiate." At about 2:00 p.m., the order was given to all the inhabitants to evacuate Phnom Penh, in order to escape bombing by the imperialists, which was only a lie.

Three young Khmer Rouge soldiers, aged 14 to 16 years, came to my parents' house. They were dressed in black and wore sandals cut from old tires, and were armed with machine guns. They threatened us with their weapons and made us pack up.

Because we left so fast, we had nothing with us. On National Route 5 near the Pepsi-Cola factory, a Khmer Rouge girl was questioning three young men of 20 to 24 years of age, ordering them to stand to one side. She shot a machine gun burst while she joked with her comrades that anyone who wears long hair is a blackguard, a degenerate, a vestige of imperialist civilization.

We trembled in fear. My mother nearly fainted. We kept going, not daring even to look at corpses bathed in blood that we saw beside the road.

I figured out that the Khmer Rouge soldiers were people who had come straight out of the forests. They did not know how to distinguish between good and evil. They obeyed only their instinct to destroy. At Prek Kdam, I saw the distress of women who were giving birth along the road, hiding themselves as well as they could with mats and blankets full of holes, under the leaden April sun. And I saw the distress of the frantic husbands as they ran to find a midwife. Out in the open, without medications, without a doctor, how could they make it?

After Prek Kdam, all the cars and means of transportation were confiscated. After that, anything round was used for makeshift carts to carry people's belongings. Because of the hardship, the lack of medicine and food, and because of exhaustion, many people died along the road.

We took twenty-two days to get to Chihe, in Kompong Cham province. We worked there eight months. On December 22, 1975, there was a new exodus to the north. The Khmer Rouge took us to Staung village, in Kompong Thom province. There we had to begin work right away. The young people and the unmarried were put into collective mobile work brigades where they were subject to strict discipline, like soldiers.

To escape death, I had to live under a false identity. I told the village chief that I was a travelling salesman during the day, and in the evening I worked in a movie theater as a ticket taker.

The Pol Pot–Ieng Sary clique uses the policy of "divide and conquer." Angkar is the incarnation of an absolute and arbitrary militarist power exercised by the Khmer Rouge. They had the right of life and death over the people. To sow dissension between the city people and the peasants, Angkar divided the people into three categories: the old people, the new people, and the enemies. The first were those who lived in the liberated zone or in the zone that supported the Khmer Rouge before the fall of the Lon Nol regime. The second were those forced out of Phnom Penh and of other provinces. The last were considered to be slaves and were subjected to all sorts of humiliations by the old people. The old people had more rights and privileges than the new people.

The new people had to do forced labor. Six months a year, Angkar made them build dikes and dig canals. It made them work thirteen hours a day, from 3:00 to 10:30 a.m., from 1:30 to 5:30 p.m., and from 7:00 to 9:00 p.m., in exchange for 150 grams of uncooked rice per day per person. They got no days off. Even when sick they had no right to take off from work. Under penalty of death, they had to work without stopping at any time of day, both day and night, rain or shine. The third category of the population was made up of military personnel and civil servants of the old regime, all intellectuals and school children from the seventh year and up. All these were doomed to death because they were their enemies.

The land was arid, the living conditions difficult. There was not enough food or medicine. Starvation led to many deaths: in Sang Khat Samproch subdistrict, there were four to six deaths every day. The inhabitants were so weak that they did not even have the strength to bury the bodies; instead they dumped them onto an oxcart to abandon them in the forest.

My mother died of starvation. She was a soft-spoken woman, modest, likable. She was only 45 years old, but she looked like an 80-year-old grandmother because she was exhausted by sadness, forced labor, malnutrition, and lack of medicines.

I was sent to a dike work site for five months, and when I returned, she was at the point of death. She cried: "Give me something to eat! I am hungry!" I hurried out at the risk of my own life to find her a bowl of rice. Unfortunately, she could no longer eat. Her voice had become weaker and weaker to the point of being inaudible. Crying, I shook her gently and asked her if she recognized me. She opened her eyes and looked at my face. She blinked her eyes as a sign that she knew me, her hand touched my arm, and she died at 4:00 p.m. I cried so much that day, I was so sad. Around me, everything was empty; even death was meaningless to me.

All modern goods were confiscated: bicycles, radios, watches, bracelets. All means of production belonged to the community. All the workers were equal, but the Khmer Rouge were better fed and better dressed than the people. They kept us from having any pharmaceutical products, but they kept them for the needs of their own families. Medicines were made of different kinds of roots and bark that they proudly called "revolutionary medicines." There were no doctors. There were only incompetent apprentice nurses selected from among children fourteen to sixteen years of age who, instead of healing anyone, damaged the health of the sick. Of the sick, 92% became infected because of improperly prepared vaccinations or medicines, or because of the mistakes of the health care personnel. To cut the umbilical cord, the midwives of the Pol Pot clinics used rusty, unsterilized scissors. The newborn often got tetanus. Infant mortality shot up.

The Khmer Rouge broke off all relationships of children with their parents, between spouses, between brothers and sister, and even between neighbors.

We were malnourished, dressed in rags, and reduced to slavery. Human rights were trampled under foot. The right to have family meals and free choice in marriage were replaced by "communal marriage" and forced collective marriages of 50 or 60 couples at a time. We, the "undesirables," had no right to go back to our native areas or to set up family life in happiness. The right to settle, to move freely around the country, the freedoms of opinion, association, and belief, the right to work, to rest, and to learn, all these were totally suppressed. Not all the citizens were equal and free; whereas the people were imprisoned in forced cooperatives and died of hunger, the Khmer Rouge representing Angkar moved around freely and ate well. They destroyed nearly all institutions of learning and made all the children abandon their studies. Children of thirteen to fourteen years of age were conscripted into the army. Children of six to twelve years of age worked tending cattle or collecting manure to be made into fertilizer.

The Khmer Rouge despised all the traditions, the manners, and customs of our people. They destroyed or made prisons out of the pagodas and temples, and they made the monks abandon their robes.

Angkar wanted to develop agriculture, but it killed the technicians, the agricultural engineers, and they closed factories one after another because of lack of raw materials and workers. There was no currency, no market. Angkar practiced a "closed economy." Commerce was with only one country, China, which did not understand the interests of the Khmer people, knowing only the interests of Peking.

Executions were frequent. Every night, two or three "new" people were called to a meeting and disappeared without a trace. No one dared ask the village chief about these unfortunate people, even the families could not grieve over the disappeared for fear of being accused of complicity. Whenever anyone was called out at an odd hour, especially at night, it inevitably meant death. We lived in perpetual fear, like fish in a net, not knowing when our turn would come to be killed. To survive, you had to be very cautious. Everyone mistrusted everyone else, because spies were among us. The Khmer Rouge set up an efficient espionage system: children of six to eight years of age had to spy on their parents.

Village chiefs who made up officialdom were selected from ignorant people who, seeking to maintain their authority, acted out of an excess of zeal.

Justice was speedy. A clumsy person who, not being careful, broke a plate could be accused of being an agent of the CIA, KGB, or Vietnam.

The most significant instance of killing came in June 1977. My friend Seng Meng Tech was the first victim that June. Just as he was beginning to have lunch with his family, two men from the police came to his house and took him away and executed him with blows of sticks under a palm tree a kilometer from the village. His only crime was that he wore eyeglasses for nearsightedness.

At that time an oral order was sent around to the people: "For lack of cultivable land," Angkar would have hundreds of model houses built for the "new" people. They would have to move to different villages to go work new lands. Every night, families selected to switch villages were called together. Convoys of ox-drawn or buffalo-drawn carts and of boats took these unfortunate families to "new villages" from which no one returned. My village alone had 36 families with 202 persons, which included women, men, the elderly, children, and infants. All of them were taken in convoys and up until now we do not know their fate. I thought that one day I too would meet the fate of those who were sent to Angkar from which there was no return. Every night we saw this boat and these carts, and we could get to sleep only when their sinister sounds moved far away from the village. "Another day's reprieve!" my wife would mutter.

We lived in constant anxiety. My wife and I had about twenty hazelnuts with strychnine in them that we always kept in our pockets. If we were to be called out, we would poison ourselves. That was the only way to escape the suffering. All these "new" people transported by carts and boats were taken to the school at Staung, which had been turned into a prison and a torture center. From there, any trace of these unfortunate people was lost. The killing was done in stages: at first the military personnel and police officers; next came the turn of the civil servants, intellectuals, technical people, doctors, teachers, and professors; then it was the turn of the students and school children.

I was made to do all kinds of jobs. I was in turn a laborer, a butcher, a fisherman, and a cabbage planter. Finally, I was made a preparer of "number 1 manure." My new function was to empty latrines and to take the fecal matter and mix it with dirt to make fertilizer. I suffered this life until December 1978, when I was switched into a fishing team on Tonle Sap.

When I left the fishing team to go back to Staung village after liberation, I found no one there. Everyone had left to live along the highway under the protection of the National United Front for the Salvation of Kampuchea, for fear of being taken away by the Khmer Rouge into the forest. No one could tell me just where my wife and my child had gone. Until now I have no news about them.

Phnom Penh, May 22, 1979

2.1.1.19
Pham Van Ngoc (Little Ngoc)
(For an explanation of this document, see Editors' Note.)

Mr. Pham Van Ngoc, 14 years of age, was born in Steng Treng district, Kompong Cham province. His parents, who were Vietnamese, were all killed by Pol Pot's troops in 1977. Ngoc testified before the court that his parents and neighbors, who were Vietnamese by birth, were tricked and killed by being invited for a half-hour meeting. As soon as they arrived, they were all tied up. Ngoc himself escaped. He was alive because he ran away and hid in a big water jar. With help from his neighbor, Ngoc was taken to be hidden in the forest. Now Ngoc and his younger sister are orphans, and they also lost two older siblings who were killed. At the end, he told the court that he saw with his own eyes how all of those Vietnamese people were put onto a boat and taken away to be killed.

2.1.1.20
Dr. Tin Yusuf Abdul Koyum
(For an explanation of this document, see Editors' Note.)

Dr. Tin Yusuf Abdul Koyum, 36 years of age, is a Muslim. He was a medical doctor at the Preah Ket Melea Hospital in Phnom Penh. He testified before the court how he was driven out of Phnom Penh, and he described his suffering and the barbarous torture that the Khmer Rouge inflicted on him. He also testified that his father was murdered on May 10, 1976, and his uncle was murdered in January 1976, because they were unable to conceal their nationality. He also stated that the Muslims were suppressed by the Khmer Rouge and said that no Muslims were allowed to keep their traditions or customs.

As for forcing all Chams to eat pork, he said: "Every Cham had to eat pork, absolutely. They would be punished if they resisted. The food was arranged on the table with all Muslims sitting in a row. There was a person who kept watch over Muslims and had a book to write down names every time pork was used for food on special occasions like New Year's or other festival days. If anyone resisted eating pork, his or her name was written down; therefore, everybody tried to eat even though it was hard to swallow. Sometimes, it made them throw up because they were not able to eat it. An 85-year-old Muslim lady, whose name was Sas, died after many days of being tied up to a pig pen with no food because she vomited after eating pork."

Dr. Koyum also testified about the way the Khmer Rouge killed people by telling them, falsely, that they were to go to work in a different place. The Khmer Rouge killed people by hitting them with a large stick or axe, or tied them up and dropped them into water, or forced them into a forest and starved them to death. Dr. Koyum confirmed that all Chams in his village were killed. No one survived. Furthermore, he described the strategy that the Khmer Rouge used to achieve its ridiculous plan.

At the end of his testimony, Dr. Koyum said that of 700,000 Chams in 1974, only 200,000 now remain alive, so that two thirds were killed.

2.1.1.20a
Mr. Pen Bun Piv, The Killing of Assistant Professor (Mrs.) Tip Man and the Pharmacist Mr. Ty Ngoy Peng Hy

The two victims lived in the same village, which was Phlov Leav, Prasath subdistrict, Preah Net Preah district, region 5, Battambang province.

I, Pen Bun Piv, a pharmacist, witnessed this killing, because our village, Ta Am, is near Phlov Leav.

The Pol Pot men ordered Mrs. Tip Man and Mr. Ty Ngoy Peng Hy to make natural fertilizer (fertilizer prepared from human and animal waste).

Despite their diligence in their work and their passivity, these two innocent persons were continually harassed physically and mentally by these savages. In July 1977, which was a period in which they got rid of intellectuals, the two victims were taken away in a Peugeot 404 family-type car for unknown reasons.

But I had often met Mr. and Mrs. Ty Ngoy Peng Hy, who told me about the hardships and anxieties of their life.

The kidnapping of her husband and of Mrs. Tip Man was also related to me by Mrs. Ty Ngoy Peng Hy, who is also called Ottara. She had not heard anything about her husband after this kidnapping. A month later she also died of a disease.

Three months later, according to secret information from the village chief, whose was named Pong, these two persons were killed at the Phnom Trayaung prison. Pong let this information out to his friend and his family. Later all the villagers heard it.

Pen Bun Piv

2.1.1.20b
Mr. Pen Bun Piv, Pol Pot Methods of Killing; the Yoke of Men

The Khmer people were quite enthusiastic and quite happy when they saw the April 17, 1975, victory of the Revolutionary Army of Kampuchea that crushed and eliminated the American imperialists, the greatest power in the world. This historic victory brought out emotion and joy, not only from our people, but from the people of the whole world.

At that time, I, Pen Bun Piv, 33 years of age, a state pharmacist who had long lived in difficult circumstances in Phnom Penh in the third ward under the yoke of the American imperialists, believed that our people would become happy and prosper after this victory. But to the contrary, on the first day, along with the other residents of the city, my family was forced by the Pol Pot clique to leave our house.

My wife, a ten-month-old baby on her arm, and my parents despite their age, walked sadly and in fear towards unknown destinations, on April 18, 1975.

There were eight in our family. All settled in Kraing Svay, District 51, Kompong Speu province, for two months, and then at Chiv Neak, Wat Phnom subdistrict, District 52, in Kompong Speu province, a mountainous area twenty kilometers from Kraing Svay.

During that time we were subjected to all sorts of physical and mental harassment (ten to thirteen hours of work a day with 100 grams of rice a day). To supplement our meager ration, we had to eat edible plants, palm fruits, snails, crabs, etc.

Despite having such a miserable existence, we always worked hard. At that place my wife's parents and my younger sister all died of starvation and disease in August 1975.

On September 15, 1975, at 5:00 p.m., in a violent rain, the other members of our family were taken by truck to Pursat, and then by train to Battambang, and finally on foot to a village called Ta Amp, in Prasath subdistrict, Preah Net Preah district, region 5, Battambang province. This was a hell and a place of real disaster for our family and for the other residents. The work was unbearable. They forced us to make natural fertilizer (fertilizer from human and animal waste). My wife built dikes, and my younger brothers and sisters built dams.

They made me hitch myself up to the cart to transport paddy rice.

In the rainy season, it was the same hitching up; I had to pull the plow to work the fields under their torture, threats, and close surveillance, with my six companions in June 1976, even though there were many domestic animals (cows, buffalo) in the village.

Those who were hitched up were:

1.	Pen Bun Piv	pharmacist
2.	Ry	a final-year school child
3.	Phan	a teacher in Kompong Speu
4.	Sieng	a nurse in Kompong Speu
5.	Khom	a school child in the third year class
6.	Phat	a worker.

Despite the hard work, for food we got one bowl of soup in which you could see only a few grains of rice floating around (a ration of one kilogram of rice for one hundred persons).

Everyone had to eat rats, grasshoppers, lizards, toads, thousand leggers, earthworms, etc., and various edible plants. There were about four thousand living in Ta Amp village, but as a result of this tragedy three thousand more or less died, and only one thousand were able barely to survive.

In our group of six, I, Pen Bun Piv, alone survived; the five others died during this time from various causes: The first and second causes were extreme physical overwork and starvation and lack of medicine. The victims of this were Mr. Phan in October 1976, and Mr. Sieng and Khom in November 1976. The third cause was simple annihilation after they protested (refusing to keep pulling the plows). The victims of this were Mrs. Ry and Phat in October 1976.

During that time, I was sick and overworked like my companions. I caught several diseases simultaneously: malaria, inflammation, and amoebic dysentery.

As extra work, I had to bury the dead of the village, both day and night.

After my time doing simple labor, I was put into various kinds of work, as a carpenter, a woodcutter, and as an oarsman. Despite my weakened condition, the Pol Pot people did not stop making me work, until one day when I fainted in the work field. I was, however, able to hide a dozen special medicines, and I used them to fight off the different diseases.

I was compliant and did not protest, despite this physical and mental pressure.

Luckily on January 7, 1979, the army of the National United Front for the Salvation of Kampuchea, united with the solidarity of the people of Vietnam, came in time to our village and saved our lives.

Pen Bun Piv

2.1.1.22
Mrs. Khem Maly Chan
(For an explanation of this document, see Editors' Note.)

Mrs. Khem Maly Chan, 35 years of age, was born in Kompong Cham province. She used to be a history professor, but now she is head of the tourism department in Kompong Thom province. She testified very clearly about the cruel torture that the Pol Pot government committed on herself and other people who were all imprisoned. They accused her of being an intellectual because she wore glasses, and they also accused her of being an agent of the KGB and CIA. They accused her husband of being a Lon Nol soldier and accused her of concealing her true identify and of lack of honesty with the government.

She confirmed clearly how the Pol Pot government took prisoners for experiments. They did not follow modern technological experimentation techniques at all. Their experimentation involved operating on people alive and cutting out their gallbladders. She confirmed that in such situations they had a good time committing these cruel acts. They killed people at night; they never killed in the daytime. They were afraid that people would see these killings because many people walked past the prison during the day.

A man named Hieng, the leader of the local soldiers, and a former Buddhist superior at the Shang pagoda, showed her gallbladders that he got from dead bodies. He said that gallbladders of healthy people were full of liquid inside, but that gallbladders of unhealthy people had only half the liquid. The bad gallbladders cannot be sold at a high price. When they were drying those gallbladders I heard them say that this time we got only one hundred gallbladders. It is much less than the previous time, because that time they handed in more than one thousand gallbladders to the government. Then they asked each other how much each gallbladder is worth, and they whispered that the government took those gallbladders to sell in China because they are very good as medicine. They took gallbladders from every dead body. They did not want people to die for nothing.

She also described the corruption of the village chief. Had she not had jewelry and gold, she would not have been able to get out of the prison, and she would not be alive today. She also explained about the food in prison; all the prisoners got only a small bowl of boiled rice. Most of them died of hunger.

She also saw with her own eyes the cruel torture that they committed on Professor Sen Ki. She said that 250 prisoners out of 300 were killed. At the end of her testimony, she told how the Pol Pot government chose medical workers. They chose only young people and trained them for only three days, and the government let those medical workers work and treat patients at various locations.

Religious Issues

2.1.2.01

Report by Kampuchean Clergy on the Situation in Kampuchea After April 17, 1975 (Reviewed by the Committee of Phnom Penh Monks)

For many centuries the Kampuchean people have followed Buddhism. Generation after generation, Kampucheans have found refuge and inspiration under the roofs of our pagodas. Furthermore, the pagodas are the places where the Kampucheans have received their cultural and religious education in the spirit of Cakya Muni's teachings aimed at making civilized men with proper manners and respect for the canons of Buddhist morals. However, on April 17, 1975, the government fell into the hands of the traitorous and anti-religious Pol Pot–Ieng Sary clique. From that day, Buddhist clergy, as well as the Kampuchean people, were condemned to a life of inexpressible suffering. The crimes of the Pol Pot–Ieng Sary clique were without precedent in world history. The following facts establish their vile crimes with regard to the Buddhist clergy and with regard to the Kampuchean people in general.

From the first days of their occupation of the capital, Phnom Penh, they drove the monks and nuns and other people from the city by deceiving them under the plausible pretext that one would be allowed to return after two or three days. All their words were lies. In reality, their policy was to chase the monks and people from the cities and direct them to distant regions in the countryside and forests where a great many perished due to diseases, above all, malaria. What is more, those who did not obey them were either threatened or killed by their weapons. This clique was more barbaric than the Hitlerite fascists. In the history of the world, as in the history of religions, there was not one clique of similar monstrosity.

After having driven them out of the towns, this clique forced the monks and nuns to give up their religious life to become ordinary citizens. Any of the clergy who disobeyed were immediately put to death: they received a blow from the handle of a pick or a bamboo stick that smashed their skulls. Most of the Kampuchean clergy loved Buddhism and they did not want to give up their yellow frocks to put on vests and pants. But they could do nothing against the injunctions ordered by Pol Pot's men. It was with bitter tears that they followed. Thus, the sublime love of Buddhism by our clergy was stifled, as was our national religion, which for centuries had permeated our people's habits and customs. In the course of these operations to compel the monks to become unbelievers, many of the monks were killed in barbaric ways. One of them was plunged into a Leyden jar filled with water where he died, drowning. Those whom the Pol Pot agents had not yet had time to kill were saved by the National United Front for the Salvation of Kampuchea.

Under the Pol Pot regime, the monks had to raise pigs, tend to the cows, and make wood cases. The plan was to force the people to do cruel acts contrary to Buddha's teachings. On the other hand, the clergy was subjected to a regimen of exhausting labor with no rest and very little food. Sometimes, ten people only had the right to a bowl of 300 grams of rice. In Kampuchea, there were around 20,000 monks and nuns. All were forced to put an end to their religious practice. Once one became aware of the condition of things, the question was asked of the Pol Pot men: Where are the numerous clergy of Kampuchea? The Pol Pot men answered with this fallacious argument: The monks are sons of the people, they are patriots and that is why they voluntarily gave up their religious life so they could join the armed forces to defend the Fatherland. Those beautiful remarks hide their disgraceful act; forcing the Buddhist clergy to abandon their religion. The ex-clergy who were able to survive until now have returned to their religious life. In our pagoda at San Sam Kosal, there are, at this time, 68 monks who are new servants of Buddha.

Our pagoda and articles of worship belong to our cultural legacy of which the entire Kampuchean people can be proud but were burned down and destroyed by the Pol Pot–Ieng Sary clique. Statues of Buddha were broken at the neck and thrown into the mud. Several principal temples of our 26 pagodas in Phnom Penh were sacked. In others, statues of Buddha were broken and putrid material, like cow dung, was stored in the temples in defiance of the people's wishes.

Now, a radiant morning has returned to Kampuchean soil. Our religion enjoys benefits of the valiant work of the National United Front for the Salvation of Kampuchea. What is more, in Point 6 of its program, the People's Revolutionary Council has decided to repair the pagodas so that Kampuchean believers may find places to worship Buddha.

San Sam Kosal Pagoda, June 13, 1979

The following have signed:
Soc Chem, Tum Lang, Pech Som, Prak Phun, Prok Chno, Kim Phay, Chhung Dem, So Di, Hoang Puk, Mop, Dok Reah, Sek Seak, Uon Cong, Ke Dang, Ich Sum, Nuon Di, Nuon Loas, Cheng Sang, Dinh Sarun, Prom Tinh, Khieu Di, Ua Som Ah, Um Chin, Kol Mrech, Hong Tich, Vong Sum, O Bung, Mech Chhua, Un Bang, Hun Som, Thong Veng, Pak Sin, Bo Rin, Ner Pok, Chok Chrok, Phun Koi, Nu Um, Mau Sim, Don In

Confirmed after examined, I certify that the crimes related in this report conform to the truth.

Le Khech Thoms Nol Moni, Buddhist Clergy Representative

2.1.2.02

Speech by the Delegation of the Buddhist Association for the National Salvation of Kampuchea at the 5th Congress of the Asian Buddhists' Conference for Peace, Ulan Bator, June 1979

Esteemed members of the Presidium, esteemed delegates: From a country just recovered from the danger of genocide, the Buddhist delegation of the People's Republic of Kampuchea is very elated to participate in the 5th Congress, the historic Congress of the Asian Buddhists Conference for Peace, held in Ulan Bator, the beautiful and heroic capital of the fraternal People's Republic of Mongolia.

On behalf of all Kampuchean Buddhists and people, we would like to convey to the Most Venerable President S. Gombojav, venerables and distinguished guests, my greetings of great solidarity and great success.

We sincerely thank the Asian Buddhists' Conference for Peace for its constant and wholehearted support to our Kampuchean Buddhists and people's just cause and for sending its delegation to visit recently our country, which greatly encourages our Buddhists and people. We also sincerely thank its Executive Committee for having admitted and recognized the Buddhist Association for the National Salvation of Kampuchea as a member of the Asian Buddhists' Conference for peace. This is a great encouragement to our Kampuchean Buddhists and people.

Esteemed delegates, enslaved for nearly 100 years under colonial and imperialist yoke, the Kampuchean people had joined efforts with the peoples of Vietnam and Laos subjected to the same yoke, risen up in struggle, endured countless hardships and sacrifices before winning victory on April 17, 1975, completely liberating our country. But right after that, a sudden disaster befell our people: Chinese big nation hegemonic expansionism imposed on Kampuchea an extremely brutal regime which brought to our nation a genocide as never before seen in history.

Peasants and city dwellers were driven into concentration camps to do hard labor until exhaustion and death through hunger, cold, and overwork. Intellectuals, specialists, writers and artists were ill-treated and murdered en masse. Schools were turned into places to detain, torture, and kill people. Hospitals and cultural works were destroyed. Buddhism was banned, religious believers were not allowed to go to pagoda or to support monks. These were stripped of their yellow robes, compelled to do hard labor, and murdered. Buddhist prayer books, articles of worship were burned and statues of Buddha smashed. Pagodas were either destroyed or turned into warehouses or stables. In the past, there were 2,800 pagodas and 82,000 monks throughout Kampuchea. However, under the Pol Pot–Ieng Sary regime no pagoda was left and only a very small number of monks managed to flee to revolutionary bases. All of Kampuchea was turned into a huge concentration camp, without currency, schools, hospitals, markets, religions, or families, and without any contact among family or friends. The people were forced to do hard labor or were murdered en masse with rifles, knifes, hoes, hammers, and other medieval barbarian means. In less than four years, the Pol Pot–Ieng Sary butchers massacred three million of the seven million people of our country.

Alongside that genocidal policy, the Pol Pot–Ieng Sary executioners pushed our youths into a savage war, well known around the world, against the Vietnamese people, causing untold suffering and mourning to the Vietnamese people in the Vietnam-Kampuchea border areas, undermining the age-old friendship and the militant solidarity between the Kampuchean and Vietnamese peoples.

The deep-rooted cause of the above-mentioned situation was the intervention by the Chinese expansionists who schemed to turn Kampuchea into a giant military base as a springboard for them to annex the Indochinese countries and expand to Southeast Asia. To this end, after May 17, 1975, China brought into Kampuchea tens of thousands of military advisers and personnel, and tens of thousands of tons of weaponry and military equipment.

Oppression begets struggle. Unable to live a human life and facing the threat of extermination, the Kampuchean people had no choice but to rise up against the Pol Pot–Ieng Sary clique that was in the pay of Peking, to save themselves and the country.

Recently, Kampuchea has seen two wars: one waged by our people in coordination with the separatist forces against the genocidal regime and the other waged by the Vietnamese people and army in self-defense along the Eastern border of Kampuchea.

The setbacks of the Pol Pot armed forces in the border areas encouraged and stepped up the Kampuchean people's uprisings which, in turn, led to heavier losses for the Pol Pot army at the Vietnam-Kampuchea border. Those were the objective factors which facilitated the rallying of the Kampuchean revolutionary forces throughout the country, led to the foundation of the National United Front for the Salvation of Kampuchea on December 2, 1978, the total collapse of the genocidal Pol Pot–Ieng Sary regime on January 7, 1979, the birth of the People's Republic of Kampuchea on January 8, 1979. That is a dismal setback for the genocidal expansionist policy with which the Peking reactionary ruling circle experimented in our country for nearly four years.

The situation in our country at present is irreversible, the Kampuchean people are masters of their destiny once and for all. The People's Revolutionary Council of Kampuchea, the sole authentic and legal representative of the Kampuchean people, which has been recognized by many countries, is really managing all the internal and external affairs of Kampuchea.

Esteemed Delegates, although the Chinese hegemonic expansionists have suffered heavy setbacks in our country (as well as in Vietnam and Laos), they have not given up their wicked design of annexing the three Indochinese countries to expand to Southeast Asia. They are doing their utmost to breathe life into the Pol Pot corpse and maintain the latter's presence in the United Nations and other international organizations. With the aid of Thailand, they keep sending military personnel and weaponry via Thailand into Kampuchea to help the remnants of the Pol Pot army to undermine the independence and sovereignty of Kampuchea. They do not take the negotiations with the government of the Socialist Republic of Vietnam seriously but only use the negotiations to foul public opinion and cover up new military adventures against Vietnam. They increasingly threaten the independence and sovereignty of Laos. Obviously, in league with the U.S. and other reactionary forces in southeast Asia, Peking hegemonism is posing a threat to the independence and sovereignty of the Indochinese countries, sabotaging peace and stability in southeast Asia.

In light of this situation, on behalf of the Kampuchean people and Buddhist believers, victims of the Peking hegemonic expansionist policy, we urgently call upon Buddhist believers and peoples in Asia to strengthen our solidarity and intensify our struggle to foil Peking's hegemonic expansionism in collusion with U.S. imperialism, for the defense of the independence and sovereignty of each country and to safeguard peace and stability in Asia, thus contributing to the defense of world peace and resolutely to prevent another genocide in Kampuchea.

We call upon you to strongly support the national defense and construction of the Kampuchean Buddhist believers and people and to press for an early recognition of the People's Revolutionary Council of Kampuchea.

The Kampuchean Buddhist believers and people are confident that under the banner of the National United Front for the Salvation of Kampuchea and under the wise leadership of the People's Revolutionary Council of Kampuchea, with the coordination and assistance of the Vietnamese and Lao peoples, the help of the Soviet Union and other brotherly socialist countries, the sympathy and support of friends around the world, including the Asian Buddhist Conference for Peace and its member countries, we will successfully defend and build a peaceful, independent, democratic, neutral, nonaligned Kampuchea, advancing to socialism.

We wish our fifth congress of Asian Buddhists for Peace great success.

Thank you very much.

Copy verified, July 11, 1979

2.1.2.03
Tep Vung, Buddhist Superior

My name is Tep Vung, 49 years old. I was a Buddhist superior priest at Bos pagoda in Siem Reap city, Siem Reap district, Siem Reap province. As a Buddhist, I have only one desire in my life: to be a completely loyal follower of Buddhism. Unfortunately, in 1975 I became a victim of the genocidal regime under the reactionary Pol Pot–Ieng Sary clique, henchmen for the expansionist and hegemonistic Peking government, allies to the imperialists hoping to turn China into a "super power." To this end, they have destroyed Kampuchean Buddhism and killed a great number of Kampuchean people. What has taken place in our province, Siem Reap, constitutes concrete proof of this.

Since the Pol Pot–Ieng Sary reactionaries came to power, they have killed so many Buddhist priests and plundered and destroyed so much property in gold, silver, and precious objects contributed by Buddhists, such as: sacred books, objects of worship, such as banners and golden parasols. Since April 17, 1975, they have murdered Buddhist priests by various methods: in April 1975, they killed 57 priests at Prey Look village, in Chan Sar subdistrict, Sotr Nikum district, Siem Reap province. (Among those killed were my three nephews, named Han, Tek, and Mon, who had taken their vows of priesthood at the Esley pagoda, in Bang Kong subdistrict, Sotr Nikum district, Siem Reap province. My nephew Mon was about to be named to Superior Priest in charge of the Roka pagoda, in Ro Lour district, Siem Reap province.)

Later on, Pol Pot agents seized and burned all the books of the Buddhist canon and other cultural works of national importance that were found in the pagodas. What most afflicts priests and Buddhists was the destruction of two bronze statues, Preah Ang Chek and Preah Ang Chom, carved by our forefathers in the Angkor Wat period, which had been maintained for thousands of years. In 1978, after Dap Chhuon, a bandit leader, was killed in the capital of Siem Reap, people frequented a beautiful and ancient pagoda, which was considered the most beautiful and sacred pagoda and a symbol for the entire country. The Pol Pot–Ieng Sary executioners, having figured this out, immediately sent their men to destroy the pagoda. But the wrath of Buddha was such that some of them lost their lives. Giving in to their hatred, the men used hammers and axes to break the arms and ears off the statues of Buddha, and threw them in a well behind the Damako pagoda in town. This act was witnessed by the local inhabitants.

In 1976, the Pol Pot–Ieng Sary executioners used mines to blow up two 5-meter-high stone statues at the Angkor Thom Temple (Puah An Tep and Puah Ngok, also carved by our forefathers). They also broke the neck of the statue of Koh Thlok, a genius who was the namesake of ancient Kampuchea—"The Koh Thlok Country." After January 7, 1979, the Buddhists restored and returned it to be used for worship by our people. The Pol Pot–Ieng Sary executioners also partly destroyed the well-known ancient Angkor Wat Temple. They destroyed or pillaged hundreds of Buddha statues carved from stone and precious wood on the third floor of the temple. There are now fewer than 20 statues left. Still more perfidious, the Pol Pot–Ieng Sary clique wanted to destroy all pagodas and temples, which they regarded as the symbols of the Khmer people's soul and sacred feelings. They used mines to blow up the main door. . . and on the third floor, on the southern side, causing heavy damage. The Southern Angkor Temple and the Northern Angkor Temple, which used to have more than 100 priests each, were overtaken by the forests after three years, their priests chased away, their pagodas and towers destroyed, and the articles of worship pillaged. All nine pagodas in the capital of Siem Reap were either turned into offices for the local security service (as was the Thoamayutt pagoda, because of its proximity to the local prison), or transformed into arms depots, or schools for training officers (as was the Preah Rom Roeut pagoda), or workshops to repair military vehicles (like the Nos and Damnak pagodas), or into barracks for mobile troops (like the Svey pagoda). Meanwhile, the Monisovan, Pour Angkor Sey, and Sour Angkor Sey pagodas were abandoned, left to be overgrown by wild grass. Those nine pagodas were used or adapted by the local rulers according to their whim.

There were 173 pagodas with 4,800 priests in the province of Siem Reap before 1970. In 1975–1976, the Pol Pot–Ieng Sary reactionaries compelled those priests to give up their religion and do forced labor, all the while saying to them: ". . . For more than 1000 years you have exploited the people, so now you must work and earn a living. . . ." Those who opposed them were labeled enemy agents; those who resisted were "made into ghosts." They forbade the people to have contact with the priests and from visiting the pagodas to make offerings of rice to Buddha — under penalty of being qualified as "enemies, plotting against the state," subject to eventual elimination.

Therefore, the priests were forced to leave their pagodas and do what they were ordered to do. There were, however, superior priests who, for survival purposes, dared to defend Buddhism and waged a revolutionary struggle. They were sickened and indignant at the crimes committed by the Pol Pot–Ieng Sary assassins against the priests. Here are a few examples: In Siem Reap province, a priest name Tit Phan, 78 years old, was forced to renounce his religion and do hard labor. From morning until night, he was obliged to build hen houses. He had very little food to ease his hunger and no medicine when he was ill. He left this terrestrial life to rejoin Buddha in 1977. The superior priest of the Tabeng pagoda, in Roun Taek subdistrict, Sotr Nikum district, Siem Reap province, was imprisoned for no reason, in the office of the local security service, and later taken to an unknown destination. The superior priest, Mit, of the Preah Angkor Sey pagoda, in the capital of Siem Reap, was accused of having illicit relations with women and jailed in the Damrey Con Forest, in Sotr Nikum district, Siem Reap province, where he later died.

As for myself, I was a superior priest at the Bos pagoda. I was also detained without any pretext. On May 6, 1975, they forced me out of my pagoda and they took me to the Chi Kreng pagoda. After three days and nights of marching, I was condemned to forced labor at the Russey Lok pagoda. Then, after another 10 days of marching, I spent one night in the Koh Thlok pagoda, and then we were off to the "Sro Nghe Cha" pagoda. After three days of imprisonment, they took me to the Kbal Dam Rey pagoda, in Pongro Leu subdistrict, Chi Kreng district, Siem Reap province, where I was forced to do hard labor receiving beatings from my executioners. One day in November 1975, they stripped me of my priest's robe, ignoring my request for a 10-day postponement so that I could get some clothes from the local inhabitants. One day, 10 security agents came, out of nowhere, to threaten me: "Take off your robe. If you don't, you'll be shot." I had to take it off and they led me away. On November 14, 1975, I was taken to a commune that was set up in my native village, south of the capital of Siem Reap, and I did hard labor there.

Later on, they transferred me to a mobile production group of young people. I was, during my time there, mistreated, tortured, and then imprisoned for 84 days without reason. I saw, with my own eyes, the same fate befall more than 100 other people. (My brother, Phnom Phoeun, was among them.) Each day, we had to work very hard but received only 900 grams of rice for 40, 50, and even 70 people. This quantity was insufficient to make even rice soup for that many people. As a result, many workers died of exhaustion, one after another.

Here are the names of the local reactionary leaders: Hom and Kheng, respectively head and deputy-head of the security service; Soth and Sien, respectively president of the region and president of the province; Da, district leader; Soi Pho and Khoun, members of the district Party Committee. Their policy toward Buddhism consisted of seizing all pagodas, stripping off the priests' robes, and eliminating them step by step. They burned the canonical books, books of Buddhist morality, and works of national culture. Then they plundered or destroyed articles of worship, blew up temples and tombs, and turned pagodas and temples into arms depots and army barracks. Brick, stone, or cement constructions were leveled to the ground by bulldozers. Such was the case for the Pra Dak pagoda, northeast of Angkor Wat.

In February 1976, the Pol Pot–Ieng Sary agents forced the priests there to take off their priests' robes and then turned the pagoda into a stable, a hen coop, and a pigsty. At the beginning of 1978, they used bulldozers to level this pagoda, and the ground was turned into a rice field. The Ba Kong pagoda in Sotr Nikum district, Siem Reap province, had many beautiful towers, surrounded by beautiful lakes and shaded alleys. In late 1977, early 1978, the pagoda was turned into an office of the security service, where the inhabitants followed reeducation courses. The local people informed me that more than 100 people died from starvation or were killed there. The Pokey pagoda with its great towers was turned into a place of torture and killing following April 17, 1975: a large number of people were beaten to death with clubs or hammers, or were shot there. The Prey Prok pagoda in Songvor subdistrict, Chi Kreng district, Siem Reap province, was turned into a reeducation center. Since September 1977, more than 1,000 families (about 7,000 people) were detained there until January 1979, when the revolutionary armed forces of the National United Front for the Salvation of Kampuchea came to free them. According to some Buddhists, the executioners had declared that the population had to be trained into disciplined people of the Party. . . . In fact, the people had to work hard day and night with their hunger and thirst, not even a sufficient amount of soup to eat. Because of this, many children and elderly became sick, and many died. From 1975 to 1979, the Troung Bat pagoda in Kompong Thkau subdistrict, Kra Lanh district, Siem Reap province, was transformed into a place of detention to jail people and Buddhists. At the entrance and exit of the pagoda there were posted signs of a skull and crossbones, forbidding entrance to the public for security reasons. Many people were killed there through barbarous methods to which I would like to draw the attention of the world's people, far and near: . . . burying alive people who were tied up in advance, herded into ditches, covered with paddy husks, and then burned to make fertilizer.

One has the right to wonder, "Who, if not the Pol Pot–Ieng Sary assassins, burned these men and women to make fertilizer?" Has there existed in all of history any leader of a country that has eradicated religion, massacred their monks and even their fellow countrymen, plundered sacred articles of worship, destroyed pagodas, temples, and Buddhist tombs—all sacred and antique works, composing the pride and substance of Khmer civilization and the Kampuchean people?

I have given a concrete account of the crimes of the Pol Pot–Ieng Sary clique, those traitors to their country who have exterminated the Khmer race and destroyed our religion. May I, in the interest of the people, propose that the competent authorities prosecute them immediately, for such is the desire of the Kampuchean people, a people deeply attached to peace, national traditions, and Buddhism. According to Buddhist principles, with these crime, the Pol Pot–Ieng Sary group may be considered to have lost their "human nature"; these savage beasts should be turned upside down like bats, with their legs in the air above their heads, and once they have fallen they will be condemned to hell, deprived forever of the sight of the sun or moonlight. I would like to draw the attention of world opinion to this: those who still carry on relations with these villains, Pol Pot and Ieng Sary, who continue to regard them as friends, as brothers, and who give them food and lodging, should consider themselves as "men who burn their own homes."

The facts I have related before public opinion are well-founded, and conform to Buddhist principles and with the eleven-point political program of the People's Revolutionary Council of Kampuchea, which includes the right to believe in Buddha and the protection of national traditions. It is in my capacity as a Kampuchean citizen, under the correct judicious guidance of the People's Revolutionary Council of Kampuchea, an organization fully capable of leading Kampuchea to socialism and ensuring an everlasting peaceful life for the Kampuchean people, that I have presented these facts.

Done at Siem Reap, June 1, 1979
Tep Vung

2.1.2.04
Monk Seng Khuon Uon

My name is Seng Khuon Uon. I am 68 years old and I am practicing Buddhism at the San Sam Kosal pagoda, Bang Tompoun village, Phsar Doeum Thkao district, Phnom Penh.

On April 19, 1975, I was driven out of the Langkar pagoda by the Pol Pot clique under the threat of force. They pointed a B-40 gun at me saying: "The whole country has already been liberated. Everyone has left. Why do you still remain here?" I was compelled to leave the city together with the people in exodus. After a ten day journey, I was taken to Talun village, Prek Sleng district, Kandal province, where I stayed until the seventh day of the first month (Kampuchean calendar). The village and subdistrict leaders, and other members of the subdistrict committee ordered: "All monks and nuns who have come here must renounce the practice of Buddhism." On the fourteenth day in the same month, I was given a black suit and ordered to abandon all religious practices from that day forward.

Four or five days later, by their order, I had to cut bamboo and braid baskets, to take care of the gardens and birds, etc.

During these three years, under the Pol Pot regime, I was sent to a re-education course once, and another time I was threatened with imprisonment. The whole family of Chong Y, young and old included, living in Prek Chrav village, Talun subdistrict, Saang district, Kandal province, were killed on August 14, 1976.

These acts of barbaric vandalism perpetrated against religion caused me profound pain. So much so, I was prepared to take part in the armed struggle against their regime if such a movement had appeared (before January 7, 1979, the day of liberation).

Although I am a monk, I could not stay with my arms crossed if the Pol Pot clique would return. I would not hesitate to push aside the sacred books to participate in combat and defend the religion.

July 12, 1979
Seng Khuon Uon

2.1.2.05
Monk Uch Phon

My name is Uch Phon. I was born in 1917, at Chheu Til village, Thnot district, Takeo province. Before 1975, I worshipped Buddha in Keo Preah Phloeun pagoda, Phnom Penh.

On April 17, 1975, around 5:00 p.m., Pol Pot–Ieng Sary agents opened fire against our pagoda to drive us out. Taken with fear, the monks ran away in all directions, several were wounded by their bullets. After having left the Keo Preah Phloeun pagoda, like the other monks, I was to go to the Preah Ta Duong pagoda in Koh Thom district, Kandal province. However, in 1976, I was driven out of this pagoda, again by Pol Pot agents, to the Kong Sombour pagoda in Koh Thom district, where they ordered the population to stop offering meals to monks while, with repeated threats, they forced us to work very hard and to stop practicing our religion. Under threats of these people, all the monks, myself included, gave up our saffron robes. In this way, they transformed the Buddhist monks into ordinary citizens. At the same time, we were ordered to remain with the confines of the pagoda. For my part, after four days in this situation of arrest, I ran away to Preah Ampil subdistrict, Saang district, Kandal province. Five months later, the subdistrict authorities sent me to Kon Chea village in the same subdistrict and forced me to pedal irrigation wheels long days and even at night. After four months of this forced labor, they transferred me to Khsach Cha Lea island. Here too the work was debilitating, but as food they gave me just a little soup with stems of water lilies. The Pol Pot–Ieng Sary agents are barbarous people who have no respect for the monks, and who have destroyed the Buddhist religion as well as the national Khmer traditions, just as they have destroyed our country.

After the victory of the armed forces of the National United Front for the Salvation of Kampuchea, I could again devote my life to the worship of Buddha. Our religion has been restored. This is one source of joy for myself and I swear to defend the new regime until my final days.

Phnom Penh, June 15, 1979
Uch Phon

2.1.2.07
Monk Nil Moni

I am Monk Nil Moni. I was born January 1, 1920, in So Yon village, Baray district, Kompong Thom province. Before 1975, I was at the Onalom pagoda, Phnom Penh city. At present I am at the San Sam Kosal pagoda, Phsar Doeum Thkao village, Phnom Penh City.

On the day the Pol Pot–Ieng Sary troops occupied Phnom Penh city, I was forced out of the pagoda, April 17, at 9:00 a.m., on the pretext that our absence of four or five days was necessary to let them restore order and security, after which time we would be permitted to return again to our pagoda. However, they directed me towards Ang Krong village, Kung Pisey district, where I stayed for three months. Then the hamlet chiefs, guerrilla fighters, and the president of the village administrative committee gave me an ordinary suit of clothes and ordered me to give up my saffron robe. They said that the Buddhist clergy was a class of exploiters living on the sweat and tears of others. I had therefore to put an end to my religious life, or they would kill me as a measure of eradicating a class of exploiters.

Once assured that I would comply with their demand, they put me in production units, forcing me into doing extremely hard work: hoeing the land, digging canals, and building dikes. I had to work with groups of young people, all of them girls. The Pol Pot agents used shocking terms offensive to the teachings of Buddha and to the dignity of religious people. One monk was forced to wear trousers and was subsequently killed in a most cruel manner. This monk was named Hom, and he was from Ang Krong village, Kung Pisey district, Kompong Speu province. He struggled heroically to defend Buddhism. The people whose hands are red with the blood of religious figures and of the people were village officials and guerrilla fighters in the pay of Pol Pot and Ieng Sary, this clique of immoral dictators who betrayed the nation, religion, and the national Khmer traditions. These savage people tried to wipe out our race.

They forced Buddhist believers to destroy pagodas, and to throw statues of Buddha into pools of water. They turned pagodas and monks' houses into pigsties and cow stables. That is why, as for me, I am determined not to let them return to power.

After my liberation by the National United Front for the Salvation of Kampuchea, who gave me my life back, and which restored religion and let me practice it, I feel a great joy. With all my heart I will restore Buddhism and at the same time defend the new government, to which I wish eternal life.

Phnom Penh, June 15, 1979
Nil Moni

Military Issues

2.1.4.01
Mr. Nhek Houn

This evidence was recorded at the office of the First Brigade, responsible for the defense of Phnom Penh, on June 10, 1979, at 2:00 p.m., in the presence of Prum Chien, an official of the Ministry of the Interior; Ouk Chandara, clerk in charge of recording statements; and Nhek Houn, the declarant.

Question: Your personal data, please.

Answer: I am Nhek Houn, 33 years of age, from Romeas Hek district, Svay Rieng province. I was a deputy political commissar of the autonomous artillery unit, sector 21, of the army of Democratic Kampuchea, stationed in Kompong Cham province. My current position is as deputy commander of the First Brigade.

Question: According to your previous statement, the Pol Pot–Ieng Sary clique betrayed the country and committed many crimes against the people and army. Please give us some specific details.

Answer: The crimes committed by the Pol Pot–Ieng Sary clique were innumerable and extremely barbarous. After April 17, 1975, they betrayed the Kampuchean people and killed people en masse to carry out China's expansionist policy. Here are the crimes they committed against my unit.

In 1975, my company had 160 men, and sector 21 had about 3,000 troops. By various means, the Pol Pot–Ieng Sary clique killed nearly all of them. Only three survive in this one artillery company, and sixteen or seventeen (including Mr. Hun Sen) from among the sector 21 troops.

After the country was liberated on April 17, 1975, the army was always hungry. Every day, each soldier was given half a tin of rice, just enough to prepare a pint of soup, but was forced to work hard. Each soldier had to hoe an area of 900 square meters a day. If anyone did not finish his work during the day time he had to work at night to finish it. That is why we had to work from ten to twelve hours a day. Anyone who fell ill had to prepare concoctions of roots or herbs gathered in the forest.

To kill army men, the Pol Pot–Ieng Sary clique used the following method. They summoned officers, allegedly for advancement courses, and then liquidated them. In 1976, I do not exactly remember the date, they called batches of 20 or 30 soldiers in my unit to work for a dam project, but when they got three kilometers away from the camp, they had to hand over their weapons and were beaten to death with hoes and shovels. On June 20, 1977, at 4:00 p.m., they sent three trucks to the camp and took dozens of officials into them, allegedly for an advancement course. But the officials never returned. Later on we learned what had occurred while talking with the drivers. Therefore, together with other comrades, we fled to the forest to look for genuine revolutionaries to wage a liberation struggle against the Pol Pot–Ieng Sary clique.

Question: Do you have anything more to say?

Answer: The army men were eliminated in stages. As for the ordinary people, they were killed under various pretexts. Thus the people at Cosoma pagoda were forced to eat pork. More than one thousand people who refused were taken away and executed at Svay Rieng, in Kompong Cham province. The crimes of the Pol Pot–Ieng Sary clique are abominable, particularly the mass killings to exterminate the Kampuchean people. I ask the Revolutionary People's Council to put them on trial and denounce their crimes before world opinion.

Question: Can you vouch for your statement? What you have said is true?

Answer: I vouch and bear full responsibility for it.

Completed at 4:00 p.m., read over, confirmed and signed by the declarant.

Investigator	*Clerk*	*Declarant*
Prum Chien	Ouk Chandara	Nhek Houn

2.1.4.02
Mr. Vang Pheap

At 7:00 a.m. on July 14, 1979, at the office of the Military Command of Kandal province, we, Mien Chieu, official of the Ministry of Interior in charge of the interview, and Mr. Ouk Chandara, secretary, recorded the following testimony by Mr. Vang Pheap.

Question: Please let us know in brief your curriculum vitae.

Answer: My name is Vang Pheap, 29 years old, born in Kompong Cong village, Kompong Cong subdistrict, Cok Thom district, Kandal province. I am Chief of Staff of Kandal province's Military Command.

Question: What did you do under the Pol Pot regime?

Answer: From December 23, 1975, to June 1977, I was commander of the second company of Unit 212 of S-21, and warden of Tuol Svay Prey prison in Phnom Penh.[1]

1. Tuol Svay Prey is the name of the secondary school that was converted into the prison that was called Tuol Sleng. See Document 2.4.10. — Eds.

Question: Do you know of atrocities committed by the Pol Pot–Ieng Sary clique in that prison?

Answer: Yes, I know of some.

Question: Could you tell us in detail about these atrocities?

Answer: My unit was in charge of guarding the prison and at the same time had to carry out orders from the Pol Pot–Ieng Sary clique to execute prisoners. This is why I am aware of what happened. This prison detained mostly factory workers from Phnom Penh. Among the prisoners there were engineers, intellectuals, army commanders, and administrative officials, together with their families, from the company and district level upwards. During the years 1975 and 1976, this prison detained more than 1,200 people. The prisoners included children who were savagely tortured. The prisoners were given electric shock, clubbed on the back or limbs, or forced to drink large quantities of salt water each time 2–3 liters and then to throw up the water.

After being interrogated, all the prisoners, whether they confessed or not, were killed on the spot, either just outside the prison, or in a paddy field in Prey So village, Don Cao district, Kandal province. To kill the victims, they ordered pits to be dug ahead of time (my unit dug such pits a number of times), each pit being 4 meters long, 2 meters wide, and 1.5 meters deep. They ordered us to take the prisoners one by one to up near the pits, where they were hit on the neck or on the head with iron bars that were nearly one meter long. After that, Pol Pot men cut the victims' throats or ripped their bellies open to pluck out the liver. Then the bodies were thrown into the pits and covered over. At first, 5 or 6 people were killed each day, but the number shot up day by day, and by 1977 the Pol Pot–Ieng Sary gang had killed from 130 to 150 prisoners a day.

When the area just outside the prison was full of corpses, they took prisoners to Prey So and Takhmau to kill them. I still remember the places and I can take you there if you want. I can't give an exact figure, but one might estimate that from December 1975 to June 1977, the Pol Pot–Ieng Sary clique killed from 10,000 to 12,000 prisoners, including children, in Tuol Sleng and Takhmau prisons.

The prisoners were killed on orders from a man named Duch, the prison chief. The company commander Proc, the assistant company commander Pay, and the company political commissar La Ruon ordered us to bring the prisoners to kill them ourselves. I beat 3 or 4 people to death in the month of March 1976. I did not cut anyone's throat, nor did I disembowel anyone.

Question: Do you know for what purpose the Pol Pot–Ieng Sary clique disembowelled prisoners after killing them?

Answer: They did so to take the bile. They dried the bile. After that, they put the bile in a room of the prison. I do not know how many, nor the use they made of them.

Question: What have you done since June 1977?

Answer: In June 1977, I do not remember exactly the day, my unit was on guard. Taking advantage of a moment of inattention on our part, a prisoner hung himself, committing suicide. The leaders suspected us of treason and they threw me and my soldiers in prison. After ten days of detention, I escaped. After July 1977 I met genuine revolutionaries and joined them in the struggle until Liberation Day (January 7, 1979).

Question: Have you any suggestions or proposals to make?

Answer: The Pol Pot–Ieng Sary clique committed extremely barbarous crimes against the Kampuchean people. They betrayed our people and our country. Their biggest crime is the genocidal crime against the Kampuchean nation serving the Chinese expansionists in a treasonous way. I ask that the Revolutionary Council of Kampuchea bring them before a court and denounce their crimes before the entire world.

The interview was completed at 9:00 a.m. the same day and was read back to Mr. Vang Pheap, who confirmed that what he said is correct.

Witness	*Interviewer*	*Secretary*
Vang Pheap	Mien Chieu	Ouk Chandara

P.S. After signing the statement, the witness showed us around the prison, where we found 19 mass graves full of bodies, and we found ten other graves in Takhmau. The exhumation of these graves is continuing.

Issues of Ordinary Citizens

2.1.5.01
Mrs. Ay Nasoeun

Today, June 26, 1979, at 2:00 p.m., we, Prum Chien, an official of the Ministry of the Interior, and Sang Nim, assistant secretary, interrogated one witness, who was also a victim, Ay Nasoeun, a female, as follows:

Question: What, briefly, is your biography?

Answer: My name is Ay Nasoeun, 25 years old, born in Pak Nam village, Maha Liep subdistrict, Koh Sotin district, Kompong Cham province. My profession is that of a weaver, but I was a farmer in the Khmer Rouge era. My educational level is 7th grade. I am of Khmer Nationality, a Buddhist.

The condition of my family is that my parents and all of my six siblings disappeared and are missing. My husband died in 1976, and in 1977 another ten died.

Question: Can you tell us the specifics about the criminal activities that Pol Pot and Ieng Sary committed on you and your own family?

Answer: The criminal activities of Pol Pot and Ieng Sary committed on me are as follows:

On March 17, 1976, my family and other people in the village were evacuated to Mondul Kiri province. When we arrived at the new area, my husband and children were separated to live in different places, and I was not allowed to meet my husband.

Right after I delivered my baby, I was forced to do hard labor. My husband also worked hard and beyond his energy. Therefore, he and my children had to get into the hospital to treat his illness. My husband died in the hospital on February 17, 1977.

In May 1977, I was placed in a mobile team, and I worked really hard all day without any rest. They forced each woman to carry 30 kilograms of dirt on average, but they gave us only a bowl of rice.

In 1978, I was really ill and I asked them to stop. They did not allow me to stop and said that I, like my husband, was a traitor.

As for my family, they arrested all of my family members and put them into the hellish collective. My child got sick, but they did not give any medicine to treat the sickness. My child died after my husband's death. My parents and my siblings all disappeared. My family consisted of seven siblings, and I am the only one alive.

Question: Besides those criminal activities that Pol Pot and Ieng Sary committed against you and your family, do you know about criminal activities against others?

Answer: I saw many younger and older women, who lived at the same collective with me, and suffered the same conditions as I did. Their children died of starvation and had no medicine to cure illness. I do not remember those people's names; therefore, I cannot describe clearly. Moreover, I lived only in the collective. I knew about conditions in other places, when I was sent to those places.

Question: What suggestions do you have for all of the criminal activities of Pol Pot and Ieng Sary that were committed against your family and the Kampuchean people in general?

Answer: Pol Pot and Ieng Sary committed severe crimes on the nation of Kampuchea. Blood debt must be compensated by blood. I suggest to the government of People's Republic of Kampuchea that it take a decision to arrest Pol Pot and Ieng Sary, to sentence them in front of the people, reveal their criminal activities of killing, betrayal to the nation, and betrayal to the people, and to let both local people and all people around the world see clearly what occurred, in order to rehabilitate the Kampuchean people and Kampuchea.

Question: Do you have any further comments?

Answer: I do not have any further comments, but I confirm that all the events I described above are true.

These remarks were finished at 4:00 p.m. the same day. We read it back and let the witness listen. She acknowledged that the remarks correctly reflect her answers, and she was willing to sign with us.

Secretary	*Witness*	*Interrogator*
Sang Nim	Ay Nasoeun	Prum Chien

2.1.5.01a

Denunciation Letter by Mrs. Ay Nasouen

A condemnation of the criminal activities of Pol Pot, Ieng Sary, and their associates committed on my family and the Kampuchean people. This is to request the approval of the relevant ministry of the People's Revolutionary Council of Kampuchea to prove and punish the crimes of Pol Pot, Ieng Sary, and their associates.

My name is Ay Nasoeun, 25 years old. Khmer nationality. Buddhist religion. Education: 7th grade. Occupation: hand weaver. Birthplace: Pak Nam village, Maha Liep subdistrict, Koh Sotin district, Kompong Cham province. Present address: Srey Sangkum subdistrict, O Reang district, Mondul Kiri province.

I have six older siblings:

- My first older sister is Kim Sean. Prior to 1976, lived in Pak Nam village, Maha Liep subdistrict, Koh Sotin district, Kompong Cham province.
- My second older sister is Nai Chean. Prior to 1976 lived the same place as my first sister.
- My third older sister is Kim Lean. Prior to 1970, lived in Prek Sambour subdistrict, Koh Chek district, Prey Veng province. She disappeared in 1970 and has not been seen since then.
- My fourth older sister is Kim Luon. At the end of 1975, she fled to Vietnam with her husband.
- My fifth older brother is Eng Ly, who worked as a teacher. At the end of 1975, he was evacuated to the northern zone.
- My sixth older brother is Eng Long, who worked as a mechanic in the army. On April 17, he was evacuated from Phnom Penh, and he disappeared from Prek Po district.

My father is Ay Kri. In late 1975, he was evacuated to the northern zone. At present, I do not know the whereabouts of my dad or six siblings, or whether they are dead or alive. They all disappeared.

My mother is Chim Aun; she died of an illness in 1972. My father-in-law is Lay; he had a step-wife who died of an illness in Vietnam in 1972. My mother-in-law is Seng; she died of an illness in 1974.

My husband, Heng Va, was tortured and was forced to do hard labor beyond his energy, without enough rice. He was sent to difficult work sites. He was separated from wife and children. When he got sick, there was no rice, porridge, or medicine for him. The hospital had a lot of fleas, black like sesame. Wife and children were not allowed to take care of husband. They said that normal people must work. There is no need for relatives to take care of a patient, because there are medical practitioners to take care of them. Death or life depends on medical practitioners. Visiting a patient will not cure that patient. They killed my husband because a tribal medical practitioner vaccinated him. The real medical practitioner felt sorry for me and said that if my husband had not been vaccinated, he would not have died. After saying that, the real medical practitioner was arrested and disappeared. My husband died February 17, 1977.

My child, Bun Than, male, 2 months old, was tortured by not being allowed to drink milk. They asked me to work far away from 5:00 to 11:00 a.m., and from 1:00 to 5:00 p.m. They let old people take care of my child without maintaining proper hygiene. Every time I came back from work, I saw my child crying and he was very dirty. When my child was 14 months old, they did not allow me to breast-feed him anymore, because they said that I could not go to work on time. My child was starved. When I asked for food, they said this person or that person is responsible. They allowed us to eat only at the time allowed, and no medicine.

After 1975, I should have reunited with my parents and all of my siblings, so that we could know about each other. What they did was totally contradictory to the goal of the people, who wanted independence and peace. All of the people consolidated, fought, and expelled the American imperialist without fearing death. We only wanted the American imperialist out of Kampuchea. After the victory, with independence and peace, Pol Pot and Ieng Sary betrayed the nation and sold Kampuchea to China for the benefits of their own families and associates.

In 1975, just months after I delivered my baby, I was forced to grow rice and to cut grass on a farm far away from home. I could not breast-feed my baby because I had to work from 5:00 to 11:00 a.m., and 1:00 to 5:00 p.m. When I got ill, they did not give me any medicine. On March 17, 1976, they forced me to go to Mondul Kiri province; they said that Mondul Kiri is abundant with rice, vegetables, and meat. They said that people should look for rice, rice does not look for people. I want to inform the responsible ministry that in Koh Sotin district, since I was born, we never grew rice at all, we grew only crops; but we never had a shortage of rice. When Pol Pot and Ieng Sary were in control of those distant lands, land that was never used before, such as the bottoms of the small rivers and lakes, was used to grow rice. But there was still not enough rice. After I was pressured repeatedly, I decided to leave my birthplace for Mondul Kiri. I was forced to work beyond my energy without enough food. There was no medicine when I got sick, and they did allow my niece or nephew to visit me.

On March 15, 1975, they put me into a special group. They forced us to work far away. They sent us to difficult work sites like broken dams and made us carry rations. They set quotas when we carried soil. We had to carry 30 kilograms of soil each time. The working time in 1977 was from 5:00 to 11:00 a.m., from 1:00 to 5:00 p.m., and from 6:00 to 10:00 p.m. In May, when I had my period, I asked them for a rest, they did not say anything, and I took a rest. However, in the meeting at night, they criticized me strongly. They said that I just had a period, why did I have to stop working. They also said that I still held the way of living as under the Sihanouk regime without attending to the urgent task.

In 1978, the work became even heavier. We started at 4:00 a.m. and worked until 11:00 a.m. We did not have enough time to eat, and then we had to work again from 1:00 to 5:00 p.m., and from 6:00 to 10:00 p.m. There was no sanitation at all when we ate. I was also criticized even when I changed my dirty clothes and washed my hands before eating. They said that I was still a noble woman. They didn't care if we all ate with dirty clothes and hands. From October 1978, they ordered us to harvest early rice in the water really fast, and in November, we had to harvest middle rice. All men and women were competing and working both day and night. In December, I got ill. I asked them for a rest. They did not allow me to rest and criticized me, asking why, when I got just a little sick, I had to stop working. They said that we were busy harvesting rice because the Vietnamese were coming. If the Vietnamese arrived, they would steal all of that rice, and we would have nothing to eat. I should look into the battlefield. Soldiers who got injured might be bleeding, but they did not stop; they still went to fight. They said that if you did this, you want to cooperate with Vietnamese or what. On January 1, 1979, I was evacuated into the jungle. I had to carry rice from department 11 in the province into the jungle. I got lost in the forest because I did not know the way. On the night of January 9, 1979, they forced me to be a soldier. I said that I did not want to be a soldier. They said that the Vietnamese would torture me. In the morning, all the commune leaders fled. I escaped from them back to the village. Until now, I have not seen any Vietnamese do any harm.

Criminal activities of Pol Pot and Ieng Sary committed against the people:

(1) In the economy, there was no food, no clothing, no materials, no communication from one place to another place or internationally. They accepted only China.

(2) In culture and politics, they got rid of schools. All the young people were illiterate. They turned schools into fertilizer warehouses, or cow or buffalo pens. They got rid of Khmer literature. They broke solidarity between Khmer and Khmer. They divided old people and new people. They made one Khmer not want to look at another Khmer's face. They created distrust between Khmers. They created divisions between ordinary people and soldiers who had served in the war of expelling the American imperialist. They made Khmer hate Khmer. They made children dare to kill their parents. They forced husband to criticize wife. Anyone who did not dare to do that would be killed. They broke down the feelings among family members. They eliminated human rights. They made people kill other people. They eliminated belief. They performed marriage like herding cattle. They did not respect pagodas.

(3) Hospitals had no sanitation. There were lots of fleas in hospitals. It dripped all over when it rained. In villages, housing was not appropriate. Food was like pig food. We ate with dirt like a recently awakened demon.

In Mondul Kiri province, their technique for killing people was: first, to call them up for a study course, second, to charge them as enemies, and third, to use medicine mixed with 100 kinds of gall. Places used to kill people are: (1) Trapeang Pring, (2) Kbal Khmoach bridge, (3) Otok, (4) O Kreang, (5) O Te. At Sok San they cut people into three pieces and put them into the bottom of a hole and grew a coconut tree in that hole. They killed people by shooting, stabbing with a bayonet knife, and hitting with hoes. After they killed, they did not bury the bodies; they just left them for the tigers to eat.

I would recommend to the responsible ministry and the People's Revolutionary Council of Kampuchea to arrest Pol Pot and Ieng Sary, to sentence and punish them for their killing of the Kampuchean people.

Written March 15, 1979.

Ay Nasoeun

2.1.5.02

Miss Touch Sakun

Today, July 14, 1979, at 8:00 a.m., at the office of the people's revolutionary committee of Kompong Cham province, we, Saes Chhon, official of the Ministry of the Interior, and San Kiri, official in charge of recording statements, heard the declarant Touch Sakun, a victim of the Pol Pot–Ieng Sary clique. Here is his testimony.

Question: We ask you to tell us your name, age, occupation, place of birth, and domicile.

Answer: My name is Touch Sakun, but people usually call me Ros. I am 23 years old. I was born and live in Koh Sotin village, Koh Sotin district, Kompong Cham province.

Under the Pol Pot regime, I lived in zone 22. I was assistant to the youth organization chief who had twelve zonal youth teams under his direction. I was a nurse, but at the same time I was responsible for writing reports for my superiors about the production work of the young people.

Question: You made a statement denouncing the crimes of the Pol Pot–Ieng Sary clique against the people and against you personally. Can you tell us specifically how you were mistreated?

Answer: The gist of it is in what I communicated to the local authorities. As for me, the Pol Pot clique accused me of having subversive ideas. I was expelled from the youth organization and was sent to a farm in Sanh Tho Kanda district, Prey Veng province. Six days later I was ordered to take a political course of study. In fact they took me to a hospital in Pom Ko Reo subdistrict, where they interrogated me about the activities of rebel organizations.

Since I knew nothing, I had nothing to say. One of the butchers, the chief, then said to me, "Since she didn't talk, she will have to be suppressed." They tied my hands with a handkerchief, and at 10:00 p.m. they took me to a ditch near Pom Ko Reo commune. They hit me two blows in the head with an axe. I fell unconscious. When I came to, I realized I had serious injuries. Then they hit me in the neck with the axle of an automobile. Against I fainted. When I regained consciousness it was raining and I was in a ditch with decaying corpses all around me. I think they wanted to kill me and bury me in the ditch. As fast as I could, I crawled out of the ditch and got away from there.

Question: Did they chase after you, and how did you escape?

Answer: I thought about going back to the farm to hide there. When I was crawling up near my house, I found a woman who was going to the bathroom, and she told me that the Pol Pot agents were looking for escapees. I turned around and went to hide in seven different hamlets, one after the other. In Ba Ra hamlet, I was given shelter by Mrs. Du, who fed me. I stayed there until the day Prey Veng was liberated by the revolutionary forces. Then I got some care in a hospital. The blows that I received have left scars on my head and neck.

Question: Do you have anything else to say?

Answer: I have given all my testimony.

The session ended at 10:00 a.m. on July 14, 1979. The statement was read back to the victim, Touch Sakun, and she approved it. The signatures follow.

Recorder	*Declarant*	*Investigator*
San Kiri	Touch Sakun	Saes Chhon

2.1.5.03

Mr. Yeng Tinh

Today, June 22, 1979, at 7:00 a.m., at the office of the Ministry of the Interior, we, the undersigned Mien Chieu, official of the Ministry of the Interior, and Ros Rokha, secretary, are taking the statement of a victim named Yeng Tinh.

Question: Can you tell us briefly about you and your family?

Answer: My name is Yeng Tinh. I am 38 years old. I was born in Pdao Chum village, Pdao Chum subdistrict, Cheung Prey district, Kompong Cham province. Now I live in Veal Ri Kaeut village, Svay Teap subdistrict, Chamkar Leu district, Kompong Cham province. I am a fisherman by trade. I am of Khmer nationality and a Buddhist. As for schooling, I finished the third-grade class.

My father is Yeng Chhang. He died long ago. My mother is Ke Nhem. She is still alive. I have six brothers and three sisters. My wife, Ky Rot, is dead. My two children, Yeng So Heng and Yeng Sok Hien, are dead.

Question: We have received your letter denouncing crimes of the Pol Pot–Ieng Sary clique. Could you provide more detail about these crimes?

Answer: The crimes of the Pol Pot–Ieng Sary clique against members of my family are as follows. After April 17, 1975, the Pol Pot–Ieng Sary men forced me to do fishing for them on the Tonle Sap in Kompong Thom province. For nearly four years, I was separated from my family. The Pol Pot thugs put my wife and my two children in another part of the province. For our everyday food, they gave us only vegetable soup. We got a rice meal only two or three times a year.

On January 7, 1979, when the country was liberated of the Pol Pot people, the 29 members of my fishing brigade decided to go back to our native village. I first rejoined my family and then we set out for Kompong Cham province. However, at the Kdong Akom village, in District 16, Kompong Chhnang province, we were all stopped and arrested by Pol Pot–Ieng Sary soldiers. They tied us up and beat us. They hit us on the chest with iron sticks, and they knocked us on the head with a bamboo stem. They took my children by their feet and bashed them against the bank of a canal. My wife, then four months pregnant, was kicked in the stomach and lost consciousness.

The Pol Pot men took two other families from my group off somewhere. After the torture, they locked us up in a jail in Kuy village, District 16, Kompong Chhnang province. The next day, January 8, the Pol Pot thugs took fifteen women and children up Chnau mountain and killed them. My wife, Ky Rot, and my children, Yeng Sok Hien and Yeng So Heng, were among them.

That same day I tried to escape, but the Pol Pot men caught me. They tied me up and beat me on the head with a gun butt. I lost consciousness. The thugs thought I was dead. They kicked me twice in the leg before leaving. When I came to, I saw two patriotic soldiers who took me to a hospital. Now I have scars on my head and legs.

So the Pol pot men killed my wife and my two children. Besides that, when she was still alive my wife told me that her sister, Uon Hen, was tied up and dragged along the ground and beaten to death with the handle of a hoe on August 28, 1978 in Svay Chanti village, Svay Teap subdistrict, Chamkar Leu district, Kompong Cham province. Six of my nephews and nieces were also killed by the Pol Pot–Ieng Sary men during 1978: Chan Sok Leng, San Muoi Kheng, Khieu Samon, Kham Kthoy, So Pon, and Ong Sia. Kham Kthoy was killed before my eyes. I learned of the deaths of the others from my brother and my mother. All six were killed in the same way, with sticks and hoe handles. The Pol Pot men beat them to death after accusing them of thoughts and acts of opposition.

Question: Besides these crimes of the Pol Pot men against your family, do you know of other criminal acts?

Answer: I know about the following cases.

• *First case.* In 1976, in Oc Mot village, Pon Tea Chey subdistrict, Chamkar Leu district, Kompong Cham province, the Pol Pot–Ieng Sary men killed 1237 (one thousand two hundred thirty-seven) persons who were tied up. After the killing, the thugs got all the inhabitants of the village together to tell them that those killed had been enemies. I was in the crowd and saw the representative of the subdistrict committee, whose name was Duan, tell that to the inhabitants.

• *Second case.* Also in 1976, the Pol Pot men took 75 people to Ka Chap mountain in Ta Ong subdistrict, Chamkar Leu district, Kompong Cham province, and killed them, saying that they were people "of a different nationality." We passed by there on our way to work and saw 75 bodies of women and men, all of them naked.

• *Third case.* Also in 1976, 45 inhabitants of my area who were called opposition elements were taken away. The torturers took the clothes off these unfortunate people, none of whom returned. I knew some of them, such as Mrs. Ne De, Chhou, and Khom Nosey. The torturers accused these people of having been connected to Lon Nol.

• *Fourth case.* In August 1977, a village leader named Huong Chrac said that city dwellers would have to be moved to different regions. The Khmer Rouge tied up 5318 (five thousand three hundred eighteen) inhabitants of Svay Teap subdistrict, Chamkar Leu district, Kompong Cham province, put them into ten Chinese-made trucks which took them to the So Pheas forest. Then bulldozers ran over them while they were still alive. The ten Chinese trucks took seven days running to transport these 5,318 (five thousand three hundred eighteen) persons to the place of the killing. Huong Chrac was one of the drivers, and he told us all about it. Other survivors in the village are also aware of this case. If you need, I can take you to them.

• *Fifth case.* In 1978, on August 28, 39, and 30, nearly three thousand persons were beaten to death in Svay Teap subdistrict, Chamkar Leu district, Kompong Cham province. On August 28, the Pol Pot people killed men. On August 29, they killed women. On August 30, they killed elderly and children. Pok, a member of the eastern zone committee, ordered this killing. He entrusted the job to Yan, a leader of Svay Teap subdistrict. Yan was later killed by the Pol Pot people. All the three thousand victims were beaten to death with bamboo stick blows to their heads. The bodies of the men were then thrown into B-52 bomb craters. The women were stripped naked before being beaten. With the children, the thugs took them by the feet and knocked their heads against trees. The site was only five hundred meters from my house in Svay Teap subdistrict. I saw the killing with my own eyes. The bodies were thrown into four holes whose locations I have not forgotten. I could take you there. All the survivors in Svay Teap subdistrict know about this. During the killing, the Pol Pot people used three loudspeakers to try to drown out the cries of the victims, but the cries could still be heard. I still remember the names of two of the murderers. They are Soy Tuch and Chhuon. Since the liberation one can still find them in Svay Teap subdistrict.

Question: Besides these cases, do you know about any others?

Answer: No, I don't know of any others.

Question: Given the crimes committed by the Pol Pot–Ieng Sary clique against you, against your family, and against our people, what do you think should be done with this clique?

Answer: The Pol Pot people have committed so many crimes. I think that their crimes should be denounced before the entire world, and that those responsible should be prosecuted at all levels to avenge our people.

The inquiry was completed at about noon on June 22, 1979, and the minutes were read in the presence of the undersigned, who confirm that the minutes are correct and who have affixed their signatures.

Secretary	*Witness*	*Interrogator*
Ros Rokha	Yeng Tinh	Mien Chieu

2.1.5.04
Mr. Thun Saray

Statement About the Crimes Committed by the Pol Pot–Ieng Sary Reactionaries Against the Kampuchean People

I am Thun Saray, 28 years of age, a Khmer. I was born in Ampil Tapot subdistrict, Koh Sotin district, Kompong Cham province. My father (now dead) was Ngoy Thon. My mother (still living) is Nhoung Neang. I have a university degree in economics. Before April 17, 1975, I was a student.

I am married, the father of two children who are living with their mother, stepmother, and three young orphan brothers. My domicile before April 17, 1975, was the third ward of Phnom Penh city.

At 9:30 a.m. on April 17, 1975, after its long struggle against the American imperialist aggressors, the people's revolutionary army of Kampuchea gained final victory, taking Phnom Penh, other cities and towns, and finally the entire country. Like the entire population of the capital city, my family and I were very enthusiastic. We hoisted flags to commemorate this victory and greeted the people's revolutionary army as it entered the capital city, taking it gifts and refreshments as a sign of deep sympathy for the revolution. This welcome was also an indication of disapproval of the oppressive and corrupt imperialist, feudal, and bourgeois regimes and for their murderous war against the people. Like the other people of the city, I thought that, under the new flag of the revolution, we would lead a life of well-being and happiness in equality, and that any oppression or killing would definitely be outlawed.

However, the realities were completely the opposite of the thoughts and aspirations of the people. At 4:00 p.m. on April 17, 1975, the new rulers began chasing out the residents of the southern part of the city and suburbs, making them leave right away, even though night was about to fall. On the morning of April 18 came the turn of my family, which lived in the city center. We were chased out, threatened with guns. Leaving so quickly, I was able to take only a few personal effects, because the authorities made us go as fast as we could, saying that it would be for three or four days, so that they could mop up the enemy, reorganize the city, and avoid American bombing against Phnom Penh.

For transport, I had only one bicycle for my entire family, my wife who was six months pregnant, and my mother and mother-in-law. These two were quite elderly and unable to help. The four of us left under these circumstances. En route, along Monivong Boulevard to National Route 1, I could see the ruins of a Phnom Penh formerly alive with industrial, commercial, cultural, and social activity. These activities were all on hold.

Along the way sorrowful and piteous scenes came before our eyes of residents leaving in great difficulty. Some carried baggage in their arms, on their heads, or on their shoulders. Others pushed whatever means of transport they had. Others carried their babies in their arms or on their backs, while the kids their parents could not carry ran behind them.

Sick people who still had relatives were being carried in hammocks while those separated from their families had to drag themselves along, stopping from time to time to catch their breath. Residents who delayed leaving their dear homes were chased out by guns shot into the air. Hearing these gunshots so close by, my family and I got away from that dangerous place as fast as we could.

A few moments later, we were disheartened to see with our own eyes how two young men with long hair were stopped en route, and then taken away. Despite our fatigue and the heat of the day, we stepped up our pace. Pol Pot men went into houses whose owners had left and broke everything: refrigerators, television sets, dishes, etc. They seized anything they needed, like watches, radios, clothing, and fine quality cloth. Books and school notebooks were heaped up and burned because they thought that the basic theories of the capitalists and oppressors were to be found in them. I thought about the books I had left at my house, which doubtless found the same fate. By noontime, we had gotten only as far as Chbar Ameou. The slow pace was a result of the mass of people leaving the city on narrow roads and under the threat of the guns of the soldiers of the new dictatorial rulers. We stopped there a short time to eat lunch. At 9:00 p.m. we arrived in Prek Eng, and that night we had to sleep in the open among the people at Prek Eng market. That was the first day passed by the Kampuchean people and by me under the new government in a deportation of a kind never before seen in history.

The next morning we got back on the road. At Koki, I again saw my mother, my brothers, and my elder sister with her five little kids. Her husband had gone no one knew where. We settled there for a time to await our return to Phnom Penh. This wait lasted three days, then a week, then two weeks without any news. Finally we decided to go back to our native village, because we were short on rice and had no way to resupply. A week later, we were in our native village of Oreng Euv, in Kompong Cham province.

There, our family of seventeen persons lived together. Luckily, three days later my brother-in-law returned to rejoin his wife and his children. But after scarcely a week of reunion, the family was separated again. Labelled as intellectuals, my wife six months pregnant, my brother, and I would have to take some courses. My brother-in-law, who by occupation was a driver, was spared. For these courses, we were taken to a prison called Balak Ong, where there were hundreds of civil servants, soldiers, police officers, school children, students, teachers, and professors, etc., who had recently left cities after the April 17, 1975, victory. Balak Ong was a large prison with several branches, like the prisons of Tuol Sleng, Pauch Bay Doeum, Sre Spey, and Ampil Tapok.

According to their plan, all persons held as prisoners of war were first put into the big Balak Ong prison. From there they were later sent out to the different branches depending on their social class. The Tuol Sleng prison was reserved for school children, students, and former soldiers. The Pauch Bey Doeum prison was reserved for other former soldiers. The Ampil Tapot prison was reserved for civil servants. The Sre Spey prison was reserved for officers and noncommissioned officers. After lunch, my wife, my younger brother, and some other persons were taken to the Tuol Sleng prison, which was about ten kilometers from the large prison. I felt very sorry for my wife, six months pregnant, forced to leave in the heat of the day for an unknown destination.

I led a miserable existence in this prison, where one could not eat to satisfy one's hunger, and one lived in repulsive conditions: no hygiene, rusty bowls, etc. Under gunfire to threaten us, we had to do hard labor, like carrying dirt on our shoulders, or digging ditches. When we would rest, we would be all tightened up and could scarcely move. For lack of handcuffs for so many persons (hundreds), the soldiers had to stand guard during the night. After one week, one of my acquaintances let me know that my wife and brother had been set free with more than one hundred other persons, mostly school children and workers. I was so happy at this news that my own sufferings seemed to evaporate.

A week later, I too was taken to the Tuol Sleng prison. I thought with joy that they would soon release me to see my family. However, day after day, no such thing happened, and life there was no different form that in the other prison. Two weeks later, a number of school children, students, former soldiers, and I totaling about sixty persons had to carry dirt to build a two-kilometer-long road at the height of the rainy season. We spared no effort, however, because they promised to set us free as soon as the road was finished. Every day we worked in the morning from 5:00 to 10:30 a.m., and then in the afternoon from 12:00 to 5:30 p.m., under armed guard. At night they did not dare make us work for fear we would escape, so they shut us all up (sixty persons) in a small house on stilts, with their men standing guard below.

When the road was completed in twenty days, far from being allowed to rejoin our families as they had promised, we were taken to different cooperatives nearby, and every family took in one of us. I lived in Oulath village, Chok subdistrict, in a peasant family of seven persons. The existence I led there was both physically and mentally painful. We had to work harder than the other members of the cooperative, day and night, never daring to rest. To that was added all the housework such as carrying water, looking for wood and kindling, husking and pounding rice, etc. In a word, I became a lowly slave of my overlord. I felt for him the same fear one has for a tiger, because since he had the right to report all my activities to his superiors, he could call me out to be executed at any time if he did not like me. My mind was in permanent tension. My boss watched me and reported frequently to his superiors the least detail about my daily activities: whether I slept with the others or at my house, my comings and goings, my words, my work, etc.

Such an existence was much like that of the slaves of ancient times. My life being in the hands of others, I could be killed if someone did not like me. I suffered as well from being separated from my family and for not knowing where they had taken my mother, my wife, and my brothers. I lived in this condition for seven months without knowing that my mother and my brother, who had been separated from my wife, were living in a village only one kilometer away from my own. However, I had no news of them since I could not speak with them or meet them. As for my wife, I was about four kilometers from her but was not allowed to meet her. I found out where she was living only two months after confinement. I asked permission to go see my wife and baby for a short time, but they refused, saying that it was not necessary to go there or even to think about it, since Angkar was taking good care of them. I was disconsolate. These people were truly inhuman and cruel. Like all the residents recently departed from the cities, and being deemed their prisoner of war, I had no rights.

I was able to see my mother, my wife, and my baby only five days before the forced exodus of all the new arrivals to Kratie province. When this exodus was completed, we (my family and I) were in Taing Prasath village, Sambon subdistrict, Sambon district, Kratie province. At first the new arrivals and the local people lived separately from each other, the local people being forbidden to make contact with the new arrivals. During this time we lived in the grasp of the local people. We were insulted and shouted at whenever we made a misstep or a mistake either at work or during meals. They spoke ill of people with school learning and degrees, saying such persons were oppressors of the people, good for nothing, and useless to the revolution. These people needed only manual labor. Unlike the local people (the old people) who did not have to work much but who ate rice and were not threatened by anyone, the new arrivals had to work night and day and got only rice broth to eat. That was so for everyone, even the elderly, regardless of their age. For the Khmer Rouge, the important thing was to leave no one unoccupied.

Because of the eyeglasses I had for nearsightedness, they insulted me so much that I did not dare wear them at work or in my other daily activities. I began to wear them again only on the day of liberation, January 7, 1979.

Only one year later did the new arrivals gain the right to live and eat together with the old people, but still without the right to say anything at meetings. This designation of new citizens and old citizens was later replaced by a division of residents into three categories: local people in cooperatives, who were called official citizens; local people in production groups but not yet in cooperatives, who were called "reserve citizens"; and new arrivals, who were called sheltered citizens. The reservists and the sheltered, with the exception of the "right" to work more than ten hours a day and to eat only broth, had no right to speak or make criticism during meetings. Children over the age of six years got no schooling but lived in work units and had to work night and day like adults, under the slogan "prove your spirit" in work to meet the Party's plan. Some residents, unable to work any more, said with irony: "The people is the master of work, and Angkar is the master of rice." Some famished cattle herders sang in the fields: "Thank you a thousand times to Angkar, thanks to you, I suffer so from not eating my fill." The people, by what they produced, could have had enough to live on, but they got only broth the whole year long because of the annual levy by Angkar of thousands of bushels of paddy rice (a unit of measure that varied from 35 to 40 liters) under the pretext of national construction and defense, but in fact it was for their masters in Peking.

How many crimes they committed against our people, mostly against the sheltered citizens who were deemed political detainees. Whatever you might say, you would be branded with having made incitement. For the Khmer Rouge, a lack of ardor at work meant not loving the revolution, and sticking to the particularism of your social class, wanting to stay with the exploitative class. Making, even by accident, a mistake at work was serving the enemy in the destruction of the revolution. Such was the case of my friend Sok, who was imprisoned for so-called reactionary propaganda. His wife and his baby were, unknown to him, imprisoned as well. An old man in my village was imprisoned and then killed for having burned little sacks of incense and for saying a prayer to cure the sick. For that he was accused of putting impediments in the way of the revolution. My friend Pon Ya of Phnom Srok village, Sambon district, broke his plowshare while working and was accused of intending to undermine the revolution. He and his wife and their one-year-old baby were beaten to death with a pickaxe handle and were buried in the same ditch. His mother was deported to a remote region where there was danger of getting malaria.

My wife and I escaped thanks to our great efforts to work night and day, except for those days when we were knocked out by serious illness and really had to stay in bed. Also, we took great precautions everywhere, and whenever we spoke at meetings, when we worked in the fields, and when we engaged in other activities of daily life. However, beyond the great suffering we bore every day, prison and death loomed over us at all times. We barely existed, waiting for the day when the armed forces of the National United

Front for the Salvation of Kampuchea would come liberate our family and the entire Kampuchean people held in this giant prison without bars that was Kampuchea, and whose jailers are traitors who sold out our country to the Chinese imperialists who turned it into military bases for their expansionist aims and who took all the rice of Kampuchea.

Thun Saray

2.1.5.05
Mrs. Khem Nary

Today, June 23, 1979, we, Mat Ly, vice minister of the interior charged with taking witness statements, and Ouk Chandara, secretary, take the statement of the witness Mrs. Khem Nary as follows:

Question: Please tell us who you are.

Answer: My name is Khem Nary, 28 years old, of Khmer nationality, a secondary school graduate. I am from Sla village, Voll Sa subdistrict, Somrong Tong district, Kompong Speu province. During the time of Lon Nol, I was an official of the Red Cross in Phnom Penh. As for the condition of my family, seven members of my family were killed: my father, my husband, one of my children, and my four brothers and sisters. Only my mother and my second child are left. I will say what happened to each of them further along.

Question: Please tell us about the crimes of Pol Pot and Ieng Sary that you mentioned in your letter of accusation.

Answer: Yes. After the victory over American imperialism in April 1975, when the city of Phnom Penh was calm and was getting ready to welcome the victory, the Pol Pot–Ieng Sary clique gave the order to all the families to leave the city immediately. The population evacuated in great numbers. Only a handful of their henchmen stayed in the city. Many families had to leave the city without having time to eat (the order was given at 7:00 p.m.). Everyone had to leave their belongings in the city to evacuate right away, because the Pol Pot men said that planes would bomb the city. That night, their troops fired on certain areas of the city. As a member of the Red Cross, I saw women who had just given birth, or were about to give birth, leave the city in great haste. Sick people died along the way.

After that night I was in terrible shape. I did not have enough to eat or drink. It took me twenty days to walk to Region 55, Kompong Speu province. On my arrival, I met my mother, who had been sent there from her native area. In Region 55, we had to cut down trees to build huts. For our very hard work, at each meal we got only one bowl of rice for three or four persons. After ten days, the Pol Pot people sent us to a "people's commune" in the Prey Lvea subdistrict, Prey Kabbas district, Takeo province. People from various parts of the country worked in this "people's commune." Some Pol Pot men came and held a big meeting, and the speaker said that, according to documents he had, 28,000 persons had come here to clear land and to work. I, and others as well, frequently heard them say there were 28,000 inhabitants, but on liberation day in January 1979, there were only 5,000. That means that they killed 23,000 persons. They used various methods to kill people: forcing people to do hard labor, letting people die through privation, beating people to death, burying people alive near the commune, taking people away to unknown destinations, or make them "disappear" at night.

Now I will tell how the Pol Pot–Ieng Sary agents killed my father, my husband, and my child.

My father was named Khau Song, and he was sixty-five years old. He was forced to work in the commune till midday, and again until late at night, and he would be given only a few spoonsful of rice broth to eat. The Pol Pot–Ieng Sary men considered my father a dissident. That is why in June 1977 they beat him in the neck with gun butts and tied him up and led him away, all of which made him spit up blood until he died. When some child cattle tenders told me about my father's death, I went to his grave and I found there his clothes stained with blood. It was a horrible sight.

My husband was named Sa Moeun, and he was thirty-eight years old. He was tortured and killed by the Pol Pot–Ieng Sary men in December 1978. His body was thrown into a ditch.

My child was named Sam Nang, and he was ten years old. He was forced to work, and he was killed. Left quite hungry, he stole a banana, and for this the Pol Pot men killed him with gun butts.

Seven members of my family were killed. Only my younger child has survived, and she is afraid to recognize me as her mother. The Pol Pot–Ieng Sary men also killed forty out of forty-five members of the families of my uncles and aunts. My uncle was named Tuy Sam, and he was thirty-seven years old. He, his wife, and four of their seven children were killed. Fourteen out of fifteen members were killed in the family of my aunt, Van Ron, 38 years old, who is from the same village as I am. My other uncle, Khim Sa At, had twelve in his family, of whom ten were killed; the family of his younger brother suffered a similar fate.

Now I will tell about my detention in jail. In the commune, I was put in such a bad situation that I expressed objections and was branded as a dissident. They arrested me and put me in a prison at Thlok Russey, which was one kilometer from the commune. In this prison they tortured me savagely. They poured water into my nostrils, drove a stick into my ears, and passed an electrical current through my body. After torture sessions, they made me pick up corpses they had thrown into ditches, to make manure out of them. I was so horrified that I frequently fainted. My colleagues and I dug up ditches and found human skulls and bones. They made us burn the human bones to make manure. If we found bodies that had not yet decomposed completely, we had to tear the flesh off and mix it with manure to fertilize the ground. One day as I was getting manure in a ditch of human bones, some women told me that the bodies of my husband and child had been thrown there. I was so horrified that I fainted.

I was kept in this prison starting in July 1977, and I saw ten or so ditches of this type. In each of them we picked up about thirty to forty bodies.

Question: Do you have anything else to ask about, or to say?

Answer: The Pol Pot–Ieng Sary clique killed millions of innocent people. It killed my family in an extremely savage way and undertook genocide against the entire Kampuchean people. I ask the authorities to try these two ringleaders, and to make them pay their blood debt towards millions of Kampucheans. I ask the authorities to condemn these reactionaries who have overturned Kampuchean society.

This record has been prepared according to the statement of Khem Nary. She has reviewed it and has affixed her signature below.

Secretary	*Deponent*	*Interrogator*
Ouk Chandara	Khem Nary	Mat Ly

2.1.5.06
Mrs. Duong Mala

Today, June 26, 1979, we, Saes Chhon, an official of the Ministry of the Interior responsible for this inquiry, assisted by Mr. Ouk Chandara, secretary, draw up the record of the statement of Mrs. Duong Mala, the witness, as follows.

Question: Please tell us briefly your personal history.

Answer: I am Duong Mala, 24 years of age, of Khmer nationality. In school I completed the eighth year of the twelve year system. I used to live in Phnom Penh, but during the time of Pol Pot I was forced to live in Baray district, Kompong Thom province. My father was killed in 1971. My mother, husband, and five brothers and sisters were killed by Pol Pot–Ieng Sary.

Question: According to your statement of denunciation, and to a report by the authorities, the Pol Pot–Ieng Sary clique committed crimes against you and your family. Please tell us what they did.

Answer: In 1974, before the liberation, I was a student in the capital at the School of Letters and Arts. With my school friends, we were studying when the order was given to leave the city immediately. Terrified, we had to leave. After walking for two weeks, I came to live in Thnong Thmey village, Baray district, Kompong Thom province. It was a hard journey. Once we got there, I, like all the others, had to do forced labor. Of the one hundred families who had lived in my section of Phnom Penh, only ten remain now after the liberation.

I know this number, one hundred families, but I do not know how many persons that includes, but it is quite a few. Those in the ninety other families were killed in different ways, but most were killed at night and then thrown into wells. I know this because the area commanders used to threaten us, saying "whoever protests or is lazy, we will kill them and throw them into the wells."

One day, I was there and found some wells, one meter in diameter, and in the wells corpses were still floating, and the smell was nauseating. I was quite frightened at the sight. I found two wells there, but I don't know if there were any more. They covered the wells with coconut leaves. The wells were about one kilometer away from the village.

Once, when I was doing forced labor, I saw a boy about thirteen years old who had gotten lost and could not find his parents. Being quite hungry he had to beg. He was suspected of being a spy for the revolutionary forces, and so he was tied to a coconut tree by his neck and killed with hammer blows. That happened in 1977.

Here is how they killed my mother, my husband, and my brothers and sisters. My mother was 48 years old, and her name was Tep Sen. She was a small trader. They classified her as an opponent. They arrested my mother, my three brothers, and my two sisters, pushed them into a truck and took them away to kill them in 1977. They said at the time that they were going to kill my mother and my brothers and sisters.

My husband was named Prak Sokhon, and he was 29 years old. He was a second-year medical student. He was arrested. He tried to escape but was arrested again and was killed in 1978. Others who were incarcerated with my husband succeeded in escaping. Once they were free, they told me that my husband was beaten, that his legs were broken, and that he was hung from a roof beam and tortured.

Out of the thirty-one members of my family, I am the only survivor. Thirty were killed. My husband's family had eighteen members, of whom fifteen were killed, and only three survived. So in my family and my husband's, forty-five persons were killed out of a total of forty-nine.

I also know of cases in which they took couples and stripped them naked, burned their bodies in a fire, beat them, and then killed them. This happened with a young man named Chea, who was thirty years old, and a young woman named Ya Kach, who was thirty-one years old.

Question: Do you know of other crimes committed by the Pol Pot–Ieng Sary clique?

Answer: I have an uncle whose name is Chem. He was arrested. He is still alive. He knows how they kill people, what they do to them in prison, and how they torture them. Also, I saw them cutting open the bodies of people that had been killed to take out the liver. Ten Tuch, the village chief, once had five or six livers in his hand. He showed them to us. The livers were dry and as big as your thumb. My husband was a physician. Sometimes Ten Tuch brought five to seven livers to show my husband.

Question: Do you have any requests?

Answer: The Pol Pot–Ieng Sary clique caused great suffering and losses to the Kampuchean people. We hate them for it. I ask the authorities to denounce their crimes before humanity, before the United Nations, and to bring them to justice. They should have to pay their blood debt to my family and to the Kampuchean people. Pol Pot and Ieng Sary should be sentenced to death. My wish is that these two ringleaders should pay the blood debts they owe to millions of Kampucheans.

This document was drawn up and read to the witness, who found it to conform to her statements. She has signed below.

Secretary	*Interrogator*	*Witness*
Ouk Chandara	Saes Chhon	Duong Mala

2.1.5.07
Miss Bun Chantini

Today, June 22, 1979, we the undersigned Saes Chhon, an official of the Ministry of the Interior responsible for taking statements, and Ouk Chandara, secretary responsible for writing this record, are taking the statement of Miss Bun Chantini, a witness as well as a victim who is a civil party.

Question: Can you tell us something about who you are?

Answer: I am Bun Chantini, 26 years of age, of Khmer nationality and a second-year student in the Pharmacy Faculty. In the times of Sihanouk and Lon Nol, I was a student in school. In the times of Pol Pot, I worked the land in a people's commune in Kandal province, and later in Kompong Thom province. I am from Phnom Penh, from the fourth ward. My father died in 1974; my mother is still alive. I have twelve brothers and sisters, of whom four were killed by the Pol Pot people.

Question: In your statement, you say that the Pol Pot men committed many crimes against your family. Can you speak about these crimes?

Answer: (1) After their entry into the city, the Khmer Rouge people ordered the population of Phnom Penh to evacuate the city in anticipation of aerial bombardment. My family was quite large and found the displacement quite difficult because my parents were already very old and weak. We were in considerable hardship when the Khmer Rouge came and made us leave everything to go to an unknown destination.

After walking several days, we got to a people's commune in Kandal province. From there we went to another people's commune in Kompong Cham province before being moved to another people's commune in Kompong Thom province. In these three people's communes, we led a terrible life: hard labor until late into the night, one bowl of rice for four persons per day. Being young, I was assigned to the shock brigade that did hard labor such as building embankments. At times I had to flounder about in the mud for days at a time. I still experience the effects on my health.

From Phnom Penh to Kandal, the road was filled with people, and along the way I saw five bodies in a state of decomposition. Rumor had it that they died of hunger.

(2) During my work in these people's communes, I observed the following crimes:

• In An Dom Po village, An Dom Po subdistrict, Tang Kok district, Kompong Thom province, a 24-year-old woman named Khim was brutally killed by the Pol Pot people. She had the misfortune to be overheard criticizing the regime. The Khmer Rouge people pretended they were taking her to rejoin her family, but scarcely were they out of the camp when they set upon her, took all her clothes off her, and cut her body into three parts.

• Of twenty members, all women, in my mobile brigade, only two have survived, including me. The others were either executed or killed little by little through forced labor.

• At the beginning, my little hamlet in the people's commune had seventy families. But starting in late 1977, trucks came at night from time to time to take away two or three families to an unknown destination. They never returned; the village people whispered that they had been killed. On the eve of liberation, forty families in the hamlet disappeared in this way.

• One resident of the village named Pun Hon secretly ate four ears of corn. He was brutally beaten in front of me by Khmer Rouge people, who accused him of being a traitor. He died from the repeated brutal blows. I was witness to this ignominious act.

• One of my uncles, Lam Long On, whom the Khmer Rouge suspected of the theft of beef was also killed under blows.

Question: Can you describe just what crimes the Pol Pot people committed against your family?

Answer: I will speak more concretely about the crimes that the Pol Pot men perpetrated against my family:

• One of my brothers, Bun Saidavan, 32 years of age, had a great deal of pain from being overworked. In July 1976, under pretext of taking him to a hospital for an operation, the Khmer Rouge people took him away and killed him.

• Another of my brothers, Bun Monivan, 28 years of age, also died of hard labor in 1977.

• My sisters Nophia Moni, 30 years of age, and Channari, 23 years of age (Channari had just gotten married) were taken away, and no one knows where. My family thinks that they were killed.

• My maternal grandmother Bon Ngan, 70 years of age, died from overwork.

• One of my sisters lost her mind following torture by the Pol Pot people.

Question: Are you aware of other crimes of the Pol Pot people?

Answer: The crimes of the Pol Pot–Ieng Sary men are so numerous that it is impossible to relate them all. I described these crimes in a more detailed manner in my denunciation statement.

Question: Do you have anything to add?

Answer: The crimes of Pol Pot and Ieng Sary and their associates are higher than the mountains. The Pol Pot clique spread the catastrophe of genocide in Kampuchea. I have a strong hatred for them. I was condemned to hard labor, and my family suffered irreparable losses. I ask the authorities to bring the executioners Pol Pot and Ieng Sary to justice to make them pay their blood debt toward the Kampuchean people, and to denounce before world public opinion the monstrous crimes of these two ringleaders of the executioners.

This record was read to the witness, who affirmed the recording of his statement as accurate and signed it along with us.

Secretary	*Witness*	*Interviewer*
Ouk Chandara	Bun Chantini	Saes Chhon

2.1.5.08
Mr. Sok Chhoy

Today, June 23, 1979, we, Saes Chhon, official of the Ministry of the Interior, and Ouk Chandara, secretary, conduct an interview with Mr. Sok Chhoy.

Question: Could you please tell us briefly about yourself?

Answer: I am Sok Chhoy, 38, of Khmer nationality. Birth place: Domrey Slap village, Sasor Lao subdistrict, Baribor district, Kompong Chhnang province. Education: 6th grade. Occupation: farming. Family background: Father, Konpa, 68, alive; Mother, Uch Kon, 65, alive; Wife, Nang Chien, farmer, still alive; Children: 5, all are alive. The oldest is 13 years old.

Question: According to your letter of denunciation, Pol Pot and his clique have committed many crimes against your family. Could you please tell us about their crimes?

Answer: After the liberation in 1975, while the people were carrying on their farm work in peace, suddenly an order from above came, according to which the people had to leave immediately for other places where they could earn their living easily. Whoever refused was beaten, threatened to be killed. My elderly parents and all my children had to go, leaving behind all our property. On the way to the commune, about 20 kilometers from our village, whoever showed any signs of protest was considered as reactionary. Therefore, despite all the sufferings, people had to go on. The commune was in Vil Thom village, Kibi Thom subdistrict, Baray district, Kompong Thom province. In this commune there were 82 families, with 400 persons.

We had to build our huts. Two or three families shared each hut. The commune was divided into hamlets. Digging an irrigation canal was our work, each man had to remove four cubic meters and each woman three cubic meters of earth a day. For daily meals we only had rice soup. Due to the hard labor and starving ration, many suffered from diseases.

Because of the hard labor, many people died, others were killed therefore only 206 persons out of 400 in 32 families survived. 194 persons were thus killed.

Question: Apart from the merciless killing of people in the commune, do you know any other acts of barbarity taken by them?

Answer: The crimes committed by the Pol Pot–Ieng Sary clique were extremely heinous. Many entire families were killed savagely; one among them was Mr. Kit's family. Eight members of his family were considered opponents to the Pol Pot government. As a result, they were taken away and bashed to death with hoes. Their clothes were stripped off and given to the commune members. Three or four people were thrown into a hole. This happened in June 1977. After a trip to the forest to collect firewood for the commune, Mr. Kit's family had been so hungry that they secretly took some rice to eat. But they were discovered and accused of taking rice for the liberation fighters. For this, none of Mr. Kit's family escaped death. Death also befell the family of Mr. Chinh Leng. This family consisted of seven members. They were also accused of opposing the government. Mr. Chinh Leng, who could not bear the charge, hanged himself on a sugar palm tree. His wife, who was too weak to do hard labor, was also killed. Their five children were stripped of their clothing and bayoneted to death. This happened in May 1977.

A relative of mine named Theng was pregnant so she could not work to the satisfaction of the authorities. Her family was accused of opposing them. As a result, they slashed her throat and bayoneted her to death. It was in 1977.

Another case was a woman whose name I cannot remember. While she was delivering her child a leader of the commune came and promised to call a midwife for her. Instead he went and got a hoe and beat the woman to death with it.

Question: Were you yourself maltreated by them?

Answer: I was imprisoned and maltreated. As I reported before, when an acquaintance of mine was beaten to death before the eyes of her shrieking child, I felt pity and cried. Some leaders threatened to beat me, then I was taken to a prison at Kandal pagoda in Tang Koh district, Kompong Cham province, in June 1978. I was considered an opponent, so I was subjected to the following forms of torture:

- I was put in chains together with 12 other people.
- Four times a day they pushed my head into a plastic bag until I suffocated.
- They hung us by our feet with our heads submerged in water tanks. I was tortured in this way 14 times.

About 142 persons were detained in this prison. Most of them died. Only 60 of them survived. I was put in this prison in June 1978. One day, two friends of mine and I beat the jailer to death and then escaped to the forest, where we called on the local people to fight against the Pol Pot–Ieng Sary clique until liberation.

Question: Now what can we do for you?

Answer: I denounce the extremely brutal acts of Pol Pot and Ieng Sary before the world and progressive mankind. I demand the setting up of a court to try Pol Pot and Ieng Sary and make them pay their blood debts to my family and the Kampuchean people.

The transcript of the interview has been confirmed by the witness, who hereunder affixed his signature.

Secretary	*Witness*	*Interviewer*
Ouk Chandara	Sok Chhoy	Saes Chhon

2.1.5.09

Mr. Yeng Mara

Today, June 22, 1979, we, Saes Chhon, official of the Ministry of the Interior, with the assistance of Mr. Ouk Chandara, secretary, composed a transcript of testimony given by Mara, a witness and also a victim.

Question: Would you please tell us your personal history.

Answer: I am Yeng Mara, 29 years old, of Khmer nationality, native place: Kompong Chun village, Baribor district, Kompong Chhnang province. Education: 8th grade. Occupation: farmer. Family background: Father, age 55, killed in August 1978; Mother, age 50, killed in June 1975; Wife (living), farmer; Two children, one dead and one living. My parents had four children, of whom two are dead, one is missing, and one is living.

Question: We know the Pol Pot–Ieng Sary clique committed many barbarous crimes against you and your family. Would you please give us a detailed account about their brutal acts.

Answer: My family shared the same fate as that of many others. I do not remember exactly the date, but one day in April when people were living in peace, Pol Pot–Ieng Sary henchmen came and ordered the people to leave, otherwise they would be killed by U.S. bombs. They told us that we had to go for only a few days, so my family together with the villagers left our native place in groups. We went into the forest and built shelters. Four people were given only about 300 grams of rice a day. We were very hungry but were not allowed to eat even leaves. About 5,600 people were herded here to set up a commune. This number was made known to us all. They were divided into different production teams. Some did irrigation work and some worked in the fields. After three years in this commune, as a result of forced labor, killings, and torture, only 3,000 out of 5,600 people survived to liberation day in January 1979. Thus, 2,600 people were killed. In my hamlet of Kam Puos, only 106 people out of 2,000 people were living on liberation day. Killing people was an everyday task of the Pol Pot–Ieng Sary agents here. All members of the commune were expecting to be killed if they could not escape.

Question: Can you tell us anything else?

Answer: I used to go fishing, I was counted among opponents so they suspected that I might supply fish for the enemy and arrested me in August 1978. I was detained in O Russey, Kompong Chhnang province. There I was frequently beaten, hung up, and stabbed with bayonets that left many scars all over my body.

The jailer was Chen, and another was nicknamed Mr. "One Hundred" because he had eaten 100 human livers. In addition to the tortures they inflicted on me, they used one particular form of torture against me, and that is, they put my head into a plastic bag and tied it around my neck, which made me suffocate. They did this to me once a day. I was subjected to this form of torture seven times.

Unable to bear their tortures, I struggled against the jailer and urged the others to do the same. Then came the triumph of the revolution, and I returned to my native village.

My elder brother, Yeng Thanh, 34, was accused of being an opponent of the regime. He was arrested with ten others. They were hung upside down by ropes made of sugar palm tree fiber over a pond. They were all killed on April 20, 1975.

• My mother was killed in June 1975, and I was not able to see her before she died. Her name was Hon Nam, 50.

• My father Yeng An, 55, was accused of being a sympathizer of the opponents. He was arrested and imprisoned in region 16. He was hung on a tree and beaten to death in August 1975.

Immediately after killing my father, they also killed my stepmother, who had two children. One of them was named Hon Nom, and he too was hung up and beaten to death with bamboo sticks. His body was thrown into a river.

Another brother of mine, Yeng The, aged 14, was hungry and stole some sweet potatoes. For that he was beaten to death with a shovel.

My other elder brother, Yeng Uon, was taken away with his family and hasn't been heard of. His father-in-law was shot dead, his mother-in-law was hospitalized, and their two sons were killed.

Question: Have you anything more to say?

Answer: During my detention, I saw them executing Mr. Ty and a girl (I don't know her name). The two fell in love with each other. The assassins drove nails through Mr. Ty's hands and tied him to a tree then burned him alive. As for the girl, they shoved an M-79 shell into her vagina and then beat her to death. Ty's father is still alive and is living in my village. My prison friends told me that the assassins raped attractive girls and then killed them.

Their bodies were used as fertilizer for coconut trees. In my detention camp, five or six girls were killed in that way. I was also told that immediately after liberation, Pol Pot–Ieng Sary soldiers tied a dozen people together and threw them into the Porang Soc river, in Kompong Chhnang subdistrict. About 10,000 people were killed in that way.

My uncle, Mr. Tron, was buried alive for having caused a forest fire while smoking.

Question: Have you any requests?

Answer: Pol Pot–Ieng Sary caused my family and the entire nation such suffering that nothing can make up for it. The consequences are extremely serious. The Kampuchean people have lost millions of their sons. The survivors today lead a miserable life, as a consequence of their strict policy.

I ask the authorities to bring Pol Pot and Ieng Sary to justice and force them to pay the blood debt they owe to the Kampuchean people.

I declare that what I have said is true.

This transcript was read to all present, and the witness agreed with it and signed it.

Secretary	*Witness*	*Interrogator*
Ouk Chandara	Yeng Mara	Saes Chhon

2.1.5.10
Mr. Nhem Heng

Today June 25, 1979, we, Saes Chhon, official of the Ministry of the Interior responsible for the inquiry, and Ouk Chandara, Secretary, have drawn up this record of the statements of the following witness and victim:

Question: Would you please tell us briefly about your personal background?

Answer: My name is Nhem Heng, 45 years old, of Khmer nationality. My educational level is secondary school. I am from Stung Chrau village, Kompong Preah Kokir subdistrict, Baribor district, Kompong Chhnang province. My occupation is farmer. My father, over 70 years of age, died as a result of doing hard labor. My mother, over 70 years of age, also died as a result of doing hard labor. My parents had six children, two of whom were arrested by Pol Pot and then disappeared.

Question: According to your accusation and report of the local administration, the Pol Pot–Ieng Sary clique has committed many crimes against you and your family. Would you please tell us about that?

Answer: The Pol Pot–Ieng Sary clique have committed crimes against me and my family. Here are the facts about these crimes.

(1) They moved my family away from our hamlet to do forced labor at a cooperative.

(2) They robbed us of all our property.

(3) There are 31 persons in my extended family, and of these they killed 26, including my parents, my wife, my two children, my brothers and nieces and nephews.

(4) After the liberation of January 1979, out of the 80 families in the hamlet, 30 were wiped out completely.

Question: Would you please tell us about specific acts of theirs?

Answer: Here are some.

(1) In April 1975 our family was forced to go live in a "collective cooperative." Just as production work was getting regularized, we were ordered to move to another place. Anyone who refused to go was immediately beaten. Everyone had to leave behind their belongings and property. Those who asked for explanations were told that we were going to live in another place for only two or three days, no more. We were forced to leave as a group, under compulsion, and on the way we were in terrible conditions, with no rice to eat or water to drink.

We arrived at the gathering place which they called a "collective cooperative." There we found many people who had come from various places. This cooperative was located in Krang Skia village to the south of Baribor district, Kompong Chhnang province, Region 31. From what we could overhear of their conversations, about 20,000 people were brought to the commune and they divided them into hamlet groups, with about fifty families in each hamlet. In the hamlet where we had to stay to await further instructions, we lived in cabins and slept without blankets or mosquito nets. Each hamlet lived in isolation from other hamlets, and no contact between the people of different hamlets was allowed.

Regarding food. They made us work very hard, up to twelve hours a day, and sometimes at night. As for women, most were assigned either to dig irrigation canals, or collect fertilizer, or till the land. Each day each of us got soup and vegetables to eat, and only 250 grams of rice for four persons. Sick people got very little medicine, but had to continue doing hard labor with very little food.

I had to do hard labor in this cooperative from 1975 until the liberation in January 1979. As I mentioned before, from their conversations, the number of persons forced to come into the cooperative was 20,000, but on the day of liberation only 1,000 people were left, meaning that 19,000 persons had died.

At first I worked in a group producing medical extracts from medicinal herbs. I looked after the sick and objected to the treatment they got. So I was considered an opponent, and as a result I was switched to a job cutting sugar palm leaves. Every day I had to fill four ox carts with sugar palm leaves. But for me it was hard to fill two carts a day. The work was so hard that I thought I would not live until today.

The 19,000 victims in the cooperative were killed in different ways. Some died of overwork in the hard labor or died later from various diseases.

Others were beaten to death on the spot or were taken away to secluded places to be executed.

(2) During the time I worked in the cooperative I witnessed extremely brutal killings. One day in August 1977 while I was climbing a sugar palm tree to cut its leaves, I saw a couple who had been stripped of their clothes. A man named Sa Phon had a rope tied under his armpits. The local authorities lifted him from the ground and burned him with a straw fire until he died. I don't know the woman's name, but they put an M-79 shell in her genital organ and then kicked her to death. The thing charged against them was that they talked with each other without permission of Angkar. These two lovers had not been able to meet for a long time! In Kampuchea, such cases were common under the Pol Pot regime. All this happened about 11:00 a.m. on the day I mentioned.

One day, while I was working I saw Khum, 75 years of age, and Rat, about 25 years of age, the two guards of the cooperative's prison, eating human liver. They often caught people trying to escape, tied their feet and hands, and then they cut open their backs to take out the liver. Then they roasted the liver and ate it. They have eaten many human livers this way. That time they said that it was the liver of a man who had fled that morning into the forest, and whom they had managed to stop.

I have told how they killed people to eat their liver. Besides that, they also killed people to take the gallbladder to make medicine. One day I myself witnessed a Pol Pot man holding a gallbladder as big as a big toe and about four inches long. The man said that it was a human gallbladder.

Now I want to denounce their ignominious crimes against my parents and members of my family.

My father was Pot Nhem, who was in his 70s, was gentle and physically weak, but he too was forced to go work in the forest. Able to rest only a few hours a day, eating only rice gruel, and getting no medicine when he would fall ill, he died in 1976, at the foot of a tree. Although I was not far away, I learned about it only the next day. Our custom is cremation, but my father was buried naked at the foot of the tree.

My mother's name was Ruos Ploeun, and she was over 70. Old and weak, she died for the same reason.

My wife was Um Kuon, 39 years old, and she had a two-year-old child. She too was forced to do irrigation work, which is physically demanding. One day they assigned her to clear trees to put a piece of land into production. The trees were quite tall, but my wife, who got only thin soup to eat, was very weak. She met her end one day, falling down, dead, at the foot of a tree. Her body lay there more than a whole day. She died in 1976. We had six children, but the 2 eldest were called to join the so-called vanguard brigades in 1975, and since then I haven't heard from them. I don't know whether they are still living.

Here is some information about the families of my brothers and sisters. My brother's name was Lon Nhem Chuon, 52 years old, and he lived in Kompong Rumchek. There were eight people in his family, and they were all killed in 1975, he, his wife, and their 6 children.

My sister's name was Nhem Noth, 57 years old. She, her husband, and their eight children were all killed in 1976 by having their skulls crushed in Preah Smit village, Baribor district, Kompong Chhnang province.

My other sister's name was Nhon Moeun, 55 years old. Her husband's name was Hol Sam. Their whole family of four was killed in 1976 by blows to the head.

Question: Apart from the crimes you have just denounced, do you have anything else to say?

Answer: What I have told you were only the crimes the Pol Pot–Ieng Sary clique committed against my family. These are the misfortunes that my family has had to endure. As for their crimes against the Kampuchean people, those crimes were extremely savage, with serious material and moral consequences, crimes unknown in human history.

Question: Have you any requests to make?

Answer: I want the People's Republic of Kampuchea to bring Pol Pot and Ieng Sary to trial and make them pay their blood debts to my family and the Kampuchean people as a whole.

This record was read to the witness and was acknowledged by him as correct and together with us he has signed below.

Secretary	*Witness*	*Interviewer*
Ouk Chandara	Nhem Heng	Saes Chhon

2.1.5.11
Miss Chhay Ny

Today, July 9, 1979, we the undersigned Prum Chien, official of the Ministry of the Interior, and Mr. Ouk Chandara, secretary, were in charge of collecting the following testimony of a victim.

Question: Could you please give us a brief biography of yourself?

Answer: I am Chhay Ny, a 17-year-old girl, not yet married. I can read a little and have never gone to any school. My father is Sien Chon, I have not heard from him since he joined the army in 1974. My mother, Chea Ban, was killed by the Pol Pot clique. I had two brothers, Chhay Mon 15, and Chhay Moeun 16.

Prior to 1975, during the Lon Nol regime, I lived in Chheu Khmau village, Chheu Khmau subdistrict, Sani Tong district, Kandal province. Under the Pol Pot regime, I was moved to a hilly region and made to work in a commune in Pursat province, but I do not remember the names of the subdistrict or district.

Question: According to the local authorities, your family was mistreated by Pol Pot soldiers. What is the truth?

Answer: I cannot remember exactly. In 1975, my family, including my mother, my two brothers, and me, were driven into a hilly region in Pursat province. Here, we led a miserable life. Every day we had to clear from 20 to 30 square meters of trees to make rice fields. We were given about 250 grams of rice every two days.

I do not remember exactly but one day, probably three months ago, while washing some edible roots, I overheard a conversation among the soldiers of Pol Pot. The one called Ses, around 30 years old, told two others: "General Ta Mok is dead (a general of Pol Pot). Let us kill someone to eat." One of them then said cannibalism was not a bad idea. This was Seng. Later, Seng came and asked my mother if he could raise my younger brother, Chhay Mon. My mother was horrified. She protested. A few days after that, while looking for edible roots to appease our hunger, I saw them killing my brother, Chhay Mon. I was about 10 meters away from them and 200 meters from my home. My brother was beheaded. His head was on the ground, a meter from his body. With a pointed knife, Seng was carving the flesh from the bones and then wrapped it up in leaves. It was about 4:00 p.m. I hid behind a big tree and saw everything clearly. I was horrified and rushed home to inform my mother. She went to find Seng. He told her he was a meat eater, not a man eater. He then tied her up and beat her, threatening to kill the whole family if she tried to interfere.

The following morning, they came to take my mother away. My brother, Chhay Moeun, and I went to look for her and found her dead. Her belly was cut open, the liver taken away. She was covered with a layer of earth. I did not see them kill her. Frightened, my brother and I ran from this place. We took the little rice left and fled. We got to a hill and stopped for a little sleep. When we woke up and went on for a short distance, the soldiers spotted us and gave chase. I managed to escape but my brother was killed, having his head and neck bashed by gun butts. I ran on for two days and nights, until I finally got to Ro Vieng village (the name of the district escapes me) in Pursat province. There I saw several vehicles and heard liberation armymen singing. I came up to ask for food. I was fed and given some cloth (now, I am still keeping 5 meters of it).

Question: Do you want to say anything more?

Answer: That's what happened to my family. I am now being well-looked after by the state. Everything I said is true.

This report has been reviewed, approved, and signed by the witness.

Investigator	*Witness*	*Secretary*
Prum Chien	Chhay Ny	Ouk Chandara

2.1.5.12
Mrs. Ouk Sao Kan

On April 17, 1975, together with my family (my three daughters and my grandfather), I was rounded up in Preah Ampil pagoda, Saang district, Kandal province. Then my husband, whose hands were tied with a rope, was led from one place to another. My three daughters and I, and other members of my family were sent to Chheu Khmau subdistrict, Koh Thom district, Kandal province, near the frontier with south Vietnam. My husband was taken away with his hands tied behind his back.

The people in that village began to suffer from starvation. One of my daughters and my grandfather fell seriously ill with dropsy. For food, 23 persons were given two kilograms of corn for ten days.

Two months later I was sent with my daughters to the rubber tire factory at Takhmau, where I found my husband, who was working there. We all suffered from lack of food, clothing and working tools. We were forced to do hard labor.

In 1977, the workers suffered more and more from famine. They were given only hard kernels of corn to eat, and those in very small quantities, though they had to work hard.

My three daughters, living in concentration camp conditions surrounded by barbed wire fences, were so weak that they were in pain as they worked. They had to catch locusts and snails to eat. One day, driven irresistibly by hunger, I decided to catch some fish in the rice field where I was transplanting seedlings. I wanted to give the fish to my daughters. Though I crawled like a snake under the barbed wire fence, I was spotted by the Pol Pot troops who subsequently separated my daughters from me and punished me by making me stand in the burning sun with an empty stomach for one day. Then the twenty-five heads of the factory accused me of being a CIA agent and traitor, and they tied me up threw me into a truck with the purpose of killing me. I immediately fainted, and that averted my being killed.

On another occasion during land-clearing work, I was pregnant, so I was very hungry. I decided to steal a small bamboo shoot. I was spotted by Pol Pot's men, who tied me up and put me on trial before a crowd of 800 persons. During the hearing I was ordered to sit on a high chair so that everyone could see me. My husband sat among the public between two guards, and my three daughters sat near me. During the trial the Pol Pot clique gave orders to their lackeys to shout that I was a traitor, a criminal who betrayed the people, and I should die.

Hearing these cries, I could not help crying. I trembled with fear, and tears flowed uncontrollably down my cheeks. My three daughters wept at my feet, as they believed that my fate was sealed. Confronting this tragedy my husband could not keep calm, and he tried to go help his children but was prevented by his guards. I knew he was suffering very much. The crowd had pity for me but could do nothing except hide their faces to weep. At 2:00 a.m. the trial ended. On our way home, my husband and I were escorted by the guards, who kept watch around our house the whole night. As for our children, they were sent to a children's concentration camp. After that the guards forbade me to go out of the factory. During work I was watched by two guards who carried long knives.

I constantly trembled with fear of being killed at some point. Because of my suffering, I gave birth prematurely. Then I fell seriously ill. I was thin and skinny, to the point of not being able to recognize myself. Luckily, ten days later the chief and his men disappeared while I was returning to my work. After hearing that on January 7, 1979, the armed forces of the National United Front for the Salvation of Kampuchea had arrived in Phnom Penh, the Pol Pot clique made us go to Bek Chan subdistrict, in Ang Snuol district. On January 9, 1979, with the resumption of traffic on National Route 4, my family was free to return to the factory. All of us were extremely happy.

Meanwhile we grieved to know that twelve members of my family, including my father, mother, brothers and sisters who were separated since 1975, were mercilessly killed by the Pol Pot clique.

After hearing my statement, the people the world over should ponder upon the crimes committed by Pol Pot and Ieng Sary and their henchmen against the Kampuchean people.

Takhmau, July 4, 1979
Ouk Sao Kan

2.1.5.14
Miss Lat Sarat

Today June 25, 1979, at 2:00 p.m., at the office of the Ministry of Interior, we, Mien Chieu, official of the Ministry on Interior, and San Kiri, secretary, have taken the following statement of Miss Lat Sarat:

Question: Please tell us who you are.

Answer: I am Lat Sarat, 25 years old. My birthplace is Ta Dot village, Prot Via subdistrict, Kompong Ro district, Svay Rieng province. My occupation is farmer. My education is primary level. My nationality is Khmer. My religion is Buddhism. My father is Lot Phon, who died in 1957. My mother, Put Tui, is missing. I have ten brothers and sisters. Two brothers Lat Phon and Lat Chum were killed by Pol Pot gangs.

Question: You have made a written denunciation about the crimes committed by the Pol Pot–Ieng Sary clique against your family and you. Would you please tell us in detail their criminal acts?

Answer: In 1975, Pol Pot men sent me to a farm in Pim Cho district, subregion 24, eastern military zone. There were about 200 persons, most of them women. The Pol Pot clique forced women to wear short pants and start working from four o'clock in the morning. We were allowed an hour break at midday, then continued working without stopping until 7:00 p.m. or perhaps 10:00 p.m. Every seven persons had to finish the transplanting of rice on one hectare a day. We worked day after day without rest. The women were not given clothes every year. Only those whose clothes were truly rags were given a new vest and pants, but few got a whole suit. Usually each woman got a pair of short pants a year.

The Pol Pot–Ieng Sary clique's crimes against my family are as follows. My elder brother, Lat Phon, was taken away and killed in 1977. He had two children. While he was climbing on a sugar palm tree, Pol Pot's troops came and ordered him to come down and took him in front of his house. His children cried and begged, but the troops did not let him talk with them. According to what we were told by some prisoners, he was taken to Chantrea district, Svay Rieng province, where he was killed.

Another brother of mine, Lat Chum, was also killed in 1977. After killing my two elder brothers, they took my sisters-in-law to a concentration camp in Kompong Ro district. There they had to dig canals. Their children were forced to live separately from their mothers.

My mother, 70 years old, was, like other elderly women, made by Pol Pot's troops to look after children from 6 months to 2 years old. The children were hungry for lack of food, so they cried much of the time. But the Pol Pot men accused those who watched the children of not taking good care of them. In early 1979, my mother was locked up in a pagoda in Kandal province. There people were kept before being killed. Since then, I haven't heard from my mother.

I have a 10-year-old niece, Chran Sout Kha. She had to graze buffaloes in the cooperative. Once her buffaloes ate rice plants, and she was charged with sabotage. In panic, my niece crossed the river to get away, but she was carried away by the current and drowned. My nephew, Chan Tho Ni, fled into the forest, but he was captured and taken by Pol Pot's troops I don't know where.

My aunt Khieu and her husband were accused of not following Pol Pot's political line. So they were taken away and disappeared.

Question: Apart from the crimes committed by Pol Pot and Ieng Sary against your family and you, do you know of any other criminal acts of the Pol Pot–Ieng Sary clique against the people?

Answer: In 1978, Pol Pot men went to the office of the Agricultural service in the eastern zone and proclaimed a death sentence on the entire population of this region, because, as they said, this population was the opposition force against the Pol Pot regime. The one who made this announcement was Chet, an official in charge of the district.

In 1977, while I was looking for my way to escape into the forest in Dambe district, Kompong Cham province, I came upon a place full of dead bodies. The bodies were tied in pairs, a man and a woman. I went on and after a while, I heard screams of the people who were being killed by Pol Pot's troops. Afraid of being detected, I hid and ran away. Along the way, I saw many other dead bodies, some with their throats cut, others with their heads bashed. Next to the bodies, I saw bamboo sticks that had been used to crush the heads of the victims.

In this forest, after getting out of the area scattered with dead bodies, I heard more screams. I climbed up a tree and saw two trucks full of people. I am sure they were on their way to meet their death.

After spending thirteen days in the forest without food, I met a unit of the National United Front for the Salvation of Kampuchea.

Question: Do you have any suggestions as to what should be done about the crimes that the Pol Pot–Ieng Sary clique committed against you?

Answer: Pol Pot and Ieng Sary had millions of innocent Kampucheans killed. Many families were completely wiped out. Thousands of children lost their parents. Wives lost their husbands. Innocent wives and children were also killed. Those who remain alive are doomed to a terrible life, overwhelmed by forced labor and dying a slow death. I ask that the Pol Pot–Ieng Sary clique answer for its monstrous crimes.

This record was made June 25, 1979, at 4:00 p.m., and was read to the witness, who confirmed its content and signed it.

Secretary	*Witness*	*Official in charge of the investigation*
San Kiri	Lat Sarat	Mien Chieu

2.1.5.15
Mr. Thaong Chin

Today is June 28, 1979, 7:00 a.m. At the office of the Ministry of the Interior, we, Saes Chhon, the investigator, an official of the Ministry of the Interior, and San Kiri, secretary in charge of recording statements, took the following statement.

Question: Would you tell us your name, age, and place of birth?

Answer: My name is Thaong Chin. I am 43 years old. I was born in Cham Bok village, Cham Bok subdistrict, Svay Rieng district, Svay Rieng province. Under the Pol Pot regime, my family was forced out of our native village to Prey Stieng village, Svay Ta Yean subdistrict, Kompong Ro district, Svay Rieng province. My educational level is that I completed primary school (seventh grade) in 1945. My occupation is teacher, but during the Pol Pot time I worked the land. My nationality is Khmer. My religion is Buddhism. My father, Thaong Touch, died in 1968. My mother, Tak Van, died at age 70 from forced labor under the Pol Pot regime when they began to give only rice porridge to eat. My wife is Som Yeaung, 38 years of age, a farmer. I had seven children, of whom one was killed by Pol Pot agents. Six of my children are still alive, the oldest age 21, the youngest age 8.

Question: Could you please tell us, the investigation department, what crimes were committed by Pol Pot–Ieng Sary agents against you and your family.

Answer: The crimes against me are as follows. They began in 1972, in February 1972. At that time my village was in an area held by Lon Nol. The Pol Pot people imprisoned me, causing me great misery, until the end of 1972. Then they released me and I began farming.

The regime arrested me in Prey Stieng village July 1, 1977, despite the fact that I was a farmer, nothing more. I was held until November 9, 1977. At the time of my arrest they accused me of opposing the Pol Pot regime. During my detention, they beat me with rifle butts to the point that I lost consciousness three times. After I had only two days to recover, they took me to go work as part of a digging crew, working every day from 4:00 a.m. to 8:00 p.m. As food, I got only one bowl of watery rice porridge a day. At night my arms and legs were chained to the ground. The conditions of detention were very bad. They worked us to the very limit of our strength every day and gave us only watery rice porridge to eat. Those who got sick never received any medical attention. That is why, there in the place where they held me, twenty or so persons died during one twenty-day period.

As for crimes against my family. First, my family was forced to leave our house at gunpoint without being able to take any belongings. My mother, 70 years of age, was separated from my family and taken away to live alone in a collective house. Sick from forced labor, she died of hunger.

My wife and children were not able to live together. My four oldest children were sent out to people's communes. Thus, my family was broken up, each one to a different place. In January 1978, my family was again transported to another area in Kandal Stung district, Kandal province. There my wife and children were kept separated and were not allowed to meet together. A time came when my wife took ill, but there was no medicine to treat her.

Two uncles on my wife's side were named Ma Sok and Ma Yong. The Pol Pot regime accused them of improper conduct, opposing the regime, and they tortured them to death in Se An subdistrict, Pong district, Svay Rieng province, in June 1978.

Question: Other than the crimes of Pol Pot and Ieng Sary committed against you and your family, do you have any knowledge of crimes committed by Pol Pot against any other people?

Answer: I know of other crimes of Pol Pot, including the following. After Liberation Day, some time around February 1979, I went to Svay Pring village, Snuol district, Kratie province. I went there and saw two trenches. Before this, the Pol Pot–Ieng Sary regime had killed people at this place.

The trenches I saw had many bodies in them. According to the people there, they estimated that more than 4,000 people had been killed at these trenches. As for those who died there, most were from villages in the east.

The people there knew that the dead had been tied up with ropes and beaten to death, then pushed down into the trenches, which they had just dug themselves.

The second trench area, in O Kran village, Svay Chreah subdistrict, Snuol district, Kratie province, the trenches there in the areas I went to had 4000 to 5000 bodies of people the Pol Pot regime had killed. The bodies were scattered all across the area there. According to what the people there said, most of those who died there came from the village of Prek Mok.

The third trench area, at Paukaley mountain, Prey Prasath district, Kratie province, the trenches there I didn't visit myself. But from reports from there, a total of 5,500 people were killed.

As for the destruction of the schools: Around Kratie province, there are 20 schools that the Pol Pot–Ieng Sary regime destroyed, where not a single thing remains. In Kratie province, there are another 40 schools that were smashed but not completely destroyed. According to reports, the Pol Pot–Ieng Sary regime left virtually nothing there that could be used for teaching. Among the debris were books and lists of students, all burnt. After Liberation Day, I worked in the provincial committee and therefore had knowledge of these numbers.

In Svay Rieng province, Prasout district, the Pol Pot–Ieng Sary regime destroyed schools. In Chikou district they destroyed several schools also.

As for the pagodas, the Pol Pot–Ieng Sary regime abandoned Buddhism. As for Svay Ta Yean subdistrict, there are three wats: Peam Cho, Prey Thlok, and Svay Treang. They stripped the robes off the monks there and forced them to do heavy farming labor. At the wat, the monks' quarters made of wood were emptied and destroyed. The monks' quarters made of stone were used to store fertilizer. As for Prey Thlok wat, they turned it into an internment center. I saw this place for myself with my own eyes the day after it was destroyed.

As for the statues of Buddha in the wat, they were smashed to bits, and were taken and thrown down into a nearby pond. The sacred texts in the wat were all destroyed by the Pol Pot–Ieng Sary regime.

Question: Especially as to the crimes Pol Pot and Ieng Sary committed against you and your family, as well as against the people as you have recounted above, do you have any opinions to express?

Answer: The Pol Pot–Ieng Sary regime are responsible for genocide, the destruction and murder of a million people. They are responsible for the utter destruction of the nation of Cambodia, above all others. Therefore, I ask the government to search for and to capture those of the Pol Pot–Ieng Sary regime, no matter where they run and hide, to sweep away those of corrupt power who made us into their slaves to do hard labor, to take those who beat the life from the faces of the people, in order to avenge the blood of our people.

The government should display those of the Pol Pot–Ieng Sary regime for the people of the world to see their disgusting crimes, so that the world can help to save the Kampuchean people who were abandoned to the fate of Pol Pot–Ieng Sary genocide.

Question: Aside from your explanations above, do you have any additional opinions to express?

Answer: I want to assure the government of the revolution that the above acts and reports are true. If the government goes to these places to confirm these acts of the Pol Pot–Ieng Sary regime, I will always remember how to lead them to these places.

This report was completed at 11:00 a.m. on June 28, 1979, and was read back for all of us herein named to hear. It has been duly received as true and agreed to by us by affixing our signatures below.

Witness	*Ministry investigator*	*Secretary*
Thaong Chin	Saes Chhon	San Kiri

2.1.5.15a

Denunciation Letter by Mr. Thaong Chin

Respectfully submitted by the president of the Cambodian People's Revolutionary Council, Phnom Penh.

Given as information.

My name is Thaong Chin, 43 years of age, male, formerly of Prey Stieng village, Svay Ta Yean subdistrict, Kompong Ro district, Svay Rieng province. Before April 1975, my profession was that of a teacher at Chi Phou general elementary school in Svay Teap district, Svay Rieng province. After April 1975, I worked as a farmer in Prey Stieng village, Svay Ta Yean subdistrict, Kompong Ro district, Svay Rieng province. Now I work at the people's revolutionary administrative offices in Kratie province.

My father's name is Thaong Touch. He lived in Cham Bok village, Cham Bok subdistrict, Svay Rieng district, Svay Rieng province. He died in 1968 of old age. My mother's name is Tak Van. She lived in Cham Bok subdistrict, Svay Rieng district, Svay Rieng province. She died in 1978 due to the traitorous Pol Pot–Ieng Sary regime, which forced her into hard labor and fed her only watery rice porridge that did not satisfy one's hunger. She became very ill. There was no medicine with which to treat her, right up to the time of her death.

My wife's name is Som Yeuang, 38 years of age, originally from Prey Stieng village, Svay Ta Yean subdistrict, Kompong Ro district, Svay Rieng province. We have seven children.

1. The crimes of the Pol Pot–Ieng Sary regime against my family, my relatives, and me personally began in late April 1972. The traitorous Pol Pot–

Ieng Sary regime arrested me at the Chi Phou elementary school in Svay Teap district, Svay Rieng province. At that time, they tied me up and took me to an internment center at Wat Meas in Samlei subdistrict, Kompong Ro district, Svay Rieng province, keeping me there for three days and three nights. During that time, there was a district official named Sa Phon who beat me a total of three times with a bamboo stick. His way of interrogating me each of the three times was by knocking me unconscious. Afterwards, he sent me for internment in Kranyong subdistrict in Romeas Hek district, Svay Rieng province, for a total of one month.

Right after that, he sent me for internment in Suang Panya Krek district and Memot district in Kompong Cham province for an additional period of seven months. At the internment center, they put shackles on our feet at night. During the day they let us out to do work digging ponds from 3:00 a.m. until 8:00 p.m. before we could stop. They made us work exposed to the rain and heat of the day, giving us only rice porridge once a day in a small bowl that did not satisfy our hunger. This made people very ill with malaria, but there was no medicine for treatment. There were no clothes to wear. We lived in sadness and the deepest of anguish.

In 1973, they released me and allowed me to return to my family in Prey Stieng village, Svay Ta Yean subdistrict, Kompong Ro district, Svay Rieng province.

On July 1, 1977, the traitorous Pol Pot–Ieng Sary regime took me and put me in prison again in Prey Stieng village, Svay Ta Yean subdistrict, Kompong Ro district, Svay Rieng province, and accused me of having ties to the Vietnamese Army. At night, they put shackles on both my feet and made me sleep on the ground. In the daytime they let me out to go work from 3:00 a.m. until 8:00 p.m., letting me stop for just a short time. They had me and another prisoner pull a cart loaded with ten to twelve bags of paddy rice (unhusked rice). They took a rod and hit us from behind like water buffalo, whenever we were too weak to pull. They used us to do work like this and gave us only a small bowl of rice porridge once a day. From time to time we were sick, but there was no medicine for treatment. They left us to lie there moaning and yelling like animals.

These traitors committed these savage acts incessantly. On December 9, 1977, I made the difficult decision to run and escape from the prison, and sought refuge in Vietnam, arriving on December 10, 1977.

In late January 1978 the traitorous Pol Pot–Ieng Sary regime took my wife and all my children for internment west from Svay Rieng. They separated my oldest child from his mother; but the two youngest were allowed to stay with their mother. During the day they were all used to do work, exposed to the heat and rain, without any time to rest. They gave them only a small bowl of rice porridge to eat each day, which was not enough to satisfy their hunger. There was no medicine for treatment. Whenever anyone was sick, they would let them lie there moaning and yelling like an animal. There were no clothes or shoes to wear. They had them build their shelter in the middle of the field so that whenever it rained their clothes would get wet; and they made them each sleep on the ground like water buffalo also.

After July 1978, they released all of my family and allowed them to come live in Kandal Stung district, Kandal province. It was the same there as before. They separated my oldest from his mother and worked them without rest, giving them only rice porridge that couldn't satisfy their hunger. Regrettably, at that place, they used my two youngest children aged seven and nine to carry dirt and paddy rice like adults. If they didn't work, they weren't given food to eat. As for their mother, she was pregnant for many months already and they forced her to work without rest continually until she gave birth. After a week, the baby died, and my wife became thin and practically wasted away. Yet they gave her no medicine for treatment. After January 1979, following Liberation Day in Phnom Penh, my family escaped from Kandal province again.

At the end of 1976, the traitorous Pol Pot–Ieng Sary regime took one of my sons to kill him in Meas Thongok subdistrict, Chantrea district, Svay Rieng province, because he had been helping people escape to Vietnam.

In mid-1977, the traitorous Pol Pot–Ieng Sary regime took two of my uncles, named Ma Sok and Ma Chhun, who lived in Prey Stieng village, Svay Ta Yean subdistrict, Kompong Ro district, Svay Rieng province, to interrogate and kill them at the internment center in Kompong Ro district, Svay Rieng province.

2. The crimes of the Pol Pot–Ieng Sary regime committed against the Cambodian people and other conflicts:

At the end of 1978, the traitorous Pol Pot–Ieng Sary regime took a total of 20,000 people from Prek Boun village to Svay Chreah subdistrict, Snuol district, to their deaths; and from the villages of Sray Pring and Okranyong, a total of 8500 people. For certain, after Liberation Day, January 7, 1979, only 11,500 people remained there. In Prek Prasap district, the traitorous Pol Pot–Ieng Sary regime killed more than 900 people in the prison there; in Roleam Phnau, more than 600 people; and in Cheung Phnom Poa Kaley, more than 4,000 people, according to reports from the police department in Prek Prasap district, Kratie province. Most of these people had been taken from the village of Prek Boun.

In regard to the people who lived through the Pol Pot–Ieng Sary regime's most difficult and savage barbarism, it consisted of forced labor day and night, only rice porridge to eat which couldn't satisfy one's hunger, no clothes to wear, frequent sickness with no medicine for treatment, people contracting malaria, unending death, no homes in which to live but only very small shelters in the middle of fields or in the forest, made to sleep on the ground, living in sadness and the deepest of misery.

But this is not all. The traitorous Pol Pot–Ieng Sary regime destroyed various items of property with their conflict, such as:

- a total of 204 homes of people in Chhlong district and Prek Prasap district in Kratie province at the end of January 1979 and the end of 1978.
- complete destruction of 51 schools in Kratie district, Chhlong district, Prek Prasap district, and Snuol district.
- complete destruction of 12 rice threshing machines at a place in Sambon district, Snuol district, Kratie district, and Prek Prasap district.
- complete destruction of 18 hospitals in Snuol, Chhlong, Prek Prasap, and Sambon districts.

Beyond all this, there were so many other crimes that I can't recount them all.

As for the savage crimes of the Pol Pot–Ieng Sary regime committed against my family and me personally, as well as against the Cambodian people, I ask the International Court of Justice, the Cambodian people, and all peace-loving nations of the earth, and especially the nations that have given asylum to the Pol Pot–Ieng Sary regime, to send them back to Cambodia so that the court may punish them for the crimes they have committed against the Cambodian people.

Executed at Kratie this 30th day of March 1979
Thaong Chin

2.1.5.16
Mr. Rous Rin

Today, June 21, 1979, we, Saes Chhon, an official of the Ministry of the Interior charged with the investigation, along with Mr. Ouk Chandara, Secretary, have composed this record of the statement of the witness Rous Rin.

Question: Can you tell us briefly your identity and background?

Answer: My name is Rous Rin, thirty-six years old, of Khmer nationality. My profession is that I am a worker at the cement factory in Kampot. My education is through the tenth year of the twelve-year curriculum. My family situation is that in my family eleven were killed by Pol Pot. Only five survived, among them my wife, who has gone insane. As for my place of origin, I am from the Koh Khmum village, Koh Khmum subdistrict, Battambang district, Battambang province. Under the Pol Pot regime I lived at Kampot.

Question: According to your complaint and reports from local officials, the Pol Pot-Ieng Sary clique committed many crimes against your family. Can you tell us any details?

Answer: I don't remember exactly the date, but at about 7:00 a.m. on a day in April 1975, an alert was sounded that the entire population must leave the city immediately, and that anyone refusing would be shot on the spot. In the face of this threat, everyone had to abandon their houses and belongings and leave. My family and all the inhabitants of the farm had to walk five days and five nights before arriving at a woods in Kompong Thom province. There we had nothing to eat, we slept outdoors, and we were divided into three categories. Every day the first category got half a container of rice to eat, the second category got one third, and the third category got only one fourth of a container. They made us do hard labor and would not let us be in contact with the others. It was the same for those living in other communes.

One day I went to plow. It was already nighttime, and that is why I broke the plow. They arrested me, tied me up, and took me to the Koh Chon prison in Prey Nup district, Kampot province. It is a major prison for the province. They interrogated me for four days in a row, during which they covered my head with a sack, suffocating me. As a result I lost consciousness three times. That is how they tortured and mistreated me. After that, I had to go carry stones for thirty-eight days.

While I was detained in this prison, I saw torture. They tied people's hands and feet, covered their heads with a jute sack, and exposed them to the sun. Many people showed marks of torture on their stomachs, including bleeding from the stomach. I saw a woman named Khen who was accused of improper sexual relations. They tied her to a tree and let yellow ants bite her. Then they stuck a stick into her vagina and disemboweled her, taking out her liver. The name of the torturer was Tau Kea.

I was kept in this prison and let out only on liberation day. I know that in this prison the Pol Pot agents kept about four hundred persons and killed almost all of them before liberation.

In my hamlet were about five hundred young people, but on liberation day only thirty-seven were left! I know that because I became an official of the locality after liberation day.

As for my family, my father Chuk Rum, 65 years old, like me was forced to do hard labor. He was mistreated and protested, and as a result he was tortured and then killed in 1977. My mother Muk Sura, 62 years old, died in 1976 as a result of weakness from hunger. My wife Kit Seng, 30 years old, went insane from forced labor and horrible treatment. I have nine brothers and sisters, all of whom were accused of treason, imprisoned, tortured, and killed. I have three children quite young. They are all still alive.

Question: Do you have anything else to say?

Answer: The crime of Pol Pot and Ieng Sary is very great. Their aim is to exterminate the Kampuchean people. I have denounced their crimes, and I will denounce them again.

Question: Do you have any requests?

Answer: The crimes of Pol Pot and Ieng Sary are savage and cruel without parallel in history. My family was almost entirely wiped out, leaving us in a tragic situation. I ask the People's Revolutionary Council of Kampuchea to arrest the two tyrants Pol Pot and Ieng Sary and to bring them to justice so that they can pay for their crimes against the Kampuchean people.

This record has been read back to the witness, who has affirmed it and signed below.

Secretary	*Witness*	*Investigator*
Ouk Chandara	Rous Rin	Saes Chhon

2.1.5.17
Mr. Saleh Sen

We, Saes Chhon, official of the Ministry of the Interior responsible for the investigation, and his assistant Ouk Chandara, have drawn up a record of a statement of the witness Saleh Sen.

Question: Can you tell us something about your background?

Answer: I am Saleh Sen, 32 years old, of Khmer nationality. I finished primary school. I am a farmer. I was born in Reshin Non village, Co Rong Ty subdistrict, Kampot district, Kampot province. My father, Nang Saleh, 70 years old, was killed in 1977. My mother, Hap Ami Nas, 65 years old, died in 1960. My stepmother, Me Sao, 65 years old, died in 1977. My wife, Rous Ek Ses, 29 years old, was killed in 1977. Of my two children, one died of starvation, and the other is still alive. Of my five brothers and sisters, three were killed by the Pol Pot clique.

Question: According to your letter of denunciation and reports of the local administration, Pol Pot–Ieng Sary and their clique committed many crimes against you and your family. Tell us about their crimes, please.

Answer: The Pol Pot–Ieng Sary clique committed extremely barbarous crimes against my family and all the Kampuchean people. In 1975, when we were farming peaceably we were ordered to go to live in a commune. That is why, although my parents were old, being in their 60s and 70s, and I had quite a few children, we had to abandon our house and property and leave! All our property was completely destroyed. Since that time we have lived a wretched life.

During the time I lived in the commune, I had to work hard all day without a break, in the morning until noon, and in the afternoon until dark. All we got to eat at each meal was one third or one half a tin of rice. We would be accused of betrayal if we didn't fulfill our production norms. The workers were ill-treated. I went a commune in Pore Cham subdistrict, Po Ray Nup district, Kampot province. That commune had four farms with 800 people. Because of repeated killings, few of them survived until liberation. I knew assassins in that commune who killed people savagely. For example, a man named Mit bragged to several persons of having killed many people by disembowelling them to get livers or gallbladders. The gallbladders of thin people were used to make medicine, while those of fatter persons were packed and sent to China. My father also practiced medicine, so once Mit gave him human gallbladders. Mit also threatened that my turn would come, implying that one day I too would be killed so he could take my liver and gallbladder. In the farm I had a friend named Sem, who was 40 years old. Sem was accused of opposition and was beaten on the skull to death in 1977.

Later, Mit did something not to the satisfaction of his superiors and was himself killed. After being very badly mistreated, I escaped from the commune in July 1977.

Question: Please tell us about other crimes they committed against your family.

Answer: My father was 70 years old but still was forced to do hard labor. He could not live that way and complained about it, which is why they killed him in 1977. The same occurred to my stepmother. In my family there were five brothers and sisters; they killed three of my brothers. They are Saleh Koh Sem, 47 years old; Saleh Hamid, 40 years old; and Saleh Saleng Men, 37 years old.

I have two children. One of them died as an infant from lack of mother's milk, because his mother had to go do hard labor. Thus six members of my family were killed by Pol Pot.

Question: What else do you want to say?

Answer: The Pol Pot–Ieng Sary clique committed towering crimes causing the worst disaster in the history of our nation. I'll submit to you an accusation letter with more details.

Question: Have you any request?

Answer: I ask the Kampuchean government to arrest, by all means, and bring to trial the two chief culprits, Pol Pot and Ieng Sary, and make them pay the blood debt for my family and other Kampucheans. Like millions of Kampucheans, I have experienced an extremely hard life. We have deep hatred against Pol Pot and Ieng Sary.

I demand that the United Nations have a clear attitude toward these two chieftains Pol Pot and Ieng Sary. I've declared my words are true.

The record of this interview has been read again and was agreed with and signed by the witness.

Secretary	*Interviewer*	*Witness*
Ouk Chandara	Saes Chhon	Saleh Sen

2.1.5.18

Hour (Orphan Girl, Surname Unknown)

The following statement was recorded June 19, 1979, at 9:00 a.m., in an orphanage in Siem Reap city, in the presence of Mr. Saes Chhon, official of the Ministry of the Interior; Mr. Chhun, secretary responsible for recording statements; the girl Hour, the declarant; Mrs. Diak Sarin, deputy director of the orphanage, tutor.

Question: Your name, your age, please.

Answer: I have forgotten my family name, but they call me Hour. I am thirteen years old.

Question: The names of your parents?

Answer: My father was Chen Suy, and my mother was Vinh Vy.

Question: Where were you born?

Answer: Phnom Penh. I have forgotten the name of the street; I remember only that it is near the new market.

Question: What did your parents do near the market?

Answer: My father was a book seller, and my mother sold cakes.

Question: How many brothers and sisters do you have?

Answer: I have five, and I am the eldest.

Question: Did you go to school?

Answer: In Phnom Penh I was in the second class. I do not recall any longer the name of my school.

Question: Why did you leave Phnom Penh and your parents?

Answer: The Pol Pot agents took my family and everyone out of Phnom Penh. My parents, my brothers and sisters and I were displaced to Battambang. After we got to the Prasath commune, my parents died of hunger.

Question: Where are your brothers and sisters?

Answer: They died before my parents.

Question: With whom did you live after the death of your parents?

Answer: I followed people on the road.

Question: Did you know them?

Answer: No.

Question: How did you survive?

Answer: I begged to survive.

Question: Why do you have scars on your head and neck?

Answer: One day, the date I don't recall, Pol Pot agents arrested me. They hit me in the neck and poured boiling water over my head. When I cried for help, someone ran up and the Pol Pot agents let me go.

Question: Do you recall the date and place of this incident?

Answer: I have forgotten the date, but it was in Prasath subdistrict, Battambang province.

Question: Who took you to Siem Reap?

Answer: I was taken by revolutionary fighters to the Siem Reap hospital and when I got better I was sent to this orphanage.

Question: Why did the Pol Pot agents want to cut you on your neck?

Answer: They wanted to beat me to death to eat my flesh.

Question: Did you ever see them kill anyone to eat them?

Answer: Yes, with my own eyes I saw them kill two girls to eat them. One was my age, and the other was younger.

Completed at 11:30 a.m., read back, confirmed, and signed by little Hour and Mrs. Diak Sarin.

Witness	*Official*	*Secretary*
Hour	Saes Chhon	Chhun
Diak Sarin, tutor		

2.1.5.19
Mrs. Leung Lada

The following statement made by Mrs. Leung Lada was recorded June 20, 1979, at 2:00 p.m. at the office of the People's Revolutionary Committee of Siem Reap 3 subdistrict in the presence of Mr. Saes Chhon, official of the Ministry of the Interior, and Mr. San Kiri, secretary, responsible for recording statements. Here follows the content of the statement.

Question: Your name, age, and place of origin, please.

Answer: I am Leung Lada, 24 years old, from Wat Svay village, Siem Reap 3 subdistrict.

Question: What is the status of your family at present?

Answer: I was married to Nuk Kim Song, 26 years old. He was killed by Pol Pot agents in 1975 while he was finishing high school. We had not yet had any children. I have six brothers and sisters, of whom five were killed by Pol Pot agents. My father suffered the same fate. Now there are only three of us in our native village: my mother, my sister, and I.

Question: Please give the particulars concerning the death of your husband.

Answer: After Pol Pot's seizure of power, my husband and I were sent to Kok Srok village, Kok Srok subdistrict, Waring district, to build canals and dams. Some time later, the Pol Pot agents promised to send my husband back to school to finish his education. I was transferred to the neighboring village of Kok Phnau in the same subdistrict. After our separation my husband was killed in a nearby woods, as I was told, perhaps because he was considered an intellectual.

Question: Tell me about the misfortunes that befell your family.

Answer: Besides my husband and me, my grandmother, my parents, my six brothers and sisters were removed to Trey Nhor subdistrict, Puok district, Siem Reap province to farm. Most of them were killed soon thereafter. My father, Leung Seng, 52 years old, a former teacher at Siem Reap, was killed at Trey Nhour for being an intellectual.

Five of my brothers and sisters (three girls and two boys), all of them unmarried, were first mobilized for hard labor in Trey Nhour village and were then killed, apparently because they were the children of a teacher and because they had gone to school.

My grandmother, 70 years old, was also killed, for no apparent reason.

I learned all this after the liberation from my mother and from my one surviving sister.

Question: Were you forced to remarry? How were you treated?

Answer: I was not forced to remarry, but I was often beaten while at work building canals and dams in the Kok Srok cooperative.

This record was drawn up on the basis of the statement of Mrs. Leung Lada. It was read to her, and she has certified it to be accurate and has signed below.

Witness	*Official*	*Secretary*
Mrs. Leung Lada (Fingerprint)	Saes Chhon	San Kiri

2.1.5.20
Mrs. Tim Moeun

This deposition was recorded June 20, 1979, at 8:00 a.m. at the office of the People's Revolutionary Committee of Siem Reap 3 subdistrict by Saes Chhon, official of the Ministry of the Interior, and San Kiri, a clerk responsible for taking statements.

Question: Your name, age, native place, please.

Answer: I am Tim Moeun, 71 years old, a native of Wat Svay village, Siem Reap 3 subdistrict, Siem Reap district, Siem Reap province.

Question: With whom do you live at present?

Answer: I have seven children, of whom five were killed under the Pol Pot regime. At present I live with one son and one daughter.

Question: Tell us about your family under the Pol Pot regime.

Answer: Under the Pol Pot regime, I was compelled to move to Say Snom village, Chruy La Nguon subdistrict, Puok district, Siem Reap province, accompanied by only one daughter, Pieng Chhon, and her seven-member family. In 1977, my daughter was taken away by Pol Pot agents who said that she was ill and had to be taken to the hospital. In fact, she was killed, as was, later on, her whole family of seven people. At that time, due to my age, I was given the task of keeping birds away from the fields, which prevented me from knowing how they killed my daughter. Later on I was told that she was killed quite near this Say Snom village.

• My daughter Pieng Guon with her family of fifteen members was forced to settle in Svay Luo village, Chak subdistrict, Siem Reap district, where they were all slaughtered.

• My son Pieng Son and his family of eight members were displaced to Varin district, Siem Reap province, where they were all killed.

• My son Pieng Koi, with his wife and children, was driven to Riem, in

Kompong Som province. Later on the Pol Pot agents killed the couple. As for their four children, only since liberation have they lived with me.

• My son Pieng Sovan, a bachelor, was forced to enlist in the shock youth to farm in Preah Vihear province. He was also killed later on.

Now I have only two children left: a son who was displaced to Battambang and a daughter in Svay Thum district, Siem Reap province. Since liberation, they have been living with me.

Question: How were you treated during this period?

Answer: In the beginning of the Pol Pot rule, I was forced to keep birds away from the fields. Then, owing to my weakness, I was sent to look after small children in the cooperative. For food I ate rice soup mixed with sweet potatoes and banana stems. After my daughter Pieng Chhon was killed, I lived by myself. After liberation, I had to walk two weeks to get back to this village.

Question: Do you know other crimes of the Pol Pot clique?

Answer: In Say Snom village, I heard a story about a couple that was killed five days after the wife gave birth to a child. The baby was abandoned on the grave of its parents by the criminals, who threatened to kill anyone trying to pick it up. Later on, the baby died too. I personally did not see it on the grave of its parents but I heard about it.

(Finished at 10:00 a.m., read back, and confirmed by Mrs. Tim Moeun.)

Witness	*Officer*	*Clerk*
Mrs. Tim Moeun	Saes Chhon	San Kiri
(Fingerprint)		

2.1.5.21

Mrs. Khang Chiem

The following statement was taken on June 20, 1979, at 10:00 a.m. at the office of the People's Revolutionary Committee of Siem Reap 3 subdistrict, in the presence of Mr. Saes Chhon, official of the Ministry of the Interior, Mr. San Kiri, clerk in charge of taking statements, and Mrs. Khang Chiem, the witness. Here is the content of the statement.

Question: Your name, age and native place, please.

Answer: I am Khang Chiem, 74 years old, native of Wat Svay village, Siem Reap 3 subdistrict, Siem Reap district, Siem Reap province.

Question: How big was your family?

Answer: I had three daughters and five sons. Two daughters and four sons were killed by the Pol Pot agents. Now there remain one daughter and one son who are living with me.

Question: Can you give me some particulars about each of them?

Answer: After Pol Pot's seizure of power, I was displaced together with my twelve children and grandchildren to Tbong Chrey village, Siem Reap 1 subdistrict, Siem Reap district. I have lost:

- My son-in-law, the husband of my daughter Kim Din; he was executed at Tbong Chrey;
- My daughter Loeun, who first was arrested and detained in Siem Reap municipal jail, and then was executed later on. Her body was buried on the grounds of Thoamayutt pagoda, near the jail;
- My son Thim and his whole family (his wife and four children) were executed in Varin district, Siem Reap province;
- My daughter Sai and her whole family (her husband and four children) were also executed in Varin district;
- My son Thu and his four children. They were displaced from Phnom Penh and executed later on. I do not know where. I think his wife and two of his children are still alive;
- My son Y and his whole family (his wife and four children) in the same circumstances as Thu;
- My son Don, a bachelor. He is certainly dead but I do not know where.

Those who survived and are living with me now are:

- My daughter Kim Lin and her five children,
- My daughter Loeun's four children,
- My son Heng, who was displaced to Battambang and returned here after liberation.

Question: What work were you compelled to do at Tbong Chrey?

Answer: The Pol Pot agents made me chase birds away from the rice fields. As food, they gave me, at times brown rice, at times damp rice, or rice soup boiled with slices of banana stem or even soup of rice bran, supposedly because my work was of insignificant value due to my age.

(Finished at 11:00, read back and confirmed and fingerprint affixed by Mrs. Khang Chiem.)

Witness	*Officer*	*Clerk*
Mrs. Khang Chiem (Fingerprint)	Saes Chhon	San Kiri

2.1.5.22

Mrs. Mok Moeun

Today, June 20, 1979, at 1:00 p.m., we, Saes Chhon, official of the Ministry of the Interior, and San Kiri, secretary in charge of record answers, are at the Siem Reap subdistrict office. The answers are as follows:

Question: Grandmother, please tell us your name. Where is your birthplace?

Answer: My name is Mok Moeun, 63 years old. My birthplace is Wat Svay village, Siem Reap 3 subdistrict, Siem Reap district, Siem Reap province.

Question: Where and what did you do under the Pol Pot regime?

Answer: Under the Pol Pot regime, I was evacuated to Tbong Chrey village and Svay Thom village, Siem Reap 1 subdistrict. The person who stayed with me was grandmother Khang Chiem, who was questioned this morning. I was evacuated to that place with my father-in-law and my 12-year-old grandchild. There they forced me to carry fertilizer and plant rice because they said that my health was still good enough to work. Like other grandmothers, I was given porridge mixed with banana stem and rice bran.

Question: How many people are there in your family?

Answer: I have two daughters and 8 grandchildren.

Question: Can you let us know how many still live with you?

Answer: Pol Pot killed all of my family members, totaling 12 persons. Now I live with my only grandchild, 13 years old, who was evacuated with me. The rest are all dead.

Question: Can you explain precisely about each person in your family?

Answer: I have two daughters. Prior to the Pol Pot regime, we grew rice in Wat Svay village. Under the Pol Pot regime, my daughter, Sarun, her husband, and their five children were evacuated to Battambang province. My daughter, her husband, and their other four children were all killed in Battambang province. Only one of her children is still alive and lives with me at the present time.

My second daughter, Sapok, her husband, and three children were all sent to live at Koulen Mountain in Siem Reap province. Later on, they were all killed there.

My father-in-law, Kea, was 77 years old. In 1977, he was kicked and beaten by Pol Pot soldiers, which I saw with my own eyes, and then they took and killed my father-in-law east of Trapeang Chruy village. Only a grandchild and I are still alive and returned to this village after the liberation day.

This statement was finished at 2:00 p.m. the same day. It was read back and listened to by grandmother Mok Moeun. She acknowledged that it was her answer and was willing to sign as follows.

Witness	*Interrogator*	*Secretary*
Mok Moeun	Saes Chhon	San Kiri

2.1.5.23

Mr. My Sambath

Today, June 28, 1979, at the office of the Ministry of the Interior, we, Mien Chieu, official of the Ministry of the Interior, and Mr. Ros Rokha, secretary, are taking the following statement of a witness named Sambath.

Question: Please say briefly who you are.

Answer: My name is My Sambath, 40 years old, born in Kompong Svay village, Kompong Svay subdistrict, Svay Sisophon district, Battambang province. By profession I am a teacher, but in Pol Pot times I was forced to collect human excrement. My education is through high school. My nationality is Khmer. My religion is Buddhism. My father, Ky Rich, is dead. My mother, Chia Ut, is still living. I have five brothers and one sister. My wife, Non Chhai, is still living. I have two sons and four daughters, all still living.

Question: You have filed a denunciation statement about the crimes of the Pol Pot–Ieng Sary clique. Please tell us about their crimes against you and your family.

Answer: The crimes committed by the Pol Pot–Ieng Sary clique against me are as follows. After April 17, 1975, Pol Pot men arrived in Kop village. They said that the population had to move elsewhere to earn a living. My wife, my six children, and I fled into the woods. But before we had made it three kilometers, we were arrested by the guards, who made us return to Prek Lea village, Pong Sat subdistrict, Mongkol Borey district, Battambang province. There I was brutally tortured. For three days in a row, I was suffocated with a nylon sack twelve times. They poured water into my nostrils, then grabbed me by the head and banged my head against a pillar, breaking one of my incisors. They made me dilute human excrement and eat it to amuse them. They did not kill me but made me collect excrement until the day we were all liberated by the revolutionary forces and allowed to return to our native village.

The following are the crimes committed by Pol Pot and Ieng Sary against my family.

In May 1975, the Pol Pot–Ieng Sary men killed the entire family of my elder brother, including my brother, whose name was Pich Hy, his wife Huong, and their two children, whose names were Hy On and Hy Kott, because they said that the family was against the regime. I learned of these murders from a neighbor who told me about them.

In July 1976, they killed my nephew, who was named Ty Huong Tech. A village official and Pol Pot agent beat him to death with a stick. I was told this by my fellow villager Huot.

In April 1975, the Pol Pot men took and killed the family of my second eldest brother, who was named Pich Chhi. Ten were killed: my parents, my brother, his wife, and their six children.

My son, Mi Tung, 19 years old, was forced by the Pol Pot men to work for them in 1977. He was labelled a dissident and arrested at a railway station in Sisophon town, because he returned to work late from a leave. They tortured him so brutally that he became insane.

My daughter is Kun Thea, 15 years old. She was forced in 1977 to do hard labor even though she was sick. Instead of giving her medication or extending any care to her, the Pol Pot agents said that she was only pretending to be ill. My daughter's illness got worse to the point that she became insane. While she was lying under her bed one day, Pol Pot men poured boiling water on her back, causing serious burns. After liberation in 1979, she was cured by the revolutionary forces.

My two other children who are only seven and eight years old, were forced to catch shrimp to feed ducks in the people's commune, in Pun Lea village. If they did not work, they got nothing to eat.

Question: Besides these crimes committed by the Pol Pot agents against you and your family, do you know of other instances?

Answer: I am aware of the following instances. The first concerns the Suot family, in which the woman is named Mao, in Prek Lea village, Pong Sat subdistrict, Mongkol Borey district. One night in June 1976, the Pol Pot guerrilla fighters heard Mr. Suot and his wife complaining about the regime. The next day, they took the whole family to Mut Si Rong, which is two kilometers away from the village. They beat them all to death with sticks, including the two spouses and their four children, and then took all their clothes. This story was known to everyone in the area.

A second instance is that in October 1977, Panh, a railway worker at the Sisophon railway station, was arrested and detained for four days by the Pol Pot men at Chamkar Ko. Then they transferred him to O Am Boss village, Kompong Svay subdistrict, Sisophon district, and stabbed him to death with a bayonet. I saw his body in a ditch. In this ditch (at O Am Boss), which was ten meters wide and one hundred fifty meters long, there were a thousand bodies decomposing. I can take you there.

In Pung Ro village, Kompong Svay subdistrict, Sisophon district, Battambang province, the Pol Pot men, using bulldozers, dug another pit. After they finished digging the pit, they planted mines around it and led people from different regions to it: Phnom Penh people displaced to Battambang, persons who had returned from Thailand, and persons from the Battambang province districts of Mongkol Borey, Num, Preah Net Preah, Thmo Puoc, and Sisophon. The total number of persons was about ten thousand. They pushed these victims into the pit and set off the mines. Then they buried the bodies with bulldozers. I was told all this by Suon, a driver of one of the bulldozers.

One other instance occurred when I was forced to carry cement in Kilo Pek Pram Moui village, south of the railway line that crosses Kop village, O Chrau district, Battambang province. I crossed at two places a canal five meters wide and one hundred meters long and could see many human bones in it. If necessary, I could take you there.

Question: Besides what you have indicated above, do you know other relevant facts?

Answer: Besides the crimes I have mentioned above, I think that the Pol Pot–Ieng Sary clique is very cruel. It wanted to exterminate the entire Kampuchean people.

Question: In light of the crimes committed by it against your family, against you, and against your people, how do you think the Pol Pot–Ieng Sary clique should be judged?

Answer: The Pol Pot–Ieng Sary clique should be severely punished. Its crimes should be brought to the attention of the entire world.

This record was completed at 4:00 p.m. on June 28, 1979. It was written according to the statements of My Sambath, who has reviewed it and has signed below.

Secretary	*Witness*	*Interviewer*
Ros Rokha	My Sambath	Mien Chieu

2.1.5.24
Mr. Sok Li Mut

This statement was recorded June 26, 1979, at 7:00 a.m. at the office of the Ministry of the Interior, in the presence of Mr. Mien Chieu, official of the Ministry of the Interior; Mr. San Kiri, secretary in charge of recording statements, and Mr. Sok Li Mut, the witness.

Question: Tell us your identity.

Answer: I am Sok Li Mut, also known as Sok Phnon, born June 6, 1964, from Dong village, Kbal Trach subdistrict, Krakor district, Pursat province. I now work the land, but under the Pol Pot regime, I was a dock worker. In school, I completed the first grade. I am a Khmer, and a Buddhist.

My father was killed by the Pol Pot agents in 1976, and my mother in 1977. I have one brother and five sisters. Two of them were killed by the Pol Pot agents.

Question: You have denounced to the government the crimes of the Pol Pot–Ieng Sary clique committed against your family and you personally. Provide us the specifics.

Answer: In 1975, at the time of liberation, I was studying in Pursat. Since the Pol Pot clique closed the schools, I went back to my village, but on the way my bicycle was stolen. My family was evacuated by the Pol Pot agents, and I was taken to Kompong Chhnang. Once there, I tried to return to my village, but I was caught and made to unload goods in the northwest region.

At first they gave me rice to eat, but starting one week later, I got only soup. With another person forced to work with me, I had to unload fifteen trucks a day, and each truck held fifty sacks of rice. Anyone who by accident let any rice spill would be killed immediately. Ten among the sixteen unloaders were killed for that reason: Kinh, Duong, Soanh, Sen, Stay, O Ly, So Hoi, and others.

Three months later I spit up blood, but I got no medicine or food for three days. We worked from 6:00 a.m. to 2:00 p.m., then we took our meal and worked until 6:00 p.m. On days when there were no goods to unload, we got only 300 grams of rice for ten persons. After six months of this work (from April 1975 to October 1975), I was transferred to Svay Sa village, Sna Ansa subdistrict, Krakor district, Pursat province, to work the land from 6:30 a.m. to 5:00 p.m., with a ration of 300 grams of rice for ten persons. I was imprisoned for three days for supposedly opposing the Pol Pot agents. Once I was released, I had to go into the forest to cut creepers (two carts full a day) from 7:00 a.m. to 3:00 p.m. After that, I was ordered to climb sixty sugar palm trees every day and get three pans of juice. To do that, I had to climb without stopping from 4:00 a.m. to 7:00 p.m., and that is why many times I fainted after finishing work. I did this work from 1976 to 1978. According to the procedure, anyone who got three warnings would be killed; I had already been warned twice.

Here are the crimes of the Pol Pot clique against my family. In 1975, they chased my family, with my mother and elder sister, to Kompong Chhnang. One day when I was at Pursat, I was able to meet my father, who was seriously ill and who got no medicine. Later on he was arrested as an opponent of the regime and was killed in June 1976 in Tra Trao village, Sira Cha subdistrict, Krakor district, Pursat province. There I saw blood and three sticks with which my father was beaten to death. The local people told me that he then had his throat slit.

My mother worked plaiting straw mats. Twice she was warned for asking to go to Pursat to see her children. To punish her, the Pol Pot agents killed her in 1977. When they took her away, my younger sister, 10 years of age, refused to leave my mother, and she was beaten, a beating that left her blind.

My elder brother Sok Pho fell seriously ill and was taken to the hospital in Pursat. They accused him of having stolen chickens and stuck his head in water to torture him. Then they beat him to death with sticks in 1977, as patients at the hospital told me.

My elder sister Sok Bun, who cried too much over the death of her husband, was killed by the Pol Pot agents. She too was taken away and killed by them. Her body was discovered naked by my sister-in-law.

My sister-in-law said that my aunt, En Sa Run, had a husband who was accused of being an opponent. The couple were both killed in 1977.

According to my sister-in-law, another aunt, En Lo, who was sick was taken to a hospital where she was injected with poison in 1977.

Question: Are you aware of other crimes of the Pol Pot clique against the people?

Answer: Yes. *First case:* In April 1975, they killed intellectuals. To do that, they assembled the families of intellectuals and of Lon Nol soldiers (with their furniture) at Pursat and took them, about 4000 persons, in more than 50 trucks, to the O Chruy river near Mount Prey, at Con Ray village, Chheu

Tom subdistrict, Krakor district, Pursat province. There they took them off and tied them up. Since there was not enough rope, those who were already tied up were led off and were beaten to death, while the others were shot right where they were. At that time, I was an unloader and I was transferred to another place. When we got to the place of the killing, our truck had a flat tire, and I saw many corpses. Our driver, who transported the victims, told me about this case.

Second case: In the Phnom Bot cooperative in Phnom Bot subdistrict, Svay Donkro district, Pursat province, the Pol Pot agents took 10,000 persons the first time by their estimate during a six-month period, the second time 12,000 persons, of whom there remain only 200, who make up about 30 families, as they told me, and the third time about 18,000 persons, of whom I was one. Here is how they got rid of their victims: by accusing them of opposing the regime and then killing them; by making them work out in the sun without a hat, and with 300 grams of rice for twelve persons.

They set aside about three square kilometers of land where they buried their victims. Then they worked this land with a mechanical plow to make fertilizer. I worked there and I saw many human bones on the soil. Escaped families told me that the thirty families I already mentioned came from Battambang for the most part. I do not know if they are still there now, or if they went back to their native place.

Third case: At Pursat, we dug a canal through the forest from Pursat to Battambang. It was one hundred meters wide, fifty meters deep, and was about 30 kilometers from National Route 5, to the left if we were going from Pursat to Battambang. They got together there from 20,000 to 40,000 persons of all ages from the provinces of Pursat, eastern Kratie, Kandal, Svay Rieng, and Kompong Cham, I went there to unload rice for three days. In 1978, when eastern Kampuchea was liberated, the Pol Pot agents got their victims together and shot them. A large number were killed, according to those who escaped.

Fourth case: In Bakan district, Pursat province, there were twelve cooperatives, including Chai Phuc, nearly all of whose members were killed in early 1978. Only Mung and Mi were able to escape and are still living in ward 4, Pursat city. Son Kin, chief of ward 4 knows this case well.

I am prepared to show you the places of these killings so that you can understand the cruelty of the Pol Pot clique. I can also introduce Mung and Mi to you right away if you need.

I hope that the government punishes these promoters of genocide as they deserve, so that they can pay their blood debts.

Completed, read back, confirmed and signed by the undersigned.

Secretary	*Witness*	*Investigator*
San Kiri	Sok Li Mut	Mien Chieu

2.1.5.25
Mr. Sok Ros

The following statement made by Mr. Sok Ros was recorded on June 20, 1979, in the office of the Siem Reap hospital in presence of Mr. Saes Chhon, official of the Ministry of the Interior, and Mr. Chhun, clerk responsible for recording statements. Here is its content:

Question: Your name, age, native place, profession, and family situation, please.

Answer: I am Sok Ros, 51 years old, native of Bia Si Ban village, Bia Si Ban subdistrict, Kien Svay district, Kandal province. Under the Sihanouk and Lon Nol regimes, I was a cycle driver. My wife was Hong Lap, a farmer. She is dead. I have three children: two daughters and one son:

—Sok So Phia, 14 (daughter)
—Sok Maly, 11 (daughter)
—Sok Vanh Na Rich, 9 (son)

Question: What did you do and where did you live under the Pol Pot regime?

Answer: After April 17, 1975, the Pol Pot clique drove my family, together with thousands upon thousands of people of the three provinces of Kandal, Kompong Speu, and Takeo, to Battambang. There, they singled out 100 people including my own family, and marched us off to Kol Ka Che village, Kien Thmey subdistrict, Mon Sa Cot district, Battambang province, in order to establish a commune of agricultural production.

Question: Tell us in what circumstances your family was sent to be killed, after which you and your three children managed to escape death.

Answer: On January 27, 1979, the commune authorities, accompanied by 60 Pol Pot soldiers, came and arrested one hundred people, including my whole family, then took us to Mon Sa Cot, near the forest and three kilometers from the commune.

On the way they said nothing of this displacement. When we arrived, they tied our arms behind us and said to us: "Phnom Penh has been liberated. We must kill you all, otherwise you will follow the liberation front and kill us."

Then it was the execution. Each in turn received three blows of a hammer behind his head before having his throat cut. It was the same for me.

I came to the day after the killing, on January 28 about 4:00 p.m. At that time, Sok Maly, my second daughter, came and untied me. Then she went to look for her sister and brother. She found them still alive but so weak that they could not stand up. I should mention that during the execution the children were not tied or had their throats cut like the adults, but were only knocked with a hammer. Fortunately, my children were only injured. However, my wife died.

We were in a very dangerous situation. With my head seriously wounded and my throat badly bleeding, I was afraid that the butchers might come back to finish us off, so I made up my mind to escape at nightfall together with my children. When we were about to start out, two children between 9 or 10 years old, who had escaped being killed like my own children, asked to join us.

After walking ten kilometers, we reached Lip river, in Battambang province, where we met revolutionary soldiers who arranged for us to be taken by car to Kra Lanh district, Siem Reap province. From there we were taken to the Siem Reap hospital. Usually we cover ten kilometers in three hours, but we were so seriously wounded we took three days to go that far.

Question: How many men, women, and children are there among those one hundred victims?

Answer: There were 30 men, 50 women, and 20 children, including my family.

Question: How is your family's health at present?

Answer: Since the revolutionary soldiers brought us to the Siem Reap hospital where we get good treatment our health has improved.

Question: Do you have anything more to add?

Answer: I must add that I have a deep hatred against the Pol Pot–Ieng Sary clique for the atrocious crimes they have committed against our people and my family. My wife is dead, and my children and I still bear wounds. Without the revolutionary power we would not have escaped death.

I have a deep gratitude for the revolutionary power which has saved my children and me.

(Completed at 9:00 a.m., read back, confirmed, and signed by Mr. Sok Ros.)

Official	*Clerk*	*Witness*
Saes Chhon	Chhun	Sok Ros

2.1.5.26

Mr. Chan Sary

Today, June 23, 1979, at 2:00 p.m., at the office of the Ministry of the Interior, we, Mien Chieu, official of the Ministry of the Interior, assisted by Mr. San Nim, secretary, have drawn up this transcript of the statement of the victim Chan Sary.

Question: Tell us the main points in your curriculum vitae.

Answer: I am Chan Sary, born September 14, 1948 in Kompong Thley village, Kompong Thley subdistrict, Kompong Chhnang province. I am a teacher; I finished a secondary education. I am Khmer, a Buddhist. My father, Chan Son Hong, was killed in 1975 by Pol Pot agents. My mother, Sun Lean, is still alive. I have five sisters and four brothers, of whom three were killed by Pol Pot agents. My wife Chlo Maly, 26 years of age, is also called Chan Siara. I have two children of whom one disappeared, and the other is named Chan Serak.

Question: According to your request, please tell about the crimes of the Pol Pot–Ieng Sary clique.

Answer: On April 17, 1975, the Pol Pot–Ieng Sary soldiers came to our house, threatened us with their guns, and forced the whole family out of the house. We were taken to Preah Vihear province, leaving behind our belongings. Along the way to Preah Vihear, everyone went on foot; we had nothing to eat and had to beg to survive. They gave us one bowl of uncooked rice for eight persons. All the things we were able to carry with us, like watches, gold rings, clothing of any value, were confiscated from us at checkpoints.

When we arrived at our destination, no one had any more than the clothes he was wearing. My family was taken into the Ta Sanh forest, Preah Vihear province. As for me, I was suspected of being a Lon Nol soldier, so I was tied up and jailed for two days. At night, every two hours, they interrogated me, threatening me and hitting me with gun butts. After two days, I had said nothing and they had to let me go.

In Ta Sanh village, Srayka district, everyone in my family had to live separately from one another. They took me to work in a commune. I am only a teacher, but they made me go re-plant rice for three months. Later, they made me plait sieves used to catch fish in the gullies. They made me do forced labor of a kind I had never done. Forced to work without a break, my body down in the water, after 15 or 16 days of work in such conditions I contracted a fever.

My wife too was mistreated. She had to do hard work and also contracted a fever, and they gave us nothing to eat. After being sick three months, I got visibly thin. They made me climb sugar palm trees and live 60 kilometers away from my family, to get me used to working, as they told me. I did not know how to climb a sugar palm tree, but they made me climb trees three bamboos high. Once the sugar palm harvest was finished, they made me go break stones to build roads eight kilometers from Preah Vihear. We got two meals a day, and each meal consisted only of two spoons of broth. We had no rice and had to work day and night.

The sick got no medicines. In our work group, three persons died of hunger and disease. I do not know their names, because our group was made up of persons from different parts of the country. Besides, they did not let us speak to each other while we worked.

For almost four years, I had to work in rice fields or climb sugar palm trees, and after the sugar palm harvest, I had to work building roads.

In October 1977, I was suspected of hostile activities and then arrested and subjected to torture for two nights. Five other persons, Som, Sean, Ly, Viral, and Bok, were arrested with me. Then they got all the people together and announced that we were enemies who needed to be watched closely.

With regard to crimes of the Pol Pot–Ieng Sary clique against my family: My father was an engineer, and he worked at the Agriculture Institute in Phnom Penh. When Pol Pot entered Phnom Penh, my father was forced out of the city and taken to the Potot pagoda, Kompong Cham province. There they let it be known that engineers and technicians could sign up to go back to Phnom Penh to work.

Believing them, my father and forty other engineers and technicians signed up. Among them were my father, named Chan Son Heng, and my three brothers, Tinh, an agricultural engineer, Da Nao, a teacher of English, and Chan Siri, a teacher.

The Pol Pot soldiers tied up those who signed up, including the four from my family, and killed them all. In May 1975 I was not there when my father and brothers were killed.

It was only in June 1979 that I found my mother again. My family was dispersed, some being out of touch with the others since the time they were forced out of the region. In April 1975, my mother and my brothers and sisters were forced out toward Battambang, going on foot.

When they got to Battambang, my mother and my four brothers and sisters had to live separately, each one in a commune. Each day one bowl of uncooked rice was given out for twelve persons. People had to work quite hard. Unable to suffer any longer, the people rose up. The Khmer Rouge mobilized armed forces to put down the uprising, and they arrested the young people involved and killed them without a trial. Among the victims were my two brothers Chan Sokhom and Chan Sophom. It is my mother who told me about this.

I have another brother whose name is Chan Sa Pik, who was killed in August 1975. He fled with me when we were chased out of the village by the Pol Pot people. They arrested and tortured Chan Sa Pik to extract information about the political attitude of the members of my family. My brother had nothing to say, and they killed him in Ta Sanh village. The village chief, whose name was So, beat my brother in the head with a hammer. Another named Muon eviscerated him and took out his liver and spleen. Another named Nou, who was head of the Svay Raho district, hit him another hammer blow in the head.

At that time I was in the same village, and that is why I was witness to all the specific details of their crimes. Now all these criminals are undergoing a reeducation course.

One of my cousins, named Ho, contracted a fever. They gave him an injection of a medicine they themselves had prepared, not a medicine that cures a fever. My cousin protested, and that made them think that my cousin must be a medical doctor. So they pushed him in a cart and took him three kilometers from the village to kill him with a pickaxe. One of them who killed my cousin with his own hands is named Divou Leng.

After my cousin was dead, they took his clothes and wore them. They are still wearing these clothes. They now live in Ta Sanh village.

Question: Besides the crimes of the Pol Pot–Ieng Sary clique against your family and against you, are you aware of other crimes against the population?

Answer: First case: I know a person named Brit. He has one son named Ruk, who lives in Ta Sanh village. His family has nine persons. Two in his family were killed, charged with activities hostile to the regime. Two weeks later, the commune authorities gave an order to the guerrillas to arrest the seven remaining persons and kill them. When they came to arrest them, they said that these seven persons had to go to the commune to be reeducated.

When they reached a point three kilometers from the Ba Sak forest, they made them dig a ditch. Once the ditch was dug, they beat to death an elderly woman and the other persons of my family, using a wood club 80 centimeters long. They took what clothes were still usable from them and then pushed their bodies into the ditch.

Everyone in the village knows about this crime. I too was witness to this crime, and I still remember the ditch.

In the Ba Sak forest, they killed many other people, especially inhabitants of Kompong Thom province. After liberation, the revolutionary army took these assassins to reeducate them.

Second case: Phon, who was head of the medical station of Phi village, Prasath district, Preah Vihear province, killed 183 persons by giving them intravenous injections of some kind of liquid. I know this because after liberation Phon confessed his crimes to the authorities.

Third case: A man named Chlai of Rum Chek village, Chey Thom district, Preah Vihear province, was extremely cruel. A member of the Pol Pot–Ieng Sary party in Rum Chek, he directed the village's guerrilla fighters in the killing of 227 persons, which included eviscerating them and taking out their livers to eat them. His eyes were always quite red. Over the two years 1975 and 1976, he killed 227 persons. In 1977, he moved to Ta Sanh village, and there he killed twelve persons more. After liberation in January 1979, he was turned over to the revolutionary authorities and he confessed his crimes to them.

Fourth case: In Kroun Duon village, Chey Sen subdistrict, Chey Sen district, Preah Vihear province, 235 women were put together whose husbands were killed by the Pol Pot clique. They are still alive. Some have children, others do not. Their ages are from 18 to 20 years and higher. After liberation, while going to work, I passed by that village and met them.

Question: Do you recall the locations of the killings?

Answer: I could take you to the places of these crimes to show you what happened and to show concrete evidence of the horrible crimes of the Pol Pot–Ieng Sary clique.

This transcript was drawn up June 23, 1979, at 4:00 p.m. The witness read it over and acknowledged that it conforms to the testimony given above.

Secretary	*Declarant*	*Investigator*
San Nim	Chan Sary	Mien Chieu

Statements of Former Agents of Pol Pot and Ieng Sary

2.2.01
Mr. Men Khoeun

(Done May 23, 1979, at Phnom Penh prison, before Mr. Saes Chhon and Mr. Ong Makan, secretary.)

Name:	Men Khoeun
Date of birth:	1951
Place of birth:	Thmey village, Chaong Maong subdistrict, Toek Phos district, Kompong Chhnang province

"My father is Men Phom, 58 years old. He lives in Thmey village, Chaong Maong subdistrict, Toek Phos district. He was a farmer. My mother is Sok Ho, 40 years old. She worked the fields with my father. My parents have five children: Men Khen, 30 years old, who used to farm but was killed by the Lon Nol clique; Men Hoeun, 21 years old, Men Khen's sister, who died of an illness; Men Khol, 19 years old, who now works the fields with my parents; Men Kheam, 17 years old, who also works with my parents; and I. My wife is Sey Nol. She also works the fields with my parents. We have a three-year-old child named Hen Ol.

"Under the Sihanouk regime, I attended school through the tenth grade. I could read and write with difficulty. Under the Lon Nol regime, I worked the fields. Under the Pol Pot regime, I was ordered to direct groups that cultivated rice. Later on I was accused of having secret relations with a girl that I had loved before my marriage. I was arrested and sent to the security service of the subdistrict to study for three months. In 1975 and 1976, I took part in the agents' committee in Choang Maong subdistrict after confessing my wrongdoings and promising to mend my ways.

"From 1976 to 1979, I worked the fields. After the liberation on January 7, 1979, I reported myself and have been under arrest up until now. I was arrested because I took part in the murder of two thousand and five Lon Nol soldiers. Personally, I killed only five soldiers. I was arrested by the revolutionary forces to be reeducated.

"The killing of the two thousand and five soldiers was carried out upon an order of Pol Pot and Ieng Sary to celebrate the April 17, 1975, victory. After April 17, 1975, the head of Toek Phos district, who is named Meak Vy, got together fifty agents of all the subdistricts of the district. He declared that it was Pol Pot's order that all the Lon Nol soldiers are our enemies, and that we must kill them all to celebrate the victory of April 17, 1975. Those failing to comply with this order would be tried themselves. After hearing that, we had no choice but to obey. If we failed to kill, we would be killed. But I did not see Pol Pot's directive, which was issued ten days after April 17, 1975.

"These two thousand and five persons were all Lon Nol soldiers. They were garrisoned in Kompong Chhnang province. After the victory on April 17, 1975, Pol Pot ordered that all the Lon Nol soldiers be brought together at a certain place. I know only that in my subdistrict there were two thousand and five soldiers; as for other localities I do not know. I swear that all these two thousand and five persons were Lon Nol soldiers.

"I remember that these two thousand and five soldiers were put in an open air concentration camp. Formerly it had been a camp to which people came to work the fields. Four days later they were taken away to be killed.

"Fifty agents drawn from each subdistrict of Toek Phos district dug ten ditches to bury the bodies. The high command did not use civilians for fear that word would get out. The two thousand and five persons were killed in ten groups, one group each day for ten successive days. We killed them during daylight hours. Our commanders said that these soldiers were being taken away for a few days of reeducation. When we got one kilometer away from the camp, we tied them up and led them to the place of the killing, which was five kilometers from the camp. We began each session of killing at 7:00 a.m., and at 9:00 a.m. we stopped to eat. On the first day we killed fifty persons, and later on sometimes five hundred, sometimes one hundred persons per day.

"After ten days, we had killed two thousand and five soldiers and the last day we killed one hundred fifty soldiers. We led them to the ditches we had prepared to bury them in the Ko Prich wood.

"We killed each one with blows of a bamboo stick. After killing them, we pushed them into the ditches. We avoided killing them with guns to save bullets. Before doing the killing we determined the method to use: we would strike them three times on the neck. As for the uniforms on the bodies, we did not take them off, because our chief had forbidden us to wear the uniforms of the Lon Nol army.

"There were ten large ditches, each ditch five meters on a side, and two and a half meters deep. These ten ditches were then filled with dirt. Even though this wood has now become a potato field, I can show you the ten ditches if you like.

"The one who received the directive of Pol Pot was the district chief, Meak Vy. In 1977 Meak Vy himself was killed as result of being accused of aiding the enemy. Among the fifty agents who participated in this crime with me (each time each of the fifty agents killed one victim), I know only two, who were from my subdistrict: Phal and Neng. These two men were in Ta Deng village. These two men were also killed later on by Pol Pot men from other subdistricts and whose identity I do not know. I killed only five people, one each day. I did the killing for only five days, and then I stayed at home to do the cooking for the other agents.

"After I married, the high command let me live as a civilian. Now I think a great deal about the offense that I committed by order of Pol Pot, who thereby forced me to commit genocide.

"After acknowledging my past misdeeds and after gaining an understanding of the just political position of the National United Front for the Salvation of Kampuchea, I promise to respect the National United Front for the Salvation of Kampuchea."

This record was written according to the statement of accused, Men Khoeun. He has listened to it and has certified it as accurate and has signed below.

Done at Phnom Penh, May 19, 1979

Secretary	*Investigator*	*Declarant*
Ong Makan	Saes Chhon	Men Khoeun

2.2.02
Mr. Mien Sem

My name is Mien Sem, 50 years of age, born in Dey Chhnang village, Hong Sam Nam subdistrict, Tbong district, Kompong Speu province. My father (deceased) was Sok Mien. My mother (deceased) was Svay Long. My brother, Mien Suor, 54 years of age, is a farmer in Kompong Speu province. My sister is Mien Sok, 47 years of age, a farmer in Dey Chhnang village, Kompong Speu province. My wife is Chea Chan, 41 years of age, a farmer in Kompong Speu province.

I had five children, the eldest being 13 years old, and the youngest 3 years old. During the Sihanouk regime, and during the Lon Nol regime as well, I cut wood and cultivated rice in Dey Chhnang village, which is where I still live. Under the Pol Pot regime I was a member of a commune in 1974, in charge of production. In the month of November 1976 I became deputy chief of the Hong Sam Nam commune, and I did that until liberation by the National United Front for the Salvation of Kampuchea in 1979.

Under the Pol Pot regime, I was deputy chief of the commune in charge only of production. But not in charge of security. I did not commit crimes against the people.

But I did take part in the arrest of thirty persons in the commune, under pretext that they had avoided work because of laziness. This arrest was agreed upon first at a collective meeting in which six persons participated, namely, (1) Ngang, the chief of the commune; (2) Khot, secretary in charge of registration; (3) Sok, in charge of finances; (4) Phat, chief of Kraing Tava village; (5) Kem, chief of Taing Bar village; and I, deputy chief of the commune.

The thirty persons were first sent to concentration camp No. 99 at Mount Bar Seth, in Tasa village, Tasa subdistrict, Tbong district, Kompong Speu province, and then they were killed.

I can tell you that nineteen of these people were killed in 1977, and eleven in 1978. In fact I took part only in the arrest of the thirty persons.

This transcript was drawn up to conform to the statement of the named person, Mien Sem. He listened to it, certified it to be correct, and signed below.

Person charged	*Interrogator*	*Secretary*
Mien Sem	Saes Chhon	Ong Makan

2.2.03
Mr. Cheo Chin

We the undersigned, in the interrogation section of Phnom Penh prison, draw up this interrogation transcript as follows:

I am Cheo Chin, 26 years of age, born in Prek Dach village, Tahing subdistrict, Leuk Dek district, Kandal province. I was a pupil for one year at the Vat Sleng school. In 1974, I was in the people's army unit of the subdistrict. From 1975 to 1979, I was put in the defense security service of the subdistrict.

My father is Sieng Cheo, 54 years of age, a farmer in Tahing subdistrict. My mother is Chum Phan, 50 years of age, a farmer. My brothers and sisters are: Cheo Chuon, 30 years of age (male), a farmer; Cheo Huoy, 22 years of age (female), a farmer; Cheo Chea, 20 years of age (male), a farmer; Cheo Tha, 18 years of age (male), a farmer; Cheo Lan, 10 years of age (female), a farmer; Cheo Lon, 8 years of age (female), a farmer. My wife Saret is 24 years of age.

During the Pol Pot period, I worked in investigation groups from 1974 to 1975, and then I was in the security service of the subdistrict. During this time I personally killed twenty persons. That is why I was arrested by the revolutionary power that liberated the territory of Kampuchea.

This murder of twenty persons took place in 1978 by a firm order of Juoy, the Leuk Dek district security chief, at the Kantheay housing block in Prek Dach village, Kandal province.

It was easy to kill them because they were already in prison. When the security chief ordered me to eliminate them secretly along with five other families, he understood that these people were sympathetic to the Vietnamese friends, who were enemies of the Pol Pot regime.

Before killing them, I tied the victims' hands behind their backs and led them to the edge of the river, where I hit them with iron bars, and then I threw them into the river.

The distance between the prison and the place where these murders were carried out is about twenty meters. Among the twenty persons I killed I recognized some of them. The oldest was 50 years of age, there was a child eight years old, sixteen boys, four girls, and five families.

I remember still that my act of butchery was carried out at the time of the Independence Day celebration, April 17, 1978. Also, these persons had their eyes blindfolded with black cloth at the time they were killed.

During the time of the Pol Pot regime, I only killed twenty persons, and it was done under the strict order of the security chief of the district. Now I understand that I am a criminal against the people, because I served the militarist and genocidal regime of Pol Pot.

This transcript was drawn up in conformity to the statements of Cheo Chin. He listed to it, certified it as correct, and affixed his signature below.

Phnom Penh, May 29, 1979

Declarant	*Investigator*	*Secretary*
Cheo Chin	Saes Chhon	Ong Makan

2.2.04
Mr. Hem Yan

On May 29, 1979, at 8:00 a.m. in the Phnom Penh prison, the accused Hem Yan, in the presence of Mr. Saes Chhon and Mr. Ong Makan, officials of the Ministry of the Interior, made the following statement:

"I am Hem Yan, 36 years old, born in Trapeang Tung village, Soeng Preah subdistrict, Ba Phnom district, Prey Veng province. I now live at Praol Toek village, Toek Thla subdistrict, Prey Veng district, Prey Veng province. I know how to read, but I do not know how to write. I was a farmer under the regimes of Sihanouk and Lon Nol. Under the Pol Pot regime, starting from the beginning of 1978, I was named deputy chief of the Toek Thla subdistrict.

"My father, named Hem Yen, is dead. My mother, named Thy, is also dead. I have six brothers and sisters. My wife is named Srey Cheang, 37 years old, a farmer. I have four children.

"During my service in the Pol Pot regime, my superiors (district chiefs) assigned me the job of drawing up lists of persons who were to be killed. These lists included approximately six thousand persons. I had to make up these lists each week, under the pretense of having a precise number in order to get clothing and food. But in fact I did it to send the exact number of persons who were to be killed. These six thousand persons were taken away in several batches. For the first three times, twenty or thirty Pol Pot soldiers came to the village to take people to the place designated for the killing. I do not know where they took them, but I know that they killed them.

"And I know that almost all the six thousand persons were killed. I can say honestly that I never killed a person. I made the list on order of my chief named Run, the district chief. Later on I was assigned the job of assembling the entire population for deportation to Pursat. At Pursat, I stayed at O Tapav, Leach district, Pursat province, where I drew up a list of fifty persons, of whom ten were killed.

"Among the six thousand persons to be killed were my own child, and other villagers whose husband or wife had been killed.

"That is why, after the liberation of January 7, 1979, when I returned to my native village, the villagers who had seen me draw up the list and who thought that their wife and children had been killed by my superiors and me arrested me, beat me, and were ready to kill me. Among these villagers I know Mr. An, whose wife and children were killed. I express my deep thanks to the revolutionary forces that intervened and saved me from death."

This record was drawn up according to the statement of Hem Yan, who has reviewed it, certified it as accurate, and signed below.

Accused	*Interrogator*	*Secretary*
Hem Yan	Saes Chhon	Ong Makan

2.2.05

Mr. Siv Samon

Before Mr. Saes Chhon and Mr. Ong Makan, the person charged makes the following statement:

"I am Siv Samon, born in 1946 at Sampor, in Svay Ang subdistrict, Meanchey district, Svay Rieng province, the son of Mr. Siv Saing and Mrs. Tep Ley (who is deceased). I have three sisters: (1) Siv Samen, a farmer at Thmar Pon, in Angtasor subdistrict, Meanchey Thmey district, Svay Rieng province; (2) Siv Samy, a farmer at Thmar Pon, in Ang Tasor subdistrict, Meanchey Thmey district, Svay Rieng province; (3) Siv Samoeun, who is deceased.

"My wife is Sek Saphal. I have one child named Siv Sokha (a son). In February 1978, I was named security chief of Meanchey district. I served in this position until the end of the Pol Pot regime. On August 12 and 13, 1978, by order of the district chief, my seven comrades, the district chief himself, and I beat 250 persons, among whom I recognized 110 women, 80 old and young people, and 60 small children about one year old, and two other children. These people were accused of being agents of the K.G.B. or the Vietnamese, or were family members of soldiers of Lon Nol or the C.I.A. These persons were beaten to death with iron pipes and bars, after having their hands tied and their eyes blindfolded.

"A few days before we dug five large ditches, 5.7 meters long, 3 meters wide, and 2 meters deep. We buried fifty bodies in each ditch. But a few days later, this region flooded, so I think the bodies must have gotten bloated and floated away somewhere. We carried out this killing near Veal Mring village, Kauron subdistrict, Kompong Trabek district, Prey Veng province.

"After the liberation, I turned myself over to the revolutionary forces on January 9, 1979, and I have been in temporary detention until now."

This transcript was drawn up in conformity with the statements of the person charged, and it was read back to him. The person charged certifies the transcript as accurate and has signed below.

Done at Phnom Penh, May 22, 1979

Person charged	*Interrogator*	*Secretary*
Siv Samon	Saes Chhon	Ong Makan

2.2.06
Mr. Sao Soeun

On May 23, 1979, at Phnom Penh prison, in the presence of Mr. Saes Chhon, an official of the Ministry of the Interior, and Mr. Ong Makan, secretary, the accused, Sao Soeun, makes the following declaration.

My name is Sao Soeun, born in 1948 at Bos village, Svay Ta Yean subdistrict, Svay Rieng province. I was arrested on March 4, 1979, while trying to flee from Thmey village, Thmey subdistrict, Kandal Stung district, Kandal province. Arriving near the Khmer-Soviet Friendship Hospital, I was recognized by a soldier of the revolutionary forces as a soldier of Pol Pot.

At first, I lived in Bos village and was then transferred, by Pol Pot, to Thmey village. I was arrested because I had killed approximately one hundred people. I, and four other killers, worked under the direction of Prak Sambo, head of security for the district. I was an agent in the district. I was working in the rice fields when I was called to the site of the killing. The four others and I were ordered by Prak Sambo to tie the victims before killing them. Prak Sambo threatened us, saying: "If you do not kill them, I will kill you." We had to obey.

The slaughter took place in a concentration camp which held 100 people. Nearby, ditches had been dug to bury the bodies. There stood a group of guards and it was they who led out the prisoners for us to kill. The place of the massacre was 100 meters from the camp. There was a rumor that the killing would not be done with firearms, because we must not make a lot of noise. The massacre was a secret.

The one hundred victims were all men from the ages of 20 to 50 years old. They were all soldiers and students. Before killing them, we tied their arms behind their back. They were killed at 3 o'clock in the afternoon. There were three ditches: two big ones and a smaller one. The big ones were 10 meters long, 1 meter wide, and 1.5 meters deep. The smaller one was 6 meters in length. These ditches were dug in Dong Khum village, Tbong Reach subdistrict, Kompong Ro district, Svay Rieng province. We did not remove the clothes from the bodies, but the victims' belongings were taken by the head of security. Those who took part in these crimes were:

1. Prak Sambo, age 50, head of security of the district, native of Ksetr, in Kompong Ro district, Svay Rieng province. He was arrested without explanation in April 1978, by the Pol Pot-Ieng Sary clique.
2. Saran, age 27, district security deputy, native of Tlak, in Svay Ta Yean subdistrict. He was killed by a mortar shell.
3. Tom Kak, age 27, district political chief, at Kspoy Leap, in Kompong Ro district, Svay Rieng province.
4. Phan, age 37, district political deputy, in Samlei subdistrict, Kompong Ro district.

I feel remorse for what I have done.

I believe that the current political line of the Revolution will be to show clemency to me.

These minutes were done on the basis of the statements made by the accused, Sao Soeun. It has been reread to him and its correctness confirmed by him, who gives his signature below.

Accused	*Interrogator*	*Secretary*
Sao Soeun	Saes Chhon	Ong Makan

Reports of Field Investigations

Crocodile Pit

2.3.1.01
Mr. Mit Narin

This statement was recorded June 19, 1979, at 3:30 p.m., at the office of the crocodile cultivation center, in Siem Reap city, in the presence of Mr. Saes Chhon, official of the Ministry of the Interior; Mr. San Kiri, secretary responsible for recording statements; and Mr. Mit Narin. The content of the statement follows.

Question: Your name, your age and place of work, please?

Answer: I am Mit Narin, 23 years of age, from Sapien Thmey village, Siem Reap 1 subdistrict, Siem Reap district, Siem Reap province. I currently raise crocodiles in the cultivation pool of the Siem Reap zoo.

Question: How long have you done this kind of work?

Answer: Since liberation (January 1979).

Question: What does one feed crocodiles, and how many crocodiles are there in this pool?

Answer: The crocodiles are fed fish from Tonle Sap, about five tons at each feeding. The pool has three sections for the three categories of crocodiles: large, medium, and small. Just now there are 130 large ones, 160 medium-sized ones, and 600 small ones.

Question: In addition to the fish from Tonle Sap, what else do you give the crocodiles to eat?

Answer: Under the new regime, only fish. But under the Pol Pot regime, I saw with my own eyes that they gave the crocodiles human flesh to eat.

Question: Can you speak about that in detail?

Answer: It was in June 1976. Our shock youth team was building roads and bridges in one section of the zoo. We were authorized to visit the cultivation pool only twice, under the supervision of our team chief, each time for fifteen minutes.

One day, about 6:30 p.m., after work, two friends and I got permission to go swim in a pond one hundred meters away from the pool. From there I saw a GMC truck drive up to the edge of the pool. Four soldiers jumped out. After looking around to make sure no one was there, they made a young man about 20 years of age, with his hands tied behind him, get out of the truck. The young man cried "Help." The Pol Pot agents immediately hit him to shut him up, then they pushed him toward the pool and threw him in. They stayed there fifteen minutes looking into the pool before they left. Ten days after this incident, our team was transferred to a different location. As for my two friends who were with me that day, I have not seen them for several years.

Question: How could you see this incident since it took place in the evening?

Answer: At night that section of the zoo and the pool were lit by electric lights, and that allowed us to see clearly from outside.

Completed, read back, confirmed, and signed by Mit Narin.

Witness	*Official*	*Secretary*
Mit Narin	Saes Chhon	San Kiri

2.3.1.02
Mr. Sim Phia

This evidence was recorded on June 19, 1979, at 2:00 p.m., at the crocodile breeding center in Siem Reap city by Saes Chhon, official of the Ministry of the Interior, and San Kiri, clerk in charge of recording evidence.

Question: Your name, age, and place of work, please.

Answer: I am Sim Phia, 23 years old, a native of Wat Po village, Siem Reap 1 subdistrict, Siem Reap province. At present, I am an employee at the crocodile breeding center in Siem Reap city.

Question: How long have you been working in this center?

Answer: I was recruited by the revolutionary power after the liberation (January 1979).

Question: Do you know when the center was built, and do you know anyone who worked there under the former regime?

Answer: The center was built by the Pol Pot clique early in 1976. All its former employees, I was told, have been clubbed to death.

Question: Do you know the reason why?

Answer: The employees, so I was told, were killed because they knew that the Pol Pot clique fed human flesh to the crocodiles. So after working there for a time, the employees would be killed and replaced by others.

Question: Do you believe that human flesh was fed to the crocodiles?

Answer: Twice I saw human beings thrown into the crocodile pool with my own eyes.

Question: When and how did that happen?

Answer: After the seizure of power by the Pol Pot clique, my family was compelled to go and settle in Pho Ri Dum Ray village, Loot subdistrict, Siem Reap district, while I myself was forced to enlist in the shock youth forces. In February 1977, one team was sent to the fifth sector of Siem Reap province to build roads and bridges. The crocodile breeding center is near the site where we were working, but we were not allowed to go there (it was only opened to Chinese, Romanians, and Koreans). Once, however, one team leader brought us to the pool to see the crocodiles. At that time, Mr. Thanh (who was killed later on) looked after the beasts.

One day in July 1977, at 9:00 a.m., as our brigade was working, two GMC military vehicles came up. Some soldiers alighted and drove us to a point some distance from the crocodile breeding center, a point that was 500 meters beyond the river. I was intrigued that we were not chased away when the trucks brought fish for the crocodiles. Therefore, I asked permission to go bathing in order to return to the river. Hidden behind a coconut tree, I saw the soldiers take nine children from 10 to 13 years of age out of the trucks. The children's arms were tied. The soldiers pulled them up to the bridge over the pool. No matter how much they cried and shouted for help, they were thrown into the pool as prey to the crocodiles. The soldiers stayed there for a while before withdrawing. I was very upset but did not dare tell anyone for fear of being killed. Nobody may have known about this, because the Pol Pot clique had forced the inhabitants out of the town.

Again, one day in August 1977, at 9:00 a.m., a military vehicle came and the soldiers drove us far from our work site. This time, I told my friend Som to go back to the river under the pretense of catching fish. There we saw the soldiers push out of the truck ten children from 8 to 10 years of age, half naked and with their arms tied. The children cried, but they were beaten and brought onto the bridge, then thrown into the pool. That night, acting on information they had gotten from someone, the Pol Pot soldiers rushed into our team and took away Som and Sa Ruon, a native of Tuc Quyn village. They arrested Sa Ruon by mistake instead of me.

Question: Did you see this a third time?

Answer: No. Our team worked in that sector until November 1977, when it was transferred to Pho Ri Dum Ray, then to Kra Lanh.

Question: Have you anything more to say?

Answer: After the liberation of Siem Reap on January 18, 1979, I was given a job at this crocodile breeding center. On January 19, 1979, as we were cleaning the pool to change the water, we found human bones on its bottom. I picked up nine ribs, including two that were broken, and three dorsal vertebrae. I threw them onto the bank, and later Mr. Ul Sem threw them onto a heap of garbage to be burned.

Question: Do you vouch for the truth of your statement?

Answer: I give my word for what I have said and I bear full responsibility for it.

Finished at 3:00 p.m., read back, confirmed, and signed by Mr. Sim Phia.

Witness	*Officer*	*Clerk*
Sim Phia	Saes Chhon	San Kiri

2.3.1.03
Mr. Ul Sem

The following statement was taken on June 19, 1979, at 7:00 p.m. at the office of the Seam Reap Crocodile Breeding Farm in the presence of Mr. Saes Chhon, an official of the Ministry of the Interior, Mr. San Kiri, a clerk charged with taking down the statement, and Mr. Ul Sem, the witness. Here are the contents.

Question: Your name, age, and place of work, please?

Answer: My name is Ul Sem, 25 years old, now working at the Siem Reap Crocodile Breeding Farm.

Question: How long have you been working there?

Answer: On January 14, 1979, that was immediately after the liberation of Siem Reap, I was appointed to the center to feed the crocodiles who were then starving. I still work there.

Question: Why were they left without care?

Answer: Owing to the hostilities, the Pol Pot agents only thought to escape for dear life, but in the past it was reported that they fed the crocodiles, sometimes with human flesh.

Question: Have you seen that with your own eyes?

Answer: No. Before the liberation I did not work there. However, on January 19, 1979, while cleaning the center, I found a score of human bones at the bottom of the breeding basin. I burned them and threw them into the river.

Question: Are you sure they were human bones?

Answer: Yes, I am. There were radials, cubitus, and ribs. They couldn't be animal bones. Moreover, about two months ago, a revolutionary soldier named Cheap Kim Heng, 23 years old, came to the center to look at the crocodiles. Seeing that I was involved in crocodile breeding, he told me that in 1976 he worked in the shock youth building local roads and culverts. Once, he saw Khmer Rouge people throw a girl with arms tied, to the crocodiles. He has written all that on a sheet of paper that I still keep with me. If you need it, here it is.

(Thereupon Mr. Ul Sem handed over to us Cheap Kim Heng's note. We requested him to confirm it by notation on the other side of the paper which the representative of the administration countersigned.)

Question: Do you know anything more?

Answer: I have not seen it with my own eyes, but I found human bones at the bottom of the rearing basin and heard Heng's story about it. Recently, two newly appointed workers, Mr. Sim Phia and Mr. Mit Narin, also said they had seen Pol Pot soldiers throw arrested people to the crocodiles. That's all.

Completed at 8:00 p.m., read through, confirmed, and signed by Mr. Ul Sem.

Witness	*Official*	*Clerk*
Mr. Ul Sem	Mr. Saes Chhon	Mr. San Kiri

Crematories in Siem Reap Province

2.3.2.01

Mr. Kung Sary

This statement was recorded on June 23, 1979, at 7:00 a.m. at the office of the People's Committee of Chon Buon Cau subdistrict, Kra Lanh district, Siem Reap province, in the presence of Mr. Saes Chhon, official of the Ministry of the Interior, Mr. Ouk Chandara, clerk in charge of recording statements, and Mr. Kung Sary, the witness. The following is the content of the statement.

Question: Your name, age, native place, and profession, please.

Answer: I am Kung Sary, 25 years old, native of Dong Treng village, Chon Buon Cau subdistrict, Kra Lanh district, Siem Reap province. Under the Sihanouk and Lon Nol regimes, I completed the sixth grade before leaving school. At present, I farm the land and participate in the communal militia. My wife is Chun So Phi, 22 years old. She also farms the land in her village. We do not yet have children.

Question: What did you do and where did you live under the Pol Pot regime?

Answer: I farmed the land in So Soan Rieng cooperative, On Sung village, Tri Chum subdistrict, Kra Lanh district. In 1976, I enlisted in the shock youth forces and farmed the land in the same cooperative.

Question: Under the Pol Pot regime, were you aware of crimes committed by this clique against the people?

Answer: Under the Pol Pot regime, my family suffered arrests and massacres like the entire Kampuchean people.

Question: Give us some particulars.

Answer: On July 6, 1978, we were at home when Pol Pot agents came and arrested my parents, my wife's parents, my younger brothers, sisters, and me. They then sent us to prison in Dong Treng village.

Question: How many people were arrested and for what reason?

Answer: There were nine in our family who were arrested: my parents and my wife's parents, my two younger brothers, my wife's two younger sisters, and I.

At the time of the arrest they gave no reason. But when they sent us to prison they said that we were indolent and lazy. Then, they tied our arms and took away eight members of my family to kill them and then buried them in a grave dug in Dong Treng village, Chon Buon Cau subdistrict, Kra Lanh district.

Question: How did they kill them?

Answer: They proceeded in two batches. On July 8, they took away five persons and the next day three. The victims had their arms tied, they were beaten, and led away by five soldiers armed with three rifles. Twenty minutes or half an hour later, the soldiers came back to the prison.

Question: How do you know that they killed and burned the victims in the grave at Dong Treng?

Answer: I know that because in both circumstances the Pol Pot agents came back with the still presentable clothes they took from my family members and shared them between their living quarters three meters in front of my detention place. Moreover, before my detention in 1976, while I was still working in the cooperative, village people told me that the Pol Pot agents had dug graves to burn the people they killed and make of them fertilizer for the fields. That immediately suggested to me that my eight relatives were killed and burned there.

Question: How long were you detained and do you know whether others were taken away and killed during this period?

Answer: I was incarcerated on July 6, 1978, and released on July 11, 1978. On July 10, four days after my arrest, I saw Pol Pot agents taking away 15 people imprisoned before me. They were tied by their arms, bound to each other and led off by three armed soldiers. Half an hour later, the soldiers came back to the prison with good clothes to share between them.

Question: Do you know how many men and women were among these people?

Answer: I remember that there were 10 men and 5 women. Two of the men were about 50 years old. There were no children.

Question: During your detention, were you ever outside the prison?

Answer: I was incarcerated for six days, with shackles during the first three days. From July 5 to 11, 1978. Thirty detainees including me were sent to mend a fence near the crematories.

Question: How far between the fence and the crematories?

Answer: This distance is five meters. I do not know how many graves there are in this region but I have seen two. One of them, to the left of the main path, was unearthed because on July 9, 1978, I saw four men squatting among the human bones.

On July 10, 1978 while I was mending the fence, I saw two trucks bringing 60 people. They were clubbed to death and hurled into the grave, from which came a fire of paddy husk fueled with oil. Then paddy husk and oil were again poured in to finish off the cremation.

Question: Do you remember the site of these graves?

Answer: Yes. I am ready to show them to you if you like.

Question: In what circumstances were you released?

Answer: I was arrested with my family, but I am the only one to be released because Dut, the head of the cooperative, as he told me, asked his superiors not to kill me since I was young and very hard-working. Thus, in the afternoon of July 11, 1978, I was released after being warned to work hard on pain of death.

Question: Do you have anything more to say?

Answer: No.

Question: Can you vouch for the truth of what you have said?

Answer: I pledge my word for what I have said and I bear full responsibility for it before the law.

Finished at 10:00 a.m., read over, confirmed and signed by Mr. Kung Sary.

Witness	*Officer*	*Clerk*
Kung Sary	Saes Chhon	Ouk Chandara

2.3.2.02

Mrs. Mun Ny

This evidence was recorded on June 22, 1979, at 9:30 a.m. at the office of the revolutionary people's committee of Kompong Thkau subdistrict in the presence of Mr. Saes Chhon, official of the Ministry of the Interior, Mr. San Kiri, clerk in charge of recording evidence, and Mrs. Mun Ny, witness. Here follow the contents.

Question: Your name, age, and place of work, please.

Answer: I am Mun Ny, 30 years old. I farm in Phnom village, Kompong Thkau subdistrict, Kra Lanh district, Siem Reap province.

Question: What did you do and where did you live under the Pol Pot regime?

Answer: After April 17, 1975, when the Pol Pot clique seized power, my husband, our two children, and I were compelled to settle in Sapien Sary village, Takhmau subdistrict, in the same district to farm the land in the shock forces, while my parents were displaced to another location. In late 1976, we were arrested for no reason and imprisoned in Phnom village. My husband was then taken away and killed. As for me, I had to do hard labor in the prison until the liberation (January 1979). One of my children was taken by a recurrent fever for lack of medicine.

Question: Give us some particulars about this prison, please.

Answer: Before 1975 there was no prison in this village. Once in power, the Pol Pot clique moved the inhabitants out of three houses at the foot of a hill and turned the three houses into a place of detention. Ten people came from other communes to staff it, including Nhan, who was chief of the prison, Pail and Nhoi, who were the two deputy chiefs, and Puol, At, Cay, Choof, May, Nuon, and Vuoi, who were torturers and guards.

The torturers occupied one of the three houses as a residence and place of torture, using another to detain men and the third to detain women and children. They brought in prisoners from other villages in the district, by carts and sometimes by military vehicles, one or two and even four or five times a day. They would take them to the foot of a hill where they would club them and throw them in a hole. Then they would cremate their corpses with paddy husks and kerosene and use the ashes as fertilizer.

It should be noted that the prisoners were tied up in groups on the way to the killing site.

Only women and children were spared hard labor.

Question: Tell us in detail about these cremation sites, please.

Answer: They were only 200 meters from here. We were forbidden to go there and they could not be seen because trees screened them at both ends of the entrance. Every day, as we went to work, we would see white smoke rising up and could smell human flesh.

Question: Did you ever happen to see with your own eyes what you have just told us?

Answer: I did not see them club and throw people into the graves and burn them with paddy husks and kerosene, but I heard the butchers talk about their acts. It is only after the liberation (January 1979) that I have been able to reach this place and have found many graves in which there have remained ashes and even human skeletons. On the edges of these graves, piles of ground bones are still lying.

Question: Do you know who did the grinding and packing of this fertilizer?

Answer: I heard the torturers say that the prisoners were compelled to do the work and that these prisoners were killed after that.

Question: Do you know how many people were brought to the prison and were burned up to make fertilizer during the period from your detention to your release?

Answer: The day I arrived at the prison, there were about thirty men, five women, and ten children with me. After that, every day there were newcomers and some departed, so that I could not reckon. I was told that somebody found in the prison a notebook left by the Pol Pot agents recording as many as 8,600 prisoners. I did not see the notebook, and I do not know who keeps it.

Question: Were there many survivors after the liberation day? Do you know any of them?

Answer: I do not know the number of men, but I know there were 30 women and 10 children: Mrs. De from Kendool village, Mrs. Nhat and Mrs. Mau from Samrong village, which is also called Chum village, Mrs. Hiep from Ta An village, Mr. Dut Thi from Cuc Don village, Mrs. Che Van Thon from Kompong Thkau village, and the two children Son and Set, from Phoc district.

Question: Do you know anything else?

Answer: Every day we were compelled to hard labor. Often we heard things when the butchers were speaking among themselves. I have had a nervous breakdown, so I cannot recall everything now. Later on, when my memory comes back, I will tell you more.

Question: Do you guarantee that all you have said is true?

Answer: I give you my word. The graves are still there and many inhabitants nearby are aware of it. I bear full responsibility before the authorities.

Completed, confirmed, and signed by Mrs. Mun Ny.

Witness	*Official*	*Clerk*
Mun Ny	Saes Chhon	San Kiri

2.3.2.03
Mrs. Che Van Thon

The following testimony was recorded on June 22, 1979, at 2:00 p.m. at the office of the People's Committee of Kompong Thkau subdistrict, Kra Lanh district, Siem Reap province, in the presence of Mr. Saes Chhon, official of the Ministry of Interior, Mr. Ouk Chandara, clerk in charge of recording evidence, and Mrs. Che Van Thon, witness.

Question: Your name, age, occupation, and native place, please.

Answer: I am Che Van Thon, 25 years old, a farmer in Kompong Thkau village, Kompong Thkau subdistrict, Kra Lanh district, Siem Reap province.

Question: What did you do and where did you live under the Pol Pot regime?

Answer: After they arrived in our village, the Khmer Rouge forced my family to go and live in Kanso village, Sam Bo subdistrict, Kra Lanh district, and to till land in the shock team of that village. On May 5, 1978, under the pretext of displacing several families to other villages, they gathered nine families comprising 18 adults (9 men and 9 women) and 15 children, whom they carried in carts to a camp in Phnom village, Kompong Thkau subdistrict. There, all the victims were tied to house pillars, tortured with sticks, and falsely accused of being CIA agents before being executed. I was beaten all that day, tied to a pillar for two days, and then sent to do hard labor at the camp until liberation. My husband was executed by Pol Pot agents.

Question: What kind of hard labor were you forced to do?

Answer: We women were forced into groups of 10 to go every day, under our hangmen's orders, to clear virgin land, grow cotton and vegetables, and gather firewood for them.

Question: What did you see and hear when you were being detained at the camp and forced to do hard labor?

Answer: At the camp I saw such hangmen as Nhoi, Puol, At, Choof, May, Nuon, and Nuoi beat and torture many people with big sticks. Pol Pot agents led their victims to a crematory, knocked them on the skull, threw their corpses into pits, poured rice husks and kerosene on them before setting fire to char the bones and turn them into fertilizer. Sometimes when I would be working nearby, I would see white smoke rising and smell the odor of burned human flesh.

Every day, one or two, sometimes four or six cart loads of people were brought to the camp, and all of them were killed and burned up.

Question: Did you ever work near the crematory?

Answer: No, access to it was forbidden to us. It was screened by trees at both ends and surrounded by three rings of barbed wire. Those who came and picked up the charred bones which they ground into powder fertilizer were common law prisoners who were also executed and burned to ashes after having done their jobs.

Question: How is it that do you know all the workers' names?

Answer: While leading us to hard labor they inquired about us, and so did we. Thus we know their names and native places.

Question: What else do you know?

Answer: That is all I know.

Question: Were there many people executed and burned up?

Answer: I don't know exactly because they were so many. Every day there were victims, so I cannot remember their number. People say since liberation that 8,000 to 9,000 people were burned in this crematory.

Question: Can you vouch for what you said?

Answer: I give you my word. The four or five crematories are still there, not to mention the charred bones waiting to be picked up. I can show them to you and I bear full responsibility for what I have said to the authorities.

Official	*Clerk*	*Witness*
Saes Chhon	Ouk Chandara	Che Van Thon

2.3.2.04
Crematories in Kra Lanh District

Today, June 24, 1979, at 9:00 a.m., we, Saes Chhon, official of the Ministry of the Interior, and San Nim, secretary, having learned from the local administration that the people of Kra Lanh district, Siem Reap province, discovered crematories left by the Pol Pot–Ieng Sary clique in the district, have conducted a field investigation, together with three witnesses: (1) Mr. Kung Sary, (2) Mrs. Che Van Thon, (3)[1]

Present at the investigation were (1) Mr. Mien Chieu, representative of the provincial authorities, (2) Mr.,[2] chief of the Kompong Thkau subdistrict, as a representative of the local administration, (3) Mr. Che Som, (4) Mr. Do Lung. Here follow the results of the investigation, with film and photographs as supporting material.

I. General View of the Sites

The site of the ditches containing numerous partially burned human bones is located in Kompong Thkau village, Kompong Thkau subdistrict, Kra Lanh district, Siem Reap province. It is 57 kilometers northwest of Siem Reap city. Specifically, we left Siem Reap city and followed National Route 6 toward Sisophon-Battambang. At the intersection of National Route 6 and Interprovince Route 68 that connects Kra Lanh to Oddar Meanchey province (54 kilometers from Siem Reap city), we turned right and followed Route 68 for 1.8 kilometers, and then we took a path to the left for 600 meters and that brought us to the site of the ditches.

The site begins with three wooden houses with tile roofs on both sides of the path, at a distance two kilometers from the intersection of National Route 6 and Route 68. The site is bordered on the far side where the path reaches the foot of Mount Trong Bak, 3.2 kilometers from the intersection of National Route 6 and Route 68. The perimeter of the investigation site is 1.57 kilometers in circumference at the foot of the mountain with ten locations at which the investigation was carried out, including eight ditches, one pond, and one well.

II. Specifics About the Sites

The three houses on the two sides of the path leading to the foot of Mount Trong Bak are located 2.2 kilometers from National Route 6, and 200 meters from the site of the ditches. These are one-story houses with tile roofs: one large house and one small house 50 meters to the right of the path, and one small house 30 meters to the left of the path.

Continuing 100 meters along the path, we found a small ditch and a broken wooden post along the path. The remains of a similar railing are found on the far side of the site.

The eight ditches, ponds, and wells that make up the main part of the site

1. The name following number 3 was omitted.—Eds.
2. The name following number 2 was omitted.—Eds.

have been moved because the people and the local authorities are building a "Monument of Hatred Against the Crimes of Genocide" in the middle of the site. According to the witnesses, and to people who work there, they buried piles of partially burned human bones and filled many ditches to ease their excruciating suffering and to ensure conditions of good hygiene for those building the monument.

1. *First ditch:* 7 meters to the left of the path that leads to the foot of the mountain, 500 meters west of Route 68, 60 meters south of the foot of the mountain. This ditch is 3 meters wide, 5 or 6 meters long, and 1.7 to 0.7 meters deep. The bottom of the ditch is already returned to red dirt, letting one see only a few ashes. The walls are partially blackened from smoke. On the edge of the ditch ashes are scattered about, and partially burned bone fragments, and piles of husks of yellow paddy rice.

2. *Second ditch:* 4 meters to the left of the path, 15 meters north of the first ditch, 45 meters south of the foot of the mountain. This ditch is 9 meters wide, 14.5 meters long, and 1 to 1.5 meters deep. West of this ditch, a channel stone 1 meter on a side and 0.5 meters deep leads to the foot of the mountain. At the bottom of this ditch, on the west side (the side toward the path) there is a large heap of ashes with many bone fragments more or less black, and half burned.

Numerous clumps of ashes of bright black show that they come from burned paddy rice husks. A few strokes of a hoe uncover a thick layer of ashes with bone fragments and black, burnt skulls.

At the bottom of the ditch, on the west side, we found under the ground many fragments of white bones not turned black, and fragments of grayish bones half burned, as well as fragments of black and red bones that were not burned. There are nine skulls, half of them not burned.

On the edge of the ditch (the side toward the path), there is a pile of ashes of the husks of paddy rice with partially burned human bones. The pile is three meters wide and 8.5 meters long. At the top there are three fragments of blackened burned skulls, and 13 skull fragments not burned. The volume of this pile is about 3 cubic meters.

To the left is another pile of grayish, partially burned bone fragments without ashes of paddy rice husks. One can readily recognize many joints and dorsal vertebrae fragments, and side vertebrae. The volume of this pile is about 0.5 cubic meters.

On the pile we found two metal screens with the screening broken, rusty, and covered in ashes. The dimensions of the screen are 30 by 40 centimeters. To the right of the pile there are several pieces of cloth, dirty with earth, obviously from used clothing.

As well on the edge of the ditch, on the side toward the path, but to the left, there is a pile of unburned paddy rice husks scattered as far as the pile of partially burned bone fragments and to the pile of ashes on the side. The volume of this pile of paddy rice husks is about 1.5 cubic meters.

3. Third ditch: 7 meters from the second ditch. This ditch is 3 meters by 3 meters on a side, and 1 meter deep. There is no particular indication in this ditch.

4. Fourth ditch: 200 meters to the left of the path, as one passes by the site of the hate monument, and 30 meters farther to the left heading southwest. This ditch is 2.4 meters wide, 3 meters long, and 1 meter deep. One meter southeast of this ditch, there is a channel stone 18 meters long, 1 meter wide, and 0.5 meters deep. At the bottom of the ditch, already covered with red earth, there are a few ashes mixed with the dirt.

The wall of this ditch on the southeast side is blackened with smoke, from top to bottom, with several parts already hardened and rather smooth, as well as indentations also blacked with smoke. On the edge of this ditch, on the eastern side, there is a pile of grayish, half burned, bone fragments, without any husks of paddy rice. The volume of this pile is about 0.3 cubic meters.

5. Fifth ditch: 2 meters to the northwest of the fourth ditch, this ditch is 3.2 meters wide, 9.3 meters long, and 1.2 to 1.6 meters deep. One meter to the west of the ditch there is a channel stone already covered with earth. At the bottom of the ditch are many ashes, with, notably, some very black clumps sticking out of husks of paddy rice crowded together. The walls of this ditch on the western side and the northern side are blackened from smoke and hardened, with smoke-blackened cracks.

At 1.5 meters north-northwest of the ditch is a pile of grayish, partially burned bone fragments with no ashes of paddy rice husks. One can readily recognize fragments of dorsal vertebrae and side vertebrae. The volume of this pile is about 0.5 cubic meters. Near this pile, on the eastern side, near the ditch, there is also a pile of partially burned ashes some blackened, and some yellowish, obviously from the unburned husks of paddy rice.

6. Sixth ditch: 2.5 meters west of the sixth ditch near the pile of bone fragments on the edge of the fifth ditch, there is a ditch 2.5 meters wide, 3 meters long, and 0.5 meters deep. Its bottom and walls have no particular indication.

7. Seventh ditch: 200 meters from the path, on the northwest side, at just over 50 meters from the three last-mentioned ditches, on the north-northwest side (walking from the three ditches to the foot of the mountain), this ditch is 2 meters wide, 3 meters long, and 0.6 meters deep. At 1 meter from the ditch, on the western side, there is a channel stone 1.5 meters long already grown over. The walls of the ditch are covered in partially burned wood planks on all four sides. They are still there. On the bottom already covered with dirt there are many ashes.

8. Eighth ditch: 4 meters from the path and opposite the second ditch at 40 meters from the foot of the mountain on the southern side, this ditch is 3 meters by 3 meters, and 0.9 meters deep, with its walls caving in. In the bottom of the ditch, on the side toward the path, there are many ashes mixed with dirt. On the edge of the ditch there are many piles of husks of yellow paddy rice.

9. Earthen well: 13 meters to the left of the path, 15 meters from the eighth ditch, on the eastern side. The opening of the well is covered with square wood planks 1.2 meters on a side. The well is 9 meters deep, the water is briny, and one sees nothing in particular down in it.

10. Large pond: 3 meters east from the eighth ditch, and 30 meters from the foot of the mountain, there is a dry pond. The pond is dug out well: 11 meters wide by 31 meters long, and 2.5 meters deep (3.5 meters counting the embankment. There is nothing in particular to note about its bottom and mouth. From the statements of the chief of the subdistrict and from the witnesses, it appears that used clothing has been piled up on the edges of the ditches and gathered in one spot, along with skulls that are not burned. Before beating their victims to death, the Pol Pot agents took all their clothing and chose the best items, leaving older items behind.

Significantly, in particular, the commune chief told us that after liberation, someone from Kompong Thkau village found a notebook near the three houses with pages torn out containing the names of the persons killed. Many persons in the village and in Kompong Thkau subdistrict read the notebook, which contained names of 600 persons who were arrested and were set on fire. At present, the notebook is lost.

Many people said that the earthen well used to be 20 meters deep and that it formerly was dry. After liberation, they saw many human bones in the well. The large pond was dug for a mass killing.

The field investigation was completed at 4:00 p.m. on June 24, 1979. This transcript has been read back, confirmed, and signed by the undersigned.

Certifiers	*Witnesses*	*Investigators*
Mien Chieu	Kung Sary	Saes Chhon, official
Chief of Kompong Thkau subdistrict	Che Van Thon	San Nim, secretary
Do Lung		

2.3.2.05

Report on the Collection of Human Bones in Pits, Trenches, and Cremation Sites, Kompong Thkau Subdistrict, Kra Lanh District, Siem Reap Province

Today, June 29, 1979, at 11:00 a.m., at the office of the people's committee of Kompong Thkau subdistrict, Kra Lanh district, Siem Reap province, we, Saes Chhon, official of the Ministry of the Interior, and San Kiri, secretary, drew up this report on the basis of statements made by witnesses Mun Ny, Che Van Thon, and Kung Sary.

We were taken by all the witnesses to the location of the pits where the Pol

Pot–Ieng Sary clique burned the bodies of their victims to make fertilizer. There we conducted examinations. We took film and photographs of the items of evidence that are attached to this report.

Having composed these documents in the field, we collected a quantity of burned bones that we piled up near the cremation sites to use as evidence. The collection consists of one fragment of a skull bone, one piece of a foot bone, one piece of an arm bone, one piece of a rib, two pieces of back bone, and a pile of ashes.

Present at the said collection were the chairman of Kompong Thkau subdistrict and the other witnesses.

Secretary	*Subdistrict Chair*	*Witnesses*	*Official*
San Kiri	Pan Rop	Kung Sary Che Van Thon Mun Ny	Saes Chhon

Common Graves in Siem Reap Province

2.3.3.01
Mrs. Nuon Thok

This statement was recorded June 17, 1979, at 8:00 a.m., at the office of the People's Committee of Siem Reap province in the presence of Saes Chhon, an official of the Ministry of the Interior, San Kiri, secretary responsible for recording, and Mrs. Nuon Thok, witness.

Question: Your name, age, and present domicile, please.

Answer: I am Nuon Thok, 26 years old, from Chet Sat village Kra Lanh subdistrict, Kra Lanh district, Siem Reap province. I am currently a tailor at the military headquarters of Siem Reap province.

Question: Under the Pol Pot–Ieng Sary regime, what did you do and where did you live?

Answer: At the age of 18, in 1971, I volunteered to join the Khmer Rouge armed forces (July 6, 1971), and I was assigned the job of mobilizing the masses in the liberated area of Siem Reap province. In 1974, I was transferred to the headquarters of the military command of Banteay Srey district. After the liberation (April 1975), I was transferred to the tailors' cooperative of the district. In November 1975, when shock brigades of young people were set up, I was appointed chief of a brigade of three hundred girls in the district.

In June 1977, I was pressed to marry an officer of the district military command, but I refused. Another time, we were lined up opposite a group of war invalids, and I was pressed to take a crippled man with no legs as my husband. For disobeying orders of the authorities, I was detained in the Siem Reap prison until my release in January 1978.

Question: How were you treated in prison, you and the other prisoners?

Answer: Quite cruelly. As for myself, I fainted three times under the blows of bamboo sticks and iron rods during the interrogation. Another time, they tore off my clothes, trying to rape me. We were exhausted as a result of forced labor, hunger, and illness. Many of us were tortured and raped to death while others died of hunger, not to mention those who were taken away and never returned.

Question: How do you know all that?

Answer: I worked in a group of vegetable gardeners, and from time to time I was assigned to take soup to the other prisoners. That is how I could move about within the prison compound. Many times I went by the torture room. Prisoners who died of torture or hunger were buried behind a pagoda in the prison compound. I can show you dozens of common graves in the prison. Sometimes we were forced to dig up human bones and to grind them with urine to make manure for the fields.

Once, when our team was cutting grass two kilometers from the prison, we smelled a horrible odor coming from a one hundred meter long trench filled with dirt. At that location there were still four or five pits where you could see human bones, and a well full of bodies. I can take you there. The dead were prisoners from our prison, who had been taken there to be killed, a fact I heard from the mouths of the butchers themselves.

Question: Do you remember the location of these pits, and can you show them to us?

Answer: I remember them well, and I can show you them, as well as the trenches, and some wells where there were bodies and human bones.

Question: Can you stand behind what you have said? Are there other prisoners from the Siem Reap prison who are aware of these matters and who are still alive?

Answer: I stand behind what I have said, and I take full responsibility before the investigative agencies. Mr. Thi, who now works in the provincial military headquarters can confirm it.

Completed at 11:00 a.m., read, confirmed, and signed by Mrs Nuon Thok.

Witness	*Official*	*Clerk*
Nuon Thok	Saes Chhon	San Kiri

2.3.3.02
Mr. Chum Rithy

This statement was recorded June 17, 1979, at 2:00 p.m., at the office of the provincial authorities of Siem Reap province, in the presence of Mr. Saes

Chhon, official of the Ministry of the Interior, Mr. San Kiri, secretary responsible for recording witness statements, and Mr. Chum Rithy, the witness. The content of the statement follows.

Question: Your name, age, and present domicile, please?

Answer: I am Chum Rithy, 25 years old. I am from Roka Koy subdistrict, Kang Meas district, Kompong Cham province. I am now serving in the 30th battalion of the 3d division, in Siem Reap province.

Question: What did you do before, and where?

Answer: My profession is repairing Hondas. Since 1974 I have been at Siem Reap. After April 17, 1975, I was forced by the Pol Pot agents to leave Siem Reap city and to live in Khnat village, Siem Reap district. There I worked the land in a youth shock team until early December 1977, when I was arrested for unexplained reasons and thrown into the Siem Reap provincial prison. I was tortured three times; once they poured boiling water on my body, which left scars that I still have on my arms.

About three months later, since they knew I was only a Honda repair person, they put me in a different room with six other mechanics who were under arrest. Every day they had us repair and clean Hondas and automobiles and left us to move freely within the confines of the prison.

Question: Where is that prison?

Answer: The prison is in the city quite close to the Thoamayutt pagoda that the Pol Pot agents occupied and turned into a place for torture, for killing, and for making fertilizer.

Question: How were the prisoners treated?

Answer: During the time I was repairing cars in the prison, I saw with my own eyes how many prisoners died of hunger or as a result of torture. They were often thrown by the dozen into ditches dug behind the pagoda. There were several dozen ditches.

Every week, or every four or five days, three or four GMC military vehicles brought in prisoners from who knows where and took others away to an undisclosed location.

Before taking prisoners away, the prison authorities prepared knives, hammers, and iron bars. Those who were to depart had their jackets taken off, and they were tied up and pushed in a group of fifty into each vehicle. When I would clean the vehicles after their return, I would see that the instruments were stained with blood. Also, we had to wash the jackets of the disappeared prisoners before they were distributed to others. This shows that the unfortunate prisoners had been killed. The authorities, moreover, bragged about it. One of them boasted of having taken a liver out of his victims.

Question: Do you know where they killed the prisoners?

Answer: I did not know when I was in prison. After liberation (1979), I asked to enlist in the provincial armed forces. One day when our unit was looking for firewood in the jungle on Route 6 that leads to Angkor Wat, at about three kilometers form the prison, I found five or six wells in which there were many human bones, and that confirmed that the Pol Pot agents killed the prisoners there.

Question: Do you remember where these wells are located?

Answer: I can take you to the ditches in which prisoners are buried at the Thoamayutt pagoda that was part of the Siem Reap prison, and to the wells three kilometers from there.

Question: Do you vouch for what you have said in this statement?

Answer: I give you my word. I take complete responsibility before the law for what I have said.

Completed at 7:00 p.m., read back, confirmed, and signed by the witness.

Witness	*Official*	*Secretary*
Chum Rithy	Saes Chhon	San Kiri

2.3.3.03

Field Investigation in Siem Reap 1 Subdistrict

On June 18, 1979, at 8:00 a.m. we, Mr. Saes Chhon, an official of the Ministry of the Interior Mr. Sang Nim, clerk, Mr. Nuon Thok, the first witness, and Mr. Suon Marak Thi, the second witness, have visited the places to make an investigation into the evidence of killing perpetrated by the Pol Pot–Ieng Sary agents against our fellow countrymen under their regime.

The following were present during the investigation: Mr. Bu Sa Ruong and Mr. Mien Chieu, both representing the Siem Reap provincial authorities; Mr. Dut Pron, head of Siem Reap 1 subdistrict, Mrs. Dinh Sa Rom, Mr. Dot Suon, Mrs. Khak Ay, and Mrs. Kong Rinh, all four representing the authorities of Siem Reap 1 subdistrict; Mr. Muong Suot, representing Shakou Say village, Siem Reap 1 subdistrict; and Mr. Ing Som, representing the authorities of Ta Phuot village, Siem Reap 1 subdistrict. Here is the result of the investigation (with film and photos attached).[1]

A. General View of the Site

The site is part of Siem Reap 1 subdistrict, Siem Reap district, Siem Reap province, northeast of Siem Reap town, along National Route 6 connecting Siem Reap to Angkor Wat.

The site starts with the Siem Reap provincial prison and the Thoamayutt pagoda, about 500 meters northeast of the town on the left of the road to Angkor Wat and on the right of National Route 6 as it goes from Siem Reap to Sisophon and Battambang.

1. This material is not available. — Eds.

The site ends in the vicinity of milestone No. 3 on the road to Angkor Wat (from Siem Reap town). The site has a perimeter of nearly 2 kilometers. The investigations were made in three places: (1) trenches and graves containing many human bones, (2) the Thoamayutt pagoda containing many graves, (3) wells containing many human bones.

B. Sites Investigated

1. Trenches and graves containing many human bones (with sketch attached):

• The site is about 2 kilometers northeast of the town of Siem Reap and 2 kilometers northeast of the Siem Reap provincial prison. It is a rather level place, uninhabited for a long time, on the left of National Route 6 as one is headed for Angkor Wat.

• Concretely, we left the main road of Siem Reap town in the direction of Angkor Wat. Arriving at milestone No. 2 (already overturned) we turned left for 500 meters, then to the right for 500 meters, following a trail. There the trenches and the graves under investigation are found within 500 meters from west to east and 400 meters from north to south.

• The site comprises two overlapping trenches: one is parallel to the trail (this trail leads to the prison), the other makes a curve cutting the trail and the first trench. Both are filled up and covered with grass, almost at ground level.

• Along the trenches we saw skulls and fragments of limb bones scattered on the ground or hidden in the grass.

For example, at 50 meters from the crossing of the two trenches, on a trench parallel to the trail, we saw seven skulls and many white limb bones as well as bone fragments in the grass (here the grass is quite green).

• In the circular trench cutting the trail, at about 200 meters from the intersection of the trenches going westward, we saw ten skulls and many limb bones, as well as bone fragments hidden in the grass. Almost all the skulls were fractured or broken.

• In the circular trench, at about 350 meters from the crossing of the trenches, going westward, between the old and the new asphalt roads toward Angkor Wat, we saw seven skulls and a large number of bone fragments.

• We unearthed three graves in the circular trench 50 meters from the place where the trench cuts the trail and the other trench, and where the grass is green we saw many corpses buried under the earth.

• At 0.2 meter deep, we found many fragments of bones of limbs and broken skulls.

• At 0.5 meter deep, we found a great quantity of skulls and limb bones.

• At 1 meter, we found many limb bones with rotting human flesh, also pieces of cloth and black and red strips of cloth stuck to bone fragments and (mixed) with damp earth.

After unearthing three graves two meters in length and one meter of depth, we picked up 40 skulls and a great quantity of bones of all kinds. Several skulls still had hair. Most of them are fractured and a number of them broken.

• Each skull is bound with a strip of black cloth over the eye sockets, tied behind.

• Beside the trail, near the excavations, we also discovered two graves of about two meters in diameter where the grass is green. At the bottom of the graves, there are many bone fragments and a skull. A stinking smell emanates from the graves.

• Moreover, we have seen, here and there, skull fragments or limb bones beside the trenches and the graves.

2. Wells containing many human bones (with sketch attached)

We made investigations in two places which have wells containing many human bones:

• 4 wells in Ta Chen village, Siem Reap 1 subdistrict.

• 7 wells and culverts at Klolek Bay (belonging to a secondary school), Siem Reap 1 subdistrict.

(a) The four wells:

They are in Ta Chen village, Siem Reap 1 subdistrict, about 800 meters west of the two trenches mentioned above. To get there one starts from the site of the excavations, takes the trail to the west (toward the prison) for about 700 meters and then to the right for about 70 meters. The four wells are in an abandoned orchard of mango trees, behind a one-story house covered with grey stone and a roof of broken tiles, with a brick kitchen in the back. The well on the west is 30 meters from the one on the east and the distance from the southern to the northern one is the same.

• Concretely, the well nearest to the trail is 70 meters west of and 40 meters east of the house (behind the kitchen). The well was built of prefabricated concrete tubes of one meter diameter and was about 3.5 meters deep. We saw bones among innumerable worms at the bottom of the well. A very terrible smell emanates from it.

• Another similar well is found 30 meters west of this well (behind the kitchen, 25 meters southward). We saw many human bones: skulls and limb bones at a depth of 3.8 meters. A very fetid odor emanates from it as well.

• Between these wells, 20 meters northwards from each other and from the kitchen to the southeast, there is a third similar well surrounded by a wall. At a depth of about four meters, we saw water and many worms. A very frightening smell emanates from it.

• A fourth well lies 13 meters north of the third one and 15 meters from the wall of the house. The well wall has partly crumbled at a depth of four meters. We saw a great quantity of dry bones: six skulls and a half of a broken skull of brown color, a pelvis bone and two thigh bones leaned against the wall of the well. Here the odor is less fetid.

• According to the local authorities, these wells normally are more than ten meters deep.

To ensure a minimum of hygiene in the excavations, we confine ourselves to these discoveries.

(b) The seven wells and culverts:

The site is part of Siem Reap secondary school, Klolek Bay village, Siem Reap 1 subdistrict, Siem Reap district. To get there, one starts from Siem Reap town by the main road to Angkor Wat, passing the excavations of trenches (kilometer No. 2) and the former high school, then turn right about 200 meters from milestone No. 3 and arriving to abandoned one-story houses, for the most part beyond repair.

• To be more precise, at about 150 meters from the road, toward Angkor Wat, on the left of the trail leading to these houses, there is a grave 1.5 meters in diameter, the opening of which has crumbled. This may be the opening of a culvert. The well lies about 20 meters northeast from a four-room house with a completely caved in roof. At 1.5 meters we saw many bones in the wet earth.

• Hidden by the bushes, 4.5 meters from this grave, and about 2 meters from the above-mentioned house, there is a well of 1 meter in diameter made of prefabricated concrete with a crumbled opening. At 2.5 meters in depth, we saw many skulls at water level. A very stinking odor emanates from it.

• On the left of the trail, about 30 meters northeast of the four-room house and 15 meters from the front of a heavily damaged three-room brick house, there is another well one meter in diameter similar to the others but with an earth wall.

About two meters from its opening, we saw many skulls and white bone fragments, many of the skulls being fractured.

• Starting from the third well toward the northeast of the trail, and at about 50 meters from the four-room house and 1.5 meters from the kitchen of another three-room house on the east, there is a square culvert, 1.2 meters wide, made of ferro concrete without a cover. At two meters depth, we saw many limb bones and three skulls.

• From about 500 meters southeast of the trail and at 25 meters south of an abandoned four room concrete house with a flat roof, there is an already filled up grave, 2 meters wide, where the grass is quite green. There we saw many skulls and bone fragments.

• About 4.5 meters eastward from the above-mentioned house, we saw a well made of prefabricated concrete of 1.5 meters wide the brink of which is covered with grass and bushes. At 3 meters deep, we saw many bones among which there were five skulls with pieces of cloth stuck to them.

• About 70 meters southeast of the above-mentioned house we saw a well similar to the others, with a crumbled cement opening. At three meters deep, we saw many white bones, specifically two skulls and a strip of white cloth entangled in limb bones. The well is easy to spot from a distance because the grass around its opening is lush.

(c) Graves containing human bones in Thoamayutt pagoda (with a sketch attached)

Thoamayutt pagoda lies in Ta Phuol village, Siem Reap 1 subdistrict, Siem Reap district, 10 meters on the left side of National Route 6 leading to Battambang. Behind the prison of Siem Reap (400 meters to the west), the pagoda consists of three buildings.

• The main building is 30 meters from the right side of the entrance. It has five rooms with a roof of broken tiles, its damaged doors and walls are replaced by barbed wire. A heap of grayish fertilizer lies in the center.

• A concrete house with a flat roof and iron door, 15 meters to left of the entrance.

• A house on stilts with a curved roof at the center of the pagoda.

We made excavations in a few places in the orchard of the pagoda:

(a) We dug a one-meter by two-meter ditch, 20 meters from the concrete house and 25 meters from the enclosure of the pagoda. Here is the result:

• At a depth of 0.5 meter, we found many bone fragments, limb bones and skulls, many bones stuck to pieces of black cloth.

• At the depth of 0.8 meter to one meter, we discovered many skulls of bright chestnut color (one skull still has hair on it), limb bones with rotting human flesh. A foul odor still emanates from it.

• At about 60 meters from the left side of the entrance, 2.5 meters from the enclosure, beside a young coconut tree, there is a grave of one meter by two meters where the earth caves in. At the depth of 0.5 meter, the excavation reveals many bones, some wrapped in cloth and mixed with red mucus, very smelly.

(b) In addition to these graves, we found, in the trenches and gutters in the orchard of the pagoda, many bone fragments and skulls. In a section of a trench, we collected and buried seven skulls, some already broken.

• In the orchard of the pagoda, there are places where the grass is lush. According to the representative of the local authorities and the witnesses, there are graves and trenches where men were buried.

The investigation finished at 4:00 p.m. on the same day, June 18, 1979.

This report was read, confirmed, and signed by the witnesses and the representatives of the local authorities.

Persons present	*Witnesses*	*Official*	*Secretary*
Bu Sa Ruong	Nuon Thok	Saes Chhon	Sang Nim
Mien Chieu	Suon Marak Thi		
Dut Pron			
Dinh Sa Rom			
Dot Suon			

2.3.3.03a

Sketch Map of the Area of Wells and Graves Full of Bones in the Area of Siem Reap Secondary School, Siem Reap 1 Subdistrict

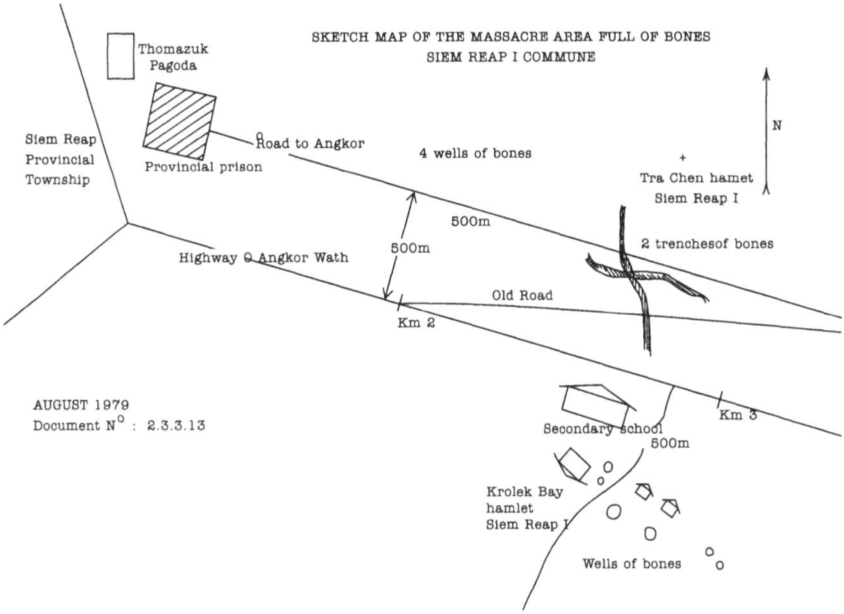

"Klolek Bay hamlet" is rendered in the text as "Klolek Bay village." "Siem Reap commune" and "Siem Reap I commune" are rendered as "Siem Reap 1 subdistrict." "Sieam Reap Secondary School" is rendered as "Siem Reap Secondary School." "Thomazuk Pagoda" is rendered as "Thoamayutt pagoda." "Angkor Wath" is rendered as "Angkor Wat." The number of this document given on the sketch map is "2.3.3.13." This should read "2.3.3.03a." —Eds.

2.3.3.03b
Sketch Map of the Massacre Area Full of Bones, Siem Reap 1 Subdistrict

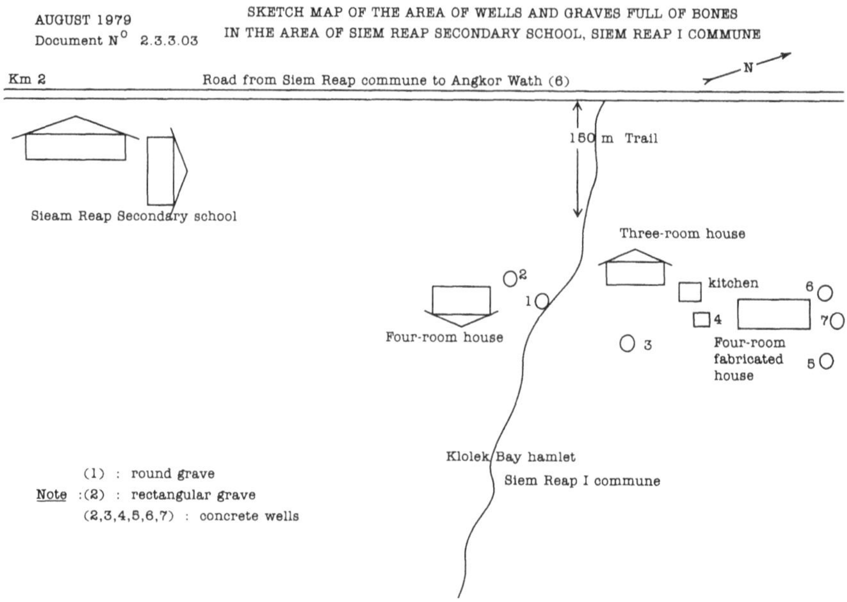

"Klolek Bay hamlet" is rendered in the text as "Klolek Bay village." "Siem Reap I commune" is rendered as "Siem Reap 1 subdistrict." "Tra Chen hamlet" is rendered as "Ta Chen village." "Angkor Wath" is rendered as "Angkor Wat."—Eds.

Common Graves in Sre Seam Village, Chiro 2 Subdistrict

2.3.4.01
Mr. Min Ban

Today, July 15, 1979, at 2:00 p.m. at the office of Chiro 2 subdistrict, Tbong Khmum district, Kompong Cham province, we, Saes Chhon, official of the Ministry of the Interior, and San Kiri, secretary, take the statement of a witness named Min Ban as follows:

Question: Please tell us your name, your age, your place of origin, and your occupation.

Answer: I am Min Ban, 26 years of age, born and living in Sre Seam village, Chiro 2 subdistrict, Tbong Khmum district, Kompong Cham province. My occupation is farmer.

Question: When was it that the Pol Pot men took people away from Chiro 2 subdistrict to kill them?

Answer: In late June and early July 1978 the Pol Pot men took many people away from Chiro 2 to kill them.

Question: Were the victims people originally from Chiro 2 subdistrict, or were they people who had been brought in from other regions? How were they taken away?

Answer: Some of the victims were workers at the Chup rubber plantation. Others had been brought in from Mi Mut, Ka Rach district, Kompong Cham province. Some were soldiers of the Pol Pot army, or subdistrict officials from the eastern zone. The victims were transported in large groups by truck, and there were more than ten thousand of them. These people were confined during the day in the former Japanese breeding center of Chiro 2 subdistrict. I saw the Pol Pot men take these persons away to kill them.

Question: Do you know how the Pol Pot men killed these people. And where they killed them?

Answer: The Pol Pot men took the Chiro 2 victims to the villages of Tu Luy, Hia, and Sre Seam and killed them at night, from 4:00 p.m. until morning, for ten consecutive days. The victims were tied up and transported in trucks. When they were taken out of the trucks, the executioners blindfolded them and led them in groups to the place where they would kill them. They were killed with blows of sticks and hammers, and those who managed to survive these blows were pushed by the executioners into the ditches. In Chiro 2 subdistrict, there are forty ditches full of corpses; some of the ditches were craters of bombs dropped in 1973 by the Americans. There are ditches 2.5 to 4 meters deep, 10 meters long, 5 meters wide, dug by the Pol Pot men using bulldozers. Some of the people were buried in dirt by the executioners using the bulldozers, others were left out in the open among the human bones and the decomposing flesh.

The victims let out mournful cries that the people could clearly hear 500 meters away from the place of the killing. I heard these cries while I was tending buffalo 300 meters from there.

The Pol Pot men kept the people away from these ditches for a month. The carnage in Chiro 2 subdistrict is known by the entire local population.

Question: Do you know other things?

Answer: No, I don't know anything else.

This transcript was completed at 4:00 p.m. July 15, 1979. It was drawn up in conformity to the statements of the witness named Min Ban. He read it over and affixed his signature below.

Secretary	*Declarant*	*Interrogator*
San Kiri	Min Ban	Saes Chhon

2.3.4.02a
Field Investigation in Chiro 2 Subdistrict

Today, July 16, 1979 at 2:00 p.m., we, the undersigned, Saes Chhon, official of the Ministry of the Interior, and Ros Rokha, secretary, met with the witness Min Ban at pits full of the remains of persons killed by Pol Pot–Ieng Sary men in Sre Seam village, Chiro 2 subdistrict, Tbong Khmum district, Kompong Cham province. We were accompanied by Pi Chey, a representative of the Kompong Cham provincial administration, Chan Mon, a representative of the Tbong Khmum district administration, and Chap Som Bat, president of Chiro 2 subdistrict. The results are as follows.

I. General View

Located near the Chup Rubber Plantation, the site of the pits is nine kilometers northeast of main town of Kompong Cham province. Specifically, from the main town of the province, one takes the ferry to cross the Bet river, then National Route 7 for seven kilometers, then turn left, eastward, on a dirt path leading to Bang Kro Chap. After going six hundred meters, one turns again to the left, heading south, and the place of the investigation is five hundred meters farther, large pits in an unwooded area. The site of the investigation is one hundred meters on a side, with two large pits twenty meters apart.

II. Site of the Investigation

1. Pits full of uncovered bones

Separated from the big dirt path to Bang Kro Chap by a former Japanese cattle-breeding center five hundred meters to the east, the pit is on uncultivated land covered with bushes and grass, right up to the pit.

The pit, bordered by a large dam of dirt, is round with a diameter of nine meters at the top, and a depth of 1.6 meters. The floor of the pit is six meters in diameter.

Wild plants and grass grow on the floor of the pit and around its edge. One can see white bones in the grass.

After picking the grass, one sees on the floor of the pit some bones, all white, some from arms and legs, and some skulls. Amidst the bones one discerns small pieces of electrical wire, and a piece of large white plastic wire with its ends twisted. One sees as well a large piece of cloth that one guesses is a shirt, a piece of thin cloth in the form of a scarf, and many other small pieces of disintegrated cloth. There are also black rubber shoe soles.

Among the human remains on the floor of the pit, one can count twelve skulls, and two halves of another skull. The flesh is completely decomposed and leaves no trace on these skulls.

2. A levelled pit

Covered by grass and small wild plants, and twenty meters west of the first pit, the second pit can be discerned by a round depression nine meters in diameter. The depth of the depression is 0.4 meter (forty centimeters) before the exhumation.

Just west of the pit, there is a trace of a depression that now forms a weak depression covered with grass. We projected digging a hole half a meter in diameter, and one meter deep. We found sticky black dirt that at a depth of thirty centimeters gave off a nauseating odor.

At a depth of 0.5 meter, the ground was strewn with white bones covered with black soil with something similar to white and pink paste. A strong nauseating odor came from the hole and water gushed forth from the hole at that depth. It was impossible to continue digging as planned because of the unsanitary conditions.

According to the witness and the people in the area, these two graves were bomb craters from American B-52s, made in 1973. Their average depth before the killings was between 6 to 7 meters.

In Chiro 2 subdistrict, there are around 40 graves filled with murdered bodies. Some of the 40 graves were made by bulldozers. The butchers, after having thrown the bodies of the victims into the graves, covered some of the graves but left others uncovered.

The number of victims transported by trucks in Chiro 2 subdistrict, according to the witness, was more than 10,000 people. Among them were workers from the Chup rubber plantation killed in Sre Seam village.

The on-site inquiry concluded at 5:00 p.m. on the same day. The minutes were read in the presence of the aforementioned; Min Ban, witness of the killings, and Pi Chay, Chan Mon, Chap Som Bat, witnesses of the investigation who affix their signatures below.

Observer	*Witness*	*Official*	*Secretary*
Pi Chay	Min Ban	Saes Chhon	Ros Rokha
Cham Mon			
Chap Som Bat			

Note: The interrogating official, the witness, and those who accompanied them have signed the original document drawn up in proper form in the Khmer language.

2.3.4.02b
Sketch Map of Graves of Bodies of Workers at Chup Rubber Plantation

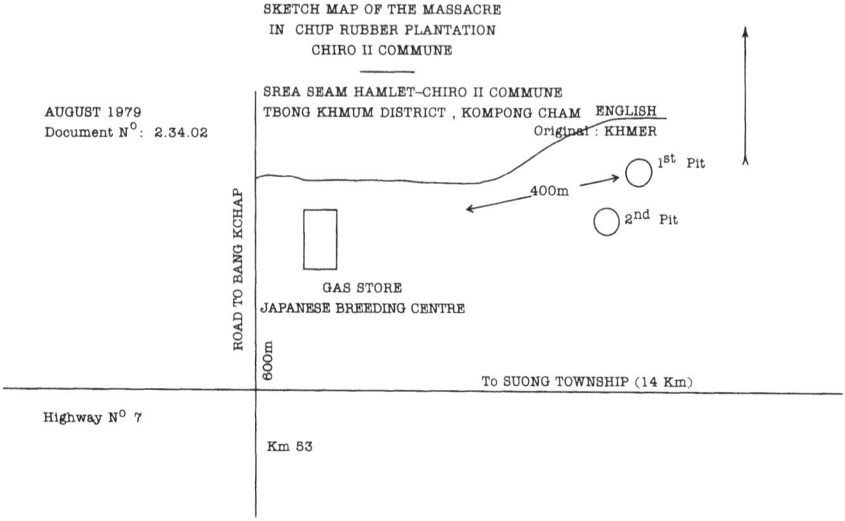

"Chiro II commune" is rendered in the text as "Chiro 2 subdistrict." "Srea Seam hamlet" is rendered as "Sre Seam village." "Highway No. 7" is rendered as "National Route 7." The number of this document given on the sketch map is "2.34.02." This should read "2.3.4.02b." — Eds.

Common Graves at Chup Rubber Plantation

2.3.5.01
Mr. Long Lai

Following is the testimony given by Mr. Long Lai at 10:10 a.m. on July 15, 1979, at the office of Chup subdistrict, Tbong Khmum district, Kompong Cham province, in the presence of Mr. Saes Chhon, official of the Ministry of the Interior, and Mr. San Kiri, secretary. The contents of the minutes follow:

Question: Could you tell us your name, your place of birth, and profession, please?

Answer: My name is Long Lai, 46 years old, and I was born in Chup Krau village, Chup subdistrict, Tbong Khmum district, Kompong Cham province. I am a farmer.

Question: Mr. Sieu Sien, who lives in Cham Bok village, said that you picked up a hammer and an iron stick left by Pol Pot agents after the killing of people on the Chup Plantation. Is that right?

Answer: That's right. I found them next to the graves in Chup subdistrict. They were left there by Pol Pot's agents after the killings.

Question: When did you pick them up, and how did you know that Pol Pot's agents used them to kill people?

Answer: Because there were traces of blood and hair stuck to them, and they were left very close to the graves. I picked them up some time in October 1978. At first, I dared not take them to my house, because of our local customs. When the blood disappeared, I took them home and used them to chop wood. As a result, the handle was damaged. If you need them, I can bring them to you.

Question: Do you know for certain about the killings committed by the Pol Pot agents on the Chup plantation?

Answer: Some time in July or August 1978, I saw some convoys of trucks filled with about 100 people each. Everyday they killed them on the plantation, from 4:00 to 5:00 a.m. and from 5:00 to 6:00 p.m. I can't tell how many vehicles per day, but the killings lasted from July until December 1978. Sometimes the agents of Pol Pot forbade people from entering the plantation, in order to keep the killings secret.

The victims were men and women, most of them workers from the plantation. There were also some of Pol Pot's officials and guerrillas. Also, many other people were brought from other places, I do not know from where, coming from the direction of O Rang Au village.

Pol Pot's agents loaded the people, tied up, into cars, to drive them to the plantation. When they got off the cars (wagons), they had their eyes blindfolded. The killers smashed their heads with hammers and iron bars. The executioners were so young, from fifteen to eighteen years old, that they sometimes did not have the strength to kill their victims with one blow. They sometimes had to strike two or three times. The victims were then buried, including the dying.

Though it was forbidden to go near, those who were at a distance of 500 meters could hear the victims crying for help. The victims were buried in five common graves on the Chup plantation. There were craters made by American bombs that were 5 to 6 meters deep and 20 meters wide. The executioners filled the craters with corpses, then covered them by leveling the earth. At present, the graves are visible because the corpses have been rotting. Besides, there were also many other smaller graves of about ten corpses each, which were flattened by rain.

I know this because I tend cows and cut the grass in this area of the plantation. On many occasions, I saw Chinese advisers come to the place of the killings, by car. Sometimes they were accompanied to the grave sites by Crut, the security chief for the district.

Question: How do you know that the Chinese advisers went to the place of the killings?

Answer: I know because the Chinese advisers came and lived in the plantation house. They were seen coming in and out by cars, wearing blue coats with stripes or white coats. They spoke Chinese. They arrived in early 1978, and not long after that, the killings began.

Question: Do you have anything else to add concerning the Chinese advisers' participation in the massacre of our people?

Answer: Bo and Ma Long, president and vice-president of the people's committee of the village, informed the people of the village that the Chinese advisers came to direct the killings in order to populate Kampuchea with the Chinese. Later on Ma Long and Bo were also killed by Pol Pot's agents.

Question: Do you have anything else to say?

Answer: No.

The minutes were finished at 12 noon on July 15, 1979, and read to Mr. Long Lai, who confirmed it to be true by signing his name below.

Secretary	*Witness*	*Questioner*
San Kiri	Long Lai	Saes Chhon

2.3.5.02
Mr. Sieu Sien

Following is the testimony given at 8:00 a.m. on July 15, 1979, by Mr. Sieu Sien at the Office of the people's committee of Chup subdistrict, Tbong Khmum district, Kompong Cham province, in the presence of Mr. Saes Chhon, official of the Ministry of the Interior, and Mr. San Kiri, secretary. The contents of the minutes follow.

Question: Tell us your name, age, place of origin, and occupation, please.

Answer: My name is Sieu Sien. I am 40 years old, and I am a native of Cham Bok village, Chup subdistrict, Tbong Khmum district, Kompong Cham province. I used to collect rubber sap on the Chup plantation. When the Pol Pot regime came to power, I returned home to farm and to collect sugar palm juice.

Question: Is your house near the Chup plantation?

Answer: Yes, it is in the area of the Chup rubber plantation.

Question: Did you see the Pol Pot–Ieng Sary agents kill people in this area?

Answer: I saw Pol Pot–Ieng Sary agents bring people to the plantation for mass executions.

Question: Were there many victims? Where did they come from? When did the killings take place?

Answer: The victims were workers on the Chup rubber plantation, or inhabitants of other regions that I do not know. The killings began in July of 1978 and continued until December of 1978. The killings did not cease until the National United Front for the Salvation of Kampuchea had been founded and the Pol Pot agents had fled.

Every day, seven or eight trucks, full of victims, arrived. The executioners killed people from 4:00 to 5:00 a.m. and from 5:00 to 6:00 p.m., when there was no one working on the plantation. During those times, no one was allowed to come near. I estimate that there were about 20,000 victims, because the convoys full of people arrived continually, but no one came back.

Question: Were you ever in that area during the killings?

Answer: My house is about 1000 meters from the places where the killings took place. Sometimes I was 100 meters from those places, when I was tending the cows and cutting the grass. Thus, I could see everything that happened, and hear the cries for help and the pleas of the victims.

Question: Do you know how the executioners killed the victims?

Answer: All the victims, with hands tied, were driven by truck to these places. When they got off the trucks, they were blindfolded and taken to the pits. The assassins smashed their skulls with hammers or iron sticks. They started up two tractors, to drown out the victims' cries during the killings. In the beginning, they killed and buried the victims near the road in bomb craters made in 1974 by American bombers. Later, they killed the victims farther away to keep the killings secret.

After the killings, the executioners threw the bodies of the victims into the bomb craters of the American B-52s. On the plantation, there are many mass graves, of which five are quite large. One of them is 5 to 6 meters deep and 20 meters wide. When all these graves were full of corpses, they were leveled and hidden by rubber tree branches. People were not allowed to walk there for one month after the killings. Around September 1978, Mr. Mo Rang and Mr. Long Lai found a hammer and iron stick left by the assassins, stained with human hair and blood, when they were allowed to go past the place.

Question: How old were the victims? Were they male or female?

Answer: I didn't see them killing old people and children in this place. They were all adults, including many women.

Question: Do you have other things to tell concerning the killings on the Chup plantation?

Answer: Just before the killings, I saw Chinese advisers come on to the Chup plantation, and they even went to the scene of the killings.

Question: How did you know they were Chinese?

Answer: I used to tend cows and cut grass on the plantation; sometimes I was 50 meters from their house. They usually came in and out of the plantation by car, and they even went to the places of the killings. Some of them wore shirts with blue stripes; some wore white ones. They spoke Chinese. They lived in the house of the former plantation owner. It was generally known that there were more than forty Chinese advisers.

Many persons are aware of this. I myself also noticed that Crut, the security chief for Tbong Khmum district, who was in charge of the killings, often accompanied the Chinese advisers to the killing scenes.

The statement was finished at 10:00 a.m. on July 15, 1979, and the transcript was read back, confirmed, and signed by Mr. Sieu Sien.

Secretary	*Witness*	*Officer*
San Kiri	Sieu Sien	Saes Chhon

2.3.5.03
Field Investigation at Chup Rubber Plantation

On July 16, 1979, at 8:00 a.m., we, Saes Chhon, official of the Ministry of the Interior, and Ros Rokha, secretary, were taken to Chup rubber plantation, Kompong Cham province, to conduct a field investigation into the killing of plantation workers by Pol Pot–Ieng Sary men. We were guided by two persons, also witnesses, namely, Long Lai and Sieu Sien.

Present at the investigation were Mr. Pi Chay, a representative of the Kompong Cham provincial administration; Mr. Cham Mon, representative of the Tbong Khmum district administration; Mr. Mia Luon, chair of Chup subdistrict, Tbong Khmum district; and Mr. Chenh Lieng, deputy chair of Chup subdistrict. The results of the investigation are as follows (the work was filmed and photographed).[1]

I. General Location of the Site:

The area under investigation is 139 kilometers northeast of Phnom Penh, 15 kilometers east of Kompong Cham town and on National Route 7. The area is in Cham Bok village, Chup subdistrict, near the seventh lot of rubber trees off National Route 7. We studied an area 500 meters long, from north to south, starting from the edge of the rubber plantation that abuts National Route 7.

II. Specifics of the Investigation Site:

1. First Pit:

The pit is 70 meters southwest of National Route 7 at Kilometer 60, and at the edge of the rubber tree grove.

• The pit is round, 9 meters in diameter at the top, 6 meters in diameter at the bottom, and 2.3 meters deep before exhumation.

• Around the edge is an earth work about 0.3 meter high, the wall of this

1. This material is not available. —Eds.

pit is worn out by rain, leaving some new soil marks. Dried rubber tree leaves scattered on the soft soil at the bottom. The surface sinks easily under foot.

We dug a square hole 1.5 meters on each side:

• At a depth of 0.1 meter, one sees quite a few bones mixed in with the soil.

• At a depth of 0.2 meter, one sees skulls and pieces of disintegrated cloth among bone fragments that are hand and foot bones that have turned dark yellow.

• At a depth of 0.4 meter, one sees nine skulls, six of which still have locks of hair stuck together with dirt. Organic matter is completely decomposed, and two jawbones are detached. One skull has a hole on top, 1.5 centimeters by 3 centimeters in size. This break in the skull is old, being brown in color. Inside this hole one sees a small amount of whitish matter.

• There are two leg bones 35 centimeters long which are tied with an electric wire, also 35 centimeters long, in black casing, and some other wires of the same type among the bones and dirt.

• Among the bones is a round-shaped cord tied to a piece of white cloth with blue stripes. There is also a cloth belt with a rusty buckle. One also sees two black shirts stuck to bones and dirt and other pieces of disintegrated cloth.

2. Second Pit:

This pit is 40 meters south of the first, inside the rubber plantation, covered with wild grass and plants, but the edge is clearly visible.

• The pit is round, about the same size as the first one. It is 9 meters in diameter at the top and, 7 meters in diameter at the bottom, and 2.8 meters deep before excavation.

• Water erosion in the walls has exposed traces of new dirt, brown in color, which mixes in with red dirt around it. The soil of the bottom is spongy and gives way under foot.

We dug a one meter by two meter hole in the middle of the pit.

• At a depth of 0.2 meter, one can see arm and leg bones and skulls.

• At a depth of 0.5 meter, the bones are still sticky and whitish, and stained with black dirt. Among these bones are clumps of black dirt with specks of white, some heaps of damp cloth, wet and shiny inside.

• At this same depth, there are 6 pieces of cloth that are still in the shape of shirts, damp and shiny, with bones inside. Another piece of cloth looks as if it may have been a pair of underdrawers, with a rubber band on it. There are also several pieces of semi-decayed cloth.

• There are ten dark yellow skulls, which still have little locks of hair on them. Two other skulls are stained with something like paste, and the flesh on these skulls is not yet completely decomposed. One skull is broken at the upper jaw that must have been hit by something hard.

• Most important, there are four bones tied in two pairs with electrical wire. We also discovered a shirt mixed with the bones and soil with a rope knotted on the two sleeves and tying them together. In addition, there are many pieces of detached rope among the bones. A terrible stench emanates from the hole.

3. Third Pit:

This pit is 250 meters south of the second pit, also in the rubber plantation, near the seventh lot.

• This pit is of the same diameter as the others, nine meters, but is only 1.5 meters in diameter at the bottom. Half of the bottom has been covered by grass. On the northern side of the bottom, there are many exposed bones, whitish in color. One can clearly discern hand and leg bones, ribs, and pelvic bones.

Because the bones were exposed, we did not need to excavate this pit.

(1) According to the local administration and to witnesses, these pits were craters made by U.S. B-52 aircraft. The depth of these pits varies between 6 and 7 meters. When the Pol Pot agents killed the victims, they tied them up and threw their bodies into the holes, then leveled them. The decomposition of the bodies and rainfall have left depressions in these holes.

• The witnesses said that the Pol Pot agents threw the bodies into five large pits and into several smaller ones in the rubber tree groves in Chup subdistrict. The victims numbered nearly 20,000, most of them workers from two rubber enterprises in the Chup plantation. That happened in June 1978.

(2) In addition to the evidence found on the site of the killings, the witnesses have shown us one axe, 51 centimeters long with an 8.5 centimeters wide blade; a pair of pliers for taking out nails that is 55 centimeters long and 0.7 centimeter in diameter.

According to the witnesses, this axe and these pliers were taken from the edge of the second pit. They knew very well that these tools, along with others, were used to smash the victims' skulls. We are keeping these two items of evidence.

The field investigation was completed at 1:00 p.m. the same day. This report was read in the presence of Messrs. Pi Chay, Cham Mon, Mia Luon, Chenh Lieng, Long Lai, and Sieu Sien, who acknowledged it and signed below along with our signatures.

Observers	*Witnesses*	*Official*	*Secretary*
Pi Chay	Long Lai	Saes Chhon	Ros Rokha
Cham Mon	Sieu Sien		
Mia Luon			
Chenh Lieng			

Note: All the officials, witnesses, and persons who participated in the investigation signed the original text that was done in proper form in Khmer.

2.3.5.03bis

Sketch Map of Graves Full of Human Bones at Chup Rubber Plantation, Cham Bok Village, Chup Subdistrict, Tbong Khmum District, Kompong Cham Province

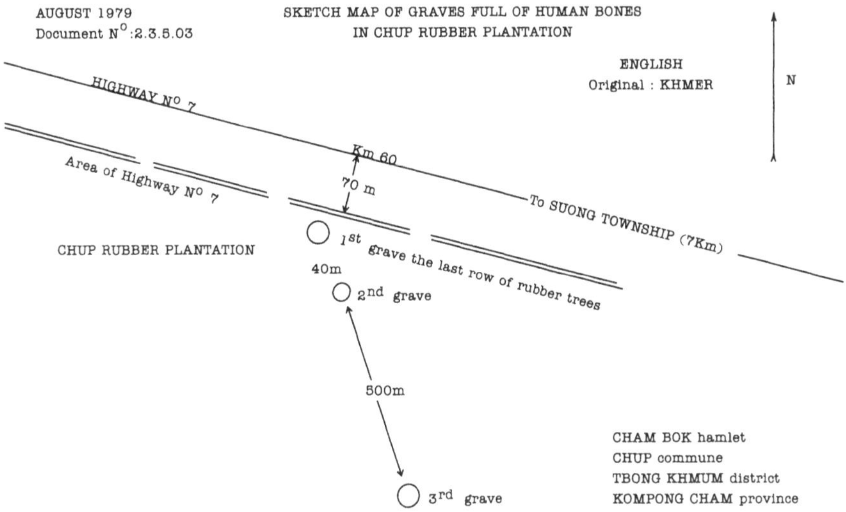

"Highway No. 7" is rendered in the text as "National Route 7." "Cham Bok hamlet" is rendered as "Cham Bok village." "Chup commune" is rendered as "Chup subdistrict." —Eds.

Common Graves in Kompong Speu Province

2.3.6.02

Letter from Officials of Am Leang Subdistrict

To the United Front for National Salvation of Kampuchea:
To the People's Revolutionary Council of Kampuchea:

We, officials representing the people of Am Leang subdistrict, Tbong district, Kompong Speu province, on behalf of 5,614 villagers here, denounce the Pol Pot–Ieng Sary clique for having carried out a genocidal policy against the Kampuchean people and having subjected them to all forms of oppression and exploitation, thus plunging the whole people into suffering never before known.

In February 1979, the Pol Pot–Ieng Sary clique concentrated the workers of Kompong Chhnang airport and of various Phnom Penh enterprises and a group of their soldiers. In an 8-kilometer stretch near Am Leang subdistrict, many pits full of bodies have been found. These pits measure about 3 meters long by 2 meters wide by 1.5 meters deep. Some of these pits measure 4 meters × 8 meters × 1.5 meters. Thus, early in 1979, in Am Leang subdistrict alone, 12,000 people were killed. There are even some pits, excavated by bulldozers, measuring 15 meters × 20 meters × 2 to 3 meters in which around 4,600 corpses were found; four pits of this size and one well were located to the north of Route 114. Among the people killed were soldiers of Mr. So Phim, using an alias Yan, a member of the Party central committee, Commander of the eastern zone, and was considered a traitor by the Pol Pot–Ieng Sary clique. As for its wounded soldiers and factory workers, their skulls were smashed and their corpses were scattered in jungles and rice fields to be devoured by wild animals.

From 1975 to early 1979, the Pol Pot–Ieng Sary clique committed extremely barbaric crimes. Over 20,000 people were brought to the Am Leang area and killed. They were buried in the villages of Thmor Cap, Reng Thom, Pong Cropeu, Thnol Bambek, etc. All the people of Am Leang subdistrict—many of them witnessed the massacres—denounce this monstrous crime perpetrated by the Pol Pot–Ieng Sary clique, henchmen of the Peking expansionists. During the past three years, from 1975 to early 1979, this clique used Marxism-Leninism as the basis for false propaganda and to cover up its deception and maneuvers from world public opinion and to deceive the Kampuchean people and patriots. It destroyed pagodas, abolished the age-old national religion. It stripped the people of their freedom of belief and wiped out a whole national culture.

As if this was not enough, it forcibly subjected children from the age of seven to hard labor, thus draining them of their strength. It even brainwashed children who were given no education and youths to serve its interests and to facilitate its war of aggression against Vietnam, a faithful friend of Kampuchea, sowing enmity and discord between the two peoples.

In face of the above situation, we ask the United Front for National Salvation of Kampuchea and the People's Revolutionary Council to call on international public opinion and peace and justice-loving people in the world to extend warm support and assistance to our people.

All the survivors of Am Leang subdistrict earnestly aspire to peace, freedom and happiness and wish to tighten the bonds of friendship with the socialist countries in the world and especially to strengthen the close unity between the three Indochinese peoples—Kampuchea, Vietnam and Laos.

The blood debts owed to the Kampuchean people must be repaid. We, the suffering victims, would like to ask the United Front for National Salvation of Kampuchea and the People's Revolutionary Council of Kampuchea to put on trial, punish and condemn the Pol Pot–Ieng Sary genocidal reactionaries—the obedient henchmen of Peking.

Lastly, in the name of the entire population of Am Leang subdistrict, we wish for the future of the United Front for National Salvation of Kampuchea and the People's Revolutionary Council of Kampuchea good health and success in all circumstances and long life in order to lead the Kampuchean people to build the country and to advance everlasting independence, freedom, happiness and prosperity.

Done June 22, 1979 for 5,614 Am Leang subdistrict residents
Huot Kim Srun, Pen Kuol, Nien Nem, Ek Oanh, Hem Mory

2.3.6.03
Mr. Bui Bun

Today, July 3, 1979, at 3:00 p.m., Saes Chhon, official at the Ministry of the Interior, and San Kiri, secretary, made the following report of the witness' statement at the Am Leang subdistrict office, Tbong district, Kompong Speu province:

Question: Would you please tell us your name, first and last, age, place of birth, and residence?

Answer: My name is Bui Bun. I am 43 years old. I was born and have been living in Ta Kong village, Am Leang subdistrict, Tbong district, Kompong Speu province.

Question: What is your occupation and where have you been working?

Answer: I have always been a farmer. However, beginning in 1975, when the Pol Pot–Ieng Sary clique came to power, they compelled people to work and live together in cooperatives. I was a cooperative member. In 1978, the Pol Pot–Ieng Sary agents gave me a gun and forced me to be a watch guard in the village sentry unit.

Question: What do you know of the criminal acts of Pol Pot and his agents committed against the people of this region?

Answer: Beginning in 1975, this region was placed under the control of Pol Pot's agents. They forced the population to join cooperatives and to work very hard. At the beginning, each person was given about 300 grams of rice per day, but later, every ten people shared a mere 900 grams. The people, including those who came from Phnom Penh and other places, were organized into "shock units" and sent to different places to clear land in overgrown areas. A very large number of these people, who were children, women, and the elderly, were killed. The method of killing used by the Pol Pot agents consisted of tying the people up and clubbing their skulls. . . . The bodies of the victims were buried in bomb craters, trenches and sewers.

In February 1979, after Phnom Penh was liberated by the revolutionary forces, the Pol Pot clique continued its mass killings in other places, killing about twelve thousand people who were buried near the Kosal Sam pagoda in four pits and at the foot of a mountain.

Question: Can you tell us more about the massacre near this pagoda?

Answer: In February 1979, I was on sentry duty for two consecutive days. I was 70 meters away from these four pits from 7:00 a.m. to 4:00 p.m., and so I was able to witness this event.

Most of these victims were Pol Pot soldiers, including the wounded and civilian citizens who were forced to accompany them. They were mostly from the East. Each day, one could see 5 or 6 trucks, loaded with people, each with more than 50 people. All of them were men, aged 18 to 40 years old. Upon arrival at Kosal Sam pagoda, the soldiers forced them off the trucks, one after another, and tied with their hands behind their backs. They were then forced into groups of twenty men each, and they were chained to a long bamboo reed. Later, they were led along a path, across a small stream, into the jungle where the pits had already been dug. At the edge of the pits, they were hit on their heads until they were dead, and then thrown down into the pits. The slaughter continued as truck after truck carried the victims there. At the end of the day, bulldozers were used to fill in the pits. The same thing was repeated the following day. I stood guard and thus, witnessed the killing for two days.

Question: Can you tell us how many men took part in this massacre?

Answer: They had a company, including escorts and executioners. A group of three executioners were responsible for a group of 20 victims. The remaining soldiers, who did not participate in the killings, transported and guarded the victims.

Question: What did the assassins use to smash the victims' skulls?

Answer: They used hard bamboo trunks, 80 to 90 centimeters long, as thick as one's wrist. Some of them used wooden clubs of the same size. These tools were prepared and brought in advance, as were the bamboo trees for chaining the victims. They were about 6 to 7 meters long and the knots in the wood were not cut off yet. They were still left around the burying pits.

Question: When were the pits dug and by what means?

Answer: They used bulldozers to dig these pits several days earlier. I saw a large, yellow painted bulldozer; however, I do not know if it was left in the area of the Kosal Sam pagoda. The four pits, dug in advance, were 20 meters long, 2 meters wide and from one to two meters deep.

Question: Do you know of any other location where the victims were killed and buried?

Answer: Yes, I know some people were killed and buried in an underground basin about 200 meters away from the four pits that were mentioned earlier. This basin had existed for a long time and measured about 3 meters wide, 5 meters long and from 5 to 6 meters deep. The victims were killed in the same way as I told you, thrown into the well and covered by the bulldozer in the same month of February, 1979.

Question: Were they undressed before being killed?

Answer: The victims, before being tied, were undressed. The clothing that was in good condition was removed in advance. When they were hit on the head they screamed.

Question: Apart from you, did anyone else in the village witness this event?

Answer: Yes, many villagers witnessed this because they attended a meeting in which they were informed that these people were declared pro-Vietnamese and would be killed. Like myself, several other villagers were on sentry duty during these days, among them, I remember, were Mr. Yeam Ich and Mr. Muon Mooun.

Question: Can you assure us that your testimony is true and can you take us to the above-mentioned pits?

Answer: I declare that my testimony is true. I will be responsible before the law if it is not true. I am ready to take you there to prove that my testimony is true.

Question: Do you wish to say anything more?

Answer: No.

These minutes were completed at 5:00 p.m. on July 3, 1979, and read to Bui Bun, who confirms that it is correct by signing his name below.

Official in charge	*Secretary*	*Witness*
Saes Chhon	San Kiri	Bui Bun

2.3.6.04
Miss Nhim Sokha

Today, July 3, 1979, at the office of the Am Leang subdistrict committee, Tbong district, Kompong Speu province, we, Mien Chieu, official of the Ministry of the Interior, and Ros Rokha, secretary, conducted an interview with Miss Nhim Sokha. The contents follow:

Question: Can you tell us briefly about yourself?

Answer: My name is Nhim Sokha, 25 years old. I was born in Popea Khe village, Koly subdistrict, Kien Svay district, Kandal province. Now I live in Thkau village, Am Leang subdistrict, Tbong district, Kompong Speu province. I was brought here by Pol Pot's agents in 1975.

Question: What was your occupation under Pol Pot?

Answer: Under Pol Pot, I worked as a rice farmer at a commune in Ta Kong village, Am Leang subdistrict.

Question: Do you know of any crimes committed by the Pol Pot clique against your compatriots?

Answer: I know that Pol Pot's clique has killed many people.

Question: Could you tell us in more concrete terms of the killings? Could you tell us when or where?

Answer: They carried out the killings without letting up for more than one week. Everyday, they made people come to the vicinity of the Kosal Sam pagoda, in 7 or 8 trucks, each truck transported 50 to 60 people, many people were piled onto the hoods. They were transported to a place in Am Leang subdistrict called Koma Meas village, to be killed in the early days of 1979.

I saw their trucks coming to the Kosal Sam pagoda, situated in the ancient village of Koma Meas. They ordered these people to get off of the trucks when they arrived at the pagoda. In the meantime, soldiers came out of the pagoda, pointed their guns at them and tied them up. They were then led in groups across a stream to a ditch which had been previously dug. They were then beaten to death with bamboo clubs of an arm's length. Their heads were smashed. In this way, they killed all the victims who came by truck, and pushed them into the ditch, which they then covered with dirt. While the blows from their sticks rained on the heads of the victims, they uttered heart-rending screams but the soldiers stifled their screams.

Question: Do you know from which social class the victims came from? Where were they brought from?

Answer: From the conversations held between the smashing of the skulls, I was able to learn that the victims were all soldiers of Pol Pot, male, between the ages of 15 to 35 years old. "They are traitors," they said. They brought them here from Kompong Chhnang airport to be executed. Besides these victims, I do not know whether they brought anyone else from other places to be killed here.

Question: Were you an eyewitness to these killings or were you told about them?

Answer: I saw it with my own eyes because at that time I was working on a clearing about 200 meters away from the scene. I clearly saw the trucks come with the victims, inside, tied with their hands behind their backs and I very clearly heard the screams of the victims who succumbed to the strikes to the head. To keep the killing a secret, they kept the local inhabitants from coming near this place. It was only due to my work there that I was informed.

Question: Do you know of anyone else besides yourself that knows this? And their whereabouts?

Answer: Besides me, there are others who know about the killing. They are Miss Houn, Miss Chon, and Miss Hourn. They all now live in Koma Meas village, Am Leang subdistrict. They were working with me on the clearing, so they know about these people who were killed and buried in that ditch. I still remember the place where these people were killed. I could take you there if you think it is necessary.

These minutes were completed at 4:00 p.m., July 3, 1979, and reread to Miss Nhim Sokha, who confirmed that they conform to her statements and signed her name here below.

Secretary	*Witness*	*Official*
Ros Rokha	Nhim Sokha	Mien Chieu

2.3.6.05

Mr. Yeam Ich

Today, July 5, 1979, at 6:00 p.m. at the administrative office of Am Leang subdistrict, Tbong district, Kompong Speu province, we, Prum Chien, official of the Ministry of the Interior, and San Kiri, official charged with recording, took the statement of Mr. Yeam Ich.

Question: Could you let me know your age, birth place and occupation?

Answer: I am Yeam Ich, 37 years old. I was born in Ta Kong village, Am Leang subdistrict, Tbong district, Kompong Speu province. Occupation: Agricultural worker. Nationality: Khmer, Buddhist.

Question: What did you do in the Pol Pot times?

Answer: I did farm work and was forced to join a defense unit of the village.

Question: Have you seen Pol Pot men committing crimes against the people?

Answer: In February 1979, I saw them bring a number of people to Am Leang subdistrict to be killed.

Question: Have you any idea about the number of people brought here, and do you know the location where they were held here?

Answer: I heard the people who were being held here say that they were from Kompong Chhnang province. Among them were prisoners of war, airport workers.

Question: What is the number of these people and where were they killed?

Answer: I saw people being held along a stretch of road from Koma Meas village to the Klong Bet intersection in Am Leang subdistrict. After that they were put into trucks and taken to Koma Meas and Krang Dom, in Am Leang subdistrict, to be killed.

Question: Were you then assigned any duty?

Answer: At that time, I was forced to patrol and to defend the village. I was not permitted to go to the killing places; I had to stand guard at about 700 meters from those places.

Question: From during the time of your guard duty, do you know exactly where and how people were killed?

Answer: I only know that these people were killed at Kosal Sam pagoda, Koma Meas village. I saw them bring trucks full of people, each truck carrying sixty to seventy people. People were brought in over a four-day period. When the trucks arrived at Kosal Sam pagoda, people were taken off, tied and led across a stream to the killing places. Some who came here knew that they were to be killed. They tried to escape, but the majority were recaptured. Those who tied and killed people were regular soldiers. Volunteer troops, militiamen, and vanguard youths were guarding outside.

I heard the executioners on their way back say that at the area of Kosal Sam pagoda, 4,600 people had been killed. These people were buried in four places and covered with earth by bulldozers. The victims were tied to bamboo trees, struck in the head, and then pushed into a pit. Later I saw the sticks that were used to kill people there.

Question: Do you know anything more?

Answer: No.

Question: Does anyone else here know about these killings?

Answer: The killings were known to everyone. Because people here belong to the first category, soldiers were not cautious about their secrets and often chatted about the killing.

This report was completed at 10:00 p.m., July 5, 1979. It was read back to Yeam Ich, who subsequently signed it.

Recorder	*Witness*	*Official who takes statements*
San Kiri	Yeam Ich	Prum Chien

2.3.6.06

Mr. Chea Cham

Today, July 4, 1979, at 2:00 p.m., at the subdistrict committee office in Am Leang subdistrict, Tbong district, Kompong Speu province, we, Mr. Mien Chieu, an official of the Ministry of the Interior, and Mr. San Kiri, an official responsible for writing down this report, took the testimony of Mr. Chea Cham. The contents follow:

Question: What is your name and age? Where is your birthplace?

Answer: My name is Chea Cham, 35 years old. I was born and lived in Koma Meas village, Am Leang subdistrict, Tbong district, Kompong Speu province. I am a farmer and an extractor of sugar palm juice.

As for my education: sixth grade. My nationality: Khmer. My religion: Buddhist.

Question: What did you do under the Pol Pot regime?

Answer: Under the Pol Pot regime, I worked at Commune No. 2, in Am Leang subdistrict. My daily work was to climb the sugar palm trees to extract the juice.

Question: What do you know about the crimes committed by the Pol Pot–Ieng Sary clique?

Answer: I know they brought people to Am Leang subdistrict to kill them.

Question: Will you tell us from which places they were brought to be killed here and when?

Answer: In February 1979, when the area around the Tbong district was liberated, I saw Pol Pot's henchmen herd a great number of people there. They gathered these people along a three-kilometer stretch of a road coming from Ka Pot, at Koma Meas village, at the Klong Bet intersection, situated in Am Leang subdistrict.

According to what they said amongst themselves, the people gathered here were defeated Pol Pot soldiers, soldiers and workers working at the Kompong Chhnang airport and also ordinary people. The victims were all men, from 16 to 40 years old.

These men were brought to Am Leang subdistrict, but to my knowledge, the place where they killed most of the people was in the vicinity of Trapeang Shao in Koma Meas village, near the Kosal Sam pagoda.

When they brought these people to the place of the killings, I was working at a place just 70 meters away, where I was forced, daily, to climb the sugar palm tress to extract the juice used in making sugar. When I was on top of the sugar palm tree I could clearly see them killing people; and according to what the Pol Pot soldiers said among themselves, they used bulldozers to make the four ditches in the vicinity of the Kosal Sam pagoda, and also used them to bury the victims. Each layer of corpses was covered up with earth. After the four ditches were full they used bulldozers to cover them up with earth.

There was a well near where I used to climb the sugar palm trees every day. I could see that they had used bulldozers to make it larger and deeper and used it as a tomb. However, I could not tell exactly how deep and large it was because I was not allowed to go near it. The soldiers moved the men who were gathered along the highway onto their trucks and transported them to Kosal Sam pagoda, each was loaded to capacity with as many as 60 to 70 men. At the pagoda, they were taken down from the trucks, and were ordered to hold up their hands and were tied. The victims were then taken to the ditches to be beaten.

A great number of the victims were taken, in groups, to this place, but I could not observe well the groups that were taken to the edge of the well, where they used bamboo clubs to hit them on the head, and they were then thrown into the well. On the days I climbed the sugar palm trees, I only worked from 7:00 to 9:00 a.m., therefore, I could not see them cover up the well with earth and I do not know how many people were killed near the well. But according to the conversations in the village, I was able to learn that they killed and buried 4,600 people in these ditches and in the well near the Kosal Sam pagoda.

Question: Besides these killings, do you know about other killings perpetrated elsewhere?

Answer: I do not know anything more.

Question: Who else knows about these facts other than yourself?

Answer: Many people from the village know about these killings of the people gathered and executed in Am Leang subdistrict. But I do not know if there is anyone else besides me who saw the killings near the well.

I assure you of the accuracy of my account of the facts. I still remember where the well is and if you find it necessary, I will take you there.

This report was done at 3:00 p.m. on July 4, 1979, and was reread to Mr.

Chea Cham, who confirms that it conforms to the testimony and he signed his name here below.

Recorder	*Witness*	*Official*
San Kiri	Chea Cham	Mien Chieu

2.3.6.07
Mrs. Sa Houl

On July 4, 1979, at 7:00 a.m., at the office of the Am Leang subdistrict committee, Tbong district, Kompong Speu province, we, Mr. Mien Chieu, official of the Ministry of the Interior, and Mr. San Kiri, secretary, recorded the following testimony of Mrs. Sa Houl:

Question: Will you please tell me your first and last name, age, birthplace and occupation?

Answer: My name is Sa Houl, 32 years old. I was born in Takeo. Since 1962, I have lived and worked in Koma Meas village, Am Leang subdistrict, Tbong district, Kompong Speu province, where I work to earn a living.

Question: From the time of Pol Pot, do you know of any crimes committed against the people by this reactionary clique?

Answer: Yes, I do.

Question: Can you tell us more concretely about the killings?

Answer: In February 1979, when the revolutionary forces had already liberated many regions of the country, the Pol Pot–Ieng Sary clique was frightened of the situation and they concentrated a large number of people in Am Leang from Kompong Chhnang province and other places, and they killed them all.

When these people were forcibly brought in by the Pol Pot— Ieng Sary clique, they were gathered on the road coming from Koma Meas village to the Klong Bet intersection in Am Leang subdistrict for a distance of nearly three kilometers. I heard the troops tell one another that these gathered people included defeated troops of Pol Pot and workers at the Kompong Chhnang airport and civilians. All were male from the ages of 15 to 40 years old and they were led away to be killed.

Question: Do you know the precise place in Am Leang subdistrict where they were killed?

Answer: I know of only one, in a forest in Koma Meas village. On that day I was working in a field with Miss Nhim Sokha and Miss Houn, about twenty meters from the place of the killings.

I saw two trucks, packed full, carrying them to Kosal Sam pagoda. The victims were forced to get off the trucks. Two armed soldiers, after having tied the victims' hands behind their backs, brought them to the graves, which had been previously dug, where they were connected to one another by way of a bamboo trunk. The other soldiers then used bamboo clubs, 90 centimeters long, to smash their heads until they were dead and then they were pushed into the graves. There were four graves in this area dug by bulldozers, but I don't know how deep they were.

The soldiers who participated in the killing said that the victims of each of the killings were transported in the four trucks. The people, once executed, were buried in the four graves. There were several massacres per day. So, 4,600 people were killed, then buried in those four graves. They had planned to do this in ten days but they had done it so quickly that they finished in four and one-half days. When these four graves were filled with bodies, they used the bulldozers to cover them with earth.

At present, the bamboo trunks, to which the victims were tied, and those that were used to smash the skulls of the people, were left on the graves. Everyone in this village knows about this. If you wish, I will take you there.

Question: Besides the above-mentioned facts, do you know anything else about the people killed in Koma Meas village?

Answer: I only know about the killings of the victims who were buried in the four graves which I have just told you about.

These minutes were completed at 9:00 a.m., July 4, 1979, and read back to Mrs. Sa Houl who confirmed that it is all true by signing her name below.

Secretary	*Witness*	*Interrogator*
San Kiri	Sa Houl	Mien Chieu

2.3.6.08
Mrs. Em Huan

At 2:00 p.m. on July 4, 1979, in the administrative office of Am Leang subdistrict, Tbong district, Kompong Speu province, were present Mr. Mien Chieu, official of the Ministry of the Interior, and Mr. San Kiri, clerk, taking down what Em Huan was stating. The content is as follows:

Question: Could you please let me know your age, birth place, and occupation?

Answer: I am Em Huan, 36. I was born in Koma Meas village, Am Leang subdistrict, Tbong district, Kompong Speu province. Occupation: agricultural worker, and during the Pol Pot period I lived on a state farm at Koma Meas village. Khmer nationality. Buddhist.

Question: During the Pol Pot period, did you see them killing people in Am Leang subdistrict?

Answer: During the Pol Pot period, on one occasion, I saw people being detained and killed.

Question: Could you tell precisely where the victims came from, and when and where they were killed?

Answer: The Pol Pot clique brought them here in February 1979. The victims said they were war prisoners, workers at Kompong Chhnang airport, and civilians. There were so many brought here that they sat along a three-kilometer stretch of the road from Potkma Mia to the Klong Bet intersection in Am Leang subdistrict. Then the Pol Pot clique took them away in trucks to another place to kill them. These people were killed at various places in Am Leang subdistrict. But I know of only one exact place in Koma Meas village where the Pol Pot clique killed victims, and that was near the Kosal Sam bridge.

Question: How did you know that the Pol Pot clique killed them at Koma Meas village?

Answer: During that time period I was clearing land, two hundred meters away from the place where the victims were killed. I saw trucks carrying people to the Kosal Sam pagoda. The trucks were full of people, about 50 to 60 people in each one. The people under detention were taken from the trucks, tied and led across a stream. The victims were held together with a bamboo stick and then were beaten with sticks on their heads until they died. They were shouting and cursing the executioners. Each day several batches were executed. Each time after the killing, bulldozers were used to cover the bodies over with earth. I saw four batches of them killed in this way.

Question: Do you know anything else?

Answer: No.

Question: Does anyone besides you know about the killing here?

Answer: The killing of the people in this village is known to many, particularly Nhin Soc Khang, Em Huan, and Chuon, who were clearing land with me.

This report was completed at 5:00 p.m. on July 4, 1979. It was read back and Em Huan agreed with the content. She also signed it.

Recorder	*Witness*	*Interrogator*
San Kiri	Em Huan	Mien Chieu

2.3.6.09

Mr. Cao Lui

Today at 3:00 p.m., July 4, 1979, we, Saes Chhon, official of the Ministry of the Interior, and Ros Rokha, secretary, drew up this transcript of a witness' testimony at the office of the Am Leang subdistrict committee.

Question: Would you tell us briefly your personal history?

Answer: I am Cao Lui, 35. I am a native of Koma Meas village, Am Leang subdistrict, Tbong district, Kompong Speu province.

Question: What was your occupation and where did you work?

Answer: I was a farmer in my native place.

Question: Did you ever witness any cruelties committed by the Pol Pot–Ieng Sary clique during their rule?

Answer: Yes, the Pol Pot–Ieng Sary clique was extremely cruel. Their men brought many people here from Phnom Penh and the eastern provinces to kill them, especially at the beginning of 1979, when they killed and buried 12,000 people at different places in Am Leang subdistrict. I happen to know the place where they killed and buried 4,600 people in ditches in a forest north of the Kosal Sam pagoda in Koma Meas village. Here is the story.

One day in February 1979, after the liberation of Phnom Penh, Pol Pot–Ieng Sary clique men drove many people to the Kosal Sam pagoda and killed them all. Four deep ditches had already been dug by two bulldozers. One of them was 20 meters long, 4 meters wide, and 3 meters deep. Groups of about 20 people were forced out of the trucks and were tied to bamboo poles about 5 meters long. Those people who were wearing good clothes were stripped. The groups were led one by one to the four ready ditches and were hit on the head to death by the soldiers with bamboo clubs and then thrown into the ditches. The slaughter lasted from 7:00 a.m. to 4:00 p.m. Trucks one after another brought people to the Kosal Sam pagoda for four consecutive days. I do not know how many trucks were used. I was told by some soldiers that 4,600 people were killed and buried in those four ditches and in a well nearby.

The murdered were mostly men of Pol Pot's regular army defeated in battles, including wounded soldiers. Some of them were workers at the Kompong Chhnang airport. One battalion and an Am Leang militia unit took part in the killing. The militiamen kept watch while the troops were doing the slaughter. I still remember several names, such as Mr. Houm, Mr. Mang Moeun, militiamen of Koma Meas village. Mr. Hon and Mr. Hoeun from Ta Kong village fled with Pol Pot to the mountains. Mr. Hon is now taking a reeducation course.

I was ordered by them to go there and fetch palm tree juice for them. I saw them hitting those people to death with bamboo clubs. Before doing the killing they all had drinks. They all had flushed faces and smelled strongly of alcohol as they came to me for water. I worked there for them for only four days, therefore, I could witness the killing only on those four days.

Question: Were there women, children, and old people among the murdered?

Answer: No, there weren't any women, children, or old people but only adult men aged from 16 to 40. They were mostly their own soldiers.

Question: Did you hear screams among the murdered?

Answer: Yes, they were screaming, shouting and cursing. Some people shouted "long live the revolution" which caused them to be immediately hit on the head to death.

Question: Do you know when the killing happened at the well?

Answer: All this happened on the above-mentioned days. After they killed and buried people in the well, they went on killing and burying people in the mentioned four ditches.

Question: Have you witnessed killing anywhere else?

Answer: No, I only heard about similar killings in other places.

Question: Have you anything else to say?

Answer: I think the Pol Pot–Ieng Sary clique was extremely cruel. What I want now is that the government arrest all those savage murderers and denounce their heinous crimes to public opinion in Kampuchea and the world. They should be eliminated for the sake of the safety and peace of the Kampuchean people. Otherwise, the whole nation will be annihilated.

Question: Are you sure that your words are true?

Answer: I swear that my words are true. I hold myself responsible to the law for anything wrong in my account.

This document was completed at 5:00 p.m., July 4, 1979 and approved by Mr. Cao Lui after the full text was read to him.

Witness	*Secretary*	*Official in charge*
Cao Lui	Ros Rokha	Saes Chhon

2.3.6.10
Field Investigation in Am Leang Subdistrict

Today at 7:30 a.m., July 5, 1979, we, Mien Chieu, an official of the Ministry of the Interior, and Ros Rokha, a secretary, arrived at the site where the Pol Pot–Ieng Sary clique carried out mass executions in Am Leang subdistrict, Tbong district, Kompong Speu province, as reported by the local population and administration.

Accompanying us were the following witnesses:

1. Mr. Bui Bun of Ta Kong village, Am Leang subdistrict.
2. Miss Nhim Sokha of Koma Meas village, Am Leang subdistrict.
3. Mr. Yeam Ich of Ta Kong village, Am Leang subdistrict.
4. Mr. Chea Cham of Koma Meas village, Am Leang subdistrict.
5. Mrs. Sa Houl of Koma Meas village, Am Leang subdistrict.

Field investigation witnesses were:

1. Mr. Ou Dong, representative of Kompong Speu provincial administration.
2. Mr. Um Chhuon, representative of Kompong Speu provincial administration.
3. Mr. Huot Kun Srin, Chairman of Am Leang subdistrict administrative committee.

4. Mr. Peu Kuon, Vice-Chairman of Am Leang subdistrict administrative committee.

The result of the investigation is as follows:

I. Site (sketch map attached)[1]

The entire area is in Koma Meas village, Am Leang subdistrict, Tbong district, Kompong Speu province, 90 kilometers northwest of Phnom Penh. The specific details of the area are as follows:

Following National Route 5 from Phnom Penh, we reached Oudong district. Route 114 (unpaved) took us to the direction of Oral mountain. Milestone No. 59 on Route 114 marks the territory of Koma Meas village, Am Leang subdistrict. At Milestone No. 59 we turned right, passed Kosal Sam pagoda and crossed Krang Ponley stream 500 meters from the road. We continued our journey to the north and reached a natural forest 350 meters from the stream. In the forest an open space had been cleared by bulldozer. This clearing was the main site for the investigation.

The investigation covered a one kilometer long area from the courtyard of Kosal Sam pagoda, to the clearing in the forest. Three specific sites were examined:

1—The clearing in the forest, which has large pits containing many human remains.
2—The Sno Pond well, containing human remains and leveled by bulldozers.
3—The pagoda courtyard with a number of bulldozers.

II. Detailed Description

1. *The area with huge pits containing human remains:*

The clearing is 850 meters north of Route 114 on a dirt path that goes by Kosal Sam pagoda. The clearing measures about 80 meters by about 40 meters. On the right were traces of three large pits leveled by bulldozers.

a) *Pit 1:* Lying in an east-west direction, measuring 7 meters by 53 meters. Around the pit to the north, east and west there were 11 tracks made by bulldozers when the pit was leveled.

b) *Pit 2:* Lying in a north-south direction and running across pit 1 and recognizable by the upgraded margin of earth that was moved when the pit was leveled. This pit was thus divided into two halves, one on each side of pit 1.

The first half, on the left side of pit 1, measured 4.5 meters by 13.5 meters. Around this half there were 3 bulldozer tracks.

1. This sketch map is not available.—Eds.

The second half, on the right side of pit 1, measured 4.5 meters by 7 meters. There were 2 bulldozer tracks around it.

c) *Pit 3:* Lying nearly parallel with pit 1, about 2 meters south of pit 1. The open space between the two pits was not leveled; shrubs and grass still remained there. Pit 3 is 8 meters wide and 27 meters long, measuring from the bulldozer tracks to the edge of the pit. Around the pit we found 6 bulldozer tracks in three directions, east, west, and south, covered with earth.

On the surface of the three pits, the earth was still soft and mixed with stones. Many parts are depressed and wet. There are only some small patches of green grass on the surface of the pits, and when we stepped onto these filled pits, our feet left footprints. This shows that the levelling had been done recently and in haste.

In particular, around the edges of the pits and in the space between pit 1 and pit 3, we found bamboo sticks of from 0.6 meter to 0.9 meter long and 4 centimeters in diameter which were found in the soft earth mixed with grass. We found 13 such bamboo sticks. We also found two long bamboo logs 7 centimeters in diameter; one is 4 meters long and the other is 1.5 meters long.

Excavation was done in four places in these pits, and the results are as follows:

a) *In pit 1:*

A 1.5 meter wide ditch was dug along the whole width of the pit at its west end.

Another ditch, 11 meters long and 1.5 meters wide, was dug along the length of the pit at its north end.

At the depth of 0.4 meter, we found, in the blackened earth, many bones in pieces and fragments with reddish wet material stuck to them, and they could still be recognized as upper limbs, lower limbs, hip bones, etc.

We found some skulls which still had patches of hair which slipped off while being unearthed. The holes of these skulls were filled with earth. Almost all skulls had lower jaws and teeth with them, many skulls were broken at the back showing grayish thick matter.

At a depth of 0.5 to 0.8 meter, more bones and skulls were seen. There were also many pieces of blackened and rotting cloth. When pulled up, fragments of bones fell out. They were recognizable as rib bones or leg bones and had moist reddish matter stuck to them.

At a depth of 1 meter, in two spots in pit 1, we found 14 skulls with patches of hair stuck to them, and 6 large pieces of clothing, recognizable as clothing of the victims, with bones inside.

The earth was sticky and was blackened with yellowish and pinkish spots. The stench was horrible.

b) *In pit 2:*

A one meter square hole was dug at the north end of pit 2.

At a depth of 0.2 meter there were pieces of small bones.

At a depth of about 0.5 meter, there were two pieces of skull, still with hair on them, and a piece of cloth, which was wrapped around a bone. The cloth was still covered in a sticky pinkish matter. When pulled out, three pieces of bones still attached to each other, not yet rotten, and clearly recognizable as hip bones.

c) *In pit 3:*

We dug a trench of 4.5 meters long, 2 meters wide. The middle of the uppermost layer of the filled pit was sinking and there was grass.

At a depth of about 0.5 meter, we saw many pieces of bones. These bones were mixed with pinkish sticky liquid mixed with black mud.

At a depth of about one meter, we saw some pieces of skull bones with some hair twisted in a paste of sticky liquid and mud. Four skulls were counted at this depth. There were long pieces of black cloth which were wet and swelling up. Inside these long pieces of black cloth there were also bones and sticky liquid.

2. *At the Sno Pond well containing human remains:*

The well lies at more than 250 meters southwest of the pits mentioned above, and 650 meters northwest of Route 114.

In the surrounding area there were traces of bulldozers forming low tracks converging at the well. The circumference of the well area including the bulldozers tracks is about 25 meters.

The well was already filled, some places on its surface sank and some wild grass appeared here or there.

Around the area of the well, there were two bamboo trunks of 0.8 meter long.

About 70 meters west of the well, behind sparse forest trees and bushes, there was a tall sugar palm with a ladder still tied to it.

A hole, 2 meters long and 1.5 meters wide, was dug in the middle of the well.

At a depth of 1 meter, we found some pieces of bones mixed with earth in very black mud.

At a depth of about 1.5 meters, many pieces of bones were mixed with pinkish sticky liquid and bones of yellowish color.

At a depth of about 1.8 meters, three pieces of rolled up, swollen cloth were found. When the cloth was torn, white and pinkish liquid mixed with black mud leaked out laying bare many pieces of bones of various types. At this depth, there was already considerable water, and a bad smell emanated from it.

3. *The Kosal Sam pagoda courtyard with many bulldozers:*

This is the site of our additional investigation, which is considered to produce supporting results for the main investigation above.

In the pagoda compound, about 30 meters to 150 meters from Route 114, there were 20 yellow bulldozers in disrepair. All the bulldozers were big and made in Japan. The blades of the bulldozers are 2.5 meters long.

III. Notes on Statements of the Witnesses and of Assistants

• The bulldozers used by the Pol Pot clique to fill up the pits and well for burying people had been allotted to water conservation and road projects and had been placed on the scene before the events happened.

• The pits were dug out according to the Pol Pot clique's order, so as to bury people, in Koma Meas were about 3 meters deep.

• Before the events took place the well had a circumference of around 4 meters and was 4 meters deep.

• The sugar palm 70 meters away from the well is the tree from where a witness who happened to be climbing it to collect palm juice saw Pol Pot agents dragging people to the well beating them on their heads, then throwing them down the well.

• Lacking minimum hygienic facilities for excavating works, we could only dig down to a depth of 1.8 meters. As human remains were rotting, we had to stop digging. We were then unable to investigate the entire depth of the pits and well as planned.

The investigation was completed at 2:00 p.m., on the same date as mentioned above.

This report was read to all the undersigned. They approved the correctness of this report and hereunder affixed their signatures.

Persons present	*Witnesses*	*Official*	*Secretary*
Ou Dong	Bui Bun	Mien Chieu	Ros Sokha
Um Chhuon	Nhim Sokha		
Huot Kum Srin	Yeam Ich		
Pen Kuon	Chea Cham		
	Sa Houl		

Investigation at Wat Champuh Kaek

2.3.7.01

Mr. Chum Sary

Made by Mr. Chum Sary, at the office of the Ministry of Interior at 2:00 p.m. on July 23, 1979, in the presence of Mr. Prum Chien, official of the Ministry of the Interior; and Mr. San Kiri, secretary.

Question: Your name, birth place, and occupation?

Answer: My name is Chum Sary, 41 years old, born in Prech Tanum village, Koh Sotin district, Kompong Cham province. Before 1975, I lived in Phnom Penh and earned my living as a car mechanic.

Question: What did you do and where did you live under the Pol Pot regime?

Answer: Following April 17, 1975, I was employed at a prison camp located at Wat Champuh Kaek, where I repaired vehicles and taught the sons of the guards to repair cars.

Question: When was the prison established in the pagoda?

Answer: The pagoda at Champuh Kaek became a place of detention in June of 1975 until January 7, 1979.

Question: A pagoda is a sacred place. Why do you call that pagoda a prison camp?

Answer: Many detainees were sent here. They were tortured for some time and then were killed. All of them. Prisoners kept coming all the time. Tens of thousands of people were detained and executed there between 1975 and January 7, 1979. The prisoners included soldiers, officers, and bureaucrats from the Lon Nol regime, monks, and even people who had inadvertently damaged tools while working in people's communes. The Pol Pot–Ieng Sary people went so far as to imprison young people here, young boys and girls who loved one another without the authorization from Angkar.

Question: How did Pol Pot men treat the prisoners?

Answer: Prisoners were treated in an inhuman way. There were times when each was given only a corncob to last the day. They were also beaten savagely. Torture was inflicted in three places: in the tower near the main shrine, at the foot of a longan tree by the steps leading out from the main shrine, and in the shrine itself.

Prisoners were tied up and left hanging on that tree. The shrine was reserved for monks, who were tied up and forced to pray before the Buddha statue.

"Bow to your Buddha and ask for his help," the guards would tell them, accompanying their words with blows. "Let's see if your Buddha could be of any help to you now." Some of the monks were clubbed to death on the spot. All told, almost 300 monks were killed at the pagoda. The guards made the prisoners dig their own graves before bashing their heads with wooden clubs or iron bars. At first, the dead were buried at some distance from the pagoda. Later they were buried close to the building and banana trees were planted on the graves. That's why the banana garden at the pagoda is full of graves now.

They even imprisoned and killed women and children, some of whom were only 3 or 4 months old, still breast-feeding on their mothers. There were almost 200 men, women, and children at the pagoda on the morning of January 7, 1979. Just before the flight of the Pol Pot men, Huon, the deputy chief of Kien Svay district (formerly District 16), personally put to death all these prisoners. There was no time to bury the bodies. This was told to me by Huon's aide. On that day, I had to drive Huon and the district chief—a woman called Bo—to their hideout on Mount Urang in Kompong Speu province. They attempted to dispose of me, but I managed to escape and return to Champuh Kaek.

I know all this because I was working in a place located only 15 to 20 meters from the place of torture, sometimes I passed by there many times a day fetching tools and parts.

Question: What was the state of the pagoda when you were first taken there in 1975?

Answer: It was in good condition then. But with the arrival of the prisoners the buildings were turned into cells and torture chambers. Statues were smashed. All the big trees at the entrance were cut down. The main shrine where monks were tortured was finally demolished.

Question: Would you like to add anything else?

Answer: No.

Question: Can you vouch for the truth of your statement?

Answer: I swear that my statements are truthful and I bear full responsibility before the law if they are false.

The interview ended at 4:30 p.m., July 23, 1979. Transcript confirmed by Mr. Chum Sary.

Witness	*Secretary*	*Interviewer*
Chum Sary	San Kiri	Prum Chien

2.3.7.02

Mr. Chung Nhet

Today, July 22, 1979, at 8:00 a.m., at the office of Prek Thmey subdistrict, Kien Svay district, Kandal province, we the undersigned, Prum Chien, official of the Ministry of the Interior, and San Kiri, secretary, are making a transcript of the statement of a person named Chung Nhet.

Question: Your family name and given name, and your place of birth, please?

Answer: I am Chung Nhet, 50 years of age, born and living in Champuh Kaek village, Prek Thmey subdistrict, Kien Svey district, Kandal province.

Question: Do you live near the pagoda at Champuh Kaek?

Answer: My house is only a few hundred meters from that pagoda.

Question: Do you recall the date of the construction of the pagoda, and can you tells us if the pagoda was visited by Buddhists?

Answer: The pagoda was built before I was born, and according to the records it was built 80 years ago. Before the Pol Pot regime, Buddhists from different regions came to the pagoda in great numbers. But since Pol Pot came to power, the pagoda has had to close its doors and stop having worship. The Pol Pot men forbade the people to visit pagodas. The residents of my subdistrict were sent by force to various destinations: some went toward Battambang, others toward Pursat, and still others toward Saang district, Kandal province. My family was in the third group. Only after the liberation of the country on January 7, 1979, could we go back to our former place of residence.

Question: The residents of the subdistrict said that you were among the first to enter the Champuh Kaek pagoda after the villagers returned. What did you see there?

Answer: At first I found everything in awful disrepair. The row of ancient trees by the gate of the pagoda had been knocked down. In back, in the pagoda's classrooms, I saw strewn about the corpses of women and children. And in the monks' living quarters there were rows of iron bars stained with blood. And the walls were stained with blood. Behind the residence, I saw a pile of men's corpses. The pagoda's meeting rooms had been turned at various times into a kitchen, a rice granary, a storehouse for human excrement, and an automobile repair shop. In the sanctuary, the statues of Buddha were thrown down to the floor, shattered. The wall hangings were in tatters. The floor stones were raised up and the ground had been dug up in several places. In one corner, I saw a pile of cassocks. According to Chum Sary, who was a mechanic at the automobile repair shop there under the Pol Pot regime, the sanctuary was used from April 1975 to January 7, 1979, by the Pol Pot people as a place to torture and kill monks. Here the executioners killed many monks who were arrested in the region.

After looking around the pagoda, I went to see some neighbors, Ta Muon, Ta Lo, and Ta Suon, who then helped me to gather up the bodies, of which there were 173. We found two men and one woman still alive, and soldiers of the National United Front for the Salvation of Kampuchea took them to the hospital as fast as they could. The woman did not survive her mortal wounds, but the two men were healed. I do not know where they are now.

All the victims had their hands tied behind their backs, their skulls were broken, and their throats slit. Some of the victims were completely decapitated. And there were even babies three to four months old. We made a notebook list of the names of the victims, and it came to 10,609. The residents of the region passed this notebook of misfortune from hand to hand looking for names of their relatives. I do not know who has the list now.

After gathering up the corpses, we burned them according to tradition and put the ashes in the burial stupa of the pagoda.

Question: Can one still see traces of the criminal destruction of the pagoda by the Pol Pot people?

Answer: With the coming of people's power, the pagoda has been restored to accommodate Buddhist believers once again. We also cleared out, cleaned, and repaired the buildings. The iron bars were taken outside. We put new statues of Buddha in the sanctuary and repainted the drawings inside the pagoda.

There remain as evidence three rows of iron bars, one iron pipe that was found when gathering up the bodies (at that time you could see fresh blood and hair on one end of the pipe), shattered statues of Buddha, destroyed towers on one of which there were blood stains, steel wires hanging from the ceiling, etc. If you come to the pagoda, I will show you all that.

The transcript was completed at 10:00 a.m. on July 22, 1979, in conformity to the statements of the above-named Chung Nhet, who read it over and affixed his signature below with ours.

Witness	*Secretary*	*Official in charge*
Chung Nhet	San Kiri	Prum Chien

2.3.7.03
Mr. Bun Sath

The following interrogation was conducted at the prison camp in Kandal province, at 8:00 a.m. on July 19, 1979, by Mr. Saes Chhon, official of the Ministry of the Interior, and an interrogator, and by Mr. San Kiri, secretary, with regard to Bun Sath, born in 1954, at Woa Koh Thom village, Koh Thom subdistrict, Koh Thom district, Kandal province, and a resident of Prek Sdei village, Prek Sdei subdistrict, Koh Thom district, Kandal province. Occupation: farming. Education: Primary school. Nationality: Khmer. Religion: Buddhist. Rank in the Pol Pot army: company political officer.

Question: Tell us about your places of employment and your jobs under the Pol Pot regime.

Answer: I joined a production team in my village in June 1974. In September, I joined the Pol Pot army and in May 1975 I became deputy squad leader. At the end of 1975 I was promoted platoon commander, and became company political officer the following year. Starting in September 1976, I was in charge of the Security Section at Prey Ksay prison camp, Koh Thom district. I was transferred to Putaly camp in April 1977. In August I was assigned to the agricultural farm where prisoners worked, which supplied food to the prison camp. I worked there until January 7, 1979, when I fled to Prey La Via, where I lived four or five days in a pagoda near the market. Then I returned to my native place in Prek Sdei village, Prek Sdei subdistrict, Koh Thom district, Kandal province. After four days, I took shelter at the house of my uncle at Prey Kabbas village, Prey Kabbas subdistrict, Prey Kabbas district, Takeo province. I stayed there just for four days and then fled to Prey Kdao village in the same province. I was arrested by the liberation forces, and attended a one-day reeducation session at Say Qua market. Then, I was allowed to return to Prey Sdayko, my native village. On February 22, 1979, I was sent to a reeducation course in Koh Thom district. On June 26, 1979, I was sent to the Kandal provincial reeducation camp.

Question: Please speak about your concrete jobs during the time you worked at the district military committee and at the prison camp under the regime of Pol Pot and Ieng Sary.

Answer: Training new recruits was my principal task during the time I worked at the district military committee. In the security force at Koh Thom prison in 1976, my job was to supervise prisoners at work. Work began at seven in the morning and continued until midday. Then the prisoners were allowed to have a break. For food they were given bran mixed with corn, cassava, or, on rare occasions, a little rice. There were only sixty or seventy prisoners in 1976, but the number increased to six hundred in 1977. I beat the prisoners sometimes when taking them out to work. Between the beginning of 1978 to August that year, I worked as a supervisor of working prisoners and head of the patrol unit.

Question: In your previous confession, you mentioned your participation in killings. Speak more about that.

Answer: About three hundred prisoners were killed at Koh Thom camp at the end of 1977. I myself killed five of the prisoners. The rest were executed by the guards and also by the camp commander and his deputy. The victims were army officers and administrative personnel under the Lon Nol regime, and former inhabitants of Phnom Penh driven out of their homes on April 17, 1975. In 1978, I took part in the execution of three thousand people at Po Tuan Le in Ko Thom subdistrict. It took five months to do the job, from May to September.

As the day of liberation came near, the remaining thirty-five prisoners in the camp were all killed. I killed fifty of the three thousand prisoners who were executed at Po Tuan Le. There were a score of other executioners including the camp commander Thi, and Sum, Khuan, Muan, Uon, Coong, Phac, and Mien, who were camp officials.

Question: What sort of people were those victims. Where were they killed?

Answer: The prisoners executed in 1977 consisted entirely of Lon Nol army soldiers and civil servants. Those put to death in 1978 included Khmers having family ties with Vietnamese or Chinese. We also killed persons who were considered hostile to Angkar.

The victims were taken to the area of Po Tuan Le village in Ko Thom subdistrict, Ko Thom district, about one kilometer from the Po Tuan Le prison. They were buried in pits, each containing three hundred or four hundred bodies. I remember the place very well.

Question: How did you kill the prisoners?

Answer: The prisoners were tied together in pairs, and were taken to the pits, bashed on the napes of their necks, and pushed into the pits. Iron bars were used for the killing. Each time, we killed from two hundred and fifty to three hundred persons. We began at 6:00 p.m. and continued steadily until 9:00 p.m. or 10:00 p.m. That was the best time because the area was deserted.

Question: What were your instructions before each killing?

Answer: There were no special instructions at all, except the order for the killing by Thi and Sum, who were in charge of the camp. The list of prisoners to be executed was read out by Coong and Sotak. We tied up the prisoners and led them out for execution.

Question: Why didn't you shoot the prisoners?

Answer: To keep people from knowing and, as explained by our supervisors, to save ammunition.

Question: Did you participate in other killings besides the ones in 1977 and 1978?

Answer: I didn't take part in any other killing.

Question: Do you guarantee the truth of your confession?

Answer: What I said was completely true. If you suspect my statement I'll accept any punishment you may think fit to give me.

The interrogation was completed at 10:00 a.m. on July 19, 1979. The transcript was read out for the defendant for confirmation.

Defendant	*Secretary*	*Interrogator*
Bun Sath	San Kiri	Saes Chhon

2.3.7.04

Field Investigation at Wat Champuh Kaek

Done at 8:00 a.m. July 23, 1979, by Mr. Saes Chhon and Mr. Prum Chien, officials of the Ministry of the Interior in charge of preparing documents, and Mr. Ouk Chandara, secretary in charge of recording transcripts. In attendance were Kum Dan, a Buddhist personality; Superior Monk Ke Dan, a representative of the Buddhist monks of the pagoda; Sam Nang, a representative of the Kien Svey district committee; Dak Tit, head of the public security services of Kandal province; Chum Sary, a witness (and who was a mechanic working in the pagoda under the Pol Pot regime).

We conducted this field investigation as follows. This pagoda, which was once named Moni Sovan, and was later changed to Champuh Kaek, is located in Prek Thmey subdistrict, Kien Svay district, Kandal province. It covers one hectare of land and includes the main pagoda, a meeting hall, living quarters for the superior monks, and three buildings for the pagoda's primary school. There are a dozen rooms for other monks and believers, and around these residences are low concrete stupas. There are also rows of large koki trees, and at their feet a thick stand of banana trees covering more than one hectare of land.

After the date of liberation, April 17, 1975, the Pol Pot–Ieng Sary gangs turned the pagoda's complex of buildings, a sacred place of worship for the Kampuchean people, into a prison, and a place for torture and killing. Here follows a description of the layout of the buildings in the pagoda.

Near the entrance one finds the primary school, which is made up of three buildings with a capacity of 180 pupils. Pol Pot and Ieng Sary used the school as a prison for women and children. Holes were made in the partition walls of the school, and long iron bars were inserted into the holes and were used to manacle prisoners. The doors of the cells are locked from the outside. On the right-hand side is the meeting hall, a place where, when the pagoda was still functioning, monks, nuns, and believers assembled to say prayers and to profess their religion. The meeting hall was turned into a shop for repairing machinery, and into a granary and a kitchen for the prison. All the statues of Buddha were destroyed or thrown down.

We next went to the living quarters of the superior monks. These living quarters had become detention cells. Inside these cells we found a hundred or so pairs of handcuffs attached to a 7-meter-long iron bar that was used to fetter groups of prisoners. Around the pagoda, cement stupas were turned into a place for torture, where one can still see blood stains, gallows, and ropes used to tie up prisoners.

Chung Nhet took us farther, in the company of other villagers, to a stupa, a kind of small mausoleum built over a tomb. This little house was 2 meters long by 1.8 meters wide.

In the stupa was a pile of human bones: skulls, arm and leg bones, and skeletons.

From Chung Nhet and Chung Sarek, who are local residents, we found out that after liberation, January 7, 1979, the executioners, before fleeing, killed the prisoners, who numbered two hundred, including thirty women and children. The local residents gathered up the corpses of the victims who had been thrown around the pagoda and buried them. The bones found in the stupas are those of these two hundred victims. Photographs and film are attached as evidence.[1]

Chum Sary pointed out a longan tree to us and explained that the enemy tied victims to it and beat them to extract statements. At the foot of the tree there are still dried blood stains, and a rope that was used to tie the hands of the victims.

The witnesses and local residents also showed us the grave area around the pagoda. Nearly all the graves are covered with banana trees or other trees.

We dug up one grave. It is 1.2 meters long, 0.45 meter wide, and 0.4 meter deep. Inside we found a human body.

We dug up a second grave 5 meters from the first. This grave is 1.5 meters long, 0.5 meter wide, and 0.4 meter deep and has two human bodies inside (these two tombs were photographed and filmed).

According to local officials, monks, and witnesses, this area of the pagoda became a detention center where large numbers of people were incarcerated. The number of persons killed is written in a notebook: about 10,600 persons, including two hundred monks. We asked for this document but,

1. This film is not available. — Eds.

out of fear of being held as material witnesses, several witnesses replied that they had burned it. All that remains is a small notebook, half burned. We took this notebook. The monks showed us as well an iron bar 0.78 meter long and 0.04 meter in diameter, that was still stained with blood.

During this field investigation, Dak Tit, a representative of the province government, Sam Nang, a representative of the district government, and Superior Monk Kum Dan gave testimony and participated in the above-mentioned acts.

This transcript was completed at 11:00 a.m. the same day. The persons whose names are written in this transcript have looked at it again and have affixed their signatures below.

Persons attending	*Witness*	*Officials in charge*
Kum Dan	Chum Sary	Saes Chhon
Ke Dan		Prum Chien
Sam Nang		Ouk Chandara
Dak Tit		

Reports on Various Aspects of Social Life

2.4.01
Report on an Investigation into Crimes of the Pol Pot-Ieng Sary Clique Against the Population of Phnom Penh

I. Introduction

Prior to April 17, 1975, the people of Phnom Penh lived through a number of unstable political regimes. The population of this administrative, economic, and intellectual capital city in the period between 1970 and 1975 grew from 2.4 to 2.8 million inhabitants. This demographic growth stemmed from the massive exodus of rural dwellers in the last three years of the Lon Nol regime, an effect of the neo-colonial war, conducted by the Americans and their henchmen. This unpopular war, which only served the cause of one faction and foreign interests, gave rise, among all social sectors, to an earnest aspiration for peace, a lasting peace based on social justice. Some of the factors that led to increasingly unbearable social injustice were systematic corruption among the rulers, the enormous gap between living standards, forced unemployment arising from the paralyzed economic infrastructure and the exploitation of the weaker by the stronger, various economic undertakings that benefited big business at the expense of poor wage-earners, and all sorts of prostitution born of misery.

Nonetheless, the Khmers, always talented and highly capable in their productive and creative labor, are a hard-working people endowed with perseverance and wisdom, whose ancient civilization was among the most prestigious. A number of monuments, among the best renowned in the world, the celebrated vestiges of Angkor, as well as numerous artistic and literary works and handicrafts speak volumes on this subject.

Therefore, faced with this degeneracy, this degradation of their society during the last years, they craved for the advent of another political regime capable of creating a new society and of meeting their wishes. This aspiration for a lasting peace, a definitive political stability, was all the more ardent as the decadence of their country was obvious. Their sole salvation lay in the Khmer socialist revolution upon which rested all their confidence and hopes. Thus, they impatiently looked forward to its victory, and in the near future. The news of the forthcoming final triumph of this revolution filled them with joy.

II. The First Days of the Arrival of the Pol Pot–Ieng Sary Army in Phnom Penh

On April 17, 1975, at dawn, the black-clad troops of Pol Pot's revolutionary armed forces entered Phnom Penh. Rudely awakened from their sleep by the shooting and explosions from the B-40s which destroyed public buildings, the residents of Phnom Penh came out of their houses to welcome them, applauding, jumping, smiling, so great was their joy. From time to time, these bursts of joy were interrupted by bomb explosions. Soon their jubilation was mixed with astonishment. Armored vehicles flying white flags and carrying Lon Nol troops side by side with black-clad men, passed along streets and avenues of Phnom Penh. They shouted in chorus: "It is peace. The war is over: no more fighting!" Following their example, the residents of Phnom Penh also waved white flags. Then, in their turn, foreign embassies hoisted the colors of their respective countries. Hospitals displayed their Red Cross banner.

It was then that the order to evacuate the capital rapidly was given out under the pretext of avoiding losses in lives which might result from U.S. air attacks and the wiping out of remnants of the Lon Nol army. Everyone was astonished beyond description.

Within a few hours, they discovered that these "black-clad" men were cutthroats and looters. To their consternation, the latter opened fire on those who refused or were not fast enough to comply with their orders. Others, armed with B-40s, began to ransack stores and houses.

There was no electricity that night. Phnom Penh had become a dead city. The national radio did not broadcast. From time to time, in the depth of the night, explosions broke the agonizing silence. The following day, "black-clad" men grew still more numerous in streets littered with the bodies of people recently killed for taking too long to evacuate. By noon, they started driving people out of their homes, threatening to destroy everything if the orders were not obeyed immediately. Volleys of AK-47s fired in the air punctuated their orders. "It is for three days only," they affirmed. In point of fact, that was only the first of the measures taken by Pol Pot's "revolution" in implementation of his radical policy, a principle of which is as follows: all city dwellers must become farmers. Only those who know how to plant rice have the right to eat and those who do not have no reason to live. This accounts for the indirect killing of Phnom Penh people, whose first trial was the hellish exodus during which more than 500,000 people were eliminated.

At the same time, is not the destruction of the libraries, including the

National Library, and of the bookshops, and the systematic destruction of books, evidence of a deliberate effort to obliterate creative intelligence, culture, civilization and sciences? And this systematic destruction was carried out in accordance with a system, an ideological principle easily recognized by the world.

From the first day of the arrival of the Pol Pot troops, the major part of the Phnom Penh civilian population saw with their own eyes how they destroyed, by B-40s, hospitals, surgical rooms, the Pasteur Institute. Patients were pushed away from their beds. Those who could not get up, or walk, or even move, were hauled together with their beds to the streets. Some of these unfortunate people were being given serum. Most of these patients died within a few hours.

On the major highways, along which the Phnom Penh people were driven to the countryside and the outlying areas plagued with malaria, the living conditions were appalling: no food allowances or medicine for a population deprived of everything. The sanitary conditions were revolting. Massive and long caravans of deportees, progressing at snail's pace, advancing one kilometer a whole morning, even a whole day, trekked along aimlessly, from place to place, pressed on by the rhythm of warning shots. Families then started being shattered: children strayed away, wives lost their husbands. Moreover, they could neither begin nor finish their meals without being disturbed by these terrible rhythms. Every time they tried to get a little rice, dried fish, or salt from villagers by trading fine clothing or valuable objects, warning shots would chase them away. All along the way, there were searches of suitcases and luggage, obviously for looting purposes (transistor radio sets, jewelry, new clothes, etc.).

Along with this indescribable disarray, the "purge" of intellectuals began. For this purpose, Pol Pot resorted to a system of detection merely based on appearances. Those who looked like intellectuals, especially those who wore eyeglasses for nearsightedness or farsightedness, were listed as suspects and could be arrested at once and sent to the security service. Many of them did not return to their families. The intellectuals were all regarded and treated as outlaws and parasites. If a few of them managed to survive, it was because they had not revealed their real identity and had lived under disguise with borrowed names. Those who did reveal their true identities and survived owed their good luck to having anti-regime "rebels" as heads of their cooperatives. The latter protected them by declining to denounce them to higher authorities and by sending them to work far away from the villages to keep them away from the watchful eyes of informers.

The purge of intellectuals started when the Phnom Penh population was driven out of the capital city. It began simultaneously with the purge of the Lon Nol army men. Pol Pot and Ieng Sary used a very simple yet quite infamous trick: dispatching vehicles equipped with loudspeakers to broadcast an urgent appeal that they needed intellectuals (professors, technicians, physicians) for the reconstruction of the country, and the former military men for the national defense.

In their long journey to the most out-of-the-way corners of the country, large numbers of Phnom Penh civilians, mostly elderly, children, women in childbirth, pregnant women, the sick, the disabled, died in atrocious conditions: without food, medicine, or midwives. Those who walked along the Mekong River during this long march through rice fields, forests, and swamps were eyewitnesses to other killings: trains of corpses floating in the river, swept away by the current. This ghastly scene lasted several months.

III. The Cruel Fate of Phnom Penh People and Intellectuals in Deportation Camps

The population was divided into three categories. The Phnom Penh people belongs to the last one, i.e., "citizens" deprived of all rights, "war prisoners," in other words, the vanquished. They were called "new inhabitants" and were treated as parasites.

The coercive system applied to the Phnom Penh population consisted of a kind of automation of men, in that they were forbidden to think, to express anything contrary to the principles of the "Revolution," to maintain interpersonal contacts, to criticize, to show emotions and feelings, or to move from one village to another. From the beginning of 1977, eating and cooking at home (apart from boiling water) was also forbidden. Failure to comply with these orders to the letter was deemed thinking, and this mental activity was considered a culpable act. Any delay in implementing the order amounted to an act of rebellion that might be intensively investigated. If this continued, the suspects would be sent to "reeducation" centers and, in a great many cases, it was capital punishment decided by the head of the cooperative. At home, especially in the evening or at night, husbands and wives dared not talk, lest spies and informers denounce them. The husband would fear that his wife might let slip something about her former profession under Lon Nol. Many had lost their lives because of this kind of imprudence. He would fear that she might tell him of her petty larceny the previous day (some fish, rice, salt, cassava, sweet potatoes, or a few bananas for their children).

Angkar, this Organization of the Revolution, always omnipresent, had its eyes and ears everywhere. It was the terror personified of Phnom Penh people. The victims, before being done away with, were usually sent away to fetch something. If in the evening, the husband did not return, his wife could be sure that he would never return. She should keep herself, above all, from crying or showing her sorrow during her working hours, for that would be regarded as an act of rebellion against the political line of the "Revolution," seriously endangering the "Revolution." The punishment varied with the degree of gravity: either sending them to a deportation camp located, most likely, in a malaria-infected area, or simply a clean disappearance. When there was public accusation, if the head of the cooperative did not mete out any punishment, he himself would disappear. Angkar was omnipresent, indeed.

How were the Phnom Penh people treated when ill? Under the Pol Pot regime, only those whose diseases were evident by sight, such as wounds, influenza, etc., were considered ill. Those who suffered from diseases of the lungs, heart, liver, kidneys, stomach, in brief, from what was invisible, were regarded as fakes, lazy, rebels and subjected to close scrutiny. Many of them disappeared. Those held to be too sick were finished off and thrown into wells. Pol Pot's henchmen told their families there were so many such wells that Korean and Chinese advisers in Phnom Penh dared not drink Khmer water: they only drank coconut milk.

Those considered to be sick were hospitalized, whether they wanted to be or not. Hospitalization was a dreadful thing: apart from the lack of hygiene and cleanliness, the diet was horrible and medical treatment, more often than not, turned out to be fatal. Some died of avitaminosis, malnutrition, others from poisoning. The luckiest were those who came out with some infirmity resulting from an abscess caused by unsanitary injections. For the "imaginary sick" and old people, deemed to be lazy or serious saboteurs, the punishment went from reduction to total deprivation of food rations (the luckiest got a handful of rice for one or two meals).

To the daily working hours was added extra work called "socialist labor." Right after the midday meal, everybody was given other jobs: planting vegetables, weeding, etc. At 1:00 p.m., as the bell rang, the ordinary work, called "basic work," resumed. At 5:00 p.m., the "basic work" was suspended and they were shifted to "socialist work" till dusk. After a quick bath, they were allowed to dine. When there was too much to do, especially in the replanting season, women worked until 10:00 p.m., sometimes 11:00 p.m. Those women who had babies under one year of age breastfed them before going to bed, utterly exhausted. At 4:30 a.m., the dreadful bell sounded all over the village. All the Phnom Penh survivors, even now, still shudder when they happen to hear something resembling that sinister bell.

There were practically no days off. The so-called holidays were devoted to indoctrination, to brainwashing, if not to other work even harder than the everyday work. So, holidays were undesirable and even abhorred. During periods when there was not enough work, sessions of mutual criticism were organized every evening. It was a kind of self-inflicted moral punishment in public. Those who were not diligent enough in working, those who spent too much time caring for their families or were late for the farm work, were virulently stigmatized, or even subject to investigation. These sessions, presided over by the chairman of the cooperative, usually ended very late in the evening.

There cannot be anything more inhuman, more shocking than this regime of working, this coercive system, this robotization that bled human beings white, overtaxed human capacities, and diminished men physically and intellectually. In a nutshell, that is a system really hostile to man in general and, in this case, to the Phnom Penh people in particular. This work of slaves, of war prisoners, imposed upon the Khmer people in general, and the Phnom Penh population in particular, had two aims: one of an economic order, and the other of an ideological order. These two aims were intertwined. The major concern of the leaders of the regime was to increase the production of paddy rice (from 1 to 3 tons per hectare and, in the last two years, from 3.5 to 7 tons per hectare). The second aim was to achieve the robotization of men so that they would have no other thoughts than those permitted by Angkar. All this had its origin in Maoism and the political principles preached by the Peking leaders who wanted to turn the Khmers into rice-producing machines who consume no fuel and not too much rice.

Spying organization and system based on the principle of "Angkar's Omnipresence"

To judge by his system of coercion, Pol Pot aimed at systematically rooting out the former feudal and capitalist society as well as the ancient Khmer family. The new society would be one composed of robots whom he could manipulate at will. The division of the population into three categories was designed to sow dissension between Khmer city dwellers and other citizens. All relations between these three categories of "citizens" were forbidden, gatherings were absolutely banned, talks between two or more people were closely watched. Denunciation was encouraged with rewards. Children were taught to spy on and to denounce their parents. In other words, Angkar made everyone distrust everyone else so that they entertained adverse feelings for each other. This famous organization of the Revolution of Pol Pot sowed panic and spread division among the population. The slightest manifestation of unity to oppose this policy was savagely repressed. At Koh Phal, in Kompong Cham province, a general uprising started by Malayans ended in a bloodbath: the whole village was massacred by Pol Pot.

Repression against the elderly, women, and children

(a) Pol Pot did not want women to be pregnant, because women constituted a very important pillar in agricultural production. Any request for maternity leave deemed too early was very ill taken and would lead to substantial reduction of the woman's daily food ration. Tormented by hunger, expectant mothers would decide to keep working. If such indispositions as vomiting or fatigue became too frequent, the women would be sent to the hospital. They would implore their team leaders not to force them there. Their husbands would be authorized to see them only two or three times a month or, if they were sent to work in remote places far from villages, once every three months. Very few men were given the favor to work in a village within reach of their wives. For this, they must work as servants to power-vested people in the village. Those poor pregnant women lacked everything: no special diet, necessary for the coming baby's health, nor affection, nor comfort. Some of the husbands were driven to commit illegal acts in order to alleviate their wives' plight. It was then that the tragedy began: picking fruit without authorization amounted to stealing socialist property, which entailed one or two days of imprisonment. In many cases, the culprit simply disappeared: the penalty depended on the local authorities.

One month after delivery, a baby's mother would resume work. Any delay would be frowned upon for lack of determination in her role as "revolutionary." It goes without saying that under such conditions, the newborn was far from being in good health. According to a study by Dr. Nouth Savoeun on the matter (see his report, Document 2.4.03c), the height, weight, and intellectual development of Phnom Penh children born under Pol Pot and Ieng Sary has been impaired permanently, as well as that of those who are now below 15 years of age. Indeed, the latter, driven out of the capital city together with their parents in the midst of the hottest season, were poorly clothed, undernourished, and had no medicine, yet they had to walk a long distance on foot to get to their destinations. In the camps, they were never given enough to eat, on the rationale that they did not work.

(b) The elderly underwent a slow death. Angkar made them work hard, despite declining health and physical capacity, and at the same time gave them only starvation rations. If they fell short in their work, the penalty went from a reduction to a total loss of food rations. The solution adopted by local authorities to do away with unproductive aged consumers was simply to ignore them. If they grumbled or shouted about their treatment, the authorities would beat them.

(c) "Children are the pillar of this new society," said the Pol Pot people, and they gave them certain privileges over the adults and elderly. These privileges, however, had to be justified by their endurance in labor, by the quantity and quality of their work. Not only did Angkar make them work as hard as grownups, but even harder: they had to build dikes, dig canals, clear trails under the scorching sun, without flinching. Many succumbed from delirious fever and in their rare moments of lucidity, were nonetheless, aware that they were being skillfully exploited. Sent to build huge dikes in remote, malaria-infested locations, they would cry together at night in their huts, battered by rain and storm, thinking of their parents, in particular of their mothers to whom they had no time to bid farewell before their hasty departure. They had almost nothing, no mosquito nets or bed covers. They quivered like birds, not daring to show their mental collapse in this "edifying struggle" to rebuild the country. The Organization of the Revolution told them that it is for their parents' welfare, so that their parents would no longer be being dying of hunger, that they are the real pillars of the nation. They wanted to send letters to their parents but unfortunately could not because they did not know how to read or write. They brought what little they had of tobacco to those Phnom Penh youths with whom they secretly kept friendly relations so that the latter would write for them to their loved ones. They wanted to write to their brothers and sisters, but did not know their whereabouts, the latter being in other mobile brigades and sent to unknown places. They regretted not having had the time to learn to read and write, and in this new society where they had run aground, the Organization of the Revolution had told them over and over again that the most efficient school was manual labor.

Repression of Buddhist monks: destruction of religious faith

Monks were forced to give up their frocks. Representatives of Angkar shamelessly humiliated them by compelling them to work like the others, produce like the others and for the others. They didn't realize how ridiculously awkward they looked with their shaved heads in those awful black clothes. This double humiliation could only drive them to suicide according to the Buddhist tenets in the sense that even though Buddhism does not accept suicide, it preaches indifference in the face of death. They continued their meditation and refused to carry out the humiliating forced labor imposed upon them: to kill oxen, buffaloes, or pigs.

Apart from the destruction of the pagodas and Buddha statues, let us examine how Pol Pot destroyed religious faith. Each time Pol Pot's militiamen surprised old women praying before the Buddha statuettes they kept in secret, they would say: "If Buddha is really mighty, he must protect you. And suppose I kill you now, are you sure he'll come to your rescue?" Thereupon the thugs would throw the statuettes into nearby ponds or rivers, or stomp on them, grinning. Take, for instance, these slogans of Pol Pot: "Buddha is useless to human society; he does not help to produce at all. Mao does help produce to support men," "Pray to god and you'll see if he gives you something to eat or not. Pray to Angkar and you'll see whether you are given food to eat or not." Of course, children who prayed to Angkar and showed their gratitude to it got their food allowances. Whereas old people, facing the choice between Buddha and their stomach, had to opt for the latter. In this way Pol Pot destroyed the Buddhist faith.

Medical care

The hospitals Pol Pot set up and the physicians he trained were merely places and means to carry out the killing of the Khmer population in general and of Phnom Penh people in particular. It is true that some scientific medicines were used, but they were reserved exclusively for the rulers. Those considered to be living under a suspended death sentence, that is, the people in general, and even more so the Phnom Penh population, had no right to use these medicines. For them, empirical medicine, so-called national medicine, was substituted for scientific medicine. In some cases, the two went in tandem or were mixed dangerously. Medication was administered without prior diagnosis. Physicians with, at best, 3 months of training, sometimes children aged 14, having no theoretical knowledge, took the liberty of performing scandalous surgical operations, as well as monstrous experimentation on patients they used as guinea pigs. Any Phnom Penh person who refused to serve as a guinea pig would be charged with instigation of rebellion against the medical science of the Khmer Revolution, in short, contempt of the Khmer Revolution.

Never before in the history of mankind had there been such a demented medical system. Never before had the people of Phnom Penh seen such a horrible, monstrous spectacle. What is more, it was they who were at the same time victims and participants, that is to say, guinea pigs. Those who dared declare themselves sick were sent to these slaughter houses. In fact, it was a purge aimed at eliminating those physically unfit for the hard work of agricultural production, because the sick consume but do not produce. As a directive to physicians to kill these unfortunates, the Pol Pot authorities used this famous slogan: "Keeping them alive, one gets nothing; killing them, one loses nothing:" (*Touk Ka Min Cham Nenh, Dak Chenh Ka Min Khat*). Small wonder those hellish hospitals were nests of lice, bugs, fleas and mosquitoes. Naturally, the mortality rate in some of those establishments reached 90 percent. To be sure, the job of Pol Pot's physicians, in those hospitals, consisted essentially in burying corpses, acting as both assassins and grave diggers. Such was the task of the physicians trained by Pol Pot.

How can one understand and interpret this unusual attitude of Pol Pot's medical personnel, which brought scientific medicine down to the empirical level through atrocious, murderous experiments, and through therapeutic procedures based on sadistic fantasy? Coconut milk was administered as glucose serum. Newly concocted solutions were injected into patients' veins without prior diagnosis, merely to observe the effect. Solutions which should be administered intramuscularly were injected intravenously, out of lack of professional knowledge and experience.

How could they help from committing those errors, those so called physicians 14 and 15 years of age who did not know how to read, either in their mother tongue or in foreign languages? To patients suffering from malaria, those child physicians administered either Chinese-made quinine, any fruit, or tree bark with a bitter taste similar to that of quinine. When they ran short of these ingredients, they gave out aspirin. If there was no aspirin, they gave whatever was available, even products meant for other diseases.

Every morning, the Pol Pot nurses distributed to all patients the same medication, mostly those prepared by Pol Pot's druggists according to their own fanciful invention and techniques. It goes without saying that fatal reactions were frequent. If, occasionally, they gave proper medication, it was because they were tired of burying corpses. The holes they dug to bury their victims were only half a meter deep because they had to dig so many.

The victims' parents and relatives were never given an opportunity to see the face of their loved ones for the last time before burial. This was forbidden. It was a heartbreaking tragedy unforgettable for all the survivors. Many other atrocious images remain engraved forever in their memory, scenes of utter despair in which their wives, husbands, and children died from misused medicines, mothers sobbing by the side of their children who died without uttering a sound. Many hospitalized Phnom Penh people witnessed ignominious acts performed before the burial of the dead: the grave diggers stripped them of all belongings: clothing, wristwatches, gold teeth, etc. And Khmer tradition requires that the dead be well dressed and perfumed!

Surgical equipment and the conditions and places where operations were performed in the subdistricts and districts were quite scandalous. It was as if children were playing: rudimentary material, patchwork, no operating rooms. It is useless to talk of anesthesia and antiseptic. Apart from the horrible dissections without precise techniques, there was acupuncture. But acupuncture was applied in an empirical manner, at an extremely low level of biological knowledge, if not a nonexistent level of biological knowledge. Acupuncture was done by children 14 or 15 years of age.

Destruction of Khmer mores and customs

Pol Pot and Ieng Sary's destruction of Khmer mores and customs painfully affected the whole Kampuchean population except those who were taken by Pol Pot's cause.

Religious celebrations, traditional festivals, artistic performances, and demonstrations of Khmer traditional art were totally banned, as were various beliefs and traditional wedding ceremonies. The ban on Prachum Ben (Festival of the Dead) plunged the Kampucheans into the most anguishing moral abyss of their lives, for the celebration of this festival is believed to lead to an absolution of the sins they had committed. Also suppressed were burial and incineration ceremonies. Khmer tradition requires that bodies be incinerated, whereas Pol Pot had them buried, and this in atrocious, shocking, and scandalous conditions: without coffins, or clothes, or religious ceremonies. All minute details of the incineration ceremonies to which the Khmers are faithfully attached were brutally trampled. For the Khmer, this violation of the traditions of incineration was an eternally unpardonable offense.

Forced marriages (Pol Pot style marriage)

Pol Pot hated marriages of love and children born to Phnom Penh people who were mentally well-balanced and sensible. The forced weddings he organized all over the country seemed to arise from two causes: hatred of attractive girls and an aversion to the mores and customs of all civilizations in general and of the Khmer civilization in particular. So he very often paired the most reluctant and proud beautiful girls with his horridly ugly, crippled or one-eyed soldiers. These very frequent forced weddings usually ended up in total failure and resulted in suicides of the wives, passive resistance, and all but provoked a general rebellion among women.

Mrs. Nguon Vuoch Ny, whose youngest sister is Miss Nguon So Pheap, 23, now working at the Ministry of Information and Culture, was one of the victims of this tragedy. She was a widow whose late husband had been dispatched to Phnom Penh by the authorities of Krala subdistrict, Kompong Siem district, Kompong Cham province, to which she herself had been deported. The holder of a master of arts degree and the mother of two children, Mrs. Nguon Vuoch Ny and 19 other widows in the village were forced to marry Pol Pot's crippled soldiers. Of course, these 20 widows refused to comply, which got them locked up in a horrible cell. In the depths of their pain and despair, they vowed to choose death rather than accept this kind of marriage, if again they were forced to the same fate after release from prison. The poor Mrs. Nguon Vuoch Ny, attractive and well educated, was a faithful wife and in full control of her faculties. Certain that she would not be able to avoid this kind of marriage, she poisoned herself with "Sleng" grains (*Stychnos vomica*). She died, leaving behind two little girls, who are still alive. The latter are now 10 and 12 years old, which means that they are able to bear witness to what occurred.

The 19 other widows were killed after being raped by Pol Pot's police. Before those 20 widows, who were all "new inhabitants," i.e., citizens of the third category, were forced to remarry crippled soldiers, a group of girls from a mobile brigade had been chosen for these marriages. They had offered resolute resistance and two of them, both "new residents," hanged themselves to avoid these forced marriages.

If some women decided to comply, it was because they feared for the safety of their relatives: their refusal could endanger the latter's lives. That they sacrificed their bodies to those savages was a gesture of self-renunciation, a philosophic attitude.

Inhuman treatment of intellectuals

Phnom Penh people, especially intellectuals, were closely watched, both during working hours and in their daily lives. They were considered undesirables, culprits and, so to speak, persons sentenced to death with the sentence suspended. Intellectuals were the incarnation of the exploiting class and consequently, corrupted beings by nature and evildoers. The authorities of every village, every subdistrict, could kill them whenever they felt like it, once they were discovered. At Prek Kak, in Steng Treng district, Kompong Cham province, Mr. Chan, a former teacher, and many other civil servants, including a former office clerk, and large numbers of students, were, all in one day, killed with axes on boats that had taken them out into the middle of a river. This crime followed an urgent order from higher authorities who decided that intellectuals still infested the country. The higher authorities gave every head of a cooperative a quota of fifteen to condemn to death. This formal order had to be carried out within the view of Organization inspectors.

Physical torture was common. People were made to pull ploughs and harrows in the rice paddies in the place of buffalo and oxen, which, in the rulers' eyes were more useful to the Revolution than those city dwellers who ate a lot and tried to work as little as possible. We only mention, for the purpose of later inquiries, that this took place in Battambang province. An eyewitness, who lived at that time in Praneth Preah district, is ready to testify. Moreover, other survivors still living in various places in Kampuchea are also willing to bear witness.

It was absolutely forbidden to keep books of the prior regime, and still more to read them. Love novels, in particular, were considered the most harmful source of corruption. "Man's feelings impede the advance of the socialist revolution," said cooperative heads over and over again.

On the other hand, if by inadvertence an intellectual used some French or English term, he seriously jeopardized himself. His relatives and friends would then worry, would be afraid, and would expect the worst. The unlucky ones lived like hunted beasts until the day the subdistrict authorities might send for the culprit to dispatch him for a special work assignment to an unknown destination from which he would never return. That was the case with many Phnom Penh youths working at the Steng Thom construction site (Karathan), in Prek Kak; they disappeared after having accidentally said words in French. They committed this unwise act during private conversations in their huts before going to bed. Despite the many precautions they had taken, a secret agent of Angkar, posted outside the hut, overheard them, and the next day, those who let slip a few French words disappeared. In the same Steng Thom construction site, another young man, overcome by deep nostalgia and great distress, started humming a French song before his friends, and a few meters from him, a young man, a "local inhabitant," heard in exasperation this capitalist song. Despite his friends' pleading, the young Phnom Penh man kept on singing defiantly and more and more loudly. When he finished, thus having somewhat alleviated his anguished heart, he said: "Now I can die." Naturally, the following day, Angkar men came to take him away. After that, his parents said nothing and avoided all human contact. The mother, consumed by gnawing inconsolable sorrow, died a month later, leaving the father in deep and absolute solitude. Someone found him hanged in his cottage one day. He wrote a few words before he hanged himself: "May my soul never fall again on this cursed land."

Treatment of artists

No less shocking was the fate reserved for artists by the Pol Pot–Ieng Sary clique, which vowed an implacable hatred against them, less as individuals than as the incarnation of aesthetic values. Movie and theater actors and singers were considered as corruptors on the same footing as intellectuals.

Apart from a few songs and other pieces of music composed by Pol Pot men, all other musical compositions, especially Western ones, were absolutely prohibited in the whole territory of this Democratic Kampuchea. To ensure the strict implementation of this ban, Pol Pot ordered all the singers done away with. Without the protection of the villagers, no singers would have survived. Movie and theater actors did not escape from this purge either. The artists too famous and too well-known were the first ones done in, especially the karate and judo champions, whom Pol Pot soldiers invited to compete in velocity with bullets of their AK-47s. Bell-bottomed trousers hidden in suitcases were considered as hidden "arms of corruption," an attempt against the Revolution.

Faced with such unbearable physical and moral torture, many people, including intellectuals, tried to flee. Flight from a concentration camp, as everybody who lived under the Pol Pot regime knew only too well, was not an ordinary adventure, but an act of suicide, and this suicide was collective because it would reverberate on the families of a fugitive. As soon as the flight was discovered, the man's wife and children were killed within a few days. Villagers of the various subdistricts of Steng Treng district and in nearly every corner of the country often saw carts carrying entire families to be killed in the woods outside their villages. All the villagers of Steng Treng district and of Kompong Cham province could serve as witnesses. If an exhumation is ordered, the Phnom Monty wood, one kilometer from Prek Kak, will amply prove this assertion.

Crimes perpetrated in Phnom Penh under the Pol Pot–Ieng Sary regime

According to statements of a number of workers living in Phnom Penh under the Pol Pot regime, the total population of the capital city at that time was estimated at just over 32,000, including 12,000 to 13,000 workers. From 1975 to 1977, only 37 workplaces functioned. These minor workshops, pompously called "factories," were in fact a few sawmills, a tobacco plant, small cement plants, tire plants, and paper plants. From 1977 on, a number of those workshops stopped functioning, being short of raw materials. Phnom Penh workers sometimes worked 20 hours a day, and their food rations were hardly higher than those of city dwellers evacuated to the countryside. Many workers feigned illness to try to catch up on their sleep. This resulted in their being considered lazy, or rebels, and harsh punishment was inflicted on them. At the slightest sign of discontent, the rulers saw CIA or KGB agents everywhere in the ranks of their subordinates. Suspects were sent almost daily to the security service, where they were tortured before being killed. The horrors in the Tuol Sleng concentration camp, which will be spoken of below, are typical of the system of torture adopted by Pol Pot.

According to a statement by Mr. Ung Pech, now a mechanical engineer in Phnom Penh, who lived there under the Pol Pot regime, over 1,000 students and personalities residing abroad before 1975 returned to Phnom Penh in 1975, 1976, 1977 and even 1978. Many of them, of whom we have a list discovered in the Tuol Sleng concentration camp together with reliable evidence, were tortured before being killed. Others were sent to do hard labor in factories or administrative offices, and put under close surveillance. Those who seemed to be critical or too vociferous were sent to be tortured in "reeducation" houses or at the security service. Many of them never returned to their jobs. If a number of them (85 out of 1,000) survived, it was because they kept their thoughts and feelings to themselves. They very rarely talked to one another or not at all. The surveillance and discipline on this matter were extremely severe.

In the Tuol Sleng prison, in reality a concentration camp and torture center, we discovered important documents concerning the elimination by torture of eminent intellectual personalities in Kampuchea, those who were still in Phnom Penh on April 17, 1975, and the 1,000 intellectuals who returned from France on the Pol Pot–Ieng Sary clique's request to take part in the reconstruction of the country. According to two students who returned from France in 1977 and who have survived, the National United Front of Kampuchea Committee in Paris, organized by Hing Un and Ok Sakun, was responsible for the repatriation of these 1,000 personalities and students. Also according to them, the latter were flown from Paris to Peking by the regular China Air Lines and from Peking to Phnom Penh by Chinese Boeing 707s.

In the Tuol Sleng concentration camp, now open to all visitors, there were rooms of interrogation and torture equipped with monstrous devices: electric shock devices, suspension devices on the ceiling, iron bars, choppers, chains, fetters on the beds, etc. On the floor, one finds tufts of hair ripped out from the scalp and traces of coagulated blood. Blood stains can still be seen on the walls and ceilings. The school's garden was turned into a burial ground where the almost flat earth suggests that the dead were carelessly buried: indeed, each hole was only half a meter deep. In two workshops, busts and portraits of Pol Pot were seen everywhere. One can imagine under what constraints painters and sculptors were forced to do this work. We also found mountains of clothing, without doubt clothing from the victims who were stripped naked before their interrogation.

Mr. Ung Pech has stated that the Pol Pot authorities sent him to Kompong Som to repair and operate machinery. There, he happened to see Chinese cargo ships unload countless boxes of arms and ammunition. This confirms the plan to establish a Chinese logistic base in Phnom Penh, where we have found a large stock of arms and ammunition far exceeding the needs of national defense of Kampuchea. Undoubtedly, this was in preparation for a major offensive against Vietnam and Laos. The Pol Pot–Ieng Sary preparations for a war of aggression against the neighboring countries and treason toward the Indochinese revolution, as well as toward the nation and people of Kampuchea, are more than evident. With regard to the Khmer people, this act of treason of Pol Pot and Ieng Sary consisted of exporting an enormous quantity of rice and rubber of the Khmer people to China. According to documents we have discovered, rice exports in 1977 totalled 480,000 tons, as compared to the figure of 400,000 to 430,000 tons planned by Pol Pot. The same document says that China demanded no less than 625,000 tons. We give, below, the conclusions of a scientific study of annual rice production under the Pol Pot regime in relation to the diet so scandalously imposed by the traitors upon the Khmer population.

The gross production of paddy rice during the 1975–1976 rice planting campaign is estimated at 3.36 million tons, and the diet of porridge plus three months of cooked rice given to the less than 6 million inhabitants, gradually reduced to 5 million inhabitants, is far below 1.2 million tons, as 1.2 million tons for 6 million inhabitants would amply cover domestic consumption with an annual quota of one ton for every five inhabitants. Where did the remaining 2.4 million, or at least 2 million tons, of Khmer rice go every year? What kind of trade with China is this, with, as importation, two Chinese bicycles per village, even per district, and the Chinese medicine that was very rarely found? The part allotted to the Khmer population in 1975–1976 is estimated at only 600,000 tons, i.e., one ton for 10 inhabitants per year; 500,000 tons in 1976–1977, and 400,000 tons in 1977–1978. And the Khmer population was being steadily reduced from 6 to 4 million over the 3-year period. The birth rate under the Pol Pot regime was insignificant, since children were often born only to die a few days later.

In 1976–1977 and 1977–1978, the exportable volumes varied from 2.14 to 1.76 million tons, while according to documents discovered by us, China demanded at least 480,000 tons and at most 625,000 tons for 1977. Unquestionably, the difference constituted an important reserve to prepare for a major offensive against Vietnam and Laos. Unfortunately, before his departure, Pol Pot took along with him part of these stocks and destroyed the rest, together with almost all the economic infrastructure.

The Phnom Penh people who have returned have been able to see huge stores of rice burning for weeks. According to their estimate, those stocks of destroyed rice would easily suffice for four or five million of the country's inhabitants for two years. Take for example the important granary of Tonle Bet near Kompong Cham city, which burned for more than a month. Phnom Penh people passing by were able to salvage only a little rice that was almost completely burned and, therefore, unusable. The first arrivals in Phnom Penh could see, at the Phnom Penh railway station, carriages full of provisions which Pol Pot troops had not enough time to take away. The troops had taken the road to the Cardamoms on the first days of the collapse of the regime. On the other hand, Mr. Vandy Kaonn, who took care of cassava fields in the rubber plantation at Meak, in Steng Treng district, Kompong Cham province, in 1977 and 1978, reported that he saw quite a few trucks taking rice northward. Without doubt, those unusual nocturnal transports, carried out for some months, were aimed at hiding provisions in strategic stockpiles located at various locations around the country.

Pol Pot's ameliorative measures were designed to remedy the general political situation. They were not as easy to implement as he had believed. Accustomed to their despotic rule, the Pol Pot people could not smother the tacit rebellion of the population this way. Concern over threatened disorder made them take other parallel measures: to eliminate the "tough heads." These measures were far from being politically effective. Rather, they "boomeranged": orders were not carried out and the "local inhabitants" deemed them improper and irrelevant because their families found themselves more and more anxious.

By the end of 1978, higher authorities, exasperated by their own powerlessness, ordered their cutthroats to kill everyone. Realizing that more than 90 percent of the population was waiting for the right moment to coordinate their actions with the National United Front for the Salvation of Kampuchea, Pol Pot had large common graves dug all over the country and had mass killings carried out, killing all but a few families in a village. (At Prek Kak, in Kompong Cham province, only seven families, deemed completely faithful to the regime, were spared.) It was widespread terror.

In every village, there was talk of a secret decision of Pol Pot: "They are going to replace the Khmer population with millions of Chinese." This was confirmed more and more with every passing day. In fact, those ditches, dug everywhere, began to be filled with corpses. The one dug at the Steng Treng pagoda, in Kompong Cham province, was the most terrifying: over five thousand bodies were buried there. In other places, in smaller ditches, people discovered choppers, anvils, barrels of alcohol, indisputable instruments of crime. At "Daun Moine," in Prek Kak subdistrict, Steng Treng district, those instruments were discovered before the crime was committed and Chim, chairman of the district committee, who was suspected of organizing crimes of this kind, was arrested by local people who already enjoyed the protection of the National United Front for the Salvation of Kampuchea. However, in other villages, those crimes were carried on at an accelerated tempo. The order was to kill, in time, those people who were going to overthrow the regime with the support of the National United Front for the Salvation of Kampuchea. The traitors included in their plans to kill even their own crippled soldiers and workers who were now useless to their revolution. Prey Veng province is now almost empty: not a living soul. In the sewers of the market, human skulls and bones were discovered. This market had been turned into a torture center under the Pol Pot regime.

IV. Conclusion

After the proclamation and promulgation of the eleven principles of the National United Front for the Salvation of Kampuchea, stating, among other things, that all deportees may return to their native areas, Phnom Penh people began to come home. However, because supplies were still inadequate to ensure regular distribution, they had to stay temporarily in villages near the capital city, waiting for Phnom Penh to become habitable again.

Indeed, after more than three years, Phnom Penh has changed beyond recognition: heaps of garbage and rubble, rampant vegetation, public buildings destroyed, religious monuments wrecked. There is no water supply. Junk cars littered the streets or lay abandoned in hallways. The many cars and trucks in good repair had almost all disappeared. One wondered where they went. In libraries, books were scattered everywhere: more than half of them were lost or lay ruined in the gardens. Inside splendid villas now crumbling after three years, and in apartments, television sets, refrigerators, and furniture lay broken or smashed.

With a superhuman effort, the Government of the National United Front for the Salvation of Kampuchea has been gradually reactivating the public services: hospitals, ministries, and various public offices.

Several thousand people have been authorized to live in the city to take part in this task of reorganization. They are technicians and former functionaries called in urgently for this difficult reorganization. Hospitals still lack adequate equipment and medicines, especially antibiotics. Only a few factories have begun to operate.

Over thirty high-ranking monks have retaken their frocks and are now living in their broken down pagodas that were almost completely destroyed or turned into storehouses for arms and ammunition. Almost all the means of transportation and telecommunication are unusable. In brief, all the economic infrastructure was destroyed by the Pol Pot–Ieng Sary clique.

In the field of culture, damage is immense. Many objects of great value disappeared, or were destroyed where they were. The five main libraries in Phnom Penh, and important university libraries, as well as objects of art and books of the Maison de France were savagely ransacked. The large National Library was turned into a warehouse for crockery, and more than 75 percent of its books disappeared. At present, only a small number of technicians, artists, physicians, and intellectuals have returned to Phnom Penh.

Statistics on this matter are now being compiled. According to the recent partial census based on samples, we have gathered the following initial results, concerning the number of Phnom Penh people killed under the genocidal regime of Pol Pot.

It is objectively impossible, for the time being, to take a general census of surviving Phnom Penh people. We have counted eighteen medical doctors, out of 500 before 1975, who have already come back to Phnom Penh. These include leading specialists, and ranking professors among others. In any case, until now, no prominent Khmer personalities of national and international standing have returned to Phnom Penh. Apart from some ten advanced degree graduates and about twenty political personalities now residing abroad, we discovered in Tuol Sleng a fairly long list of well-known persons, of whom many were killed in cold blood, and others were tortured and then condemned to death.

The written statements of those murdered people are extremely eloquent on the matter. This speaks volumes for the fate of other victims and opens the door to no less important documents on Pol Pot–Ieng Sary's policy of genocide and high treason.

Following are the names of some well-known persons executed by them:

- Huot Sambath, a diplomat, executed Sept. 9, 1976,
- Y Sup Kunthy, a diplomat, executed Sept. 9, 1976,
- Mouk Savuth, a United Nations official, executed Sept. 23, 1976,
- Chim Kok Hue, a diplomat, executed Oct. 23, 1976.

Personalities who were to be interrogated and were probably executed include:

- Phung Ton, Director of Higher Education and Rector of the Phnom Penh University,
- Chea San, former Kampuchean ambassador to the USSR,
- Chhuk Heng Mao, an education specialist affiliated with the U.N. Economic and Social Council (UNESCO),
- Rath Kuth, Professor of the Faculty of Medicine in Phnom Penh,
- Chou Savon Han, doctor in physics,
- Nou Phon Ton, Professor of Secondary Education, and a UNESCO fellow,
- Miss Ap Meng Chheng Im, Master of Arts
- Tea Meng Teck, an inspector of primary education, attached to UNESCO.

The consequences of the innumerable crimes perpetrated by Pol Pot and Ieng Sary on the Kampuchean people are uncountable and disastrous for both the present generation and for posterity. The Phnom Penh people who were the most affected inherit from this barbarous regime lasting diseases which will affect them for life, and extremely cruel recollections forever engraved in their memories. They are determined, more than ever before, to build a new life, and a new society based on humanitarianism. They all have special physical or intellectual needs and require urgent care.

Phnom Penh, August 15, 1979

Vandy Kaonn

Doctor of Sociology, Masters of Arts, Professor of Philosophy

2.4.01a
Mr. Kaing Tong Heang

It is true that April 17, 1975, is the historic day of the revolutionary victory of the people after a long struggle filled with sacrifices. From that day the colonialist, feudal, reactionary regime that had been in power in our territory for centuries was eliminated once and for all. It is very regrettable, however, that instead of continuing to defend and guard the revolutionary gains, Pol Pot, Ieng Sary, and their clique turned the dear homeland away from the truth and the internationalist spirit that are the aim of the Kampuchean people. They betrayed the nation, the people, and the revolution, and they applied a policy of exterminating the Khmer race, a policy more wicked and savage than that of Hitler, in order to serve the expansionist ambition of Peking.

To show the proof that this treason, being one of the people who seeks a pure revolution, and taken with justice and humanity like other peoples of the world, I take this opportunity to write this statement, and I submit it to the People's Revolutionary Council of Kampuchea after having survived the period of the perpetration of the crime of genocide by the Pol Pot–Ieng Sary clique for three years, nine months, and ten days. This statement is as follows.

I. Savagery During the Deportation of the Residents of Phnom Penh

Taking advantage of the liberation day, April 17, 1975, the Pol Pot clique deported all strata of the population from Phnom Penh, under the pretext of allowing the entry to the capital of its forces, which would mop up there within three days. In fact, that was a trick to deport the entire population in order to be able to kill the intellectuals, students, and civil servants in their strange concentration camps.

That same day (April 17), I saw with my own eyes that the Pol Pot troops shot at unarmed, innocent people who took too much time in evacuating. For me as for others, on April 17 I was duped by the so-called revolutionary Angkar that urged me to explain honestly my background. I was interned in Tapoy concentration camp in Sangkep village, which is along National Route 7. Among the victims were students, intellectuals, soldiers, and civil servants who, numbering in the hundreds, were mistreated in the so-called courses of political education. Every night there were families transported out on carts from this village under the pretext of being sent for more training. Once I understood the sinister aims of Angkar, I was able to overcome many obstacles to escape from the concentration camp with my family in the middle of the night.

After surviving this mortal abyss, I changed my statement, declaring that I had been a peddler of the lower class. With this false biography I could continue my way. Along the way I was quite moved upon seeing the wives and children of former civil servants, soldiers, teachers, and intellectuals who had left the city before me, crying over having lost their killed husband and father. At this stage I grasped clearly the fascist nature of the Pol Pot–Ieng Sary clique, which had first had the former intellectuals, soldiers, police officers, and civil servants, etc., killed. The other classes of the population were also in poor condition. People died during the trip for lack of food, or because of disease, as the Pol Pot clique by design let them perish, depriving them of transport, of medicines, of the basics of life. During this long trip, we were searched by the Pol Pot troops and our belongings were confiscated, in particular, jewelry, watches, radios, etc. Anyone who resisted these confiscations was tortured in a savage and cruel way. In light of this scene, I had to give them all my belongings to save my life and my family's. That is the tragedy that confronted the April 17 people during their journey.

II. Absolutism and Fascism in the Cooperatives

After walking 28 days to get to my native village in Kratie province, I arrived at Speu Ka village, Cheyo subdistrict, Chamkar Leu district, Kompong Cham province. There I was held by the all powerful Angkar, and I was forced to settle in this village.

In this new situation I could not falsify my past as before, because here there were others deported from Phnom Penh who had told my secret to the murderous Angkar in order to demonstrate their loyalty. That was bad luck for my family. I knew that my life was in jeopardy because everyone knew what I had been before. Even after we settled in the village, they still would lead away people suspected of being former military or former civil servants or intellectuals, etc. We were called by the criminal Angkar "the new people" or "the 1975 people," as opposed to the village people, whom they called "the old people." In fact the latter did not desire this categorization. The traitorous Angkar forbade any relationships between the old people and the new people, and the latter were followed and closely watched. The traitors manipulated the situation so that the two groups of people could not have any contact with each other during work or at other times of the day. It was like water and oil that never mix.

In conferences or public meetings, the authorities said soft words to us, but among themselves they considered us prisoners of war, or as their enemies. We were deprived of freedom, and we became like servants. We were living dead, because we could not go beyond the line they drew.

III. Forced Labor, Daily Life, and Rules of a Changing Morality

(1) Forced labor:

The regime's slogan was written as follows: "Make a great leap forward," "a marvelous leap forward," and to accomplish this slogan people had to work from 4:00 to 11:00 a.m., and from 1:00 to 6:00 p.m. In addition, they made us do work that was beyond our capabilities, and anyone who could not carry out this forced labor would be punished, or sometimes killed.

The Pol Pot clique made us work harder than animals or machines. It did so in order not to leave any free time, because it feared an uprising by the people against it, and on the other hand it wanted to kill people by forced labor. It forced weak women to make fertilizer (human or from the farm) in the amount of 150 kilograms to 200 kilograms a day.

Little children were put in a place they called "the center for children," where they were forced to carry from 100 kilograms to 150 kilograms of fertilizer a day. If they did not meet this level, they would be punished like adults in front of their parents. Any who dared complain for their child were considered enemies and were killed.

(2) Daily life of the people:

The people lived miserably, deprived of everything except one suit of clothes in tatters. All belongings were made collective. All year the people ate clear rice soup, at times mixed with corn, potatoes, or grasses. Often people ate the plant and flowers of the banana tree as a vegetable. When there was a holiday or a ceremony, the authorities killed a cow or a pig, but they did not give us anything to eat, reserving meat for the chiefs. Anyone who tried to ask for explanations would be condemned to death.

Under the Pol Pot regime, fishing or cooking individually were done in secret, and if it was detected, those guilty would be punished with forced labor. The people lived in terror. At night we did not dare speak because the police were hidden under our houses to keep after us. If we spoke, members of our family would be taken away forever. So each family had to sleep like chickens.

(3) Changing discipline:

Relations between men and women, or between young men and young women, were strictly forbidden, and measures of persecution were taken.

Marriage was contracted without the consent of the future spouses.

At conferences and public meetings, the Pol Pot people talked about illegal relations between men and women, and between young men and young women. Anyone who committed this wrong would be condemned to fifteen years in prison. If the person was from the April 17 people, he would be killed. Marriage was also forbidden, if one of the intended spouses was from the April 17 people. Anyone who married an April 17 person would automatically be excluded form their original class and would be considered to be of the April 17 people.

IV. Methods of Killing

The Pol Pot people killed by various methods. First, they killed by secret methods, sending suspects to be reeducated. These people were killed clandestinely. Others were killed as they were going to work, half way into a forest, with a poison arrow or hacked up. For the sick, they killed them by keeping them from having food. The methods used in 1977 and 1978 were as follows:

In 1977 (twice): The first time about 60 families were killed by being beaten with sticks and then thrown into a well located near Mr. Pom's field in Svay Teap subdistrict, Chamkar Leu district. Women and children were thrown into different pits.

The second time, they killed people from their own ranks. Thirty leaders of the commune were killed secretly.

In 1978, they carried out three atrocious killings:

(1) In early 1978, forty families were killed, men, women, children, the elderly, were all stripped of their clothing and killed in separate locations. And the clothing they took from the victims would be distributed to the villagers as war trophies.

In June 1978 it was the turn of their men. But they took away only the men; the wives and children were left apart. These men themselves were formerly killers.

In late 1978 came the definitive act: to clean out all the bourgeoisie, the capitalists, the petty capitalists, former civil servants, former students and intellectuals, widows, etc. But thanks to the National Untied Front for the Salvation of Kampuchea, they were able to carry out only one part of this plan. Men were killed as they were returning from the field. Wives and children of the victims were killed near the village. This time it was extermination of the April 17 people. The Pol Pot people said to the inhabitants that they had thrown children in the well still alive and then threw large stones on top of them. Babies and the newborn were torn apart. Widows and young virgin girls were stripped of all clothing and kicked in their genital organs. This was a savage and inhuman act.

That is the tragedy that I saw under the fascist regime of Pol Pot and Ieng Sary during nearly four years in Cheyo subdistrict, Chamkar Leu district, Kompong Cham province.

It is with sadness that I write this story:

(1) to be a document for our countrymen who live abroad and did not taste life under the dictatorship of Pol Pot and Ieng Sary. And so they can do us justice.

(2) to leave a document to make matters clear for international public opinion as concerns genocide in Kampuchea, and to seek support and justice for the National United Front for the Salvation of Kampuchea.
(3) so that Pol Pot and Ieng Sary should be convicted by the People's Revolutionary Tribunal of Kampuchea, to avenge the three million inhabitants who were killed by these criminal hands.

Done at Phnom Penh, May 28, 1979
Kaing Tong Heang

Additional Statement

(1) What I saw happened in April 1975, one day after the liberation of the city of Phnom Penh, at 2:00 p.m., when the Phnom Penh residents were being forced to evacuate their homes. A young man, about 25 years old, brown-skinned, ran back perhaps to get something he had forgotten. Suddenly AK (Chinese) shots ran out, it was a Pol Pot soldier who shot at the young man, who collapsed and died on the spot. A boy who was on the hood of a car was wounded by this shot.

(2) The Pol Pot people arrested intellectuals, officers, and former civil servants, and I too was arrested. When I was arrested, we were put in the Tapoy camp, which is near Sangkep village along National Route 7. This camp was made up of several old abandoned houses whose walls were knocked down and which were enclosed by a hedge row. At night this place was guarded carefully. There was no torture in this place, because it was only a place for sorting people out. However, there were people taken away secretly at night.

(3) I know well that Mr. Khorn and his wife were killed by leaders of the Cheyo subdistrict, from information given by Mr. Lang who saw it with his own eyes. Mr. Khorn was killed along with a woman; the two were beaten with iron bars. Mrs. Tos was raped in an inhuman way before being killed.

The executioner himself, named Phann, said that he killed these victims.

There are many other locations of killing in the Cheyo subdistrict, Kompong Cham province. These locations are well known by those named Vuoch, Phin, Huot, and Lang, who still live in Speu "A" village, Cheyo subdistrict, Chamkar Leu district.

2.4.01b

Results of Investigation of 100 Workers' Families at the Takhmau Automobile Tire Factory

	Number	*Percentage*
Number of family members before April 17, 1975	947	100%

	Number	Percentage
Number of survivors at present	651	69%
Number of people killed under the Pol Pot–Ieng Sary regime	81	9%
Number of people dead of starvation, disease under the Pol Pot–Ieng Sary regime	103	10%
Number of people missing under the Pol Pot–Ieng Sary regime	112	12%

2.4.01c

Results of Investigation of 100 Families in the "100 Family Area" Subdistrict, Phnom Penh

	Number	Percentage
Number of family members before April 17, 1975	1075	100%
Number of survivors at present	442	41%
Number of people killed under the Pol Pot–Ieng Sary regime	456	42%
Number of people dead of starvation, disease under the Pol Pot–Ieng Sary regime	111	11%
Number of people missing under the Pol Pot–Ieng Sary regime	64	6%

2.4.01d

Results of Investigation of 100 Families in the Phsar Doeum Thkau Subdistrict, Phnom Penh

	Number	Percentage
Number of family members before April 17, 1975	906	100%
Number of survivors at present	425	47%
Number of people killed under the Pol Pot–Ieng Sary regime	298	33%
Number of people dead of starvation, disease under the Pol Pot–Ieng Sary regime	103	11%
Number of people missing under the Pol Pot–Ieng Sary regime	80	9%

2.4.02

Report on Crimes Committed by the Pol Pot-Ieng Sary Clique Against National Minorities in General and the Cham Muslims in Particular

Comrade Chairman of the Tribunal, Comrade Prosecutor, Comrades of the Council of Judges, Ladies and gentlemen, representatives, witnesses, and compatriots here present today:

Acting upon the order of the Prosecutor, a team was set up to conduct an inquiry into the crime of genocide committed by the Pol Pot–Ieng Sary clique against the ethnic minorities. It has reached unanimity on the content of the following report.

I. Outline of the Composition of Nationalities in the National State of Kampuchea

The total population of Kampuchea was about 7 million, according to the statistics published in 1969 by the Bureau of Tourism, whereas the figures given by the Pol Pot–Ieng Sary administration were nearly 8 million.

Apart from citizens of Khmer origin, who constitute the great majority of the population (about 90 percent), there also exist nearly 20 ethnic minorities who have long since been citizens of Kampuchea, living on the plains, the highlands, and the mountainous regions. They have been closely united with the Khmer nation and have made their contributions to the cause of nation building and defense in the course of our centuries-long history.

At present, in Kampuchea there are perhaps more than 20 ethnic minorities:

1. The Cham
2. The Lao
3. The Thai
4. The Cu La
5. The Por
6. The Kuoi
7. The Krung
8. The Prao
9. The Kavet
10. The Ta Puon
11. The Charai (Giavai)
12. The Rade (Ede)
13. The Phnong
14. The Kachos
15. The Lanam
16. The Lun
17. The Krol
18. The S'och
19. The Stieng
20. The Sam Re
21. The Choong

In addition, there are a great number of Vietnamese, Chinese, and yans (Chven) who have taken nationality and become citizens of Kampuchea.

It is due to the destruction by Pol Pot–Ieng Sary regime and other causes that we are not able to obtain reliable statistics about ethnic minorities in Kampuchea at present.

For example, with regard to the Cham population, which constitutes the most numerous of the minorities, some documents give the figure of 110,000, while other documents give 150,000, and another even 700,000.

On the other hand, there are no statistics available to distinguish the Cham, who have long been Kampuchean citizens with the Chven (also called Malay) who immigrated to Kampuchea later, having the same Islamic faith and speaking the same language as the Cham. As a legal matter, the distinction between Kampuchean citizens and foreigners is not clear. Some textbooks even consider the Cham as foreigners.

The former regimes of Kampuchea did not register among the total population some of the ethnic minorities living as nomads in the mountainous regions (about 100,000 people).

II. Some Typical Crimes Against Ethnic Minorities

We have received 22 claims from various strata of people, different nationalities, different ages, men and women, followers of different religions in 13 provinces and one city, denouncing extremely serious crimes committed by the Pol Pot–Ieng Sary clique (see annex).[1]

Based on dozens of exploratory investigation interviews with persons with a range of opinions, and on an exchange of ideas with direct witnesses who are officials or from Kampucheans who are part of an ethnic minority with a view to verifying the crimes alleged and their extent, crimes committed and guided by a policy of anti-ethnic discrimination;

Based on the results of the field investigations of the killing sites:

We affirm that the Pol Pot–Ieng Sary clique has committed criminal acts, specifically against ethnic minorities who are in fact citizens having the same equal rights as other citizens living in the national community of Kampuchea.

The genocidal regime of Pol Pot–Ieng Sary has denied, on the level of legal rights, the recognition of the factual existence of ethnic minorities in the nation of Kampuchea. At the same time, it has carried out forcible, urgent assimilation, repression, and mass extermination. In so doing, it clearly aims at committing genocide with a view toward abolishing the existence of ethnic minorities in terms of their names and numbers.

The ethnic minorities, victims of the crimes of genocide are as follows:

1. The ethnic minorities living in the mountainous regions, mainly in the provinces bordering Vietnam, Laos, and Thailand.

2. The Muslim community, the great majority of whom are the Cham minority, residing in various provinces, cities, and urban centers, mainly in Kompong Cham and around Phnom Penh.

Let us examine the crimes committed by the genocidal clique of Pol Pot and Ieng Sary.

The 1976 Constitution of so-called Democratic Kampuchea established

1. See Document 2.4.02 Annex. — Eds.

by the Pol Pot–Ieng Sary clique implicitly did not recognize the existence of ethnic minorities as part of the national community of Kampuchea.

Following the liberation of Phnom Penh, April 17, 1975, the Pol Pot–Ieng Sary administration publicly announced and strictly applied a policy of discrimination by dividing citizens into 3 categories, each having different rights and obligations, from a legal standpoint. Along with this policy the Pol Pot–Ieng Sary clique has also imposed another one specifically aimed at the ethnic minorities, and which was uniformly applied in the various provinces:

- The Kampuchean Revolution is one. And there is only one Kampuchean nation. The Khmer language is the only language.
- From now on, the various nationalities X.Y. . . . no longer exist in Kampuchea (national minorities in different regions were listed).
- Therefore, individuals must change their names by adopting new ones appropriate to the Khmer race (names could either be given by the authorities or chosen by individuals).
- The conscience, languages, ethnic characteristics, customs, habits, and religions of the former nation of origin are to be totally abolished.
- Those who do not abide by this order will reap the consequences.

Obviously, this is a fascist policy, requiring immediate assimilation under threat of severe punishment to be applied without delay, giving the ethnic minorities no time or any flexibility in preparing and adapting to the new situation.

Crimes against ethnic minorities in the mountainous region of the northeast zone, including the provinces of Preah Vihear, Stung Treng, Ratanak Kiri, Mondul Kiri, and Kratie

Although the majority of the ethnic minorities here have for many years lived in the revolutionary zone, the Pol Pot–Ieng Sary clique did not classify them in the category of the ordinary citizens, i.e., the first category citizens according to the regime's general policy. On the contrary, the minorities were separated from their former dwelling areas and dragged into concentration camps situated on the plain, together with other Kampucheans from different parts of the country. Those who refused to go to concentration camps were repressed, tortured, and usually killed.

Mr. Buon Thang, an official of Ta Puon minority, Ratanak Kiri province, declared:

After the liberation of Stung Treng province in January 1979, thousands of families from various minorities in the region have approached the revolutionary authorities seeking information about their husbands and children who were "invited to reeducation courses" by the Pol Pot–Ieng Sary clique, and vanished, partly because they were classified as citizens of the second and third categories, partly because they cannot speak Khmer or do not pronounce it correctly, or because they have surreptitiously practiced religious ceremonies according to their faith. Our officers and fighters have helped the population in searching operations in the forest surrounding Stung Treng town and have found the killing sites of tens of thousands of people with their bones uncovered in the area. A number of families have been able to identify the belongings of their vanished dear ones, notably, sandals, vests, and others.

The plan of discrimination worked out by the Pol Pot–Ieng Sary genocidal clique to exterminate ethnic minorities has also been reflected in their plan of gradually killing officials who are from ethnic minorities. These dark attempts had continuously and perfidiously taken shape since 1968, and were applied in the years 1977–1978 in an overt, massive and cruel manner, demonstrated by the killings of the following officials:

1. Comrade Seda of the Lao minority, secretary of the Party committee of the northeast zone during the war against the French and the political struggle against the Sihanouk regime.

2. Comrade Chan Den of the Lao minority, member of the zone Party branch committee, in charge of tasks related to the United Front for the National Salvation of Kampuchea.

3. Comrade Kham Phay, a member of the Stung Treng Party Committee, who was accused of being an agent of the CIA, and who was killed, together with his family.

4. Comrade Ta Kien of the Lao minority, secretary of the Voeunsai District Party Committee, Ratanak Kiri province.

5. Comrade Thong Nam of the Lao minority, Voeunsai District Chief of Staff.

6. Comrade Khvong of an ethnic minority, Assistant Staff Officer of the district.

7. Comrade Thong Samey of an ethnic minority, Assistant to the Political Department of the Northeast Zone.

8. Hundreds of ex-officials from different ethnic minorities, who were assigned to various localities far from their families, and later disappeared or openly accused of being CIA agents and killed. At present, only 4 or 5 of these people have survived and are working in administrative departments in Phnom Penh.

9. In particular, during the years 1977–1978, the genocidal clique of Pol Pot–Ieng Sary without warning organized the arrest and killing of all officials belonging to ethnic minorities, people who trained and matured during the period of resistance against the American imperialists, from the provincial level to the village level, as well as officers in the army and guerilla units down to the platoon commanders. The officers were taken to Phnom Penh and killed.

Crimes against the ethnic minorities in the Southwestern Region, especially in Koh Kong

Mr. Say Buon Thang, an official, a man of the Thai minority, related:

• The area inhabited by ethnic Thai people, in Koh Kong, was a strong revolutionary base. After usurping power in the leadership, the Pol Pot–Ieng Sary clique chose to follow a political line contrary to that previously applied by the Party. What they did was to make propaganda aimed at creating divisions between the Khmer (who are in the majority in Kampuchea but a minority in Koh Kong) and the Thai (who are a minority in Kampuchea but the majority in Koh Kong).

• In early 1974, the genocidal Pol Pot–Ieng Sary clique, using a ruse, summoned all the Thai officials working in the administration and the social organizations at the provincial level to the central headquarters for a political seminar and then killed them all. After that, they dispatched a large military unit to the area with the order to capture comrade Say Buon Thang, the commander of the regional armed forces. Orders were also given concerning the annihilation of all the regional armed forces. But their schemes were discovered and foiled. However, during April 1974, they succeeded in annihilating all the officials of the Thai minority and their wives and children, totaling 600 persons. But as the regional forces fought back relentlessly, the Pol Pot–Ieng Sary forces had to withdraw. Koh Kong province was thus fully liberated and remained under the control of the regional forces who, since mid-1974, openly opposed both the Lon Nol and the Pol Pot regimes.

• On May 25, 1975, the genocidal Pol Pot–Ieng Sary clique, concentrated their armed forces with a view of "erasing" the whole of the Koh Kong area Thai minority. The Thai minority and their separatist armed forces fought back in legitimate defense. They succeeded in holding out for several years. Finally, they coordinated their activities with general uprisings led by the National United Front for the Salvation of Kampuchea leading to the liberation of Phnom Penh on January 7, 1979, and of the whole country some time later.

• The Thai population in this area formerly numbered about 20,000 inhabitants. After the January 7, 1979, liberation, only around 8,000 people survived. In some villages which formerly had 500 to 600 inhabitants, there now remained only 5 to 7 families. A case in point was Srok Don Sima village. Nolta Khien village now has only 20 families left from its former 10,000 inhabitants; of the 700 families formerly living in the township of Koh Kapi, only 30 have survived.

• At Svay Sisophon in Battambang province, the Lao minority formerly numbered 1,800 families. Now only 800 families have survived, but all of these have lost some family members. As a whole, more than fifty percent of the local population has been killed. All the survivors in this area have a unanimous opinion: they all said that if the armed forces of the National United Front for the Salvation of Kampuchea and the Vietnamese army were one week later in liberating this area, then all the Lao people, down to the babies, would have been slain because the Pol Pot butchers had already made plans and preparations for the wholesale massacre of the population.

• Until today, no trace of the Cu La minority has been found. This minority numbered around 2,000 people specializing in the trade of polishing diamonds and precious stones and were living the Pailin area and some other places.

The genocidal fascist Pol Pot–Ieng Sary clique sought every pretext and resorted to every barbaric means in order to annihilate the Cham minority, or adherents of the Islamic religion

The Pol Pot–Ieng Sary policy of immediate forcible assimilation has been carried out on a wide scale, in urgent and bloodthirsty ways, especially among the Cham ethnic minority who are at the same time of the Islamic faith.

Mr. Sit Sakarya, 29 years old, formerly a student at the Khmer-Soviet Friendship Technical College in Phnom Penh, said:

"I was forced to leave Phnom Penh and I reached Svay Bakeo village, Ta Ches subdistrict, Kompong Tralach district, Kompong Chhnang province, on May 24, 1975. On our arrival, we were informed that all the women must cut their hair short, and that in a Khmer country, there existed no Cham minority. Therefore, I was obliged to change my name Sit Sakarya to Duon. My wife had her name Saros changed to Saray. My eldest son had to give up his name Kadaray to take that of Vuon. My second son had his name Mat Sen changed into Sy. My mother Sarvas took the name of Am.

"On October 5, 1975, they ordered my arrest, intending to give me a death sentence under two charges, being a former functionary in Phnom Penh and, at the same time, a Cham. Fortunately, all the local people in Svay Bakco went to the Pol Pot headquarters and told the mobile team that under the former regime I was only a blacksmith and also that I was not a Cham. Thanks to their testimony I was freed.

"On March 15, 1977, my elder brother, named Polydan, a former student at the Faculty of Law, was killed because he was caught speaking with my son in the Cham language, in Kok Banteay village. In this same village of Kok Banteay, on February 5, 1977, my niece, 18 years old and a former student at La Providence school in Phnom Penh, and who has changed her name to that of Matos, was arrested and killed because the Pol Pot men knew, from their investigations, that she was an intellectual and also a Cham. For the same reasons, my younger brother, who was formerly a student at the Faculty of Agriculture, was also executed.

"On December 5, 1978, Phuoc, who was the head of the agricultural commune in Ta Ches subdistrict, told my Aunt Mas, in Svay Bakao, that during the following February 1979, after the harvest, all the remaining Cham people in the place would be killed. This news threw all of our Cham into utter despair, although we tried our best to become Khmers. We told ourselves to be more and more careful. . . ."

Tin Yusuf Abdul Koyum, formerly a physician at the Preah Ket Melea Hospital, Phnom Penh, said:

"After I was forced to leave Phnom Penh on April 17, 1975, I changed my name to Soth and said that I was a dock worker and illiterate. At the same time, I tried to behave like an idiot. But on February 5, 1976, I was arrested and subjected to atrocious torture. I had to eat, drink, and defecate in the same place, my two legs being chained to the spot. My interrogators had only two queries: What did you do before 1975? and Are you Cham?

"As I stuck to my statements, they released me six months later. I returned to my village like a dead person rediscovering life.

"Unfortunately, my father said, honestly, that he was a Cham and a Muslim. The butchers took him and then killed him on February 10, 1976.

"My uncle had abandoned his name, Suleiman, and called himself San and had adopted all the manners and behaviors of a Khmer. But because he had many pupils who knew him, he failed in hiding his origin. The Pol Pot–Ieng Sary men therefore arrested him together with his wife and children, and on March 12, 1976, they killed him and his whole family of nine people and buried them in the same grave."

The facts recounted above do not reflect separate individual instances of racial discrimination. Rather, they were typical of systematic suppression as part of a state policy. The Pol Pot–Ieng Sary clique even killed all Khmer families who, out of humanitarian feelings, gave shelter to Chams.

Besides the barbaric and widespread ways of killing mentioned above, the Pol Pot–Ieng Sary clique killed Chams in the following ways:

• They tied 5 to 10 people into one group, attached heavy stones to the group, and pushed them into the Mekong River. This practice occurred in villages in Khlong district of Kratie province, and Kroch Chhmar district of Kompong Cham province, both bordering the Mekong River.

• They used armed forces to encircle villages and then used B-40s, B-41s, and mortars to destroy the villages. Adults who survived the bombardment were taken to the nearby forest to die of starvation or to become prey for wild beasts.

They threw babies in a sack, filled it with paddy, tied it, and finally threw it into the river. In this way, newborns, in certain places, like in Koh Sotin (Kompong Cham province), the agents of Pol Pot–Ieng Sary put them in plastic bags and hung them on tree branches to make games of amusement. In another place where Mr. Abdul Koyum is a witness, the torturers of the subdistrict threw 5 children, ages 1, 2, to 5 years (3 girls and 2 boys) in a dried up well and covered them with dry straw and coconut leaves, and then poured in 3 liters of gasoline and burned the coconut leaves for their amusement until the children cried pitifully and succumbed to it.

• They tied the arms of victims and made them walk on a suspended bamboo tree over an abyss 50 to 70 meters deep. This abyss, known as "Chruos Stung Treng," is located in Kompong Cham province. They also carried truck loads of bound Muslims to this abyss and threw the victims into it. Public opinion put the number of Cham people killed at Chruos Stung Treng at about 20,000.

At present, conditions do not permit us to make a total figure of deaths of ethnic Cham people as a result of the Pol Pot–Ieng Sary clique's genocidal policy. But it is certain that from two-thirds to three-fourths of the Cham population has been annihilated by this clique. Here under are some examples:

• In the Chruy Changvar area (Phnom Penh province), there used to be 1,200 Cham households. But seven months after the liberation of the whole country only 60 such families have returned.

• Miss Charya, back from Battambang, reported that out of 8 Cham families evacuated from a hamlet in Phnom Penh, there remain the following after liberation:

1. In Mr. Ly's family of seven, only one young daughter survives.
2. In Mr. Ek Min's family of nine, no survivors.
3. In Mr. Sman Chek's family of twelve, only one young daughter survives.
4. In Mr. Sles's family of seven, only two children survive, aged 10 and 12.
5. In Mr. Los's family of six, only one 12-year-old child survives.
6. In Mr. Hachi Sles Chasda's family of twelve, only one daughter-in-law survives.
7. In Mr. Suleiman Sutri's family of six, only three survive, namely the mother, a young girl named Chari Ryn and a small child.
8. In Mr. Lap Ly's family of nine, none survives.

Thus, out of 68 people, only 9 survive.

• In Kompong Siem district, Kompong Cham province, there used to be about 20,000 Cham inhabitants. So far, no survivors have been found.

• In Kang Meas district, Kompong Cham province, there used to be about 20,000 Cham inhabitants. So far, only four survivors have been found. They escaped when the mass killings were conducted against the Cham people.

• The village of Koh Phal, the name meaning "island of good luck and prosperity," in Kroch Chhmar district, Kompong Cham province, was destroyed completely by the Pol Pot–Ieng Sary clique with B-40s. They renamed the village "Koh Phes," meaning island of ashes.

Wherever the masses rose up in a political struggle, and were armed only with sticks and bars, they were mercilessly repressed, more or less in the same way as inflicted on the Koh Phal people.

• There were also killings of a genocidal character of Cham people in Chhlong district (Kratie province); Kroch Chhmar, Tbong Khmum, Ponhea Krek, Chamkar Leu, Kompong Siem districts (Kompong Cham province); Kompong Tralach district (Kompong Chhnang province); O Russey district (Pursat province); etc.

• Even those who joined the ranks of the Pol Pot–Ieng Sary clique were also subject to being killed. Realizing the danger, Mr. Mat Ly, of Cham ethnicity, a Member of Parliament under the Pol Pot regime, left their ranks and together with other Cham officials and fellow countrymen joined the National United Front for the Salvation of Kampuchea in 1978.

III. Conclusion

1. While investigating the Pol Pot–Ieng Sary genocidal crimes against the Kampuchean people as a whole, one can perceive more clearly the seriousness of their crimes perpetrated against ethnic minorities. In carrying out their criminal acts, the clique of Pol Pot–Ieng Sary either relied on its policy of immediate forcible assimilation as a legal justification or resorted to sheer armed force for extermination purposes, as in the cases of the Thai and the Cu La people, or used both forms as in the case of the Cham people.

2. Considering the irrefutable nature of the Pol Pot–Ieng Sary genocidal crimes and the legitimate demands from all letters of denunciation, we propose that the Tribunal contemplate a sentence with a most severe punishment inflicted on the two main accused, Pol Pot and Ieng Sary, who themselves represent the most odious regime in our times.

So far, we have been unable to investigate the extremely tragic fate of the Vietnamese minority who have been living for ages in Kampuchea and well-loved by the Kampuchean working people and yet considered the sworn enemy to be exterminated on sight. The survivors among them certainly are very rare.

In addition, the Khmer minority of South Vietnamese origin was also listed as the first to be exterminated by the genocidal clique of Pol Pot–Ieng Sary because, according to their calumnious accusations, these Khmer people were "Vietnamese mentally and Khmer physically," because they used to live in Vietnam and used to speak Vietnamese.

Finally, we should mention that the minorities of Chinese origin or the Chinese themselves, were also killed in 1975, as they were labeled "bourgeois elements." However, since 1976, their lives in the communes became less difficult due to the effective intervention of the Government of the People's Republic of China on their behalf.

2.4.02 Annex

List of Victims Who Have Provided Testimony to and Made Accusations to the Tribunal Concerning Crimes of Genocide of the Pol Pot–Ieng Sary Clique Against National Minorities

1. Mr. Tin Yusuf Abdul Koyum, age 35, of Islamic religion, formerly a physician at Preah Ket Melea Hospital, Phnom Penh. Letter of denunciation dated February 2, 1979.

2. Miss Soleymal, age 24, of Cham nationality and Islamic religion, former seventh-grade student. Address: Kokor Thom village, Slous subdistrict, Somrong Tong district, Kompong Speu province. Letter of denunciation dated February 1, 1979.

3. Miss To Roni Meas, age 22, of Cham nationality, of Islamic religion. Address: Prek Pra village, Chabar Ompou subdistrict, Kien Svay district, Kandal province. Letter of denunciation dated February 26, 1979.

4. Mr. Tres Du Leas Mohamad Ahsihsor, of Cham nationality and Islamic religion, former fourth-year student at the Medical University, Department of Pharmacy, Phnom Penh. Address: formerly of the third precinct, Phnom Penh, then displaced successively to the provinces of Takeo, Kandal, and Prey Veng. Letter of denunciation dated February 24, 1979.

5. Mr. Tin Prosot, of Cham nationality and Islamic religion, formerly a student in Literature and the Humanities. Address: Chrang Chonires, Phnom Penh. Back from Kratie province, to which he had been displaced. Letter of denunciation dated February 11, 1979.

6. Mr. Len Mathy, age 25, of Cham nationality. High school diploma. Address: Srok Romiet village, Chhuk Sa subdistrict, Kompong Tralach district, Kompong Chhnang province. Letter of denunciation dated February 12, 1979.

7. Mr. Sa Muhamad, age 18, of Cham nationality and Islamic religion. High school diploma. Address: Thoy village, Kampot subdistrict, Kampot province. Evacuated to Battambang. Letter of denunciation dated February 3, 1979.

8. Mr. Sit Ibrahim, age 28, of Cham nationality and Islamic religion. High school diploma. Address: Srok Romiet village, Chhuk Sa subdistrict, Kompong Tralach district, Kompong Chhnang province. Letter of denunciation dated February 1, 1979.

9. Mr. Cafor Tozep, age 20, of Cham nationality and Islamic religion. High school diploma. Address: Chamkar Samsap village, Phnom Penh. Back from Kompong Cham province, to which he had been displaced. Letter of denunciation dated February 12, 1979.

10. Miss Romilas, age 22, of Cham nationality and Islamic religion. High School diploma. Address: Chruy Chongvar, Phnom Penh. Was exiled to Siem Reap province. Letter of denunciation dated February 12, 1979.

11. Miss Sleymal Nur Hassana, age 20. High school diploma, of Cham

nationality and Islamic religion. Was exiled to Kompong Cham province. Letter of denunciation dated February 2, 1979.

12. Miss Mot Maridan, age 20, of Cham nationality and Islamic religion. Fifth grade education. Was exiled to Siem Reap province. Address: Chruy Chongvar, Phnom Penh. Letter of denunciation dated February 18, 1979.

13. Mr. Smas Mat, age 28, of Cham nationality and Islamic religion. High school diploma. Was exiled to Kompong Cham province. Letter of denunciation dated February 12, 1979.

14. Mr. Sit Sakarya, age 29, former Polytechnic student. Address: Srok Romiet village, Chhuk Sa subdistrict, Kompong Tralach district, Kompong Chhnang province. Letter of denunciation dated February 25, 1979.

15. Miss Sary Mana, age 20, of Cham nationality and Islamic religion. High school diploma. Address: Chruy Chongvar, Phnom Penh. Was exiled to Kompong Chhnang province. Letter of denunciation dated February 12, 1979.

16. Mr. Ken Sani, age 37, of Cham nationality. Bachelor's degree. Address: Tuk Chanh village, Sre Cham subdistrict, Prey Nup district, Kampot province. Letter of denunciation dated March 2, 1979.

17. Mr. Rok Sach Mat, age 26, of Cham nationality and Islamic religion. Address: Srok Romiet village, Chhuk Sa subdistrict, Kompong Tralach district, Kompong Chhnang province. Was exiled to Kompong Speu province. Letter of denunciation dated February 20, 1979.

18. Miss Mathy Zainop, age 28, of Cham nationality and Islamic religion. Former second-year student at the Faculty of Medicine (and Pharmacy), Phnom Penh. Was exiled to Kompong Chhnang province. Letter of denunciation dated March 21, 1979.

19. Mr. Sit Sakarya, Chairman of the Central Committee of the Kampuchean Islamic Association for National Salvation. Address: Kilometer 7, Phnom Penh. Letter of denunciation dated June 19, 1979.

20. Mr. Cato Tozep, age 40. Address: Chamkar Samsap village, Kompong Siem district, Kompong Cham province. Letter dated February 12, 1979.

21. Mr. Smas Haron, age 57, of Cham nationality and Islamic religion. Address: Trokang Shuk village, Bang subdistrict, Rarai district, Kompong Thom province. Letter of denunciation dated July 10, 1979.

22. Mrs. Ay Nasoeun, age 26, of Khmer nationality. Birth place: Maha Liep subdistrict, Koh Sotin district, Kompong Cham province. Present address: Srey Sangkum subdistrict, O Reang district, Mondul Kiri province.

List of witnesses who have spoken with our group

1. Miss Chari Rya, age 23, of Cham nationality. Returned from Battambang province. Address: Government Guest House, No 100.

2. Miss Na Aysoeun, age 23, Khmer nationality. Home province: Mondul Kiri. Address: Guest House of the Central Committee Secretariat.

3. Mr. Say Buon Thang, age 53, of Thai nationality. Home province: Koh Kong. Address: Organization Department of the Central Committee.

4. Mr. Buon Thong, age 49, of Ta Puon nationality. Home province: Stung Treng. Knowledgeable about the ethnic minorities in the provinces of Stung Treng, Ratanak Kiri, Preah Vihear, and Mondul Kiri. Address: Education and Propaganda Department of the Central Committee.

5. Mr. Kun Dan, age 45, of Khmer nationality. Address: Government Guest House, No 100.

Done at Phnom Penh,[1] 1979
Group investigating the crimes of genocide of the Pol Pot–Ieng Sary clique against national minorities

2.4.03

Siem Reap Province Health Service, Report on the Clinical Work of Siem Reap Hospital

In a period of six months, from the day our hospital was established, to June 18, 1979, our Siem Reap hospital treated a total of 1,158 patients. These can be classified into three categories:

		Number of cases
Common diseases		579
Beriberi, diarrhea, dysentery		378
Wounded by bullets and shells		
Men wounded in the head	35	
Men wounded in the stomach	25	
Women wounded on the feet	37	
Women wounded in the body	25	
Boys wounded in the back	25	
Girls wounded in the back	15	
Men with venereal diseases	30	
Subtotal	197	
Total all patients (diseases and wounds)		1158

These 1,158 persons were treated and cared for by our hospital with all means at our disposal; 738 of them have recovered their health and returned to productive work. However, a number of patients with serious diseases, such as beriberi, dysentery, and diarrhea, could not be cured despite our doctors' devotion, because of pernicious anemia. A total of 114 persons have thus died in these six months. There were cases in which patients in critical condition were brought to the hospital. In such circumstances, all our doctors' efforts were of no avail.

1. The date and month were omitted. — Eds.

On June 17, 1979, the number of patients undergoing treatment at the hospital was 306 persons, most of them children:

Parkinson's disease, dysentery, diarrhea	103
Swollen face	64
Beriberi	88
Subtotal	255
Wounds:	
Wounds on the feet (men)	20
Wounds on the feet (women)	16
Wounds on the feet (children)	10
Venereal diseases	5
Subtotal	51
Total	306

Siem Reap Hospital, June 20, 1979
Nhat Lay, Director of the Hospital

2.4.03bis

Report on the Crimes Committed by Pol Pot-Ieng Sary Against the People of Wat Svay Village, Siem Reap 3 Subdistrict, Siem Reap District, Siem Reap Province

Cover Note

The People's Revolutionary Committee of Siem Reap province has the honor to convey to the Minister of the Interior the enclosed report made by the people of Wat Svay village, Siem Reap 3 subdistrict, Siem Reap district, Siem Reap province.

Siem Reap, June 23, 1979
For the People's Revolutionary Committee, Siem Reap Province
Hem Bo (signed and sealed)

The atrocious crimes committed by the Pol Pot–Ieng Sary reactionaries were of a genocidal character. They were deliberate acts of savage brutalization against innocent people. Here are items of proof:

1. Prior to the Pol Pot period:

Population:	447 families, a total of 2,153 persons, of whom 1,374 were women
Old people:	278 persons, including 152 women

Young people (peasants and workers):	968 persons, including 499 women
Intellectuals:	35 teachers, including 9 women
Doctors of medicine:	3 persons, including 1 woman
Professors:	4 persons
Farmers:	2 persons
Financial employees:	1 person
Metropolitan policemen:	8 persons
Primary school pupils:	628 persons, including 452 girls
Secondary school pupils:	146 persons, including 88 girls
Children:	320, including 178 girls
Monks:	98 persons

2. During the Pol Pot period:
The Pol Pot agents killed 704 people, of whom 205 were women.

Old people:	82 persons, including 41 women
Middle-aged:	290, including 51 women
Intellectuals/teachers:	23 persons, including 3 women
Doctors of medicine:	1 person
Professors:	4 persons
Farmers:	2 persons
Financial employees:	1 person
Civil servants:	1 person
Metropolitan policemen:	8 persons
Adolescents:	83, including 57 girls
Children:	56, including 39 girls
Secondary school pupils:	98, including 53 girls
Monks:	55 persons

Their methods of killing people were smashing their heads with shovel handles, hammers, bamboo trunks, iron bars, beheading, or starving.

3. After the liberation of January 7, 1979:
The surviving people:

Old people:	196 persons, including 129 women
Middle-aged:	678, including 506 women
Teachers:	12 persons, including 6 women
Nurses:	2 women
Adolescents:	545, including 307 girls
Children:	287, including 186 girls
Secondary school pupils:	48, including 39 girls
Monks:	43 persons

The total number of survivors living by the Heng Samrin regime was 1,449, of whom 1,169 were women. Some of these came from other localities after liberation. Thus, the death toll officially recorded was still below the truth.

Done at Wat Svay village, June 21, 1979

Tan Tik
Chairman of Siem Reap 3 subdistrict

Ky Choeun
Chairman of the village

2.4.03a
On Crimes Committed in the Field of Public Health and Social Action

For nearly a century, our country was under a "protectorate" of France, by force of bayonets. The colonial administration did almost nothing to improve the state of cultural and scientific underdevelopment, in the medical field in particular. There was a great shortage of physicians, midwives, nurses, etc. in face of the ever increasing needs of a population of nearly five million.

After the Proclamation of Independence (1954) and before the events of April 17, 1975, despite some achievements, the public health sector was far from meeting the needs of the population, especially in rural areas. Unfortunately, this meager legacy was almost totally destroyed under the Pol Pot–Ieng Sary regime and replaced by a "medicine" which helped to plunge our people into the abyss of genocide.

1. The Killing of Medical Personnel:

On the morning of April 17, Phnom Penh was invaded by soldiers of Pol Pot and Ieng Sary. At 9:30 a.m. some hospitals were evacuated. Physicians in working garb were driven out and forced to march in a specific direction, together with other personnel: nurses, midwives, etc. Patients were treated in the same way. They were forced to leave the hospitals and march toward the "liberated zones." Seriously sick people were left in their beds. those being operated on were left on the operating tables, as surgeons were forced by the "black clad" people to abandon their work. On the road from the capital to the outskirts one could see a long procession of moving beds on which recently operated on people were lying; with transfusion bottles hanging on bedposts—a form of makeshift vehicles. A sergeant, whose throat and mouth were torn by an explosion, newly treated in facial surgery, was also transported in the same way, pushed along by his elderly father. Women in childbirth were also forced to leave the maternity wards with babies in their arms, walking very slowly, supported by their relatives. But other orphan babies were left in the cradles without care at the Kantha-Bopha Center of Pediatrics (in Phnom Penh). Forty of them were left there to certain death.

The pharmacies and pharmaceutical laboratories were the first to submit to the pillaging. Locks and doors were destroyed by bullets, axes and hammers. Trucks and utility vehicles were assembled in front of each drugstore. All medicine, pharmaceutical materials and other goods and instruments were loaded in those vehicles which hurried back along National Routes 1, 5, and 4 toward the East, North, and Southwest military regions.

Everyone left the capital city with expressions of defeat, bringing along just a few things, leaving to the victors their wide opened houses and bundles of keys. The "black clad" people told them, through loudspeakers: "Do not bring along anything. Angkar asks you to leave the city for three days only to enable our troops to mop up the Lon Nol forces and avoid American bombings."

Pharmacists were the greatest victims of this forced evacuation, at bayonet point as most of them lived on the very premises of their stores, which were guarded and controlled by Pol Pot troops in the first minutes of their arrival. Going away empty handed, without food or spare clothes, pharmacists and their families shared the sad plight of their colleagues of the medical profession. All were forced on a long, exhausting march on foot under the sun, rain and wind, and were subjected to the pillaging by the "black clad" people prior to arriving at a predetermined destination or to their home villages. Those city people slowly walked toward different places, unknown to them in most cases. The weak, the old, the sick, the children, the women in childbirth, the newly operated died one after another and their bodies were left on the roadside, scattered with human flotsam under the scorching April sun. People continued to march, at a snail's pace, day and night, toward another place, hoping for a better life. Alas, no one took care of us, as this was the will of the new dictators. There was no doctor for the sick, except for some self-styled ones who distributed some questionable pills which were ineffective.

During the exodus some physicians were recognized and arrested. They are now missing. Among them were the Doctors Srey Phay and Kong Chhoeurm. Arriving at their destinations, former members of the health service tried to conceal their identity in order to survive. On the other hand, Pol Pot–Ieng Sary men left no stone unturned to discover and kill them. Yes, they killed physicians, pharmacists and nurses, just because these were such. We have learned, from proof and from eyewitnesses, the death of some colleagues:

• Professor Tip Mam, a respiratory specialist (at Tuol Sleng).

• Doctor Ly Chhun Hau, a general practitioner, and Dr. So Ley, a colonel-surgeon, both arrested at the pagoda of Baray (Kompong Thom) and killed. An eyewitness was Dr. My Samedi, now at the Revolutionary Hospital in Phnom Penh.

• Dr. Phlek Chhat, a resident physician at the Preah Ket Melea hospital, arrested in July 1975 in Ngorn village, Sandan district, Kompong Thom province, tortured and killed in prison from a wound in his mouth, which was caused by a burning torch thrust into it by his torturer.

• Nurse Nin Kham Oun was 38 years old, arrested in June 1977. Killed, together with his wife and eight children aged from 2 to 14 years in Sdeung Chey village, Skon district, Kompong Cham province. Eyewitness: Mr. Kham Phean, from the Ministry of Health.

• Nurse Tit Bopha was 45 years old, from Monivong Hospital and was killed, together with his wife and three children in July 1977, accused of being a lieutenant, in Baray village (Kompong Thom), beside a well in front of the Baray supply center. Many villagers were eyewitnesses.

• Dr. Meas Samban, died after a hunger strike done because he was dissatisfied with the Pol Pot regime (his wife was an eyewitness, at the home of Dr. My Samedi).

• Dr. Vu Kim Pop attempted to kill himself by cutting his radial artery (a scar still bears evidence of the act).

• Dr. (Mrs.) Kim Line was killed in July 1975 in Kompong Cham for having said a few technical words in French during a class she was teaching to medical workers in the regional hospital of Kompong Cham. The eyewitnesses were Dr. Samedi and Mr. Tieng Oun, a dentist.

• Dr. Hong Heav Pa and his large family of 28 people were massacred in Sre Veal village, Steng Treng district, Kompong Cham province in 1977. Eyewitness: Mr. Ly Den of the Ministry of Health.

• Dr. Neang Ho Kim Hay, the head physician of the Treung Leper Center, Kompong Cham province, was killed in 1977. Eyewitness: Mr. Ro Kim Chheng.

• Dr. Kong Choeun, Dean of the Faculty of Pharmacy was murdered at Tuol Sophi pagoda. Eyewitness: Mr. Ly Den, of the Ministry of Health.

• The pharmacist Cheam Kim Heng, professor of organic chemistry at the Faculty of Pharmacy was killed during the march toward Kompong Cham. Eyewitness: Mr. Sam An.

Mr. Pen Bun Piv, a pharmacist, can testify to the murders of:

• Professor (Mrs.) Saorin Tip Man, an anatomist-pathologist was killed in Phlov Leav, Preah Net Preah district, Battambang province.

• Dr. Tea Kim Hy, a radiologist and former student in Paris, died in a village infirmary without any medical treatment in 1977.

• Dr. Lach Kalmine was killed in a prison in Preah Prasath village, Khsach Kandal district, Kandal province. His wife, a qualified midwife working at the Revolutionary Hospital, can testify to this.

• Dr. Mat Turen and his wife were killed in Bos Thlann village, Chamkar Leu district, Kompong Cham province. Mr. Tieng Oun can so testify.

• Dr. Son Qui, a great specialist in ORL was killed at Rovieng, in Preah Vihear province in August 1978. Eyewitness: Dr. Samedi.

And a large number of other colleagues were killed for having served under the "old regime" or "old society." We refrain from citing other names for a lack of clear proof.

Many pharmacists were murdered with their families including, without exception: women, children, pregnant women, old people. The "purge" of intellectuals reached its high point in early 1977, following the motto "no interest in keeping; no loss in liquidating."

Any time a member of the local authorities told you, "to go and attend a reeducation course," this meant, "You are going to die."

2. "Bare-foot Doctors": An Instrument of Genocide of the Pol Pot–Ieng Sary Regime

Thus, Pol Pot and Ieng Sary killed competent physicians and replaced them with "bare-foot doctors" some of whom were illiterate but belonged to families of the first category. They underwent some dubious professional training. We are trying to give some information to future generations related to these facts.

To become a physician, they were required to have three months of training in a hospital-college. They became doctor of medicine after a six-month refresher course, and another one-year refresher course would make them "specialists" in various medical specialties.

The "physician" had to have the indicated qualifications. The nurses, male and female, were inhabitants from the same subdistrict, aged 11 to 15. The subdistrict infirmary was located in one of the local houses, many in a bad state of repair, with leaky roofs and no beds inside.

For medical equipment, they had a few syringes and a few blunt needles. The medicines included white, yellow, and dark colored tablets. The white and yellow ones were Chinese made (aspirin, sulfaguanidine, anti-malarial, chloramphenicol, tetracycline, etc.). These medicines were reserved for officials and citizens of the first category. The dark colored ones were for people of the second and third categories, i.e., mainly for us, who were also called the "April 17" people. So when we were sick, we had to swallow, by the handful, these questionable, perhaps harmful, tablets.

Sick people lay on the ground on torn mats. They were never carefully examined, but prescriptions were given after a few cursory questions. The distribution of medicine and injections were entrusted to the "nurses," who often failed to give out the medicine or give the injections. It happened quite often that antidiarrhea tablets were given to malaria patients and vice versa. Injections were given from red, orange, or white solutions contained in old orange squash bottles. It was noticed almost everywhere that before an injection the nurse wiped the needle with his or her own fingers to disinfect it. A needle was sometimes used for ten consecutive injections, without disinfection. "Comrade" Oeurn, the governor of Province No. 42, told me in October 1978 (Dr. Nouth Savoeun is a witness) that he had only one syringe and one needle for all the patients of his liberated zone, and that there had been no cases of infection. He kept his tool rolled under the waist of his black trousers. "And," he said, "there was no need for disinfecting the instruments with alcohol"! Naturally, the outcome was quite the opposite. There was an infection rate after injections reached a phenomenal 90 percent, and people were afraid of those injections. Some even became disabled after those shots. And the treatment performed by the doctor did little good. It was designed to frighten the sick and force them to go back to work, because the barefoot doctors believed that if a person was truly sick they would have had to be carried to the hospital, instead of coming by themselves.

Many examples proved how Pol Pot had used those "doctors" for torturing the sick, who also served as guinea pigs for studies in pharmacology, physiology, anatomy, etc.

The third category of people, the "April 17" people, were the victims of this practice. An eyewitness, Mr. Tieng Oun, reported some facts that confirmed those crimes. These events happened at the Kompong Cham hospital:

A group of surgeons, named Lay, Pei, and Sen, were supposed to conduct a study on the healing of tissue and to do it on a live being. A laparotomy was made: a section of small intestine was cut off and the ends joined. A compress was squeezed in to cover the wound. Every day the "researchers" came to study the process of healing of the intestine by looking through the gaping wound of the abdomen. The condition of the "human guinea pig" got worse daily, and he died after three days.

Another group of "physicians" made an anatomical and physiological study of the heart. Procedure: a patient was anesthetized, and they made a large incision at the third intercostal space on the right side and then stretched the opening of the wound. Then they began to inspect the wound. The poor patient died immediately.

Another group made a comparative study of the gallbladders of the living and the dead. A man was tied to a stake and a large front-to-back incision was made on his body, beginning from the region of the appendix and ending in the right paravertebral area on the back, following the right edge of the rib cage. Then the two sides of the incision were stretched open. Don't forget that the poor "human guinea pig" was howling in pain with eyes wide open, struggling desperately to get out of the tight ropes that held him to the stake. The surgeon thrust his left hand into the abdominal cavity, groping while smiling and shaking his head. Then he held scissors in his right hand and cut abruptly. The poor victim no longer yelled as he was no longer able to speak. The "surgeon" pulled out the gallbladder and compared it with a gallbladder from a corpse.

For the record, we must mention again the names of these butchers, lest they be forgotten: Lay, Pei, and Sen.

Sometimes the abdomen of a patient was cut open to try to find the cause of abdominal pain.

Other crimes merit mention. The following story happened in an infant nursery. While trying to calm a crying one-year-old baby, a nurse gave him four tablets (at 0.10) of gardenal and the child went to sleep, never to wake up.

Pol Pot's "medicine" was not aimed at relieving the people's pain; it plunged them into an abyss of despair. Old people were not welcomed at hospitals. Pregnant women had to work up until their delivery date. Sick children were often sent to hospital too late and infant mortality was very high, reaching 80 percent in Koeut village, Speu subdistrict, Chamkar Leu district, Kompong Cham province, as witnessed by Dr. Nouth Savoeun, a pediatrician at Hospital 701.

Pol Pot's "pharmacy" receded centuries back in history. Peasants were favored to be chosen as directors of pharmacies. Children were recruited and trained to be "primary pharmacists" or barefoot pharmacists, who were age 13 to 15, most of them illiterate, and who came from remote corners of the country and had never used a toothbrush. Evidence of this policy can be found in a report by Pol Pot's Ministry of Social Action dated July 15, 1978, which reads in its third Chapter, third paragraph: "Given the capabilities of the new recruits, most of whom are illiterate, the number of illiterate people is now very high in the Ministry of Social Action."

We can infer from this that pharmacists under Pol Pot were completely ignorant of pharmaceutical science.

Mrs. Kho Vanny, a French-trained pharmacist, who took part in the liberation movement with Pol Pot beginning in 1971, ran the PAK factory from 1975 to 1977 and then was sent away to be a teacher of primary school.

With regard to preparation of medications, they had no use for pharmacists or technicians, and preparation was done all over the country.

Lacking sterilizing equipment or thermometers, the peasants of remote villages prepared injectable solutions and put them in orange squash bottles; 90 percent of people receiving injections got infected. These fever reactions were often deadly. Patients were thus used as guinea pigs.

In Kompong Cham province in 1976, a barefoot doctor by the name of Chit gave two lepers some chicken soup in which the fruit and leaves of Datura stramonium (jimson weed) served as vegetables. The two patients died three days later from reaction to this poison.

In the "people's communes," old people, sick people, disabled people who could not work in the fields (especially those with infected wounds and tuberculosis) were asked to help traditional healers in preparing medicines.

Bark, roots, and leaves of medicinal herbs cut into fine pieces were dried in the sun on a mat where poultry, pigs, children, and the healers themselves might walk on them.

Preparations were made without any measurement of dosage. Most of those medicine-making houses had no scales, no test tubes or any other measuring instruments.

Most often, a given medicine was a "cocktail for a hundred diseases."

We have not found any documents on the analysis of pharmaceutical products. Since laboratory instruments and materials had been destroyed, no testing or analysis was done for the products they made.

Here are some examples of medicines widely made during the Pol Pot years:

(a) *Quinine*
strychnos nux vomica
tinospora crispa
azadir acta indica

(b) *Aspirin*
First formula:
- potash alum
- calcium sulfate (gathered from the sea)

Second formula:
- Garnicia laureiri
- Hephilium lappaceum

(c) *Vitamin C*
- Soluble injections of lemon juice

(d) *Vitamin B1*
- Distilled water from rice bran

(e) *Antipyretic*
First formula: Powdered human bone and coconut milk
Second formula: Leeching in honey

According to the professional ethic under Pol Pot, all barefoot doctors were also pharmacists.

In that period, the barefoot pharmacists never used narcotic (Table B) products, poisonous (Table A) products and dangerous (Table C) products.

Returning to Phnom Penh, surviving pharmacists have been able to pick up from the ground several dozen kilograms of opium powder and extracts of morphine and pethidine left about among herbal remedy products in unlocked rooms.

Poisonous products of Table A were scattered in hundreds of places. Insecticides were left within reach of everyone.

Not only did Pol Pot fail to take care of the people's health, he destroyed the old hospital facilities, medical equipment and instruments, pharmaceutical works and medical documents.

3. The Destruction of the Health Care Infrastructure:

Since the great victory of January 7, 1979, we have been able to gather a great deal of evidence showing Pol Pot's aim of destroying all health care facilities.

All hospitals in Phnom Penh, the provinces, and districts were destroyed along with their modern medical equipment. Medical instruments were found scattered on the ground, heaped in corners or thrown about in the courtyard. Laboratory equipment from the Phnom Penh Medical School was thrown onto the sidewalks.

Hospital furniture, hospital bedding, and sanitary receptacles (e.g., spittoons with lids) disappeared and were replaced by rudimentary beds with dirty mats.

Revolution Hospital (formerly Calmette Hospital) had no running water or electricity, and no sanitary facilities. Clean lavatories were replaced by latrines covered with sheet metal built along the fences.

The same sort of destruction befell the glass windows, doors and locks, and flooring.

The operating rooms of the Khmer-Soviet Friendship Hospital, where the great Khmer surgeons used to do heart and lung surgery and other operations, are in ruins. The electrical generator, expensive refrigerators for medicines, and health care equipment have been destroyed.

Green, well-tended lawns and beautiful walking lanes for patients were turned into wild brushwood which the barefoot doctors used as bathrooms.

The Langkar pagoda (directly south of the former Independence Monument) was turned into a warehouse for medical equipment. This valuable equipment was simply dumped there, was not cared for, and is now useless.

In January 7 Hospital, we found seven dental apparatuses out of order because of poor maintenance. The official slogan "economize everywhere" was never observed. Pol Pot's physicians did the exact opposite with regard to the protection of medical equipment.

The large library of the Medical Faculty, with valuable manuscripts, books, and periodicals patiently gathered since 1946, was simply ransacked. Evidence of the destruction of this famous library could be found in the heaps of burned paper in the backyard of this establishment.

The Troeung Leper Hospital with its 800 beds was destroyed in May 1976, and its 800 patients were condemned to death. These were lepers and syphilitics and they were taken out of the hospital by force. The killing was ordered by one Pok, who was governor of the northern zone. The order was carried out by Chit, the political commissar of the northern zone hospital and Sen, chief physician of the Leper Hospital. Mr. Ly Den and the villagers who lived in the neighborhood can testify to what occurred. The crime was one of the many examples of how the Pol Pot clique carried out their slogan: "Those who do not work will not eat."

Boils were removed by making a crude incision, without local anaesthesia, with a palm-juice gatherer's knife. The resulting wound was left open, without proper treatment, to the mercy of flies.

Rice paddies were fertilized with human manure. Women from the third category of the population had to walk in this infested mud when planting rice and even to drink the polluted water as there was nothing else to drink. Cases were common among those women rice planters of allergic and infectious skin diseases, intestinal parasites, microbial and parasitic vaginal infections.

4. Conclusion

Let the whole world know the whole truth, the tragedy that we have just experienced. As we all know, food deprivation alone undermines people's health and can lead to the invasion of the body by micro-organisms that may cause deadly infection. Exhausting labor in the working sites, fields and rice paddies make people prematurely old. Food deprivation also kept children from developing their intelligence. Apart from that, the Pol Pot–Ieng Sary clique intentionally lowered the standard of medical care to an extremely low level to raise the morbidity rate: Those who could not meet the work norms had to die. Professors of medicine and pharmacy, doctors and pharmacists, and other medical personnel were harmful to them. They were the first to be killed.

With these monstrous crimes of the Pol Pot–Ieng Sary clique, what will be our country's demographic future if the mortality rate is ten times the birth rate? (Studies made by the Ministry of Health.) One can easily predict that the People's Republic of Kampuchea will be depopulated if urgent measures are not taken. Forty-five percent of the four million surviving people are in poor health. In particular, the future of children aged one to five is in jeopardy. They all constitute an overwhelming burden for the health service. Our service will have to solve this distressing problem of seriously sick people as soon as possible.

What can we do when all the health care facilities have been practically destroyed? For those two million who are seriously ill, we now have 54 doctors and a few hundred paramedics, and the remains of medical clinics, equipment and instruments that have been 95 percent destroyed. And with what can we treat sick people when we lack pharmaceutical technicians and pharmaceutical factories, which have also been ransacked?

Shortages in everything haunt us day and night. We have to solve this equation with empty hands. What tremendous difficulties we have to overcome! We shall never be able to forget that Pol Pot medicine has left innumerable and sometimes unpredictable consequences, ranging from birth defects to carcinogenic effects that in the future will cause tumors or specifically Khmer pathologies. Indeed what Pol Pot and Ieng Sary did was like dropping a large atomic bomb in the middle of the country, with the explosion killing three million people, and radioactive fallout among the four million survivors, 45 percent of whom have a very bleak future. The pillar of our nation is also undermined, as a whole generation of children who lived under Pol Pot is at risk. Unless they receive particularized, urgent, and effective care, these children will not become healthy and balanced citizens, but rather sick, mentally handicapped, or outcast people before reaching a mature age.

In short, Pol Pot managed to implement his Satanic plan, engineered by the Chinese hegemonists and expansionists. He has left us a thousand difficulties to overcome right now and in the future.

So we must unite closely around the National United Front for the Salvation of Kampuchea to defend our imperilled nation, and to counter any new attempts of subversion by the Pol Pot–Ieng Sary clique. We must remember, and make our children remember, what the Chinese-backed genocidal Pol Pot–Ieng Sary regime has been. Let world opinion, let people dedicated to peace, happiness, and justice, condemn the genocide of Pol Pot, Ieng Sary and their accomplices that aimed at exterminating our people and that managed to kill more than 40 percent of Kampuchea's population! Let Pol Pot, Ieng Sary, and their accomplices be brought to trial and punished by our people's court under our law and international law. The poor victims, men, women, pregnant women, children, and the elderly, buried in tens of thousands of common graves, are crying for justice and demand that the world's people pillory the genocidal regime of Pol Pot and Ieng Sary and their Peking masters! Let such a regime never appear again on our planet!

Phnom Penh, August 1979

2.4.03b

Report of the Orphans Relief Center of Siem Reap Province

The People's Revolutionary Committee of Siem Reap province wishes to submit to the Minister of the Interior the following document: "Report of the Orphans Relief Center of Seam Reap Province."

Siem Reap, June 23, 1979
For the People's Revolutionary Committee, Siem Reap Province
Hem Bo (signed and sealed)

Report of the Orphans Relief Center of Siem Reap Province

The Orphans Relief Center of Siem Reap province was established on February 18, 1979. Situated along a lake about 100 meters from the provincial town, the Center has two rows of houses. It now has 152 orphans, of whom 70 are boys and 82 girls. By age, they number as follows:

1) Under 4: 2 boys, 4 girls.
2) From 4 to 10: 26 boys, 24 girls.
3) From 10 upwards: 42 boys, 51 girls.

Most of them were born in Phnom Penh, Kandal, Takeo, and Svay Rieng. The majority of the orphans were taken to the Center by the Kampuchean army who found them wandering along the Siem Reap—Battambang highway.

Under the Pol Pot rule, most of the orphans lived in Phnom district of Battambang province. Some had no idea where their parents were, and with others their parents had been killed by the Pol Pot soldiers.

When they were brought to the center, they were very weak and suffered diseases, the most common being beriberi. They were only skin and bone. They could not walk far and thus could not attend a class. Now they are much better. They are as healthy as their parents' care can achieve. They are now able to go to schools and to work in accordance with their ability. Some of them, however, still need further treatment.

Our Center takes in all the orphans of the province provided that their orphanage is confirmed. After a period of treatment in the hospital to get them healthy, they are to be organized into small groups. A school has been set up to educate them and teach them practical work. It now has four grades.

Ill orphans continue to receive appropriate care or are sent to the hospital.

For their moral education, our center fosters among the orphans a spirit of solidarity, comradeship and mutual help; at the same time we teach them to distinguish friends from foes. All our children strictly abide by our Center regulations.

As far as their food and clothing are concerned, they are provided with rice, foodstuffs, and clothes by the provincial administrative committee. However, few orphans go to school because the school is newly set up and lacks textbooks, teaching materials, and chalk.

The staff of the Center consists of 9 persons (3 men, 6 women). They are: (1) Mr. Van Roeum, director, (2) Yim Sary, teacher, (3) Chup Ou Ses, teacher, (4) Ou So Chieu Ta, teacher, (5) Uk Sary, teacher, (6) Mrs. Ch Tha, cook, (7) Mrs. Vat Sa Roeum, cook, (8) Chan Luk, worker, (9) Pou Khinh, worker.

Above are the activities of the Orphans Relief Center of Siem Reap Province since its establishment.

Done at the Orphans Relief Center, June 20, 1977
For the Managing Board, Doup Sau Ry

2.4.03c

Future Physical and Intellectual Development of Phnom Penh Children After the Fall of the Khmer Capital in 1975 as Seen by a Pediatrician: A Report

Before the fall of Phnom Penh on April 17, 1975, children in the city accounted for 45 percent of the total population (figure supplied by the former head of the Anti-Tuberculosis Service in Phnom Penh). This would represent 900,000 children under 15, out of two million total inhabitants in the city. These children were evacuated from the city with their parents in the hottest season of the year; they were poorly clad, ill fed, and without medicines. In addition, the poor things had to go on foot a long distance before arriving at their destination. While en route, they contracted many diseases, of which several were quite bad.

In the well-known "Pol Pot–Ieng Sary cooperatives," these children were divided into labor groups: from 15 to 13 years of age they worked in mobile teams, from 13 to 8 years they tended oxen and buffalo, from 8 to 5 years they were sent to "rural schools" with an astonishing curriculum of "collecting cow dung" from dawn to dark in exchange for a bowl of lightly salted and poorly prepared thin broth. Hygiene was denied to them during these gloomy years. At the work sites and elsewhere, "savings" were achieved by compelling them to work hard and giving them little food to eat. This same measure was applied to women in the first to seventh month of pregnancy. So even a fetus must be subjected to a restricted diet!

Hygiene was something unknown to children: they wallowed naked in a pond or in a lane, swallowing from time to time a pinch of earth or dirty leaf. A succulent mouthful it might be! In this way they swallowed larva of all manner of intestinal worms. How many deaths were caused by these parasites in our cooperative? One village doctor said, "Cases of mortal intestinal perforation and colic due to these worms were common."

Besides, Phnom Penh children were to die because they had lived in the capital, or because their parents were "traitors to the country," because they belonged to military families or the royal family, or because they were born to intellectuals.

Now, after liberation by the National United Front for the Salvation of Kampuchea, the surviving children returning to the capital fall into three categories:

1. Category A—Children aged around 3 years, 8 months, and 20 days (in round figures, 4 years).
2. Category B—children above 4 years of age.
3. Category C—children born after January 7, 1979.

Children belonging to category A were the worst hit by all kinds of measures taken by the Pol Pot–Ieng Sary clique against the Kampuchean people. Since intelligence develops when the child is two years old, his food must meet the needs of the rapid development of the brain. Psychological development requires the presence of a mother, or at least of some sympathetic person. Unfortunately, our children never enjoyed this privilege; they had to be content with a septuagenarian grandmother who looked after ten children at the same time: this is a catastrophe. Besides, physical development depends heavily on a balanced diet composed of proteins, fats, sugars, mineral salts, vitamins, and milk products. Hygiene is important for children in avoiding intestinal parasites very harmful to their good intellectual, spiritual and physical development.

All these considerations allow me to predict that the children of category A will have height and weight inferior to those of children of the same age living under the previous regime. Also, the poor little ones will have a lower intelligence quotient (IQ), 100 at the highest (a physician should have an IQ of 120), with perceptible emotional difficulties.

As for category B children, only their physical development will be affected.

Finally, category C represents the future people of the People's Republic of Kampuchea. These children will be the subject of our next study. Only the future will tell us whether these children will be tall, intelligent and freed from emotional disorder. However, what is most regrettable is that for the next sixteen years we shall have a people of small stature, less intelligent, listless, and ill-tempered. But this is not to say that they won't be hard working.

Dr. Nouth Savoeun, Pediatrician
"January 7" Hospital, Phnom Penh

Harmful Effects of a Restrictive Diet on Children One to Four Years Old Who Lived Under the Infernal Rule of Pol Pot and Ieng Sary

Our work in the "January 7" Hospital lets us make some assertions about the causes of death of children in an "age sample," and to make some clinical observations on the psychology of these children.

The children treated in our hospital were all newly liberated and had lived for a longer or shorter time, from one to four years, under the genocidal regime of Pol Pot and Ieng Sary. We notice that the death rate is higher for girls than for boys (a ratio of 12 to 11), and that the older the children are, the higher their death rate. On 28 cases of death, there were 8 children of 4 years of age, 8 children of 3 years of age, 5 children of 2 years of age, and one one-year-old. The children died of infections that came on top of chronic deficiencies. Among the diseases causing children's death we must mention infectious diarrhea, food diarrhea, parasitic diarrhea, various microbial diseases, intestinal infections, ear, nose, and throat infections, fevers of undetermined etiology, and recurring and lethal convulsions.

Amoebic and bacillary dysentery, however, was the main cause of child mortality. We know that a diet poor in protein cannot provide a sufficient quantity of eighteen essential amino acids, chiefly lysine and tryptophane, whose role is to regenerate tissues corroded by the lytic action of germs. Hence, the infected tissues would be a door wide open for invasion by microbes, and the body's weakened defenses would let it be invaded. The undernourished body would have an inadequate system of defenses. As a consequence, the malnutrition during the dark period of Pol Pot and Ieng Sary weakened the health of children, allowing even a nonserious infection to cause death. A great number of children lost their lives for lack of a proper diet. The survivors of this generation (aged from one to four years) will necessarily have a highly reduced intelligence potential, with IQs no higher than 95. An IQ of 120 is necessary to be a physician. This figure will enable us to predict the intellectual and professional future of these children.

Even though we lack specialized materials needed to do psychological evaluations of children, we are trying, with the means we have available, to make some determinations.

As of July 7, 1979, our pediatric service is treating 73 patients, all of them severely malnourished. In addition, they are apathetic and indifferent to others. Only food could draw their attention: they are bulimic. Some are shying away from animation, an abnormal behavior worthy of notice. They like to cluster silently in a dark corner: this is the instinct of a wild animal fond of the jungle and silent in nature. The sight of a toy makes some of them crazy. They are even afraid of a doll or a toy motorcar. In short, Pol Pot and Ieng Sary have transformed the future pillars of the nation into wild beasts living a vegetative life, having no consciousness, no affection, no feelings.

Finally, with the few materials in our possession, we are trying to show civilized people, who seek peace and happiness just how unfortunate the children of Kampuchea really are. What will be their future, and that of the entire Khmer nation? Pol Pot and Ieng Sary not only killed the poor defenseless and innocent children, but they have ruined a whole generation of still living children, aged from one to four. These children will suffer retarded growth; their lives will be marked by long stays in hospitals and sanatoria; they will hardly be able to fulfill the duties of citizenship. Such is the gloomy prospect for this category of children who have lived through the bloody and savage Pol Pot–Ieng Sary regime.

Phnom Penh, July 7, 1979
Dr. Nouth Savoeun, Pediatrician, "January 7" Hospital

Infections and Diseases During the Infernal Years Under Pol Pot–Ieng Sary Rule

All the infections and diseases were due to lack of food and a beastly work regime imposed on the people.

1. *Dropsy* contracted at any age and by both sexes, caused by the absence of all daily nutritive elements: protein (meat), glucose (rice), lipids (animal or vegetable fats), and vitamins. Dropsy can provoke a secondary infection, in which case death is inevitable.

2. *Microbial infections* were common, but left untreated they would become mortal, for instance, different kinds of abscesses, furunculosis, anthrax, malignant staphylococcus.

3. *Seasonal viral diseases* affecting a subject poor in amino acids, sometimes causing an epidemic with a high death rate, even though a few aspirin tablets would have cured them in 48 hours.

4. *Bacterial lung diseases* and tuberculosis were quite common.

5. *Vaginitis, inflammation of the uterus, inflammation of the Fallopian tubes, and prolapsed uterus* were frequently found, chiefly in women who wallowed in rice paddies fertilized with human waste.

6. *Irregular menstruation or cessation of menstruation* was common in young women and girls.

7. *Malaria* was endemic, causing the death of tens of thousands of people every year.

8. *Lepers and syphilitics*, considered products of the old society, were all, so to say, condemned to death.

9. *Intestinal parasites* show that there was a general absence of hygiene and a return to the "stone age."

10. *Yaws*, formerly eradicated in Kampuchea, began to reappear everywhere in the country.

11. *Cases requiring surgery* are seen very frequently but often the stage of operability has passed.

12. *Cases of anemia* of all kinds were numerous.

13. *Cirrhosis of the liver* is also common, directly caused by lack of protein in the diet.

14. *Blindness* is frequently found in children due to the absence of secondary vitamin A, or to chronic diarrhea.

Dr. Nouth Savoeun

2.4.03d

Policy of Pol Pot and Ieng Sary on Humanitarian Organs

The Pol Pot–Ieng Sary clique broke off all relationships with international humanitarian organs. Our humanitarian organ called Khmer Red Cross was put under the supervision of the Ministry of Public Health.

After April 17, 1975, the reactionary Pol Pot–Ieng Sary gang forced the delegates of Swiss nationality of the International League of the Red Cross to leave Phnom Penh. The League has its headquarters in Geneva. At the beginning of the war, a delegation of the International Committee of the Red Cross set up in Phnom Penh in cooperation with the Khmer Red Cross to help our people with its good offices. This delegation intended to remain neutral and not to interfere in the internal political affairs of the country.

In early April 1975, the International League of the Red Cross gave its agreement with the Khmer Red Cross on philanthropic aid, stating that at the end of the war, the League would help resolve the problems of refugees. Refugees numbered 30,000 families that would have to go back to their native villages, but this plan could not be carried out because all the members of this organ were expelled from our country because the Pol Pot–Ieng Sary clique did not recognize the International Committee of the Red Cross.

On the morning of April 17, 1975, as President of the Khmer Red Cross, I was preparing aid packets for refugees. I was surprised to see soldiers in black clothing come and ask me to leave our office with all my staff. They took us out by force, and we had to spend the night in the open, along the sidewalks in front of the Monorom Hotel, which was their headquarters. I was alone, separated from all the members of my family.

After the liberation of January 7, 1979, I had an opportunity to return to Phnom Penh, and I was able to establish that the central office, the dispensary, and the warehouses where aid provided by the various Red Cross international organs is kept, all medicines, and all illustrated photographs of the International Committee of the Red Cross were completely sacked and pillaged.

At present if we need documents in our work regarding the Khmer Red Cross, we must request them from the International Committee of the Red Cross in Geneva.

Later we found out that the Pol Pot–Ieng Sary leaders killed the Vice President of the Red Cross and members of its administrative council, such as Mr. Thor Peng Thong, Dr. Long Nget, Dr. Ber Keng Hean, and Dr. Teck To (only the name of Dr. Teck To is found on the list of those condemned to death at Tuol Sleng).

To verify the damage in the building of the Red Cross, I noted that no medical material or pharmaceutical products were left; even the Red Cross symbol from the front of the office was removed.

In the countryside, where I spent my life in captivity, the Pol Pot–Ieng Sary leaders made me do forced labor day and night but gave me only a meager food ration. That is why I got so thin and aged so much. I am now only 56 years old, but my face is that of an old woman of 70 years.

To escape death I had to conceal my identity and to say that I was illiterate.

In sum, the disappearance of the Khmer humanitarian organs was a great loss for the Khmer people in terms of aid from international humanitarian organs.

Mrs. Phlek Phiroun

2.4.04
Report of the Ministry of National Education Concerning the Crimes Committed by the Pol Pot–Ieng Sary Clique in the Field of National Education

After the April 17, 1975, victory against the neo-colonialist war of aggression waged by U.S. imperialism and its lackeys, the people of Kampuchea placed all their hopes in the carrying out of the people's democratic revolution on the path to genuine socialism. However, their legitimate aspirations were betrayed by the new masters of the regime. During the three years, eight months and twenty days of the genocidal regime of Pol Pot and Ieng Sary, dictators practicing nepotism and militarism, the Kampuchean people fell into an indescribable and immeasurable disaster, entailing a calamity never known before in the history of the world. Under the false banner of socialist revolution, the Pol Pot–Ieng Sary traitors, puppets of the Peking expansionist reactionaries, sowed among the Kampuchean people crimes and damage of all kinds and in all fields. With regard to national education, they killed professors, teachers, and students along with their families, destroyed all the infrastructure of education. At the same time, they worked out a new plan of teaching whose essence was obscurantism.

1. Premeditated Crimes

Immediately after victory had been won, the militarist Pol Pot–Ieng Sary dictators expelled by force of arms the whole population from the capital city, provincial capitals, and other urban centers. Loudspeakers mounted on motor cars called on the intellectuals to report to the new authorities in order to take part in the reconstruction of the homeland. Those who came during the first days were immediately sent to unknown destinations. Others, more distrustful, returned to their native villages along with other strata of the population. There they had to state their identity. Most of the teachers and their families revealed their true identities; they were sent to concentration camps separated from the population. We have attached to this report a list of eyewitnesses.

With regard to the students, they were formed into mobile teams for special work and grouped according to their level of education.

After being chosen, teachers and students were sent to their death one after another according to their level of education, without being informed of their misdeeds. The first victims were people with the highest level of education. In those cases, their families were killed too. In some provinces, the traitors gathered together the teachers, students, and other civil servants in one place and killed them in groups.

2. Crimes Perpetrated by Any and All Means, and of Unimaginable Cruelty

The traitors used such means as no one could imagine being used in the twentieth century. We are appending an attachment to this report that explains how the teachers and their families were killed, the names of some witnesses, and the names of some of the executioners.[1] I will give only a few examples:

1. This attachment is not available. — Eds.

Pursat province: In a barn serving as a prison at Khal Chhoeupouk, the traitors had the victims go out one after another to be killed. Pretty young girls were stripped naked, raped until they lost consciousness, and then killed. The same thing happened at Preah Chrey and Bak Chunk Ching in Bakan district to teachers and civil servants.

Siem Reap province: The teachers of Kompong Thkau subdistrict, Kra Lanh district, were killed in furnaces built for this purpose, and turned into fertilizer. Such "furnaces for fertilizers" existed in great numbers in Varin district. Other people at Svay Sar in the same district were killed and thrown into a pit.

Takeo province: Seventy teachers and their families were killed from the village of Prey Kabbas and they were buried in a pit five meters from the prison. The adults were beaten to death with a metal bar, and the children and babies were taken by their feet and had their heads smashed against a tree trunk. Even pregnant women among the teachers were not spared.

Kampot province: All male and female teachers of Touk Meas district were pushed over a precipice.

In Kandaul village, Totung subdistrict, most were killed and covered with earth in bomb craters. The children's bodies were torn apart by the legs. In O Sleng village, Damnak Kantuot subdistrict, Kompong Trach district, over 300 people had their stomachs cut open and their gallbladders taken out. These infamous executioners were encouraged and congratulated by the district chief.

In addition to these violent methods, the traitors also used indirect, "milder" ones, such as letting people live without shelter, without medicine, without hygiene, without clothes, and with only one or two ladles of rice broth during the preharvest season. In Siem Reap, in September 1977, the teachers and their families, totalling 460 people, received only 2.5 kilograms of rice per meal. A witness to these meager rations is Mrs. Chuop Ose, 32 years old, former teacher in Siem Reap city, and Mrs. Diep Sao Ry, 34 years old, a former teacher in Siem Reap city.

At Cham Roa, in Mong Russey district, Battambang province, from March to December 1976, 100 people received only 250 grams of rice to be mixed with banana tree trunks cut into small pieces to make a kind of soup. Mr. Chhay Yi Heang can serve as a witness.

Twelve- to fifteen-year-old children were forcibly drafted into the army. As for the April 17 children, they were compelled to do forced labor, they were forced to carry dirt all day long, overworking them terribly, both physically and intellectually. Young people had to carry out work according to increasingly higher norms. Should they fail to furnish the required quantity of work, they were deprived of the daily ration.

On the other hand, teachers, students, and other intellectuals, whatever effort they might make, could not escape death because their mistake, if they had one, was their intellectual level. Even those who were comparatively less educated had the same fate. Similar to the extermination of those teachers whose identity was known to those in the concentration camps, the traitors were constantly looking for educated people who were not yet discovered, with a view to totally eliminating them.

Those who managed to escape death are those who could feign ignorance or disguise themselves or who were hidden by patriots.

The following statistics show the crimes committed by the Pol Pot–Ieng Sary clique against teachers and students.

Higher education	*1968 census*	*August 1, 1979*
Professors, teaching assistants	725	50
Students	11,000	450
Secondary education		
Teachers	2,300	207
Students	106,000	5,300
Primary education		
Teachers	21,311	2,793
Students	991,000	322,379

Of the 1,000 teachers, students, intellectuals, and political personages who came back from abroad between 1975 and 1978 in response to the deceptive call of Pol Pot and Ieng Sary, many were killed in cold blood at Tuol Sleng, formerly Tuol Svay Prey secondary school in the capital city. Of these, let us mention Tea Meng Tek, Inspector of Primary Education; Kit Chhe, professor; Ing Sokhom, professor; Tram Kim Youy (f), professor; Chung Chhum Leang, engineer; Sok Cham Nang, medical student; Lam Viri, engineer; and Huot Sambath, diplomat.

At the Tuol Sleng prison the victims were subjected to electric torture, hanged, or beaten with shovels, picks, axes or had their throats cut, or their stomachs opened, or were cut to pieces and thrown to pigs. By July 11, 1979, there remained only 85 out of the 1,000 people who had come back from abroad. (Please see the statement of Mr. Chea Kong, former professor of technology now working in the Teaching Committee of the Municipality of Phnom Penh.)[2]

2. This document is not available.—Eds.

3. Crime of Destruction of Education-Related Property

Almost all school buildings were destroyed after April 17, 1975, under the Pol Pot–Ieng Sary regime. In particular, in different provinces like Stung Treng, a model primary school was completely demolished; in Prey Veng, the secondary schools of Ba Phnom and Kompong Trabek districts were destroyed, and the bricks and stones were broken up and used in road construction.

In Svay Rieng Province, seven secondary schools were completely destroyed, while two others could only be used after major repairs. Two hundred primary schools were totally destroyed.

The primary school of the city of Kampot, and the four secondary schools of Kep, Tani, Touch Meas, and Kompong Trach were razed to the ground.

In Kompong Thom province, only two primary schools out of a total of 180 can still be used: as for the eight secondary schools, only that of Kompong Thom city can still be used.

In Kompong Speu province, not a single primary school has remained in existence. The situation is the same for secondary schools with the exception of the secondary school of the province capital, which was turned into a car repair workshop and an arms and ammunition depot.

How much time and work will be required to reconstruct these precious and useful buildings?

In addition, there remain no benches, no tables, no school materials or books. The provincial libraries are empty.

The damage caused in the capital city is less than that in the provinces, in that the existing school buildings still have their walls intact. But inside, there are no longer any doors, windows, or ceilings. The wooden floors were removed.

The Arts and Trades College, and the Khmer-Soviet Friendship Institute of Higher Technology have been greatly damaged. Other school buildings were turned into prisons, workshops, stables, and mechanical workshops, storehouses. Here are some examples:

The secondary school of Tuol Svay Prey was turned into a prison; the teachers training college into a storehouse for motorcycles and beer bottles; the girls primary school into a pigsty and a goat stable.

School equipment and materials were thrown in disorder on the ground or broken up. The laboratories of the various colleges are unusable. For instance, at the laboratory of the Teachers' College there remains only glass debris. The laboratories of the Faculty of Sciences and Pharmacy were completely destroyed.

The books and documents in the National Library, the Buddhist Institute, and various other establishments have been seriously damaged. It is now impossible for us to reconstitute a complete set of some masterpieces and even of some collections of textbooks, not to mention scientific books necessary to teachers and students.

4. Education Under Pol Pot and Ieng Sary Was Merely a Smoke Screen to Deceive the Masses

Since the buildings constructed in accordance with pedagogical norms had been destroyed, the students were taught in "dining rooms" or in empty granaries.

Once teachers possessing genuine knowledge had been killed, they were replaced by people who hardly knew how to read and write, whose role consisted primarily in interrogating the students to collect information on their prior conduct and activities of their parents, and also on those of other people in the cooperative. This way of proceeding provided the authorities with plenty of truthful information. Questions were asked regarding the parents' behavior at home: "What have you to eat as additional food?" And the children answered without lying.

Pupils were divided into classes according to their age, regardless of their level of education; this was done to be able to send them out for manual labor. They had no notebooks, no chalk. All were seated on the ground and a number of them, both girls and boys, were naked. There were some books about reading and arithmetic, the same books for all grades; there was nothing else.

Besides manual labor, such as collecting manure, and embanking rice fields, the content of that education consisted in promoting hatred for former city dwellers, finding and wiping out hidden foes, and the traditional enemy, Vietnam. The students were taught that the true friend of "Democratic Kampuchea" was Peking, and that Angkar, the administrative apparatus of the Pol Pot–Ieng Sary regime, was the benefactor of children, etc.

The classes were open only half-an-hour a day, between noon and one o'clock. Besides the lesson hours, the children were used for tending the cows and buffaloes, digging earth, collecting dung (20 to 30 kilograms a day for each 8- to 10-year-old child). In Kompong Speu province, they had to carry dirt, making 100 trips in the morning and 70 in the afternoon. Each trip covered a distance of 50 meters. In Mong Russey district, Battambang province, the children were made to dig water ponds and channels and to take part in the building of dikes and embankments. Several hundred died because the work required from them was beyond their strength. At Chieb, in Toek Phos district, Kompong Chhnang province, 200 out of 300 children died. Witness: Mr. Nuth Sen, 36 years, a former teacher now in Kompong Chhnang city. The sad atmosphere in the classes, where there was no play and no song, drove children to desert the schools, but no one paid much attention.

The teaching methods used under the Pol Pot–Ieng Sary regime involved committing sentences and slogans to memory without any understanding of their meaning. In other words, the education of our children consisted of making them love Angkar, of forgetting the sacred links between them and their parents, and of making them capable of killing their fathers, mothers and other relatives with their own hands, if they were suspected of actions likely to harm the revolution. The traitors wanted to turn our children into robots who thought only about what was taught to them by Angkar, and who acted only on the order or slogans of Angkar.

It is to be noted that if the children failed to fulfill the required norms, they were refused food rations, whipped, and punished by any means available, in the presence of their friends. Sometimes, a guilty child was killed in front of the others, to serve as an example. His stomach was opened; his gall-bladder taken out, and put into alcohol. Sometimes, the breasts of young girls were cut off and made into food for Angkar in the cooperative.

Future officials, between 12 and 15 years old, were given orders to execute tens and even hundreds of people.

5. Aims of Education in the People's Republic of Kampuchea

Education in the People's Republic of Kampuchea is of a revolutionary type and democratic in character, aimed at achieving true socialism. We are strongly fighting against the great dangers of illiteracy among both adults and children.

But we are facing a critical situation created by the Pol Pot–Ieng Sary clique. Beyond the grief and suffering caused to the teachers and their families, the killing of students, a policy of obscurantism carried out against the people, we must add the immense destruction of school buildings, laboratories, and school materials. Several decades will be required for us to rise again from the ruins: training of new teachers and professors, publication of new textbooks, training of a new generation of primary and secondary pupils, pupils in practical subjects, and university students in various fields, construction of buildings, and supplying of materials. The task is a gigantic one, but under the clear sighted leadership of our Party, Government and Front, our people will make the necessary sacrifices so that the teaching given may, in time, meet the requirements of the rebuilding of our beloved homeland, the People's Republic of Kampuchea.

2.4.06

Report on Social Problems Under the Dictatorial, Fascist, and Genocidal Pol Pot–Ieng Sary Regime

I. Social Aspects

Under the Pol Pot regime, citizens were put into three categories. The first category was mainly high officials of the regime and of the inhabitants of the former liberated zone. The second category included the other inhabitants of the zone liberated before April 17, 1975. The third category consisted of persons expelled from Phnom Penh and cities liberated beginning in early April 1975, these people being called either parasites or "April 17, 1975" people.

At the same time, there was a systematic mixing, from north to south, from east to west and vice versa, of the inhabitants of border zones. Peasants in the east of the country had to move to the west because they were suspected of being pro-Vietnamese. Peasants in the west of the country were forced to go to the east. This was an enormous social dislocation initiated by the leaders of the regime, who wanted to build a society on entirely new bases, with no deep attachment with the environment in which people lived before April 17, 1975. Pol Pot and Ieng Sary boasted that in only three days they destroyed the parasitic social classes in the cities and urban centers. One must add, however, that during the months following their "revolution," most inhabitants changed domicile; this was thorough-going social dislocation. Family dislocation came a short time later in the agricultural cooperatives.

Apart from a few differences in treatment among the persons of the first and second categories, these residents were favored in all aspects of life (work, food, clothing, shelter . . .). The third category was considered to be traitors and were also called prisoners of war.

II. Subjection to Forced Labor

They made everyone work hard in the field, because their policy was that when one has rice one has everything. No one had a choice of line of work based on their capabilities and their inclination. It was ill fortune for any men or women who revealed their true identity. All intellectuals, students, secondary school pupils, that is, anyone who thought, anyone capable of judging the genocidal regime, is killed sooner or later. Those with higher university degrees are first in line, along with their families. The reports of the investigation commission on public health and education provide irrefutable proof of this. They deemed each and every third category person a slave, and not a citizen. Children beginning at the age of six years, pregnant women, women two months after delivering a baby, the elderly, the sick, and convalescents were required to go to the work sites like everyone else. The workers were frightfully mistreated by their group chiefs. Most of the time people replaced cattle and buffalo in plowing and tilling. One would often see six people harnessed to a plow (Witness Pen Bun Piv, a pharmacist and victim).

Even pregnant women in their eighth or ninth month were required to do hard labor, and this often caused difficulties in childbirth. Some women miscarried. (Doctor Mrs. Pen Prinman can testify about this.) Pregnant women who did not work in the fields had their food ration immediately reduced; they were put on a ration of broth, and it was the same for women during the time they nursed a baby. It was not rare to find cases of prolapsed uterus, of irregular menstruation, or of a cessation of menstruation among young women and girls in the mobile work teams. Many women were toothless.

III. The Issue of Shelter and Clothing

As concerns shelter, there was no appropriate housing. The Pol Pot people dismantled large wood houses to build smaller ones (3 meters by 4 meters). The "parasites" lived in shelters infested with bugs and mice, and where there was no sanitation system. Two or three families (15 to 20 persons) lived in a single ramshackle straw hut of 20 to 25 square meters. At the work sites (drainage, dike construction, land clearing, work in the fields, etc.) the workers had nowhere to sleep but under the trees or under the stars.

There was a general lack of clothing, because at the time of the expulsion from Phnom Penh, each person had only the jacket or pants he was wearing. The annual distribution of low quality black cloth to make new clothes barely sufficed to make one pair of pants and one jacket for one member of the family, if it was a large family. Only one member of each family had the right to get a new pair of drawers. That is why the clothing of the inhabitants was pieced together with many scraps of cloth of different colors, even though the workers were required to work rain or shine, day after day, without any real rest.

IV. Food Rations

Under the Pol Pot–Ieng Sary regime there was no such thing as a wage for the members of "production cooperatives." Each worker got only a ration that varied in amount according to the work done. Workers were divided into two categories: the vanguard, or shock, workers, and rear-guard workers. The former had to work very hard 12 to 15 hours a day, for 350 grams of rice per person at harvest time. At other times the daily ration was lowered to 250 grams for eight persons, a quantity that sufficed to make rice broth. Rear-guard workers had the right to a reduced ration (half that of the other workers). When rice was in short supply, people ate a little corn, potato, and especially banana stalks. In regions of persistent scarcity because of the requisition of rice (Battambang, for example), one would eat any weeds that were edible. Meat figured in the menu once or twice a year in the cooperative, and then in small quantities. Although there was a slogan: "Those who produce, eat; those who work a lot, eat a lot," it was precisely the opposite of that. Workers worked hard but unfortunately did not get enough to eat to fill them up. They worked without breaks or rest. There was no such thing as a day off: it was work, work more, and keep working. When by chance there was no work to be done on a particular day, that day was used to study the policies preached by Pol Pot and Ieng Sary, followed by a session of criticism and self-criticism.

V. Family Life

The Pol Pot–Ieng Sary clique wanted to destroy family ties: the husband was separated from his wife, and children from their parents. Each one worked at a different work site even if there was work for all members of the same family at one work site. Families could see each other only once a month, for a period of 12 to 24 hours at most. Pol Pot made children deny the existence of their parents, and he sabotaged the respect and love that is due to parents. It often happened that a child, or a nephew, would kill his own father, or his own uncle, on orders of Angkar. Examples abound. Comrade Sim Kok Noy witnessed events that took place at the Keas Uralar prison (Battambang).

VI. Activities Of Humanitarian Organs

Pol Pot suppressed all the activities of the Red Cross of Kampuchea and severed all connections between the Red Cross of Kampuchea and the International Committee of the Red Cross. As well, all orphanages were closed, and orphans were left to their sad fate.

VII. Customs

The policy of the Pol Pot–Ieng Sary clique was to try to eliminate all Khmer customs deemed inimical to their society "without rich or poor," and in which any human feeling, any love between members of a family, any love between two young people, was strictly forbidden. Everything was decided by Angkar, even marriages. So forced and collective marriage was instituted throughout the country as a measure of economics! Young people to be married were chosen by the village committee, which had full power to decide which girl should marry which boy. They decided blind. The intended spouses did not know each other at all before the wedding ceremony. Only the combatants of their "revolution," and those of their soldiers who were wounded in battle had the right to marry the prettiest girls, those in the best health, the prettiest widows! Refusal on the part of the intended bride was the same as a death sentence. Parents did not even have the honor of attending the ceremony, which might involve 50 to 100 couples. Suicide after marriage was quite common. In many cases, the couple accepted the cruel situation created for them in order not to jeopardize the lives of their parents. For them, especially for the women involved, this was a sacrifice of their emotional life.

Religion was completely abolished. Pagodas were more or less destroyed, as well as Catholic churches and mosques. Ecclesiastical books were all destroyed, and the statues of Buddha were decapitated. Many statues dating from the 8th to 12th centuries were destroyed. The shrine west of the Hotel "Phnom" literally "evaporated." One sees not a trace of it. Adherents, especially those following Islam, who were caught worshipping were killed.

As for traditional holidays, they were totally modified and replaced with Pol Pot–Ieng Sary holidays.

VIII. Conclusion

Pol Pot and Ieng Sary achieved their aim of dislocating the social life of the Khmer people. Half a million corpses were strewn about the roads that took the city people to concentration camps, or they were thrown into rivers. Two and a half million were killed because they were intellectuals capable of judging the horrible crimes that the Pol Pot–Ieng Sary clique perpetrated against their people, or because they allowed themselves to have feelings a bit different from those that Angkar had inculcated in them, or because they did not fulfill the required work norms, or simply because their life was not useful to the so-called socialist revolution. Kampucheans were reduced to a condition of slavery, worse than that of the slaves of ancient times because they did not have the right to have a single thought other than that of Angkar, and they had no family life. They were deprived of religion, of traditional customs and habits, of civilization. They became robots who had to trudge from early morning till late at night, without an hour of rest, while in return they got little to eat. Many died at the work sites. It was like living in the stone age!

The intellectual level of the Khmer fell markedly, as well as their general level of knowledge. The residents had no newspapers, and no political or scientific magazines. As for national feeling, the Khmers lost a sense of solidarity and instead mistrusted each other.

Most people were illiterate.

The mortality rate shot up substantially, in particular among males, and among children under the age of two years. The main causes of mortality were hunger, disease, and killings, all of which left a considerable number of orphans and widows. As for the other Kampuchean citizens, most were seriously malnourished.

Fortunately the liberation of Phnom Penh and of Kampuchea on January 7, 1979, put a end to this genocide of an entire people. The social problems we must face are many, and are difficult to resolve. Our people, however, are determined to surmount these problems so that our People's Republic of Kampuchea can prosper in independence, peace, and happiness.

2.4.07

Report on the Pol Pot–Ieng Sary Clique's Genocide Related to Kampuchea's Economy and Social Welfare

April 17, 1975, marked our people's victory in the struggle for Kampuchea's independence and freedom. Our people showed indescribable joy at this victory and were ready to make the greatest efforts to restore the national economy and meet the material and spiritual needs of the population. However, the Pol Pot–Ieng Sary clique abused its power and worked against the socialist political line it had promised. It was bent on carrying out numerous measures which undermined national independence and destroyed the country's independent and sovereign economy, by applying internal and external policies modeled on China's.

Looking back at the period 1969–1970, we find that Kampuchea had an arable acreage of 2,427,000 hectares yielding a total output of 2,503,000 tons of paddy rice. The acreage of maize was 85,300 hectares with a total output of 99,300 tons. The acreage of pepper was 66,666 hectares with a total output of 2,250 tons. Fishing in the Tonle Sap, in rivers and in the ocean, plus farm fishing, supplied a considerable source of food. Some industries, in particular light industry and handicrafts produced consumer goods that satisfied some of the people's needs.

Goods were moved on public transportation. There was an upward trend in the use of money, of the postal service, in the circulation of goods through markets. Although under the Lon Nol regime, stooge of U.S. imperialism, certain sectors of the economy receded in comparison to the preceding period, the population, on the whole, and especially those living in rural areas, had enough to eat. It is to be stressed, however, that the general well-being was not commensurate with the labor supplied for there was much inequity in the distribution of social income.

Instead of the realization of a great dream, a horrible misfortune began to befall our country right after the liberation, just a few hours after the march of the "black clothed" people into Phnom Penh. For nearly four years, the Pol Pot clique almost destroyed the very foundations of our economy.

1. In 1968–1969, Kampuchea boasted more than 100 industrial enterprises owned by the state and by private companies, and more than 3,700 units of handicraft production, located in various provinces.

Under the Pol Pot–Ieng Sary regime, handicraft production was totally eliminated; many factories were closed, or left in disrepair; many workshops, stores and warehouses were overrun with grass. Only a few factories continued to operate, turning out products for daily consumption of the leaders in Phnom Penh, the Chinese advisers and for export to China, such as power plants, distilleries, soft drinks factories, tire factories, glass works, etc. Nothing was produced by industry and handicraft for the most elementary needs of the laboring public.

2. As for transport, there existed in 1969 in Kampuchea 9,700 trucks, 1,300 motorcars, and more than 25,000 tourist vehicles. Passengers and goods used the ports of Kompong Som and Phnom Penh, the railway, and river transport. Under the Pol Pot–Ieng Sary regime, transport was used mainly, if not exclusively, for military purposes or for the conveyance of export goods. Public transport for the civilian population was abolished.

When our people recovered their independence, transport, meaning train engines and train cars, trucks, cars, and tourist vehicles, were either in ruins or were taken by the traitors in their retreat; the docks and bridges were destroyed.

3. No traces of telephone and telegraph lines can be found. There was no mail delivery.

4. Markets and shops were all closed down because products belonging to or produced by private persons no longer existed, "commodities" were banned and money was nonexistent.

5. Concerning agricultural policy, the so-called basic policy of the Pol Pot–Ieng Sary clique asserted that rice was to be the basic capital of the economy, other products being secondary, and that producing and exporting rice would provide the means to accumulate capital for industrial development and national defense.

In fact, the clique could only grow rice on 1,650,000 hectares (a decrease of over 700,000 hectares in comparison with 1969–1970). It figured that there would be two kinds of rice fields—those with one crop yielding three tons per hectare, and those with two crops yielding six tons per hectare. It envisaged a total output of 5,600,000 tons a year, of which 2,300,000 tons would be exported, and 3,300,000 would be left for domestic consumption. It was, however, obvious that the means put to use not only could not produce such results but gave rise to a tremendous waste of manpower.

Let us take some examples. Concerning water, the Pol Pot–Ieng Sary clique forced people to a kind of slave labor to dig canals, and, as nearly all technicians had been killed, there was a shortage of workers with the skills needed to plan agriculture and building large infrastructure for it. That was why the dikes and irrigation canals that had been built or dug were of no practical use, although millions of people died because of this exhausting labor, of starvation, of diseases, often right on the construction sites. It was an unspeakable disaster for Kampuchea which, thus, suffered a needless loss of millions of lives for no gain in terms of irrigation.

Concerning fertilizers, although the Kampuchean soil was fertile, it used to yield only a little over one ton of paddy rice per hectare, whether it was a good year or a bad one. The Pol Pot–Ieng Sary clique wanted to use only about 5,000 to 10,000 tons of chemical fertilizers for the 1,650,000 hectares (about 5 kilograms per hectare) and 300 kilograms of organic manure per hectare. Experience in other Southeast Asian countries has shown that to get two and a half to three tons of rice per hectare per crop, you need 100 to

150 kilograms of chemical fertilizers and 10 to 12 tons of organic manure per hectare. One can see that the Pol Pot–Ieng Sary clique was very far from reaching such average figures.

There was no improvement in the quality of seeds used to grow rice.

Because handicraft was altogether abandoned while industry was not yet developed, farm tools were so lacking that people had to dig the soil with their own hands. Draught animals were also in short supply; men had to take the place of oxen for drawing the ploughs.

In such conditions, how could the Pol Pot–Ieng Sary clique achieve a yield of three tons of rice per hectare, let alone six tons? The figures they produced were sheer eyewash.

And yet, during a meeting of officials to study the 1978 state plan, Pol Pot said: "In 1978 we have to export to China from 100,000 to 150,000 tons of rice and from 20,000 to 25,000 tons of rubber. Having signed, we have no right to renege. Failing to fulfill these contracts would negatively affect our overall policy. . . ."

That was why the Pol Pot–Ieng Sary clique grabbed all the rice it could: not to break the promise it had given to its masters in Peking. For them, it mattered little that the Kampuchean people ate thinner and thinner soup during preharvest periods, that pregnant women, women in childbirth, children, and old people had to obey Angkar orders and ate only diluted soup or died of starvation, provided that there was enough rice for delivery to the Peking expansionists in exchange for guns and ammunition that could be used to repress the people's discontent or wage wars against neighboring countries. The minutes of the meeting of the Party organization of the eastern zone noted: "As of May 1977, the living conditions of the population have worsened, especially in the districts of Kroch Chhmar, Peam Chileang, Koh Sotin and Muk Kampoul, where they have seriously worsened, so much so that people only eat diluted soup. Even with weakened strength, people still have to dig canals, to dredge waterways, to raise output and fulfill the plan."

On the other hand, industrial and other food crops such as cotton, maize, beans and sugar cane were abandoned. With regard to rubber, an important source of income for the country, it was left uncared for, which is causing great problems for its rehabilitation and exploitation. The population of oxen, buffaloes and pigs has been reduced nearly by half as compared with the figures of April 1975.

Fishing could have been done in very favorable conditions, given the great density of fish in the Tonic Sap, one of the most densely populated fishing lakes in the world; fish is also abundant in the rivers and the sea. But fishing instruments were partly destroyed and fishermen were sent to work the land in concentration camps. That is why, under Pol Pot and Ieng Sary, fishing only yielded about 25,000 to 30,000 tons a year while the annual output had been previously 100,000 tons.

6. The last and most important question concerned manpower. Out of a total population of more than 7 million people on April 17, 1975, more than 3 million had been exterminated (i.e., 43 percent) in the most varied and barbaric ways, by the Pol Pot–Ieng Sary clique. Among those killed were 80 percent of our technical personnel in economic fields (engineers, technicians, skilled workers, teachers and students of higher and secondary technical schools). Among them were also many engineers and technicians returning from Europe after 1975 responding to the appeal of the Pol Pot–Ieng Sary clique. This loss of technicians is irreparable for us because the reconstruction of such a ravaged country as ours requires many technicians and modern technology. How many decades will it take us to train new technicians, professors, engineers, managers, foremen, and skilled workers, only to fill the vacuum left by the massacres committed by that clique?

It should be stressed that of the 4 million inhabitants who have survived, the active population is not large. The large majority of these, who for four years have been deprived of the bare minimum necessary for preserving their physical strength and working capacity. Their labor productivity is well below their capacity and it will take a long period to reach it again. Concerning the children who will succeed us, we don't know yet what their physical and intellectual development will be, given the extreme and cruel hardships they have been subjected to in their early infancy.

The picture we have just sketched, above, reflects the economic situation and living conditions of our people under the Pol Pot–Ieng Sary regime and leads to the following conclusions: the genocidal regime of Pol Pot and Ieng Sary bears absolutely no relation to scientific socialism, which they claimed to be. On the contrary, they brought Kampuchean society back to slavery. We were faced with a neo-slavery system: the masters were Pol Pot, Ieng Sary and their accomplices; all the others, whether they were workers, peasants, or intellectuals, were reduced to a state of slavery, were treated worse than animals, worse than any slaves known in history. It was a backward turn of the wheels of history, contrary to the law of evolution, with the immediate consequence being the total destruction of production and other unpredictable, serious consequences. The Pol Pot–Ieng Sary clique have, thus, committed the crime of economic genocide against the Kampuchean people, a crime defined in Articles 1 and 2 of the Decree Law of July 15, 1975, issued by the People's Revolutionary Council of Kampuchea.

2.4.08
Report on the Crimes Committed by the Pol Pot–Ieng Sary Clique Against Culture, Information, and the Press in Kampuchea

Kampucheans have always been great artists. The descendants of the builders of the Angkor temples have continually enriched the culture of the

Khmer people with contributions in the various domains of culture: architecture, music, sculpture, painting, dance, literature, and theater. Since the introduction in Kampuchea of film, radio, and television, the creative spirit of the Khmer people has brought these means of entertainment and education to the masses of people. Our people anticipated as well the implementation of the socialist revolution that Pol Pot and Ieng Sary promised. The new regime will certainly let the masses of people be exposed to the great acquisitions of culture that our ancestors have amassed, as well as the treasures of world culture.

Unfortunately, the Pol Pot–Ieng Sary clique despised our national cultural patrimony and the people who maintained this national culture. Their aim was to eliminate Khmer culture and Khmer artists. They wanted to impose on the Kampuchean people the "cultural revolution" imported from China, and to bring into being new propagandists, not new artists. Their policy was defined as follows: "In the four-year plan for 1977 to 1980 on culture, literature, and art, all vestiges of imperialism, colonialism, feudalism, and other former ruling classes must be eradicated from culture and art." Translated into terms accessible to the public, that meant killing, or at least mistreating, artists and all those who had any closer or more distant connection with Khmer culture. It meant as well the destruction of monuments, libraries, television and radio studios, in brief, the infrastructure.

Let us review their killings and their destruction, committed on a scale never before known in world history.

1. The Arts

In the field of art, we can mention traditional music, Pin Peat Mohori music, classical music, modern music, "Bassac" theater, Yike, ayay, Chheu Pei, Chhay Yam, ballet, the "trott" folk dance, all known throughout the world. They are the symbol of our national culture, the soul of Kampuchean civilization. Once in power, the Pol Pot–Ieng Sary clique had all musical instruments destroyed, all traditional costumes used in the theater, and all documents about the arts. The venues in which artists practiced their trade, such as the theaters in Phnom Penh and in the provinces, the College of Fine Arts, the faculty of music, were almost all destroyed or damaged, with rare exceptions.

Artists, men and women, young and old, were mercilessly beaten to death with hoes, bamboo sticks, or metal rods. Some were run through with bayonets, or iron spears. Many were blinded, or disemboweled, or buried alive. The least unfortunate, if one can say, died a slow death from the forced labor that was demanded of them in exchange for inadequate nourishment. Well known actors died in horrible conditions, as, for example, M.M. Sin Sisamuth, Neang Huoy Meas, Hal Salan, Poeuv Sipho, and Voy Ho.

Mr. Ly Kim Uong, a renowned dramatist, professor at the faculty of dramatic arts, was beaten to death with a hoe in the O Samrong forest, near the Romduol cooperative, Phnom Leap subdistrict, Preah Net Preah district, Battambang province. The murderer was named Luy, a militiaman in the security service of the subdistrict. Mr. Mao Keng, now an artist at the artists' quarters on the Bassac Front, was an eyewitness to this murder.

Mr. Ay Savouth, a musician, was tied up and beaten to death with a stick by this same Luy at O Romchek, Phnom Leap subdistrict, Preah Netr Preah district. The artist's wife was raped by five Pol Pot men before being killed. Mr. Sot, living in the same quarters as Mr. Mao Keng, was an eyewitness to the crimes.

Mr. Hing Bunthon, professor of arts, having studied in Czechoslovakia, an actor in the well-known film "A Chey," former technical director of television, could not accept for long the slave work imposed on him and decided to kill himself by cutting his tongue in Chek village, Chen Choeung subdistrict, Stung district, Kompong Thom province. The eyewitness was Mrs. Malay, now living at the artists' quarters on Bassac Front.

Other women artists were raped by this band of traitors then buried alive. For example, that was the case of Mrs. Mom Sarem of the drama theater. The murderer was a militiaman in the security service of Prasath subdistrict, Svay Teap district, Svay Rieng province. The victim's step-brother, Mr. Nou, now living at Phnom Penh's central market, was a witness.

Of the 30 musicians, 74 dance students and 77 dancers of the folk-dance group, only 38 dancers and 9 musicians escaped the massacre. Of the 195 classical dancers, men and women, only 48 remain alive. Of the 54 dancers of the ballet corps, only 4 escaped death by a miracle. Of the 416 students of the faculty of plastic arts, only 14 have survived.

In total, of the 1,241 artists, only 121 have survived, i.e., 10 percent.

2. Cinema

The 34 movie theaters in the capital city and all those in the provinces were closed as soon as the Pol Pot–Ieng Sary clique came to power. The projecting materials of those theaters and of the 8 mobile projection teams were destroyed or seriously damaged. Film making companies were liquidated. While about 50 to 60 films were made every year, under Pol Pot–Ieng Sary, they were all short, color propaganda films, destined for foreign consumption. For obvious reasons, they were not shown to the population in concentration camps.

Naturally, most of the technicians and actors who had worked under the "old regime" were mercilessly persecuted, murdered or forced to hard manual labor in the fields or in fishing cooperatives on the Tonle Sap. Of the 75 persons connected to film companies of the information service, only 6 have been found alive so far. Of the 40 men and women artists, two are still living. Only 7 cinema halls in Phnom Penh can be restored to operation after considerable repairs.

3. Television

The only television station in the capital city was destroyed, including the transmitter, the studio, and most of the buildings. With the destruction of 40,000 TV receiver sets, there are virtually none in Kampuchea.

Of the 66 technicians and employees of the TV service, only seven are alive.

4. National Broadcasting System

Radio broadcasts continued to operate under the genocidal Pol Pot–Ieng Sary regime. They served as a means for timely transmission of directives to local authorities. Receivers were in the hands of Angkar people. The contents of broadcasts mainly referred to the tasks which the authorities should require from their subjects and the hatred they should entertain against the Socialist Republic of Vietnam which was called the hereditary enemy of Kampuchea. There was no intention to use the radio as a means of entertainment for the workers; music would be fatal to them. Their lot was to work like robots and to think of nothing, in this prison with millions of inmates was our Kampuchea!

5. The Press

Under Pol Pot and Ieng Sary, this service catered to local rulers and foreign propaganda needs. The simple citizen had to be left in total ignorance of what was going on in his own country and abroad. Angkar saw to it that this order was strictly obeyed, as reading would have helped some citizens to form personal opinions, and this was formally forbidden.

The new newspaper and magazine published by the clique disseminated only ideas and ideologies slavishly copied from the Chinese "cultural revolution." This press was against the profound feelings of the Kampuchean people who wished to be well and quickly informed, to live in harmony with the brotherly Vietnamese people.

The revengeful spirit emanating from this press and this so-called national radio was the cause of numerous deaths among soldiers who were forced to wage a war of aggression against Vietnam.

Journalists and newspaper editors, even those who were against the Lon Nol regime, were mercilessly eliminated. Mr. Hem Vanarith, former director of "Samleng Phnom Penh," who had taken part in the struggle against U.S. imperialism and its stooges, and who had been imprisoned by the Lon Nol clique at Prey Sar, was murdered by Pol Pot–Ieng Sary men in Andaung Po village, Andaung Po subdistrict, Tang Kauk district, Kompong Thom province in 1978. His daughter Mom, now living at the village of Andaung Po, was an eyewitness. Mr. Chou Thany, director of "Koh Sante Pheap," who supported the revolutionary cause against the US imperialists, was killed in a village in Saang subdistrict, Koh Thom district, during the exodus from Phnom Penh in 1975. Before killing him, the murderers forced him to dig his own grave at dusk. An eyewitness was his step-brother.

Of the 300 journalists and printing workers of the newspapers, only 5 journalists are living.

In short, all means of information were put in the service of an ideology that aimed at transforming people into robots.

Thus, instead of creating favorable conditions for man, this "thinking reed," to blossom freely and fully, all possible means, including torture and mass murder, were used for destroying this will to think and to reflect. People had to work like machines which were made to produce more and consume less. All Angkar orders had to be executed at once: any delay was punishable often by the only applicable penalty: death by a stroke of a hoe on the nape.

6. Libraries and Museums

Spending time in libraries and museums was not only considered to be useless and a waste of time, but also illegal, as it would allow readers and visitors to acquire unorthodox ideas. That was why hundreds of thousands of books in the National Library in Phnom Penh, the libraries of the Buddhist Institute, the Khmer-Mou Institute, the Pedagogical Institute and other academic establishments were ransacked and thrown out into gardens and on the pavements. Library staff were murdered: 35 out of the 41 employees of the national library were killed.

The museum which is found in the confines of the old royal palace, of the Silver pagoda and of various provinces, in particular the Battambang and Wat Po Weal museums, were destroyed. Of the antiquities of the glorious Khmer civilization, those made of gold and silver were all stolen by the ruling clique. Seventy percent of those made of bronze and other alloys were seized. The same happened to stone statues and sculptures. Very fine monuments were destroyed, together with the faculty of archaeology, a training and research institution. Most of the researchers, sculptors, and students of the faculty of archaeology were murdered. Mr. Ly Vou Ong, dean of the faculty of archeology and curator of the National Museum, was killed at Kien Svay right after leaving Phnom Penh. The victim had to dig his own grave before being killed with a hoe. Mr. Kem Nou, who now works at the National Museum, was an eyewitness.

7. Religion, Traditions, and Customs

The 3,254 pagodas were either destroyed, left uncared for, or used as prisons or manure dumps. . . . Valuable antiquities were either thrown into ditches or stolen. Treasures of old civilizations were lost forever. The 63,000 Buddhist monks (one percent of the population) had to shed the religious frock and return to civilian life, contrary to age-old customs. The rulers were afraid of their influence among the believers, of people meeting in pagodas. The mosques were also destroyed and Muslim followers killed. The Phnom Penh grand cathedral has disappeared; nothing remains there where once was a great building.

Khmer traditions and customs were despised as products of former exploiting classes. Annual festivals were no longer celebrated: such time was considered as wasted forced labor of digging soil. However, in their hearts, Kampucheans could not forget their traditional Prachum Ben (Festival of the Dead) triple anniversary, water festival, offerings to the monks, traditional agricultural festivals, etc.

8. Conclusions

The list of crimes committed by the Pol Pot–Ieng Sary clique against Khmer culture is a very long one. This clique carried out an obscurantist policy advocated by Peking in its "great cultural revolution." Their masters taught them how to suppress all human feelings, all human relations. All inhabitants had to become robots who would automatically execute all orders. A Kampuchean had to cease being human: death would befall him immediately if he only tried to become a human being again. The notions of freedom of the human being, of personal rights and liberties were old-fashioned in Kampuchea as well as in China because they belonged to the bourgeoisie. They had to be banned if a new society was to be built on entirely new basis, without any links with Kampuchea's glorious past. This social breakup went together with the breakup in family relations. School "masters" taught children to spy on their parents to loosen ties with them and even to kill them if they are suspected of rebelling against the policy of Pol Pot and Ieng Sary.

Under such conditions, all culture had to be abolished and was in fact abolished during the Pol Pot–Ieng Sary years. The consequences were numerous. Besides the great loss in artists, men of science, and a considerable loss in material, it should be stressed that the losses in human terms are incalculable. The children and young people who have been seriously intoxicated by Pol Pot–Ieng Sary's cultural revolution must become again Kampucheans with genuine Khmer culture.

August 1979

2.4.09

On the Crime of Genocide of the Pol Pot–Ieng Sary Clique Against Religions and Believers in Kampuchea, April 17, 1975 to July 1, 1979

Honorable President of the Court, Honorable Prosecutor, Honorable Members of the Court, Esteemed Delegates: On order of the Honorable Prosecutor, an inquiry and investigation team has been formed with a view to shedding light on the crimes of genocide against religions and believers, committed by Pol Pot, Ieng Sary and their associates. In order to present evidence for the record, we wish to present the Court with the initial results of our work, which will reveal the scope of the criminal acts and devastation that befell the believers all over the country. Our report is comprised of four parts: Crimes against Buddhists, Crimes against Muslims, Crimes against other beliefs, and Conclusion.

Part I: Crimes Committed by Pol Pot, Ieng Sary and Their Associates Against the Buddhist Religion

A. On the social role of Buddhism in Kampuchean society

Kampuchean citizens of Buddhist faith constitute nearly 90 percent of our population. In 1975 there were more than 3000 pagodas and more than 100,000 Buddhist monks.

In Kampuchea, the pagoda is not only a place for worshipping Buddha but also includes a primary or secondary school. It is a work of architecture, usually the largest building in a village. It is also a common heritage for the whole village, built and embellished by contributions from many generations of Khmers, as some pagodas are more than two centuries old. Furthermore, the pagodas serve as museums and exhibition halls for architecture, sculpture, and painting, and concurrently as storehouses for national musical instruments, a library with the richest collection of classical and contemporary literary works in the village. Finally, the pagoda is the place of cremation and a depository of the ashes of believers and their families, and most importantly of the ashes of successive generations of Buddhist monks.

In brief, in the eyes of Buddhists who constitute an overwhelming majority of Kampuchea's population, the pagoda is not only a place of worship but also a popular cultural center, indispensable to the people's spiritual and moral life, especially in the countryside.

B. *Serious crimes committed by the Pol Pot–Ieng Sary clique against Buddhism and the Buddhists.*

1. *In conjunction with their plan of driving people out of Phnom Penh, the Pol Pot elements swiftly wiped out Buddhist leadership throughout Kampuchea*

Here are the facts:

• Starting from the afternoon of April 17, 1975, just after their march into Phnom Penh, the Pol Pot men ordered all Buddhist monks to leave the city at the same time as the other strata of the population. A young officer came personally to tell the Reverend Huot Tat, Superior of the Mahanikay Buddhist order to leave the city with the other people.

• On April 18, 1975, the Reverend Huot That, accompanied by a number of monks close to him, got into a car. According to different sources, he was taken to Oudong. After being insulted and beaten, he was killed in Prang pagoda, Oudong district, Kompong Speu province. Thus the Superior of the Mahanikay Buddhist order was promptly eliminated.

• To date, nothing is known of the fates of the Buddhist Superiors Preah Thamma Likhet Kimto, Preah Vannarot Von Sompheas and Preah Pothivong Sohay. The Buddhist Superior of the Thoamayutt order and his associates are missing.

2. *Between April 17 and 19, 1975, the Pol Pot men liquidated the whole Buddhist hierarchy in terms of organization and personnel, together with centers for research, dissemination of Buddhist teachings, and training of priests from the national level down*

At the national level, the research centers, centers for the dissemination of Buddhist teachings, and seminaries comprised:

1. The Phnom Penh Buddhist Institute.
2. The Phnom Penh Buddhist Institute library, which contained 30,000 valuable classical and contemporary works of Buddhist literature in many languages: Khmer, French, English, Thai, Sinhalese, Burmese, Sanskrit, Pali, etc., and a small museum of cultural works and natural history related to Buddhism in Kampuchea.
3. The research commission on Kampuchean traditions and customs.
4. The commission for the translation of the *Tripitaka* (holy books of Buddhism).
5. The Buddhist high school, founded in 1955.
6. The Buddhist university, founded in 1954.
7. All monasteries attached to the 24 great pagodas, which accommodated thousands of believers coming from all corners of the country to Phnom Penh to pursue religious studies.

To the above list should be added a number of other general education or art institutes. All this Buddhist heritage and the whole Buddhist system throughout the country was destroyed in one day by official order and injunctions of the Pol Pot–Ieng Sary administration. Buddhism institutions in our country were quickly paralysed and simply ceased to exist.

3. *The Pol Pot clique insulted, tortured, and persecuted, individually and collectively, more than 100,000 Buddhist monks among whom the backbone of the Buddhist hierarchy, comprising four to five thousand Buddhist superiors, Buddhist monks, and other Buddhist clergy, achars (Buddhist preachers), and elder clergy*

According to witnesses from various provinces, the Pol Pot army and administration, when occupying new areas in the country, proclaimed everywhere in the same way this official view of "Angkar" concerning Buddhism.

(a) Buddhism is a politically reactionary religion to be eliminated.

(b) Buddhist monks do nothing but eat and sleep and have exploited the population for more than 2,000 years. They are leeches sucking the people's blood.

(c) Angkar's order to be rigorously applied can be summed up as follows:

• Monks must shed their robes, quit their religious life to go back to a secular life. Those who refused to comply were to be considered enemies and sent to the nether world. (In Khmer: Lok na ta thlay, chat touk chia Khmang. Lok na prochhang, chat touk chia Khmoch).

• Believers of both sexes must stop all religious practices at the pagoda and at home, such as praying, genuflecting, and making offerings to the gods. It was strictly forbidden to offer food to monks.

• Anyone who violates these orders of Angkar will be considered an enemy from within. To them the following slogan was applied: "no advantage in leaving them alive, no loss in killing them."

Apart from the order to shed the saffron robes, one of the most draconian measures, and one of the most difficult for the monks to follow, was an order to raise and kill poultry for food. This would be a sin strictly prohibited by Buddhist precepts, and would make the monks lose, forever, their quality of Buddha's disciples.

After having rid them of their religious capacity (especially by stripping them of their saffron robes), the Pol Pot men continued to persecute the Buddhist monks by forcing them to do exhausting labor, which caused pitiful deaths among elder monks.

In early 1976, the Pol Pot–Ieng Sary clique decided to liquidate the remaining monks. Those few who by the end of 1975 still refused to give up their religious life were all condemned to death. These are a few cases among thousands of others:

1. The Reverend Sin Um, Superior of the Ratanamuni pagoda (who had supported Pol Pot and Ieng Sary during the resistance against the Americans and Lon Nol) in Prey Veng province, was harassed, persecuted, and savagely beaten because he refused to abandon the religious life. In the end, he could not endure and gave up the saffron robe (June 1975). He was then submitted to forced labor. He narrowly escaped death in an accident.

The reverend is now 78. He has gone back to his former place at Ratanamuni pagoda. He was particularly lucky.

2. The Reverend Prok, Superior of Kam Prou pagoda, was forced to give up his saffron robe for a threadbare vest and pair of trousers, then subjected to forced labor. He died in 1977 from exhaustion and lack of food. (Testified to by Ros Keo, who was formerly a Buddhist superior in a pagoda in Phnom Penh.)

3. At Pothisal pagoda in Prey Veng province, in July 1975, the Pol Pot–Ieng Sary men forcibly took off the robes of six old priests. Among them was the Superior of Pothisal pagoda, by the name of It, and the Superior of Mongkol Ratanaram pagoda of Prey Kduoch village, by the name of Khuon. They made them put on black, patched clothes. The six were tied up, taken to Pothi Boray prison, Ben Dorl village, Peam Chor district, and subjected to hard labor and a miserable diet, which killed them all. (Testimony given by Mr. Kan Man, a former archaeology student and currently Director of the Phnom Penh Museum.)

4. In Siem Reap province, there were 173 pagodas and 4800 Buddhist monks in 1970. In early 1976, nearly all the monks had been expelled from the pagodas and returned to a secular life. The Pol Pot men made them take wives, even though some of them were already seventy years old. The Superior Tit Phan, the highest Buddhist figure, was subjected to hard labor. In spite of his old age (he was 78) he was forced to build hen houses. He died in 1977.

• Superior Bor of Tbeng pagoda, Roun Taek subdistrict, Sotr Nikum district, and Superior Mit of Preah Ankosey pagoda, Siem Reap city, were summoned to the Security Service and disappeared. Since then, nothing has been heard of them.

• The Superior Bao, 87, the highest figure of Peam Preah Phnuoh pagoda, Koh Sotin district, Kompong Cham province, almost blind, was summoned to the Security Service. He was beaten there and had to agree to abandon the religious life. He died in 1977 in miserable conditions. (Testimony by the Buddhist monk Sey Ros Keo, 65, a former student at the Pali Institute and formerly the Superior of Preah Put pagoda, Phnom Penh city.)

• In January 1976, the Pol Pot men came to Pothi Vong pagoda, Kandieng district, Pursat province, and forced the Superior Prouch to quit the religious life. The Superior refused. A few days later, those men came back again, seized him, tore off his robe, beat him severely and drove him out of the pagoda. A hut was built for him, 300 meters away, by people who loved and pitied him. But owing to the blows he had received, he fell ill, could not eat and finally died. The Pol Pot men came again with many ox carts, plundered valuable articles, ransacked the pagoda and burned many wooden Buddha statues and other objects of worship.

In some regions where Pol Pot's henchmen were particularly bloodthirsty, Buddhist monks were killed en masse in 1975. Here are a few examples: As early as April 1975, Pol Pot's men killed 57 monks in Loeuk forest, Chan Sar subdistrict, Sotr Nikum district, Siem Reap province. About 200 monks coming from Phnom Penh or from other regions in Kandal province were taken to Wat Champuh Kaek in Kien Svay district, Kandal province, where they were executed in the following manner: each of them was taken to the Main Temple, in front of the Buddha statue. The torturers sneeringly said, "You will see what good you can get from being a priest. Try now to call Buddha to your rescue." Saying so, they struck the poor monks in the back of the head with an iron bar. The victims fell and died while writhing in pain. Their bodies were thrown into a ditch. Those who did not die were, again, thrown into prison.

4. Pol Pot–Ieng Sary and their associates liquidated any who refused to forsake their religion

Buddhist believers were not only prohibited from visiting and worshipping in pagodas to whose construction they had contributed and which they venerated, but still they were forced to categorically express their will to carry out Angkar's order which ordered them to abolish Buddhism and participate actively in the destruction of the pagodas, to retrieve building materials and Buddha statues to show their will to give up religion definitively. This constituted a punishment that cruelly tormented the believers in their spiritual life.

Mr. Kan Man, the former university student of archaeology, was driven out of the museum. He left Phnom Penh for his native village of Lvea, located in Kompong Trabek district, Prey Veng province. Upon arriving he, along with the other village residents, was made to destroy pagodas and all the objects of worship, particularly the Pothi Lvea pagoda in Prey Kduoch village. Mr. Kan Man said: "I did not have the courage to do it. I hesitated to lift the hammer. However, the fear of being killed made me close my eyes and do the destruction work in a mechanical way. . . . But since I am still quite attached to historical objects and relics, I have hidden the pieces of some precious objects and some religious books at my house. Unfortunately, the reactionaries got wind of this. On January 27, 1976, they organized a meeting to denounce me and to condemn me. They ordered that I be locked in the toilet and they tortured me brutally until I lost consciousness." (From the affidavit of Mr. Kan Man, head of the Phnom Penh Archaeology Museum.)

Mr. Sang, 60 years old, who lived in Sang Khat Memot, Memot district, Kompong Cham province, was compelled to leave the religious life in 1975. He later got married, but some time later his wife died of exhaustion. At night, he would say prayers and take candles, incense sticks, and flowers to his wife's grave. The Pol Pot agents discovered that, arrested him, and released him after severe warnings. Then when they spied on him and found out that he continued to visit his wife's grave, they seized him and took him out and killed him. (From the affidavit of Miss Kong Rasmey, born at Sang Khat No. 5, Phnom Penh.)

Even more barbarous was their treatment of Mr. Hi, 65 years old, and his wife Mrs. Tuch, 63, who lived in Sras Pring village, Cheung Prey district, Kompong Cham province. They were spied on by the Pol Pot agents who saw them as they were worshipping, saying prayers at night in their home. They were immediately arrested, tortured and given stern warnings in the premises of the Security Service. The Pol Pot agents also arrested 34 of their relatives, and killed them, including children of two or three years of age. (From the affidavit of Mrs. Pheari, also known as Mrs. Ren, 34 years old, residing in Kompong Siem, Kompong Cham province, who now works at the Phnom Penh trade bureau. She is Mr. Hi and Mrs. Tuch's surviving daughter.)

5. *Pol Pot, Ieng Sary and their associates closed down 3,500 pagodas and partially or totally destroyed the buildings, infrastructure, and other valuable items in these pagodas, in particular, many invaluable historical objects and relics.*

(a) All of the pagodas were used for other purposes such as storehouses for building materials, or headquarters for administrative or security services. A large number of pagodas were turned into concentration camps, some of which were centers for internment, torture and murder on a frightening scale, especially the Otakuon pagoda at Sang Khat Angkorban, in Kang Meas District, Kompong Cham Province, or the Champuh Kaek pagoda in Prek Thmey subdistrict, Kien Svay District, Kandal Province, where the Pol Pot agents killed thousands of people, including about 200 Buddhist monks.

(b) More than 95 percent of the Buddha statues and precious objects belonging to the pagodas were nearly or totally destroyed. Those made of gold and silver were lost forever, except for some which were hidden in the beginning by believers.

(c) Buddhists books and other books were collected and burned or otherwise destroyed. Among them were very valuable ancient books of historical value, made of sugar-palm leaves. Of particular value was the translation of the *Tripitaka*, a monumental work of 110 volumes, each of 400 to 900 pages, translated from Pali into Khmer.

(d) Most of the pagodas are still abandoned. Weeds grow in the yards. The walls are dilapidated. The roofs, carpentry, and columns have almost disappeared as they were taken away for other uses.

(e) The Pol Pot–Ieng Sary clique destroyed numerous historical monuments and relics, artistic works, a number of ancient temples and buildings which even the Siamese aggressors did not dare to touch during past centuries. The most serious destruction happened in Siem Reap province. The Reverend Superior Tep Vung (Siem Reap province) testified: "Two bronze Buddha statues, Preah Ang Chek and Preah Ang Chom, made during the Angkor Wat period and greatly venerated by the people, were seriously damaged as the Pol Pot agents blew them up with explosives."

In 1976, the Pol Pot agents blew up a number of large stone Buddha statues in the Angkor area, in particular the Preah Antpu and Preah Ngok statues sculpted thousands of years ago. The Preah Kok Thlok statue was also mined, but it sustained the blast without much damage and has been restored by our people. At Angkor Wat Temple, in the area called Preah Ang Preah Porn, more than a hundred small statues of stone or precious wood had been preserved, of very fine sculpture. The Pol Pot men broke them into pieces with hammers or iron bars, and threw them away. There now remain about twenty of these statues. These barbaric men also blew up and greatly damaged the second flight of stairs at the main entrance to the Angkor Wat Temple.

Part II: Extremely Serious Crimes Committed by the Pol Pot–Ieng Sary Clique Against Islam and Its Followers

After Buddhism, Islam is the second largest religion in terms of followers. Nearly all the followers of Islam belong to the Cham ethnic minority.

Carrying out the directive aimed at abolishing all religions in the most savage and speedy fashion, the Pol Pot–Ieng Sary men took on Islam and its followers with the same rigor as they did Buddhism. In general, the suppression of Islam and its followers was seen as more urgent, more rigorous and more violent than the repression of Buddhism. This extremely serious crime was carried out as follows:

1. *When the population was expelled from Phnom Penh, Pol Pot, Ieng Sary, and their associates created conditions for the total liquidation of the Islamic leadership at the national level, the Islamic leadership at the provincial and district levels, and Islamic clergy in general.*

1. The Imam Hachi Res Los, whose home town was at Chroi Changvar (Phnom Penh), was forced to leave Konhom village, Peam Chor district, Prey Veng province. He was identified, imprisoned and savagely tortured by the Pol Pot agents, who threw him into a vat of hot water. Finally, they broke his skull with an iron bar, killing him on October 8, 1975.

2. The deputy Imam Hachi Sleyman Sokri also died under the blows of the Pol Pot men and was thrown into a deep ditch in Kohs village, Prek Anh Chanh district, Kandal province, in August 1975.

3. The vice deputy Imam Hachi Mat Sles Sleyman was expelled to Battambang. He was later arrested, tortured and disembowelled on August 10, 1976.

4. The President of the Islamic Central Committee in Phnom Penh, Mr. Hachi Matly Haron, was forced to go to Onlong San, Kandal province, where he was arrested and died of starvation on September 25, 1975.

5. Mr. Hachi Srong Yusuf, professor of Islam at Chrang Chamres, was killed at Peam Chor, Kandal province, on October 19, 1975.

Everywhere, the Pol Pot–Ieng Sary agents worked quickly to identify Islamic figures at all levels in order to execute them later, without waiting for orders from higher authority and without proceeding stage by stage as they did with Buddhist monks.

The Muezzin Srang Yusuf, residing at Kilometer 7 at Chrang Chamres, was arrested, imprisoned, and tortured in June 1975. He was killed later by hard blows to his head and had his throat slashed.

The dignitary Hachi Yusuf at Trapeang Chhouk was forced to live and eat with pigs until his death in July 1975.

Very few of the Islamic dignitaries have survived, only some who managed to conceal their identity.

Mr. Sit Sakarya, the former secretary-general, is the only survivor of the Central Organization of Islam. He managed to conceal his identity, and, finally, in January 1979, he was liberated by the armed forces of the National United Front for the Salvation of Kampuchea while he, like thousands of other Muslims, was digging a ditch that was to be his grave.

2. Closely linking the policy of abolishing religions to that of discriminating, pressuring, and assimilating the Cham ethnic minority, the Pol Pot–Ieng Sary clique created pretexts and conditions for their plan of genocide against Muslims in a horrible way in Kampuchea.

Pol Pot, Ieng Sary, and their associates ordered that: "The revolution is the only one. There is only one nation in Kampuchea and only one language, Khmer." Hence, on Kampuchean territory belonging to the Khmers, no Cham nation can exist.

"Consequently, it is imperative to abolish Cham awareness, Cham ethnicity, the Cham language, Cham manners and customs and also Cham religious beliefs. The Cham must change their names to those similar to the Khmers.

"Those who do not carry out the order that has been given shall bear all consequences for their opposition to Angkar."

The following facts illustrate this policy.

• The young Muslim Samu Hamas, age 18, a high school student at Kampot, was forced to go to Mount Bade, Sisophon district, Battambang province on April 17, 1975. During the journey, his father and his brother died in a wagon. Arriving at the new place, his family planed to hold funerals with minimal Islamic rites, but they were criticized and threatened, then searched and stripped of their luggage. The Pol Pot men seized from them the Koran and other holy books and burned them or tore them up in front of the whole family.

• Mr. Len Matly, age 25, a Muslim living at Srok Romiet village, Chhuk Sa subdistrict, Kompong Tralach district, Kompong Chhnang province, declared the following:

His family was forced to go to Kompong Speu province, Khtum Krang subdistrict, Thloy village, on April 28, 1975. First, the Pol Pot men made his family abandon their religion, eat pork, give up their Cham origin and Cham language, as well as all their Cham manners and customs. Women had to cut their hair short, as Khmer women do. On May 5, 1975, the Pol Pot agents killed his father, his elder brother and his younger sister after catching them saying Islamic prayers and speaking Cham. They were given blows on the back of the neck with bamboo sticks and thrown to the edge of the Kros Kropo Forest situated in Khtum Krang subdistrict. Mr. Len Matly managed to survive for several reasons: he took the Khmer name of Son, stopped talking in his mother tongue, and stopped saying prayers and worshipping Allah. He ate pork, managed to do all sorts of miserable jobs to earn a livelihood, and, for the sake of form, hailed the "very just revolution" of Pol Pot, Ieng Sary, and so on.

• Mr. Rok Sanh Mat, age 26, a Muslim from Chhuk Sa subdistrict, Kompong Tralach district, Kompong Chhnang province, was forced to go to Yea Ang subdistrict, Tbong district, Kompong Speu province, on April 21, 1975. He reported that his father and brother were killed by Pol Pot agents on May 5, 1975 because the latter found out that they did not eat pork, as ordered.

• To discover followers of Islam, they served meals with pork and made them eat it under the watch of guards armed with rifles pointed at their victims. Those who refused to eat or who vomited after eating were taken away for punishment. In most cases they were executed.

• Mat Ly Zaiyub, age 28, a second-year student at the Phnom Penh Medical Faculty, who was expelled to Kompong Chhnang, related that on the anniversary of the foundation of the Kampuchean Communist Party, they discovered two old Muslims who would not eat pork. (It should be noted, by the way, that it was the sole occasion in the year when all inhabitants of the commune got some meat to eat.) The two old Muslims were taken directly to the execution ground.

The Pol Pot men not only tried to discover Muslims who had integrated into the Khmer population, in order to kill them individually or by their entire families, they also carried out mass executions of Muslims. Here are some examples:

• In Kang Meas district, Kompong Cham province, on the shores of the Mekong, about 1200 families of Muslims lived in the villages of Svay Ta Hen, Sach So, Anlong Sor, and Angkorban. A number of the inhabitants had been forced to go away and had disappeared. Others were beaten to death and thrown into the river on August 1, 1978. The only survivor was a man named Chuk.

• Many Muslims lived in Kompong Siem district, especially in the villages of Kompong Krabey, Chamkar Samsep, Korkor, Koh Rokar, Koh Prak, Rokar, and Ro Ang. There were nearly 1000 families. All have perished.

• Children from Muslim families in Kang Meas district were captured and thrown into old wells. The Pol Pot men threw dry hay over those unfortunate children, poured in petrol, and burned them.

• In March 1977, the Pol Pot men seized babies from Kompong Siem district, put them into plastic or jute sacks and hung them on trees without giving them anything to eat or drink. The babies struggled in those sacks until their death.

• Other mass executions of Muslims of an utterly genocidal type occurred in various places in the provinces of Kompong Cham, Kompong Chhnang, Pursat, Kampot, and Kompong Thom.

3. All 108 Islamic mosques existing before April 17, 1975, were either destroyed or turned into pigsties or storehouses for manure. Some large mosques, like the Grand Mosque in Phnom Penh or the one at Kilometer 7 in the suburbs of the capital city, were blown up and leveled with bulldozers: the Pol Pot men wanted to eradicate the last traces of Islam.

The Koran and all the holy books which were discovered in the mosques or individual houses were destroyed or thrown into latrines or pigsties.

In brief, it is thanks to the arrival of the National United Front for the Salvation of Kampuchea forces, and Vietnamese troops that liberated the followers of Islam in time that those who remain in the Muslim community of Kampuchea survived and narrowly escaped imminent and total extinction. Our citizens of Islamic faith, together with other sections of the population, witnessed unprecedented large-scale preparations for liquidating the last Muslims, even though they had, willingly or by force, given up Islam, at least in appearance, long ago (from 1975 to 1979). In fact, in communes where Muslims lived, the Pol Pot men had worked out plans and mobilized people for digging large wells for burying the victims. Sit Sakarya, a former student of the Higher Technical College "Khmer-Soviet Friendship" at Phnom Penh, recounted:

"On December 5, 1978, a man named Phuoc, head of Ta Ches subdistrict, told my Aunt Mas, who lived in Svay Bakeo, that an order had been given by Angkar that all remaining Chams living on Kampuchean soil were to be exterminated after the next harvest in February 1979. The news spread terror in our hearts as we had tried every means to become true Khmers. It also heightened our vigilance.

"While the revolutionary forces advanced swiftly, having liberated Phnom Penh on January 7, 1979, the Pol Pot men in my region, on January 20, 1979, summoned all Moslems in Svay Bakeo village and took them to the western side of the railroad tracks and made them dig their own graves at the foot of Mount Ach Sat (Ta Ches subdistrict, Kompong Tralach district, Kompong Chhnang province). However, a unit of the forces of the National United Front for Salvation, in coordination with the Vietnamese forces, launched a surprise attack and liberated all the Muslims in our region."

According to estimates from various sources, at least two-thirds to three-fourths of Muslims in Kampuchea had been murdered either individually or collectively for the sole reason that they were Muslim.

In some villages of certain districts, all the Muslims have disappeared. The few inhabitants living there at present are new villagers who came there during the Pol Pot–Ieng Sary period or after their overthrow. In other villages, the number of Muslims who survived was less than 50 percent of the previous Muslim population. Most of the survivors are children and women. In one of the petitions presented by the victims, they estimated the number of survivors to be 200,000 people, as compared to 700,000 Muslims from before, which means at least 450,000 Moslems died. We are in no position to verify these figures concerning the pre-1975 Moslem population, but the estimate that about two-thirds of the Muslims were killed by the Pol Pot men seems well-founded.

Part III: Crime of Genocide Against Other Religions, Against Christianity

Catholic missionaries arrived in Kampuchea in the mid-16th century. According to the 1970 statistics, there were about 60,000 Christians, of whom 90 percent were Vietnamese residents.

After April 17, 1975, all Christian churches were ransacked, most of them demolished. In particular, the Grand Cathedral of Phnom Penh disappeared without a trace: bricks, tiles and even the floor were all taken away.

All holy books, statues of Christ, and objects of worship were destroyed, in the same manner as those of other religions.

As far as Christians were concerned, a most cruel fate awaited them. A majority of them, being Vietnamese residents, were of course put in the category of Enemy Number One, to be exterminated on sight. A small number of Christians were Khmers, or Chinese residents. None of the Christians thus far have indicated their survival or tried to restore the churches, unlike surviving Buddhists and Moslems who have undertaken efforts to renovate their pagodas and mosques.

One may presume that as a consequence of the policy of genocide pursued by the Pol Pot–Ieng Sary clique, all Christians and their clergy in Kampuchea have been exterminated.

Against Protestantism

In Kampuchea, Protestantism was still at the initial stage of its evangelical work. The activities of the Protestant Church were limited to preaching and distribution of the New Testament (in Khmer language "Sanha Thmey") and other prayer books or literature in Khmer under the aegis of the "Samakum Preah Kumpi" (Evangelical Society) in Phnom Penh.

One may presume that the number of Protestants was small, that, being inhabitants of Phnom Penh, they were put in the class of "new citizens" under Pol Pot, and that all of them have been liquidated, except perhaps a few who managed to conceal their identity until the arrival of the liberation forces of the National United Front for the Salvation of Kampuchea and the Vietnamese troops.

Against Other Faiths

The Pol Pot men even turned against the primitive religions of some ethnic minorities in mountainous areas. They imposed on those minorities the same policy of forced assimilation. However, to our knowledge, our brothers in the highlands sustained less severe losses than those in the plains, thanks to the difficult terrain in their regions and their determination to oppose the Pol Pot–Ieng Sary regime, and also thanks to the favorable conditions that enabled them to establish early contacts with the genuine revolutionary forces of Kampuchea and join their ranks.

Part IV: Conclusion

1. The crimes covered in this Report are by no means isolated cases, but rather constitute an illustration of a large-scale criminal policy applied throughout the country with increased intensity, which reveals an aim of deliberate genocide.

2. This premeditated policy of genocide directed against all religions and faiths necessarily encompassed both "new" and "old" citizens among its victims, which resulted in the fact that many Buddhists, and Muslims who had taken part in the revolutionary fighting against the Americans and Lon Nol, and those who had sided with the Americans and Lon Nol against the revolution were indiscriminately persecuted by the barbaric torturers. In fact, Pol Pot's genocide targeted the entire population of Kampuchea.

3. Thus, the policy of genocide by Pol Pot and Ieng Sary against the Kampuchean people, against the lives and property of the followers of various religions, has been a horrible national disaster as well as a violation of the laws of the revolutionary state of Kampuchea, and also a serious violation of international law.

4. Consequently, given the irrefutable evidence of their crime of genocide and in the name of the millions of victims, we ask the Court to judge these criminal acts of Pol Pot and Ieng Sary properly and to impose well deserved punishment on them.

Kum Dan, Rapporteur
Official
National United Front for the Salvation of Kampuchea

2.4.10
Report on the Tuol Sleng Extermination Camp

The extermination camp of Tuol Sleng, the name of a residential quarter in the southern part of Phnom Penh, occupies an area 600 meters long and 400 meters wide, surrounded by a fence of corrugated sheets with barbed wire.

The Tuol Sleng prison was a school known under the Sihanouk regime as Ponhea Yat High School, and then in the Lon Nol period, that is since 1970, as Tuol Svay Prey High School.

Behind this high school was another school, the Tuol Sleng primary school, which was one of the oldest schools in the capital. When it was founded in the mid-1950s, it was called Boeung Keng Kang school, but it was renamed Tuol Sleng after 1970, under the Lon Nol regime.

Around these two schools were dwelling houses of the Tuol Sleng quarter. These sad dwellings, abandoned, like city homes all over Kampuchea, housed, in the time of Pol Pot, the agents responsible for the organization and functioning of the extermination camp.

Organization of Tuol Sleng

Tuol Sleng became an extermination camp at the end of 1975. It was one of the most important centers, if not the main center, of imprisonment, torture, and killing in Kampuchea under the Pol Pot regime. There were other camps which were to some extent dependent on Tuol Sleng, notably the camp of Takhmau, formerly a psychiatric hospital, the camp of the former National Police Headquarters south of the New Market, the Vat Phnom camp set up in the former Navy officers building, the camp of the former Sangkum High School, and the camp of Prey Sar west of Phnom Penh in Kandal province. All these dependent camps were placed under the command of Tuol Sleng and were also known under the abbreviation of "S-21," that is "Security 21," which reported directly to the Defense Ministry of the Pol Pot–Ieng Sary regime.

The classrooms were transformed into cells with the windows solidly barred. All the cells in the basement and on the first floor of the four buildings had been turned into small individual compartments 2 meters long and 1 meter wide. In each cell there were 18 such compartments. The second floor was used for collective imprisonment.

The prisoners were divided into 3 categories: leadership figures and the civilian elite; military officers; workers, peasants, and ordinary soldiers.

The small compartments were reserved for prisoners of the first two categories, whereas prisoners of the last category were herded into the cells on the top floor of the building.

In order to ensure the security and functioning of the central camp and the dependent camps, Pol Pot used one army division, of which a regiment of more than 1,000 men served in the Tuol Sleng camp. This regiment, bearing the number 703, was divided into several units: a liaison unit, an interrogation unit, a torture and killing unit, a typing unit, and a security and surveillance unit.

Each unit was also divided into small groups which recruited children of 12 to 15 years of age.

The communications between the different units were transmitted by telephone. Pol Pot had a telephone center with 100 lines installed in Tuol Sleng.

Almost every day the security unit dug graves 4.5 meters long, 2 meters wide, and 1.5 meters deep for the bodies of the detainees who would be killed, usually at midnight.

Treatment of Prisoners

The prisoners were from all strata of the population of Kampuchea. The civilians: from simple peasants to ministers, including blue-collar workers, technicians, intellectuals, professors, physicians, and engineers. The military: from soldiers to division commanders, including all the ranks in between. Among the prominent persons detained at Tuol Sleng were:

- Hou Yuon, government minister at the time of the Royal Government of National Union of Cambodia (GRUNK),
- Hu Nim, Minister of Information under the Pol Pot regime,
- Toch Phoeun, Minister of Public Works under Pol Pot,
- Toch Kham Doeun, diplomat,
- Chau Seng, government minister under the Sihanouk regime,
- Cheng An, Chairman of the Industrial Committee under Pol Pot,
- Vorn Vet, Second Deputy Prime Minister, in charge of Economy, Central Committee Member of the Pol Pot Party,
- Thiounn Thioeunn, Doctor of Medicine, Minister of Health under Pol Pot,
- and others.

It is significant to note that the wives and children of prisoners were also detained. Among the prisoners were two Americans, one Australian, one Briton and forty Vietnamese. These people were taken from the prison in November 1978, probably to be killed.

In 1975–76 the detainees numbered about one hundred. This number increased gradually year after year. And in 1977 the number reached over 1,200. In 1978 there were more than 1,500. This number then remained the same, but the names of the prisoners changed. The duration of detention was either 1 to 2 months, or 3 to 4 months. High officials were imprisoned up to 6 months.

Prisoners detained in the small compartments had one foot chained to the wall. Those who were detained collectively in the cell had one foot fettered by the ankle to a long iron bar. Each bar, of 6 meters long, could hold the feet of twenty persons.

Once imprisoned in their cells or compartments, the detainees had to take off all their clothes, except underwear. They slept on the floor, without mats or blankets.

Every morning, around 4:30, they had to take off their underwear to be searched by one group. After the search, there was a half hour of gymnastic exercises, but of course with one foot attached. Detainees relieved themselves on the spot in metal or plastic boxes.

In every cell there was a regulation written on a blackboard:

"(1) Speaking is absolutely forbidden.
(2) Before doing anything, permission must be obtained from a guard.
(3) Prisoners must strictly obey the rules of discipline."

Thus, while in bed, if someone wanted to change position, he had to obtain permission from a guard. Anyone who violated the regulation immediately got 20 to 30 lashes with a whip.

As for bathing, a water pipe was put between the bar of the window. As soon as the prisoner got some water on his body, the water pipe was taken away.

Any prisoner who, by inadvertence, overturned the excrement box or the urine can would be beaten and then had to pick up all the contents and put it back, and then clean the floor by licking with his tongue.

Every morning, so-called physicians went through the cells for consultation. In fact, they were sorts of charlatan kids who knew nothing about medicine. They just put routine questions and distributed to the patients a handful of medications that were locally made in dubious ways, from tree roots or plant roots.

The torture that prisoners underwent often took place during interrogations. It began by the prisoner being chained to the wall or to the table of the interrogator. The typical accusation was that the prisoner had been an agent of the CIA or KGB, or that he worked with the Vietnamese.

If the victim denied the accusation, the executioners resorted to action. For beating, they used anything they could get: different kinds of tree branches, coconut branches, bamboo, whips hurriedly made from electric wires. After some weeks, if those interrogated persisted in their position, the severity of torture increased. After the beating at a more violent level, the Pol Pot men would use electric current, wetting down the prisoner's body to increase the electric shock. They used either electromagnetic devices with high tension but weak intensity, or household current of 380 volts. The electric wire was attached either to the foot or the tongue of the prisoner, or to his ears, fingers or to his penis.

Some prisoners were hung by their feet. In this position, water, salt water or soap water was forced into their nostrils. There was another method which crushed the fingers of the victim with a vice to the point that one could easily remove the fingernails with pliers. When the nails were pulled out, alcohol was poured in. There were also cases in which alcohol was poured into the eyes. Sometimes a piece of wood was used to press the victim's stomach until it touched the backbone. Also needles were driven into the fingernails of the victims. And the prisoners were forced to drink urine or salt water. Prisoners' heads were pushed into the excrement box.

As a rule, prisoners who confessed as well as those who did not admit the actions imputed to them were all exterminated after being interrogated. Usually the killing was carried out at midnight. They were taken away one by one with arms tied behind them, eyes blindfolded, to a common grave that had been dug in the afternoon. They were put on the edge of the grave. Then they were struck violently at the nape of the neck with a one-meter iron bar. Some of the prisoners had their throats cut, or more barbarous still, they were disemboweled so that the torturers can get the liver and gallbladder which, as the Pol Pot men said, were used to make medications. Finally the corpses were thrown into the grave.

In 1975 and 1976 the number killed was 5 to 6 persons a day. But the pace increased in 1977 and especially in 1978; during these years Pol Pot had 100 to 150 persons killed a day.

Thus, from December 1975 to June 1977 the prisoners killed at Tuol Sleng and at Takhmau numbered from 10,000 to 12,000 including children and newborn babies.

Here, as a clear example, is a partial list of the killings in 1977:

March 8: 102 killed, 3 of them by blood letting.

May 12: 152 killed.

June 20: 256 killed.

October 18: 179 killed.

October 20: 88 killed, 6 of them by blood letting.

October 23: 148 killed.

December 9: 301 killed.

The prisoners were killed by order of Duch.

Items of Evidence

The extermination camp at Tuol Sleng with its notorious prison is in itself clear proof of the genocide committed by Pol Pot against the Kampuchean people. On January 7, 1979, as they fled, the murderers were unable to wipe out all the traces of their heinous crimes and left behind piles of incontestable evidence.

Arriving at the camp, first of all one is impressed by the double or triple fence of corrugated sheet iron topped with barbed wires.

The heaps of debris should also be mentioned: handcuffs, metal rings, fetters, iron bars 1.2 to 6 meters long. Building A, which in 1978 housed the prominent prisoners, has in each cell a bed with iron fetters, a table, and a chair. Puddles of congealed blood and clusters of hair remain on the floor. Ten soundproof cells with one-way glass were used to interrogate the prominent prisoners.

In each small numbered compartment there remain two fetters to chain the foot of the detainees. Barbed wire still "decorates" the front of Building C. The traces of other demolished compartments are still visible. Small plastic urine containers and metal munitions boxes marked "made in USA" which were used for the prisoners' excrement are scattered on the ground. There are 7 bars in every window.

One can see other evidence of torture: wood sticks, bamboo sticks, rattan sticks, tree branches, coconut branches, iron bars, whips made of electrical wire, electromagnetic devices, field telephones, locally made electro-shock apparatus with buttons connected to household current; cans of fish sauce; ropes; heaps of clothes left by prisoners; military clothing; black clothing of the type worn under the Pol Pot regime; civilian clothing of men, women, boys, and girls; rucksacks, satchels, belts, cans, mosquito nets, and hammocks used by the army, etc. One also finds blackboards on which are written the prison regulations, boards with the names of the detainees, and cameras.

There are documents, lists of detainees, lists of prisoners who were killed, written statements from interrogations, photographs of prisoners, and photographs of the Pol Pot agents.

Testimony of Surviving Prisoners:

Only a very few prisoners survived the genocide at Tuol Sleng. So far we have found only eight such persons; of these four are children, the oldest age ten:

• Mr. Ung Pech, a mechanical engineer, specialist on heavy engines, detained in April 1977.

• Mr. Ruy Neakong, carpenter at the former Cambodia Electricity Corporation, imprisoned March 21, 1977.

• Mr. Iem Chan, a sculptor who worked at the Siem Reap museum, detained in early 1978.

• Mr. Vang Pheap, former head of one of the groups of guards at Tuol Sleng prison, who himself was imprisoned in January 1977.

• A boy named Phal, age 10, whose parents were killed.

Mr. Chan made the following statement: "I suffered horrible punishments. The murderers beat me from morning until 11:00 p.m. My arms and legs were tied to the bed. They covered my face with a piece of cloth on which they poured water to suffocate me. When I would lose consciousness, they would press my stomach to expel the water that I had breathed in from the wet cloth. Then they would pour in more water. I suffered this torture for five successive days. Then they changed the method, using electrical current instead. Finally they got me to admit that I was a KGB agent. Fortunately, my occupation saved my life, because they chose me to work in a sculpture workshop."

In the prison, Mr. Iem Chan witnessed the cruelest, most barbarous, the bloodiest, and the most fascist things the world has ever known. "They drowned prisoners like a string of sausages," he continued. "They pierced the bodies of the interrogated with sharp knives. They let the millipedes or the scorpions bite the prisoners.

"Girls age 8 to 10 years were handcuffed, lined up, and taken one by one to be killed. Women who had just given birth were tortured like the rest. The torturers let the babies die of hunger."

Mr. Vang Pheap was chief of a group of guards called Section 212, a unit responsible for security in the prison, and he worked in the camp from December 23, 1975, until January 1977, when he was imprisoned on a groundless accusation of treason. Mr. Vang Pheap stated: "Married prisoners were imprisoned together with their wives and children. If the husband was condemned to death, the wife and children were killed as well. There are few survivors of the Tuol Sleng extermination camp, only ten or so. At first the killing was carried out near the prison. But later, when there was no more room for graves, they sent the prisoners to Chamkar Daung in Dangkor district, Kandal province, not far from Phnom Penh, and killed them there. Children were detained separately from their parents and typically were killed before their parents."

Here is the statement by young Phal: "My name is Phal, age 10. My father, Chen, and my mother Yeuv were murdered by Pol Pot. I have two brothers: Lit, who is 8 years old, and my other brother, who died in Tuol Sleng prison at the age of 5 months.

"I was taken prisoner with my mother and my two brothers. When we arrived at Tuol Sleng, the Pol Pot men separated us from our mother. As he was very hungry, my little brother cried all the time and eventually died. In the day time, they let me and Lit in the kitchen. At night we slept on the second floor of Building C, whereas my mother was chained in a small compartment on the ground floor of the same building. We each had only a dirty pair of trousers and a dirty shirt. We slept without mosquito nets or blankets. At night we were prey to hordes of mosquitoes. Each meal we were given a ladle of stew and a spoon of soup with a little salt. Each time Pol Pot men got angry they beat us mercilessly. They hit us on the head. They kicked us on the back if we did not walk fast enough.

One day we heard gunshots, my brother and I, and we hid behind a pile of clothes taken from the prisoners. At that moment I saw they were killing a boy, a little bigger than me, by bashing him against a tree near the kitchen. I don't know where they threw the boy's body. When they all left the prison, we went back to the kitchen. Since we had no way to cook rice, we ate the last of some soup that was already rotting. We also ate the rest of the food that was for the pigs.

During my time in the prison I saw the most atrocious tortures by the Pol Pot men against prisoners. They heated an iron stick white-hot and put it up prisoners' nostrils. They submerged women prisoners in water tanks. Some days before their departure, they showed me a photo of my disemboweled mother."

Following is another type of killing that young Phal described in his statement: "Once, after lunch I saw five Pol Pot men taking to the gallows a prisoner who wore white undershorts and a blue shirt. After knotting his neck, they pulled up the other end of the rope so that the poor prisoner rose in the air. They then loosened the rope and let the prisoner fall down from the top of the gallows. They did the same thing twice more and then his body was dragged to a cell beside the electroshock room. A short time later, they brought out another prisoner who had on only undershorts. They killed him the same way. After his death, I saw his tongue sticking out of his mouth. And then they led out a third man who walked slowly, because the elastic on his undershorts was worn out and he was trying to hold up his pants. They beat and kicked him in the back to make him walk faster. When they hung him up in the air, his undershorts slipped down to his feet, and the Pol Pot men broke out laughing."

Common Graves:

The common graves are one of the most convincing pieces of evidence of genocide by Pol Pot. The torture, killing, and burial of prisoners were conducted within the camp compound. Common graves have been found one after another. So far we have located nineteen graves around the prison. Most of these graves are on the western side of the camp. According to the witnesses, these graves typically measure 4 meters long by 2 meters wide by 1.5 meters deep. A few graves are 9 meters long by 2 meters wide. Each grave contains on average 30 to 40 corpses. One grave we have excavated shows that the corpses are in a state of decomposition. In Takhmau camp we have found 9 common graves.

Conclusion:

Although brief, this report will hopefully make clear to the public, both domestically and internationally, the crime of genocide committed by the Pol Pot–Ieng Sary clique. We submit this report for the decision of the Revolutionary People's Tribunal, which we hope will give us justice.

Phnom Penh, August 1979

Excerpts from Captured Documents

2.5.01

Document of the Central Committee of the Communist Party of Kampuchea Addressed to Zone Administrative Committees After April 1975

The character of our revolution is basically distinct in several respects from that of revolutions in other countries.

. . . The expulsion of the population from Phnom Penh is a measure that one does not find in the revolution of any other country. This is an extraordinary measure aimed at the total overthrow of the feudal system and the capitalist system.

In dispersing the city population to the countryside, we deal a decisive blow to the old order, and we transform all the towns of the country into worker towns. This is better than ever.

2.5.02

Excerpt from Political Education Courses Given in November and December 1975 to Middle and Higher Level Officials of the Party and the Administration

The Crime of Genocide

To wipe out the cites, to force the population to leave Phnom Penh to go to the countryside and mountainous areas, to lead a poverty-stricken life, the majority dying of hunger, sickness, or being killed[1]

(page 1)

I. Part concerning nationalities

The most important thing is that we have a policy of emigration, whose essential aims are the following:

1. This heading is not part of the Excerpt but was included in the Document to show the category of crime to which the Excerpt relates. — Eds.

- to create support points for the army
- to assure security
- to preserve the political position of officials and combatants
- to wipe out commando groups
- to eliminate subversive elements and rebels
- to avoid a situation of peaceful evolution that could corrode from within
- to fight corruption, degradation, and debauchery
- to get the urban population to take part in production
- to remove Sihanouk's support base

As concerns nationalities, the policy of emigration, of displacing the population, was adopted in 1970 by the central committee of our party. As it advanced, the army put into practice the policy of displacement of the population, but this policy is a new issue for the world and for our revolution. Once we liberate Phnom Penh, we will be fully in control of it. Enemy elements who hide in the population will be put out.

As concerns the democratic aspect, it will be desirable to evacuate 95% of the inhabitants of Phnom Penh. These inhabitants will join the liberated areas empty-handed. What they will hold as private property will be insignificant. They will be transformed into a productive force. They will be put under the control of the ordinary people, under the control of the revolutionary forces and of our cooperatives. We will be able to eliminate the petty-bourgeois and bourgeois strata and to achieve socialism. . . .

III. Situation of the democratic revolution after the complete liberation of the country

First situation:

We have evacuated the population of Phnom Penh to steep it in the work of goods production in local areas. We have completely swept away the feudal, bourgeois enemy, along with the system of private property and material goods. As for pupils, students, intellectuals, professors, they must be extricated from the filth of imperialist and colonialist culture.

2.5.03

Excerpts from Documents Used in Study Courses for Middle and Higher Level Officials of the Eastern Zone in November and December 1975 (supplied by the police)

4. Schemes of American imperialism and our measures of action

. . . We must maintain the state of war as previously.

. . . What we must do:

1. Instill revolutionary vigilance, and vigilance against military, political, and diplomatic provocations and against espionage.

2. Mount pursuits and searches on land and in territorial waters.

3. *Political and diplomatic measures*

Remove Sihanouk from power for good.

Initiate provocations, attack, and occupy the Khmer Krom territory and Saigon.[1]

2.5.04
Excerpts from the Notebook of a Zone Official, 1976

Enlarged zone meeting

3. Mobile team of youths and adolescents

• Attack forces: people from 15 to 45 years of age are grouped in the main in attack forces. Women with young children are grouped in reserve attack forces. They will also be the bulk of attack forces of work teams. Making this differentiation and managing it closely will let young people stay in work teams.

• Work teams manage the lives of the young people. They should not sleep in their families. They must sleep separately; work teams are permanent units.

• Their meals should be well prepared.

• Demgianet, an instructor at the teacher's college, was the CIA chief for the district.

• Mobile forces of young people and adolescents:

(1) Males and females from 15 to 45 years of age form the bulk of the attack forces (enroll young people from 15 to 45 years of age).

(2) Women with young children are also in local attack forces directly controlled by base units.

2.5.05
Excerpts from a Speech by Wang Shang Rhung, Deputy Chief of the General Staff of the Chinese Army, at the Talks with Son Sen, February 6, 1976

Purpose of the Talks

In keeping with the idea of military aid in principle, as discussed during the June 1975 talks between the two parties, we sent a number of officials to Kampuchea from August to October of last year to study the situation. After

1. Khmer Krom territory refers to several Vietnamese provinces claimed as Kampuchean territory on the basis of Kampuchea's precolonial control of them. — Eds.

study, we worked out a draft plan for military aid. This draft plan as well as a draft agreement were presented on October 12 of last year to the Kampuchean comrades by Comrade Ambassador Sun Hao and our military attaché Deng Kun Shan, and were favorably received by the Kampuchean comrades. Now we are presenting the text of the agreement, which has been discussed by the two parties, to ask for your approval, and, if you are in agreement, whether we can sign this text.

Now I would like to clarify certain issues:

1. The draft agreement is quite brief. It mentions only the equipment clearly necessary to organize and build up the army. As for other necessary arms and munitions that will be provided, as well as technical equipment, they could not be detailed now in the same way, given the great variety and large number of the different items. For this reason the draft agreement only clarifies the principles. In our view, we should give the chiefs of the general staff of the two armies time to discuss the details, and then to exchange instruments ratifying the agreement.

2. As regards the schedule for delivery of the equipment, arms, and munitions, we are prepared to complete delivery by the end of 1978. As to which items of equipment will be delivered at which times during the period 1976 to 1978, the following is what we think appropriate.

During 1976, we will first deliver equipment and arms to train field-level officers. This would involve:

- a delivery of equipment for an anti-aircraft artillery regiment, a delivery of equipment for a radar regime, and equipment for a military airport,
- four escort ships and four torpedo boats for the naval forces,
- a delivery of equipment for a tank regime, a delivery of equipment for a signal regiment, a delivery of equipment for three field artillery regiments, the equipment for a pontoon battalion of the army.

The other equipment and arms would be delivered as follows:

Anti-aircraft guns for the air force will be delivered in 1977. The delivery of radar will be done both in 1977 and 1978. Combat aircraft and bombers will be delivered as pilots are trained and new airports are built. Another delivery of equipment for airports will be delivered as new airports are built.

As for the six escort ships for the navy, four will be delivered in 1977, and two in 1978. As for the eight torpedo boats, four will be delivered in 1977, and four in 1978.

The equipment for the three field artillery regiments for the army, with the exception of the 130 millimeter canons, could be delivered in early 1977, and the 130 millimeter canons will be delivered in the second half of 1976. The equipment for the tank regiment will be delivered in 1977 and 1978. The equipment and arms for the signal regiment will be delivered in

1977; 300 kilometers of communication wire will be delivered in 1976, and as for the remaining 1,000 kilometers, please make a proposal and we will make arrangements.

What we have said here is only our estimate. The production of military factories depends on production in other branches of the economy, and as a result the equipment could be delivered earlier or later. The appropriateness of our thoughts on the matter requires your reaction. Please give us your views.

3. As concerns the procedure for delivery and acceptance, and the method of delivery equipment, most of the equipment involved can be shipped by boat and unloaded at the port of Sihanoukville. The aircraft will be disassembled and packed for transport by boat, and once they arrive in Kampuchea they will be reassembled. Submarines and tankers can go straight to Kampuchea, but what will need to be done to ensure safe passage and the security of the ships is rather complex and will have to be discussed in detail later.

As for coordinating the shipments, we will notify you two weeks before the ships leave port so that you can get ready, but arranging transport ships depends on rail deliveries, ports, merchant ships, etc. If any link in this chain fails, that will affect the transport. This is what happened with the recent escort ship. We planned to load the ship Da Fu at Chanchiang on January 5, but this ship was late coming back from overseas, and the unloading and loading took time. That is why the loading was delayed. In future, if this happens, we will let you know right away.

As for the procedure for delivery and acceptance, on our side the office of the military attaché will take up this matter with you. At the delivery, the itemized delivery certificate for receipt will be done in two copies, one in Chinese and one in Khmer. We can handle the Chinese, but we will have trouble with the Khmer or French, because we have few translators. Perhaps it will be enough to use Chinese. If you have no problem using English instead of Khmer or French, we could do that. We are raising this issue so that we can find a mutually satisfactory solution.

4. As for sending technicians, in keeping with the principles agreed upon by the two sides, if it is possible the personnel could be trained on the spot, and we will take care of training the core personnel. Later on, when you are ready to have more sophisticated training, we think that our technicians sent by us will arrive in Kampuchea more or less at the same time as the first delivery of equipment. So in 1976 the number of technicians arriving in Kampuchea will be: radar technicians, anti-aircraft artillery technicians, personnel to train in the air force, cargo pilots, aircraft repair personnel, in all about 320 people, including those who are already in Kampuchea. The communications service will have 32 persons, including 12 already in Kampuchea. For the escort ships, torpedo boats, and ship repair, there will be about 120 persons. For the tanks there will be 28 persons. For field artillery

there will be 25 persons. For pontoons there will be 6 persons. The total will be about five hundred persons. These technicians will come in turn to Kampuchea. In our view, once they are in your country, these comrades will help you basically to understand the technical features and manner of using and handling these pieces of equipment and arms. As for their length of time working, we will tell them to come back when the Kampuchean comrades think they can use and handle the different pieces of equipment and arms, and their presence is no longer necessary. These technicians will come to Kampuchea to help you and at the same time to learn from you. But in our view, the number of these technicians will gradually grow, and their work time will get longer. This will doubtless lead to problems. We ask you to consider them as your own personnel, to train them and to check on what they do. If they make mistakes, we ask you to help them to make corrections. If you can't do education with them, we ask you to let our ambassador or military attaché know so that they can inform our general staff so that we can do it ourselves. As for the procedure for choosing technicians, we are not sure whether the two general staffs should exchange letters indicating they agree to particular persons. We raise this issue with you so that we can figure it out.

5. As for our accepting trainees, particularly trainees from the navy and air force, for 1976 the number of trainees needing to come to China to improve their skills will be 471 from the air force, and 157 from the navy. The two sides will confer on the selection of these trainees and on the dates of their departure for China.

6. As for the five complete projects, namely, the construction of one new naval base, of one airport, and of one munitions depot, and the enlargement of one weapon-repair facility and of the port of Kep, our government has agreed to take responsibility. From our side, the ministry of foreign economic relations is assuming the responsibility of organizing the work, because these projects are in the category of complete projects. As for the procedure for confirming implementation, our ministry of foreign economic relations will confer with you. After completing a survey of the projects, we will convey our view, conferring with you on the matter, regarding the precise scope and times for carrying out these projects. We ask you to let us know an appropriate date when our survey personnel can come to Kampuchea, so that we can make preparations.

7. As for the matter you raised of repairing and refitting certain items of military equipment you have captured, in the case of equipment you deem to be usable but in need of repair or refitting and requiring only our technical work, or our spare parts or materials, we will definitely help to the extent we can. This work can be done, in our view, as soon as the general staffs of our two armies exchange letters ratifying the agreement.

8. As for the matter of language translation, the military assistance specified above will require quite a few translators. For 1976, one hundred trans-

lators will be needed for the anticipated number of technicians and survey personnel that we will be sending, and for the number of trainees we are accepting. At present, however, we have only ten translators. We ask you to find a way to resolve a part of this problem.

These are a few points to clarify how this agreement can be carried out. One other question remains. That is the question of military assistance for 1976 on which the two sides exchanged views orally during Comrade Ieng Sary's stay in Peking in April 1975. This aid totals about 13,300 tons. In 1975 up until the date of the liberation of Phnom Penh, deliveries totaled more than 3200 tons. Thus, we have more than 10,000 tons to deliver, including 4,000 tons of arms and munitions, and 1,301 vehicles of various types. Since Comrade Ieng Sary wanted to postpone delivery, we stopped shipments. Recently you said that you need this equipment in February and March, except for 150 sea mines. We figure that, with the exception of the automobiles, of which there are too many for all to be delivered in March, since each ship can carry no more than 200, and with the exception of the one hundred 120 millimeter artillery pieces whose quality still needs to be checked and the shells for the 120 millimeter artillery pieces, all the rest is to be delivered in March. You have agreed that the remaining quantity of petrol and of oil tanks will be delivered in batches. We are conferring with our agencies in charge of these matters to find a solution.

Regarding the above-mentioned outstanding issues of military assistance for 1976, the procedure should be settled by way of an agreement. In this connection, we would like to know if it is possible to complete this procedure during this year. If you agree, upon our return we will immediately begin preparing documents that will then be discussed by the Kampuchean comrades and our ambassador to find a solution.

I am honored to convey my views for discussion. I hope to be able to learn your views.

February 6, 1976

2.5.06

Directive No. 32 of the Party Standing Committee of the Eastern Zone, September 5, 1976 (Transcribed for Dissemination by the Region 21 Standing Committee, September 9, 1976)

We must heighten our revolutionary vigilance as regards those elements who served in the administration of the former regime, such as technicians, professors, doctors, engineers and other technical personnel.

The policy of our Party is not to employ them. If, seeing their apparent submission, we employ them, they will infiltrate our ranks, each year more deeply. This will be very dangerous for us.

For the workers of the old regime, by reason of our revolutionary vigilance, we do not employ them any longer. We can employ a certain number of them only if we know their background quite well.

2.5.07
A Perspective on the Four-Year Plan (1977–1980)

Done December 22, 1976

Production targets for rice for export (page 9)

1. Total for the period 1977–1980: 3,000,000 to 3,500,000 tons
2. Value in foreign currency: $600,000,000 to $700,000,000
3. Quantity of rice to export, by year:

1977:	400,000 to 500,000 tons
1978:	650,000 to 750,000 tons
1979:	850,000 to 950,000 tons
1980:	1,100,000 to 1,300,000 tons
Total:	3,000,000 to 3,500,000 tons

Rice exported in 1976:

Northwest:	50,000 tons
East:	50,000 tons
Southwest:	30,000 tons
West:	20,000 tons
Total:	150,000 tons

Additional forecast

Northwest:	15,000 to 20,000 tons
East:	15,000 to 20,000 tons
Southwest:	8,000 to 10,000 tons
North:	3,000 to 5,000 tons
West:	3,000 to 5,000 tons
Total:	46,000 to 64,000 tons

2.5.08
General Situation in Kompong Ro District During the First Six Months of 1977

On the health of the population

During the last six months, many different diseases have been in evidence, such as cholera, dysentery, eruptive fever, whooping cough, consumption, mange, tuberculosis, typhoid fever, beriberi, and prolapsed uterus.

The diseases that are the most widespread and the most readily contracted by others are cholera, dysentery, eruptive fever, smallpox, and diseases of the intestinal tract.

During these six months, in the entire district the number of persons suffering from disease was 29,692, of whom 7,219 were men, 2,068 women, 7,628 children, 7,778 elderly, and 220 dead.

2.5.09

Report on the General Political Tasks of the Party in the Northern Zone for the First Quarter of 1977 (from the Notebook of a Zone Official)

Issues relating to future tasks

. . .

K. Among both state officials and among the people, marriage is most often dictated, contrary to the Party's political line, by the free choice of the spouses. Families should be founded in keeping with the Party's political line.

As the officials in charge, we must make a judicious inquiry about the future spouses: their political ideas, their way of thought, their organizations, and their social class. They should be allowed to form a relationship to get to know each other's view of life, to find out if they are happy to marry each other or not, and then to draw up their curricula vitae.

The future spouses must have in-depth knowledge about the Party. Therein lie both the guarantee of their happiness and the protection of the Party.

2.5.10

Report on the General Political Tasks of the Party in the Northern Zone for the First Quarter of 1977 (from the Notebook of a Zone Official)

Steps to be taken

1. To carry out purges in the cooperatives. To withdraw far from the region if the people are not loyal to the regime. To educate the people in politics and organizational ideology so that they thoroughly understand the task of defending the country, defending the sector, and building socialism. To organize properly questions of ideology and of thought. To organize well the activities of the army, both from the political and from the moral and organizational point of view.

Gangs of reactionaries. In the country, in our zone, these are:

1. First gang: that of Vietnam, almost wiped out.

2. Second gang: that of Ba and his adherents, almost wiped out.
3. Third gang: reactionaries from the north, almost wiped out.
4. Fourth gang: gang of the KGB and the USSR, almost wiped out.
5. Fifth gang: made up of intellectuals, students, monks, teachers, and people who worked for the old regime, almost wiped out.

2.5.11

The People's Service Committee of Region 25 on June 21, 1977, Dispatched a Notification Along with Circular No. 11–6-1977 to the District People's Service Committees, Military Commands, Army Battalions, and Security Organs in the Region

To the district level people's service committees, to the military general staff and the different battalions of the region, and to the security service of Region 25 of the eastern zone:

Contents of the text:

We have just received a report from the people's service committee of Romeas Hek district informing us that at 1:00 a.m. on June 16, 1977, a man named Pich Chum, 30 years of age, who formerly resided in Thmey village of Don Srok subdistrict, Romeas Hek district, and who now resides in Bak Trong village No. 1, Sambath Rean Chey village, escaped from a camp of the Nhum Sambath Ran Chey cooperative. Pich Chum is 1 meter 55 centimeters tall, of pale complexion, and of slender build, and with narrow eyes. He was wearing a short sleeved blue shirt, and carrying nothing with him.

We ask the people's service committees at all levels, all military units, and all checkpoints to be on the lookout. If he is found, he should be arrested and taken to the authorities. If this occurs, we ask that we be informed so that we can decide what measures to take.

2.5.13

Congress of the Party Committee of the Eastern Zone in 1977 (from July 17, 1977)

2. On the people's life:

1. From January to May, we have settled problems concerning the people's life according to the norms given by the Party. But since the end of May, the people's worsened living conditions have made it impossible to apply the Party's norms. People in many areas such as Chhlong, Kroch Chhmar, Peam Chileang, Koh Sotin, Muk Kampoul, and Tbong Khmum districts have been living in acute privation. The living conditions in Kroch Chhmar, Peam Chileang, Koh Sotin, and Muk Kampoul districts have worsened considerably since 1976. People are living on nothing but thin rice soup.

However, the people's spirit is still high, especially the fighting spirit is very high. They have fought day and night without complaint. Through tired, they have worked hard digging canals and waterways, increasing production, striving to fulfill the Party's plan with unabated enthusiasm.

2.5.14
Circular to the District People's Service Committees, Military Units and to All Units and Revolutionary Organizations in Region 23

We have received a report from the people's service committee of Kompong Las district informing that at 7:00 p.m. on August 2, two civilians escaped from Trapeang Treo Khor, in Koonpong subdistrict. They are:

1. Ke Chan, 50, citizen, widower, category: from the old people. Identification: dark skin, thin, gaunt face, 1.6 meters tall.

2. Te Sa Chen, 23, citizen, widow. Identification: stout, fair skin, short hair, 1.6 meters tall. Category: from the old people.

By getting married the two committed a moral offense subject to punishment (art. 8). Chen is now three months pregnant. They had escaped for fear of punishment. We ask the people's service committees at all levels, and military units and watch posts, particularly those at the border, to help us look for them. If found, please hand them over to the authorities and duly inform us for specific measures.

2.5.15
Report on the Activities of the Khmer Communist Party in 1977, November 8, 1977

1. Concerning the task of protecting Democratic Kampuchea, the gains of the revolution, the Party, and the worker-peasant rule of the party

. . .

We have eliminated enemy elements who have penetrated the army, liquidated detrimental members of the army, and improved the quality of the army.

. . .

Concerning the enemy inside the country

If we have won a great success in 1977, we owe it to the fact that we have harassed the enemy, carried out purges in our own ranks, and destroyed their network to its roots.

In late 1976, we worked out this plan, and in early 1977 we liquidated a rather large number of enemy ringleaders. . . .

. . .

This is a great victory for us.

. . .

About the situation of the enemy outside the country

It is clear that this year, fighting on a substantial scale occurred in the southwestern zone, and in the eastern zone. . . .

These are two theaters of bloodshed, because in these zones there are valleys, rice fields, and a high population. In particular, the enemy for its part has a rather high population.

. . .

At present, the fighting going on in the eastern zone is giving us new experience in carrying out the policy of the party. In the southwest, we have attacked the enemy's populated areas. That is the weak spot of the enemy, who is wavering. We must take note of this situation to draw lessons to push our political position to a higher level, to enhance our viewpoints, and to improve our combat tactics.

. . .

2. Concerning observations about and study of the results obtained in 1977 in all fields

. . .

In the field of organization, the important issues this year have been personnel selection and full purging of elements that may be enemies hiding in our ranks and entrenched in the organization. These efforts have completely purified our party.

. . .

We have undertaken purges, prevention, and annihilation of spies and enemy commandos hidden in different strata of the population to preserve the Party, the revolution, the army, and Democratic Kampuchea.

By way of accomplishments, we have discovered and liquidated several spy rings in the army in the Kandal zone, in the northern zone, and in the northwestern zone. We operated systematically there, because the enemy had hidden its agents there for a long time.

2.5.15b
Report on the Activities of the Khmer Communist Party in 1977

Page 3

. . . .

I. On the task of defending the Democratic Kampuchea revolutionary gains, the Party and the Party's worker-peasant administration

As for the 1977 political tasks, we included the task of defense in Article 3. But in February 1977, the standing committee proposed to put it in Article

1, then in April 1977 the Party central committee decided to include it in Article 1.

Page 3

On the enemy situation at home

We achieved great victory in 1977, because we decided to wipe out the enemy systematically, and wiped them out from the grass roots.

Excerpts from the propaganda book on Kampuchea (in French: *République populaire du Cambodge*):

Page 35

"Vietnam is weaker then ever. The moral . . ."

From February 28, 1978 to March 1, 1978, a Chinese delegation met them. The record of their meeting recited among other things: "Vietnam is further weakening. Troop morale is low and could not be bolstered. We are in a strong offensive posture, being backed by 800 million Chinese people. We must, then, attack Vietnam and win victory."

2.5.16

Salute to Our Party's Victory in the Liquidation of the Leaders of the Kampuchean Workers Party in the Pay of the CIA, June 3, 1978

Here are the names of the key leaders of the Kampuchean Workers Party:

1. Phum: secretary of the Kampuchean Workers Party, committed suicide June 3, 1978
2. Nhum: assistant secretary, arrested June 11, 1978
3. Keo Mias: arrested September 21, 1976
4. Ya: arrested May 20, 1976
5. Son Ngoc Minh: formerly president of the Kampuchean Workers Party, died in Peking in 1972
6. Koy Thuon: arrested January 25, 1977
7. Non Suon: arrested November 1, 1976
8. Chou Chet, also known as Sy: arrested March 26, 1978
9. Pha Sot, also known as Chong: arrested in 1974
10. Phuong: arrested June 6, 1978
11. Som Ok, also known as Poont: arrested April 28, 1976
12. Hoong: arrested January 3, 1978
13. Yi: arrested March 21, 1978
14. Phe and Prak: arrested March 15, 1978, and March 13, 1978
    1. Toch Phoeun: arrested February 17, 1977
    2. Hou Yuon: arrested in 1975
    3. Hu Nim: arrested April 10, 1977
    4. Tiv Ol: arrested June 6, 1977

2.5.17
Decision of the Standing Committee (Concluding Statement by Pol Pot, August 2, 1978)

. . .

II - *Rivalry in the east*

• This is a life and death rivalry.

• With Thailand we also have a serious rivalry, but not a life and death rivalry that has to be resolved right away as a matter of urgency.

• From 1975 to 1976, American imperialism played the main role in the attack directed against our country. American imperialism gave the order to its lackeys to attack from inside to try to take power in this period, which was a time of probing. American imperialism led a combined offensive to attack us from the outside.

• With the loss of its probing forces, American imperialism suffered a strategic defeat. After the war it thus lost its strategic forces.

• Thus it had to cooperate with Annam. This time it had to turn toward Annam.

• Since that time the main role has bee played by Annam, which enjoys the support of the USSR This is the period that began in the second half of 1977, a date at which Le Duan left to sign an agreement with Laos to take over this country. This is the time when Annam prepared to attack Kampuchea, and Annam did attack us in late 1977.

In late 1977, the Annam-USSR-USA clique hatched a strategic decision to wipe us out. But in December they suffered the first defeats, when the invasion activities led by Annam, the USSR, and American imperialism were coordinated with the internal forces led by Pheng Phin.

• The third period began in January-February and continues to the present time. Outside the country, Annam has played the main role. It has in support the USSR and the USA These have been the external forces. But inside the country the main role has gone over to the gang that in the past used external forces involving one division to bring us down. This third time, the internal gang that played the main role was the gang of Phin, and the gang of Cha Rieng. This third time was marked by their defeat.

This defeat was a joint defeat against the strategic play of Annam, the USSR, and American imperialism, a strategic defeat of the reactionary international forces. This third time one found Annam, the USSR, and American imperialism. For Annam and the USSR, this was only the second defeat, because Annam and the USSR had the main role in the second period.

Now they have gone into a fourth period. The more serious the defeats suffered by the enemy, the more it becomes wicked and savage, the more its conspiracies become wicked and savage, the more the Soviets show themselves wicked and savage, the more Cuba shows itself wicked and savage.

Here we must analyze our advantages and our handicaps. We must consider the pros and the cons, in order to be able to outdo the enemy on the road to victory.

• As for the military aspect, we can strike the enemy ten blows for every one the enemy strikes against us.

• In the southwest, we can attack the enemy mainly because our troops are pure, our local organizations are pure, not 100 percent pure but pure to the local level, which applies as well to Region 24.

The enemy can attack us there where our army is not pure, our local organizations are not pure.

That is where we are weak. Right now we have already resolved the problem of the eastern zone, but we are now in a period of transition.

• In May and June, we carried out a purge.

• In June and July, the forces that we brought in to help us turned out not to be pure.

• In July and August, we got ready to coordinate our forces.

• Our weakness is the inadequate numbers of our forces, but our strong point is that our army is pure, and our local organizations are pure.

• As for the enemy, it also lacks forces. We are in the process of destroying it in part, of annihilating it, of gathering our forces to annihilate it completely.

• The problem we need to resolve is that of getting our forces underway, to reinforce their numbers.

• To reinforce our troops that are ready to confront the present situation, and at the same time to confront our long-range strategic circumstances.

• If we succeed in resolving this question, we will in our overall strategy.

• If the plots are foiled this fourth time as well, the enemy will become strategically passive, in a defensive mode only, and we can go over to a strategic offensive that will be easy to carry out on the tactical side.

• For the immediate present and for the long-term future, the direction to take is to resolve the big problem of local reorganization. If we do not succeed in building a local base, we will not be able to defeat Annam. If we coordinate our forces well, we can defeat Annam decisively, because our society is a collective society, whereas the Annam society is a society characterized by private property, chaos, and disorder.

2.5.18
Deng Tsiao Ping's Talks with Ieng Sary on January 13, 1979

Deng Tsiao Ping:

World public opinion has taken note of several aspects of the purges you are carrying out, purges that are a bit excessive and on a bit too large a scale. I am certain that this information has reached you as well. I am raising this issue for the sake of the future struggle.

Phnom Penh, now liberated, has a population of about two million, that is, one fourth of the total population of the country. Half of these residents, that is, one million, are agents of An.[1] I am of the view that you must not ignore this state of affairs, because it is a fact that the enemy has a social base.

Only, as I have already said, the domestic counterespionage struggle has created an atmosphere that negatively affects all our activities, without mentioning other problems. You must admit that this struggle on a rather large scale has brought negative consequences that we must reverse by all possible means. This issue must be looked into more closely, both as concerns its political aspects, and as concerns the concrete measures to be taken.

Van (Ieng Sary):[2]

We all agree and we all understand that we must not abandon the socialist revolution, but, at this time, gather together all our forces.

Deng Tsiao Ping:

During the war against the Japanese, we, together with Chiang Kai Shek, turned all the revolutionary military forces into an army of national revolution, namely, the Eighth Route Army and the Fourth New Army. In doing this, we did away with the distinction between the two sides. We allied with Chiang Kai Shek so that he would wage war against the Japanese. We declared that we agreed with the doctrine of national democracy of the Kuo Min Tang, because the path of national democracy was a necessity for China.

That did not mean that we abandoned the struggle for socialism and communism. For now, Sihanouk is taking a good approach. To be sure he has made some poor statements in Peking, but he has his reasons. He tried to exonerate himself and denounced certain acts that he did not like, and people believed him. Till now he has stated that he is the representative of Pol Pot and Ieng Sary abroad. His speech at the United Nations was good, well grounded, and firm. When reporters asked him whether the communist party of Kampuchea has committed the crime of genocide, he replied that he hasn't seen the communist party of Kampuchea act in such a fashion, and that the population is happy. Now one must keep in mind the overall situation. It would be a great loss if we did not unite with him; at worst, the date of victory will be delayed a bit. So at an appropriate time in the near future, after an exchange of views on the matter, I ask you to give the position of head of state to Sihanouk. Comrade Pol Pot will be prime minister in charge of defense, as well as commander-in-chief.

As head of state, Sihanouk could conduct his international activities from Peking. Moreover, in this government, one could incorporate Kampucheans living abroad, because they cannot return to the country to wage war.

I ask you to confer on this matter seriously with the central committee of the communist party of Kampuchea, after you go back to Kampuchea.

1. An means Annam, the former name of Vietnam. (Note in original.)

2. Van is a pseudonym of Ieng Sary. (Note in original.)

If you think our suggestion is a good one, we will help you. But for now don't speak yet with Sihanouk about it, because it is not certain that he will accept. Deal with the matter on the international level. That will bring changes. The struggle in the international arena will take a new approach, and that will be very useful for the struggle inside the country.

So you have a decision to make that is of strategic importance. The greater the unity, the more it will result in good consequences for the struggle at this difficult time. And as for your proposals, there are no obstacles.

1. *A radio broadcasting transmitter.* We are ready, but we must tell you that public opinion around the world is not favorable to the broadcasts of our radio, or to those of the radio of the communist party of Thailand or the communist party of Malaysia. Your broadcasts will be ridiculed as not reflecting the truth. For now, don't talk a lot about the communist party. Talk about patriotism, nationalism, and democracy. The flag of patriotism, of nationalism, and of democracy is more important. Everything for the radio broadcast transmitter is ready.

2. *The issue of finances.* How will we get money to you? Send money to Bangkok? To Kriangsak Chamanond?[3] To the Bank of Thailand? Five million dollars will be available to you, and you can get it at any time. This money will be deposited either in the Bank of Thailand, or at the Chinese embassy, or at the Kampuchean embassy in Thailand.

Van (Ieng Sary):

We prefer that it be deposited at the Chinese embassy in Bangkok.

Deng Tsiao Ping:

You can use this money right now. We will give you more when it runs out.

3. We need to maintain contact with you by radio.

Keng Biao, deputy prime minister:

We would like to install the radio broadcast transmitter on the Thai border. There will also be a mobile broadcast transmitter because the central committee of the communist party of Kampuchea is in transit. That is why there is a need for a mobile transmitter, and a stationary one on the border. It should be easier to set it up in Thai territory.

2.5.20
Excerpts from Minutes of an Enlarged Conference of Region 21 Party Committee, Early 1977

I. Assessment of the enemy's situation

1. General political problems

2. . . . .

3. Head of the Thai army.—Eds.

3. . . . .
4. . . . .
5. . . . .
6. . . . .
7. On the problem of refugees after April 17, 1975

. . . .

Some said wherever he went Angkar went, it sent people into prison. The Angkar prison is a large prison, without walls or iron fetters, but no one can escape!

2.5.21
Excerpts from Instructions by Party Standing Committee of Region 203, November 26, 1975

Permission for movement is given by the village administrative committee. It is absolutely forbidden to displaced persons to go about on their own. They are authorized to go only from their lodgings to their places of work, as worked out by the cooperatives. The cooperatives, therefore, should keep strict control of displaced persons.

Su Danh

2.5.22
Materials of the Fifth Congress of the Pol Pot–Ieng Sary Party, November 1978 (from a Pol Pot Agent's Notebook)

. . .

Decisions

(1) Communes should be consolidated and expanded . . .
(2) . . .
(3) The building of vanguard cooperatives should be promoted.

How to build a vanguard cooperative.

A. Economic features

(1) On agriculture.
(2) Professional skills.
(3) On social and health affairs, and living standards: . . . a new increase of population 6/100 killing from 0.5 to 1 percent, family built according to set lines (politically, ideologically, and psychologically). Politics should continually hold supremacy.

B. Political features

2.5.23
Excerpts from Minutes of the April 11, 1977, Meeting of the Standing Committee of the Party Central Committee

Present: Pol, Muon, Phim, Mok, Won, Van, Nhim, Ke, Khieu[1]

I. Assessment of the situation in the country

. . .

Every unit, service, and ministry should take the initiative, within its organization, to continue to purge and sweep away adversaries, and at the same time carry out normal activity.

. . .

2.5.24
Important Culprits (Arrested from 1976 to April 9, 1978)

No. (1)	*Names (2)*	*Other Names (3)*	*Sex (4)*	*Age (5)*	*Rank (6)*	*Imprison Date (7)*
Regiment 152						
1	Panh Siem	Sol	M	29	Regiment Political Commissar	26-4-1977
2	Huc Nuon	Cha	M		Regiment Deputy Political Commissar	26-4-1977
Division 164						
1	Chay Hean	Chhann	M		Division Deputy Political Commissar	19-10-1976
2	Hang Doeun	Dam	M	33	Division Deputy Political Commissar	21-4-1977
3	Mum Chan	Kann	M	33	Division Staff member	28-4-1977
4	Men Nghet		M	42	Division Staff member	2-6-1977
Division 170						
1	Chan Cahc Kray	Mean	M		Division Political Commissar	19-5-1976
2	Ly Vai	Sua Su Phan	M		Division Political Commissar	20-5-1976
3	Ruas Phuon		M		Division Staff Member	9-7-1976
4	Su Cheat		M		Political Commissar of Regiment 73, Division 170	20-5-1976
5	Ke San	Sok	M		Division Political Commissar	4-3-1978
Division 310						
1	Sbau Hkm	Uon	M		Division Political Commissar	4-3-1978

1. These are pseudonyms of Pol Pot, Nuon Chea, So Phim, Ta Mok, Vorn Vet, Ieng Sary, Moul Sambath, Ke Pauk, and Son Sen. — Eds.

No. (1)	Names (2)	Other Names (3)	Sex (4)	Age (5)	Rank (6)	Imprison Date (7)
2	Diem Soeun	Voeung	M	29	Deputy Political Commissar	17-2-1977
3	Su Sonn	Sonn	M		Division Staff member	25-9-1977
4	Sau Khuon	Kim	M		Ex-Deputy Political Commissar of Division 310	1-3-1977
Division 450						
1	Chea Nun	Suong	M		Division Political Commissar	19-2-1977
2	A Chhoi	Khean	M		Division Deputy Political Commissar	17-2-1977
Division 502						
1	So Tuon	Mau	M		Division Staff member	29-3-1977
Regiment 377						
1	Khe Heng	Ne	M		Regiment Political Commissar	29-3-1977
2	Chai Han		M	38	Regiment Staff member	29-7-1977
3	Tu Nim		M		Regiment Political Commissar	11-3-1977
Division 801						
1	Keo Saruon		M	39	Division Staff member	25-3-1977
Division 920						
1	Men Meng	San	M		Division Political Commissar	19-3-1977
2	Ia Chu	Soi	M	38	Division Commander	17-2-1977
Regiment 488						
1	Sau Mun		M	33	Regiment Deputy Political Commissar	4-6-1977
2	Ben Youm	Chay	M	29	Regiment Staff member	4-6-1977
General Staff						
1	Siet Chhe	Tum	M		Regiment Staff member	29-4-1977
2	Pech Chhon	Som	M		Assistant to Chief of General Staff	14-3-1977
3	Soc Sau		M		Staff member of the Office area "KH-62"	1-11-1977
4	Uc Teh		M		Chief of Staff of the Office "V-66"	25-9-1977
5	Svai Khat		M	45	Deputy Chief of Staff of the Office	7-4-1978
6	Oi Ren	Mau	F	25	Regiment 75 Logistics	11-5-1977
P-98						
1	Sua Sa Ret	Pang	M		P-98 Hospital Director	29-3-1977
2	Thoong Sam Un		M		Hospital Staff member	6-1-1977
3	Yuang Nut		M		Hospital Staff member	6-1-1977

No. (1)	*Names (2)*	*Other Names (3)*	*Sex (4)*	*Age (5)*	*Rank (6)*	*Imprison Date (7)*
Southwestern Zone						
1	Som Chia	Chia Sdong	M		Party Secretary of Region 25	15-3-1977
2	Koong		M		Zone Office's Chief of Staff	1-10-1976
Western Zone						
1	Chou Chet	Si	M	52	Zone Party Secretary	26-3-1977
2	Tep Hai	Hom	M		Former Party Secretary of Region 15	14-3-1977
3	Boc Pin	Sau	M	40	Executive member of Region 37, Party	19-7-1977
4	Moc Men		F	30	Executive member of Region 31, Party	10-5-1977
5	Am Mun	Hon	M	28	Chief of Staff of the Zone Party Office	28-3-1978
6	Am Nen	Ly	F	43	Party Secretary of Oudong district (Chou Chet's wife)	26-3-1978
7	Nhem Cho	Keo	M	43	Formerly Party Secretary of Region 15	2-1977
8	Sau Kong	Nhac	M		Member of the Zone Agricultural Service	12-1976
9	Sum Kim Eng	Suon	M	34	Secretary in charge of the Zone agricultural Service	30-8-1977
10	Chap Nom		M	31	Head of Region 23 Security Service	29-7-1977
11	Seng Phon		M		Deputy Secretary in charge of the Zone Social Welfare	30-3-1978
12	Chau Van	Kham	M	37	Military Commander of Region 32	31-8-1977
Northwestern Zone						
1	Ruas Mau	Thon	M	44	Zone Party's Chief of Staff	26-6-1977
2	Chea Huon	Vang	M	36	Executive member of Region 1	12-9-1977
3	Sray Iem	Ven	M	40	Party Secretary of Region 2	28-3-1977
4	Um Sam Uon	Sawe Ret	M	37	Executive member of Region 2 Party Committee	4-8-1977
5	Hom Chhal	Vang	M	45	Executive member of Region 2 Party Committee	4-8-1977
6	Duoc Pheach	Nup	M	48	Executive member of Region 1 Party Committee	12-9-1977
7	Von Chet	Cu	M	48	Deputy Secretary of Region 3 Party Committee	18-12-1977
8	Thin Tham	Hieng	M	46	Party Secretary of Region 4	18-12-1977
9	Sun Kun	Sui	M	31	Deputy Party Secretary of Region 4	23-6-1977
10	Khec Bin	So	M	44	Deputy Party Secretary of Region 4	22-7-1977

No. (1)	*Names (2)*	*Other Names (3)*	*Sex (4)*	*Age (5)*	*Rank (6)*	*Imprison Date (7)*
11	Toch Much		M	45	Execution Member of the Region 4	5-8-77
12	Men Thun	Hung	M	36	Party Secretary of Region 5	20-8-1977
13	Xnung Len	Le	M	34	Executive member of Region 5	2-9-1977
14	Sieng Ngan	Thun	M	34	Formerly Executive member of Region 5 Party Committee	2-9-1977
15	Um Chhuon	May	M	42	Formerly Executive member of Region 6 Party Committee	23-6-1977
16	Ke Kuom Huot	Sut	M	46	Party Secretary of Region 7	13-7-1977
17	Oum Tuoi		M	40	Party Secretary of Region 7	28-6-1977
18	So Nau		M	31	Member of the Zone's Staff	13-6-1977
19	Sa Rum	San	M	36	North-Western Division Political Commissar	20-6-1977
20	Uc Suong	Son	M	30	North-Western Division Command Staff member	22-6-1977
21	Ly Mi Suon	Khleng	M	42	Deputy Political Commissar of Division 2	18-12-1977
22	Kum Then	Khoi	M	47	Member of the Division 2 Command Staff	21-9-1977
23	Em Nut	Sung	M	34	Deputy Head of the Zone Security Office	16-1-1978
24	Vai Huon		M	36	Head of Zone Committee for Agriculture	18-12-1977
25	Van Nhup		M	34	Head of Zone Committee for Agriculture	23-10-1977
26	Muon Mau		M	43	Head of Zone Committee for Agriculture	30-7-1977
27	Sin Eng	Suon	M	37	Head of the Zone Committee for Commerce	30-8-1977
28	Tea Dam		M	31	Head of the Committee for Commerce in Phnom Penh	30-7-1977
29	Keo Can	Doeun	M	37	Assistant Head of the Zone Committee for Commerce	3-8-1977
30	Hy Sary	M		44	Head of the Committee for Construction	10-8-1977
31	Cheach Chu	Puch	M	40	Head of the Zone Hulling Rice Service	3-8-1977
32	Nup Soeun		M	29	Head of the Zone Hulling Rice Service	11-6-1977
33	Yun Chan		M	32	Head of hulling for Committee for Commerce	1-7-1977
34	So Pham	Chet	M	46	Director of the Zone Textile Mill	28-6-1977
35	So Sanh	Mean	M	38	Head of the Zone Food Store	16-7-1977

No. (1)	Names (2)	Other Names (3)	Sex (4)	Age (5)	Rank (6)	Imprison Date (7)
36	Hyot Keo		M	32	Deputy head of the Zone Food Store	16-7-1977
37	Kao Sam On	Saravyth	M	37	Director of the Zone Packing Factory	2-9-1977
38	Kao Sa Nat	Rit	M	46	Deputy Head of the Zone Cotton Farm	16-10-1977
39	Neang Nau	Se	M	49	Executive member of the Zone Coffee Farm	25-9-1977
40	Som Hang		M	49	Head of the Zone Coffee Farm	25-9-1977
Northern Zone						
1	Cho Chhan	Seeng	M	44	Deputy Secretary of Zone Party Committee	18-2-1977
2	Com Chan	Chon	M	44	Party Secretary of Region 43 Party Committee	20-9-1977
3	Chum Chhum	Tang			Secretary of Region 41	[1]
4	Chau Mul	Tul	M	37	Party Secretary of Region 42 Party Committee	20-9-1977
5	Soi Srun	Say	M	32	Party Secretary of the Division 174	13-8-1977
6	Chum Lach	Veng	M	30	Deputy Political Commissar of Division 117	19-2-1977
7	Tep Su Vong	Ven	M		Chief of Staff of Region 43	
8	Di Chhon	Khan	M	32	Deputy Director of the Zone Rubber Plantation	24-10-1977
9	Yang Chheng	Heng	M	21	Deputy Director of the Zone Rubber Plantation	25-1-1977
10	Ban Sarin	Phen	M		Head of the Zone Security Office	9-1-1978
11	Chan Phat	Phok	M	27	Head of the Zone Security Office	26-10-1977
12	Suong Sut	Nghin	M	44	Head of the Zone Office for Agriculture	19-12-1977
13	Chac Saron	Kung	M	48	Deputy Head of Zone Office for Agriculture	11-3-1977
14	Kham En	Va	M	29	Head of Zone Industrial Service	19-5-1977
15	Kung Luong	Prap	M	68	Executive member of Zone Industrial Service	18-2-1977
16	Hem Sut	Sean	M	28	Head of Zone Industrial Service	4-10-1977
17	O Oong	Phan	M	27	Deputy Head of Zone Industrial Service	14-11-1977
18	Nuon Khieu	Keo	M	41	Deputy Head of Zone Industrial Service	1-5-1977
19	Phen Soon	Lon	M	25	Head of Zone Committee for Commerce	4-10-1977

1. An imprisonment date is not given for this entry and for some subsequent entries.—Eds.

No. (1)	*Names (2)*	*Other Names (3)*	*Sex (4)*	*Age (5)*	*Rank (6)*	*Imprison Date (7)*
20	Prat Chhean	Nuon	M	23	Head of Zone Committee for Commerce	19-3-1977
21	Chan Pa To	Bo	M	38	Deputy Head of Zone Commercial Service	19-3-1977
22	So Them	Chey	M	33	Deputy Head of Zone Commercial Service	14-11-1977
23	Lam Kim	Kim	M	25	Executive member for Commercial Service	14-11-1977
24	Chaay Chuo	Loeun	M	37	Executive member for Commercial Service	16-6-1977
25	Xong Soc	Nguon	M	39	Executive member for Commercial Service	21-3-1977
26	Seng Heam	Chum	M	57	Executive member for Commercial Service	10-5-1977
27	Dan Lam	Loon	M	42	Executive member for Commercial Service	10-5-1977
28	Yak Hung	Kham	M	35	Head of Zone Public Transport Service	18-2-1977
29	Yap Yon		M	36	Head of Zone Public Transport Service	20-9-1977
30	Me Nuon	Chet	M	35	Deputy Head of Zone Public Transport Service	19-3-1977
31	Chan Srang	Cheat	M	35	Director of Zone Hospital	18-2-1977
32	Kim Sun	Pep	M	46	Director of Zone Hospital	1-3-1978
33	Pol Puon	Pruong	M	27	Director of Zone Hospital	26-10-1977
34	Sam Sarum	Man	M	32	Director Zone Rubber Plantation	26-3-1977
35	Say Saroeun	Pech	M		Member of the Zone Rubber Plantation's Director Staff	24-2-1977
36	Prean Khen	Khen	M	41	Member of the Zone Rubber Plantation's Director Staff	26-9-1977
37	Re Sim	Reap	M	33	Political Commissar of Regiment 901, Division 174	20-9-1977
Region 106						
1	Pa Thol	Sut	M	33	Party Secretary of Region 106 Party Committee	21-2-1977
2	No Chhon	Hien	M	34	Deputy Party Secretary of Region 106 Party Committee	26-2-1977
3	Nup Sa Kum	Sean	M	35	Executive member of Region 106 Party Committee	1-3-1977
4	Chan Thul	Pol	M	37	Deputy Political Commissar of Regional Division 335	26-2-1977
5	Ke Huon	Huon	M	27	Member of Division 335 Staff	2-3-1977
6	Yong Pau		M	26	Head of the Regional Security Office	1-3-1977
7	Nuon Tet	Cheap	M	37	Head of Regional Committee for Commerce	3-3-1977

No. (1)	*Names (2)*	*Other Names (3)*	*Sex (4)*	*Age (5)*	*Rank (6)*	*Imprison Date (7)*
8	Chey An	Chum	M	50	Executive member of Regional Committee for Commerce	5-3-1977
9	Suon Chhean		M	41	Head of Regional Transport Service	2-3-1977
10	Lach Chhon		M	43	Deputy head of Regional Transport Service	20-3-1977
11	Siv Vun	Poong	M	25	Member of Regional Transport Service	2-3-1977
12	Yum Yat		M	32	Director of the Regional Handicraft Service	3-3-1977
13	Kam Tich	Vuth	M	31	[2]	2-3-1977
14	Ui Suong		F	27	Director of the Regional Sewing Service	6-3-1977
15	An Hieng	Soi	M	35	Head of the Regional Art Service	5-3-1977
Eastern Zone						
1	Pen Chhe	Chhan Sa Vat	M	53	Executive member of Region 23 Party Committee	8-9-1977
2	Tam Srun (Van)	Mut (Suon)	M		Formerly Party Secretary of Region 22	31-5-1977
3	Bun Kung	Sam Boc	M	45	Deputy Secretary of Region 22 Party Committee	8-6-1977
4	Un Sa Van	So	M	45	Party Secretary of Region 23 Party Committee	17-3-1978
5	Men Diec	Muon	M	53	Deputy Party Secretary of Region 23 Party Committee	26-3-1977
6	Suas Nau	Chhuk	M	53	Party Secretary of Region 24 Party Committee	28-8-1976
7	Pot Un	Nav The	M	65	Deputy Party Secretary of Region 24 Party Committee	12-7-1977
8	Ly Phel	Den	M		Member of the Zone staff	8-7-1977
9	Pen Cheap	Chuon	M		Political Commissar of Zone Division 3	29-3-1977
10	Soc San		M		Director of Zone Rubber Plantation	8-9-1976
11	Bun Sa Ni		M		Director of Zone Rubber Plantation	10-7-1976
12	Yun Suon	Yos	M		Director of Zone Handicraft Service	4-11-1976
13	Ui San	Kun	M	36	Head of the Zone Commercial Service	4-11-1976
14	Pech Phean		M	45	Director of Zone Rubber Transport	2-3-1977

2. Rank is not given for this entry. — Eds.

No. (1)	Names (2)	Other Names (3)	Sex (4)	Age (5)	Rank (6)	Imprison Date (7)
15	Veng Ky	May Pho	M	45	Director of Zone Rubber Transport	1-6-1977
Northeastern Zone						
1	Men San	Achar Sieng alias Ya	M		Party Secretary of the Zone Party Committee	20-9-1977
2	Bun Than	Chan	M		Former member of the Zone Party Committee	31-2-1978
3	Sim Soi	Om	M	32	Executive member of Region 102 Party Committee	
Region 105						
1	Su Kum An	My	M	44	Deputy Secretary of Region 105 Party Committee	24-3-1977
2	Kheam Krud	Cham	M	31	Executive member of Region 105 Party Committee	27-3-1977
Region 505						
1	Ban Sa Nuom	Coong	M	32	Former Deputy Secretary of Region 505 Party Committee	22-4-1977
2	Bon Nat	Di	M	38	Party Secretary of New Region 505	21-3-1978
3	San Bun Hy	Kuon	M	38	Deputy Party Secretary of New Region 505	23-3-1978
4	Kheant Hung	Muc	M	30	Executive member of Region 505	23-3-1978
5	Thach To Net		M	30	Assistant to Region 505 Party Committee	30-10-1976
State Commerce						
1	Koy Thuon	Khuon	M		Party Secretary of the Commercial Branch	25-1-1977
2	Sua Vasi	Doeun	M		Party Secretary of the Commercial Branch	12-2-1977
3	Tit Sun	Nhiem	M		Executive member of the State Commercial Branch	25-11-1976
4	Tan Tri	Suong	M		Executive member of the State Commercial Branch	17-2-1977
5	Nin Kim Hung	My	M		Executive member of the State Commercial Branch	25-10-1976
6	Nghet Du	Hong	M		Executive member of the State Commercial Branch	12-3-1978
7	So Pha	So	M	48	Chief of Staff for Foreign Trade	13-3-1978
Public Transport						
1	Toch Phoeun	Phin	M		Party Secretary of the Ministry for Transport	26-1-1977

No. (1)	*Names (2)*	*Other Names (3)*	*Sex (4)*	*Age (5)*	*Rank (6)*	*Imprison Date (7)*
2	Huot Sean	Thon	M		Executive member of the Ministry for Transport	15-7-1977
3	Sea Pa	Pa	M	48	Director of Chamkar Mon Water Pumping	8-3-1977
Energy Service						
1	Eng Me Heang	Chhun	M		Deputy Party Secretary of the Ministry for Energy Service	26-1-1977
2	Yong Sim	Hac	M		Executive member of the Ministry for Energy Service	2-2-1977
3	Uong Suong Hang	Hong	M		Executive member of the Ministry for Energy Service	2-2-1977
4	Kim Srung		M	29	Executive member of the Ministry for Energy Service	9-3-1978
5	Di Min		M	32	Assistant to the Ministry for Energy Service	15-1-1978
Ministry For Foreign Affairs						
1	Hak Sieng Lanni	Lonn	M		Secretary of the Central Committee of the KGB Party	18-12-1977
2	Cheam Sam At	Ruon	F		Executive member of Ministry for Foreign Affairs	17-2-1976
3	Thach Suong	Ti	M		Ambassador to Yugoslavia	19-12-1976
4	Sieng An		M		Ambassador to Hanoi	29-12-1976
5	Suoc Mang Mau		M		Ambassador to Sweden	8-12-1976
6	Tep Sam An		M		Embassy 3rd Secretary	23-10-1976
7	Phang Coc Hua		M		Chargé d'Affaires ad interim	23-10-1976
8	Y-Sum Kunthi		M		Ambassador	8-9-1976
9	Huot Sam Bat		M		Ambassador	8-9-1976
10	Soc Khcang		M	38	Ambassador to Vietnam	25-3-1978
11	Van Pi Ni	Tit	[3]	37	Vice-Minister for Foreign Affairs	20-11-1977
12	Meak Toch	Kem		42	Ambassador to Laos	20-11-1977
13	In Su Phon			36	2nd Secretary Kampuchea Embassy in Albania	1-6-1977
14	Kim Ren	Sun Trinh		43	2nd Secretary of Kampuchea Embassy in Egypt	15-6-1977
15	Ngo Tang Ti Kea			32	2nd Secretary of Kampuchea Embassy in Rumania	1-6-1977
16	Hua Su Meth			30	2nd Secretary of Kampuchea Embassy in France	1-6-1977

3. Sex is not given for this entry and for some subsequent entries. — Eds.

No. (1)	Names (2)	Other Names (3)	Sex (4)	Age (5)	Rank (6)	Imprison Date (7)
17	Tan Chhai Heng			34	Kampuchea Embassy's Secretary in Yugoslavia	16-5-1977
18	Iv Se Na Ras			37	Kampuchea Embassy's Counsellor in Soviet Union	16-5-1977
19	Hy Bun Heng	Sau	M	37	Ambassador to Korea	5-7-1977
20	Toch Kham Doeun	Toch	M	42	Ambassador to China	14-3-1977
21	Chau Seng		M		Executive member of the Front Abroad	18-11-1977
Propaganda						
1	Hu Nim	Phos	M		Party Secretary of the Ministry for Propaganda	10-7-1977
2	Tiv Ol	Som	M		Staff member of the "C-33" Office	6-6-1977
3	Chay Chum	Ko	M	60	President of Phnom Penh Capital City's Front	16-3-1977
Social Welfare						
1	Leng Sim Hak	Sei	F	37	Director of the P-17 Hospital and Party Secretary of the Ministry for Social Welfare	17-12-1977
2	Sin Phol Kun	Su	F		Executive member of Ministry for Social Welfare	3-3-1977
3	Chan Sam Ul	Muon	F	30	Executive member of Ministry for Social Welfare	18-2-1977
4	Sim Nhok	Van	F	31	Member of the P-17 Hospital Staff	10-4-1977
5	Tui Chih	Mau	F	28	Member of the P-17 Hospital Staff	
State Sewing Enterprise						
1	Long Sam Ua	Kun	M		Director	17-2-1977
2	Eng Kim Teng	Keo	F		Member of the Enterprise Staff	3-2-1977
3	Sim Minh	Cau	M		Member of the Enterprise Staff	28-4-1977
4	Ban Si Vat	Khon	F		Member of the Enterprise Staff	
State Agricultural Service						
1	Chey Suon	Chey	M		Party Secretary of the Ministry for Agriculture	1-11-1976
2	Duong Thuon	Neng	M	32	Deputy Party Secretary of the Ministry for Agriculture	20-3-1977
3	Loch Pot	Ret	M		Member of the Technician Service of O Dan	30-11-1976

No. (1)	Names (2)	Other Names (3)	Sex (4)	Age (5)	Rank (6)	Imprison Date (7)
River Transport						
1	Hong At	Mon	M	38	Party Secretary of the River Transport Service	11-2-1977
2	Sim Mey	Srun	M	30	Deputy Party Secretary of the Branch	30-3-1977
3	Tuch On		M	34	Executive member of the Ministry for River Transport	30-3-1977
4	Vong Thon	Kri	M	32	Executive member of the Ministry for River Transport	30-3-1977
5	Va Lim		M	44	Executive member of the Ministry for River Transport	30-3-1977
6	Lai Hua	Ley	M	36	Formerly Deputy Party Secretary, subsequently Assistant to Economy Service	13-3-1978
State Store						
1	Thim Srau		F	28	Member of State Store Staff	15-3-1977
2	Tep Su Phean	Phean	F	27	Deputy Head of the State Store No. 774	9-6-1977
3	Sray Vong	Do	F	23	Assistant to Division 72 of State Store	6-5-1977
Railway Service						
1	Mias Nil		M	45	Staff member	1-4-1977
Kompong Som Port						
1	Chhun Sok Nguon	Som	M		Deputy Director of Kompong Som Port	19-10-1976
State Fishing Service						
1	Min Suon	Duon	M		Director of the State Fishing Service	1-1-1977
2	Phan		M		Deputy Director of the State Fishing Service	1-11-1976
State Industry						
1	Bun Hua	Kho Mau	M		Deputy Party Secretary of the Ministry of Industry	12-3-1978
2	Prum So	Sai	M		Staff member of the Ministry	28-1-1978
3	Sin Kim Ien	Pon	M		Director-Manager of the Salt Producing Field	23-2-1978
Office 870						
1	Mau Khem Nuon	Phun	M		Deputy Chief of Staff of "S-21" Security Office	8-4-1977

No. (1)	Names (2)	Other Names (3)	Sex (4)	Age (5)	Rank (6)	Imprison Date (7)
2	May Son	Chhan	M	51	Member of the People's Representative Institute	17-2-1977
3	Phot Chhai	Toch	M		Official of Office 870	14-3-1977
4	Sem Ki	Benh	M	27	Chief of Staff of the "KO-1" Office's Bank Service	28-3-1977
5	Ket Chau	Sen	M	34	In charge in the "KO-1"'s Guard Unit (Commander of the Guard Unit of "KO-1" Office)	18-2-1977
6	In Voon	Su Voon	M	27	Commander of the Battalion for Guarding "Office 870"	26-2-1977
7	Keo Mu Ni		M		Former member of the Central Committee of the People's Revolutionary Party	15-10-1976
8	Keo Mias		M		Party Secretary of the Workers' Party	20-9-1976
9	Op Poong		M			22-4-1978

2.5.25a
Bill on Arms and Other Military Equipment Sent by China as Nonreimbursed Aid to Kampuchea, 1976–1978

I. For the Army

1. Equipment and arms for three artillery regiments, one anti-aircraft battalion (36 each of: 85 millimeter artillery pieces of type 56, 122 millimeter mortars of type 54, 130 millimeter artillery pieces of type 59-1; 18 double-barrelled 37 millimeter anti-aircraft guns of type 65).

Artillery shells: 85 millimeter artillery of type 56, 8640 pieces, National United Front for the Salvation of Kampuchea No. 3-1-336/338(13); 130 millimeter artillery of type 59, 4320 pieces, National United Front for the Salvation of Kampuchea No. 3-1-335/353(13)

2. Arms and equipment for a tank regiment: 72 light tanks of type 62, and 32 amphibious tanks of type 63.

Shells for 85 millimeter tank guns of type 56, 10,058 pieces, National United Front for the Salvation of Kampuchea No. 3-1-333/335(7).

3. Arms and equipment for a communications regiment: 459 radio transmitters, 2203 telephones, 910 kilometers of wire of different kinds, and 1300 kilometers of antenna wires. Also, 885-type radios, 360 sets, National United Front for the Salvation of Kampuchea No. 3-4-1.

II. For the Navy

Equipment and arms for a platoon of chase submarines, one company of torpedo boats, and one company of escort boats: four rescue boats of type 037, 10 escort boats of type 62C, 12 high speed torpedo boats of type 026, one 80 ton mine sweeper, and one 300 ton tanker. Also, type 533W torpedoes, 48 units, National United Front for the Salvation of Kampuchea No. 3-3-506.

III. For the Air Force

1. Equipment and arms for a regiment of fighter planes: 30 model 6 fighter planes, 6 model 6 training planes.

2. Spare equipment and arms for one regiment of bombers: equipment and arms for 17 bombers and 3 model 5 bomber training planes.

Type 5A turbines, 20 pieces, National United Front for the Salvation of Kampuchea No. 02.

Shells for the type 23-2 anti-aircraft artillery: 36,720 pieces.

3. Equipment and arms for two anti-aircraft regiments, 48 guns of 100 millimeter caliber, type 59; 48 guns of 57 millimeters, type 59; and 36 double-barrelled anti-aircraft guns of type 65.

4. Spare equipment and arms for one radar regiment, for 20 sets of search and guide radar.

2.5.25b

To the General Staff General of the Revolutionary Army of Democratic Kampuchea

Acting under Article 2 of the agreement between the government of the People's Republic of China and the government of Democratic Kampuchea on unreimbursed aid from China to Kampuchea in arms and military equipment, signed by the two governments on February 10, 1976, at Phnom Penh, we have drawn up a draft of a detailed bill of arms and military equipment provided by China as unreimbursed aid to Kampuchea (attached herewith). If you agree, this letter of ratification (including the detailed bill) will become part of the agreement.

We extend highest revolutionary regards.

October 5, 1977
The General Staff of the
People's Liberation Army of China

Annex: Military Material Delivery Bill

Provider: The general staff of the Ministry of National Defense of the People's Republic of China.

Delivering party: The military attaché in Kampuchea of the army, navy, and air force of the People's Republic of China.

Signed: Meo An Lam

Party for whom material is destined: the military general staff of the government of the United National Union of Kampuchea.

Recipient: Comrade Nat, division commander, on behalf of the head of state Major General Son Sen.

Signed: Nat

October 17, 1975

2.5.26

Excerpts from the Minutes of the Conference of the Northern Zone, July 15, 1977

There are no key personnel, or if there were, they are reactionaries and cannot continue in their positions. That is why we must pay great attention to the question of key personnel, a question of great importance. . . . Even children can be key personnel. Only in this way can we build the party, because the children will grow up in the movement.

2.5.26a

Excerpts from the Minutes of the Conference of the Western Zone, July 15, 1977

. . . The first six months of this year are the six months we have used to struggle against the enemy inside us. It is also the first time that we have dealt with the entire reactionary system in the zone, within the party, in the army, and in the public services and commissions. . . . But in our party ranks, purification has not yet been achieved. We must take radical and thorough measures.

2.5.27

Excerpts from the Conference of "S-21" on Conduct of Interrogations, July 23, 1977

. . . In interrogations, we analyze the background of each enemy individual in order to learn about his political leaning, the nature of his activities, his relationships, his trade, and his family. We study the influences that changed him, over time, at first quantitative and then qualitative, into becoming in the end an agent of the Central Intelligence Agency.

. . . As for the methods of torture, lessons must be drawn to avoid means of torture that cause death.

. . . Shortcomings: we are not working particularly well, we have not made much progress, meaning that we have not made a great leap forward, and we have not achieved greatness.

2.5.28
Excerpt from the Sino-Kampuchean Meeting of September 29, 1977

Kampuchea was represented by Pol Pot, Ieng Sary, and Vorn Vet. China was represented by Hua Kuo Feng, Deng Tsiao Ping, Li Sionan, Kong Piao, and Han Nianlong. Pol Pot spoke about the situation in Kampuchea: "In our discussion early this year, President Hua Kuo Feng stressed that there was a group opposing us. I confirm this reality. There were spies who caused problems in several ways in our country. There were three main networks.

"In 1976 we liquidated the Vietnam agents in the main. In June 1977 we similarly liquidated in the main the forces of the CIA.

"We estimate that the morale of the Vietnamese army is low; it will not be able to endure the hardships as it did in the past. . . . Its shock troops in the South are weakened.

"If the revolution in Southeast Asia takes this opportunity to step up the offensive, the situation will improve and we will be able to resolve our problems. We have exchanged views with our friends in Burma, Malaysia, and Indonesia and find we hold the same views. Thailand as well agrees with us. That is a great political success. To be sure, in the details there remain complications, but in the north we are supported by our Chinese friends, while in Southeast Asia there is unanimity among our friends. This strategic light gives us encouragement. If before we were sure of the friendship of the Chinese, today we are even more sure of it. . ."

2.5.29
Excerpt from Document No. 45-P5-CP of the Permanent Meeting of Office 870 of January 26, 1978, and February 1, 1978[1]

During the war we had about 80,000. But we have switched some into various other posts and have purged a certain number, so that by early 1977

1. Office 870 is the central apparatus of the Communist Party. — Eds.

there remained 50,000. Another 20,000 have been added, making a total of 70,000. These 70,000 we have equipped with Chinese weapons.

2.5.30

Excerpt from the Proceedings of the Conference of Office 870 on August 5, 1978[1]

We must understand our present predicament. Our corps of leading officials is very weak. They are not up to the task. There are too few of them. There are more and more tasks all the time. There exists a major contradiction in that 60 percent of the leading officials have to push to the limit to keep the organization afloat. . . It is only possible to exert oneself so hard for a given time period. But if this situation goes on, it would become unbearable. For now we can hold on, incurring only some damage. But a continuation of this situation could bring the danger of a collapse.

1. Office 870 is the central apparatus of the Communist Party. — Eds.

Excerpts from Published Accounts

2.6.01
The Military Aid Given by China to Pol Pot Is Basically Arms for the Offensive Against Vietnam, by Miyamoto Taro, Special Correspondent of the Newspaper *Akahata* in Phnom Penh, June 14, 1979

The document on arms supply to the Pol Pot clique by China that I saw this trip in Phnom Penh is printed in Chinese characters. This document of thirty-eight pages, including the cover, bears on the cover this inscription: Act regulating military equipment furnished gratis by China to Kampuchea from 1976 to 1979. It is the list of arms furnished gratis by China to "Democratic Kampuchea" (the Pol Pot–Ieng Sary administration) in the years 1976, 1977, and 1978.

Along with this document are papers on the delivery and receipt of arms furnished that bear the signatures of the highest official of the general staff of the People's Liberation Army of China, and of the highest official of the general staff of Pol Pot. These military officials say that by all appearances these are documents having an important connection to the secret military agreement signed by the two parties.

The first part of this list deals with land forces, the second with naval forces, and the third with air forces. In each part there are two chapters indicating clearly the designation of the armaments, the quantity furnished, and the types of arms. For example, in the first chapter of the part on land forces are inscribed the name, number, and label of large caliber cannons distributed to "three artillery regiments," and to "a battalion of anti-aircraft defense."

According to this list, over three years, China furnished to Pol Pot 36 85-millimeter type 56 cannons, 36 130-millimeter type 59-1 cannons with a range of 30 kilometers. In all, counting only large-caliber cannons, China furnished 108 pieces. In addition, it furnished to Pol Pot 18 37-millimeter type 65 anti-aircraft cannons. It also furnished all the equipment for these three artillery regiments and this anti-aircraft battalion: the shells for the four types of cannons mentioned (a total of 40,310 shells), equipment such as 36 tractors for heavy artillery, 12 command cars, three trucks, and such equipment as artillery scopes, clamps, batteries, generators, and training projectiles, etc.

In the second chapter of the part on land forces one finds 72 type 62 light tanks, 35 type 63 amphibious vehicles, 545,058 projectiles, including 85-millimeter projectiles for tank cannons, and other equipment for tank units such as traction vehicles.

In the third chapter of this part one finds radio transmitters and receivers, 1,300 kilometers of electrical wire, and other equipment for a communications regiment.

In the second part on naval forces one finds a total of 28 boats of different types: one company of submarine chasers, one coastal defense battalion, one torpedo launching battalion, and a total of 205,240 torpedoes, underwater engines, and projectiles for these boats.

In the third part on the air forces one finds a total of 56 planes of different types, such as combat aircraft, reconnaissance aircraft, transport aircraft, and training aircraft, and a total of 132 anti-aircraft cannons of different types for two anti-aircraft regiments, as well as projectiles and other arms for airborne units.

The above items are only a part of the list of arms furnished by China to the Pol Pot administration. According to the military experts, besides this secret agreement, other agreements on arms supply for the air and sea forces include two destroyers, and for the infantry such arms as guns, machine guns, anti-tank cannons, etc. These agreements were signed separately.

Regarding the supply of these arms by China to the Pol Pot administration, the military experts made the two following points. First, one sees immediately that China's military aid to the Pol Pot administration is aimed basically at furnishing arms with which to attack Vietnam. For example, regarding the land forces, this aid focuses on arms and munitions for artillery and tank units, and this shows clearly the aim of Chinese military aid.

Second, the size of Pol Pot's army as of the liberation of Kampuchea, April 17, 1975, was only six divisions. (One Kampuchean division is generally made up of 4,000 men, and usually 6,500 men if one adds special forces, such as an artillery regiment.) This number grew to 11 divisions by April 1977, to 16 divisions by January 1978, to 22 divisions by September 1978, and to 23 divisions by December 1978.

Because of the heavy losses suffered in the war of aggression against Vietnam, Pol Pot had to recruit children aged 12 and 13. The secret of the rapid growth of the size of the army is the large arms shipments by China. The rapid growth of fully equipped forces made the Pol Pot–Ieng Sary clique more aggressive against Vietnam. That is why Chinese arms aid to Pol Pot is quite dangerous.

2.6.02

Reckoning with the Past, by Dragoslav Rancic (excerpt), (*Politika*, Belgrade, March 31, 1978, p. 5) (Interview with Yun Yat, Minister of Culture and Propaganda)

Under the old regime the peasants believed in Buddhism, which the ruling class used as an instrument of propaganda. With the development of revolutionary consciousness, the people stopped believing, and monks left the pagodas. The issue is gradually fading away. As a result, there is no issue.

2.6.03

Excerpt from Pol Pot's Speech to a Press Conference in Peking, September 29, 1977, During His Visit to China, Published in *People's Daily*, October 3, 1977[1]

We have studied the experience of world revolution, particularly the works of Comrade Mao Tse Tung and the experience of the Chinese revolution of the period (1957) that has an important impact for us. After assessing the specific experience of Kampuchea and studying a number of instances of world revolution, and particularly under the guidance of the works of Comrade Mao Tse Tung, we have found a way appropriate for the realities of Kampuchea. Thus, our Party committee set the Party's line, and this line was debated and approved by the first congress, held at Phnom Penh on September 30, 1960.

2.6.04

Excerpt from Pol Pot's Speech at a Party in Honor of Hua Kuo Feng During Pol Pot's Visit to China September 29, 1977 (Published in *People's Daily*, September 29, 1977)[2]

We have creatively and successfully applied Mao Tse Tung's thoughts to the realities of Kampuchea. With our bare hands from the start, we won victory on April 17, 1975. . . .

For our revolution in Kampuchea, Mr. President Mao, the communist party, and the Chinese people have provided us the most precious thing, the thought of Mao Tse Tung. President Mao always gives us support and encouragement.

1. Full text in Foreign Broadcast Information Service (China), October 3, 1977, p. A20. —Eds.

2. Full text in Foreign Broadcast Information Service (China) September 29, 1977, p. A16. —Eds.

2.6.05
Excerpt from Hua Kuo Feng's Speech at a Party in Honor of Pol Pot, September 29, 1977 (Published in *People's Daily* in Peking the Same Day)[1]

". . . the heroic Kampuchean people have succeeded not only in doing away with the old world, but in building a new one . . .

". . . They have persistently maintained independence and sovereignty, and the spirit of self-reliance, and managed to foil all subversive and sabotage schemes of the enemy, in Kampuchea and abroad."

2.6.06
A Glimpse into the Houses of Death, by Wilfred Burchett (*Afrique-Asie*, No. 188, May 28, 1979, p. 10)

It is hard to find words to describe the nightmare that lasted nearly four years of life, torture, and death in the Kampuchea of Pol Pot. Are there any remotely possible comparisons, or precedents? Tied with irons hand and foot, their eyes and hair pulled out from blows of iron bars, bamboo sticks thrust under their nails, suffering atrocious torture before being finished off with axes, hammers, or knives, the victims of the former school Tuol Sleng in Phnom Penh converted into a house of detention and execution, they number as many as those who perished at Hiroshima.

In every provincial capital there were similar torture and death chambers.

Among the victims were not only diplomats and high officials of the former regime of Lon Nol and of the previous regime of Sihanouk, but as well anyone with education beyond high school. Doctors, lawyers, engineers, nurses, monks. The mountain of clothing taken from the victims before they were dragged into the torture chambers includes even clothing of children, dresses of women, and the saffron robes of monks.

The families of former officials of the Sihanouk and Lon Nol regimes, or of the officers of their armies, were killed with them. The torture was aimed at extracting confessions, an admission of having been an agent of the C.I.A., the K.G.B., or the Vietnamese, or to get the names of accomplices who could be "treated" in turn.

Travelling in the provinces, one can conclude that the essence of the "activities" of the Pol Pot government was to seek out systematically, torture, and execute anyone who might be suspected of being a potential political opponent. That meant the extermination of more than 90 percent of the

1. Full text in Foreign Broadcast Information Service (China), September 29, 1977, p. A13. —Eds.

educated Kampucheans. Phnom Penh and the provincial capitals that I visited, Prey Veng, Kompong Speu, and Svay Rieng, were centers for the extermination of intellectuals. But the murder of former urban residents continued in the villages and countryside until only a few hours of the crushing of Pol Pot's army and government.

The Milk of the North Koreans!

This was confirmed to me by Chung Van, a manufacturer of small farm tools, 59 years old, who returned to the city a few hours before the arrival of the troops that overthrew the Pol Pot forces. Executions continued until the early morning of January 7. At noon that day, Phnom Penh was liberated.

The main torture center in Prey Veng was a former house of prostitution that was camouflaged under the Lon Nol regime as a "sewing factory." The women who had attracted clients were put into special rooms from which they never returned. Or if they were found to be too sick, they were thrown into deep cellars in the part of the city where sewage water passed through. One understands today why the North Korean "security advisors" who helped the several hundred Chinese "military advisors" in Prey Veng drank only fresh coconut milk!

President Heng Samrin, who is in charge of the new government, told me that the current population is estimated at some 4.5 million. Compared to seven to eight million when the Pol Pot regime took power on April 17, 1975, the difference is made up by those who were killed or who died of hunger and exhaustion. (Seven days of work a week, twelve to thirteen hours a day, with only a bowl of sticky rice twice a day.)

The population of Prey Veng province declined from 857,336 at the fall of Lon Nol to 446,357 today. In Kompong Speu, it went from about 250,000 to 150,000; in Svay Rieng from 290,000 to 220,000. And the figures showing the number of survivors do not reflect the incredible loss in manpower caused by the killings. Quick checks in several dozen villages showed that 70% to 85% of the adult survivors are women, and among the others, the children are mostly below the age of twelve years.

The most typical scene when one travels today on the roads in Kampuchea are small groups of people, survivors of one or several families, pushing primitive carts with wooden wheels. Women pulling in front, children pushing in back, they transport a few miserable goods with, always, the most vital item, a blackened pot for cooking rice.

Each of these small groups has a tragic story to tell. They represent another aspect of the nightmare: the forced evacuation of the three million inhabitants of Phnom Penh on April 17, 1975, which was reported by the world press at the time because there were still many Western journalists there to describe what happened.

What Is to Be Done?

What was not known was that this was followed by a generalized forced migration of nearly the entire population. Because of an obsession with "contamination" of the Kampucheans by the Vietnamese, nearly all the inhabitants of the provinces bordering on Vietnam, especially those of Svay Rieng, Prey Veng, and Takeo, were sent to the distant provinces of the west, such as Pursat and Battambang, whereas those living near the Thailand border were sent to the eastern provinces.

The policy of the new government, President Heng Samrin explained to me: "If you want to stay in your new region and have a house and the means to engage in farming, do it. If you want to go back to your native village, we will help you."

Most have chosen to go back, and in the first weeks after the fall of the Pol Pot regime, there were still some trucks to transport them. But now, trucks are needed for work that is literally a matter of life and death. As much rice as possible must be planted during the rainy season, which starts in late May.

Then some dozens of thousands of people push their carts on the roads, making ten to twenty kilometers a day, hoping to find their houses intact at the end of the voyage.

It is almost impossible to imagine a society so profoundly destroyed and broken up by its own leaders. Phnom Penh, so beautiful in former times, is no more than a phantom city, most of its former residents being presumed dead. Because they were the main victims of the death houses.

The situation is worse than one can think or imagine, and it is hard to see even how international aid could come in time where it is most needed.

2.6.07
The Country Is a Torture Chamber: The Crimes of the Pro-Peking Regime in Kampuchea (*Pravda*, Moscow, January 25, 1979, p. 4)

". . . In front of all the inhabitants of the village, the chairman of the cooperative, one of his assistants, and the head of a production brigade were shot. . . . These were 'traitors,' we villagers were told. . . . Then a short time later, in front of everyone, they beat to death a woman who was the mother of two children."

". . . Thirty families of my fellow villagers were forced to go to the outskirts of the village, where they were shot. I saw the ditch: fifteen meters long by two meters wide. The corpses lay there a long time, in water in between grass used as fertilizer and manure . . ."

Such is the testimony of people who miraculously survived the genocide in Kampuchea, which was carried out there during the horrible years of the rule of the Pol Pot–Ieng Sary regime. The first statement was by Yich Som-phol, recounting events in 1977 in his native village of Prek Norin. The second was by San Kanda, a farmer, about a tragic incident of last year, 1978, on the other side of the long-suffering country of Kampuchea.

And here is one other eyewitness account reported by a correspondent of the French newspaper *Le Monde*. It is by Prok Sam, one of the Kampucheans forced out of Phnom Penh. In the place he was resettled, Phnom Srok district, he was forced into a work brigade of 230 men. "The brigades," he said, "were either for men, or for women. Men and women always had to work separately. I got married in 1976. After our first night together, they separated us for four months."

In a country turned into a huge concentration camp, where with the active participation of Peking an export variant of the cultural revolution was cultivated, the only people who had free access were the thousands of Chinese advisors. Peking in fact was behind the experiment of implanting a "new society" in a population hostile to the idea. As for what this "new society" was to be, one can judge from what Pol Pot himself revealed in the spring of last year, just at the time the fellow villagers of San Kanda were being taken to the outskirts of the village to be shot. "To build a new society we need only one million Kampucheans," declared this advocate of the Chinese model for the political structure of the country. Facts show what they planned to do. Over the three and a half years of the management of the pro-Peking clique in the country, many hundreds of thousands of people were physically liquidated.

To the question of how the puppets could hold power so long in the face of the people's anger without the help and support of Peking, there is only one answer. The *New York Times*, which is far from sympathetic to the patriotic elements of Kampuchea, calling the Pol Pot–Ieng Sary regime "another Auschwitz," "the darkest period in the history of the twentieth century," had to acknowledge, "The Pol Pot butchers sadistically killed a huge number of the inhabitants of Kampuchea. And China gave its Kampuchean vassals the instruments of murder and torture." It is curious that even former Prince Sihanouk, whom Peking sent to New York to play the role of representative of the "legal" government of Pol Pot, himself condemned this regime. More than that, he declared that he was its prisoner.

Let us recall how a military dictatorial regime was forced on Kampuchea, how the country was turned into a springboard for international provocations. In the spring of 1975, after five years of armed resistance, Kampuchea was fully liberated from the management of the pro-American puppet authorities. Guerrilla forces entered Phnom Penh. The capital cordially welcomed the liberators. But a week later, Pol Pot was delivered to Phnom Penh in a Chinese airplane, and he began to carry out a "cultural revolution" on Kampuchean soil.

From the stories of refugees, with whom I have had the opportunity to meet, one can imagine how this was done. More than three million city residents were forcibly dispersed to rural areas. Travel from one populated area to another was forbidden, and many families were separated by force. With a stroke of the pen, the Phnom Penh rulers "abolished" currency. The doors of institutions of learning were closed, as well as hospitals. The civil postal and telegraph services were "abolished." The whole population from the age of 12 or 14 years was organized into work brigades. As encouragement for forced labor they got only scant food rations. Millions of people labelled "agents" or "reactionaries" became the victims of mass terror. Reprisal awaited anyone who refused or was unable to comply with the orders to resettle elsewhere. National minorities, hill tribes, and the small Cham national group became the objects of genocide. Many Kampucheans saved themselves by fleeing to the neighboring countries of Vietnam and Thailand. Among the victims of the pro-Peking regime were those who took gun in hand in the ranks of the guerrillas or underground groups that recently fought for the freedom and independence of Kampuchea.

The country was artificially isolated from the outside world and turned into a springboard for spreading tensions in Southeast Asia. The Pol Pot regime, complying with orders from Peking, made Kampucheans shed their blood in confrontations with their former allies in the liberation struggle, the Vietnamese. Kampuchean troops landed on the Vietnamese island of Phu Quoc. Armed attacks were launched on the Vietnamese border provinces: Tay Ninh and at Ha Tien. A network of clandestine schools was set up, to teach sabotage and espionage to agents who then were sent to neighboring countries.

In early 1978 the Pol Pot regime formally broke diplomatic relations with Vietnam and stepped up provocations against its neighbor. By no accident this came just as Peking began an open campaign against Vietnam. Recently in liberated Phnom Penh, in a school that the clique turned into a torture chamber, the following slogan was found: "With China's help, we must crush Vietnam!" Is there any more convincing evidence that the now overthrown regime worked hand in hand with the Chinese hegemonists?

And only a people's opposition movement was able to drive the bloody dictators from Kampuchean soil. The Chinese "experts" are running away behind them. Such is the ignominious ending. Those guilty of this genocide will not escape the judgment of the Kampuchean people or of the peoples of the world.

2.6.09
Account of Jarai Nirat, a Refugee

UPI (Buriram, Thailand, June 19, 1978) —A refugee speaks today about the workers at naval construction sites of the government of Kampuchea, who work hard to convert fishing boats captured from Thailand into powerfully armed patrol boats. Jarai Nirat, 24 years old, a former boat construction worker who left Kampuchea two months ago, tells the UPI correspondent that for more than a year he belonged to a group of forty to fifty people who worked on armaments and motors of fishing boats that had already been converted. The norms set by the Khmer Rouge were quite high. The Khmer Rouge gave the workers little time to get the work done. When the workers could not meet the norms, the Khmer Rouge would cut the food ration.

Jarai said that ten patrol boats were converted during the year. He said that he worked at a naval construction site in a coastal town in Koh Kong province, on the Gulf of Thailand.

According to Jarai, these boats are fitted out with recoilless 75 mm mortars set up on reinforced bridges.

In some cases more powerful motors, up to 300 CV are put on fishing boats 15 to 20 meters long, replacing the old motors. These boats were taken from Thailand fishermen, Jarai said.

He said that he does not know what happened to the crew. Some boats converted into patrol boats lie at anchor in nearby ports; they don't operate regularly for lack of fuel. Some motors are in need of spare parts. Fuel for the motors is limited.

Jarai added: "It is like being in jail. Exhausted by hard work, we get two meals a day, some rice with vegetables. From time to time they cut our food ration as a punishment.

"I was under suspicion because I am not Kampuchean. When I found out one night that there was a conflict with Thailand, I decided to escape because to stay would be quite dangerous."

With three of his friends, Jarai left the naval base and fled into the forest.

Two weeks later, all four crossed the sea and got to Thailand. At present they are being held in the Center for Illegal Foreigners in Buriram, which is 320 kilometers northeast of Bangkok.

2.6.10
Testimony of a Former Resident of Pailin: Forced Labor Under the Gun (Testimony of a Former Resident of Pailin, a Town in Northwest Cambodia), *Le Monde* (Paris), May 21, 1976, p. 6 (excerpt) and Summary of a Series in *Aurore* by Denis de Dumoulin, 1978

On April 17, 1975, at 11:30 a.m., Radio Phnom Penh broadcast the news that since 9:30 a.m., the city had been in the hands of the Khmer Rouge. With the announcement of this news, the whole town of Pailin was in ferment. That evening the governor of the town, the department heads, and other high-ranking officials fled to Thailand in their cars. They took their families.

On April 18, about thirty Khmer Rouge came into the town in a truck. Their chief was named "Bun." Over the next three days more and more Khmer Rouge came to Pailin. Their chiefs were named Say, Pom, and Ngen, whose surname was Sou. They ordered all the heads of the government army who had not fled to come to headquarters. There they told the officers: "We ask you to help Angkar (the Organization). You will go to Battambang to teach our soldiers to drive tanks and airplanes, and to operate radios and mortars, our people don't know these things."

The next day, about forty officers presented themselves. The Khmer Rouge took them out west of Stung Treng and killed them. Among them were Lieutenant Colonel Oeum Akkaseri, and Lieutenants Lav Song and Khoun Sabin. The truck drivers who took the officers secretly told us about this. The Khmer Rouge then took enlisted personnel and shot them at Trapeang Ke, near the bridge on the Battambang—Pailin road.

On April 26, the Khmer Rouge ordered all the people to evacuate the town within three days. My wife, my five children, and I left Pailin on foot, walking day and night toward Battambang. At night we got to Trapeang Ke, where we smelled corpses of people killed by the Khmer Rouge and left along the road. The women and children were very frightened and did not want to go any farther. We saw many corpses on both sides of the road.

The people of Pailin, deported in this way, left on National Route 10, which leads from Pailin to Battambang. They entered the forest toward Treng, Chak Chha, Ronua Ngea, Roung, Kompong Kol, and Boeung Trasai. Another group of people who left Pailin went north, toward Sala Krav, Sre Antea, Khay, etc.

After walking six nights, we came to a pagoda near the Snoeung village market. There I met many people from Pailin, including Mr. Eng, who used to be the customs inspector. He told me that he was the last person to leave Pailin. He told me that Deputy Governor of Pailin Pauch Pa, Pailin Department Chief Po Man, Pailin Bureau Chief Tek Rovvi, Ward Chief Miet Thairak, Deputy Director of Primary Education Pi Kom Su, and nineteen other people were taken to Higher Angkar (the Organization) and were shot at the Samlaut road intersection. He also said that the Khmer Rouge were looking for all the civil servants and all the military personnel to kill them to the last person. My family and I went and asked some villagers to take us in, and they did. This village was about five kilometers from Snoeung, and no one there knew me.

At first the Khmer Rouge split the people up into groups of ten families, and each group had a chairperson, a vice-chairperson, and a secretary chosen by the Khmer Rouge to run each group. In our village there were five groups. From the time we left Pailin until July 1975, the group we were in got nothing from the Khmer Rouge. We lived on a broth-type soup, one bowl in the morning and one in the evening. We exchanged our suits, watches, and sarongs for rice in order to survive.

For more than two months we built little dams in the rice paddies, and cleared the forests without a single day of rest. There were no medications for us to use. We had only salt to go with our rice, and in the last few months we didn't even have salt. One could trade gold for salt, because gold was the only thing the Khmer Rouge would take. During the hard period, for seven persons we ate every day a soup that had the equivalent of only one tin of rice (250 grams), into which we mixed some roots and sweet potatoes. In August the group chief gave out two sacks of rice for each ten families. That came to fifteen kilograms of rice per family. Often we went to bed with nothing to eat, because we had nothing.

The group to which I belonged farmed more than twenty hectares of rice paddies. When we worked, the group chief spread the rice seeds himself. He said that at harvest time we would have to pay him to buy the rice plants. From May until the rainy season (December) the Khmer Rouge on four occasions gave us two sacks of unhusked rice, or eight sacks in all. They told us that as for anything else we would have to fend for ourselves. So we never ate sugar, or meat, or fat, but only rice soup mixed with tree leaves, and salt when there was any. Everyone was sick.

From time to time, the Khmer Rouge killed a man and left his body in the village to put fear in the villagers, because no one had any confidence in them any more. In August, the Khmer Rouge sent me, along with another person from the same group, to cut down trees at the Battambang hospital. There were nine of us in all. Since there was no transport, we had to walk to Battambang, which was about thirty kilometers. At Boeung Trau, we saw large quantities of human bones strewn about on both sides of National Route 10, which leads from Snoeung to Battambang. On the rice paddies between Phnom Krapeu and Phnom Sam Peoun, one of the people who was taking us said, "In this rice paddy, the Khmer rouge killed many people." East of Phnom Sam Peoun, in the village of Chhang Kdar, we saw many human bones in a rice paddy.

At Battambang, along the Sangkar River, in front of the school, south of the city hospital, the Khmer Rouge piled up high quality furniture and left it there. Along the stone road by the river, they planted banana trees, because they wanted to turn Battambang city into countryside, and to turn the countryside into city! The whole city was bathed in a silence of death. We slept at the hospital while we were cutting trees there. We got more to eat there: one tin of rice per person per day, one tin of salt for ten people. After seven days, the Khmer Rouge sent us back from where we had come, to Canton No. 4.

* * *

Starting February 25, the newspaper *Aurora* published a series of articles by Denis de Dumoulin, special correspondent in Thailand, about the cruel regime of the Phnom Penh authorities as told by refugees who were Kampuchean soldiers who had fled to Thailand to escape repression and terrorism. The newspaper writes: On April 17, 1975, the Khmer Rouge marched into Phnom Penh, giving orders to carry out the most thorough-going terror of the twentieth century, to kill all the soldiers of the Republic army and their families, to kill all the high-ranking military people and non-communist intellectuals. This genocide undertaken by the Khmer Rouge has lasted nearly three years. Of the seven million Kampucheans as of 1975, it is estimated that one to two million have died from summary execution, disease, or exhaustion.

The newspaper reproduced an account told by a Kampuchean soldier named Seng, 29 years of age, who just fled to Thailand a few weeks ago. "One day in 1973, the Khmer Rouge came into my village at Bankem, in Kompong Thom province. They asked me to follow them. I was only fifteen years old and was still studying in school. I had to follow them, because otherwise my parents, who were simple farmers, would have been killed. I was not the only one to whom this happened. Fifty young people from the village were arrested the same way I was. In forcing me to go with them, they gave me a gun. Since I did not know how to handle a gun, I had to imitate what the others did. Our commander was a Kampuchean who returned from Vietnam after going through education there for twenty years or so."

For two years, Seng's unit operated in Kompong Thom province, and later in Siem Reap province. Seng says that after April 17, the life of the Kampucheans got worse and worse. Seng's unit controlled the "new people," that is, city people who had been forced out of cities to work in the countrywide, to clear land, and to dig ditches. It was also given the mission of executing anyone the officials labelled "obstinate." "They made us arrest and kill people without there being any real reason for doing so. We killed people with sticks to save bullets and to keep others from hearing. I don't know who is in charge in Phnom Penh. Recently I learned that it is Pol Pot who heads the government. I never heard of Khieu Samphan, Ieng Sary, or Nuon Chea."

Seng says as well that in February 1977 there was a major purge in Kampuchea. Commanders were taken to the south, labelled as traitors. First it was those at the level of battalion chief down to district chief. Then they arrested company chiefs and below. Civil officials as well as military were arrested, along with their wives and children. High ranking officials were taken by car to Siem Reap, away from their families. They made them talk before killing them. Since then most of the commanders are between twenty and thirty years old. The soldiers from Preak Vihear are twelve years old and up.

No longer able to live under the tough regime of the Phnom Penh authorities, Seng, along with other soldiers from his company, took off under the leadership of a group of soldiers who revolted. With five other soldiers, Seng fled to Thailand. All the refugees gave similar accounts with similar details:

continuing brutalization, forced labor, little food, disease, lack of medications, mass executions, the "old people" being separated from the "new people." The uniform conclusion is that all the villages of Kampuchea are wastelands and dismal places.

2.6.11
Statement of Senator George McGovern

Reuters (Washington), August 25, 1978—Today Senator McGovern again called on the nations of the world to take collective action to "stop the killing of innocent people" in Cambodia.

In a speech in the U.S. Congress, McGovern said that the mass killing carried out by the Cambodian authorities has forced the world community to act in a more reflective fashion. He called on the United States to take up this issue in the Security Council of the United Nations.

He added that the Cambodia issue should at least be put on the agenda of the next meeting of the U.N. Security Council.

2.6.12
Schools Closed

Reuters (Belgrade), March 11, 1978—The Tanjug news agency announced today from Phnom Penh that all the schools in Kampuchea are closed except in the primary grades.

Quoting the minister of culture, education, and information, Tanjug said that the main aim of the Kampuchean authorities is to get everyone able to read and write.

The Tanjug correspondent said that university departments and high schools will be opened after a time if it is necessary.

2.6.15
Account of Khem Sou, a Refugee[1]

Vietnam News Agency (Berlin, February 22, 1978)—The magazine *Der Spiegel* that comes out in the Federal Republic of Germany published in this week's issue an account by a Khmer named Khem Sou, who fled Kampuchea and now lives in Austria. His account relates to the situation of Kampuchea from the time of the entry of the Khmer Rouge into Phnom Penh until his flight to Thailand. According to an editor's note in the maga-

1. From *Der Spiegel*, vol. 32, February 20, 1978, p. 142.—Eds.

zine, the terrible news about Kampuchea for the past three years was only rumor, but now for the first time, the magazine *Der Spiegel* has published an article by a Khmer eyewitness who survived the first two months of the terrorism of the Khmer Rouge.

The magazine also published the biography of the author of this article. He is the son of a general loyal to the King and of a woman professor of literature at the University. Khem Sou was born in 1951 in Phnom Penh. The war interrupted his studies when he was in the fourth year at the Faculty of Medicine and the Faculty of Law. He then became a lieutenant in Public Security. During his studies at the University, Khem Sou tried his hand at writing literature and published several literary and philosophical essays. Of these, one titled "The Blackened Sky," an article of a pacifist tendency, led to the author's being imprisoned by the pro-American regime of Lon Nol. By the end of the war, Khem Sou was a worker at the stone quarry in Pailin (a town of 10,000 population) in the north of the country, near the Thailand border.

In April 1975, denounced by the residents of the area, Khem Sou was forced out of Pailin and after that lived in the forest to which he and all the other inhabitants were driven.

After fleeing to Thailand, Khem Sou sought political asylum in Austria. What follows is the text of Khem Sou's article.

Right at midnight on April 17, 1975, Radio Phnom Penh announced that the communists had won the war. The new government, which included some capable people, came to power. This news made many people happy, but it frightened others. The chief of Pailin province, the only province that had not fallen into the hands of the communists, fled to Thailand by helicopter with military officers and his staff. Some still thought that the former head of state, Prince Norodom Sihanouk, would take power again. But I realized that this would not happen. I advised my close friends, especially those in the government staff, to flee immediately to Thailand, whose border was not far away. Few people followed this advice, however. As for those who remained, some did not want to leave because of their children and houses, while others wanted to wait to see what the new regime was like, thinking that a better and more peaceful time might ensue. As far as they were concerned, any government is good if it gives them peace.

April 18: At first, I wanted to go to Thailand, but a family matter concerned me. I still had my parents, and my brothers and sisters in Kampuchea. If I were to flee, I could never return to Kampuchea, which will always be my native country regardless of what government it has.

It was especially the Khmers of wealth who took advantage of this opportunity and fled the country, but people of lesser means did not follow their example. On the contrary, everyone was enthusiastic and hung white flags in their windows to welcome the new authorities.

April 19: The communists came. They occupied the entire province. But there were still not many, and no shooting. There was no more resistance anywhere. To the contrary, the communists were welcomed. But some incidents are still worth mentioning. Anyone who wore a wrist watch, rings, or other jewelry of value could expect to be forced to turn them over to the communists: "All property belongs to everyone; your jewelry is mine too(!), your wrist watch is also mine; you have worn your jewelry for a long time and that is enough, now let me try it."

On the same day, the Khmer Rouge announced that all civil service people, and all officers and soldiers would have to register with the regional commander. They would be reeducated; they would be initiated in the principles of communism. Most of these persons complied with these recommendations. After taking down their family names and given names, the Khmer Rouge let these people go back to their houses. They told them that in a few days they would be taken to a reeducation camp at Battambang. As for me, I did not go to the regional commander; I concealed my past as a civil servant of the former government.

April 20: Everything seemed to return to normal. I took up my work again at the quarry. In the previous few days, even people who had fled to Thailand came back to the country, certain that a time of peace had begun, because the price of goods dropped, something that had not happened in the prior few years. But more and more communists arrived by the day, and little by little they showed their true colors.

April 25: The Khmer Rouge announced that all soldiers, police officers, and civil servants of the former government had to go to a reeducation camp at Battambang. Trucks would take them there. On a particular day everyone would leave their houses and land to go to Battambang where they would get new houses.

Because the program of the communists said so, a completely new society would have to be established in Cambodia. Each person was supposed to create a new life, right from the beginning. Those who weren't capable, they should die miserable deaths, since they weren't needed in this new society. Forests were supposed to be cleared and turned into fields.

At first, they used the threat of American bombing as a pretext to evacuate villages and cities. The idea of leaving left many people aghast. The Khmers were steeped in their traditions, and attached to the past, but now they were forced to abandon their houses and their familiar surroundings, their native village, and often as well the birthplace of their ancestors. One can understand that many people, especially the elderly, broke down in tears upon hearing an order of a mass departure.

But another deception made even the most optimistic cry. It was not Prince Norodom Sihanouk who took the reins of power, not he, the one who, returning from exile in Peking, called the people "my children." From radio discussions, it became clear that the communists were in power, and no one knew who they were.

Any request for special treatment for the elderly, for the sick, or for pregnant women was refused with such remarks as: "We spent five years and one month in the forest; during this time we fought for your freedom and we had not even the basics of life."

April 28: On this day I got ready to leave for Battambang. The period in which all inhabitants of Pailin had to leave ended on April 30.

April 29: People who had a car or some other means of transportation used them. I had a motorcycle, and I took a neighbor on the back of it and towed behind it a two-wheel cart full of rice and other necessities.

In Dei Kraham, three kilometers away, I noticed we had forgotten the frying pan. I drove back once more. Shortly before I reached my village I made a gruesome discovery. I went past the hut of a family who had fled the takeover by the communists toward Thailand, but then because of the initial rejoicing had been deceived into returning to Cambodia. The family was obviously no longer to be trusted by the communists. They had shot them. The husband was hanged by his feet from a ladder and had been killed by a couple of bullets to the body. The wife and two children lay at the entrance to the hut, also dead.

The Khmer Rouge people did not bury their victims. I made another half-turn and headed for Die Kraham, but before I got to the hill, I found along the road the body of a sick old man whom I knew. Unable to move because of his illness, the old man asked the Khmer Rouge to let him stay. The Khmer Rouge granted his wish in their own way; they shot him and would not let anyone bury him. His death was an example.

April 30: At 4:00 a.m., we had to get up to go farther. The road was full of people, of mothers crying for children lost in the crowd, of children in tears who had lost their mothers. To restore order, the communists fired into the air.

The cruel nature of the Khmer Rouge was shown clearly: in order to break up the bottlenecks, the Khmer Rouge pushed the crowd back, sending the men in one direction, and women and children in another. I was sent west toward Sala Krav. Spurning family feelings, the Khmer Rouge thus separated from each other spouses, parents and children, and brothers and sisters. Any show of opposition could bring a rain of bullets.

2.6.17
Facts About the Vietnam-Kampuchea Border Question (Excerpts from a Document Released by the Foreign Ministry of the Socialist Republic of Vietnam, April 7, 1978)

. . . The fact is that as early as May 1, 1975, the Kampuchean authorities ordered their armed forces to encroach on Vietnamese territory in a number of places in border areas from Ha Tien to Tay Ninh, causing great human and material losses to the local population.

On May 4, 1975, Kampuchean troops landed on Phu Quoc Island, and on May 10, 1975, they launched attacks from the mainland and from Hon Troc (Way Island) on Vietnam's Tho Chu Island and occupied it. Tho Chu Island lies far south of the Brevié line.[1] The Kampuchean authorities launched repeated attacks on this island with their armed forces, destroyed villages, killed many people and abducted 515 inhabitants of the island. In spite of the protest made by the Vietnamese side, the Kampuchean troops maintained their stance.

. . . The Kampuchean troops' encroachments upon Vietnamese territory were admitted on June 2, 1975, by Pol Pot, Secretary of the Central Committee of the Communist Party of Kampuchea, when he received Comrade Nguyen van Linh, representative of the Vietnam Workers' Party, but he argued . . . that the Kampuchean troops' "ignorance of local geography" had been the cause of these "painful and bloody clashes."

. . . Far from taking steps to stop this activity, the Kampuchean side launched continuous military attacks against Vietnam and encroached on Vietnam's sovereignty and territory. April 1977 marked an increase in the Kampuchean authorities' mobilization of a very large force, of several divisions with the strong support of artillery clusters and mortars based in Kampuchea, to carry out concerted attacks on almost all border areas, from Ha Tien in Kien Giang province to Tay Ninh, to loot, to burn houses, and to kill people in a most savage manner, causing very great losses to the local inhabitants, and committing extremely barbarous crimes of the type described in detail in the White Paper published in January 1978 by the Department of Press and Information of the Ministry of Foreign Affairs of the Socialist Republic of Vietnam. At the same time, the period January-May 1977 saw the Kampuchea side successively cut all relations between the liaison committees of Kampuchean and Vietnamese border provinces. . . .

2.6.18
The Massacre on January 28, 1977: Relations Between Thailand and Democratic Kampuchea (Information Department, Department of Foreign Affairs, Bangkok)

At 11:00 p.m. on Friday night of January 28, 1977, large units of the armed forces of Democratic Kampuchea, numbering approximately 300 Khmer

1. The Brevié line is a boundary line between Kampuchea and Vietnam, drawn in 1939 by Jules Brevié, French governor-general of Indochina, the line extending over the maritime area. The line has been a source of dispute between Vietnam and Cambodia. — Eds.

Rouge soldiers armed with powerful and deadly weapons, intruded into Thai territory and, without giving any warning, launched three-pronged attacks on three Thai villages, namely Baan Nong Dor, Baan Klong Kor, and Baan Noi Parai of Aranyaprathet district, Prachinburi province, in southeast Thailand. The said Khmer Rouge soldiers fired their guns at the innocent Thai villagers and burnt all houses to the ground. These murderers did not only gun down everybody in sight, including helpless women, they also disfigured the bodies and slashed the throats of children and babies. Before they were driven back across the border, the Khmer Rouge murder squad managed to set fire to the crops and slaughtered animals to complete their bloodthirsty mission.

The degree of unprecedented savagery displayed by the attacking Cambodian forces on the innocent unarmed Thai villagers was a great shock to all those who witnessed the scene after the attack. The *Asiaweek* correspondent, who arrived at the scene after the attacks, reported that the smell of death was everywhere — ten families who made up the population of Nong Dor had been obliterated and their bodies, slick with rot, lay singly and in clumps amid the long grass and stunted trees of the rugged border areas. The body of one woman lay ten yards from her shack in a curiously hunched position, just as though she had been praying for mercy as machine gun bullets ripped through her chest. A few yards away lay a pregnant woman and the body of her baby son. The mother was stripped naked and a gaping wound could be seen in her inner thigh. Her little boy was sprawled beside her dead body, his throat had been slashed and there were numerous knife wound in his body (*Asiaweek*, issue of February 11, 1977, pages 14–16).

The *Time* magazine correspondent wrote that "the Khmer Rouge soldiers came to the Thai villages having the intention to kill everyone in sight. The communists gunned down fleeing villagers, bayoneted others and mutilated many victims. The massacre was worse at Nong Dor, where 21 of 60 inhabitants were murdered" (*Time* magazine, issue of February 14, 1977, page 11). *Newsweek* magazine's correspondent reported that "in the late evening, about 300 Khmer Rouge soldiers emerged from the darkness and simultaneously struck three Thai hamlets along the Cambodian border, burning houses to the ground, killing everyone in sight, and even taking babies away from their mothers and slashing the infants' throats" (*Newsweek*, issue of February 14, 1977, page 11).

The Times, in its issue of Wednesday, February 2, 1977, published an article under the title of *Communism shows its brutal face once more*, criticizing that "totalitarianism is what it sounds like: a system in which the state is everything and human beings are its raw material." The said article further described the scene, as told by rice farmer Cherd Rongland, of the slaughter of his wife and five of his eight children that "a Khmer Rouge soldier shot her through the right shoulder, seized a month-old baby from her arms and cut its throat. In almost every case, their throats were slashed with a jagged knife edge" (*The Times,* issue of February 2, 1977, page 12).

The *Daily Telegraph,* reported by John McBeth who visited the places, headlined, *Babies' throats cut, women shot in Thai massacre.* Mr. McBeth, who reached the area after the raid with the investigation group, told the story that "at Klong Khor, a rice-growing hamlet, half-a-mile from the border, the Khmer Rouge displayed the type of brutality that was unleashed on Cambodians which ended in the slaughter of at least 800,000 people." He further described the scene that "in every case, their throats were slashed with a jagged knife edge . . ." (*Daily Telegraph,* issue of February 1, 1977, page 10).

The Thai authorities have made a survey of the results of the terrible carnage perpetrated by the Cambodian soldiers in the said villages. The casualties and damage are as follows:

1. At Baan Nong Dor, 21 Thai residents were killed including a pregnant woman, children and babies who were badly mutilated; all the houses were burnt down.

2. At Baan Klong Kor, 8 Thai residents were killed and all houses burnt down.

3. At Baan Noi Parai, all 200 residents were forced to abandon their homes and a large number of people were seriously wounded.

On January 31, 1977, the Government of Thailand lodged a strong protest with the Government of Democratic Kampuchea for the barbaric acts committed by the latter's forces which constituted a flagrant violation of Thai national sovereignty and territorial integrity in contravention of international law and the Thai-Kampuchean Joint Communique of October 31, 1975. Furthermore, the Government of Thailand regarded the incident as grossly inhuman and a serious breach of civilized morality.

The Government of Thailand accordingly demanded that the Government of Democratic Kampuchea assume full responsibility for the incident and make a prompt and just compensation for the loss of life and damage to property incurred as a result of the said incident.

On February 7, 1977, the Government of Democratic Kampuchea sent a note to the Government of Thailand stating that the three villages in question were in the territory of Kampuchea and that the measures taken by the Government of Democratic Kampuchea in its own territory were answerable to the sovereignty of Kampuchea.

In this connection, the UPI reported from Bangkok on February 16, 1977, that "Cambodia has admitted that its forces killed 30 villagers in a brutal attack near the Thai border last month, but dismissed the incident as arranging its internal affairs.

"The note was significant because it marked the first time Cambodia has admitted using massacres as a means of arranging its internal affairs.

"Tales of atrocities by victorious Khmer Rouge have been told since the day of their victory April 17, 1975, but until now there had been no reply to the charge by refugees and others.

"Most observers believe that well over 1 million persons have perished in Cambodia since the communist victory. Some refugee workers, diplomats and correspondents have estimated a death toll of more than three million attributable to brutality, starvation and sickness brought about by the communist victory.

"Newsmen who visited the villages found survivors who were clearly Thai, and who said they had lived there for 10 years or more," reported UPI.

It is to be noted that in its reply note, the Government of Democratic Kampuchea did not deny the atrocities perpetrated by the Khmer Rouge forces on the night of January 28, 1977, which resulted in the brutal and barbaric massacre of Thai nationals and cruel destruction of their properties in the three Thai villages. On the contrary, the reply note constitutes an official admission of the grave crimes committed by the Khmer Rouge forces in complete disregard of human rights and human decency, which the civilized world cannot ignore but can only find downright repugnant.

Democratic Kampuchea maintains that the three villages were within its territory and hence the Government of Democratic Kampuchea had the right to "rearrange" its own internal affairs. However, according to all available evidence, including the map, it can be conclusively shown that these villages are located on Thai territory. The inhabitants of these villages are Thai by nationality, speak Thai as their native tongue, and own allegiance to Thailand. Foreign correspondents who were on the scene also shared this view and have already reported the gruesome incidents to the world at large.

Thailand has already made an official proposal to Democratic Kampuchea to appoint a joint committee to inspect the sites of border incidents, and to commence negotiations on the question of border demarcation between the two countries. Indeed the purpose of this proposal is to prevent such border incidents between the two sides. However, the Government of Democratic Kampuchea has thus far refused to agree to the Thai proposal.

The Government of Thailand has consistently and patiently pursued the policy of trying to maintain friendly relations with all countries that sincerely wish or show the genuine intention to reciprocate, irrespective of differences in the political, economic or social system.

Accordingly, Thailand has endeavored to convince the Government of Democratic Kampuchea that all existing problems between the two countries can be satisfactorily resolved by peaceful means, especially through diplomatic negotiation, and to appreciate the utility of such processes as a means of settling international disputes. The Government of Thailand for its part, will never cease in its earnest endeavor to work toward a durable peace within the region, and to forge peaceful coexistence with Democratic Kampuchea and other neighboring States on the basis of international law and international practices, mutual respect of each other's sovereignty and territorial integrity, and mutual non-interference in the internal affairs of each other.

The international community views the Cambodian raid on the three Thai villages as an act of savagery, unprovoked and cold-blooded. Thailand, as the Thai Minister of Foreign Affairs told the press, is not demanding an eye for an eye, which means that the Thai armed forces have no intention of taking retaliatory measures against Cambodia unless the latter makes a new attack on Thailand or Thai people. In such an event, the Government of Democratic Kampuchea must be solely responsible for all the consequences.

2.6.19
Genuine Revolutionary Forces in Kampuchea Call for People's Uprising Against Pol Pot Regime

Leaflets have been distributed most recently in many areas in Kampuchea, calling for the uprising of the population and army to overthrow the reactionary Pol Pot–Ieng Sary clique, according to sources from the liberated zones. Following the statement made by Samrin, a member of the Party committee of the eastern zone and commander of Division 20, here is a statement made by Chea Sim, Party Secretary of Region 20 and a former member of the Assembly of People's Representatives of Kampuchea:

Statement in protest against the Pol Pot–Ieng Sary clique

I am Chea Sim, Secretary of the Party Committee of Region 20 and a former member of the Assembly of People's Representatives of Kampuchea, make the following statement in protest against the reactionary actions of the Pol Pot–Ieng Sary clique fostered by the Chinese rulers:

As every administrator, fighter and fellow countryman has seen, the reactionary Pol Pot–Ieng Sary clique, which took power after the liberation of our country on April 17, 1975, has drowned our country and people into a sea of sufferings. Kampuchea, under the Pol Pot–Ieng Sary regime, has been turned into a land of mass murder.

They have subjected our Kampuchean people to massacre that amounts to a genocide unprecedented in the history of mankind. They are killing everyone, except their own families and accomplices, even those in the Party Central Committee and Government. At present, Phnom Penh is reserved only for their families and clique. In other localities, they kill officials from regional down to grassroots levels. They kill the population without discriminating between ages or sexes, and including lepers and the insane. They do not spare the lives of those who have done good serve to the country and people. To take an example: Bo village in Don Tei subdistrict, Ponhea Krek district, Kompong Cham province, was a revolutionary base during the struggle against the French and U.S. aggressors. During the time of underground activity, Pol Pot and Ieng Sary could survive only thanks to the cover and care of the local people. They, however, have shown their gratitude by killing all the 400 inhabitants in Bo village, including Mrs. Num, who was a standing member of the Assembly of People's Representatives of Kampuchea and had personally sheltered and fed Pol Pot and Ieng Sary.

In the army ranks, Divisions 280 and 290 of the main force are subject to repression. They sent truck loads of officers and men for execution. Many were killed at once, the others were detained, kept on a starvation diet and forced to do hard labor or killed daily in groups. So were divisions 3, 4, and 5 of the eastern zone, divisions of regions 20, 21, 22, 23, and 24 and regiments of the various districts. They killed all, from division commanders to private soldiers, even invalid soldiers who had been wounded during the five years of war and had done good service to the working class and the peasantry.

Under the Pol Pot regime, those who do not approve its reactionary policy are accused of serving foreign countries as secret agents. Crops and cattle are also destroyed. The history of Kampuchea has never witnessed such cruel butchers as the Pol Pot clique. At heart, they are traitors to the country, the people and the cause of revolution.

To carry out their reactionary lines, and encouraged and backed by the Chinese authorities, the Pol Pot–Ieng Sary clique unleash a war against Vietnam. They slander that "Vietnam makes aggression against Kampuchea" and pressure her to join Federal Indochina, using this as a pretext to send their army to attack Vietnam, kill the Vietnamese people, and destroy their crops and property. They indoctrinate the Kampuchean people and armed forces with the false idea that "Vietnam is their enemy number one." In their armed intrusions into Vietnamese territory, the Pol Pot clique carry out the policy "kill all, burn all, and destroy all," committing barbarous atrocities against the population in Ta Not, Ta Dai, Sa Mat, and other areas in Vietnam.

At these heartbreaking facts, administrators, fighters, and people throughout the country have risen up to fight them: In many areas, army units, mass organizations are waging their struggle in various ways.

I, therefore, appeal to all fellow-countrymen:

1. In the face of the nationwide people's uprisings, the Pol Pot–Ieng Sary clique are seeking all means to repress this movement. At the same time, they are resorting to persuasion and deception to mislead the people, in order to carry on their policy of murder. Let everyone not be fooled by the enemy tricks.

2. Let those who still serve in the army of the Pol Pot–Ieng Sary clique soon awake and not join in raids to repress the people, because their own families are now being tortured, slandered as traitors and killed daily by the Pol Pot clique.

3. Let those in the Pol Pot army, together with the people, rise up and turn their arms against the clique of traitors and their agents and join the genuine revolutionary forces and fight once more to overthrow the Pol Pot–Ieng Sary clique, smash their barbarous regime, and build a new society in Kampuchea, a society endowed with equality, freedom, democracy, independence, peace, and happiness for the whole nation and every family.

It is time to act; let everyone start unhesitatingly. The just and progressive forces are always at your side and always support you. With my warmest fraternal and revolutionary feelings,

Chea Sim, Party Secretary of Region 20

2.6.20
A Moment in the History of Kampuchea, by Prak Sok, Former Student, Department of Economics and Finance, National School of Administration

Division of the Population into Categories

The socialist revolution is a revolution that foresees the suppression of class contradictions, those between landowners and farmers on the one hand, and those between capitalists and workers on the other, in order to create a new classless society. The Khmer Rouge, instead of creating a classless society, divided the population, after liberation, at first into two categories: one was before April 17, 1975, and one was after April 17, 1975, that being the date of the complete liberation of Kampuchea from the yoke of the American imperialists.

The population of after April 17, 1975, was divided into two classes: the civil servants and military personnel, who were treated as prisoners of war; and the nonofficial civil population, which was scorned and continually cursed. The population of the period prior to April 17, 1975, was primarily peasants. They in turn were divided into three categories: higher class, middle class, and lower class. Those in this latter category were given quite a few privileges.

A bit later three new categories emerged: provisionally liberated people, people ready for full rights, and people enjoying full rights.

In the first category were prisoners freed from concentration camps to become members of cooperatives, but they could be arrested at any time if they did something wrong. The second category was those ready for full rights. The third category enjoyed considerable freedom of action, and the state conveyed to them secrets not divulged to the other categories that were not together with them.

This complex structure was later rendered more simple. Knowing that the people on the eastern bank of the Mekong River would not stand for being treated in a barbaric manner, and knowing that if they kept killing people the regime would be threatened, the Khmer Rouge devised a new policy with significant implications.

Around July 1978, equality of rights was given to the entire population, that is, there were no longer three categories of people as before. In early August 1978, a general amnesty was given to former CIA agents, KGB agents, and Vietnamese agents, on condition that they renounce any activity hostile to the Khmer Rouge party from the date the amnesty was declared. In reality, there were no Khmers who were agents of the Americans, Soviets, or Vietnamese; this was invented to satisfy a political need.

This easing of political rigor made the people feel a bit more relaxed. The suspension of executions was not a product of the good faith or sense of justice of the Khmer Rouge, but rather a consequence of the struggle and rebellion within the country. If the people relaxed their struggle and allowed themselves to be led about, as in 1975, the Khmer Rouge would resume repression of the most severe kind. In fact, despite the relaxation, the people did not forget the horrible past that could one day return.

This was for me a great piece of fortune, because without the directive giving a general amnesty I might have been killed by August 1978. In July 1978 I was forced to leave Kompong Ro district to go to Kien Svay district on the west bank of the Mekong River. The head of the cooperative in which I lived was reputed to have killed intellectuals, and as a student I could not expect to be an exception. By good luck, however, the directive from above arrived, suspending killings, at an opportune moment.

The people displaced from Kompong Ro district at the same time as me were spared, and none of them were killed. The directive continued to be applied, and just at that time the army of the National United Front for the Salvation of Kampuchea arrived. On January 7, 1979, amnesty directive was still in effect. The Khmer Rouge were attacked everywhere and fled in disarray. Not only that, but their plan to kill people was aborted three days before the date set for its application, which was January 10, when they planned to kill the entire population of Kien Svay district.

Extinction of Freedom

We had no freedom, no freedom of speech, no freedom of movement, no freedom to hear.

(1) Freedom of speech

At every monthly or annual meeting, and at every meeting of the cooperative, they always talked about the population having broad liberties. However, if we dared express an opinion, we would be noticed. If we expressed something favorable to the regime, we would be considered intellectuals, or as persons able to express themselves well, and who therefore needed to be removed. If we expressed something unfavorable to the regime, we would be labelled enemies and would be hounded every day. In case of a wrong committed three times, we would be arrested and killed as an example to others. Any talk between two persons who were walking side by side was suspect, and any private encounter for any reason was forbidden.

(2) Freedom of movement

We were not allowed to move from one province to another, from one district to another, or even from one village to another, and at times from one house to another. At night a strict curfew was in effect. Only the Khmer Rouge people could move around to carry out investigations along the roads, from house to house, and at times even under our beds. To make it easier for them to move around, dogs were eliminated, because they barked and disrupted their work.

(3) Freedom to hear

They didn't let us hear or learn. They took radios away from us. We knew nothing from abroad, or what is going on inside the country. If we heard anything of a type that contradicted the revolution, we could not talk about it. When we heard machine gun fire, we had to say that someone was shaking straw mats. When we heard cannon shots, we had to say that it was thunder, etc.

In sum, as for freedom, we had our mouths shut, our eyes blindfolded, our ears stuffed up, our hands and feet tied, just like what one sees on advertisements distributed on the anniversary of human rights every year on December 10.

The Dictatorship of the Khmer Rouge

The Khmer Rouge declared loudly that Kampuchea follows democracy. That is how they gave the name Democratic Kampuchea to our country to deceive national and international opinion. In fact, the regime of the Khmer Rouge was a dictatorship. This dictatorship was a combination of the two absolutisms of the world.

They used trickery and appearances suggested by Machiavelli, the theoretician of absolutism of the area around Florence in the sixteenth century. A striking example is that they asked the elite people of Phnom Penh to go back to the city from which they were forced out on April 17, 1975. They said that the new regime needed them to help it. The authorities did not kill the Khmer "blood brothers" for fear of being ridiculed by foreigners. In fact, the Phnom Penh leaders of this period killed many elite Khmers, including some decent people like Mr. Chan Sau of the National Bank, Assistant Professor Phuong Ton, and other intellectuals, victims of the rulers of the Khmer Republic. We did not feel sorry about the lives of those elite people who killed the people and worked the rice paddies on the backs of someone else. But we were sorry about those who wanted to help the country without socialism, and who were patriots hostile to the former corrupt regime.

Another example of Machiavellian trickery and hypocrisy was that the Khmer Rouge told the widows of military people that they were sorry for them. They freed them from the feudal regime and gave them everything they didn't have before. All that was only a lie, the reality being quite different. In documents that they made their soldiers study and that I had a chance to see with my own eyes, they said that the widows were quite disaffected with the Khmer Rouge, that they wanted their husbands back if they were taken prisoner, and that they told their children not to forget their fathers and to avenge them. So we all, the Khmer Rouge, had to strengthen our attention and vigilance about the widows.

At certain times, they did not use trickery and hypocrisy. They used direct threats, arrest, and even death following fascist trial procedures like those of the great murderer of the Second World War, Germany's chief of state, Hitler. But what is more striking still is that the Pol Pot–Ieng Sary clique was even more fascist than Hitler.

The aim of Pol Pot and Ieng Sary was to kill millions of people of the same race and same blood as themselves.

Divide and Conquer

The European colonialists who carried out territorial expansion in Asia used a theory of divide and conquer. They favored a privileged few in each country, giving them broad powers. Once they were in power, they became faithful followers of the expansionists and followed policies that worked against the majority of the people. When we were divided, we were weak. Then it was easy to repress any nascent struggle movement.

The Khmer Rouge took the example of this division and applied it to the Kampuchean population. They gave more rights to the people of before April 17, 1975, than to those of after April 17, 1975, more rights to poor farmers than to middle and upper class farmers. They made lower class peasants into administrators, and these latter were faithful to the Khmer Rouge and carried out repression against all the social classes of the population. Finally after having purged Kampuchean society, keeping only lower class peasants, they brought in a new major division.

That was to make the people of the southwest military region rivals of the people of the east and to have the soldiers of the southwest kill those of the east and of the rest of Kampuchea, letting only the Khmer Rouge of the southwest live, because the native village of Pol Pot is in the southwest.

2.6.21
Prisoner of the Khmer Rouge for Three Years (April 15, 1975 to January 9, 1979) by Denise Alfonso

Biography:

Before beginning my story, let me draw a short sketch of my life. My name is Denise Alfonso. I was born November 22, 1944, in Phnom Penh (Kampuchea). I am Eurasian. My father, Maurice Alfonso (deceased), a Frenchman from Pondicherry[1] who came to Kampuchea about 1930, was a teacher at the Sisowath Lycée in Phnom Penh. My mother, Truong Thi Le, is Vietnamese, from Saigon.

Born in Phnom Penh, I did all my education there: primary education at the Norodom school, and secondary at the Lycée Descartes. When my studies ended in 1964, I married a Chinese from Kampot, half Vietnamese, named Phou Teang Seng. We had two children: a boy Jean Jacques Phou Mino born August 25, 1964, and a girl, Jeannie Phou Dong born May 30, 1967 (deceased). Both of them hold French nationality and were educated at the Little Lycée Descartes in Phnom Penh. After getting married, I began to work.

- From 1964 to 1966, I was a French-English typist at the Consulate of the Republic of South Korea.
- From 1967 to 1969, I was a nurse-trainee at the Calmette Hospital but could not complete the training period because for extended periods (about two months) I was assigned to the pharmacy to look after its stock of medicines.
- From 1970 to 1973, I left Calmette Hospital to take a job as a secretary in the bilingual French-English management board at Sokilait, the condensed milk factory.
- From 1974 to 1975, I left Sokilait to work as a secretary at the Cultural Service of the French Embassy in Phnom Penh, a position that offered me social advantages. I stayed in this job until the arrival of the Khmer Rouge.

As for my husband, from 1965 to 1968, he was manager of the Pochentong Royal Inns, under Mr. Ang Kim Khoan, deputy secretary of state for Tourism. From 1969 to 1975, he became a contractor and earned a good living.

* * *

Over the last nine years (1970–1979), the political situation in Kampuchea has changed more than once. In 1970, Lon Nol overthrew Samdech Sihanouk's regime and set up the Khmer Republic that he governed for five years (March 18, 1970, to April 17, 1975). As soon as Lon Nol seized power,

1. A town in India. —Eds.

he launched an operation to repatriate Vietnamese residents from Kampuchea to South Vietnam by boat. Very few of the Vietnamese however were able to return to their Motherland, for a great number had been killed by Lon Nol's soldiers. These killings were similar to those perpetrated later by the Khmer Rouge, except that the Khmer Rouge killed people of any race: Khmers, Krom Khmers,[2] or Chinese.

In early 1975, the Lon Nol government began to crumble. Rockets rained down on the city from morning till night, sowing panic in the population. The shells hit schools, hospitals, cinemas, and marketplaces, killing people like flies.

The rich hastened to gather up gold and foreign currencies and send their families abroad. An exit visa cost about 700,000 riels (about 700 new francs). Even reserving a seat on a plane required an extra payment, since everybody wanted to leave.

The French Embassy repatriated French residing in Kampuchea (specialists, teachers, physicians, etc). On March 15, 1975, the first batch embarked on the Transal, coming from Bangkok. On March 15, 1975 a second batch departed. Then shortly before April 15, 1975, a third batch. Before leaving, the chargé d'affaires, Mr. Pavec, and the cultural officer, Mr. Prunières, advised me to leave Kampuchea as soon as I could. But I did not listen to them because my husband, whose ideas were redder than the Rouges' themselves, remained sanguine. "Don't worry," he said, "once the Rouges are in Phnom Penh, if Lon Nol's troops hoist the white flag, there will be no street fighting and everything will go as smoothly as roller skates." How sorry I am to have listened to my husband, who did not want to let me leave. Today I am still angry at him; because of him I risked my life in all this business.

I carried on my job in the Cultural Service until Saturday, April 15, 1975, the eve of the Chaul Chhnam (Khmer New Year). When I went home, I learned that the American Embassy was also repatriating its staff by helicopter. Obviously things were getting worse. On Sunday, April 16, 1975, as we were still celebrating the Chaul Chhnam with a group of Khmer friends, that morning, the general staff was bombarded, and there was panic and a round-the-clock curfew. On Monday, April 17, 1975, I tried to get to the Embassy to see how things stood. But as soon as I got into the car I heard firing from all directions. It was the Khmer Rouge who were marching into the city and were firing salvoes to announce their arrival. My stupid husband was the first to go out to welcome and cheer them in the street. Everybody was wild with joy, and shouted: Long live the liberation soldiers! I will never forget this word "liberation," for after they freed us from the yoke of Lon Nol, they threw us into prison again and subjected us for three years to an even more atrocious slavery.

2. Khmers inhabiting several Vietnamese provinces claimed as Kampuchean territory on the basis of Kampuchea's precolonial control of them. — Eds.

A few hours after their arrival, the soldiers went from house to house to ask the Phnom Penh populace to evacuate the city. Angkar (the government) asked us to leave our "homes" for a few days, only for the time needed to establish a bit of order in the city. I tried several times to get to the French Embassy but it was impossible. Highways leading north were all blocked, no one was allowed to go north. The people had to evacuate the city to the South. I had to do as other people. We (that is my husband, my two children, myself, my sister-in-law and her four children — three girls and a boy) packed up our things, piled up clothes and the whole stock of foodstuff (rice, fish sauce, dried fish, milk, sardines, coffee, tea, sugar, etc.) in the car and left the house on April 18, 1975, heading south. But scarcely had we started down the street than I was overtaken by fear at what I saw, and I cried like a baby. Effectively all the houses were deserted, and the drug stores, groceries, secondhand shops, and the orange squash factory (FUP) had been looted. These premises had been locked up by their owners when they left. The soldiers were the first to force the doors open and grab whatever they wanted, and anyone who came later on could help themselves. All the streets were blocked; people labored along them in the heat, bent under the weight of their heavy luggage.

Have you ever heard of such a thing as emptying a city of two to three million people in a matter of days on the pretext of setting it in order? Strange as it might seem, this nevertheless was taking place. Those people who were used to being evacuated from place to place took with them as much rice as they could and foodstuffs, but the wealthy of Phnom Penh instead took radio and TV sets, records, tapes, gold, and money (money that later would cause many a suicide as nobody knew that Lon Nol's money was no longer in circulation in the liberated zones).

Because of the traffic, we could not go forward or backward, so we had to wait. Just then two soldiers in green uniforms carrying bags containing medicines and other items they had taken from a secondhand shop stopped our car and asked for a lift. My husband, who was not at all ungrateful to his liberators, gladly agreed. "How far are you going?" he asked them. "About 40 kilometers south from here," they answered. On learning that we were running out of petrol, they went themselves to fetch some. When the tank was full, they cleared the road, so we could go through the traffic without getting blocked. As we went past Chamkar Mon (State Residence), I felt a strong smell of rot; it was not astounding; dozens of dead bodies, all swollen and rotten, lay scattered about the garden ground.

We continued our trip. Wherever we hit traffic jams, our two passengers cleared the way for us. When we got to Takhmau, about 10 kilometers from Phnom Penh, there was a roadblock and a search, and our identity documents were confiscated. One astounding fact should be mentioned here. The streets of Takhmau were littered with bank notes of all denominations (1, 5, 10, 20, 50, 100, 500 riels), making a thick carpet. Asked about the reasons for this phenomenon, which was something I had never before seen, the soldiers answered that from April 17, 1975, the currency of "A. Nol" (Lon Nol) was no longer in circulation anywhere on Khmer territory. It was incredible. We still had 500,000 riels that my husband had kept, in the hope that the situation might change.

One other strange occurrence should be mentioned. A few days after we arrived at the first place we stayed, we found out that at Kien Svay (located in the Kandal province) money was still in circulation and one could still buy vegetables and some foodstuffs. Out of curiosity, my husband went there with a friend, taking 100,000 riels. He came back with 200 grams of soy sauce that he got for 50,000 riels, one kilogram of cucumbers for 20,000 riels, and 300 grams of pork for 30,000 riels. At first I thought it was simply a joke, but it was real.

Once the search was finished, we set out again, but the journey got harder with the overwhelming heat, and with roads and bridges out. At these spots, we had to get out of the car and push it. The children got tired and cried. I was so discouraged that I too was in tears.

At Svay Rolum, 25 kilometers from Phnom Penh, the two soldiers invited us to eat with them (rice and dried fish mixed with green mangoes dipped in fish sauce), and to share a bottle of alcohol to wash the meal down. After the meal, they thanked us and before taking leave advised us to continue southward, where Angkar (the government) would welcome us. At first, as I did not understand exactly what the word "Angkar" meant, I wondered: "Who is Angkar?," "Where does he live?," "How are we to find him?"

We drove on, but now the journey was even harder, because we had to tow the car of a friend of ours we had met in Svay Rolum who was having engine trouble. At about 3:00 p.m., we got to Prey Tauch, where a whole group of soldiers (this time in black uniforms) searched us again. They confiscated anything written in a foreign language, and any schoolbooks, magazines, identity cards, birth certificates, radios, tape cassettes, and wristwatches. I showed them my passport and tried to make them understand I am of French nationality. But to no avail; they confiscated my passport and in answer to our questions said that there were no longer French, Chinese, or Vietnamese, that now everything was Khmer.

When the search was finished, they told us to continue our way to the south where Angkar was waiting for us. At 5:00 p.m., we got to the Prey Tauch pagoda, where we were given a meal (rice mixed with yellow ground corn, plus a beef and green papaya soup).

There were hundreds of refugees, and we had to wait over an hour to get our shares. After the meal, we resumed our trip. Around 6:00 p.m., we stopped at a small village to spend the night. The village chief, a Khmer who had been living in the liberated zone since 1972, greeted us nicely and offered us food and drink. The next day we set out again. The village chief gave us some ripe fruit (several bunches of bananas and three ripe papayas) and advised us, "Go a bit farther, Angkar is waiting for you and will welcome you." With the friend's car still in tow, we left. At 11:00 a.m., we arrived at Tukvil (48 kilometers from Phnom Penh) where we spent the rest of the day and the night in the pagoda (called Tukvil pagoda). Facing the pagoda was an island called Koh Tukvil.

In the morning of the next day, as we were getting ready to leave, the chief of the village on the island, a Mr. Thien, came to greet us, accompanied by three body guards. Mr. Thien too had been living in the zone liberated by the Khmer Rouge since 1970. Koh Tukvil was to be our first stop. First we had to leave the car at the pagoda; canoes would ferry us across the river with our luggage. But before we got on, they wanted to search our belongings as a precaution. Of course, they took whatever they wanted: eau de cologne, perfumes (which they used as an ear lotion), toilet soap, dolls, jewels, medicines, syringes, thermometers. My son's school books escaped notice. The search done, they helped us load our luggage into the canoes. After we got to Tukvil Island village, Mr. Thien put us up in a straw house on stilts near his own.

A few days after our arrival, the "Anniversary of the Founding of the Red Liberation Army" was celebrated. Each village was ordered to slaughter a cow for a three-day feast. On the first day, after he killed a cow, Mr. Thien offered us two kilograms of meat. In the evening, he invited us to the pagoda where a dinner was served (rice mixed up with ground corn, and beef soup). After dinner the village chief made a short speech. Then the children began to sing and dance (everybody, including the children, were in black clothes). Then they performed plays until dawn. We were shown new paper money displayed on a board (bills of 5 cents, and 1, 5, 10, 20, 50, and 100 riels). But never did I see any of these bills in circulation during the whole period of my imprisonment.

After the festivities, a meeting was held of the entire village. At this meeting, we were asked not to think about Phnom Penh anymore, because we could never return there. Angkar[3] had turned the city into a warehouse. On the first day of our arrival, everything seemed fine; we were free to do as we pleased.

But gradually, Angkar's face would appear in its true color. In fact, soon came a host of prohibitions:

- Speak no language other than Khmer: if you do not speak it fluently, you should learn it.
- Girls and young women were not allowed to keep long hair. Hair should be cut quite short (in the bob style of little Chinese girls of Peking). In the village there was a woman hairdresser for everyone. She offered service to men,

3. Only when we got to the island did I figure out just what Angkar was. Angkar means the government. Anyone empowered to direct a village or a work team can always speak in the name of Angkar. Angkar is everywhere. (Note in original.)

women and children free of charge and never asked for anything, but if you were kind you would give her something like dried fish or used clothing.

• All clothing should be black. If you did not have black clothing, you had to dye your clothing black. There was a kind of green fruit called "makhloeur" for the purpose.

• At dusk go to bed and do not speak too much (spies made rounds and eavesdropped under the houses).

Tukvil village received five or ten families of refugees every day. Each village was ordered to take 100 to 150 families, depending on its situation. I noticed that Mr. Thien, my village chief, only chose families he believed to be well off.

In Tukvil village, the main crop was corn, but the island was small, and land for cultivation was scarce. So the village set up 2 and 3 hectare fields to the west. The second major crop on the island was tobacco, a commodity in keen demand. During the dry season, people from the west rich in palm sugar came to exchange their palm sugar for tobacco; trade was always carried on by the barter method.

To earn one's daily rice ration, one had to work hard. I took part in every kind of work: clearing rice paddies, transplanting rice plants, harvesting, weeding corn fields, planting corn, etc. This is how corn was planted. First the field was well plowed and furrowed. Then each of us, the women, with a handful of seeds wrapped up in a kerchief, walked between the furrows and dropped four or five seeds, no more, at regular intervals, meaning every meter, and covered them with earth. The work was simple enough but on the first day I found it hard to walk between the furrows because I was not yet used to walking barefoot. The older women laughed at me as they watched me doing so badly. When all the fields on the island were planted, we had to go to the fields in the West. Since these fields were rather far away, we had to set out at dawn, taking our lunch with us. We usually put rice in small baskets made of palm leaves (called smocks). Those smocks were handy and very commonly used by the people of the South. The work day ended at 5:00 p.m.

The laborers were divided into categories according to their strength, and rice was distributed according to these categories.

First category: men, young men (*Yuvachuon*), and girls (*Yuvaneary*) received 500 grams of rice per day and per person.

Second category: married women in good health, 400 grams per day and per person.

Third category: children, elderly, the sick, 300 grams per day and per person.

For these savages, only people enjoying a good health and able to work were to be properly fed. The elderly, children, and the sick were more or less abandoned. When a man or a youth was addressed, if he was not called by his name he was called *Mith* (which means comrade), and for married women *Mith Neary*, and for girls *Neary*.

Each group was under a chief or chairperson responsible for everything. If someone fell ill and could not go to work, the chief had to be informed.

As for my husband, he had to go to reclaim flooded forest land in the west. He would leave the house at dawn taking his lunch in a smock and would come back home only at dusk. Had he been less talkative, he would not have been sent to the reeducation camp, poor husband. Alas! He had a blind trust in those cursed Rouges.

Mr. Thien formed a friendship with my husband. Every evening, he came over and they chatted. My husband told him all about his life from A to Z. Mr. Thien was always kindly. Whenever we ran short of rice, for instance at the end of a rice distribution round, he would send us one or two extra kilograms. When he fell ill, my husband got him medicines (at the time, we still had a stock of drugs to last us for about three months).

My husband's second blunder was to ask that one of his friends who had just arrived be admitted to the island. (A month after our arrival, refugees were still flowing in.) That fellow was the owner of our house in Phnom Penh. He was boastful and spoke too often in French or English. Two months after he came (July 1975), he was the first to be "admitted" to a reeducation camp. One evening after dinner, they took him away, telling him that Angkar needed his services. Two weeks later (July 15, 1975) it was the turn of 20 other people, including my husband, of course. They left after lunch. I was not there when they left, because that day I went to the West to harvest corn. When I got back home that evening, Mr. Thien told me: "Don't worry, he'll be back in two days. Angkar simply needed some information because your husband's friend denounced him." Days, months and years have passed, but up till now I have not seen my husband again. Those who were taken away with him have not come back either.

In June 1975, Angkar had a kind of "brainwashing" course given to the refugees. They got us together in a pagoda five kilometers to the west. We left at dawn taking our lunch with us. First of all we were requested to fill out information sheets, a kind of curriculum vitae, and we were asked to tell only the truth. It was made to appear that Angkar was recruiting personnel for factories in Phnom Penh (factories turning out dry cells, fishing nets, condensed milk, etc.). Then the Kanak of the Damban (chief of the locality or district) began a lecture that lasted from 9:00 a.m. to 5:00 p.m. with half-an-hour pause at noontime for lunch. I cannot remember in detail what he told us, but I found his talk interesting on certain points. After recounting the history of Kampuchea from the time of Samdech Sihanouk until the triumph of the Khmer Rouge, he said: "Dear brothers, do not forget that you are regarded as war prisoners. Before the entry of the Khmer Rouge to Phnom Penh, you had been asked to leave the city. Why didn't you leave?" His words made me shudder. In fact, during the years that followed, we were treated as prisoners.

According to this Kanak Damban, Angkar no longer needed aid from anyone. We were to learn to produce everything by ourselves. For instance, from now on for a train run by diesel fuel there would be no need to purchase this fuel abroad, because firewood would be used instead. I thought to myself, "If this is the situation, this is some kind of idiot, and Kampuchea was moving backward." The sick will be cared for using herbs; there will be no occidental medicines. As regards money, he said that new bank notes had already been issued and would soon be put in circulation. He gave us an idea of the value of the new money. One kilogram of rice would cost around 3 riels; one kilogram of salt, 5 cents. As I was leaving the lecture, I began musing about the possibility of returning to Phnom Penh as a worker (Kamakar)[4] at the condensed milk factory (Sokilait). But my dream would not be realized.

Another annoying thing was the violation of private residences. Angkar had the right to search your house at any time, even in your absence. That is what happened to me two weeks after my husband left. That day, my sister-in-law and I had to leave the house at 3:00 a.m. to transplant rice in a two-hectare paddy. This rice paddy was of great importance to the village because it was on land that was not flooded, but it was rather far from the village (around 7 kilometers to the west).

When I got back in the evening, the children told us that two informers had come, along with the village chief, and searched our house. It was the second search they had carried out since my husband left for the reeducation camp. The first time, they had not been able to search everything because I had been there and had managed to hide some items. But this time, everything was carefully inspected and confiscated: my little address book, my checkbook, my consular card, two syringes with needles, a thermometer, some little bottles of Becozyme and vitamin B12, a bottle of eau de cologne, two cakes of toilet soap, a laundry iron, a portable radio set, and all the books that I still had. On counting up the things they took, I cried in despair, I was the most sorry about the little address book.

A few words about the informers. They were a kind of spy who when night came would go around the houses to eavesdrop. Be careful if you did not speak Khmer! In daytime you ran the risk of coming into contact and talking with these "dirty scorpions" without realizing it. Everything you might say to them would immediately be reported.

That was what happened to my husband. A lad of the village (he was perhaps 25 years old), a little hunchbacked dwarf, made acquaintance with my husband. They became friends and spent a lot of time together. Finding him sympathetic, my husband told him all about his good old days; he told him that his ideas were always red (as a matter of fact, they were redder than the Rouges). Soon after those confidences, my husband was on the list of people to be "admitted" to a reeducation camp. One day he confided to the

4. The feminine form is Kama Karini. —Eds.

dwarf that he often listened to Radio Peking and asked for permission to listen to that evening's broadcast. The permission was granted by Mr. Thien. For two evenings he was able to listen. On the third day, Mr. Thien came and asked him to tune into the domestic station because his own radio was not working. On the fourth day, he came and borrowed our radio, and I never saw it again.

The next evening, toward midnight, two fellows from the west came to Mr. Thien's house. As I was still awake, I could hear what was said: listening to Radio Peking was to be strictly prohibited; all portable radios were to be confiscated; all Vietnamese were to be repatriated. So that was the reason for the confiscation. No one except the village chief ever saw those fellows' faces, because they only met at night, between midnight and 2:00 a.m.

In late August there were rumors of Angkar authorizing people to return to Phnom Penh. And as if to confirm those rumors, boats were seen sailing down the Tonle Sap and sailing up it again loaded with refugees. Nobody knew for certain where they were to be landed. Some people said they were going to Phnom Penh, others said they were going to Kompong Chhnang. Then notices were distributed in all the villages announcing that Angkar was resettling the population in the following provinces: Kompong Cham, Kompong Chhnang, Kompong Thom, Svay Rieng, and Prey Veng. Natives of those provinces were requested to leave. This news brought great joy. Everyone wanted to leave right away, especially the Phnom Penh residents, most of whom still hoped to return to Phnom Penh. But alas, we were all fooled by Angkar. No one could go back to their native place. The boats kept sailing up and down. Rumor had it that people would not be allowed to take too much luggage with them. (This was a trick played on us by the Moulathans,[5] so that we would leave behind some of our belongings.)

On September 15, 1975, there appeared a list of names of families from Phnom Penh. We were to leave the island that very day. I was not at all anxious to leave, because the night before the village chief's mother asked me not to leave. "It's not to Phnom Penh that you are to go," she said, "you will be taken to mountain areas, I don't know exactly where. Phnom Penh is reserved for the soldiers' families. Ask my son for permission to stay here with us. I love you like my own daughter, and we need people like you who are so willing to work."

I asked her to speak to her son on our behalf, but it was hopeless because we had no Moulathan families (residents of the island) as friends who could be our guarantors. Besides our names were already on the list, so there was nothing to be done. I therefore resigned myself and got ready to leave; I got rid of most of my belongings (clothing, pans, pots, folding chairs, a bicycle, etc.). Around 2:00 p.m., the canoes took us to the pagoda opposite the island; it was full of people.

5. Inhabitants of the so-called liberated (before 1973) zones. —Eds.

That evening, the village chief came and distributed rice. We had to spend the night in the pagoda but no one could sleep. Everyone was happy, joyful, because we were almost sure we were to return to Phnom Penh.

The next day, September 16, 1975, military trucks stood waiting in a line. The Pol Pot agents made note of the names and number of persons in each family and then searched the luggage. Bags were emptied of their contents. And this time we lost another part of our belongings. They confiscated a large family photo album that I loved dearly. They said, "No souvenirs. Everything connected to the old regime should be wiped out. Lon Nol's was a regime of rotten, corrupt people." By insisting, I was able to get back my father's photo, which I valued most among the things confiscated. The 500,000 riels we still had were scattered in little pieces on the roadway. "Why keep all this rotten money?" they said.

The search over, the soldiers loaded us up. We were packed in like beasts of burden. Around 9:00 a.m., we started off. An hour later, we got to Takhmau. Joy showed on everyone's face, but it did not last long, because the trucks made a long detour in the direction of Kompong Kantuot (about 20 kilometers from Phnom Penh) to go into Phnom Penh on the Pochentong road. This was a new gleam of hope, but then the trucks continued on without stopping. We crossed Phnom Penh on Monivong Boulevard, which was quite deserted, not even a cat in the street, then through Russey Keo and we headed north. Bitter disappointment. Nobody knew the exact destination. In answer to our questions, the soldiers simply said, "We haven't arrived yet." So we kept going without a break. The children cried because they were hungry. A sick old woman could not help relieving herself right in the truck, and we had to stand the smell. The driver did not stop until one passenger was about to faint because he needed to urinate.

The main province towns we went through were also deserted; not a living soul was to be seen. At midnight, we reached our first destination, Pursat. As soon as we got off the trucks we received a ration of rice and salt (two tins per person). I looked for a good place to spend the night; makeshift shelters of wood and corrugated iron had been set up for us. We spent three days at Pursat, waiting for the train which was to take us to our second destination. During these three days, we were given rice and medicines.

On September 15, 1975, the train came at 5:00 p.m. We were asked to load on our luggage, but the train did not leave until September 20, at 6:00 a.m. The trip took one day. We went through Battambang, Svay Chot Samrong, and Mongkol Borey, and at 4:00 p.m. we arrived at our second destination, Svay Sisophon. Svay Sisophon was also filled with people, but some organization was already on foot. Krums (groups) of ten families were formed each led by a krum chief chosen among the members of the families involved. A slip listing the names and number of persons in each family was handed to the people in charge, who noted down the information and gave a number to each krum. Ours got number 62. Once these formalities were completed, we were allowed to enter the town, where housing had been found for us to spend the night. On the basis of this slip, the krum chief went to fetch rice and salt, which he then divided among the ten families. On September 22, 1975, tractors took us to our third destination. The krums were loaded onto the tractors by number: three krums (that is, 30 families) per tractor.

At last we reached the foot of a mountain range located in Battambang province (this range is made up of three mountains: Phnom Leap, Phnom Trayon, and Phnom Tralach). We were dropped off at the Phnom Leap hospital, and from there ox carts took us to a pagoda located three kilometers from Phnom Leap.

There the chiefs of the three villages around Phnom Tralach were waiting for us. They were: Ta Chen ("Ta" means elderly uncle, or more exactly old uncle; the titles Mr. and Mrs. were no longer used), Ta Svay, and Ta Kroch. Again, I had bad luck and landed on a bad number, because I was chosen by Ta Chen, whose village was the poorest of the three and whose residents were greedy and ate a lot.

The krums were thus divided up by the three village chiefs. Each took fifteen families for his village, and ox carts carried our luggage to our destination.

The village of Ta Chen got five krums. Each krum had a chief. I was made a member of Krum No. 2, whose chief was Pouk San ("Pouk" means father or dad. As was the custom in those regions, men were called "Pouk," and women were called "Meir," which means mum or mother). The village people immediately made a clear distinction between the refugees and themselves. We as refugees made up a colony of the "new people."

They called us "the new people." To their way of thinking, they were the "old people." We had no "private homes." Each family of "old people" shared its thatched hut with one, two, or three deportee families, depending on the size of the hut. I lived with a young woman who had two children. She was rather nice yet greedy and inclined to take food for herself. Her husband was never in the village; he was working for Angkar in a company called Chuo and came home only once or twice a year.

Soon after our arrival, these were the prohibitions in force:

1. Speak Khmer only.
2. Do not talk in the evening, because informers would go on round and listen at the doors.
3. Do not eat more than two meals a day.
4. Do not cook rice, but eat only rice soup, rice being scarce in the locality.

In late 1978, the Pol Pot people started a series of executions which spread panic among the people. In fact, in August, September, and October, 1978, when starvation was high, people, old or young, stole whatever they could lay hands on (cassava, vegetables, sugar cane, etc.), but if they were caught they could say their prayers and commend their souls to God. If they were caught it was the "forest of the West" for them.

One day a young fellow named Touch was arrested for digging up a few cassava roots. On learning this, Ta Ling simply said: "Take him to the western forest" (where a special spot had been cleared for such jobs). The condemned man was accompanied by three executioners: Ta Sok, who was in charge of manure collection, a bloodthirsty fellow coming from Kambaul; Ta Doeung, also bloodthirsty and also from Kambaul; and Ta Chea, a "new person" like us from Phnom Penh but who had turned proud and arrogant when he became Ta Ling's aide.

Gradually there were no more men to be seen, as a result of deaths from disease or execution. Those who remained and could read and write became a rare commodity. Out of curiosity, I followed the men at a distance without letting them see me. When I got to the spot, I hid in a thicket from which I could watch the "ceremony" without being seen. But I was so horrified by what I saw that I nearly fainted. The condemned man was tied to a tree, his chest bare and a blindfold over his eyes. Ta Sok, the executioner, using a large knife, made a long cut in the stomach of the poor man.

In pain, the man screamed like a wild beast. Even today his cries still ring in my ears. Blood rushed out everywhere, his insides were all laid bare, and Ta Sok cut out the liver and cooked it on a little stove that Ta Chea had just heated up. A strange fact to mention is that the human liver, cooking on the stove, made little jerks like frying pancakes. They divided up the liver among them and ate it hungrily. After they buried the body, they left looking satisfied. I did not dare leave my hiding place until they had gone far away, because if they found out that I knew about their bloody deeds, it would be all over for me. That night I could not sleep, because I was haunted by the horrors of the day.

It was not only thieves were put to death. Former Lon Nol military personnel, Krom Khmers, half-bred Chinese, half-bred Vietnamese, and Vietnamese were executed as well. Angkar, they said, was sorting the good seeds from the bad. One evening at about 9:00 p.m., Ta Ling, accompanied by Ta Sok and Ta Deoung, took seven young men away. All of them were former Lon Nol soldiers, and one was Van, Ta Chea's son-in-law. They were seen making their way to the "forest of the West." The next day, Ta Ling was seen with Ta Chea's son-in-law's silk kerchief around his head. No commentary is needed. No one ever saw the seven young men again.

There were other executions that were more gruesome. What I am going to tell you now is quite true. In October 1978, I was taken seriously ill, and I was sent to the Phnom Leap hospital for a week (although there were no medicines there for treatment). One night at the hospital no one could sleep, because we anticipated the arrival of the customary truck. At about 9:00 p.m. the truck stopped near the hospital at the foot of Phnom Trayono.

Men's voices were heard shouting orders, and then there was total silence. Then there were cries of pain that were quickly stifled: "Ay," "Oy," and then silence again. An hour later, the truck drove off. Now stifled groans were audible. They were uttered by people who simply had fainted and had been buried alive. The next day, out of curiosity, I went out to that spot. I was petrified by what I saw. There were huge trenches that could hold forty to fifty bodies; some of them had not been well covered with dirt in the darkness, and arms and legs were sticking up.

The next night shortly before the truck arrived, I went out and hid near the trenches behind a thick cluster of bamboos to be able to watch. At 9 o'clock, a military truck crammed with people pulled in near the trenches. One, two, then a third guy got out and ordered everyone to get out one by one and to walk single file behind the driver to a freshly dug trench. There were forty (I counted them), men, women, and children of all ages. The two other guys brought up the rear, carrying axes and pick-axes. When they got to the edge of the trench, the driver pushed the victims up two by two. The other two guys stood, each with a condemned person in front of him, and with a stroke of the axe and pickaxe, knocked the person down and kicked the body into the trench.

Other victims, seeing what was happening, tried to run away but were quickly caught. Once the whole group was in the trench, the three guys covered it with dirt and left. When they were gone, I slipped out of my hiding place and hurried away, because the place, now deserted, was frightening.

My god! Why were there still such atrocities in this world? What sins have they committed, those poor humans, to be punished so cruelly today? A month later, a bulldozer came and levelled the place, and the chief of a village that was nearby received orders to have it planted in cassava. Until I die, I shall never forget those horrors, for only wild beasts like the gang of Pol Pot and Ieng Sary (the Khmer Rouge leaders) are capable of such.

In the society built up by Pol Pot and Ieng Sary, there was no prostitution (a good mark to their credit). A man had no right to take two wives. If a married man or married woman had a lover, the couple at fault would be killed. But strangely enough, Nearadays, even if they were married, could make love to pretty girls. A pretty girl who pleased them might be asked, and if she refused, that meant she was looking down upon a Nearaday and thereby was courting death.

At Phnom Srok there was a case that is absolutely unbelievable, yet true. The village chief had noticed a young woman and wanted to sleep with her. She was married with two children, but the children had died of disease and her husband had been done in by Angkar in 1976. The young woman lived now with her sister and her elderly mother. She refused the village chief. He swallowed the refusal, but a few days later, two aides of his came to fetch the young woman at her house, telling her that Angkar had sent for her. They took her to a deserted place where she was undressed and tied by her arms and legs between two trees. She screamed in shame and cried out for help. And who would hear her, but her mother, worried that the men had come for her daughter, followed at a distance. Now hidden in a thicket she saw all that was happening. She wept in anguish, but what could she do? If she dared show herself, she would be executed, so she stayed hidden.

The two executioners then took a sharp palm branch and thrust it into the young woman's uterus. She fainted from the pain, and blood flowed out like water. The two executioners went away, leaving their victim like this. After they left, the mother, crying like a mad woman, went and untied her daughter, who died a few minutes later. In grief, the mother went mad and has remained so ever since. That is what manners and customs were like in the society of Pol Pot and Ieng Sary.

I was in Team No. 3. Out of 150 persons in the team, only 30 were physically able to go to the fields. Our team was assigned to uproot rice plants. The two other teams were in charge of transplanting.

In August-September I still had enough strength to work, but my health was failing rapidly, for, as I had said above, we were getting less and less rice in our soup. It was the season of cassava harvesting. Soup was cooked with cassava to make it look thicker. Only the workers were entitled to a bowl of pretty creamy soup while the elderly, children, and the sick got only a bowl of whitish liquid in which perhaps two pieces of cassava as big as your thumb were swimming.

Only those who held an important position stayed in good health and kept up their strength, for example, the village chief Ta Ling and his family (his wife was as big as a sow); the team's chairperson and vice-chairperson, who always got a double ration of thick soup; the women who did the cooking, who could eat their fill of thick soup, sometimes even of rice with the permission of the village chief who himself had rice; the fishermen, who caught fish for the whole village; the makers of palm sugar, including those who climbed trees to get the juice; and last but not least the paddy husking workers who could steal rice to add to their ration.

As for the rest of us, we grew weaker day by day. But what irritated us most of all, was the remark by the leaders of Team No. 1, Ta Vong and Ta Chea: "Your team is lazy. Why can't you work like us? We eat the same ration as yours. You get one bowl, we get one bowl." Ah, these nasty fellows, excuse the term, but even today thinking about it makes me angry. Ta Vong's wife was a cook; she kept the best pieces and ate her fill. Ta Chea's wife was a paddy husking worker, a situation that allowed the taking of rice. The husbands themselves were team leaders. Where then was the equality they talked about? In addition, Ta Ling gave them practically full authority. They took advantage of it by giving themselves and their friends all the good jobs.

To earn a bowl of rice that was a bit thicker, my son had to work every day as hard as an adult. He had to carry on a shoulder pole big bundles of seedlings from the field where they were uprooted down to the field where two other teams would transplant them (a distance of about one kilometer). It was hard work for a boy his age, because the load was heavy and he had to make about twenty trips a day. The meal we had at 10:00 a.m. in the rice paddies was very simple, a bowl of "rain" along with a ladle of bindweed soup. To fill up our stomachs, mine and my son's, every day I cooked a big pan of cassava leaves that we ate with salted water and something tart. For the tart taste I used tamarinds, but when they were not available I used a wild plant that grew in the forest. When boiled, this plant became creamy and tart, but it didn't taste very good. Our menu never changed; it was the same every day.

Cassava: cassava roots remain an unforgettable memory for me. For about a month, cassava was our staple food instead of rice. There were several large cassava fields: one in Phnom Tralach (called Field no. 500). This field could feed the whole population of "Sahakar" for two weeks and another field of the same size at Kokey. But the most important field was Koh Tral (a ten-minute walk from the village) which could feed the inhabitants of Sahakar Lite for a month. After the cassava roots were dug up, they were taken to the Sahakar store, where Mrs. Khom, the wife of the chairman of Sahakar, was in charge of the daily food distribution to each village.

When cassava digging started at Koh Tral, I would go there almost every day during my free time to pick up cassava roots that were broken, or that had been left in the ground. I had to dig deep in the ground with a pickaxe to get four or five kilograms of cassava a day. Sometimes I would go straight to Ta Khoum, the chief of Koh Tral, and he would see that I was given several large roots, around two kilograms, enough for one day. Other times, I would go pick up the "heads" of roots attached to the leaves of the cassava plant. Those little cassava tips were delicious. I peeled and washed them and then ground them up and cooked them with a little water. You got a thick white cream that I could mix with two ladles of rice water.

When there was no rice at all, we were given boiled cassava, 200 grams per person per meal, which was not enough even for a two- or three-year-old child. So everyone would go out each day to pick up forgotten roots or root "heads" to fill the empty space in their stomachs. Hunger tortured us day and night. I had never suffered so much in my life. I was so hungry that at one point I even ate cowhide. One day I was almost bitten by a dog when I tried to take a piece of cowhide it was eating. That day, at Koh Tral, a cow had been slaughtered. I got there too late, and it was all gone. Out behind the kitchen, I saw Ta Khoum's two dogs chewing cowhide. Using a stick I tried to take away the cowhide, but the dogs were hungry too. One of them jumped at my face and scratched my cheek. Oh my, that was a narrow escape. I took off without asking for anything more. Ta Khoum's wife, who saw what happened from a distance, called me back and gave me a slice of beef (around half a kilogram). I warmly thanked her and hurried home.

One morning, most of the workers were mobilized to go dig cassava in a flooded section of the Koh Tral field. I was not on the list because I was too weak. They only took people who were strong and in good health. As Ta Chea was responsible for the choice of workers, his relatives and friends were first on the list. In despair, I mingled with the group that was going to do the digging. No one noticed me, but when we got to Koh Tral, Ta Doeung, leader of Team no. 3, was surprised to see me and asked who sent me. "Ta Ling," I answered. It was not true, but when you are hungry, you can do anything. He left me alone, and I helped with the digging without any problem.

All day long I ate raw cassava. It tasted good but was hard to digest. While working I crammed my pockets with cassava roots and stuck some around my waist (roots 15 to 20 centimeters long). Before we left for home, we were each given around two kilograms of cassava. This small stock lasted us for two days. The cassava diet continued until the end of October. Meanwhile I was taken ill again and this time my strength failed me for good. Day by day I grew weaker and my knees would not hold me up.

At that time, transplanting was over, and we had to plant cassava (individual and collective planting) while awaiting the next harvest. That year I managed to plant quite a bit around my house (about 70 holes). Cassava is easy to grow. The plant would be cut into little sticks about 20 centimeters long. Then you would dig holes 40 to 60 centimeters wide and 50 centimeters deep. When the hole was ready, you would lay two or three little cassava sticks in horizontally and cover them with dirt. You needed to water for the first two months, but then you didn't need to. I was also able to grow a few patches of lettuce, spinach, and sugar cane. Watering was the hardest, because I was not strong enough. But I had to try hard because if I did not grow anything, I would have nothing to eat. Moreover, the experience of the year 1978 had affected me deeply, and I was afraid it might be the same in 1979.

In November and December the first harvests began. Once again we had rice soup, but it was as before quite watery. That was why every other day, I went to the fields to pick shafts of paddy rice that I would peel and cook. Now we had rice but I had lost my appetite. In fact the pain in my chest got worse, and I grew thinner day by day. I turned into a skeleton. There was no medicine to help me. My son was away from the village. During the time of the famine, he had gone to O Leap to work as a cowherd. Sometimes he could steal paddy rice from the threshing barn, and that helped him keep up his strength. I remember something that makes me laugh now. At times my son and I argued over a handful of grilled paddy rice (grilled paddy is like popcorn). With the hunger, we behaved like children.

My strength was really failing me and I had to stop work. At first Ta Ling said I was lazy and came every day to get me out, but soon he saw that I was really sick. The weakness was due to sustained undernutrition, and to my second near drowning that I forgot to mention earlier. It was in late September. On my way back from work, as I crossed a bridge, I lost my balance and fell off the bridge. It was still the time of flooding, the water level was high, and the current was very swift.

As you already learned, I did not know how to swim at all, and I floundered about in the water. I was swept along by the strong and fast flowing current. I can't tell you how much water I swallowed and the torment I experienced for these few minutes that seemed like an eternity. Fortunately, the team leaders Ta Sok, Ta Chea, and Ta Touy were nearby. On seeing me this way, they did not hesitate but quickly swam in my direction. Before going under and losing consciousness, I said to myself, "This is it, Denise, your last minute has come." When I came to, I saw three heads bent over me. I was on the riverbank. Once I collected myself, I thanked them very much for saving my life.

There was another strange happening that bears mention. In 1977, no one was allowed to pick paddy shafts and cook rice individually. But in 1978, we were left free to pick rice shafts and peel them and cook the rice. The harvest women came back every day with five or six bunches of rice plants. Besides, their children went to pick rice shafts too. At 3:00 a.m. working pestles could already be heard. At 6:00 a.m., the pounding stopped because it was the time to go to work. Then from 9:00 p.m. to 2:00 a.m the next morning, pestles were active again. Ta Ling let us pound paddy as much as we wanted outside work hours.

What was happening at the top? Were they sorry for us because we had been hungry for so long? Or were they concerned about the political situation? Or had they received orders to turn us all into manure in their crematoria? Who could tell?

In January 1979, being sick and staying home all the time, I scarcely knew what was happening, or what the situation was. On January 7, 1979, I was bloated again. I had to go see Mrs. Khom, the wife of the chairman of Sahakar, to ask for some palm sugar. When I got there, I realized that things were bad. All the Nearadays of Sahakar, armed to the teeth, were in Ta Soy's house, and they were looking very concerned. Four or five women seamstresses were sewing backpacks as fast as they could, and also sacks in the shape of cowhides for rice carrying. Two days now, the rice mill had been husking about 40 sacks of paddy per day.

Toward evening, they piled up luggage, rice, salt, and dried fish on oxcarts. Their wives and children got on too, and they left Sahakar heading north without so much as saying farewell to us. How impolite! We were not surprised, because they had never shown politeness. In the evening after they left, everything was plundered by the inhabitants: sugar canes behind Ta Soy's house, the rice and salt stores, and all Sahakar's pigs and piglets as well as all the paddy rice in the threshing barn. No one could stop those plunderers, people who had been subjected to restrictions for such a long time.

I tried to figure out what was happening, and I learned that liberation troops had already reached Phnom Leap. The people were urged to evacuate and head east. Everybody packed their bags without needing much urging. The Nearadays' supporters who were still there tried to stop us. "Where are you going? Who is asking you to leave? Don't you know that you will die on the way? No rice, no medicines, no transportation. You'll starve, for sure, because Siem Reap is 60 kilometers from here." But nobody listened to them. People even said, "Oh! if we are to die, wouldn't it be better to go and die somewhere else and not leave our bones here in this accursed forest?"

Nearadays' supporters told me: "You, Alfonso, stay here, you will never reach your destination; it is certain you will starve on the way." At first, I was a bit worried because I had no strength left. I was quite thin, and my swelling was bad again (both my feet were swollen).

I waited three days before leaving the village. Meanwhile, at Loti, those who remained led a princely life. They caught and slaughtered all the oxen that were wandering about unattended. Twenty persons shared a cow. I ate beef so much during these three days that I had diarrhea. We dug cassavas in the village's collective field. We found plenty of rice and vegetables.

Travelling away from Loti was very difficult. With my luggage on my shoulders, I could not walk very far or very fast. I stopped every hundred paces and wept like a child. It took me two hours to walk from Loti to the blacktop road, a distance of only about two kilometers. I spent the night beside the road. The next day some generous souls took my luggage on an oxcart.

As a result I was able to get to Phnom Leap without being too exhausted. I must say that without my son I don't know what would have become of me. He carried two containers of rice. Once we got to Phnom Leap, what a great joy and relief I felt when I saw our liberation soldiers. This time I could speak of Liberation. If the liberation troops had been only a few days later in arriving, we would all have been turned into manure in the crematorium (the Pol Pot–Ieng Sary era was comparable to that of Hitler).

Everyone, Khmers and Chinese alike, trusted the liberation soldiers; no one was afraid of them. I stayed four nights at Phnom Leap. When I left Phnom Leap, I went on foot to Ta Phon, which is five kilometers away from Phnom Leap. I stayed five nights at Ta Phon, waiting for vehicles that would take us to our destination. Those who had ox carts or hand carts did the journey by easy stages and reached Siem Reap in seven or eight days. The old and the sick had to stay at Ta Phon and wait for trucks that took a few at a time.

Arriving at Siem Reap, I had no more rice and was hungry. I wandered about aimlessly in the streets until I met a liberation soldier whom I later found out was a physician. I told him my story from the beginning to the end. Seeing that I was hungry as I spoke to him, he gave me a packet of rice.

God bless him! And seeing that I was thin and sick, he advised me to go to the hospital where I could get multivitamin tablets and B1.

Things were well organized to take care of the refugees. Paddy rice or husked rice were being handed out, and salt too. If you were ill you could go to the hospital where you would be given necessary medicines. People who were seriously ill could be admitted as inpatients at the hospital, and if they were too emaciated, they would get sugar and milk. For several days I lived on the liberation soldiers' charity. If they saw you were hungry, they would give you food (rice, dried fish, pork soup, noodles, etc.), even though they did not know you.

These liberation soldiers were not as had been described by the Pol Pot–Ieng Sary gang (the Nearadays). As they had told it, these soldiers were supposed to be murderers, killers of children, blood suckers. The liberators were mere skeleton-like figures, because they had only rice bran to eat. I couldn't stop myself from talking on and on to the liberation soldiers; they were amused as they listened to me. We who had lived with the followers of Pol Pot and Ieng Sary, we could say that the real murderers and killers were the Pol Pot–Ieng Sary gang. For instance, at Phnom Srok, they killed people who had not left in time or put out their eyes.

The liberation soldiers behaved correctly toward girls and young women. Moreover, they were not allowed to touch the fruit and vegetables of the country. They had to be satisfied with whatever their government was sending them by airplane: rice, wheat, sugar, milk, fish sauce, dried fish, salted pork, noodles in packets, etc. As vegetables, they were sent cabbage and turnips. They took nothing of what belonged to Kampuchea but rather brought commodities here as aid.

A few days later, I again met my first protector, who advised me this time to look for a job in Siem Reap while France did what was necessary to repatriate me. He advised me to go and explore possibilities at the hospital; I therefore went there with my sister-in-law. We were immediately taken on and given board and lodging. I could thus earn my three daily meals while waiting for what might come next. Seeing that I was very thin, my liberator protector put me to work in the pharmacy where, he said, the work would suit my poor health, but he gave me medicine every day. Today I must say that thanks to him, I have put on weight and am almost myself again. He even gave me sugar and milk, because, bloated as I was, I had to eat sugar and nonsalted food. Every day we had fish and vegetables at our meals, (not small fish the size of your thumb but fish weighing two or three kilograms). You could eat as much as you wanted. Rice was not rationed, and everyone could eat to satisfy his hunger.

As we had no clothing, the liberator soldiers gave us cloth. I was given two meters of black cloth, a shawl and a white blouse. Seeing that I was barefoot, another generous soul gave me a pair of old shoes. My son got five meters of black cloth, enough for a pair of trousers and a shirt. A soldier from next door gave him a pair of shoes. They all were kindhearted and helped everyone in need, irrespective of age or race.

The town of Siem Reap has come to life again. An orphanage has been set up for sixty boarders, and a school founded to answer the home's education need. Those orphans are well clothed and well fed.

Siem Reap's main hospital is functioning again and is admitting hundreds of sick and wounded (Pol Pot's and Ieng Sary's victims).

The town now has electricity and running water. From time to time people can enjoy a play or a film show. Houses are being repaired, and people are gradually resettling in their former homes. Life has resumed its normal course which was interrupted three years ago by those monsters.

I can say that I have awakened from a long nightmare. Had the liberation troops taken only a little longer in coming, I think I would have been in the grave. Let me thank the liberation soldiers and above all my several personal protectors to whom I owe more than I can repay. For the rest of my life, I shall be grateful to them all. God bless them all.

2.6.22
Leaflet Signed by Heng Samrin, Member of the Eastern Zone Committee of the Communist Party of Kampuchea and Commander of the Fourth Division

To administrators, combatants, youths, and people in the eastern zone and throughout the country:

Like the rest of our compatriots, you administrators, combatants, and youths know that in the recent five-year-long revolutionary struggle against the U.S. imperialists and their administrators Lon Nol, Sri Matak, and Son Ngoc Thanh, Kampucheans throughout the country shed their blood and sacrificed many lives to liberate the country and free our people from oppression, exploitation, and massacre by the imperialists and their lackeys.

Our people's earnest desire is genuine independence, freedom, real democracy, peace and a plentiful and happy life in the national community and in each family. But since liberation on April 17, 1975, our people have suffered greater disasters than at any time in our history. The traitors Pol Pot and Ieng Sary, the ringleaders of the executioners whose cruelty has reached a frenzy, have enforced the most barbarous fascist laws to coerce, persecute, repress, and kill civilians, administrators, combatants, and young people throughout the eastern zone and in the rest of the country. They said they "respect, love, and wholeheartedly serve the people," but in fact they acted like fascists, committing bloody crimes against our people, administrators, and other patriots.

Over the past three years, our people have led a most miserable life.

Everyone from children to the elderly, from pregnant women to recently confined mothers, has been forced to do hard labor all year round without any rest, without enough to eat or drink, without clothing or medicine, without any schooling, in short, without any freedom.

In our country, arrests and killing are daily occurrences. Worse still, on orders from the Chinese ruling circles they have pushed our people into an unjust aggressive war against the neighboring Vietnamese people who have always been friendly to us.

In particular, on May 25, 1978, the Pol Pot–Ieng Sary gang, defying public indignation at home and abroad, decreed militarist and fascist laws. They carry out arrests and public execution of our administrators at all levels, male and female combatants of all three armed services, civil servants, workers at factories, ports and rubber plantations, and members of mobile youth teams. In some areas, whole villages, subdistricts and entire families were massacred.

Let us mention some cases: The villages of Bo, Don Tei, Punlay, Chiek, Pon, Coroban, Coronhung, and Dondok in Ponhea Krek and Kamchay Mear districts; the villages of Phkar Dong, Corobey, Korek, Domnak, and Popen in Kroch Chhmar and Tbong Khmum districts, and the villages of Kantuot and Phnoeuv in Memot district. Pol Pot–Ieng Sary men killed wantonly, not sparing even newborn babies and persons with mental problems. They accuse everyone of being "agents of Le Duan," which is sheer fabrication. We may ask them: can newly born babies and the insane be traitors?

In execution of their reactionary policies and with support from the Chinese ruling circles, the Pol Pot–Ieng Sary gang have cooked up fantastic stories as a pretext to "kill all, burn all, and destroy all" so as to exterminate the Kampuchean nation.

They are essentially a gang of dictatorial, militarist and nepotic rulers. All the present members of their "Central Committee" and "Government" are their relatives or close friends. All the others have been killed.

In the present painful situation of our country, we call upon all administrators and combatants still in the Pol Pot–Ieng Sary army, all our youths, and the entire people:

1. To think and make a judicious choice on the basis of the noble national ideals and see through all the demagogic, deceptive, and treacherous schemes of the Pol Pot–Ieng Sary gang of traitors. Whatever schemes they may use, don't fall into their trap, but struggle resolutely against them in every possible way.

2. Young men and women who have been forced to bear arms to serve the traitors, to massacre our own people, and to make war on Vietnam, turn your guns on the Pol Pot–Ieng Sary gang of traitors, flee to the jungles with your weapons, and join the new revolutionary forces to fight against the traitors and destroy them.

3. Mothers and aunts, encourage your husbands, children, and nephews to flee to the jungle to avoid being killed and to join the people's genuine revolutionary forces to topple the dictatorial, militarist, and nepotic regime of the Pol Pot–Ieng Sary gang of traitors, to liberate our country and our people, and to build a new, beautiful, and equitable society.

Our slogan is: Fight or die.

We send you our loftiest revolutionary greetings.

Signed: Heng Samrin
Member of the eastern zone committee of
the Communist Party of Kampuchea and
Commander of the Fourth Division
November 11, 1978

2.6.23

Mao Receives and Greets Pol Pot and Ieng Sary

(Photo and caption excerpted from the archives of the bureau of the central committee of Pol Pot's party, numbered 870, and published in the pictorial magazine of the People's Republic of Kampuchea, May 1979, p. 15)

. . . At his reception, Mao Tse Tung greeted Pol Pot and Ieng Sary: "Comrades, you have won a great victory. With a single stroke you have gotten rid of social classes. Communes in the countryside, with poor and lower middle peasants, are our future."

Part III
Indictment and Judgment

Indictment

3.01

Mat Ly, Prosecutor of the Tribunal, Indictment for Genocide Committed by Pol Pot and Ieng Sary

The prosecutor of the People's Revolutionary Tribunal at Phnom Penh,

On the basis of Decree Law No. 1 of July 15, 1979, of the People's Revolutionary Council of Kampuchea, establishing at Phnom Penh a People's Revolutionary Tribunal to try Pol Pot, Ieng Sary, and associates on accusations of genocide,

On the basis of Article 4 of the indicated Decree Law on the tasks and powers of the prosecutor,

On the basis of point 8 of the eleven-point declaration of December 2, 1978, of the National United Front for the Salvation of Kampuchea,

On the basis of Decision No. 2 of July 25, 1979, of the prosecutor to open a case, and the Decision No. 3 of July 26, 1979, of the prosecutor calling for a search for Pol Pot and Ieng Sary and their arrest,

On the basis of the results of the investigation,

We find that,

Contrary to the deeply felt desire of our people, once the country was completely liberated, to live in peace, independence, and democracy, and to assure prosperity and happiness for Kampuchea, during these past four years the Pol Pot–Ieng Sary clique betrayed our people and pushed it to the brink of extermination. Approximately three million innocent persons were killed, more than four million survivors bear the serious physical and moral aftereffects of this inhuman regime. The national economy has been destroyed, the national culture has been eradicated, and all social strata, all families, all regions, the whole nation have borne the disastrous consequences of the policy of genocide of the Pol Pot–Ieng Sary clique.

A. Pol Pot, Ieng Sary, and their associates are charged with the following criminal acts:

1. Systematic execution of an increasingly desperate plan to kill all strata of the population

They divided the population into three categories. The first category was called "the old inhabitants," consisting of persons residing before the liberation in resistance base areas. The second category was called "the new inhabitants," consisting of persons residing in the areas under the former Lon Nol administration. The third category consisted of the personnel of that administration.

They envisaged eliminating the third category, and carrying out purges in the second. The first category initially was favored but was also subjected to purges, beginning in 1977 (Minutes of the meeting of July 7, 1977 of the Party Committee of Kompong Ro 2 district, Svay Rieng province, Document 2.5.12).

(a) They envisaged eliminating all, and in fact killed nearly all, of the officers, soldiers, and civil servants of the former regime, including members of their families.

We may cite, as examples, witness statements representative of many others, regarding killings in this category.

Men Khoeun, who was in charge of Chaong Maong subdistrict, Toek Phos district, Kompong Chhnang province, affirms that on April 17, 1975, he was told by the district head, Meak Vy, that the former officers and soldiers of Lon Nol are enemies, and that, according to a directive of the leader Pol Pot, they should be killed to celebrate the victory. Carrying out this recommendation, Men Khoeun and one of his militiamen used a ruse to get 2005 former officers and soldiers to come out of their camp and led them to a deserted location. There they tied them up, beat them with sticks on the back of the neck and threw their corpses into a ditch that had been dug beforehand (Document 2.2.01).

Sok Li Mut of Pursat witnessed as follows: In April 1975, approximately 4000 former civil servants and military personnel of Lon Nol and their families were beaten or shot to death on the banks of the O Chruy river, at the foot of Mount Prey in Con Ray village, Chheu Tom subdistrict, Krakor district, Pursat province (Document 2.1.5.24).

Bun Sath, warden of the prison of Koh Thom district, Kandal province, and Siv Samon, security agent of Meanchey Thmey district, Svay Rieng province, confirm having participated in the killing of two to three hundred officers, soldiers, and civil servants of the Lon Nol administration, and their families. Chum Sary reports that thousands more Lon Nol officers, soldiers, and civil servants were killed at Wat Champuh Kaek, where they were in custody (Kandal province) (Documents 2.3.7.03, 2.2.05, 2.3.7.01).

Many mass killings of officers and civil servants of Lon Nol at Battambang, Mongkol Borey, Sisophon, Kompong Speu, and other localities have also been confirmed by foreign sources (Document 2.6.2).[1]

1. This document number is apparently in error, as there is no document by such a number. —Eds.

(b) They envisaged and carried out a preestablished plan to kill ethnic minorities.

Immediately after April 17, 1975, according to a report of a group of Kampuchean ethnographers, they sought to carry out a policy of assimilation with the Khmer race, with regard to thirteen ethnic groups. They made them speak Khmer and killed those who refused. They made them evacuate the plateaus and mountains of the northeast and southwest of the country to live in "people's communes." Those who opposed this directive were killed en masse.

Buon Thong, an official who is of the Ta Puon minority group of Ratanak Kiri province, has affirmed that dozens of militiamen, members of the national minority of the northeastern zone, were killed near the town of Stung Treng. Many talented officials enjoying the public's confidence were killed, such as Seda, of the Lao minority, secretary of the zone Party committee, and Chan Den of the Lao minority, a member of the zone Party committee. Nearly all the officials belonging to the Lao ethnic minority have perished, including military and paramilitary officials who took part in the resistance to American aggression.

The Thai ethnic group of Koh Kong province in the southwestern zone was in large part killed by the armed forces of Pol Pot on May 25, 1975. This ethnic group, which before April 17, 1975, numbered 20,000 persons, now has no more than 8000. The number of households in the town of Koh Kapi has decreased from 700 to 30 at the present time (Document 2.4.02).

In addition, resident foreigners were killed en masse, in particular Vietnamese. Even Kampucheans having family connections with Vietnamese were killed with their entire families (statements of Bun Sath, Khieu Kola, Document 2.3.7.03).

(c) They repressed and systematically killed anyone who opposed the regime, even potential opponents.

To consolidate their power, after eliminating for all practical purposes the inhabitants of the third category, Pol Pot, Ieng Sary, and their associates envisaged mass repression of persons suspected of opposition to the regime. They carried out purges in the Party, in the state bureaucracy, and in the army.

Early in 1977, they ordered the authorities of the "people's communes" to exterminate more or less all the so-called "reactionaries," including opponents and suspected opponents (Document 2.5.10).

On April 11, 1977, they gave an order to all units, and to all agencies of various levels, to continue to carry out purges within these organizations (Document 2.5.23).

In a communication of June 3, 1978, they boasted of having killed eighteen Party officials, calling this act a great success. In a list of victims, they mentioned Son Ngoc Minh, former president of the Issarak Front (1945 to 1954), and a member of the Party Central Committee; Hu Nim, minister of information; Toch Phoeun, minister of public works; and Koy Thuon, commander of Military Region 304 (Document 2.5.16).

On another list, they gave the names of 242 officials of all branches arrested and killed from 1976 to April 9, 1978. The list includes two members of the Party central committee, four Party inter-zone secretaries, four cabinet ministers, nine senior ministerial officials, eight political commissars, deputy political commissars, and division command members, and twenty-four secretaries and members of zone Party committees (Document 2.5.24).

In an end-of-the-year report about Party activity in 1977, they affirmed, "If we have won a great success in 1977 (the killing of many high-level officials), we owe it to the fact that we have harassed the enemy, carried out purges in our own ranks, and destroyed their network to its roots" (Document 2.5.15).

Vang Pheap, a resident of Kandal province, and former head warden of the Tuol Svay Prey prison in Phnom Penh, has revealed that Pol Pot, Ieng Sary, and their associates threw into that prison and killed there a large number of officials from company commanders to division commanders, and among civil servants those from the district level up to the central level, including family members. Approximately 10,000 persons were killed in the Phnom Penh prison between only December 1975 and June 1977 (Document 2.1.4.02).

In May 1978, in order to put down an uprising in the eastern zone led by So Yan, alias So Phim, the secretary of the Party zone committee, they conducted a virtual war against the inhabitants, using troops of the Kandal military region, tanks, aircraft, and heavy artillery. They killed nearly all the officers and soldiers of Divisions 280 and 290, which were under the Army High Command, those of Divisions 3, 4, and 5 of the eastern military region, local forces of sectors 20, 21, 22, 23, and 24, including invalids who had fought during the resistance against American aggression. According to a statement by Nhek Houn, former deputy political commissar of the Sector 21 artillery company, Pol Pot and Ieng Sary, under the pretext of organizing study sessions or dike construction, killed almost all the personnel of this company, reducing its numbers from 160 to three. Sector 21, which numbered 3,000 personnel, has no more than seventeen left (Document 2.1.4.01). They completely wiped out the population of many villages, such as Bo, Don Tei, Punlay, Chiek, Pon, Coroban, Coronhung, and Dondok villages, all in Ponhea Krek and Kamchay Mear districts); Phkar Dong, Corobey, Korek, Domnak, and Popen villages in Kroch Chhmar and Tbong Khmum districts; Kantuot and Pnoeuv villages in Memot district, etc. (Documents 2.6.19, 2.6.22).

They killed not only the inhabitants and troops of the eastern zone, but as well persons originally from this zone who had been displaced and were living in other regions. This was the case with 40,000 persons of this region who had been forcibly recruited to dig the Pursat-Battambang canal; they were killed in June 1978 (Document 2.1.5.24).

According to the statements of the witnesses Kung Sary, Mun Ny, Che Van

Thon, Nuon Thok, and Chum Rithy, all of Siem Reap, tens of thousands of people's communes inhabitants succumbed in cremation ditches and pits in the Siem Reap region (Documents 2.3.3.01, 2.3.2.02, 2.3.2.03).

Similar killings were carried out at the Chup rubber plantation in Kompong Cham province (Document 2.3.5.03), and in Kratie province (Document 2.1.5.15).

At present, one finds in many other localities vestiges of this genocide: smashed skulls, limbs, bones with ropes around them, children's clothing, Lon Nol troop caps and boots, and sticks and iron rods that were used to kill, found near corpses. Thousands of pits containing hundreds and thousands of corpses each have been discovered in different localities.

2. The forced, sudden evacuation of cities and systematic displacement of rural inhabitants, causing death to many persons

(a) Forced evacuation of the inhabitants of cities to rural and mountainous areas

On April 17, 1975, using violence combined with deception, Pol Pot and Ieng Sary forced more than two million residents of Phnom Penh to leave the city. Those who refused to obey or who delayed leaving their houses were beaten or shot. Old persons, the infirm, pregnant women, even patients in hospitals, did not escape this forced exodus. They had to walk, rain or shine. Robbed of their possessions along the way, they arrived at their destinations empty-handed. Pol Pot and Ieng Sary deliberately mistreated the urban population along their route and in places of detention. They drove them to adversity and hardship. As a result, tens of thousands perished from hunger, thirst, or sickness, or died from exhaustion.

This was a calculated policy. In a document written in 1975 to train higher officials, they indicated: "The policy of displacing the population was decided upon by the Central Committee of our Party as early as 1970. Troops displace the population of cites as they occupy them. When we liberate Phnom Penh we will fully control it. The enemies who are mixed in with the population thus will be excluded and eliminated. They will go into the liberated areas, their hands empty, and they will be under the control of the cooperatives" (Directive of Central Committee, Documents 2.5.01, 2.5.02).

The above-mentioned crimes are proved by the investigation report of the crimes of Pol Pot and Ieng Sary committed against the population of Phnom Penh, and the statements of many witnesses, such as those of the San Sam Kosal pagoda monks, Thun Saray, Khem Nary, and others (Documents 2.4.01, 2.1.2.01, 2.1.5.04, 2.1.5.05).

Mrs. Yasuko Naito, a Japanese resident of Phnom Penh, and a widow of a Kampuchean man, stated: Phnom Penh, on the afternoon of April 17, the Pol Pot–Ieng Sary soldiers, using loudspeakers, ordered everyone to leave their houses. They shot at houses whose doors remained closed. They forced the inhabitants to leave the city, which, they said, would be bombed by enemy aircraft. Thinking that the evacuation was only temporary and would last but a few days, the residents of Phnom Penh took only a few items of clothing. Along the route, I met patients who had been forced out of hospitals. One of them was accompanied by his nurse, who was still giving him blood transfusion with needles. He had been operated upon only a few hours earlier. On a door panel, there was a naked man, nailed there, with a sign on his chest with the word "enemy" in large letters. In the evening, the families slept under the stars, to be led farther the next morning. Along the way, corpses of soldiers lay everywhere (Document 2.1.1.07).

Miss Bun Chantini, who was forced out of Phnom Penh to Kandal, says that the road was so crowded with people that she could hardly walk. Many succumbed on the road. With her own eyes she saw five corpses (Document 2.1.5.07).

The residents of other cities and urban centers were also evacuated and know the same sufferings and the same fate as the residents of Phnom Penh (Documents 2.1.5.16, 2.1.1.01).

The investigation report on the crimes of Pol Pot and Ieng Sary committed against the inhabitants of Phnom Penh provides the following figures:

- A survey of one hundred families that returned to the capital city after enduring the exodus and the conditions of life in the various countryside zones during these past four years, showed that 42% of the persons involved were killed, 11% died of hunger or sickness, and 6% disappeared. Only 41% survived (Document 2.4.01c).
- In the Phsar Doeum Thkau subdistrict, the number of persons killed is 33%, the number of persons who died of hunger or sickness is 11%, and the number who disappeared is 9%. The survivors make up 47%.

(b) Mixing up the population of different areas of the country in order to break up existing social relations and to keep the people from organizing opposition to the regime

At the same time as they transferred the city populations to the countryside, Pol Pot and Ieng Sary also displaced rural populations. Rural residents had to turn over all their possessions to "Angkar" and leave with their hands empty. Late in 1975, the inhabitants of the provinces of Svay Rieng, Prey Veng, and Takeo (southeast) were displaced into the provinces of Pursat, Battambang, Sisophon (northwest) and Oddar Meanchey (north). Correspondingly, the population of the west was sent to the east.

Mr. Khieu Kola states that after being driven out of Phnom Penh to Kandal, his family was taken by truck to Pursat in August 1975, with no explanation and without being able to take anything with them. When they arrived, they had to sleep in the open for lack of any lodging. A hundred or so persons underwent the same treatment. The Pol Pot soldiers searched the people every day for any goods and confiscated what they found. Four or five persons died every day (Document 2.1.1.02).

Mr. Nhem Heng and his family, of Kompong Chhnang province, were forced out of their own village and put in a people's commune where they lived with 20,000 persons from different parts of the country. There was no housing or furnishings (Document 2.1.5.10). The family of Tik How, made up of thirteen persons, was split in two; eight were taken to Battambang, and five to Kompong Thom (Document 2.1.1.05).

The statements of witnesses from various parts of the country, such as Ay Nasoeun (Kompong Cham), Lat Sarat (Svay Rieng), Yasuko Naito (Phnom Penh), Sok Ros (Kandal), Koh Chhay (Kompong Chhnang), and Saleh Sen (Kampot), show that these population transfers were done at the national level, that they were carried out over a period of years and were even more devastating than the forced evacuation of the cities (Documents 2.1.5.01, 2.1.5.14, 2.1.1.07, 2.1.5.25, 2.1.5.08, 2.1.5.17).

3. The devising of a system of repression and coercion in the "people's communes," where the people, forced to work to the point of exhaustion, were reduced to a state of slavery and to conditions of life that led to their physical and moral ruin

In order to control the population, Pol Pot and Ieng Sary put it into "people's communes," which were disguised concentration camps. That is why popular opinion had it that "the Angkar prison is a large prison, without walls or iron fetters, but no one can escape" (excerpts from minutes of an enlarged conference of Region 21 Party Committee, early 1977, Document 2.5.20).

(a) They forced the residents to do hard and exhausting work, regardless of their age or state of health.

This involved using the people to build dikes, dig canals, and clear forests, etc., with their bare hands or only the most rudimentary tools, making them work 12 to 16 hours a day or more, and imposing on them work norms beyond the normal work capacity of a person. Deprived of the fruits of their labor, the workers did not have enough to eat and wore only rags. They lived in ramshackle huts. They had no medications in case of illness. Dysentery, beriberi, cholera, malaria, tuberculosis, and mental illness were widespread. Many women could not give birth. Old people and children died in large numbers. Many people died a slow death from physical exhaustion, malnutrition, and sickness.

Mrs. Ay Nasoeun, from Kompong Cham, said that she was placed in a shock team where she had to work every day until ten o'clock at night. When she had her period, she asked to rest, but was accused of laziness and of opposition to the regime. Her children died of hunger and illness. Many women in the "people's commune" suffered the same fate (Document 2.1.5.01).

Prak Sok, a former student of the National School of Administration in Phnom Penh, who was sent to the countryside, said, regarding work conditions, that the people were treated worse than convicts at hard labor, that they had to work day and night, rain or shine (Document 2.6.20).

Mrs. Mok Moeun, 63 years old, Mrs. Khang Chiem, 70 years old, and Mrs. Tim Moeun, 71 years old, all of Siem Reap, said that they were forced to carry manure, transplant rice, care for children, and keep birds away from the rice paddies. To eat they were given only broth cooked with vegetables and sliced banana stems (Documents 2.1.5.22, 2.1.5.21, 2.1.5.20).

Many witnesses from different areas said that the daily ration for ten persons was one tin of rice. They had to eat banana stems (Documents 2.4.01, 2.1.1.07).

Mrs. Denise Alfonso, who had lived in Phnom Penh and was forced out to the countryside, says that she was always hungry and had to eat crickets, scorpions, and cockroaches. One day, dogs bit her as she tried to get a piece of meat away from them (Document 2.6.21).

During the first six months of 1977, there was a famine in the eastern zone, particularly in the districts of Kroch Chhmar, Peam Chileang, Koh Sotin and Muk Kampoul. Fed only rice broth, many members of the "people's communes" were completely wasted. Nonetheless they had to dig canals and carry out the work plan given to them (Minutes of the Congress of the Party committee of the eastern zone, Document 2.5.13).

The report on the general situation in Kompong Ro district, Svay Rieng province, during the first six months of 1977, confirmed that the inhabitants of the "people's communes" suffered from many serious diseases (Document 2.5.08).

(b) The organizing of a network of spies to inform on others in order to stop any opposition

Angkar closely controlled the least important actions and the slightest thoughts of the members of "people's communes." They were to think and work only according to the directives of Angkar. Any who showed the slightest indication of freedom of thought or an independent will, or any who complained or protested, were put on a list of "dubious elements," treated as opponents, and killed (Document 2.4.01).

Chean Phanna and Denise Alfonso said that at night, the spies eavesdropped on family conversations. During the day they mixed among the peasants. If anyone voiced a complaint, the agents reported it to Angkar (Documents 2.1.1.12, 2.6.21).

One night, Mr. Suot and his young wife complained to each other about the harsh regime in the "people's communes." The next day, the couple and their four children were beaten to death (Document 2.1.5.23).

According to Mr. Thun Saray, in the cooperative of Oulath village, Chok subdistrict, the life there was both physically and mentally painful. We had to work harder than the other members of the cooperative. To that was added all the housework in the house where I lived. . . . The owner of the house watched me and reported frequently to his superiors the least detail about my daily activities. My mind was in permanent tension. I was haunted by the fear of being called out to be executed at any time (Document 2.1.5.04).

The residents of the "people's communes" were not allowed to have any contacts with each other. On November 26, 1975, the Party standing board of Region 203, applying a directive of the permanent bureau of the Party central committee by Pol Pot, decided: "It is absolutely forbidden to displaced persons to go about on their own. They are authorized to go only from their lodgings to their places of work" (Document 2.5.21).

(c) Punishing arbitrarily and severely any breach of Angkar's discipline

The system of punishment had only two levels of penalty. The first was to require the guilty party to work two or three times harder than the ordinary norms, or to reduce or eliminate the food ration. The second was death.

Eight of the nine members of the family of Mr. Kung Sary of Siem Reap were executed for not working hard enough (Document 2.3.2.01).

Mr. Pun Hon was executed for stealing ears of corn to assuage his hunger (Document 2.1.5.07).

Anyone who tried to escape from the "people's communes" was tracked down and punished (Documents 2.5.11, 2.5.14).

The repression in the "people's communes" resulted in many deaths. Mrs. Khem Nary says that the Prey Lvea "people's commune" of Takeo province had 28,000 members in 1975, but only 5000 after the liberation of January 7, 1979 (Document 2.1.5.05).

Mr. Sok Li Mut of Pursat says that when he was employed as a dock worker in a port, he and one other worker had to load fifteen trucks a day, putting fifty sacks of rice into each truck. Anyone who inadvertently spilled rice on the ground was killed. Of the fifteen members of his team, ten were killed for this reason. In the "people's communes," anyone who had received three warnings was condemned to death. At the Phnom Bot "people's commune" in Pursat province, three different times 10,000 persons were sent in from other areas to replace losses due to starvation or executions (Document 2.1.5.24).

4. Destruction of all social relations, destruction of all thought, making the person a slave having as his only connection that of subordination to Angkar

(a) Abolishing traditional family relationships

Spouses had to live apart from each other. Children were separated from their parents (Documents 2.1.5.03, 2.1.5.04, 2.1.5.14, 2.1.5.15, 2.1.5.20).

Love among young people was forbidden. Marriage was by order of Angkar. A decision of Pol Pot and Ieng Sary of November 1978 prescribed, "The family should be built by Angkar on the basis of political and ideological considerations. Respect for this principle must be assured" (Documents 2.5.10, 2.5.22).

According to the statement of Mrs. Duong Mala of Borey, Kompong Thom province, and Mr. Nhem Heng of Kompong Chhnang province, couples caught exchanging confidences were often hanged, burned, or beaten to death. In one case, M-79 shells were rammed into the vagina of the girl involved (Document 2.1.5.06, 2.1.5.10). There were instances in which lovers who tried to run away were followed and punished like major criminals (Document 2.5.14).

Widows were forced to remarry war invalids. This happened with Mrs. Nguon Vuoch Ny and nineteen other women of the Krala subdistrict, Kompong Siem district, Kompong Cham province. Mrs. Nguon Vuoch Ny committed suicide. The others refused and were arrested, raped, and then killed (Document 2.4.01).

Mrs. Nuon Thok, of Siem Reap province, was jailed because she refused to remarry a disabled man selected for her by Angkar (Document 2.3.3.01).

(b) Eradicating personal relationships, as well as supportive relationships among relatives, friends, and neighbors

It was forbidden to show any pity or sympathy for those beaten or killed. Because she cried over her husband, who had been killed, Mrs. Sok Bun, of Pursat, was immediately executed (Document 2.1.5.24). Mr. Sok Chhoy was jailed because he cried upon seeing a relative killed in a savage way by Pol Pot agents (Document 2.1.5.08).

People were unable to help others, for fear of being compromised. They did not even take care of orphans, for fear of being accused by Angkar of helping children of enemies (Documents 2.1.5.20, 2.1.1.07).

In addition to these acts, the elimination of currency, of commerce, of the market, and of postal and telegraphic communications had the effect of putting an end to relationships between people, or to any relationship with society, and thus to isolate the inhabitants.

The elimination of social relations created a "wall of silence" separating people from each other. The individual had only one relationship, that of dependence on Angkar.

5. Elimination of monks, religious persons, and believers, the systematic elimination of intellectuals, and the elimination of religion and the national culture

(a) Elimination of Buddhism, practiced by 85% of the population

Pol Pot and Ieng Sary forced the monks and nuns to abandon their saffron robes and to work in "people's communes." They killed many of them. They destroyed pagodas, temples, statues of Buddha, and holy books. They turned pagodas into granaries or fertilizer depots. They forbade the people to observe Buddhism or to join Buddhist orders. Not one of the 2800 pagodas that adorned Kampuchea remains intact. Of a total of more than 82,000 monks, few managed to survive (Document 2.1.2.02).

The monk Tep Vung said that in Siem Reap province, 57 monks were killed in April 1975. Superior Tit Phan, 78 years old, died in 1977 as a result of ill treatment. In two years (1976 and 1977), 4800 monks were forced to abandon the religious life. Many statues of Buddha were destroyed, such as the two famous bronze statues at Preah Ang Chek and Preah Ang Cham dating from the Angkor Wat period, and two five-meter-high stone statues, Preah Ang Tep and Preah Ngak. Many pagodas and tombs, and objects of veneration, were also destroyed (Document 2.1.2.03).

The Champuh Kaek pagoda, in Kandal province, was used as a detention camp. Three hundred monks were detained there and later killed (Document 2.3.7.01).

Similar facts were attested by the report written by the monks of the San Sam Kosal pagoda in Phnom Penh, and the statements of many witnesses (Document 2.1.2.01).

Answering questions of Yugoslav journalists, Yun Yat (Mrs. Son Sen), Minister of Culture and Propaganda of Pol Pot and Ieng Sary, said, "At present, there is no longer any issue of Buddhism in Kampuchea" (Document 2.6.02).

(b) Along with Buddhism, Islam was abolished.

Pol Pot and Ieng Sary envisaged the elimination of followers of Islam. During the first months after April 17, 1975, they tracked down Islamic priests. They killed Hachi Res Los, the head of Islam in Kampuchea, and his deputy Hachi Sleyman Sokri. They forced followers of Islam to renounce their religion, and, under penalty of death, to eat pork. Those who refused were punished, often with death. According to Mr. Nhek Huon, who is now in Army Corps One, more than one thousand people were killed at Svay Rieng, in Kompong Cham province (Document 2.1.4.01).

The Koran was banned, and mosques were destroyed or turned into fertilizer depots, pigsties, or detention centers.

Mr. Tin Yusuf Abdul Koyum, a Muslim medical doctor, said, "In Kompong Siem district, Kompong Cham province, there were five villages inhabited by 20,000 Muslims, and now none are left. Of the tens of thousands of Muslims living in seven villages of Kang Meas district, in the same province, only four have survived" (Investigation report by a group of Kampuchean ethnographers, Document 2.4.02).

(c) Large-scale elimination of intellectuals, of persons having any education or technical knowledge. Destruction of the national culture, and the practice of obscurantism for the purpose of eliminating opposition.

Pol Pot and Ieng Sary envisaged eliminating all intellectuals. A directive of September 5, 1977, of the eastern zone, implementing a decision of the central committee of their party, said, "Revolutionary vigilance must be increased regarding persons who served the administration of the old regime: technicians, teachers, doctors, engineers. . . . Our party does not employ them. If we run after technology and employ them, the enemy will infiltrate our ranks, each year more deeply. This will be very dangerous for us" (Document 2.5.06). In fact, Pol Pot and Ieng Sary deemed these persons as being under a suspended death sentence, subject to being killed at any time (Document 2.4.01).

In 1975, with the evacuation of the city populations, Pol Pot and Ieng Sary forced the intellectuals to go to the countryside, supposedly to "reeducate" them in "people's communes," but in reality to eliminate them over time. Many intellectuals had to hide their background, to escape being liquidated. Such was the case of Mr. Tik How of Phnom Penh, a graduate of the Faculty of Literature of the University of Phnom Penh, who survived only because he managed to conceal his level of education (Document 2.1.1.05).

Those who let it be known that they had any education were killed. Thus Chan Sary's cousin, who caught malaria and refused to be injected with a locally produced medicine, was suspected of being a doctor and was immediately killed (Document 2.1.5.26).

Khieu Kola, a former professor of history working at the Ministry of Education in Phnom Penh, recounted the life of an intellectual in the "people's commune" of Prek Tauch village, Saang district, Kandal province. According to the explanations of Angkar officials, "Educated people like doctors and teachers are part of the ruling and exploiting class." They killed teachers without explanation. The professor saw six teachers condemned to death in the commune. Early in 1978, when Pol Pot gave an order to hunt down intellectuals and kill them, he himself tried several times to commit suicide. (Document 2.1.1.02) According to Mrs. Leung Lada, of Kompong Chhnang province, whose husband, an intellectual, was killed under Pol Pot, "teachers and even secondary school students were eliminated, together with their families" (Document 2.1.5.19).

According to many witnesses, a thousand or so intellectuals living abroad were deceived by Pol Pot and Ieng Sary into returning. All of them were pressed into forced labor. Hundreds of them were killed (Documents 2.4.01, 2.1.1.01).

Medical personnel—physicians, pharmacists, surgeons, and dentists—formerly numbered 643. Now there are only 69 (Document 2.4.03a).

Many documents from foreign sources confirm the elimination of intellectuals by the fascist regime of Pol Pot and Ieng Sary.

(d) Elimination of education at all levels

Schools were turned into prisons, torture chambers, granaries, and fertilizer depots. Books and documents kept in libraries, universities, and research institutes were burned or destroyed. According to the investigation report by the Ministry of Education, during the four years of the Pol Pot regime, 80% of the teachers were killed, including university professors and lecturers, physicians, and pharmacists. In the provinces of Kandal, Prey Veng, Kompong Cham, Kratie, Kompong Speu, and others, teachers, university students, and secondary school students were put into special camps where they were killed over time, starting with the higher ranking among them (Document 2.4.04).

(e) Abolishing national culture

According to an investigation report done by our Ministry of Information and Culture, Pol Pot and Ieng Sary, during the four years of their rule, envisaged eliminating all the material bases of our traditional national culture, and killing persons who worked to preserve and develop it.

Cultural establishments, like museums, theaters, cinemas, television, the College of Fine Arts, the Conservatory of Music, stadiums, and sport clubs, were closed down.

Ninety percent of the artists were killed, including such well-known figures as Neang Huoy Meas, Hal Salan, Poeuv Sipho, and Voy Ho. Of 1241 artists living in 1975, only 121 remain alive.

Two thousand well-known athletes who had competed internationally and three hundred coaches were killed.

Large libraries in Phnom Penh, major scientific research institutes, and famous pagodas and temples were destroyed.

About half of 1225 historical monuments and architectural treasures were destroyed. The famous temples of Angkor Thom and Angkor Wat were damaged (Document 2.4.08).

6. Killing of children, and turning the youth into thugs devoid of human feelings

Children over the age of six were not allowed to live with their parents, but were forced to herd cattle and collect cow dung. Children over the age of ten had to do hard labor, like adults. They could not go to school, or play, according to the witnesses Ung Pech, Denise Alfonso, Thun Saray, and the investigation report of the Ministry of Education (Documents 2.1.1.01, 2.6.21, 2.1.5.04, 2.4.04).

Khieu Samphan, head of state in the Pol Pot–Ieng Sary regime, praised this exploitation of child labor thus: "Our children have a good time building dikes, and digging ponds and irrigation canals."

It was forbidden to care for orphans, for the stated reason that their parents had committed wrongs before Angkar. Many orphans were homeless, because they were not admitted to "people's communes." Children caught begging were beaten to death (Statement of Duong Mala of Kompong Thom province, Document 2.1.5.06). Orphans who survived are seriously malnourished, and many contracted serious diseases of the digestive system, or became mentally deficient.

Some Pol Pot soldiers killed children and ate their flesh. Miss Chhay Ny of Kandal province, says that this happened to her younger brother (Document 2.1.5.11).

Hour is a thirteen-year-old girl who now lives in an orphanage in Siem Reap. Her parents and older brothers and sisters died during the forced evacuation. She said that Pol Pot–Ieng Sary soldiers killed and ate two young girls, and that soldiers cut her neck, but that in response to her cries someone came, and the Pol Pot men let her go. She has a large scar on her neck from this incident (Document 2.1.5.18).

Even as they mistreated and persecuted children, Pol Pot and Ieng Sary forced children under fifteen years of age into army units, or shock teams, because they considered children of this age to be pure and to be loyal to them. They trained them to be killers and used them in wars against neighboring countries and in repressing the Kampuchean population.

A document of the conference of northern zone, dated July 15, 1977, says, "Even children can be key personnel. Only in this way we can build the party, because the children will grow up in the movement" (Document 2.5.26).

Children were used as spies in the "people's communes" (Documents 2.4.01, 2.6.21).

7. Destruction of the economy, driving the people to starvation

Pol Pot and Ieng Sary destroyed the structure of the economy. Production plummeted, with disastrous consequences for the well-being of the population.

In industry, they did not use qualified personnel from the old regime (Directive of September 5, 1976 of the eastern zone implementing a decision of the Central Committee of the Party) (Document 2.5.06). Engineers and technical personnel were killed, and workers were sent to the countryside.

Although not highly developed, Kampuchean industry before 1975 counted hundreds of enterprises, including thirty-seven at Phnom Penh with 12,000 to 13,000 workers, along with 3700 units of handicraft production. These units of production were already inadequate, yet as a result of the draconian policy toward the personnel and workers, they had to shut their doors or curtail production.

A cement works with a capacity of 50,000 tons per year, and a glassware works with a capacity of 40,000 tons per year stopped functioning.

Small works like a sawmill and a textile factory had only a few workers left. All production slowed down as productive forces were destroyed.

In agriculture, our country had, in certain years, exported hundreds of thousands of tons of rice.

Under the slogan, "when one has rice one has everything," Pol Pot and Ieng Sary changed the mode of production used by the people. They displaced the farmers, or killed them, or put them into "people's communes" where they subjected them to a regimen of exhausting forced labor.

There was a shortage of the means of production. Many tracts of land lay fallow. Rice produced was in large part exported for armaments, or stockpiled to prepare for war, while the farmer-producers remained malnourished and poorly clothed.

Tracts of land used for industrial crops, like rubber and pepper, were reduced.

Fishing, which formerly yielded 100,000 to 140,000 tons of fish per year, gave no more than 20,000 to 30,000 tons.

As regards the circulation and distribution of commodities, currency and markets were eliminated. A market economy no longer existed.

As regards communications and transportation, the means of civilian transportation were destroyed to keep the people from moving about. At the same time, military means of communication, ports, airfields, and strategic roads, were developed.

The reactionary economic policy of Pol Pot and Ieng Sary and their associates ran counter to objective economic laws, to the interests of the people, and to the realities of Kampuchea. It destroyed the productive forces. Industrial production and agriculture fell. Forced to work using only their own power, producers ware condemned to a slow death.

8. Since their overthrow on January 7, 1979, Pol Pot and Ieng Sary have continued to commit new crimes and to kill en masse those people who refuse to follow them in their hideout.

In their flight, Pol Pot and Ieng Sary have forced the population to follow them to protect them as shields. Wherever they have passed, they have stolen goods, destroyed crops and granaries, and plundered the population.

In many localities, before fleeing, they have killed people en masse to keep them from joining the revolution (Document 2.1.5.03, 2.1.5.25). Yeng Mara of Kompong Chhnang province confirms that many people were tied together and pushed into the Porang So Keo river (Document 2.1.5.09). At the Champuh Kaek pagoda in Kandal province, on the morning of January 7, the district chief and his soldiers killed two hundred persons who had been incarcerated in the pagoda, including women and children. There was no time to bury the bodies (Document 2.3.7.01).

Pol Pot and Ieng Sary and their associates killed *en masse* persons who did not want to follow them. In February 1979, in the Am Leang subdistrict, Kompong Speu province, they killed 12,000 persons, among them the workers and other employees of the Kompong Chhnang airport, and their own wounded and demoralized soldiers (Document 2.3.6.02).

They accused Kampucheans sent back by the Thais of treason and executed them on the spot. They destroyed supplies they could not carry with them, thereby forcing the inhabitants to follow them and inflicting starvation on those who stayed behind.

Phnom Penh residents on their way back home could see many rice granaries burning for weeks, longer than a month, as for example the large granary at Tonle Bet, near the city of Kompong Cham.

9. Pol Pot and Ieng Sary used savage methods of torture and killing, as well as many specific techniques to terrorize the people.

(a) Methods allowing the killing of hundreds and thousands of persons at one time, methods more cruel than those used by Hitler

Using hoes, pick axes, sticks, iron rods, to strike blows to the head or the back of the neck, to break the skull.

Using knives or the sharp-edged stalks of sugar palm trees to cut people's throats, cut open their stomachs, or take out their livers to eat, or take out the gallbladder to use to make medications.

Using bulldozers to crush people, or explosives to blow up a large number at one time.

Burying people alive, burning alive persons suspected of opposition to the regime, cutting up flesh little by little to let people die a slow death.

Throwing children up in the air and letting them be impaled on a bayonet, tearing children limb from limb, shattering children's heads against tree trunks.

Throwing people into ponds used to raise crocodiles.

Killing by "swinging," which involves hanging a person by the neck, arms, or legs on a tree branch.

Injecting poison into a person's arteries, poisoning people en masse (Documents 2.3.5.01, 2.3.5.02, 2.3.4.01, 2.1.5.23, 2.1.5.24, 2.1.5.10, 2.3.7.01, 2.6.21, 2.3.1.01, 2.3.2.01., 2.2.01, 2.2.02, 2.4.01a).

(b) Savage torture to extract confessions from suspected opponents of the regimes, especially officials and Party members before killing them

Torturing innocent persons to force them to confess that they worked for the CIA (Report on a conference on methods of interrogation in the Pol Pot–Ieng Sary security services. Document 2.5.27).

Torturing people two or three months on end to get a false confession and a statement of support for the regime, then killing the person ten days later.

Disrobing women under torture, raping them, cutting off their breasts, cutting their genital organs.

Hanging persons under torture upside down, passing an electrical current through the body, ripping out fingernails with pliers, covering the head with a plastic sack, or wrapping the head with cloth and then pouring water from above to asphyxiate the person, forcing persons to drink liters of salt water (Statements of Ung Pech, Vang Pheap, file of Tuol Sleng prison, Documents 2.1.1.01, 2.1.4.02, 2.3.8).[2]

(c) Coercive methods to crush the human will and human thought

Forcing people to work all day to keep them from having time to think of rebelling, accusing sick persons who asked for time off of harboring nostalgia for the past.

Brainwashing of members of "people's communes," ordering them to tell nothing of what they know, as if they saw nothing, heard nothing, knew nothing.

Organizing a network of spies, watching people day and night, using children to spy on and denounce their parents.

Creating suspicion between the different categories of members of a "people's commune" and using the old members to repress and spy on the new members.

Establishing draconian and arbitrary discipline in the "people's communes" and killing anyone who violated it (Documents 2.1.1.16, 2.1.5.07, 2.3.2.01, 2.1.5.06, 2.4.,[3] 2.1.1.17).

B. On the aims and consequences of the crimes of Pol Pot, Ieng Sary, and their associates

1. Their acts indicate an intention of genocide.

The statement of witnesses in the country, the investigation reports of different branches of our state apparatus, the minutes of field investigations, as well as documents from abroad, all show that the criminal acts of Pol Pot, Ieng Sary, and their associates were committed in a systematic way, in various localities throughout the territory of Kampuchea, with a deliberate aim of carrying out genocide.

These criminal acts were discussed in Party meetings and were written down in resolutions that were turned into directives to the various levels of the party and state and teaching materials for officials, and explained in documents whose implementation was checked (Documents 2.5).[4]

2. The aims of Pol Pot and Ieng Sary, and the support they enjoyed in carrying out genocide

(a) Pol Pot and Ieng Sary were power hungry and spared no means to concentrate power in themselves and in their family members.

In 1960, taking advantage of the enemy's terror and repression that broke

2. There is no Document 2.3.8. The document on Tuol Sleng prison is 2.4.10. —Eds.
3. This is an apparent reference to all the documents whose numbers begin with 2.4. —Eds.
4. This is an apparent reference to all the documents whose numbers begin with 2.5. —Eds.

up many Party units and that led to the arrest or liquidation of many of its most loyal members, Pol Pot and Ieng Sary usurped power within the Party and founded Angkar, a fascist and dictatorial organization to serve their own ends.

Beginning in 1970 they tried to extend their influence and establish their personal authority.

In 1971 and 1972, they eliminated a number of figures from the anti-U.S.A. resistance government and replaced them with people loyal to them.

In 1973, they liquidated many true revolutionaries in Koh Kong province, including comrade Prasit, deputy secretary of the regional committee of the Party. They ordered the dissolution of certain units of the resistance army that they suspected of opposition to their political line.

In 1975, they liquidated cabinet minister Hou Yuon.

In 1976, they organized fake elections and set up a government with Pol Pot, secretary of Angkar, as prime minister, and Ieng Sary, a member of the permanent bureau of Angkar, as deputy prime minister in charge of foreign affairs.

In 1977, falsifying the Party's history, they brought their Angkar into the open under the usurped name of the Communist Party of Kampuchea, which had supposedly been founded in 1960, the year in which Pol Pot took power. This was done to lend prestige to themselves.

In 1977 and 1978, they continued to liquidate persons they considered an obstacle to their power, such as Hu Nim, who was minister of information and propaganda, and Toch Phoeun, who was minister of public works (1977), and So Phim, vice-president of the presidium of the so-called Democratic Kampuchea (1978).

(b) Pol Pot and Ieng Sary pursued reactionary policies that ran counter to the people's interests and aspirations and as a result led to ever increasing opposition.

During the years 1967 and 1968, at a time when the situation in the country and the balance of forces was not favorable, they nonetheless staged an armed uprising at Sam Lot (mid-1967) and at other locations (early 1968). As a result, these uprisings were severely repressed, causing heavy losses to the revolution.

During the years 1970 to 1975, they began to implement policies that ran against the interests of the people and the anti-USA resistance, such as the forced evacuation of people and their concentration in "cooperatives and people's communes."

During the nearly four years of their power, from 1975 to 1979, they implemented on a large scale their policy of repression and coercion of the population, and of major purges within their own ranks, in order to maintain their own dictatorial personal power. They forced the population out of cities and divided the people into different categories in order to kill en masse anyone suspected of opposition. They forced the population of one region to move to another and sought to suppress all familial and social relationships, transforming people into slaves, and condemning them to a slow death.

Under slogans like "a leap forward in economic development" and "make great leaps," they imposed a regime of forced labor in which people were malnourished, lacked medications, became exhausted, and were condemned to die of hunger or disease.

In foreign policy, they refused any connection with or aid from foreign countries or international organizations, aid that could have helped heal the wounds of war. They carried out a policy of hostility toward all our neighboring countries. They provoked conflicts with Thailand in mid-1975 and during 1977. They seized a dozen Mekong River islands belonging to Laos. They launched a major war against the Vietnamese people: attacking the islands of Phu Quoc and Tho Chu in May 1975, initiating a border conflict in the northeast by invading the Vietnamese provinces of Gia Lai and Kontum (late 1975), refusing many offers by Vietnam to negotiate a peaceful settlement to the border problems (1976 and 1977).

Pol Pot and Ieng Sary thought that the contradictions with Vietnam "could not be settled by political means," and that in opting for a military solution, it was necessary "to wipe out Vietnam on Vietnamese territory itself" (Document for the dissemination of Angkar's policy at the eastern zone conference in 1977).

In April 1977, they launched a war of aggression along the whole length of the eastern zone, as far as the Vietnamese province of Tay Ninh. Beginning in late December 1977, the war of aggression against Vietnam was brought into the open and intensified.

This bellicose foreign policy served as a pretext for intensifying the repression of the population, for purging their own ranks, and for slandering and eliminating persons who objected to their political line or that they suspected of obstructing their power. This policy of war and repression caused great human and material losses to our people and exacerbated the exhaustion of our economy. At the same time, Pol Pot and Ieng Sary committed atrocious crimes against the neighboring people, especially the Vietnamese people (Documents 2.6.17, 2.6.18).

Faced with the danger of annihilation, our people rose up, starting in 1976, in many localities, and this movement spread in 1976 in Phnom Penh and in the central and eastern zones, and in 1977 in the northeastern, eastern and southwestern zones. In 1978 the whole eastern zone rose up, followed by five of the other seven zones of the country.

The more they felt isolated and opposed by the population, the more Pol Pot, Ieng Sary, and their associates intensified repression and purges. The more they indulged in genocide, the more they struck out against the opposition of large segments of our people that finally overthrew them on January 7, 1979.

(c) Bereft from the beginning of any support from the people, and facing growing opposition form the people, Pol Pot, Ieng Sary, and their associates relied on reactionary forces abroad, in particular on the Peking reactionaries, to build and maintain their dictatorial rule.

At a press conference in Peking on October 3, 1976, Pol Pot admitted that ever since 1960 he had relied on "the works of Mao Tse Tung" to oppose the line of true revolutionaries and to impose his own reactionary line on the people of Kampuchea.

In the nearly four years of their rule, from 1975 to 1979, Pol Pot and Ieng Sary advanced their idea of a so-called "100 percent high level socialist revolution," a "revolution of great leaps, of great progress, of marvelous achievements," aimed, according to their own words, at "building a country without cities, without countryside." In reality the cities were wiped out, the people were concentrated into "people's communes," and there was no market, no currency, no schools, no postal service.

All social and familial relations, all interpersonal feelings were eliminated (Document on the current situation in Kampuchea, 2.5.01). This political line was welcomed and encouraged by Mao Tse Tung: "You, comrades, have won a great victory. With one blow you have put an end to social classes. People's communes in the countryside with poor peasants and lower middle class peasants all over Kampuchea, that is our future" (Talks between Pol Pot and Mao Tse Tung, June 1975, Archives of the central committee of the Angkar party, taken from the pictorial magazine "The People's Republic of Kampuchea").

Pol Pot and Ieng Sary's policy of mass killings, or repression in "people's communes," of internal purges, and of conflict with neighboring countries gave rise to opposition from our people and was condemned strongly by large segments of world opinion. It was, however, praised and encouraged by the Peking leaders. Hua Kuo Feng said, "Comrades, you have succeeded not only in destroying the old world but in building a new world. You have achieved great success in neutralizing the maneuvers of subversion and sabotage by enemies internal and external." On the same occasion, Pol Pot said, "We have creatively and successfully applied Mao Tse Tung's thought to the realities of Kampuchea. . . . For Kampuchea, the most precious Chinese aid has been the thought of Mao Tse Tung" (Document 2.6.04).

Pol Pot and Ieng Sary relied on Peking's economic and military aid to hold power. Starting in October 1975, Peking sent economic and military aid on an urgent basis: tens of thousands of military advisors, workers, and technical personnel, and a large amount of equipment to restore the operation of airfields, ports, and strategic roads, and to supply Pol Pot's army, whose troop strength was 50,000 in 1975, but went up to 70,000 in 1977, with China providing equipment and logistical services (Documents 2.5.05, 2.5.25).

Bolstered by Chinese aid, Pol Pot and Ieng Sary intensified the repression of the people in 1976 and 1977. According to witnesses, Chinese advisors were present at certain sites where mass killings took place. (Documents 2.3.5.01, 2.3.5.02) But the more Pol Pot and Ieng Sary intensified the repression, the more the people rose up and drove them into a corner. At a meeting of the central committee of their Angkar in May 1978, they had to admit, "For now we can hold on, incurring only some damage. But a continuation of this situation could bring the danger of a collapse" (Document 2.5.26).[5]

Faced with this situation, Pol Pot and Ieng Sary moved even closer to the reactionary leaders in Peking. To help them increase the troop strength of their army from 70,000 to 130,000 men in a short period, China stepped up deliveries by air and sea to Kampuchea, in order to get them arms and other military equipment right away.

From 1978, in tandem with the aims of Peking, which followed a policy of open hostility toward Vietnam, Pol Pot and Ieng Sary stepped up their war of aggression against this neighboring country, encouraged by China to do so (Talks between the Chinese leaders and Son Sen, minister of national defense of Pol Pot during a visit to China in October 1978). They concentrated on the eastern front the bulk of their elite units equipped with modern weapons and supported by tanks and long-range artillery that they had just received from China.

In addition, Pol Pot and Ieng Sary worked hand in hand with Peking in their activities in Southeast Asia. During the September 1977 talks with Hua Kuo Feng, Pol Pot said, "If the revolution in Southeast Asia takes this opportunity to step up the offensive, the situation will improve and we will be able to resolve our problems. We have exchanged views with our friends in Burma, Malaysia, Indonesia and find we hold the same views. Thailand as well agrees with us. That is a great political success. To be sure, in the details there remain complications, but in the north we are supported by our Chinese friends, while in Southeast Asia there is unanimity among our friends. This strategic light gives us encouragement. If before we were sure of the friendship of the Chinese, today we are even more sure of it . . ." (Excerpt from the Sino-Kampuchean meeting of September 29, 1977).

After he was overthrown on January 7, 1979, Pol Pot sent Ieng Sary to Peking many times to discuss a plan of action against our people. According to documents seized at Ta Sanh, Peking promised to keep sending funds, arms, munitions, and food. Peking set up a radio station for Pol Pot and Ieng Sary and worked out for them a propaganda line and a foreign policy.

A point to note is that during one of these meetings in January 1979, Hua

5. The quoted language is found not in Document 2.5.26 but in Document 2.5.30. — Eds.

Kuo Feng and Deng Tsiao Ping drew up a plan to unite the counterrevolutionary and reactionary forces and agents of the imperialists in Kampuchea, and discussed with Ieng Sary the parceling out of leadership positions as a way of pursuing their action against our people's power (Document 2.5.18).

In sum, since gaining power, Pol Pot and Ieng Sary have been close to Peking in all fields. They considered Peking as their only support from the standpoint of ideology, politics, economics, and military affairs. They colluded with the Chinese leaders and became dependent on them in their criminal aims and actions against our people and against neighboring countries.

3. The serious consequences of the criminal acts of Pol Pot and Ieng Sary and their associates, and their damaging aftereffects in all aspects of the life of the Kampuchean people

The consequences of nearly four years of rule and of genocide by Pol Pot, Ieng Sary, and their associates, have been extremely damaging for our people. They have brought our nation to the brink of annihilation.

• Some three million innocent people were killed. From investigations done on the Phnom Penh population and on the population of a subdistrict in Siem Reap province (Documents 2.4.01, 2.4.05), and data from investigations done by the Australian journalist Wilfred Burchett in three provinces, Prey Veng, Kompong Speu, and Svay Rieng (Document 2.6.06), there is good reason to estimate that during the nearly four years of their rule, Pol Pot, Ieng Sary, and their associates killed about three million people. This number included many strong patriots and true revolutionaries, nearly all the intellectuals, scientific and technical personnel, writers and artists, and a large number of students and school pupils who were both able bodied and highly cultured. All these groups represent elements sorely needed for defending and building the country. More than four million persons survived, but they are seriously traumatized physically and spiritually.

The consequences are serious and long lasting: ruined health, many serious diseases, like tuberculosis, beriberi, malaria, and mental illness, and many women who are sterile.

The proportion of widows and orphans in the population is abnormally high. In Brum Duon village, out of 1,449 survivors, 1,169 were women, or 77 percent of the population.[6] A survey conducted in several dozen villages shows that women make up 70 to 85 percent of the current population, with most of the rest being children under the age of twelve years (Document 2.6.06).

All the disastrous consequences of such a situation for the coming generation are not yet predictable. A study done after the liberation at a hospital in Phnom Penh surveyed the children there by placing them in three categories. Category A is those four years of age and younger. Category B is those over four years of age. Category C is those born after January 7, 1979. The children in Category A are the worst affected in their physical and mental development, and in their psychological and moral growth. They suffer from many diseases. The children in Category B are also affected; their height and weight are lower than average. For children in Category C, the impact will be felt in the future, and their progress needs to be monitored (Report of a medical delegation of Dr. Nouth Savoeun, July 16, 1979, Document 2.4.03).

• Pol Pot and Ieng Sary brought the national economy to ruins. Production and goods distribution were seriously disrupted. Material resources and the means of production were destroyed. In cities, most of the factories, shops, scientific research institutes, and public utilities were destroyed. In the countryside, farm implements, draught animals, manure, and seeds were in short supply. Traditional techniques that drew on long experience in agricultural production were abandoned. The work force has been impaired: technical personnel and the former workers have almost disappeared. The population in both the countryside and the cities is in a state of extreme exhaustion.

As a result of this policy of destruction of the economy, two and a half million of our compatriots are threatened with starvation. The state and our people will have to exert great efforts over many years to restore production and the living conditions of the people.

• Pol Pot and Ieng Sary destroyed the national culture and the educational and public health institutions.

As a result of their policy, our people have fallen into ignorance, and our national culture has taken a major step backward.

Cultural and scientific institutions, schools, and hospitals have been destroyed. Teachers, university students, and school pupils that our people took many years to train have been in large measure eliminated. One now finds few university professors (there were 725 before 1975), only 207 secondary school teachers are left out of 2,300, and only 2,717 primary school teachers out of 21,311. There are only fifteen pharmacists left out of 196, and 54 medical doctors, as against 487 before 1975.

• Pol Pot and Ieng Sary destroyed the social fabric, as well as the unity felt among the various nationality groups in the country. The basic units of our society, the family and the village, were torn apart. Ethnic communities living on our territory have been battered. The entire Thai minority in Koh Kong province, and nearly all the other minorities in the northeast, such as the Muslim community, have been eliminated. The destruction of the political, economic, and cultural structures of Kampuchean society has caused and will cause serious and long-lasting consequences that one cannot fully assess at present.

• In foreign policy, the prestige and position of our country in the world have been serious eroded. As a result of Pol Pot and Ieng Sary's collusion with the Peking reactionaries, our national independence and sovereignty have been jeopardized. The crime of genocide has aroused a wave of indignant condemnation all over the world. Kampuchea was a "hunting reserve" of Pol Pot and Ieng Sary allied to Peking. Closed to the rest of the world, it was isolated from the many friends who warmly supported us during the time of anti-American resistance.

Provoking conflicts and wars with neighboring countries, Pol Pot and Ieng Sary undermined the peace and stability of Southeast Asia, in the service of interests totally foreign to our country and our people. By encroaching on Laotian territory and starting a war of aggression against Vietnam, they jeopardized the militant solidarity and friendship among the three peoples of Kampuchea, Laos, and Vietnam, a factor critical to the victory of each of these peoples in the struggle to defend national independence and sovereignty and to assure prosperity.

On January 7, 1979, Pol Pot and Ieng Sary and their associates were overthrown, and our people have become master of their own destiny. Strengthened by our traditions of indominability and national vitality, and with the devoted aid of fraternal and friendly countries, our people are determined to overcome the disastrous effects of the genocide committed throughout the country by Pol Pot and Ieng Sary.

C. Penal responsibility of Pol Pot and Ieng Sary

1. In light of Article 1 of Decree Law No. 1 of July 15, 1979, of the People's Revolutionary Council of Kampuchea, and with reference to international law punishing the crime of genocide, in particular the Convention on the Prevention and Punishment of the Crime of Genocide of December 9, 1948, we consider that the conscious criminal acts recounted above committed by the Pol Pot–Ieng Sary clique constitute the crime of genocide.

The crime of genocide is also defined in Article 1 of Decree Law No. 1 of July 15, 1979, as "planned massacres of groups of innocent people; expulsion of inhabitants of cities and villages in order to concentrate them and force them to do hard labor in conditions leading to their physical and mental destruction; wiping out religion; destroying political, cultural and social structures and family and social relations."

2. Considering that the crime of genocide has been committed by Pol Pot and Ieng Sary, in the aggravating circumstances enumerated below:

- genocide on a large scale, against different social strata, carried out throughout the entire country and in an evermore savage manner,
- methods and means used were particularly cruel, aimed at destroying the victims physically and morally by inflicting severe suffering upon them,
- killing of the entire family of a victim, killing of parents in the presence of their children, and killing of children in the presence of their parents,
- genocide in collusion with a foreign power against their own people,

• genocide with extremely serious consequences for all aspects of the life of the people, putting an entire people in danger of annihilation,

• after their overthrow on January 7, 1979, continuing their collusion with the reactionary leaders in Peking to continue opposing the Kampuchean people in the hope of restoring their dictatorial, and genocidal rule.

3. As concerns the personal responsibility of Pol Pot and Ieng Sary:

(a) Pol Pot:

• As Secretary of Angkar (the party) and prime minister, he held the highest post, directed all the activities and the organization of the party and of the state apparatus, and set the political line in domestic and foreign affairs and directed its implementation.

• He personally directed domestic policy, organized and directed the implementation of genocide in those localities where the people firmly opposed the policy of repression, as in the southwestern, northern, northwestern, and eastern zones. In these zones, genocide was carried out with particular ferocity.

• Since he was overthrown, he continues to kill those people who refuse to follow him and directs the burning and destruction of state granaries and of other commodities, with the aim of provoking starvation and penury.

• He was the instigator and planner of genocide as stipulated in Article 2, paragraph 1, of Decree Law No. 1 of July 15, 1979, and must assume entire responsibility for it.

(b) Ieng Sary:

• As a member of the permanent bureau of Angkar, he participated in the general leadership and specifically directed the implementation of genocide,

• As deputy prime minister in charge of foreign affairs, he deceived about a thousand students, intellectuals, and high officials to return to the country supposedly to build up the fatherland, and then ordered them to be killed. He defended the crime of genocide of his clique in international fora. He actively maintained the collusion with the Peking reactionaries in order to be able to carry out their criminal plan,

• After he was overthrown, on January 7, 1979, he went a number of times to China to continue the collusion with the foreign power, in order to oppose the people's power and to restore the dictatorial and genocidal regime,

• He was in close collaboration with Pol Pot to take control of the party and the state apparatus and to carry out together their reactionary domestic and foreign policy,

• He was the instigator and planner of genocide as stipulated in Article 2, paragraph 1, of Decree Law No. 1 of July 15, 1979, and must assume entire responsibility for it.

For these reasons, and in accordance with Articles 1 and 2 of Decree Law

No. 1 of July 15, 1979, of the People's Revolutionary Council of Kampuchea, we decide to try for the crime of genocide before the People's Revolutionary Tribunal at Phnom Penh the following accused persons:

1. Pol Pot, alias Saloth Sar, of Khmer nationality, born in 1925 in Prey Sbau village, Kompong Thom province, a resident of Phnom Penh, former prime minister of the government of Democratic Kampuchea that has been overthrown, married to Khieu Ponnary, currently in hiding and under an arrest warrant;

2. Ieng Sary, of Khmer nationality, born in 1925 in Hoa Lac village, Luong Hoa subdistrict, Chau Thanh district, Tra Vinh (currently Cuu Long) province, Vietnam, a resident of Phnom Penh, former deputy prime minister in charge of foreign affairs of the government of Democratic Kampuchea that has been overthrown, married to Khieu Thirit, currently in hiding and under an arrest warrant.

Attached are the investigation files of this case, the list of evidence, and the list of witnesses invited to appear before the Tribunal.

Done at the Prosecutor's Office, July 30, 1979
Prosecutor of the People's Revolutionary Tribunal at Phnom Penh

Closing Statements

3.02

Closing argument of Mat Ly, Prosecutor of the Tribunal

Mr. Chairman, and Messrs. the People's Assessors, the Kampuchean people have just come out of a most terrible nightmare. Unfortunately, this nightmare is a fact. It lasted nearly four years. Although it was less than four years, under the bloody rule of the Pol Pot and Ieng Sary, more than three million of our compatriots died an extremely tragic death.

Almost all the surviving Kampucheans have come back from the world of the dead. In face of the odious crimes of the Pol Pot–Ieng Sary clique, the conscience of mankind rose up. The Kampuchean people rose up. They themselves toppled the Pol Pot–Ieng Sary executioners totally, established a government truly of the people, their sole legitimate representatives.

Today the whole people of Kampuchea raising their voice jointly with progressive mankind demand that the genocidal Pol Pot–Ieng Sary clique be tried so as to lay bare before public opinion all their odious crimes, to punish the culprits with a view to setting an example, and preventing the repetition of such crimes both against the Kampuchean people and any other people in the world.

Indeed, our tribunal meets this legitimate demand. Set up under a Decree Law of the revolutionary government, the tribunal has conducted the trial fairly and impartially. It does not give judgment on the basis of sentimentality with a purpose of vengeance, nor impose a verdict of the victor on the vanquished. On the contrary, it holds public sittings attended by well respected journalists, public figures, and jurists, and uses objective, concrete evidence, observing normal judicial procedures to guarantee justice.

The investigative agencies, with the voluntary and effective assistance of the citizenry, have managed to collect, analyze and summarize several categories of different kinds of evidence to uncover the truth about the crimes of the genocidal Pol Pot–Ieng Sary clique.

The investigative agencies have secured the statements of many victims and witnesses belonging to different strata of the population and living in different areas of our country. They have managed to get confessions of agents of the fallen regime who had a hand in the crime. They have come to the places of the crime where various methods and means of killing were used. They have studied documents, books, notebooks, and recorded tapes that Pol Pot and Ieng Sary were unable to take with them in their hasty flight before the lightning attack of the people's liberation forces. They have collected and studied books, newspapers, magazines, photographs, and films published at home and abroad about the crimes of Pol Pot and Ieng Sary. They have put together several specialized investigative files, such as the file on the crimes of Pol Pot and Ieng Sary related to the destruction of the economy, a file on the crimes against culture and education, a file on the crimes against religions, a file on the crimes against ethnic minorities, and a file on the crimes against the population of Phnom Penh capital city.

During the five days of the trial, the tribunal interrogated witnesses and scrupulously examined all these different pieces of evidence.

The evidence publicly presented to the tribunal evoked deep emotions on the part of all who attended the trial.

These pieces of evidence, and nothing other than these pieces of evidence, even though millions of other Kampucheans are equally victims and witnesses who could supply us with equally convincing and moving evidence, suffice to demonstrate clearly and irrefutably that the genocidal Pol Pot–Ieng Sary clique committed the following criminal acts as charged in the indictment:

1. the killing of various strata of the population on an increasing scale and with increasing cruelty.

2. the expulsion of the entire populations of the cities to the rural areas, and then the displacement of the inhabitants of the rural areas according to a concerted plan.

3. the concentration and oppression of the people in "people's communes," mistreating them physically and morally in such a way as to turn them into slaves.

4. the destruction of all human relationships among the Kampuchean people.

5. the complete elimination of intellectuals and the Buddhist clergy, the liquidation of religions, and the destruction of the national culture.

6. the killing and mistreatment of adolescents, and turning many of them into inhuman tormentors.

A point that draws our particular attention and arouses our indignation when we examine the criminal acts of the genocidal Pol Pot–Ieng Sary clique is the extreme cruelty and barbarity of the crime.

It is extremely barbarous not only because of the killing of millions of persons on a nationwide scale, but also because the human person has been mistreated and trampled under foot to such an extent that man is no longer a man and that life is more terrible than death. And more serious still, the genocidal Pol Pot–Ieng Sary clique destroyed the social fabric and the way of life of the Kampuchean nation.

I. Nationwide massacre of millions of people conducted in an extremely barbarous way

Each of us has suffered by losing persons dear to us. Here it is not a matter of hundreds of lives lost. At Lidice and Oradour, several hundred innocent people being killed aroused indignation in world opinion during World War Two.

Here we have lost much more. Several million innocent citizens died a tragic death. This immense human loss occurred not in a war waged by one country against another, but in the course of a bloody repression without precedent in history, inside a country subjected to a fascist regime.

Within a comparatively short span of time, barely four years, we lost three million human lives, three million of our countrymen in a population of about seven million.

The genocidal Pol Pot–Ieng Sary clique did not content itself with terrorizing and killing a single stratum of the population. Indeed it went after all social strata. It exterminated not only the general population, but also believers in religion, and particularly national minorities. It killed not only adults but persons of any age, children and newborn babies included. It killed men as well as women. The killings took place not in one locality, one city, one province or one region, but all over the country.

These nationwide killings caused deep suffering to millions of people and their families. Our entire people is still in mourning.

Overnight, our nation lost nearly half its population, a proportion of killings even higher than that carried out by the Hilterite fascists during World War II. In that war, Poland, which suffered the most from the Hitlerite killings, lost only one fifth of its population.

We are speaking here only of the number of the dead. Allow us to draw the tribunal's attention to the quality of our lost population. Indeed, a high percentage of the victims are proven patriots, true revolutionaries, scientists, people of culture, technicians, and highly skilled workers, and hard-working people in industry and agriculture. This human loss seriously affects activities in all political, economic, social and cultural fields of our national life.

The genocidal Pol Pot–Ieng Sary clique cut off the most useful arms of our homeland, arms that are precious to us, particularly just now when we have to rebuild a destroyed country, and rapidly heal the serious wounds caused by the crimes of this clique.

This loss in people and in intellectual and spiritual wealth is beyond calculation and nothing can make up for it.

The genocidal Pol Pot–Ieng Sary clique carried out its plan of killing against the people with a feverish rage. This attitude is seen in the instructions and educational documents of the genocidal Pol Pot–Ieng Sary clique and was consistently carried out in the purges and extermination activities launched against the people and the clique's own personnel.

The genocidal Pol Pot–Ieng Sary clique sees opponents everywhere, calling them "reactionaries" and "enemies," and regarding them as subjects for purge.

For the Pol Pot–Ieng Sary clique, "to purge" meant to kill, to deprive people of the right to live. They repeatedly exhorted their agents "to continue the purge," "to increase the purge," and "to purge in a fundamental way all kinds of reactionaries." Although they had carried out killings on a large scale for three years in a row (1976–1977–1978), this clique at the end of 1978 was getting ready to purge even more thoroughly.

This bloodthirsty policy was manifested in other activities as well:

1. The killing not only of an entire social group that might oppose the regime, such as the killing of intellectuals, and of all the military personnel and civil servants of the former regime, but as well the killing of their entire families, including husband, wife, and children, in order to eradicate the opposition completely.

2. The mass killing of Party committee members, of officials, and of military personnel of an entire region if any entity within the region was suspected of rebellion.

The genocidal Pol Pot–Ieng Sary clique reasoned that if the people of a locality are rebellious, the officials of the locality are under suspicion as well. When the officials at one level are under suspicion, the officials above and below them are also under suspicion. Therefore, it is necessary to purge a whole range of officials at different levels in order to purify the ranks.

This policy of generalized purging was laid down in a resolution of July 17, 1977, of the eastern military region on the selection and reorganization of the administrative committees of cooperatives and of cooperative members:

"The selection of administrative committees of cooperatives and of cooperative members has not been done well. . . ."

"Why do we need to change the selection process?"

"Because when the district committee is suspect, the subdistrict committee is also suspect. The two committees are connected. They constitute a single system. When the district becomes reactionary, the village is reactionary too. This is natural, because officials select only people they like to serve under them. . . ."

"We should be adamant against bad elements. We must cut short, and not allow them to exist."

In carrying out this policy of purging, the genocidal Pol Pot–Ieng Sary clique killed a whole series of leading officials of each military region, such as the eastern military region.

3. The killing not only of leading officials of a military unit suspected of opposition, but of the whole unit concerned. Some divisions were in effect killed off completely: for example, Division 200 and Division 290, both directly under the Central Command; Division 3, Division 4, and Division 5 of

the eastern military region; and regional units in regions 20, 21, 22, 23, and 24.

4. The indiscriminate killing of the entire population of a region in the event of indications of rebellion in some localities in the region. The killing of the population of the eastern military zone is a typical example of this. The executioners killed not only the inhabitants of the eastern zone who were still there, but they followed others to the western zone, to which they had been forced to evacuate. In fact, in Pursat province of the western zone, they collected 40,000 inhabitants of the eastern zone, and wiped them out in three rounds of mass killing in June 1978.

5. The extermination not only of the Khmer population, but also of ethnic minorities, such as the Thai minority, and particularly the Cham minority, which practiced the Islamic religion. The genocidal Pol Pot–Ieng Sary clique did not stop at these criminal acts. They also exterminated Vietnamese and the Chinese residents who had been living for a long time in our country.

6. After being overthrown, the genocidal Pol Pot–Ieng Sary clique in its flight forced masses of inhabitants to follow, leaving behind villages and property, to serve as a shield. They even killed en masse inhabitants who refused to follow them; let us mention for instance the recent massacre of 12,000 inhabitants in Am Leang subdistrict, Kompong Speu province, in February 1979. As well, they killed thousands of other Kampucheans who had been sent back to the country by the Thai authorities.

The killings have been perpetrated in an arbitrary, fascistic manner. Any agent of Angkar is authorized to arrest and kill people. Persons who were arrested, imprisoned, or awaiting execution, and their relatives had nowhere to lodge a complaint. In fact there is no agency to receive or examine complaints or claims from the inhabitants. The Pol Pot–Ieng Sary regime has no law or court system. Its law is that of the jungle, or more precisely, the whim of the blood thirsty Pol Pot and Ieng Sary. The arbitrary acts of arrest, imprisonment, and killing of innocent people have been committed in a persistent and continuous way during long years throughout the country without any remedy from the genocidal Pol Pot–Ieng Sary clique. On the contrary, such acts have been encouraged and rewarded.

The methods of massacre were extremely cruel.

Hitler's fascists used toxic gases to kill people en masse in "gas chambers." At the time, this method was strongly condemned by world opinion for its inhumane character, for causing needless suffering to the victims before death. Hitler's fascists were compelled to mask their crime; they perpetrated it secretly in concentration camps far from inhabited areas.

In our country on the contrary, the genocidal Pol Pot–Ieng Sary clique carried out their crime against their own fellow countrymen shamelessly, through official acts, in broad daylight.

The investigation conducted at the trial has allowed us to imagine the tragic scenes of killing: The executioners make the victims dig their own graves, huge graves in which dozens, even hundreds, of bodies could be buried. They line the victims up next to the graves. They use not toxic gases, but the most rudimentary means, bamboo sticks, axes, picks, or hoes, to strike at the victims' skulls as one would kill an animal. The victim does not die immediately, but turns around in place under the feet of the executioner, like a top before it spins itself out. That is why the agents of Pol Pot and Ieng Sary call this means of killing "the top method."

The executioners strike each victim in full view of many other victims. Let us imagine the fear and torment of a person awaiting his turn to suffer this torture. The wait is not just for a few minutes, but may last for hours, because they torture and kill hundreds, and even thousands of people at one time. Worse still, the victims typically do not die immediately after a few blows to the head. They turn around before collapsing. The executioners kick them into the pit and cover them with a little earth. How many victims are not struck at a vital spot and do not die at once, but suffer for hours before taking their last breath! How many others lose consciousness immediately but come to later, only to die slowly of asphyxiation in atrocious pain under the heaps of bodies and earth that cover them! The investigations have revealed a number of cases of persons surviving in this way, including some children.

This extremely inhumane method of killing was applied all over the country. The broken skulls found in large pits in various regions of the country would make a mountain.

The genocidal Pol Pot–Ieng Sary clique also came up with other barbarous means to kill people. Let us mention some: burying alive; burning alive; pouring boiling water over the body; pushing rows of victims into a river; cutting off the flesh bit by bit; cutting open the stomach and taking out the liver or spleen; cutting the throat; crushing people under armored vehicles; tearing children apart; bashing children's heads against tree trunks. And another more original method has been used: throwing victims into ponds where crocodiles are raised.

The above relates not only to innocent victims who have been massacred. What was the situation of the millions of other people who survived under the genocidal Pol Pot–Ieng Sary regime?

II. Mistreatment and extermination of the Kampuchean people, both physically and morally, in the "people's communes," driving the Kampuchean people to a slow death

The physical mistreatment was truly terrible. Millions of our fellow countrymen were forced to work twelve to sixteen hours a day with extremely rudimentary instruments. In some places, they had to draw ploughs in the place of oxen or buffalo, or to carry earth with their bare hands. They were made to exert themselves for days, weeks, or months on end, often without rest, under the threat of rifles and bayonets. Fourteen- to fifteen-year-old children had to work like adults.

What kind of food was provided to persons in this regime of forced labor? A starvation diet, to the extent that for months on end, workers ate nothing but rice soup. Tortured by hunger, our fellow countrymen had to eat wild plants, roots, even scorpions or millipedes to fill their stomachs. As a result, there were many cases of death from hunger or disease.

The food ration being clearly insufficient for the energy expended, the health of all the workers visibly dissipated. Some were unable to stand up but had to drag themselves to the fields to get their daily rations and live on.

The weakened body, losing resistance, was an easy prey to disease. Such dangerous diseases as dysentery, bloating, and tuberculosis were widespread among the workers, and every day, every hour gnawed at their bodies.

Dwellings were only makeshift huts which collapsed in the slightest storm.

To compel people to do forced labor in such conditions is to condemn them to an inevitable, slow death.

Moral mistreatment and terror are even worse than physical mistreatment.

Human relationships are a threat to the genocidal Pol Pot–Ieng Sary clique. Relationships among persons who hate or despise the Pol Pot–Ieng Sary regime are an even greater threat. That was the reason they tried hard to destroy interpersonal relationships. To that end they tried to destroy relationships within the family, to separate husbands and wives from each other, to separate children from their parents, to stop relationships among neighbors, and between villages, to eliminate all factors conducive to interpersonal relationships, such as currency, communications, and mail service and telegraphs. . . .

In particular, they held the people down under a regime that was fascistic in the extreme. They subjected the people to severe police control, even as regards private feelings and thoughts.

A cry of pain, a complaint, a word of compassion or a suggestion, the voicing of a claim or a question, even when the person involved suffers from gross injustice, could be regarded as signs of opposition. More fascistic still is that they kept watch for the expressions on people's faces. A trace of sadness or indignation could be considered a crime punishable by death.

The genocidal Pol Pot–Ieng Sary clique needed only the physical labor of people blindly obeying its orders, and not people with a heart and a mind.

The clique organized a whole network of security agents and spies to keep close watch on the population. It even organized and trained children to keep tabs on the acts, words, and attitudes of their parents, and brothers and sisters. The agents spied day and night, hiding in bushes or along a road, putting their ears up to the walls of a house, lying flat on a roof, or creeping under the floors of a house.

This is a permanent situation of oppression operating around the clock, a fascistic oppression against the Kampuchean people to a level hitherto unknown.

There are only two penalties, a warning and death. Often Angkar warns only once or kills immediately without warning.

It is as if every Kampuchean citizen were under a suspended death sentence that the agents of Pol Pot–Ieng Sary may carry out at any time.

Physically exhausted, and constantly in fear of being arrested and executed as he many times had seen or heard about, every Kampuchean led an extremely tense life.

That is why our fellow countrymen always had to be on guard, and watch their actions and words. They had to control their own feelings, thoughts, and words, as well as the expression on their faces, not to weep when they were sad, not to laugh when they were happy. Their heads did not dare to think, and their mouths had to say things contrary to what they felt and thought, to such an extent that they were no longer themselves.

People were oppressed, trodden under foot, to the point of totally losing the right to be their own masters, of becoming a slave both physically and mentally, a slave whose condition was more unfortunate and degrading than that of the slaves of the Middle Ages.

The destruction of the human personality and of human dignity was pushed to the limit.

A life of such mistreatment and oppression is worse than death.

That is why so many of our fellow countrymen died an early death.

That is why so many of our fellow countrymen went out of their minds.

That is why so many of our fellow countrymen committed suicide, sometimes together with their whole family, preferring death to a life unworthy of a man.

Moral oppression added to physical mistreatment led our people to the point of withering away.

In view of this fact, the "people's communes" were for practical purposes slaughterhouses. And on this point, the genocidal Pol Pot–Ieng Sary clique were more barbarous than Hitler's fascists.

III. Destruction to the core of the whole social structure of Kampuchea; Destruction of her national culture

The family, the village, the city are the basic elements of social organization. These elements, and a person's relationship with his family, his village, or his city, make up the life of a nation.

One of the serious crimes of the genocidal Pol Pot–Ieng Sary clique is the destruction of the family through the suppression of familial relationships.

This crime was systematically committed by several related methods. The first was the destruction of feelings between husband and wife, of the love between parents and children. Those are sacred family sentiments of any human being, and in particular of the Kampucheans.

However, the genocidal Pol Pot–Ieng Sary clique arbitrarily separates husbands from wives, forcing them to live and work far from one another, and keeps spouses from visiting each other and helping each other, even in case of illness or danger. They even forbid one spouse to show affection toward the other, or to weep when the other is killed. Indeed, many men and women have been savagely killed simply for daring to keep their faithfulness to, or to help, or to weep for, their spouses.

Children are separated from their parents. At the age of 14 or 15 years, they are forced to join mobile production brigades or the army, where they are educated in a spirit of absolute blind obedience to Angkar.

Freedom of marriage does not exist at all. Young boys and girls are forbidden to have friendships or to marry without permission of Angkar. Angkar practices forced marriage. It forces young girls or widows to marry men it chooses.

As a result, many women have killed themselves, preferring death to a union with a man, perhaps an enemy, who could not ensure their happiness, or who even might destroy their life.

The genocidal Pol Pot–Ieng Sary clique did not stop at the destruction of the family. It also suppresses the life of cities and villages.

Long before coming to power, the clique envisaged a policy aimed at totally eliminating all towns and cities in Kampuchea. After the liberation of April 17, 1975, it began immediately to carry out this scheme in a brutal and treacherous fashion. It deceived the urban population by saying that this was only a temporary evacuation of a few days to avoid American bombardment. Then by force of arms, rifles and bayonets pointed at the backs of the people, it forced all city dwellers to evacuate right away, with no exceptions whatsoever, sick people and women in childbirth included. No assistance was organized along the evacuation routes. Overnight, urban Kampucheans were deprived of all their wealth, the result of a lifetime of work and thrift. They were thrown into the streets and forced to walk day and night, for weeks, and even months in the suffocating heat of the summer sun, and to sleep in the open air or under bushes. Particularly barbarous was the expulsion of all the patients from hospitals, without exception even for those who had just undergone operations, or those confined to bed, or the infirm.

What was worst for the evacuees was their worry whether they would have food the next day. With their hands empty, what could they do? Their misfortune also lay in the fear of being killed at any time, a fear aroused by seeing killings every day, every hour, first against the military personnel and civil servants of the former regime, and against anyone suspected of opposition or who did not follow the orders of the Pol Pot soldiers, for instance, by slowing down or stopping along the way.

En route, tens of thousands of city-dwellers died of hunger, exhaustion, disease, or even from despair. Driving all the inhabitants out of the towns and cities in such conditions was practically mass murder of the civilian population.

The genocidal Pol Pot–Ieng Sary clique also destroyed normal life in the villages. It set up in the villages so-called "people's communes," which were actually concentration camps for the inhabitants in which they were condemned to forced labor, and turned them into slaves subjected to a fascistic police state that trampled all fundamental freedoms and human rights.

The regime suppressed all human relationships, with the exception of the relationship with Angkar on the basis of servile obedience. The Pol Pot–Ieng Sary agents made villagers move quite often, keeping them from harvesting what they had planted. Life in the villages thus was extremely unsettled.

By destroying families, by eliminating cities, by uprooting villages, and by abolishing the family and social relationships of the citizen, the genocidal Pol Pot–Ieng Sary clique destroyed the entire social structure of the country.

The destruction of the national culture was also a policy that the genocidal Pol Pot–Ieng Sary clique tried to carry out systematically. It abolished the entire educational system, from primary schools to higher education, and it destroyed books and libraries. It killed not only nearly all the intellectuals living in the country, but as well the Kampuchean intellectuals living abroad who responded to its call and repatriated in the hope of participating in the reconstruction of the country.

Eighty percent of the professors and teachers have been killed. Among the 11,000 students in the country, only 400 remain alive. Of 683 physicians and pharmacists, only 69 are left. In other words, nine out of ten of the physicians and pharmacists were killed. The few intellectuals who have survived are those who were able to portray themselves as not being intellectuals, and to hide their knowledge and identity.

The genocidal Pol Pot–Ieng Sary clique also went to great lengths to eliminate believers in any religion. It deliberately suppressed Buddhism, a religion that is closely connected to the lives of most of our compatriots. It made all the monks leave their pagodas and return to a secular life; it made them do forced labor in the "people's communes." It destroyed and burned all the holy books, it broke the statues, and it used the pagodas as military camps, arms depots, or cattle farms.

It particularly wiped out Islam, killing nearly all the leading figures. To add to its barbarism, it tried to kill all followers of Islam.

By making the Kampuchean people live under a regime of fascist domination that deprived them of any rights or liberties, by suppressing all their social relations, and by making each citizen live in isolation, the genocidal Pol Pot–Ieng Sary clique destroyed the beautiful traditions of the Kampuchean people.

By closing schools and destroying books, libraries, and museums, by eliminating the culture and art of the Kampuchean people, by wiping out intellectuals and religions, and by destroying the beautiful traditions of the Kampuchean people, the genocidal Pol Pot–Ieng Sary clique simply destroyed the national culture of the Kampuchean people.

The totality of the criminal acts of the genocidal Pol Pot–Ieng Sary clique has caused incredibly serious damage to all aspects of the life of our people.

Nearly half our population was wiped out.

There is no family that has no victims killed or tortured in a tragic fashion by the bloody hands of the genocidal Pol Pot–Ieng Sary clique. Many families have been totally wiped out, with no family members surviving.

Today one finds many widows and orphans in every village.

Our country is full of graves that are not at all individuals' tombs with stones inscribed with names in memory of the person, but rather collective graves for mass burial of anonymous victims and in which broken skulls piled up at random revive our long suppressed feelings of hatred.

What is most dramatic for us is that on the soil of our beloved homeland, inhabited for thousands of years by people characterized by goodness, loyalty, charity, and fraternity, and a country of the talented people who built the glorious Angkor civilization, there occurred the most barbarous mistreatment that history has ever known.

It is a case of deportation, imprisonment, and torture against a whole people.

It is a case of the abolition of all rights of all citizens, confiscation of all their property, and turning them into slaves deprived even of the right to emotions and thoughts, that is to say, of all human personality, of the right to be human.

It is a case of a "great leap" backward from civilization to the stone age. All towns and cities became deserted. All villages became mournful.

The whole economy was destroyed, as was the material base, starting with the infrastructure. As a matter of fact, a major part of industry, which had about one hundred factories, equipment, and materials, was destroyed. Handicrafts were dying. In agriculture, tens of thousands of hectares of rice fields were left to waste, with agricultural implements destroyed. Trade and goods distribution were totally abolished. The means of communication and information such as railway engines, ships and boats, ports, the mail service, telegraph, and telephones were also almost completely destroyed.

With regard to the labor force, we lost thousands of workers. Eighty percent of engineers, technicians and skilled workers were killed. The four million Kampucheans who survived have been seriously affected both physically and mentally as a result of malnutrition, suffering, and the misfortunes they endured for several years on end.

With regard to modes of production, the workers were turned into slaves in agriculture.

The education system entirely collapsed. Education did not go beyond learning to read and write. Illiteracy prevailed in the population.

Precious intellectual and spiritual values left by our forefathers for centuries were destroyed.

From the social angle, as has been pointed out by some of the special reports, there are many physical and mental diseases: general feebleness, bloating, dysentery, and tuberculosis have struck many people; women's diseases are serious, hindering the restoration and normal development of the Khmer population; physical and mental atrophy is widespread among children, particularly those who were born under the Pol Pot regime. More serious still is the moral poisoning of most of the adolescents, who have been turned into killing machines without any human character.

The far-reaching and long-lasting consequences are so serious that no one can yet assess them of the crimes of abolition of families, mistreatment of the population in the "people's communes," extermination of the intellectuals, destruction of the soul of the adolescents, and abolition of national culture.

The question which arises here and requires an explanation is: Why did the genocidal Pol Pot–Ieng Sary clique embark on such terrible genocide against its own people? The answer to this question lies in the nature of the Pol Pot–Ieng Sary regime, which was a new type of fascist regime of slavery.

With their policies of dividing the population into categories, and then eliminating them one by one, of driving city dwellers out of towns and urban centers, of concentrating the people in "people's communes" and subjecting them there to a regime of coercion and forced labor, and of an obscurantist destruction of national culture, the Pol Pot–Ieng Sary regime ran counter to, and betrayed, the legitimate interests of the Kampuchean people, thus incurring their opposition. However, the leaders of the regime wanted to maintain their absolute power.

Having failed to gain the backing, sympathy, or support of the people, the genocidal Pol Pot–Ieng Sary clique was driven to a position of weakness and isolation. It had to seek the backing of the reactionary ruling circles of Peking to maintain its dictatorship and embark on a bloody repression to eliminate the people's opposition, and to wipe out any hint of opposition. Although they had to kill a part of the Kampuchean people, their radio impudently boasted of their frantic genocidal aim: "Even if we have only two million Kampucheans left, that is enough for us to rebuild the country."

The more Pol Pot and Ieng Sary stepped up their repression and terror, the more they encountered the opposition and uprising of the people. That is why they had to cling to and seek the unfortunate backing of the leaders in Peking. The latter increased their support and aid so that Pol Pot and Ieng Sary could expand the scope of terror, and carry out even more savage persecution and extermination of the people.

The genocidal Pol Pot–Ieng Sary clique leaned on Peking to stay in power. For its part, Peking used the clique to carry out its policy of big-power expansionism and hegemonism in Southeast Asia, and in the immediate future, to carry out this policy with regard to our country and the other countries of the Indochinese peninsula. Close collaboration developed between the genocidal Pol Pot–Ieng Sary clique and the reactionary ruling circles of Peking. And the genocidal Pol Pot–Ieng Sary clique became a perfect instrument of China's big-power expansionism and hegemonism.

Holding a monopoly on military and economic aid, and using a network of dozens of advisers exerting both military and administrative leadership, the Chinese reactionaries put Pol Pot–Ieng Sary under their sway, and actually turned our country into a new-type colony and a base for provocation and aggression against the neighboring countries such as Thailand, Laos, and Vietnam.

But Peking's massive military and economic aid could not prevent the danger of collapse of the genocidal Pol Pot–Ieng Sary regime. To maintain their position, to divert the people's struggle, and at the same time to find a pretext to step up repression against the people, the genocidal Pol Pot–Ieng Sary clique, directed and encouraged by Peking, resorted to a perfidious approach. They aroused hatred between our nation and the Vietnamese nation, provoked border conflicts in order to launch a war of aggression against Vietnam, an unjust war running counter to the national interests of Kampuchea, thereby destroying the traditional friendship and fraternal, militant solidarity between our people and the people of Vietnam.

The collusion between Pol Pot and Ieng Sary and the hegemonist expansionists of Peking has been a key factor behind the genocidal Pol Pot–Ieng Sary clique on the one hand carrying out genocide against the Kampuchean people, and on the other, waging a war of aggression against the people of Vietnam.

In a word, the genocidal Pol Pot–Ieng Sary clique betrayed the people and nation of Kampuchea, usurped the revolutionary accomplishments of our people, established a fascist and dictatorial regime such as has never been known before in history, turning our whole country into a hell of blood and tears, threatening peace and stability in Southeast Asia, and furthering expansionism and hegemonism of the reactionary Peking rulers.

The Charge:

Considering the totality of the criminal acts of the genocidal Pol Pot–Ieng Sary clique which have been clearly and precisely demonstrated before the tribunal,

On the basis of the declaration of January 10, 1979, proclaiming the establishment of the People's Republic of Kampuchea, and condemning the dictatorial, fascist and genocidal Pol Pot–Ieng Sary regime that drove the Kampuchean people to slavery and the threat of extermination,

On the basis of Decree Law No. 1 of July 15, 1979, of the People's Revolutionary Council of Kampuchea, defining and punishing the crime of genocide,

On the basis of the International Convention of December 9, 1948, on the Prevention and Punishment of the Crime of Genocide,

We find that the criminal acts committed by Pol Pot and Ieng Sary contain all the elements of the crime of genocide.

Genocidal intent is shown by the policy and action plans for each category of criminal acts of genocide, committed by Pol Pot and Ieng Sary, and listed in the indictment. This policy and these plans were included in the study and teaching documents for Pol Pot–Ieng Sary officials, or made public in radio broadcasts.

In particular, genocidal intent was clearly manifested in the acts of genocide taken as a whole. These acts were perpetrated systematically, and repeated many times with similar methods and means, on a large scale throughout the country, against our whole people. This shows a policy and a concerted plan from the central administration, that is to say, a deliberate intention of genocide.

Concerning the acts of genocide, the genocidal Pol Pot–Ieng Sary clique committed all the acts of genocide defined by the Decree Law of July 15, 1979:

- killing innocent people en masse and systematically,
- driving the inhabitants out of towns and villages and throwing them together and forcing them to work in physically and morally exhausting conditions,
- eliminating religion, and destroying economic and cultural institutions, and family and social relationships.

The above-mentioned acts brought our nation to the brink of extermination.

Thus we have adequate factual and legal grounds to conclude that the genocidal Pol Pot–Ieng Sary clique committed the crime of genocide against the Kampuchean nation.

This crime of genocide is shown to be extremely serious by the following aggravating circumstances:

1. driving the entire people into slavery, destroying all rights and human dignity.

2. carrying out the genocide through a state apparatus with its armed forces and police. That state's main function was to repress, terrorize, and kill the people.

3. using extremely barbarous methods to kill the people.

4. not only to exterminate the population, but to compel it to live in conditions leading to a slow death by making living conditions impossible.

5. carrying out genocide while forbidding the victims and their loved ones to show compassion or pity. To close the country to all foreign contact,

except for China and some partner countries, in order to keep the Kampuchean people's cries for help from being heard in the outside world.

6. carrying out genocide according to a criminal escalation with regard to scope and barbarity, in spite of the warnings, vehement protests and condemnation of progressive mankind.

7. Extremely obstinate, the genocidal Pol Pot–Ieng Sary clique is continuing and intensifying the genocide in spite of the strong opposition of progressive mankind. Moreover, since being overthrown, they continue to commit other criminal acts against our fellow countrymen.

Examining the individual responsibility of the genocidal Pol Pot–Ieng Sary clique, we find that:

- Pol Pot was secretary of Angkar and prime minister.
- Ieng Sary was a member of the standing committee of the central committee of Angkar, and vice-premier in charge of foreign relations.
- Pol Pot and Ieng Sary are brothers-in-law, and sons-in-law in the same family.

Pol Pot and Ieng Sary are men loyal to Peking.

Pol Pot and Ieng Sary have colluded with each other for a long time, since soon after plotting together to seize the monopoly of leadership over the party and state in 1960. This close collusion has continued during the whole period when the crime of genocide was being carried out in Kampuchea. In fact, these two individuals forming a dictatorial clique of nepotism together worked out a reactionary policy in both domestic and foreign affairs.

With regard to Pol Pot, in his capacity as secretary of Angkar and prime minister, he chaired the meetings of Angkar and of the government at which decisions were taken on domestic and foreign policy, in particular, on the policy and plans of genocide against the Kampuchean people. He personally ordered the execution of these policies and plans.

With regard to Ieng Sary, in his capacity as a member of the standing committee of the central committee of Angkar, he ordered the carrying out of the crime of genocide inside the country. In addition, in his capacity as vice-premier in charge of foreign relations, he actively promoted the collusion between Pol Pot and Ieng Sary and the reactionary Peking ruling circles. The genocidal Pol Pot–Ieng Sary clique's close ties with Peking to seek its aid and leadership constituted an important and indispensable condition for perpetrating the crime of genocide against the people of Kampuchea. In addition, Ieng Sary actively defended before international institutions the criminal acts committed by his clique against the Kampuchean people.

As a result, Ieng Sary's crime is no less serious than Pol Pot's. Both culprits are responsible as instigators and perpetrators who set the policy and plans for genocide and ordered their execution. Neither culprit can be deemed to benefit from any mitigating circumstance. Both criminals showed great obduracy.

A whole people must bear the particularly serious consequences, both physical and moral. The restoration, repair, and reeducation work will require great efforts, over a dozen or so years, perhaps even over a whole generation.

However, at the present time, the reactionaries within the ruling circles in Peking, in collusion with imperialist forces, are working for a return to power of these great criminals to let them repeat genocide at a level of savagery that defies human imagination, for a return of an enemy regime opposed to the people and their civilization, allowing the criminals once again to spread misfortune.

This judgment shows the determination of our people and of progressive mankind definitively to eliminate from our planet this monstrous genocidal regime.

Millions of widows and orphans, millions of fathers and spouses in Kampuchea, and millions of people of conscience the world over have been raising their voices to demand that the criminals be duly and severely punished, and to demand that this terrible danger to the people and to human civilization be checked.

Public opinion at home and progressive opinion around the world will not be able to forgive us if we let the lead executioners escape punishment. Human civilization could not survive if this crime of genocide of a new type were not punished and could be repeated.

This judgment is the verdict not only of the Kampuchean people, but also of all mankind.

For these reasons, we have the honor to ask the judges, under Article 2 of Decree Law No. 1 of July 15, 1979, to condemn Pol Pot and Ieng Sary to death, with total confiscation of their property.

3.03a

Closing Argument of Hope R. Stevens, Defense Counsel (Attorney and Counsellor at Law, Member of the Bar of the United States Supreme Court, Co-Chairperson of the National Conference of Black Lawyers of the United States and Canada)

Honorable Chief Justice, the Honorable Court, permit me to thank the Revolutionary Court for allowing me to appear before you as an advocate for the defense of the accused. I have not come from halfway around the world to give approval to monstrous crime or to ask for mercy for the criminals. No! A thousand times no! Not at all! I would never be found in such a position. The reasons for my presence include the following points:

1. I belong to a minority in my own country whose present members and

whose ancestors have been the victims of the same crime of genocide that has decimated the people of Cambodia during the past few years.

2. My ancestors were kidnapped by force and violence, transported across the oceans from Africa, subjected to forced labor by the so-called civilized Anglo-Saxon white majority and irrespective of their high culture my people were deported to a strange and inhospitable environment to plant not rice, but cotton and sugar cane.

3. In order to accomplish that program the oppressors had to abolish the national culture of the victims, my people, and by the most horrible forms of torture, raping the women, mutilating the men, cutting off their feet, toes or hands when they tried to escape, tracking them down with blood hounds, and killing them when they refused to submit to the degrading life of slavery.

4. I am therefore by my history an expert on the subject of the crime of genocide, murder, rape, torture, mutilation, lynching, and deprivation of human rights.

5. And up to now, neither the Supreme Court of my country nor the Congress which makes our laws has ever ordered a trial condemning the criminal institution of slavery or the genocidal behavior of the society that practices that horrible criminal system. Nor have the criminals who used those disgusting and inhuman methods against my people ever been "posthumously" tried, condemned, convicted, or denounced in absentia. So you see, Honorable Chief Justice and the Court, I could not be present here to defend, condone, or approve the awful crime of genocide against the beautiful and noble people of Cambodia.

Then, Honorable Chief Justice and the Court, you may ask me "Why are you here?"

"Why am I here?" "Why do I permit myself to speak as advocate for the accused?"

The people of Cambodia and you are entitled to a further explanation: I am here as the Co-chairperson of the National Conference of Black Lawyers of the United States and Canada. In my country this organization exists for the purpose of making sure that every person accused of crime has the opportunity of defending himself? the right to a fair trial before a court of competent jurisdiction. It exists to compel the Courts to hear what the accused has to say in his own defense or in mitigation of the crime with which he is charged before being convicted, or to hear what facts or testimony anyone else may have to offer in defense of the accused. We exist to see that the law is applied to all without fear or favor, so that each accused may have "Equal Justice under Law." I do not intend you to understand or to believe that we always succeed in this effort. Quite often in my country, the elements of racism and prejudice interfere to defeat our goals and to pervert and make mockery of justice and to condemn the innocent while the guilty go free.

But above all, I am here because the world is struggling to achieve the

"Rule of Law." This means that we all work to dissolve and defeat the misrule of violence, terror, barbarism and the effects of unjust laws. Because only through just laws, impartially enforced, can justice ever be guaranteed to those accused of crime, be they guilty or innocent, and the cause of world peace advanced.

So that I, with many other lawyers from all parts of the world, am here to seek to ensure that those accused of the unspeakable crimes that have been alleged against them receive a fair trial. This trial here in Phnom Penh is being observed and will be analyzed and discussed all over the world. Particularly will the enemies of world peace and those who seek hegemony over the people of Cambodia in particular, and all of Indochina in general, be looking to point out errors in the process of the trial. To defeat that opposition:

1. The trial must be shown to be by legally recognized means, before a court of competent jurisdiction. What more original authority can there be than this Court appointed by the sovereign Revolutionary People's Council of Kampuchea? So this first important requirement of all recognized legal systems has clearly been met.

2. The proceeding must be conducted with "Due Process of Law." The rights of the accused must be respected; the trial must be in accordance with the law of the land; the testimony must be from persons having knowledge of the facts constituting the crimes; there must be proof satisfactory to the Court that the accused were connected with the facts alleged either by personal participation or as principals of agents acting by their orders or in keeping with their policy or instructions.

3. The evidence must be deemed by the Court to be competent; it must be relevant; it must be material. It must be of a quality to establish the proof for the Court beyond a reasonable doubt, in the opinion of the Court, about the guilt (or the innocence) of the accused.

Honorable Chief Justice and the Court, you have been listening for three days to the testimony of witnesses. You have heard the charges as set forth in the indictment. At this point there should be no doubt, in fact there can be no doubt, that one of the most disgusting and one of the most unspeakable series of crimes in the history of the world has been committed. Indeed, long before the date of this hearing, long before the success of the overthrow of the previous government of Cambodia by the people's revolutionary forces, the world knew and understood the enormity of the shameless crime of genocide that had been carried out in the massacre and murder of some three million people in Cambodia. So that the fact of the crime was and is clear and overwhelming. But only you have the duty and the authority and the obligation of deciding by law now, "Who are the criminals?" The places where the accused would stand in this Court are vacant. The accused are being tried in absentia. You and you alone must now name the criminals whom you find guilty of the crimes as charged or otherwise. You! Not the sorrowing people of Cambodia, not the mothers and fathers left childless, not the thousands of children made orphans, not even the witnesses who called the names of the accused so often, not the stricken survivors who mourn their dead, not the holy men whose few members escaped extinction, nor the homeless wanderers and refugees whose lives have been forever broken, not the freedom-loving people of the world who have shared the suffering and travail of the tortured Cambodian citizens. No! Although they doubtless have already reached their own verdict, the responsibility now falls on you legally to name the perpetrators of these crimes, for, Honorable Chief Justice and the Court, I must call your attention to the important principle of law enshrined in most of the legal systems of the world that to accuse the defendants is by itself not enough. They are protected by the "presumption of innocence," and this "presumption of innocence" continues right down to the moment when you, the Honorable Chief Justice and the Court, render your verdict. Until that moment the Rule of Law requires that in spite of the feelings, the sorrow, the disgust, the impatience, the opinions of anyone or all who suffer the agony caused by the holocaust of Cambodia, all must await your decision. You and you alone will announce to the world the names of those who are responsible for this monstrous outrage against humanity whom you find guilty.

It is now clear to all that Pol Pot and Ieng Sary were criminally insane monsters carrying out a program the script of which was written elsewhere for them.

So that, if it were left to me and the other lawyers of the world who are present here, you would not have only Pol Pot and Ieng Sary and their agents and willing vassals standing judgment here; in fairness to them we would have besides them as fellow-accused the manipulators of world imperialism, the profiteers of neo-colonialism, the fascist philosophers, the hegemonists, who are supporting Zionism, racism, apartheid and reactionary regimes in the world, all these would be standing there with the false socialist leaders of fascist China awaiting the verdict and sharing the sentence of your decision.

In the meantime, Honorable Chief Justice and the Court, we will entertain the hope that soon, and very soon, a wind of change will blow across the Gobi desert to where once a hundred flowers were invited to bloom; that land where flowers have dried up, where one ugly, spiny cactus has survived to be nurtured, not only by a "Gang of Four," but also, it seems, by a group of despots of the kind of the former celestial emperors who have for the moment grasped and hold unscrupulous power for their own selfish ambition to extend regional and world hegemony by force and brutal violence, ready to sacrifice hundreds of millions of their own and other people to achieve their goals and who used the accused with success as their willing agents in perpetrating this awful crime of genocide against their own people of Cambodia and who also used this poisoned cactus of fascism masquerading under the false cover of socialism directed by "thoughts" so twisted that not only many of the peace-loving people of China, committed to decency and the respect for freedom and human rights, have been deceived by it, but all of them are for the moment enslaved by it. The traitors of Cambodia were also ready victims to this false doctrine, guided and blinded by their power-hungry leadership.

Our hope must be that another revolution, the revolution of true socialism, will soon again respond to the wind of change and restore China to the ranks of the freedom-loving progressive people of the world in search of world peace.

Then, and only then, will it be possible for Cambodia and her valiant people, together with Laos and the brave Vietnamese nation, to join hands with their peace-loving neighbors from the north and work with love for genuine and lasting friendship.

Honorable Chief Justice and the Court, the burden in the days ahead falls on all of us to forge the links of solidarity through world opinion and action to prevent such a shameful and terrible challenge from ever again being presented to people anywhere. Only thus can true world peace be assured and its benefits brought to all mankind.

Honorable Chief Justice and the Court, we and the world await your verdict. "Let justice be done."

3.03b

Closing Argument of Attorney Yuos Por for Pol Pot and Ieng Sary, Accused of Crimes of Genocide

Mr. Chairman, People's Assessors, Article 5 of the Decree Law of the People's Revolutionary Council of Kampuchea of July 15, 1979, states, "The defendant is entitled to represent himself or to be represented by a lawyer or by a Kampuchean citizen. If necessary, the presiding judge of the People's Revolutionary Tribunal may appoint an advocate for the accused."

This article reflects the democratic character of the revolutionary power. A person charged with even the most serious crimes has the right to present all the arguments he deems necessary for his defense, and to seek the assistance of a defense lawyer of his choice. The presiding judge of the tribunal, if he deems it necessary, with respect to serious crimes, may appoint a defense lawyer for a defendant who has not found one.

In this case, despite the absence of the defendants, the presiding judge of the tribunal, under the above-cited Article 5, has appointed Comrade Dith Munty and me to defend Pol Pot and Ieng Sary, in order to ensure democracy and justice.

In our judicial system, a defense lawyer, in order to guarantee respect for legality and to preserve the interests of the people and the country, must try to shed light on the truth concerning the crime, so that the court's decision will be just and will punish a guilty party only as is appropriate under the law.

In pleading this case before the tribunal, our task is extremely difficult, because the criminal acts of the defendants were committed against their own people, and these acts have been strongly protested by all our fellow citizens and by world opinion.

From the defendants' point of view, we find that the tribunal has carried out the necessary procedural formalities to try the defendants in absentia.

As for the evidence, the tribunal has examined all the necessary evidence regarding both the acts and intent involved in genocide.

At the court's sittings, all aspects of the crime of genocide have been clearly shown by the victims, by witnesses, by persons who carried out the acts, by material evidence, by documents, by photographs, by films, etc.

As defense attorneys, we find no basis for denying the criminal acts charged in the indictment.

We must acknowledge the extreme seriousness of the crimes in terms of their character and their scope, and that the defendants were fully aware of their criminal acts and had the deliberate intention of committing them. These are undeniable facts.

However, allow us to draw the attention of the tribunal to one other truth: the objective causes leading to the crime.

Behind the defendants are unacknowledged forces that incited, encouraged, pressured, and protected them. These unacknowledged forces, despite all their efforts to conceal themselves, have shown their ugly face on the immense crime scene that is our country.

This criminal, this highly dangerous abettor, is a mystery for no one. It is the hegemonist expansionists of Peking.

Alongside the defendants Pol Pot and Ieng Sary, the expansionists-hegemonists of Peking should have appeared before the tribunal to respond for the countless murders, suffering, and destruction that they caused on our soil.

They supplied to Pol Pot and Ieng Sary the entire ideological base and the entire material base to commit their crimes.

The ideological base is Maoism and the expansionism and hegemonism of Peking.

Pol Pot and Ieng Sary are persons who departed from the revolutionary struggle of national liberation of the Kampuchean people. They joined Maoism at a time when its reactionary character had not clearly shown itself. Pol Pot declared on September 28, 1977, in Peking that the most precious Chinese aid is the thought of Mao Tse Tung.

Pol Pot and Ieng Sary found in Maoism the ideological banner and the maneuvers to maintain their dictatorship, namely, the banner of class struggle and suppression of classes, and the maneuvers of repression, terror, and extermination of the people and of their own ranks.

The facts show that the policies and plans of repression, terror, and extermination against true revolutionaries, and against the Kampuchean people were modelled on the policies and plans of Maoism, despite the ravages caused by Maoism in all aspects of the lives of the Chinese people, especially the loss of hundreds of thousands of human lives and the destruction of the Chinese economy.

We recognize that Pol Pot and Ieng Sary were the perpetrators of their criminal acts, that they voluntarily applied Maoism in Kampuchea and that they must, as a consequence, assume full responsibility.

However, we feel that we must stress for the tribunal the fact that it was precisely under the strong influence of Maoism and through a blind, nearly insane, obedience to the dogmas of Maoism that Pol Pot and Ieng Sary perpetrated acts no person with a conscience and normal mental state would ever have committed.

The juxtaposition of Pol Pot and Ieng Sary's activities and their crimes with facts and events in China in application of Maoism allows us to conclude that the diabolical society that Pol Pot and Ieng Sary erected in Kampuchea is a product of Maoism. Sun Hao, Chinese ambassador to Kampuchea, recognized that the acts of the genocidal clique of Pol Pot and Ieng Sary were those of China as well.

As for the material base of the crime of genocide, the expansionist hegemonists of Peking provided all the financing, the means of repression, killing, and torture, and the means and weaponry for the carrying out of genocide against the Kampuchea people and for the war of aggression against the Vietnamese people, and provocations and armed conflicts against Laos and Thailand.

As Comrade Prosecutor has correctly noted, Pol Pot and Ieng Sary needed the backing of the Peking reactionaries, who took advantage of the situation to use them as an instrument of their expansionist and hegemonist policy in Southeast Asia, in particular in Kampuchea and in the other countries of the Indochinese peninsula.

Our country was a base for provocation and aggression for the aims of annexation and domination of the Peking reactionaries against the neighboring countries, and an ideal base of experimentation in applying Maoism in other countries and realizing their dream of world hegemony.

The relationship between the genocidal regime of Pol Pot and Ieng Sary and the Peking reactionaries in political line and personal ties, as well as a number of important documents in the case file of the crimes of Pol Pot and Ieng Sary, prove that in the perpetration of the crime of genocide against the Kampuchean people, the Peking reactionaries have played the role of an extremely dangerous abettor.

Without their collusion with the Peking expansionist hegemonists, Pol Pot and Ieng Sary, weakened and extremely isolated in a vast sea of hostile people, could not have carried out their crime of genocide against the Kampuchean people.

In order to ensure equity in this case, we ask you to examine this objective element of the crime.

I yield to my colleague, Attorney Dith Munty, who will present other arguments for the two defendants.

3.03c

Closing Argument of Attorney Dith Munty for the Accused Pol Pot and Ieng Sary

Comrade Chairman of the People's Revolutionary Tribunal, Comrades People's Assessors, I fully concur in the arguments presented by Comrade Yuos Por concerning the reactionary expansionist hegemonists in Peking, whose blood-stained hands actively promoted, incited, and aided Pol Pot and Ieng Sary to put Maoist doctrine into practice in our country. I have no dispute with Comrade Prosecutor regarding the criminal acts and criminal intention of the two accused. I would like to elaborate on the arguments of Comrade Yuos Por by analyzing the situation as it stood when Pol Pot and Ieng Sary took power, their aims when they decided to put Maoism into practice, and the congruence between their aims and those of the reactionary expansionist hegemonists in Peking, who wanted to use our country as a base for expansion in Southeast Asia.

Since 1968, there had been many changes on the battlefields of Indochina, changes favorable to the three countries of Kampuchea, Laos, and Vietnam. The aggressive forces of America and its satellites, as a result of the defeat suffered in Vietnam, were gradually retreating to their countries of origin. After 1973, the revolution in Kampuchea found itself in increasingly favorable conditions, and finally our people achieved complete victory on April 17, 1975. We then had ideal conditions to unite to restore our destroyed economies after five years of war, and to suppress on a gradual basis the inequalities of the old society, thus responding to the most earnest desires of our people, namely, to build an independent, peaceful, and happy Kampuchea.

However, disaster befell our people. Since the early 1960s, Pol Pot and Ieng Sary had often gone to China and had become increasingly strong adherents of Mao Tse Tung thought. They were taken to visit several of the farming regions in China, and from then on, they admired the "great leap forward" and the "great cultural revolution" in China. They quickly understood the importance of the "people's communes," as the places most appropriate for holding every inhabitant in submission: workers from large factories, artisans, artists, and intellectuals, all must come back to the countryside to be reeducated by the poor and lower-middle-class peasants. There no one could eat to assuage his hunger, no one could be warmly clothed.

The cultural revolution created the conditions most favorable to the men who held power to strike at the internal organization of the party, the state, and the army, to purge all their opponents.

Pol Pot and Ieng Sary thought that if they used both of these weapons, the "people's communes" and "cultural revolution," these weapons would help achieve their goal of bringing about the conditions necessary to concentrate power in their hands, since they had no confidence in the people, since they were not supported by the masses of the people, and especially since they did not enjoy the political confidence of the true revolutionaries of Kampuchea.

These were the reasons they decided to apply to Kampuchea Mao Tse Tung thought and the Chinese experience with "people's communes" and "cultural revolution."

In implementing these goals, Pol Pot and Ieng Sary found important and effective backing from the expansionist, hegemonist reactionaries in Peking in all fields: ideological, political, military, economic, and in the international arena. The reason was that the reactionary expansionist hegemonists in Peking lacked any prospects but wanted nonetheless to extend their domination in the world. They wanted to apply Maoism in a southeast Asian country with a new and more radical approach, after drawing lessons from the experience of grave losses suffered in China, as for example the economic decline in the years 1960 to 1962 when ten million persons died of hunger each year, or the factional fighting during the cultural revolution that had killed thirty million people.

It was also the case that the goals of Pol Pot and Ieng Sary coincided with those of the reactionary expansionist hegemonists in Peking. For the one side, the monopoly over government and the state was assured by the many forms of aid from China, while the other side had a good territorial base for aggression to dominate Southeast Asia. In other words, the two sides entered into close collusion. And since 1975, our infrastructure was almost entirely destroyed and three million innocent persons were killed. Had the Maoist experiment conducted in Kampuchea by the reactionary expansionist hegemonists in Peking succeeded, our country would have become an excellent base for aggression for Chinese expansion in Southeast Asia, in keeping with the view expressed by Mao Tse Tung in 1965: "We must retake Southeast Asia, which includes Vietnam, Kampuchea, Laos, Thailand, Burma, Malaysia, and Singapore. . . . Southeast Asia is a rich region, with many minerals. It is worth expending considerable effort to recover it. In the future this region will hold great interest for the development of Chinese industry. And this might fully make up for the losses suffered. . . ." Along with becoming a base for aggression, Kampuchea would be used as a model for other countries.

In fact, Pol Pot and Ieng Sary got all they needed to dominate Kampuchea and to have support in the international arena. From the Chinese side, Pol Pot and Ieng Sary were used as an instrument of the reactionary expansionist hegemonists in Peking. Early on they were assisted in a despicable affair, the assassination of their political adversary, Comrade Son Ngoc Minh, a true old revolutionary, who was then undergoing treatment in a hospital in Peking. The reactionary expansionist hegemonists in Peking supplied arms to Pol Pot and Ieng Sary, sent them advisors to turn Kampuchea into a logistical base, into a counterrevolutionary assault force in this region, a first step in the realization of their goal of expansion in Southeast Asia. They also warmly received Pol Pot and Ieng Sary, as in the words spoken on September 28, 1977 by Hua Kuo Feng: "Comrades, you are not only capable of destroying the old society, but as well of building a new society. . . . You have won great success in the repression of the enemies' attempts at subversion and sabotage. . . ."

On the other hand, since Pol Pot and Ieng Sary had completely closed Kampuchea to the outside world, for example by breaking diplomatic relations with nearly all countries, and had decided to take aid, principally military aid, only from China, they depended more and more on China and consequently were increasingly roped to the chariot of the reactionary expansionist hegemonists in Peking.

I allow myself to draw your attention to one other matter, namely, international public opinion. Right after the expulsion by force of all the inhabitants of towns and cities, after the widespread killing of people belonging to all strata of the population, international public opinion, justly shocked, severely condemned such criminal acts, analyzed them, and concluded that they were the true product of Maoism. Many personalities abroad, great friends of Kampuchea, had sincerely put forward valuable suggestions. But at the same time, the reactionary expansionist hegemonists in Peking endeavored to embellish the genocidal regime of Pol Pot and Ieng Sary, which succeeded in deceiving some ill-informed people. That was one of the reasons Pol Pot and Ieng Sary rejected all the suggestions that were prompted by good intentions and heeded only deceitful but flattering words and reactionary opinions.

Comrades, I have finished. I had tried to flesh out the pleading of my colleague Yuos Por by analyzing the circumstances in which the crimes were committed, so that the tribunal may examine this case in all its aspects and weigh the penal responsibility of Pol Pot and Ieng Sary, thereby assuring that good people's Kampuchean justice will be served.

3.03d
Closing Argument of Mohammed Hikmet Turkmanee, Counsel for the Plaintiffs in the Concurrent Civil Action

Mr. President, Members of the People's Revolutionary Tribunal, allow me to thank you for giving me the right to plead on behalf of the civil plaintiffs before the honorable tribunal despite my being a foreign lawyer.

I would like as well to express my gratitude to my Khmer colleagues for having given me the opportunity to bring my modest contribution, in this historic trial, to the defense of countless widows, and orphans and victims of the Pol Pot–Ieng Sary regime, which will remain one of the bloodiest regimes ever known in human history.

As representative of the Khmer society and on behalf of the Khmer people and state, the prosecutor has pronounced a complete and convincing indictment. He has been able, with talent, competence, and objectivity, to persuade you by supplying you with a great deal of evidence on the guilt of the accused, who, unfortunately, are not sitting on the bench of the accused, having preferred to flee the country and continue their crimes.

I would like to address you both as a lawyer and as a human being for, in this case, not only are the universal principles of law concerned, but also the essential foundations of humanity. Nobody could remain indifferent to the ordeal the Khmer people went through during the terrible days and the bloody nights from April 1975 to January 1979.

Nobody could remain untouched by the systematic genocide of millions of men and women of all ages and conditions, committed with premeditation and in cold blood by the accused Pol Pot and Ieng Sary and their clique, or by the series of indescribable sufferings which ensued and the terrible consequences the genocide has caused and will cause to the martyred Khmer people.

For my part, on behalf of the plaintiffs, I will confine myself to submitting to you some general remarks about: (I) the personal penal responsibility of the two accused Pol Pot and Ieng Sary and (II) the political responsibility of certain countries in the genocidal crime perpetrated by the abovementioned accused.

I. Personal penal responsibility of the accused Pol Pot and Ieng Sary

Juridically, you have to settle two main questions, firstly that of the value of the evidence presented by the prosecution, and secondly, if your conviction is established, that of the juridical qualification of the charges brought against the accused.

You will equally have to study whether there are mitigating circumstances in favor of the accused or whether, on the contrary, there are aggravating circumstances deriving notably from the premeditation of the crime and the use of barbarous methods to perpetrate the crime.

1. Evidence of the charges against the accused given in the indictment has been obtained through all the means of evidence commonly admitted in criminal proceedings in all countries.

The testimonies by numerous witnesses during the sessions of this tribunal, perfectly sincere and sometimes so moving and pathetic, are quite clear, formal, detailed, and consistent. They can, moreover, be corroborated by all Kampuchean survivors, whether they be Khmers or members of a national minority, Buddhists, Muslims, or Christians. It would be enough to open the doors of your tribunal to have thousands of testimonies which confirm those which have been heard at the trial. Each foreign guest has heard the same stories told by Kampucheans he has met.

Furthermore, the testimonies officially recorded by your tribunal from people of various social conditions are amply confirmed by the confessions of the Pol Pot–Ieng Sary clique's agents and above all by the official documents written by the two accused, Pol Pot and Ieng Sary.

They are also corroborated by the films shown, by the investigations done at mass graves, by the objects shown as evidence, by the enquiries carried out not only by the authorities of the People's Republic of Kampuchea but also by journalists from all over the world in the camps of Khmer refugees in Thailand and in Vietnam, and finally by the latest statements made by the former Kampuchean head of state Norodom Sihanouk, who was until quite recently the spokesman of the Pol Pot–Ieng Sary regime.

Thus there exists every proof of the guilt of the accused Pol Pot and Ieng Sary. The proofs are plentiful, incontestable, and convincing.

2. The juridical status of the charges against Pol Pot and Ieng Sary is both the crime of genocide and various common law crimes.

Genocide is a crime against humanity, the definition of which derives from the jurisprudence of the Nuremberg trial and from international law, notably the December 9, 1948, International Convention on the Prevention and Punishment of the Crime of Genocide.

The decree which set up your tribunal restated the elements of that crime, such as that they are universally recognized, and notably the mass extermination of the population.

As the condemnation of genocide by international law is prior to the crimes charged against the accused, the accused cannot justifiably invoke the rule of nonretroactivity of penal legislation.

So far as the applicable penalties are concerned, Decree Law No. 1 of July 15, 1979, of the People's Revolutionary Council applies the principle found in all penal legislation under which the instigator of a crime is punishable for the offense equally, and often more severely, than the actual performer of the crime.

The evidence and the closing arguments have fully established that Pol Pot and Ieng Sary did commit the crime with which they are charged, that is, they organized and directed the execution of the crime of genocide.

Three million human beings, that is three eighths of the population of Kampuchea, were killed in particularly cruel and savage circumstances.

If a crime of such scale had been committed in France, out of the 50 million there would have been 18,750,000 victims. If it had been committed in the USA, there would have been 75 million victims.

Pol Pot and Ieng Sary are among the greatest criminals of history. They resemble Hitler and his agents both by the number of victims and by the barbarous character of the methods used. All the juridical principles deriving from the Nuremberg trial can be applied to them. But their sinister originality is that they committed their crimes in time of peace and cannot even invoke military necessity.

Moreover, they attacked not only the ethnic and religious minorities but their own fellow Khmers, who were the main objects of their crimes, and their own country, in destroying the economic, financial, social, and cultural institutions.

There is in their crimes an element that can be compared to the aggravating circumstances that exist in ordinary criminal law for the perpetrators of such crimes as fratricide or infanticide.

All their policy was based on the violation of all fundamental freedoms and rights proclaimed by the Universal Declaration of Human Rights up to and including the right of all human beings to life.

And among the revolting crimes against fundamental freedoms that the accused have perpetrated, we should stress the elimination of religions in general and the absolute liquidation of the Islamic religion in Kampuchea by the systematic extermination of Muslim men, women, and children. Only those survived who managed to hide their affiliation to Islam.

The genocidal clique of Pol Pot and Ieng Sary is banished by mankind. It is the right and duty of your tribunal to punish them for the crime of genocide that they committed and to render justice to their victims and to the Kampuchean people.

But there exists in this case one other aspect that the civil plaintiffs must invoke, that is, the political responsibility of third parties in the genocide.

II. Political responsibility

The political responsibility of the Peking leaders in the crimes of the Pol Pot–Ieng Sary genocidal clique is terrible and obvious.

Pol Pot and Ieng Sary follow the Peking ideology, whose foreign policy they took up, and certain of its domestic institutions, the "people's communes" being the most well known.

These "people's communes," veritable concentration camps of forced labor and extermination, played a fundamental role in the carrying out of the crime of genocide.

The Chinese authorities could not have been unaware of the genocide, of which millions of Kampucheans were victims, since they had an embassy in Phnom Penh with a staff of several hundred who were the only foreigners allowed to move freely throughout the territory of Kampuchea.

Although they were aware of the crimes committed, as is proved by the record of the conversation between Deng Tsiao Ping and Ieng Sary (Document

2.5.18), they continued to give the Pol Pot–Ieng Sary genocidal clique economic and military aid which allowed it to carry out its crimes of genocide and wars of aggression against neighbor countries, particularly Vietnam.

The civil plaintiffs believe that the attitude of the Chinese authorities was an encouragement for the criminals Pol Pot and Ieng Sary and played a role involving their moral and political responsibility in the crime of genocide committed by the accused.

A moral and political responsibility of a different sort rests with the western countries. They denounced the crimes of the Pol Pot–Ieng Sary genocidal clique up until January 1979, when Kampuchea was liberated by the troops of the National United Front for the Salvation of Kampuchea, with the help of the Vietnamese army.

Since that time, paradoxically, they have taken up the defense of Pol Pot and Ieng Sary by invoking the issue of legitimacy. The legitimacy of the Pol Pot–Ieng Sary genocidal clique is based on systematic genocide. To seize power they not only exterminated officers and civil servants of the Lon Nol regime but, aware that their regime lacked any popular basis, they organized the evacuation of towns and villages, and then the elimination of what they called "the enemy's societal support," that is, intellectuals, city dwellers, former revolutionary fighters, in short, the majority of the population.

In order to maintain power, that clique exterminated all the activists of the Communist Party of Kampuchea and military personnel who opposed or were only suspected of opposing its policies.

The western press is now silent about the crimes committed by Pol Pot and Ieng Sary and supports their intrigues before international bodies.

The same people who welcome the entry of Tanzanian troops into Uganda and the fall of Idi Amin Dada raise objections about the liberation of the Kampuchean people from the terror of the oppression, from the starvation and the extermination, that liberation having come with the cooperation of Vietnamese troops.

The families of the victims of genocide, and the survivors of the bloodthirsty and tyrannical regime of the Pol Pot–Ieng Sary genocidal clique, welcome with great relief the proclamation of the People's Republic of Kampuchea. They are coming back to real life.

On their behalf, the civil plaintiffs ask you not for vengeance but for justice for the three million victims by imposing a punishment that will make an example of the executioners and of the Pol Pot–Ieng Sary genocidal clique.

On their behalf, the civil plaintiffs express the wish that these two monsters with human faces, perpetrators of a holocaust unequalled outside Europe, will not find a place of refuge in the world. They must pay for their crime.

3.03e
Statement of John Quigley (Professor of Law, Ohio State University, USA)

As a citizen of the United States of America, I have found it particularly painful to listen to the testimony before this People's Revolutionary Tribunal and to learn of the atrocities committed here in Kampuchea during the past four years. The USA backed the government of Lon Nol and destroyed much of the Kampuchean countryside through its bombing. The mass influx of people into Kampuchea's cities as result of that bombing led to shortage and disease in the cities. Those conditions in the cities doubtless provided Pol Pot with a pretext to empty Kampuchea's cities, and to commit monstrous crimes.

The trial of Pol Pot and Ieng Sary before this tribunal of the Kampuchean people marks an important step in the efforts of the international community to prevent large-scale brutality by governments against their own populations. The first major step was the Nuremberg trials following World War II, where the concept of "crimes against humanity" was first applied. The second was the adoption in 1948 of the Convention on the Prevention and Punishment of the Crime of Genocide. The third is the trial of Pol Pot and Ieng Sary.

The evidence which has now been made known to the world about Kampuchea during the period 1975–1979 makes it clear that genocide has indeed been committed here. Article 2 of the Genocide Convention prohibits the killing of members of a national, ethnical, racial, or religious group with an intent to destroy that group in whole or in part. The massacres carried out by the agents of Angkar manifest an intent to use mass killings to wipe out national minorities, religious groups, and the stratum of intellectuals in Kampuchean society.

Article 2 of the Genocide Convention also considers it to be genocide if conditions are imposed on a group to bring about its elimination in whole or in part. The living conditions imposed on the Kampuchean people, beginning with the forced evacuation of its cities in April 1975, led to large-scale death from starvation and exhaustion.

The Genocide Convention does not simply make genocide a crime. It also requires states to prevent and punish genocide. Thus, by holding this trial, the People's Republic of Kampuchea is fulfilling its solemn obligation to the world community.

The nations of the world should applaud this effort by the People's Republic of Kampuchea to carry out its duty under the Genocide Convention and should assist Kampuchea in that effort. Article 7 of the Genocide convention requires any nation where perpetrators of genocide are found to extradite them so that they can be held accountable for their crimes. Article

8 of the Genocide Convention requires the United Nations to assist to facilitate extradition of perpetrators of genocide.

In Kampuchea those who have perished in the last four years are not the only victims of genocide. Those who remain alive continue to suffer from its effects. If the nations of the world are truly interested in stopping genocide, they must provide material assistance to alleviate the conditions under which the victims of genocide in Kampuchea are presently living.

But rather than provide this much needed assistance, most nations refuse to have any relations with the government of Kampuchea, preferring instead to recognize the perpetrators of genocide as the *de jure* government of Kampuchea. Certainly one of the consequences of the commission of genocide must be that a regime perpetrating genocide loses its right to govern. So it was with the government of Adolf Hitler, and so it must be with the government of Pol Pot and Ieng Sary.

The trial of Pol Pot and Ieng Sary will demonstrate to the world the sufferings of the Kampuchean people during the past four years. The world must recognize the fact that the people of Kampuchea are united in their effort to build a new nation out of the rubble left by the Pol Pot regime. The international community did nothing to help the Kampuchean people when they were being starved and slaughtered. The least it can do now is to help them recover from the effects of the genocide they have endured.

3.03f

Statement of Susumi Ozaki, Lawyer

My name is Susumi Ozaki, Japanese citizen. I worked as a judge until 1932 under the absolute emperor system. Just because I joined the Japanese Communist Party I was arrested, put on trial and imprisoned for six years. Following the defeat of Japan in 1945, the absolute emperor system collapsed and subsequently, my lawyer's qualification has been restored.

Today as a democratic lawyer I am working together with other people for peace and democracy. I have come here to collect the truth about Kampuchea through observing this tribunal and reporting it to other democratic lawyers and Japanese people who love justice, thus consolidating and developing friendly relations between the people of Japan and Kampuchea.

Modern law requires correct procedure for criminal trials. Allow me in this regard, to express my respect for the People's Revolutionary Council of Kampuchea in its efforts made to set up this tribunal and proceed with strict and correct procedure, despite extremely difficult conditions.

The Decree of the People's Revolutionary Council on the Establishment of the People's Revolutionary Tribunal in Phnom Penh to try the Pol Pot–Ieng Sary clique for their crime of genocide, dated 15 July 1979, and the decision of the presiding judge concerning the penal procedure for the judgment of the crime of genocide of the Pol Pot–Ieng Sary clique are both in conformity with the Nuremberg principles which were confirmed in the United Nations General Assembly in 1946 and the purport of the International Convention on Genocide signed in 1948.

I have witnessed that the actual proceedings till now have been strictly organized and hope that the following process continues to go smoothly. Only a few days before the opening of the tribunal, I saw some sites of massacres and destructions and heard from six victims and witnesses. I am now full of sorrow and pain. The Kampuchean people who won independence in 1975 after a long struggle and expected peace and prosperity, never supposed they would encounter such hardships as they have.

In my short tour in the city I noticed beautifully constructed houses with practically no people living there. Phnom Penh has become virtually a ghost town, which proves the Pol Pot–Ieng Sary's policy of forcible evacuation. I have heard that this policy had been applied to other cities and a number of rural centers. The destruction of modern political and social organizations and of cities means also the destruction of the economy. I have seen the Central Bank in ruins and the market closed. Currency and the market are a product of human initiative and the result of long practices of economy. Modern social and economic life is sustained by them. Otherwise, civilized life would collapse.

I have seen a newly constructed high school building turned into a prison. The classrooms are divided into small cells with an iron chain in each of them. This prison was far from an ordinary modern penal institution. Let us compare it with hell. But schools are educational establishments to bring up a young generation capable of constructing a new society.

On the walls, I saw hundreds of portraits with names on their clothes which told that a large number of people of different strata were killed after barbarous torture. I collected testimonies of a boy whose parents were killed there and a man who had been imprisoned for two years. I saw a vacant plot where once a Buddhist temple stood. Temples are a symbol of religion. Their destruction represents the devastation of traditional culture. For future development of moral culture requires the protection of cultural property of mankind.

I was given an opportunity to hear testimony from a woman student whose thirteen closest relatives were separated from each other. All but three died of hunger and disease. Also from a young girl whose mother and two brothers were brutally massacred, from a peasant whose wife was killed and who twice witnessed large-scale massacres, and from a mother of French nationality who suffered cruel persecution.

Their testimonies were too vivid for me to hear. The acts of the butchers were simply those of devils. The suffering of Mrs. Yasuko Naito is today widely known in Japan.

What I heard and saw in Phnom Penh may be only a small part compared to the whole picture in the Indictment. The Indictment has systematically and concretely pointed out the facts that the Pol Pot–Ieng Sary clique betrayed the Kampuchean people, led them to the verge of extermination, massacred three million innocent people, brought unbearable physical and spiritual pain to four million survivors, destroyed the national economy and culture, thus causing damage to every social stratum, family, regional life and the nation as a whole.

The Indictment has been endorsed by many documents submitted to this tribunal with vivid testimonies by survivors including Mrs. Yasuko Naito. These items of proof clearly show that the main aspects of the crime were: forcible evacuation from Phnom Penh, abolition of religion, persecution of the ethnic minorities and people of other nationalities, starvation, death of sickness, torture, and massacre of millions of people of every social stratum, total denial of human dignity and humanity, destruction of the social fabric.

The crime of Pol Pot and Ieng Sary violates not only the convention on genocide and other international laws but also human dignity and humanity. In this regard, I share the view with the report of the International Association of Democratic Lawyers which visited Kampuchea last May.

At this moment, I remember that the Kampuchean people has a tradition of having fought heroically for independence and liberty over thirty years, hand in hand with the people of Vietnam and Laos till 1975. This struggle enjoyed worldwide support from those who love justice. Independence and liberty are the basic rights of any nation. I believe that the Kampuchean people, guided by the National United Front for the Salvation of Kampuchea will in the end overcome the present hardship and develop their national rights to independence and liberty.

Today the Kampuchean people has a sole and legitimate government, i.e., the People's Revolutionary Council of Kampuchea.

I conclude my statement by assuring that we will do our utmost to reinforce the solidarity of the Japanese people with the Kampuchean people, and to get the Japanese government to recognize Kampuchea's legitimate government as soon as possible.

3.03g

Statement of Francisco Varona Duque de Estrada (Vice-President of the Cuban People's Supreme Tribunal, and Representative of the Cuban Association of Lawyers)

Mr. President, respected judges, on behalf of the Cuban Association of Lawyers, we express our respect for the People's Tribunal at Phnom Penh to judge the crime of genocide committed by the Pol Pot–Ieng Sary clique, as well as our gratitude for the honor given us to address the tribunal. We consider that the proceedings of the trial have proved, with all the formal legal rules, what constitutes a notorious fact known by all the inhabitants of this country who have survived the Pol Pot–Ieng Sary regime, for they have experienced it. That is to say, the accused have intentionally committed the crime of genocide against different sections of their own people, causing millions of victims. We have had the opportunity to talk with witnesses, who are at the same time victims and who have survived Pol Pot–Ieng Sary's crimes. We have had the chance of visiting centers of torture and extermination, for ascertaining what is to be proved fully in the course of the trial, that is to say, the accused have committed the crime of which they are accused. In technical terms, they are the direct authors for having premeditated the crime and for having directed the execution of the crime of genocide, as provided by international law.

There is, however, an aspect which is interesting to examine, the degree of guilt of the accused not only in the intention of genocide which was behind the carrying out of their barbarous policy of extermination and their cruel and inhuman forms of systematic execution, but also by another factor, perhaps more condemnable, that is to say their betrayal of the Kampuchean people who had brought them to power at the price of one of the most arduous and heroic revolutionary struggles. Their vile betrayal of all honest workers, peasants, and intellectuals of Kampuchea, who had confidence in them and pinned their hopes on them, and who found themselves rewarded with their own extermination.

This was a betrayal of their people, of their comrades, or the liberation movement of the oppressed people and of the Marxist-Leninist principles they claimed to profess. Instead of developing their country's productive forces, they completely annihilated them. Instead of creating a free and just society, they installed a regime of slavery without precedent. Instead of fighting for the all-round development of the citizens, they exterminated them physically, mentally, and morally. Instead of working for the glory of their country, developing its riches and culture, instead of winning for it the place that it deserves among the fraternal revolutionary countries, instead of fulfilling that noble task, that duty toward the living and the dead, Pol Pot and Ieng Sary tried to turn Kampuchea into an agricultural appendix of China, inhabited exclusively by slaves. To this end they applied a policy of genocide, they committed the most monstrous crimes, for which they are being tried today. Hence their criminal guilt which is exacerbated by perfidy and treason. Hence the well-deserved condemnation by this tribunal, by their people, by all the nations, and by history.

Judgment

3.04

Judgment of the Tribunal, August 19, 1979

The People's Revolutionary Tribunal, created by Decree Law No. 1 of July 15, 1979, of the People's Revolutionary Council of Kampuchea, has held its public sittings in the capital city of Phnom Penh from August 15 to 19, 1979. It is composed of:

Mr. Keo Chanda	President of the Tribunal and Chairman of the jury
Mr. Chhour Leang Huot	People's Assessor
Mr. Pen Navuth	People's Assessor
Mrs. Chea Samy	People's Assessor
Mr. Meas Savatha	People's Assessor
Mr. Nouth Savoeun	People's Assessor
Mr. Nouch Than	People's Assessor
Mrs. Chhouk Chhim	People's Assessor
Mr. Kim Kun	People's Assessor
Mr. Kim Kaneth	People's Assessor
Mrs. Lek Sarat	People's Assessor

The Court sessions have taken place in the presence of Mr. Mat Ly, Prosecutor-General, acting as public minister at the Tribunal, and Mr. Lim Nay, Prosecutor, with a secretariat composed of Mr. Hul Sam Ol and Mr. Ouk Chandara.

The tribunal has tried as a court of both first and last instance:

1. Pol Pot, alias Saloth Sar, born in 1925 at Prey Sbau village, Kompong Thom province, with secondary school education, former Prime Minister of the overthrown Democratic Kampuchea Government, married to Khieu Ponnary, now at large and the object of a warrant of arrest;

2. Ieng Sary, born in 1925 at Hoa Lac village, Lien Hoa subdistrict, Chau Thanh district, formerly Tra Vinh province and now Cuu Long province, Vietnam, with university education, former Deputy Prime Minister of the

overthrown Democratic Kampuchea Government, married to Khieu Thirit, now at large and the object of a warrant of arrest.

The accused Pol Pot and Ieng Sary are prosecuted for committing genocide, under Article 2 of Decree Law No. 1 of July 15, 1979, and referred to in the Indictment dated August 1, 1979, of the Prosecutor of the People's Revolutionary Tribunal.

Acting under Article 5 and Article 6 of Decree Law No. 1 of July 15, 1979, of the People's Revolutionary Council of Kampuchea, the tribunal decided to hold sessions to try the accused Pol Pot and Ieng Sary in absentia.

The decision to bring the present case before the tribunal and the subpoenas summoning the accused to appear were made known through broadcast over the National Broadcasting Station and were posted at the offices of the people's committee and the People's Revolutionary Tribunal in the city of Phnom Penh.

The People's Revolutionary Tribunal has appointed: Mr. Dith Munty and Mr. Yuos Por, Kampuchean lawyers, and Mr. Hope R. Stevens, American lawyer, to defend the two accused.

Mr. Abdul Koyum, Mrs. Denise Alfonso, and Miss Chhay Ny took part in the proceedings as civil plaintiffs. The People's Revolutionary Tribunal admitted Mr. Mohammed Hikmet Turkmanee, Syrian lawyer, as counsel for the civil plaintiffs.

After hearing the Indictment dated August 1, 1979 of the Prosecutor;

After hearing the investigation reports made by representatives of different branches of the People's Revolutionary Council of Kampuchea on the economy, culture, health, education, religion, and national minorities, and by representatives of various strata of the Phnom Penh population who have been asked by the Prosecutor to testify before the tribunal;

After hearing the statements of witnesses, of victims, and of civil plaintiffs;

After hearing the statements of witnesses from abroad, namely, Mr. Francisco Varona Duque de Estrada, Cuban lawyer; Mr. Susumi Ozaki, Japanese lawyer; and Mr. John Quigley, American lawyer;

After examining the documents and evidence in the case, including texts, documents, and photographs of the Pol Pot–Ieng Sary clique which had been seized, as well as documents and films taken during field investigations into the crime of genocide perpetrated by the genocidal Pol Pot–Ieng Sary clique;

After hearing the closing argument by the Prosecutor;

After hearing counsel for the civil plaintiffs;

After hearing the lawyers representing the accused;

After examining all the documents of the case file; after conferring and deliberating as required by the law;

The jury of the People's Revolutionary Tribunal at Phnom Penh has determined the nature of the case as follows.

After a protracted and arduous struggle, shoulder to shoulder with fraternal peoples of Vietnam and Laos, against the French colonialist invaders, and later against the American imperialists and their agent Lon Nol and his associates, our people won a glorious victory: on April 17, 1975, the territory of our dear Kampuchea was completely liberated.

The most profound aspiration of all strata of our people is to live in independence, peace, and happiness in a just and democratic society, and to unite in developing the glorious traditional Angkor civilization, and in promoting prosperity and peaceful and friendly relations with the fraternal neighboring peoples. But during their nearly four years in power, the accused Pol Pot and Ieng Sary betrayed our people and fatherland. The tribunal has found that they committed the following criminal acts.

I. Systematic implementation of a plan to kill many strata of the population on an increasingly ferocious scale; indiscriminate extermination of nearly all the officers and soldiers of the former regime; liquidation of the intelligentsia, and of all persons and organizations deemed to be opposed to the regime

Pol Pot, Ieng Sary, and their associates divided the population into three categories, in order to subject them to different treatment. The first category was "old citizens," i.e., persons who had lived in the areas of resistance bases before liberation; the second category was "new citizens," i.e., persons who had lived in areas controlled by the former regime; and the third category was those who worked for the former regime.

They plotted to kill off the third category, and to carry out purges within the second category. The first category was favored at the outset but was subjected to purges beginning in 1977 (Minutes of a meeting of Kompong Ro district Party committee).

1. Indiscriminate extermination of officers, soldiers, and civil servants of the former regime and their families

Pol Pot and Ieng Sary decided to kill all the officers, soldiers and civil servants of the former regime. Many officers of the Lon Nol army were killed, as well as many members of their families. Immediately after April 17, 1975, Pol Pot and Ieng Sary resorted to various ruses. For example, in the cities and provinces of Battambang, Mongkol Borey, and Sisophon, they summoned victims for supposed political courses and then killed them. In other cases, victims were led into a forest, then surrounded and killed by hitting them with bamboo sticks on the back of the neck.

One of those executioners is Men Khoeun, who stated before the tribunal:

"The killing of two thousand and five persons was carried out upon an order of Pol Pot to celebrate the great victory of April 17, 1975. The head of Toek Phos district, who is named Meak Vy, got together fifty agents of all the subdistricts of the district. He declared it was Pol Pot's order that all the Lon Nol soldiers are our enemies, and that we must kill them all to celebrate the victory of April 17, 1975. Those failing to comply with this order would be tried themselves. Receiving in this way an order from the district chief, we all, the fifty agents, went out to kill the two thousand and five soldiers of Lon Nol."

According to witness Sok Li Mut from Pursat, in April 1975 about four thousand Lon Nol civil servants, officers, and soldiers were beaten to death or gunned down at the O Chruy river, near Mount Prey, Chheu Tom subdistrict, Krakor district, Pursat province.

As has been admitted by Siv Samon, who belonged to the Pol Pot–Ieng Sary security service, officers and soldiers of Lon Nol and their families who had taken flight were pursued and killed. On August 12 and 13, 1978, together with eight others, he killed 250 Lon Nol soldiers and their families.

2. Liquidation of the intelligentsia

Pol Pot and Ieng Sary thought that intellectuals, students, professors, and scientists were seriously contaminated by the former regime, as reactionaries not fit for any use. Their policy was to get rid of this social stratum to "purify society."

This policy was reflected in a captured document on a directive of the permanent bureau of the eastern zone Party committee, which reads:

"We must heighten our revolutionary vigilance as regards those elements who served in the administration of the former regime, such as technicians, professors, doctors, engineers and other technical personnel.

The policy of our Party is not to employ them. If we run after technology and employ them, the enemy will infiltrate our ranks, each year more deeply. This will be very dangerous for us."

Pol Pot and Ieng Sary held that "there are still many intellectuals in hiding and they could undermine state power." They gave orders that "in every people's commune at least fifteen intellectuals must be killed."

Intellectuals and students were hunted down to be killed. Many of them had to conceal their identity and do such work as making manure or other farm work in people's communes. Those whose identity was discovered were taken to an unknown destination.

Doctor Phlek Chhat, a physician at Preah Ket Melea Hospital, was arrested in July 1975 and was tortured. He died in jail after a burning torch was forcibly driven into his throat.

Doctor Tan Beng Phoun, arrested in April 1976, was thrown into a crocodile-breeding pond at Trey Khleng village, Sandan district, Kompong Thom province.

According to a report of the investigation into crimes committed by the genocidal Pol Pot–Ieng Sary clique as presented before the tribunal by a representative of the Phnom Penh population, persons who looked like intellectuals, such as those wearing eyeglasses, were under suspicion. Those suspected of being intellectuals were closely watched in their daily activities and were considered as undesirables, as persons with a suspended death sentence over them. The authorities of a "people's commune" could kill these persons at any time, and all they had to say was that there were intellectuals in the commune.

At Prek Kak, in Stung Treng district, Kompong Cham province, Mr. Chan, a teacher, and a number of students and former civil servants were put on boats and taken to the middle of a river, where they were beaten to death with hoes by soldiers in another boat.

Dr. Yith Kim Seng, who was formerly deputy minister of health and a professor at the Medical College, has related his life in hiding in a "people's commune":

"I kept cattle for four years in a forested area in Takeo. I was not able to read a single page of a book, or to hear a news broadcast, and I didn't have a scrap of paper or a pen to write. For nearly one thousand days I did not touch a cake of soap, and I had to smoke dried forest leaves. I ate rice gruel all the year round, so that now the sight of it makes me shudder and gives me goose bumps."

Pol Pot and Ieng Sary and their associates deceived a number of intellectuals, diplomats, and students living abroad to return to Kampuchea to take part in building up the country. When they arrived at the airport, they were taken away by clique agents to concentration camps, after being stripped of foreign currency and any valuables they had.

According to surviving returned intellectuals who testified before the tribunal, under the Pol Pot–Ieng Sary regime, about one thousand intellectuals came home from abroad, but only 85 remain alive.

Mr. Ung Pech, a bridge and road construction engineer from Kompong Som, testified that when he worked at the port in Kompong Som he was entrusted with the job of maintaining the unloading cranes, but for food he was given only banana stems and salted fish, while the Chinese advisors were fed extremely well. In April 1977, he was accused of being an enemy and was jailed at Tuol Sleng Prison in Phnom Penh, together with other professors and intellectuals. He knows that about six hundred foreign-returned intellectuals and students were held there and were then killed.

Numerous articles carried by the foreign press and news agencies also confirm the elimination of intellectuals by Pol Pot and Ieng Sary.

3. Systematic repression and killing of individuals and organizations suspected of opposition to the regime

In order to consolidate their power, Pol Pot and Ieng Sary avidly purged their own organization, which involved liquidating, by savage means, individuals and organizations suspected of opposing them. Early in 1977, they ordered the authorities of "people's communes" to eliminate so-called "reactionaries," meaning opponents or potential opponents. On April 4, 1977, at a meeting of the standing committee, the following directive was issued: "All committees, and branches must actively carry on the task of purification by wiping out enemy elements."

Any official of the Party, the administration, or the army at whatever level who did not approve of Pol Pot and Ieng Sary's criminal acts could be considered a spy for foreign countries and be killed. Not only the official, but entire units, might be killed.

Early in 1977, Pol Pot and Ieng Sary accused Koy Thuon, commander of the northwest military region, of being a traitor. They had him killed. Then scores of other high-level officials were killed, including Hu Nim, the minister of information, Toch Phoeun, the minister of public works, and Duon Po, commander of the northwest military region.

In a list dated June 3, 1978, Pol Pot and Ieng Sary named eighteen high party officials killed between 1972 and 1978. It is worthy of note that on the list was the name of Comrade Son Ngoc Minh, former president of the Issarak Front, and a member of the central committee of the Kampuchea Communist Party, who was killed as a service to Pol Pot and Ieng Sary by the Peking reactionaries at a Peking hospital in 1972.

These bloody internal purges were considered by the Pol Pot and Ieng Sary clique as great victories. A captured report reads: "We have won these great victories because we have judiciously identified and systematically harassed our enemies and have methodically carried out purges in our ranks, rooting out the enemy's network."

As time passed, their purges became increasingly bloody and extensive. A captured list contains the names of 242 high-level officials killed from 1976 up to April 9, 1978. Among them were two party central committee members, four zone Party secretaries, 24 secretaries of party regional committees, four ministers, five deputy ministers, nine leading officials of ministries, eight political commissars and deputy political commissars of divisions, and a number of ambassadors who had been recalled from abroad.

In May 1978, they killed Mr. So Yan, alias So Phim, a member of the standing committee of the Party central committee, and secretary of the Party committee of the eastern zone. Following this event, a great number of officers of Military Region 203, of Divisions 280 and 290, and of divisions in the eastern zone, including even district-level units, were considered disloyal and were killed. Tens of thousands of persons, officers and soldiers were killed, together with their fathers, mothers, wives and children, and even war invalids who had served well during the war. Even eastern zone natives who had been forcibly evacuated to other areas were tracked down and killed in large numbers. The numbers killed in June 1978 ran to the tens of thousands (Statements of witnesses Sok Li Mut from Pursat, and Yeng Tinh from Kompong Cham).

Soldiers from the Kandal military region were used as executioners in these killings, with support from aircraft, tanks, and artillery. Even a close associate of Pol Pot and Ieng Sary, Vorn Vet, a member of the standing committee of the party's political bureau in charge of the economy, was killed in November 1978.

4. Together with these internal purges, from early 1978, and particularly from April 1978, the first category citizens, who had been Pol Pot and Ieng Sary's base of support, were also subjected to bloody repression

Unable to bear the harsh, coercive Pol Pot–Ieng Sary regime any longer, citizens of the so-called first category rose up. Killings on a large scale were carried out against them in Chup, Prey Veng, Kompong Cham, Svay Rieng, Ratanak Kiri, and Mondul Kiri.

Witnesses from Chup stated before the tribunal that tens of thousands of people, including workers of the Chup rubber plantation and other persons brought to Chup from other places, were killed in the Chup area in July and August 1978, and that these killings were carried out in the presence of Chinese advisors. "Their bodies were thrown into craters made by B-52 bombs. There were about forty B-52 craters filled with bodies, and this white terror caused more than thirty thousand surviving Chup workers to flee and take refuge in Vietnam." A witness, Mr. Nan Somit, who was a leader of these refugee workers, denounced these atrocious crimes before the tribunal (Minutes of a field investigation at Chup).

II. Killing of clergy and believers, and eradication of religion; systematic killing of members of ethnic minorities to force them to assimilate; extermination of foreign residents

Pol Pot and Ieng Sary ordered the shelling of pagodas and Islamic mosques and destroyed pagodas and churches. They forced the monks to give up their saffron robes, and to leave places of worship to join "people's communes" for hard labor. Statues of Buddha and objects of worship were destroyed or plundered. Many temples and pagodas were turned into depots for rice, manure, or armaments. Worse still, pagodas were transformed into jails or concentration camps or reeducation camps, and into places of torture and killing of a great number of our fellow countrymen.

Monk Long Swim, of Phnom Penh, revealed at the Asian Buddhist Congress that there had been in Kampuchea 2800 pagodas, with 82,000 monks, but under the Pol Pot regime not a single pagoda remained in operation.

A witness, Superior Tep Vung of Bos pagoda, Siem Reap city, stated before the tribunal: "Pol Pot–Ieng Sary agents killed 57 monks at Prey Look village, Chan Sar subdistrict, Sotr Nikum district, Siem Reap province. In this province there were 173 pagodas and 4700 monks. Religious men were forced to abandon their robes, to go work in the 'people's communes,' and to get married, whether they were young or old."

Many monks were tortured or beaten to death. Hundreds of Buddha statues in stone or wood were destroyed, including historical relics thousands of years old. Religious books (collections of the teachings and sayings of Buddha) were all burnt. The pagodas of Ba Kong (Sotr Nikum district), Sophy, Phnom Truong Bat (Kompong Thkau subdistrict, Kra Lanh district, Siem Reap province) were all turned into places of torture and killing.

The large cathedral of the Catholic mission in the heart of Phnom Penh was blown up by Pol Pot and Ieng Sary and completely razed.

Yun Yat (Mrs. Son Sen), who was the Pol Pot–Ieng Sary minister of culture and propaganda, confirmed this policy of eliminating religions in her talk with Yugoslav journalists. She said: "Buddhism being a tool for exploitation, there is no longer any issue of Buddhism in Kampuchea."

Suffering the same fate as Buddhism, Islam was also eliminated, and even more ruthlessly, as the policy toward this religion was closely linked with the fascist policy of forcible assimilation of ethnic minorities.

According to the investigation report on national minorities, after April 17, 1975, along with their policy of forcible and immediate assimilation, Pol Pot and Ieng Sary tracked down Muslim clergy in order to exterminate them:

• Grand Mufti Hachi Res Los, imam of the Muslim community, was killed at Sonchon village, Peam Chor district, Prey Veng province.

• Mufti Hachi Sleyman Sokri, first deputy iman, was killed with his skull smashed.

• Mufti Hachi Mat Sles Sleyman, second deputy imam, was killed in Battambang province.

• Hachi Matly Haron, former president of the central committee of the Muslim Society of Kampuchea, was killed in Kandal province.

All the 114 Islamic mosques were plundered and destroyed. Some of the more beautiful mosques were razed to the ground by explosives or bulldozers.

To force the Chams and Malays to forsake Islam and to provide a pretext to kill large numbers of them, Pol Pot and Ieng Sary forced them to eat pork, contrary to their customs and to the precepts of the Koran. Those who refused to do so were killed on the spot. Anyone caught using his mother tongue was also killed.

The Muslim population of many villages, subdistricts, and even districts was exterminated for opposing forcible assimilation.

Abdul Koyum, a Muslim and a physician, stated: "Kompong Siem district, in Kompong Cham province, had five villages with a total Muslim population of about 20,000, but not a single inhabitant survived." Kang Meas district, in Kompong Cham province, had seven villages with about 20,000 Muslim inhabitants, and only four survived.

Ninety percent of the Muslims were killed, because they wanted to keep their religion and preserve their mother tongue. To escape total extermination, some 3000 Muslims fled to Thailand and later settled in Malaysia.

Along with other ethnic minorities, the Thai minority, for example, was equally the object of extermination. Pol Pot and Ieng Sary mobilized troops to wipe them out, as was the case with the Thai population of Koh Kong province on May 25, 1975.

Formerly in Koh Kong province there were about 20,000 Thai people, but after liberation on January 7, 1979, there were only 8000. Many villages that formerly had 500 to 600 Thai families now have only 5 or 7 families. Of the 700 Thai families living formerly in the town of Koh Kapi, only 30 are left (Investigation report on national minorities).

Mr. Buon Thong, an official who is of the Ta Puon minority, Ratanak Kiri province, denounced the killing of tens of thousands of ethnic minority people in the northeastern zone near the town of Stung Treng. Many leading officials belonging to ethnic minorities who had been able and respected men were killed. Among them were regional party secretary Seda, of the Lao minority, and party regional committee member Chan Den, also of the Lao minority. Nearly all officials from ethnic minorities, from the provincial down to the village level, who had taken part in the resistance against U.S. aggression were killed.

Foreign residents like the Chinese, Vietnamese and those who were close to them, like mixed Chinese-Khmer, or mixed Vietnamese-Khmer, were killed. Pol Pot and Ieng Sary killed and deported hundreds of thousands of Chinese and Vietnamese. As a consequence, tens of thousands of Chinese took refuge in Vietnam.

The inhabitants of Stung Treng have discovered many human remains in a lake with an area of ten hectares, lying southeast of the town. Those are the bones of some two thousand Vietnamese who were killed.

III. Forcible evacuation of the population from Phnom Penh and other liberated towns and villages; the breaking and upsetting of family and social structures; mass killings and mass executions

After Phnom Penh was liberated on April 17, 1975, Pol Pot and Ieng Sary immediately ordered that the population be evacuated from the city, with no exceptions, within three days. The force of bayonets was combined with deceptive claims, such as "a few days of evacuation, enough to avoid bombings by the U.S. air force," or "to allow the revolutionary forces to wipe out the enemy in the capital city." The more than two million inhabitants had thus to leave the city. Anyone who refused to leave or procrastinated or showed any opposition was beaten or shot dead. The sick, the elderly, the disabled, children, pregnant women, patients who were being operated upon or who had just been operated upon, were not spared. A number of small children left hungry in day care centers ate their own excrement and drank their own urine, and finally died of starvation.

Without any preparations, without being able to take with them the bare necessities, and without knowing where to go or what to do, long columns of people, under threat from the Pol Pot–Ieng Sary soldiers, trekked rain or shine, toward unknown destinations. At checkpoints, Pol Pot–Ieng Sary soldiers robbed them of almost all their remaining possessions. Tens of thousands of people died on the roadsides or in the bush, of starvation, diseases, exhaustion, were shot or beaten to death by Pol Pot soldiers.

Phnom Penh, the capital city, became completely lifeless. In the days that followed, other cities and towns suffered the same fate as Phnom Penh. Such was the case of Battambang with 200,000 inhabitants, Svay Rieng with 130,000, Kompong Chhnang with 60,000, Kompong Speu with 60,000, Siem Reap with 50,000.

At the trial, representatives of various strata of the Phnom Penh population, as quoted in the investigation report on the situation of Phnom Penh residents during the first days after April 17, 1975, described the situation as follows: "In their long journey to the most out-of-the-way corners of the country, large numbers of Phnom Penh civilians, mostly elderly, children, women in childbirth, pregnant women, the sick, the disabled, died in atrocious conditions: without food, medicine, or midwives."

Mrs. Yasuko Naito, a victim of Japanese nationality, native of Tokyo, who was living in Phnom Penh, stated in a letter addressed to the tribunal, "on the afternoon of April 17, 1975, Pol Pot's soldiers used megaphones to tell everyone to go outside. They fired at any doors that were closed. . . . Along the way, we met patients who had been forced out of the Calmette Hospital and other hospitals. Some who were weak walked with the help of nurses, having been operated upon only a few hours before. The places where the operation had been performed were still bleeding, with flies swarming around. They all wore hospital clothing. It made me think of a painting I had seen somewhere depicting scenes of hell." During this forced evacuation Mrs. Yasuko Naito lost her entire family: her husband and her two children.

These acts by Pol Pot and Ieng Sary were premeditated and planned in advance, as may be seen in a captured document which states that the evacuation of the population of the cities could serve as an example in revolutions in all the other countries. It was a question of the total destruction of the feudal regime and the capitalist regime by dispersing enemy forces to the countryside to wipe them out.

At a press conference in Peking on October 2, 1977, Pol Pot said: "This policy had been worked out before the victory, meaning before April 1975. We were not strong enough to defend the revolution against attacks by enemy intelligence organizations of all kinds. . . . The enemy forces were dispersed to the cooperatives under our control, and in this way we had the situation in hand."

After emptying the cities and urban centers of their inhabitants, Pol Pot and Ieng Sary used deceptive slogans, such as, "We are clearing land to enrich the country," to forcibly relocate the population of the rural areas, especially from the areas formerly occupied by Lon Nol. In this way a forced transfer to the west and north was carried out of inhabitants of the eastern provinces near the common border with Vietnam, who had friendly relations, built up over the years of common struggle against the French and American imperialists and their lackeys, with Vietnamese on the other side of the border. Inhabitants of the provinces of Svay Rieng, Prey Veng, and Takeo were forced to move to the provinces of Pursat and Battambang in the west, while inhabitants in the west near the Thailand border were also under suspicion and were transferred to the east.

Like the population of the cities and towns, the rural population of several provinces was also transferred. They were forced to leave their homes and were separated from their loved ones. They were robbed of their belongings by Angkar and forced to move to other provinces.

Mr. Khieu Kola in Kandal said that in August 1975 he was put on a truck and sent to Pursat without any explanation. He was not allowed to take anything with him. At Pursat he had to sleep in the open. The same thing happened to hundreds of other people. The Pol Pot soldiers searched them and took their belongings. Each day four or five persons died, he said.

Mr. Tik How's family of thirteen persons was split into two: eight were taken to Battambang, five to Kompong Thom.

IV. The herding of the population into "people's communes," which were disguised concentration camps, where they were forced to work and live in physically and morally destructive conditions that caused deaths in large numbers

1. Physically, the people were put to do hard labor like slaves. They were left hungry and wearing rags. They were condemned to a slow death from exhaustion and disease.

The urban population and the rural people in the newly liberated areas were expelled from their localities. And after a long and bloody journey, they arrived in new places where they were sent to the so-called "people's communes." Under the slogans "all-round socialist revolution" and "to have rice is to have everything," Pol Pot and Ieng Sary made the people work like slaves.

The labor force was divided into male and female groups living and working separately in collective style. Everyone had to work ten to sixteen hours a day, using rudimentary tools, sometimes only bare hands, and this included even young children, the elderly, and people who were too sick to work. The prescribed daily ration was one bowl of rice with salt, but most of the time they got only thin rice gruel. The "people's communes" were placed under the control of people many of whom had lost all human feelings. The people had to work hard all day. Any violation of labor discipline would result in a beating, or in a reduction in rations, or in an increase in work norms, or even in being killed in the forest. The "people's communes" became large concentration camps in which the majority of the Kampuchean population were imprisoned. This regimen of starvation and deprivation, this life in tiny huts that provided no protection from the rain or sun, a life with no medications or medical care in case of illness, a life with constant tension and threats, all this brought a slow death, both physically and morally. The largest number of dead were among the elderly, the ill, and women who were about to give birth or were nursing their babies. These women, since they could not work, received reduced food rations. Many women became sterile.

According to captured documents, even some units of Pol Pot and Ieng Sary's party and government at various levels could not cover up this tragic reality. The minutes of the party conference in the eastern zone, held in 1977, had to admit: "Since May 1977, the living conditions of the population have worsened, especially in the districts of Kroch Chhmar, Peam Chileang, Koh Sotin and Muk Kampoul, where they have seriously worsened, so much so that people only eat diluted soup. Even with weakened strength, people still have to dig canals, to dredge waterways, to raise output and fulfill the plan."

The report on the situation in Kompong Ro district, Svay Rieng province, for the first half of 1977 recognized that the population in the people's communes suffered from many diseases such as cholera, dysentery, typhoid fever, asthma, lung infections, convulsive tuberculosis, smallpox, and beriberi.

Mrs. Denise Alfonso of Phnom Penh, who was sent to a people's commune, stated that because she never had enough to eat she had to catch crickets, scorpions, and cockroaches to survive. One day after a long period without meat, a small amount of meat was given out, but she arrived late and got none. When she saw two dogs fighting over a piece of rawhide, she tried to take it from the mouth of one of the dogs, but it bit her.

She also testified that a man named Touch in the same people's commune one day stole a cassava plant to assuage his hunger and was beaten to death. Those who murdered him then cut out his liver, and fried it and ate it on the spot.

Mr. Sok Chhoy of Kompong Chhnang stated that one day in June 1977, the family of a Mr. Kit, numbering eight persons, also stole some cooked rice, and all of them were put to death for it.

2. With regard to the moral side of life, all social relations were eradicated among the Kampuchean people. They were turned into slaves living in isolation. Even the right to freedom of ideas and independent thinking was eliminated.

The fact that men and women were separated from each other for work and for daily life completely destroyed the family structure. Children above six years of age were separated from their parents. When they reached the age of thirteen or fourteen, they were sent to mobile shock brigades for building irrigation networks or clearing land outside the commune.

Children were taught to be loyal only to Angkar. Some were assigned to eavesdrop on their parents' private conversations and report to Angkar.

If a family member disappeared, relatives dared not ask for information about their loved ones, because anyone who expressed feelings toward disappeared persons would suffer the same fate. According to Sok Li Mut of Pursat, the husband of Mrs. Sok Bun was killed, and because she cried over him, she was put to death. Those in love with each other were strictly forbidden by the Pol Pot–Ieng Sary regime to exchange confidences, even though such behavior is normal in all other societies.

According to Pol Pot–Ieng Sary directives, marriage in the "people's communes" and in the army was to be carried out upon designation by Angkar or army unit commanders. A number of captured directives and resolutions of the Pol Pot–Ieng Sary party committees were quite explicit in this matter. An example is the resolution of November 1978 which provided: "Families should be formed by designation . . . This method has proven to be best and should be continued. . . ."

All freedom was eliminated in the choice of a spouse, since young men and women were separated from each other in work units. Abandoning natural traditions regarding marriage, Pol Pot and Ieng Sary organized collective marriages of couples designated by Angkar. Those who refused to comply would have their throats slashed in public to serve as an example to others. Young lovers who ran away from the "people's communes" had arrest warrants issued for them and were considered major criminals.

According to the investigation made by representatives of various social strata in Phnom Penh, Pol Pot and Ieng Sary forced widows to marry soldiers who were war invalids. Such was the case with Mrs. Nguon Vuoch Ny, who held a bachelor of arts degree in literature, whose husband was killed, leaving her with two children, and who was required, along with nineteen other widows, to marry soldiers who were war invalids. They all refused, and they were all jailed. Mrs. Ny committed suicide to remain faithful to her husband, while the nineteen others were raped and then killed by Pol Pot–Ieng Sary soldiers.

On one occasion, girls in a shock brigade were lined up face to face with a group of soldiers who were war invalids, and each girl was ordered to marry the man in front of her. This time, forced marriage by designation of Angkar led two of the girls to commit suicide.

In order to isolate the citizens even more in their daily life, immediately after April 17, 1975, Pol Pot and Ieng Sary decreed the abolition of currency, of trade, and of postal communications and transport services. In effect, each person was placed under house arrest. All relations with the outside world, or with family and friends were cut off, as were cultural relations. The inhabitants were surrounded by a network of agents who spied on them day and night. Persons who uttered a careless word might be invited "to a meeting," after which they would disappear.

Mr. My Sambath, a witness, told the tribunal: "One night, Mr. Suot and his young wife complained to each other about the harsh regime in the 'people's communes.' A report was made to Angkar, and the next day the couple and their four children were beaten to death." This level of physical persecution, of coercion, and of threats led many entire families to commit suicide by eating poisonous leaves or drowning themselves in rivers.

Mrs. Khem Nary, a witness, denounced the harsh life in Prey Lvea people's commune in Takeo province. The commune began with 28,000 members in 1975, but in January 1979, at the time of the liberation by the National United Front for the Salvation of Kampuchea, only 5,000 remained.

V. Massacre of small children, persecution and moral poisoning of the youth, transforming them into cruel thugs devoid of all human feelings

The genocidal Pol Pot–Ieng Sary clique did not allow children over six years of age to live with their parents. The children were forced to tend cattle and collect cow dung. Children over ten years of age had to do very hard work, just like adults. They were not allowed to go to school or to play (according to witnesses Ung Pech, Denise Alfonso, Thun Saray, and an investigation report by the Ministry of Education).

Khieu Samphan, head of state in Pol Pot and Ieng Sary's regime, praised this exploitation of child labor in the following terms: "Our children enjoy themselves by building dikes and digging ponds and irrigation canals."

It was forbidden to take in orphans, on the ground that their parents had committed wrongs toward Angkar. Many orphans had to live as vagabonds, because they were not admitted into "people's communes." According to the testimony of Duong Mala of Kompong Thom province, children caught begging were beaten to death.

Some Pol Pot–Ieng Sary soldiers killed children and ate their flesh. Such was the case of the younger brother of Miss Chhay Ny of Kandal (Document 2.1.5.11), and of Hour, a thirteen-year-old girl who now lives at the Siem Reap orphanage, and whose parents and elder brothers and sisters had died during the forced evacuation. Hour said that Pol Pot–Ieng Sary soldiers killed two young girls and ate their flesh. The soldiers had already put a gash in her throat when some people ran up and the soldiers fled. She still has a large scar on her neck (Document 2.1.5.18).

Although they persecuted and mistreated children, Pol Pot and Ieng Sary sought to use children under fifteen years of age as spies in the "people's communes" and to enlist them in army units or mobile shock brigades. They considered children at that age to be pure, and loyal to them. They trained children to make killers of them and to use them in aggressive warfare against neighboring countries, and in campaigns of repression against the people of Kampuchea. A document of the conference of the party's northern zone on July 15, 1977 read: "Even children can be key personnel. Only in this way can we build the party, because the children will grow up in the movement" (Document 2.5.26).

VI. Pol Pot and Ieng Sary destroyed the structure of the national economy and destroyed the national culture, the educational system, and the health care system.

1. Prior to 1975, Kampuchea was not industrially developed but had nonetheless a significant number of factories in the state and private sectors. Phnom Penh alone had 37 factories that employed 12,000 to 13,000 workers. Through the country there were 3,700 handicraft enterprises supplying consumer goods and art goods for the home market and for export. As for agriculture, in addition to rice cultivation, animal breeding and fishing were relatively well developed.

During their nearly four years of usurped power, Pol Pot and Ieng Sary completely destroyed the structure of the national economy. Under the slogan "to have rice is to have everything," they completely destroyed handicrafts. Industrial production was in serious trouble. More than 50% of the factories had to close down, machinery and equipment became unusable, as at the cement works with annual output before 1975 of 50,000 tons per year, and the glassware works with a capacity or 40,000 tons per year. Both of them ceased production. Prior to 1975, the sawmill had 180 workers for each shift, but now only ten are left. Engineers and technicians were all put to death. Some of the skilled workers were compelled to go to the countryside to work, while others were killed. The policy of Pol Pot and Ieng Sary was not to use the personnel and skilled workers of the former regime. Some were used to train new personnel and workers but were killed when the training was completed.

Prior to 1975, fishing yielded 100,000 to 140,000 tons a year. Under the regime of Pol Pot and Ieng Sary, fishing yielded only 20,000 to 30,000 tons a year.

With regard to communications and transportation, in 1969 Kampuchea had 9,700 trucks, 1,300 buses. The ports of Kompong Som and Phnom Penh, and the railway and waterway networks functioned well. Under Pol Pot and Ieng Sary, these means of transport were used mainly for military purposes or for the transport of goods to be exported to Peking. The public transport service ceased to operate, a measure designed to keep the people from getting around.

The postal and telephone service was abolished. The same was true for currency; they blew up the Central Bank building in Phnom Penh. The people were not allowed go to market or to trade in goods.

This reactionary economic policy of Pol Pot and Ieng Sary, which ran against objective economic laws, against the interest of the people, and against the realities of life in the country, destroyed the country's productive forces. Industrial and agricultural production collapsed. The producers, poorly fed and dressed, and required to work beyond their capabilities, were condemned to a slow death. An extremely reactionary policy of Pol Pot and Ieng Sary was to concentrate and destroy almost all the belongings of the urban and rural population, which they considered as vestiges of capitalism. The population was forced to wear only black clothes. They were not allowed to wear shoes or sandals, or to possess such cooking utensils as pots and pans. (See the investigation reports on the economy and on the crimes of Pol Pot and Ieng Sary against the residents of Phnom Penh.)

While the population were living on thin rice gruel, the Pol Pot–Ieng Sary regime stored up rice for war purposes, and for export to Peking in exchange for weaponry, to build up a fascist army as an instrument for repression, purges, and waging wars against neighboring countries. The army increased from 7 divisions in 1975 to 23 in 1978.

At a meeting on implementation of the state plan for 1978, Pol Pot said specifically: "In 1978 we must export to China from 100,000 to 150,000 tons of rice, and 20,000 to 25,000 tons of rubber. The contract has been signed and we must carry it out."

2. Concerning culture and education, Pol Pot and Ieng Sary advocated total abolition of our culture and education, and destruction of the cultural and educational institutions. According to the investigation report by representatives of various strata of the Phnom Penh population, the damage caused by Pol Pot and Ieng Sary is quite serious. Immediately after April 17, 1975, five principal libraries in Phnom Penh were destroyed, along with many other libraries at universities and scientific institutes. The National Library was turned into a goods warehouse. A great number of valuable art objects in museums were destroyed or carried off. Out of 1,225 objects and relics of traditional culture, more than one half were either destroyed or carried off.

The human losses in education and culture are heavier still. Ninety percent of the artists were killed. Out of a total of 1,241 artists who were alive in 1975, only 121 survive (Report on the situation of national culture). The country had nine universities and colleges with more than thirty faculties, with 11,000 students and 725 professors. Under Pol Pot and Ieng Sary, all educational establishments were closed down and became either prisons, such as Tuol Sleng, or warehouses for weapons, fertilizer, or goods. Now there are only two or three university professors left. Out of 2,300 secondary school teachers there remain only 200. Out of 21,311 primary school teachers there remain only 2,783.

3. With regard to health care, according to an investigation report, there were formerly 62 hospitals with 6,000 beds, with services in a variety of medical specialties. Under Pol Pot and Ieng Sary all these institutions were closed down. Out of the 19 professors of medicine and pharmacology, none is still alive. Out of 462 medical doctors there remain 54. Out of 156 pharmacists there remain now only 15.

There was one medical and pharmacy college with 2,124 students and one dentistry institute with 847 students. The Pol Pot–Ieng Sary regime shut them both down. Instead, they organized a system of "barefoot doctors" selected from among persons loyal to them. After only a three-month apprenticeship, these people, having no instruction in medicine and no sense of professional responsibility, used patients as guinea pigs, as in Kompong Cham hospital where a group of surgeons opened the chest of a patient just to see his heart, though he had no heart disease. In another case, a patient died of kidney trouble. They operated on the dead body to take out the kidney, then took out the kidney of a healthy man to make a comparison.

VII. *After their overthrow by the genuine revolutionary forces, Pol Pot and Ieng Sary are still committing new crimes and are still killing those who refuse to follow them.*

In their flight, Pol Pot and Ieng Sary compelled people to follow them to serve as a shield. Wherever they have gone, they have plundered property, destroyed crops, burned down rice granaries, and pillaged from the people. In many localities, before fleeing they killed large numbers of people, fearing that they might want to return to live under the genuine revolutionary regime.

The liberation of Am Leang, a subdistrict in Kompong Speu province, set free 60,000 people. These people said that the Pol Pot–Ieng Sary people killed 12,000 persons, including wounded soldiers in their army whose morale was low, and workers and employees at the Kompong Chhnang airport.

At the Champuh Kaek pagoda in Kandal province, on the morning of January 7, 1979, before fleeing the head of the district came in together with some of his soldiers and killed some two hundred persons who were being detained there, including women and children. They fled without burying the bodies of the victims.

On January 27, 1979, in Battambang province, Pol Pot–Ieng Sary men took one hundred inhabitants into a forest and beat them to death. Mr. Sok Ros, who together with his three children survived this killing, testified before the tribunal about these crimes. Kampucheans who had taken refuge in Thailand and were sent back to Kampuchea were killed in large numbers on the pretext that they committed treason.

VIII. *During their four years in power, Pol Pot and Ieng Sary and their associates used extremely savage methods of torture and killing, as well as many techniques designed to terrorize the population.*

Pol Pot and Ieng Sary employed methods of killing that involved hundreds, thousands, and even tens of thousands of victims at a time without expending a single bullet. The executioners lined prisoners up on the edge of previously dug pits and hit them on the back of the neck with pick handles or bamboo sticks and then pushed them into the pit. When a pit was full of corpses, they used bulldozers to cover it with earth and moved on to the next pit to continue the killing.

Many savage methods were used, such as cutting a person's throat with the tooth-edged leaf of a sugar palm tree, disembowelling in order to eat a person's liver, or taking out a person's gallbladder to make medications, or using gallows. With women, they tied them naked to tree trunks and thrust sharp sticks or M-79 shells into their sexual organs until they died. To kill people in groups, they tied victims together and used bulldozers to crush them or electrocuted them or made them walk across mine fields. They buried suspected opponents alive or burned them alive, or cut them with a knife until they died, or threw them into crocodile-breeding ponds.

With children, in some localities they arrested groups of them and tied them inside plastic bags and hung them on branches to the point of suffocation. Then they threw the plastic bags into dry wells, soaked them with gasoline and set them ablaze, laughing while the children writhed in anguish. They amused themselves by throwing children into the air and catching them on bayonets as they fell, or by tearing children apart.

Not infrequently, Pol Pot–Ieng Sary agents amused themselves by cutting victims with knives to see how the bodies of the two sexes are made up.

After killing high-ranking officials by beheading them, the Pol Pot–Ieng Sary agents put the heads back on the corpses, stuck on a number and took photographs so that Pol Pot and Ieng Sary themselves could check personally that their orders had been carried out (see collection of photographs attached to the case file).

With victims killed in pits, after letting them rot under the earth, the Pol Pot–Ieng Sary agents ordered the inhabitants to dig up the remains for use as manure. With corpses that had not sufficiently disintegrated, they ordered the inhabitants to tear them up into smaller pieces.

At some places, such as Siem Reap, these agents put the bodies in the pits in layers, with a layer of corpses alternating with a layer of rice husk, and then they poured on gasoline and set it on fire. The ashes were used as fertilizer. If any bones were found to be insufficiently cremated, they ordered the inhabitants to grind them up so that they could be put through a strainer. The ashes and bone dust would be used as fertilizer. Today, those who were forced to engage in this gruesome task still shudder when thinking of it. Here are some actual cases.

Witness Yeng Tinh in Kompong Cham said that he saw Pol Pot–Ieng Sary men taking 5,318 persons in trucks to the So Pheas forest over a period of seven days to crush them with bulldozers.

Miss Chhay Ny said that Pol Pot soldiers cut the throat of her brother, sliced off his flesh and wrapped it in leaves and took it home to eat as food. She also said that they killed her mother, taking out her liver to eat it.

Mr. Sim Phia of Siem Reap stated before the tribunal that he saw Pol Pot–Ieng Sary agents throw children into crocodile pits.

Mr. Kung Sary, Mrs. Mun Ny, and Mrs. Che Van Thon of Siem Reap stated that they saw corpses burned to make fertilizer at Dong Treng village, Chon Buon Cau subdistrict, and at Phnom village, Kompong Thkau subdistrict.

The investigation report prepared by representatives of the Phnom Penh population read before the tribunal described the Tuol Sleng prison, a center for torture and detention of Phnom Penh inhabitants, as follows: "This prison was formerly a school. We saw rooms for torture and interrogation equipped with horrifying torture instruments: electric shock devices, suspension devices on the ceilings, iron bars, choppers, and chains. In these rooms, there still were on the tiled floor tufts of hair which had been pulled out of victims' heads, puddles of dried up blood. Blood stains can still be seen on the walls and ceilings. The school's garden was turned into a communal burial ground to bury the bodies of prisoners. There one can still find heaps of clothes of various types—clothes stripped off the victims before they were tortured to death."

Mr. Ung Pech said the following about torture at Tuol Sleng:

"A prisoner would be seated on the floor, his hands and feet chained to a table. One guard did the questioning, another had a stick that he would use to hit the prisoner. . . . Women who were interrogated had to take off their clothes, and they would be tortured, and the pretty ones would be raped."

Other methods of torture were: electric shock, hanging by the feet from the ceiling, pulling out fingernails with pincers, placing the head inside a plastic bag, and pouring water continuously on the face wrapped in cloth until the prisoner suffocated.

Killings of groups were carried out everywhere in Kampuchea. In nearly every village one can find common graves with heaps of corpses, broken skulls, and femur and tibia bones with ropes still attached to them. Case files examined by the tribunal, like those relating to Tuol Sleng, Chup, Siem Reap, Battambang, etc., represent but a few among countless proofs of genocide committed by the genocidal Pol Pot–Ieng Sary clique.

* * *

After examining the criminal acts committed by the accused, the tribunal can conclude that Pol Pot and Ieng Sary committed these crimes with genocidal intent.

Considering that in his well documented indictment, the prosecutor-general has presented to the tribunal original copies of documents such as resolutions, directives, teaching materials, etc., from the genocidal Pol Pot–Ieng Sary clique that prove that these acts of genocide were studied and discussed in many meetings;

Considering that, pursuant to the orders of the genocidal Pol Pot–Ieng Sary clique, these acts of genocide were carried out in a systematic way and by the same methods and procedures throughout the territory of Kampuchea and under the control of the authorities of Angkar at all levels;

The tribunal has examined the reports prepared by representatives of various departments of government, and by organizations of the National

United Front for the Salvation of Kampuchea, with figures and evidence in support: records of field investigations conducted at sites where crimes were committed; items of evidence collected; statements by Kampuchean witnesses and material from foreign countries. All these proofs show that the Pol Pot–Ieng Sary clique had genocidal intent.

The lawyers for the accused too have acknowledged that the indictment levelled against the criminal acts of the genocidal Pol Pot–Ieng Sary clique is well grounded to charge Pol Pot and Ieng Sary with genocidal acts and intent.

Considering that the criminal acts of the accused Pol Pot and Ieng Sary have had extremely grave consequences, and what is more serious still, that these acts will have serious repercussions for a long time in many aspects of the life of the country;

After April 17, 1975, our people could have enjoyed peace and happiness and lived in friendship with neighboring countries. But during their nearly four years in power, Pol Pot and Ieng Sary set up in our country a most brutal dictatorial militarist regime that betrayed the people and killed people in bloody mass killings and by methods of torture and killing as savage as those of the Middle Ages, and in certain respects, more cruel than those used by the Hitlerites. In many areas of the country, they killed the entire population of a village or subdistrict, and in some cases they killed nearly the entire population of a district, including children, the elderly, pregnant women, invalids, and the war wounded.

After examining the investigation reports presented at the hearing, the findings of a sample census conducted in a number of villages and subdistricts, and other information in the case file, the tribunal finds well founded the estimate that more than three million persons were killed or otherwise succumbed because of torture or the poor conditions of life under the Pol Pot–Ieng Sary regime.

The extermination of about forty per cent of the population has brought untold sufferings to millions of families and caused irretrievable loss to the country, an underdeveloped country just emerging from the resistance war against U.S. aggression, whose productive force consists mainly of the labor and creativeness of its industrious people. The loss is particularly great because many of those killed were genuine patriots, workers, peasants, intellectuals, patriotic personalities, technicians, scientists, artists, writers, and the youth which is the main labor force to rebuild the country. Especially the teenagers and the children were persecuted, physically ill-treated and morally corrupted; a large number were killed. The genocidal Pol Pot–Ieng Sary clique destroyed the elements that are the hope of the nation.

The approximately four million who were left alive were herded into huge concentration camps where they were forced to work like animals. Their lot was worse than that of slaves. Hungry, clad in rags and without medical care, they were doomed to physical degeneration. On the mental side, they were constantly threatened and spied upon by secret agents. They might be arrested and killed at any moment together with their close relatives.

As a result of the victory of the National United Front for the Salvation of Kampuchea and the People's Revolutionary Council with the liberation of Phnom Penh on January 7, 1979, leading to the overthrow of the criminal Pol Pot–Ieng Sary clique, these four million survivors were saved from annihilation. Now, so that the people may return to a normal life and to normal work, it will take us years to solve problems like restoring health services, eradicating dangerous diseases, caring for orphans and invalids, and in general stabilizing the living conditions of the population, etc.

Serious damage has also been done in the political, economic, cultural, and social fields.

National unity has been damaged as a result of the reactionary policy of dividing the people into three categories to kill them, and of eliminating ethnic minorities through forced assimilation and the killing of many leaders and members of these ethnic groups. The damage is the greater because of the elimination by Pol Pot and Ieng Sary of Buddhism, a religion closely connected to our people for many centuries. With the elimination of Islam and the destruction of places of worship and the burning of holy books, Pol Pot and Ieng Sary seriously offended the religious beliefs of minority ethnic groups.

With these genocidal crimes, Pol Pot and Ieng Sary have created a generation of young people many of whom have their hands soaked in the blood of their fellow countrymen. They have become executioners who have lost their human character. It will require great patience to reeducate these people.

The friendship and solidarity among the peoples of the three countries of Indochina resulting from their struggle against a common enemy to maintain peace and stability in Southeast Asia are a precious tradition and a factor ensuring independence and prosperity for each nation. Pol Pot and Ieng Sary destroyed these traditional ties. They have sown hatred among fraternal nations. They have provoked armed conflicts with Thailand and Laos and waged a large-scale war against the Vietnamese people, thereby turning friends into enemies. Waging a war of aggression against Vietnam while intensifying brutal oppression of the people and purges, they caused tremendous losses in lives and property to our people. They exhausted our national economy and drove our people into destitution. At the same time, they committed extremely barbarous war crimes against the neighboring countries.

In external affairs, they caused serious damage to our relationships, to our prestige, and to our international role. The crime of genocide committed by Pol Pot and Ieng Sary has raised a worldwide wave of condemnation and indignation, tarnishing the image and prestige of our country in the international arena.

In the economic, cultural, and social fields, all scientific and technical institutions, economic institutions, enterprises, schools, research institutes, and hospitals were destroyed or turned into prisons or fertilizer warehouses. Libraries were ransacked, and scientific books were burned. Trading and currency were forbidden. Many workers, peasants, scientists, technicians, professors, artists, etc., were eliminated. There was no school for our youth or children. Illiteracy grew. In fact, Pol Pot and Ieng Sary pushed Kampuchean society back to the age of slavery. They destroyed the conditions of Kampuchea's existence. Our nation was on the brink of extinction.

Pol Pot and Ieng Sary stopped our society's development and even set it back, leaving extremely grave after-effects that cannot be remedied overnight. The problems to be solved are restoration of production, stabilization of the people's living conditions, supplying millions of people faced with imminent starvation, construction of the material and technical bases for the economy to proceed toward industrialization, the training of scientific and technical personnel, etc.

They wiped out all fine traditions and customs of our people and destroyed our age-old great Angkor civilization. The family and the social fabric have been destroyed. Pol Pot and Ieng Sary instituted forced marriage, thereby destroying many families and causing depravity. They wanted to destroy the family, the social structure, the foundations of our economy, culture, education, health services, and religion in order to force on the people a model society that they thought to be genuine and pure socialism. In reality it was a slavery system of a new type copied from abroad. This system had nothing in common with true socialism.

During their nearly four years in power (1975–1979), Pol Pot and Ieng Sary spared no devilish or perfidious tricks to concentrate power in their own hands. They set up a fascist dictatorship and practiced nepotism. They carried out a policy of coercion and oppression of the people on a large scale. They expelled the people from towns and cities, dislodged rural residents from one region to another, and classified the population with a view to exterminating people and organizations suspected of opposing them.

They tried to eliminate their political opponents within the party. The killing of Comrade Son Ngoc Minh in Peking is a case in point. During 1977 and 1978 they liquidated those who were considered as adversaries, including Hu Nim, the minister of information and propaganda, Toch Phoeun, the minister of public works, and So Phim, the vice-president of the National Assembly.

With their extremely reactionary domestic and foreign policies which were against the interests of the people and the nation, Pol Pot and Ieng Sary provoked opposition from our people. Popular uprisings increasingly broke out in many localities. By 1978, the revolutionary movement under the banner of the National United Front for the Salvation of Kampuchea, formed against Pol Pot and Ieng Sary in the eastern zone, and later in five of the seven zones of the country.

To maintain and consolidate their power, Pol Pot and Ieng Sary had to turn to fascist methods. They increasingly carried out repression and purges under the pretext of class struggle to eliminate people and groups labelled as reactionaries or suspected of being hostile.

The more ferociously the oppression was carried out, the more the barbarous repression spread, the more vigorously our people rose up, and the more divided the followers of Pol Pot and Ieng Sary became. Politically isolated at home and in the international arena, Pol Pot and Ieng Sary had to rely more and more on Peking to maintain their power.

Pol Pot said, "We have creatively and successfully applied Mao Tse Tung's thought to the realities of Kampuchea. . . . For Kampuchea, the most precious Chinese aid has been the thought of Mao Tse Tung" (Pol Pot's speech at a reception given by the leaders in Peking, September 28, 1977).

Pol Pot and Ieng Sary have constantly been encouraged and supported by the Peking reactionaries while all progressive mankind was condemning their crime of genocide. When he received Pol Pot and Ieng Sary, Mao Tse Tung said, "Comrades, you have won a great victory. With a single stroke you have gotten rid of social classes. Communes in the countryside, with poor and lower middle peasants, are our future."

In reality, the genocidal Pol Pot–Ieng Sary clique closely colluded with the Peking big-nation expansionist reactionaries and were dependent on them. The "people's communes," huge concentration camps, places where the Kampuchean people were killed, were modelled on the Chinese "people's communes."

The use of children and young people as executioners in the killings of various strata of the population (including near relatives of the executioners) was a faithful copy of the Chinese cultural revolution. Pol Pot and Ieng Sary's policy of relying mainly on the poor and lower-middle-class peasants to carry out revolution instead of on the working class was a product of Mao Tse Tung's thought. The genocidal Pol Pot–Ieng Sary clique wrote in a letter to the Peking reactionaries: "We have studied, we are still studying, and we have determined not to stop studying the valuable experiences of the great cultural revolution and Mao Tse Tung's thought. Mao Tse Tung is a guiding star who gained great successes." Hua Kuo Feng praised and encouraged the genocidal Pol Pot–Ieng Sary clique: "Comrades, you have succeeded not only in destroying the old world but in building the new world. You have achieved great success in neutralizing the maneuvers of subversion and sabotage by enemies" (Hua Kuo Feng's speech at a banquet for Pol Pot in Peking, September 28, 1977).

The soiled hands of the Peking reactionaries seized this opportunity to interfere in Kampuchea's internal affairs. They wanted to use the genocidal

Pol Pot–Ieng Sary clique as a counterrevolutionary assault force to carry out their expansionist strategy in Indochina and Southeast Asia, in line with Mao Tse Tung's statement in 1965: "We must take back the southeast Asian region including Vietnam, Kampuchea, Laos, Thailand, Burma, Malaysia, and Singapore. Southeast Asia is very rich in mineral resources. It is well worth retaking. In the future this region will contribute much to the development of Chinese industry. Thus, we can compensate for the losses we have suffered. . . ."

The Peking reactionaries wanted to turn our country into a military base and a springboard for their big-nation expansionist scheme in Southeast Asia. They massively increased their military aid and set up a thick network of advisors to supervise all the activities of Pol Pot and Ieng Sary. They encouraged this clique to carry out a savage genocidal policy against our people. They encouraged armed conflicts against Thailand and Laos, and a war of aggression against Vietnam. Without the Peking reactionaries' assistance, encouragement, and direction, the genocidal Pol Pot–Ieng Sary clique could not have perpetrated the crime of genocide against our people on such a large scale and with such ferocity, or have provoked armed conflicts with the neighboring countries and stepped up their war of aggression against Vietnam.

In encouraging Pol Pot and Ieng Sary to carry out their policy of genocide and to destroy Kampuchea's social institutions, the Peking reactionaries aimed at tightening their control over the clique and made them more dependent on Peking. This was the extremely perfidious aim of the Peking reactionaries. We succeeded in warding off the danger of extinction of our people in time, thanks to the historic victory of January 7, 1979. Even after this date, the Peking reactionaries kept aiding the genocidal Pol Pot–Ieng Sary clique. Documents captured at the Ta Sanh base show that the Peking reactionaries have assured Ieng Sary that they will continue to supply through Thailand financial aid, weapons, and foodstuffs, and that they will supply a radio station for Pol Pot. Hua Kuo Feng and Deng Tsiao Ping have set out a plan for the Pol Pot and Ieng Sary clique to rally Kampuchean reactionary forces to oppose the revolutionary government.

To sum up, since its usurpation of power the genocidal Pol Pot–Ieng Sary clique has colluded with Peking. Together with Peking, it jointly carried out a criminal plan against our people and the peoples of the neighboring countries. It is clear that the Peking reactionaries were the invidious instigators of this plan. They used the hands of Pol Pot and Ieng Sary to commit genocide against the people of Kampuchea. It is equally clear that it was again the Peking reactionaries who used this clique to conduct a war of aggression against Vietnam, to combine with their plan of aggression against Vietnam in the north of Vietnam. In fact, shortly after the genocidal Pol Pot regime was overthrown by the National United Front for the Salvation of Kampuchea, the Peking reactionaries launched aggression against the Socialist Republic of Vietnam along its northern border with a force of 600,000 to avenge their defeat in Kampuchea, but they were completely defeated.

On the basis of Decree Law No. 1 of July 15, 1979, of the People's Revolutionary Council of Kampuchea, and with reference to public international law on the punishment of genocide (and specifically the 1948 Convention on this subject), we find that the above-mentioned criminal acts perpetrated by the accused Pol Pot and Ieng Sary were committed with genocidal intent. Consequently, the accused have committed the crime of "genocide."

The crime of genocide is defined in Article 1 of Decree Law No. 1 of July 15, 1979, in the following terms: "planned massacres of groups of innocent people; expulsion of inhabitants of cities and villages in order to concentrate them and force them to do hard labor in conditions leading to their physical and mental destruction; wiping out religion; destroying political, cultural, and social structures and family and social relations."

The crime of genocide committed by the accused Pol Pot and Ieng Sary, with its tragic and far-reaching consequences, is of a level of seriousness unprecedented in world history, being far in excess of what is required for genocide in the December 9, 1948 Convention. The accused not only wiped out the intellectuals, the officers, and civil servants of the previous regime, religious believers, and ethnic minorities for the sole reason that they were intellectuals, officers and civil servants, religious believers, and ethnic minorities, they also killed, en masse and in a planned way, innocent people of different social strata. The accused sought to exterminate their own people, their own nation, pushing the people of different social strata to the point of extinction.

The accused committed the crime of genocide not only by grouping the people in concentration camps where living conditions were such as to bring about their physical and moral destruction, but they went farther still by committing genocide as well in the cultural and economic fields.

The genocidal Pol Pot–Ieng Sary clique denied the existence not only of the Kampuchean nation, but also of our national cultural traditions, and they destroyed family and social structures, the economic system, national culture and education, and the health service. The accused Pol Pot and Ieng Sary even destroyed the national conscience and spirit of the Kampuchean people. They destroyed the conditions for the existence of the Kampuchean people.

The accused Pol Pot and Ieng Sary have committed all the acts of genocide specified in Decree Law No. 1 of July 15, 1979:

- Planned massacre of groups of innocent inhabitants;
- Forced evacuation of people from towns and villages;

- Concentrating people and forcing them to do hard labor in physically and morally exhausting conditions;
- Abolition of religions and destruction of economic and cultural institutions and of family and social relations.

After January 7, 1979, when most of those who had served in the armed forces and the government of the genocidal Pol Pot–Ieng Sary clique turned themselves in and benefitted from the policy of leniency of the National United Front for the Salvation of Kampuchea and the People's Revolutionary Council of Kampuchea, the accused Pol Pot and Ieng Sary still clung to the Peking reactionaries and continued their betrayal of the nation and their opposition to the revolution.

The accused deliberately used extremely cruel methods of torture and killing and savage means of persecution to demoralize people with a view to destroying them physically and morally. The grave consequence of their acts is that about three million persons lost their lives; over four million who survive are suffering from serious injury physically and morally. Of the victims, many are teenagers and children.

Considering that the accused Pol Pot and Ieng Sary have a record of collusion with each other to oppose the Kampuchean revolution; that they jointly mapped out extremely reactionary domestic and foreign policies and organized and directed the implementation of these policies; that they are thus instigators and planners of genocide; that they are therefore responsible for all the particularly grave consequences of their genocidal acts;

Considering that in order to defend justice and the just cause of the Kampuchean people and to respond to the wishes of various strata of our people and world opinion, which demand severe punishment of Pol Pot and Ieng Sary for their crime of genocide, and in order to prevent a repetition of such acts;

Considering that the facts presented to the tribunal by material evidence and witness testimony, including witnesses from abroad and well known lawyers, have established that an important factor in the crime of Pol Pot and Ieng Sary has been the instigation of a foreign country and collusion with this country, and that this must be denounced in order to stop it and to prevent it, and to defend the right of the people to life, independence, and liberty;

Considering that the lawyers defending the accused acknowledged that the criminal acts of genocide of which the defendants stand accused have been fully proved;

Considering that the case files and oral argument before the tribunal show no mitigating circumstances in favor of the accused, but rather many aggravating circumstances, particularly the persistence of the accused in continuing their betrayal of the nation;

Considering the personal responsibility of each of the accused:

Pol Pot, as Secretary of Angkar (the party organization) and prime minister of the government, bearing ultimate responsibility for directing the entire state bureaucracy, mapped out the general lines and orientation of domestic and foreign policy and directed their implementation. Pol Pot himself on many occasions toured different localities to direct and inspect personally the purges of forces accused of opposition. Pol Pot is an extremely dangerous criminal deserving no degree of leniency.

Ieng Sary, as a standing member of the political bureau of Angkar and deputy prime minister of the government in charge of foreign affairs, holding high offices and wielding real power, worked with Pol Pot in the leadership. He built up and conducted collusion with the Peking reactionary forces and other international reactionaries and defended the criminal acts of genocide committed by his clique in international fora. Ieng Sary ordered the issuance of the invitation to return to intellectuals and students working or studying abroad. He is directly responsible for the large-scale execution of intellectuals and students living in the country, and those returning from abroad. The accused Ieng Sary is an extremely dangerous criminal deserving no degree of leniency.

For the above-mentioned reasons,

Acting under Articles 1, 2, 7, and 8 of Decree Law No. 1 of July 15, 1979, of the People's Revolutionary Council of Kampuchea, the judge and jury of the People's Revolutionary Tribunal in Phnom Penh decides:

1. That the accused Pol Pot, alias Saloth Sar, and Ieng Sary are guilty of genocide.
2. That the accused Pol Pot, alias Saloth Sar, and Ieng Sary be sentenced to death in absentia.
3. That all the property of the accused Pol Pot and Ieng Sary be confiscated.
4. That all the items of evidence in this case be entrusted to the Ministry of Internal Affairs and the Ministry of Defense to deal with them appropriately.
5. That the accused Pol Pot and Ieng Sary are entitled to approach the People's Revolutionary Council to request a reduction of sentence within seven days from the day on which this judgment is posted at the office of the municipal people's council.
6. That this judgment be posted at the office of the municipal people's council.

This judgment is rendered in public session and as a matter of last instance.

Presiding trial judge
President of the People's Revolutionary Tribunal at Phnom Penh

3.05

Speech by President Heng Samrin at a Reception in Honor of Foreign Guests, August 19, 1979

Ladies and gentlemen, honored foreign guests, comrades, and friends: Pleased at the splendid results of the People's Revolutionary Tribunal to try the Pol Pot–Ieng Sary clique for the crime of genocide, I would like, on behalf of the Central Committee of the National United Front for the Salvation of Kampuchea and the People's Revolutionary Council of Kampuchea, to convey my warmest greetings to the foreign guests who have come from all continents to Phnom Penh, capital of the People's Republic of Kampuchea, to attend this tribunal. I sincerely thank you all for having witnessed the proceedings, for having expressed your sympathy and support, and for having made important contributions to the success of this tribunal.

After five days of sessions and with facts expounded clearly, demonstrated convincingly, and analyzed objectively, this tribunal has shed light on this truth: the crime of genocide of the Pol Pot–Ieng Sary clique is undeniable and indefensible. The proceedings at the tribunal have indicated that every Kampuchean citizen is a victim and at the same time a witness to the most horrible crimes of Pol Pot, Ieng Sary, and their associates. Everywhere on Kampuchean soil one can point out proofs of the crimes committed by these butchers devoid of all human feelings, arch-traitors who have betrayed their people and their fatherland and for whom death sentences still are too mild a punishment.

It is a shame that imperialist and reactionary forces in the world, and first of all the expansionist reactionaries in Peking, still keep trying to cover up these abominable crimes of Pol Pot, Ieng Sary, and their associates, and to extend protection to them, and, even after they have been overthrown and condemned by the Kampuchean people, there are people who loudly praise these genocidal criminals as the "authentic legitimate representatives" of the Kampuchean people. This vile action was a manifestation of the reactionary nature of both the Peking expansionists and the Pol Pot–Ieng Sary genocidal criminals. This constitutes a gross challenge to the people of Kampuchea and mankind's conscience.

The People's Revolutionary Tribunal of the Kampuchean people, with probity and uprightness and following normal legal procedure, has condemned Pol Pot and Ieng Sary to death, thus unmasking their reactionary nature, promoting the Kampuchean people's just cause, and affirming the role of the People's Revolutionary Council of Kampuchea as the only authentic legitimate representative of the people of Kampuchea. This position is supported, and will be supported in an effective manner, by the forces of peace and justice in the world. We are also certain that the tribunal of history, the tribunal of mankind's conscience, not only will join with the Kampuchean people in pronouncing its verdict against the Pol Pot–Ieng

Sary genocidal criminals but will also demand that their masters and accomplices be tried and convicted.

The achievements of the People's Revolutionary Tribunal in Phnom Penh to try Pol Pot, Ieng Sary, and their associates for the crime of genocide are a success for truth and justice. It is not only a success for the Kampuchean people, but also a victory of the conscience of mankind, of the socialist and nonaligned countries and of all forces of national independence, democracy, peace, and progress the world over.

This victory encourages the Kampuchean people to march forward confidently, overcoming the serious consequences caused by the Pol Pot–Ieng Sary regime and the expansionist reactionaries in Peking, and to do their utmost to rebuild and defend their country and be resolved to achieve an independent, peaceful, democratic, neutral, nonaligned Kampuchea progressing toward socialism.

This victory raises before international opinion an urgent appeal for granting aid to the Kampuchean people helping them to do away with the serious aftermath of the Pol Pot–Ieng Sary regime to stay the criminal hands of the Peking reactionaries and other reactionary forces who are strenuously trying to sabotage the Kampuchean people's just cause and to undermine peace and stability in Southeast Asia.

The Kampuchean people deeply understand that every success in their just cause is closely connected with the common struggle of the peoples of the world for national independence, democracy, peace, and social progress. On this occasion, in the name of the central committee of the National United Front for the Salvation of Kampuchea and the People's Revolutionary Council of Kampuchea, I would like to express our heartfelt thanks for the most valuable sympathy and support given our people by the fraternal socialist countries and the peoples and governments of other peace- and justice-loving countries, international organizations and progressive personalities.

We firmly believe that the voice of justice, probity and uprightness of the People's Revolutionary Tribunal held in Phnom Penh to judge the crime of genocide of the Pol Pot–Ieng Sary clique will resound all over the world thanks to the selfless help of our foreign guests present here today as well as of all peace- and justice-loving people of our planet.

You will leave Phnom Penh tomorrow to return to your homeland and your work. May I wish you, friends and comrades, bon voyage. May I propose a toast:

- to the health of our guests, our comrades and friends here present!
- to our common victory!

Sources for Additional Information

Abrams, Jason S., and Steven R. Ratner. *Striving for Justice: Accountability and the Crimes of the Khmer Rouge*. Washington, D.C.: United States Department of Justice, 1995.

Barron, John, and Paul Anthony. *Murder of a Gentle Land*. New York: Reader's Digest Press, 1977.

Becker, Elisabeth. *When the War Was Over: The Voices of Cambodia's Revolution and Its People*. New York: Simon & Schuster, 1986.

Burchett, Wilfred. *The China Cambodia Vietnam Triangle*. Chicago: Vanguard Books; London: Zed Press, 1981.

Chanda, Nayan. *Brother Enemy*. New York: Macmillan, 1988.

Chandler, David. *A History of Cambodia*. Boulder, Colo.: Westview Press, 1983.

———. *The Tragedy of Cambodian History: Politics, War, and Revolution Since 1945*. New Haven, Conn.: Yale University Press, 1991.

Chandler, David, with Ben Kiernan, eds. *Revolution and Its Aftermath in Kampuchea: Eight Essays*. New Haven, Conn.: Yale University Southeast Asia Studies Council Monograph no. 25, 1983.

Chomsky, Noam, and Edward Herman. *The Political Economy of Human Rights*. Boston: South End Press, 1979.

Criddle, Joan D., and Teeda Butt Mam. *To Destroy You Is No Loss: The Odyssey of a Cambodian Family*. New York: Atlantic Monthly Press, 1987.

Dith Pran, compiler, and Kim DePaul, ed. *Children of Cambodia's Killing Fields: Memoirs by Survivors*. New Haven, Conn.: Yale University Press, 1997.

Eliot, David W. P., ed. *The Third Indochina Conflict*. Boulder, Colo.: Westview Press, 1981.

Etcheson, Craig. *The Rise and Demise of Democratic Kampuchea*. Boulder, Colo.: Westview Press, 1984.

Fenton, James, ed. *Cambodia Witness: The Autobiography of Someth May*. London: Faber, 1986.

Haing Ngor. *A Cambodian Odyssey*. New York: Warner Books, 1987; and *Une odyssée cambodgienne*. Fixot: Rungis, 1988.

Heder, Stephen. *Kampuchean Occupation and Resistance*. Bangkok: Chulalongkorn University, Institute of Asian Studies, 1980.

Hinton, Alexander Laban. "Agents of Death: Explaining the Cambodian Genocide in Terms of Psychosocial Dissonance." *American Anthropologist* 98, no. 4 (1996): 818–31.

———. *Anthropologies of the Khmer Rouge: Genocidal Bricolage*. Working Paper Series

(Working Paper GS 06), New Haven, Conn.: Yale Center for International and Area Studies, 1998.
———. "Why Did You Kill? The Cambodian Genocide and the Dark Side of Face and Honor." *Journal of Asian Studies* 57, no. 1 (1998): 93–122.
Jackson, Karl D., ed. *Cambodia 1975–1978: Rendez-vous with Death*. Princeton, N.J.: Princeton University Press, 1989.
Kamm, Henry. *Cambodia: Report from a Stricken Land*. New York: Arcade Publishing, 1998.
Kiernan, Ben. *Burchett: Reporting the Other Side of the World, 1939–1983*. London: Quarter, 1986.
———. *Cambodia: The Eastern Zone Massacres*. New York: Center for the Study of Human Rights, Columbia University, 1986.
———. *Genocide and Democracy in Cambodia: The Khmer Rouge, the United Nations, and the International Community*. New Haven, Conn.: Yale Southeast Asia Studies Council Monograph no. 41, 1993.
———. "Genocidal Targeting: Two Groups of Victims in Pol Pot's Cambodia." In *State-Organized Terror*, V. Schlapentokh et al., ed. Boulder, Colo.: Westview Press, 1991.
———. "Orphans of Genocide: The Cham Muslims of Kampuchea under Pol Pot." *Bulletin of Concerned Asian Scholars* 20, no. 4 (1988): 2–33.
———. *The Pol Pot Regime: Race, Power, and Genocide in Cambodia Under the Khmer Rouge, 1975–79*. New Haven, Conn.: Yale University Press, 1996.
Kiljunen, Kimmo, ed. *Kampuchea: Decade of the Genocide*. London: Zed Press, 1984.
Locard, Henri, and Moeung Sonn. *Prisonnier de l'Angkar*. Paris: Fayard, 1993.
Metzl, Jamie Frederic. *Western Response to Human Rights Abuses in Cambodia, 1975–1980*. New York, St. Martin's Press, 1996.
Orentlicher, Diane F. "International Criminal Law and the Cambodian Killing Fields." *ILSA Journal of International and Comparative Law* 3, no. 2 (1997): 705–11.
Picq, Laurence, *Au-delà du ciel: cinq ans chez les Khmer Rouges*. Paris: Bernard Barrault, 1984. (English translation by Patricia Norland, *Beyond the Sky*. New York: St. Martin's Press, 1989.)
Pin Yathay. *L'utopie meurtirère*. Paris: Laffont, 1980.
Ponchaud, François. *Cambodia Year Zero*. London: Allen Lane, 1978.
Porter, Gareth, and George Hilbrand. *Starvation and Revolution*. New York: Monthly Review Press, 1976.
Railsback, Kathryn. "A Genocide Convention Action Against the Khmer Rouge: Preventing a Resurgence of the Killing Fields." *Connecticut Journal of International Law* 5 (1990): 457.
Ratner, Steven R., and Jason S. Abrams. *Accountability for Human Rights Atrocities in International Law: Beyond the Nuremberg Legacy*. Oxford: Clarendon Press, 1997.
Schanberg, Sydney H. *The Death and Life of Dith Pran*. New York: Penguin Books, 1980.
Sliwinski, Marek. *Le Génocide Khmer Rouge: Une analyse démographique*. Paris: Éditions L'Harmattan, 1995.
Sobel, Lester. *Cambodia: Holocaust in Asia*. New York: Facts on File Press, 1982.
Spence, Jonathan. *The Death of Woman Wang*. New York: Penguin, 1982.
Vickery, Michael. *Cambodia, 1975–1982*. Boston: South End Press, 1984.
Y Phandara. *Retour à Phnom Penh*. Paris: Métailié, 1982.

Acknowledgments

The editors are grateful to three persons who provided invaluable assistance translating Khmer-language documents: Phalla Phan of Sydney, Australia; Yuok Ngoy, acting director of the Faculty of Law, Phnom Penh; and Paul Neese, J.D. candidate at the University of San Francisco. The National Library of Australia kindly microfilmed its extensive collection of tribunal documents and made it available to the editors. Dr. Craig Etcheson of the Cambodian Genocide Program at Yale University and Youk Chhang, director of the Documentation Center of Cambodia, consulted with regard to documentation issues.

Ohio State University facilitated this project in a number of ways. It provided funds to John Quigley under a Distinguished Scholar Award and as summer research support. It also provided research support funds to Kenneth J. Robinson. Allan H. Robinson, M.D., and Jennifer Moorman Robinson assisted in editing and indexing. Michele Whetzel-Newton, of the College of Law, Ohio State University, gave unsparingly of her time in typing substantial segments of the text. Documentary materials relating to the tribunal were traced by Jennifer Larraguibel, foreign and international reference librarian at the College of Law, Ohio State University, and by Jared Ingersoll of the East European Division of the Ohio State University Library. Professor Jasna Kragalott of the Ohio State University kindly assisted with Serbo-Croatian terminology. For assistance with agricultural terminology, we are grateful to the department of entomology at the Ohio State University, and for assistance with medical terminology, to Harry A. Quigley, M.D., of the Johns Hopkins University School of Medicine.

Howard J. De Nike wishes to express his appreciation for the academic support provided by the University of New South Wales Law Faculty, where he was a visiting fellow during 1998 while studying the record of the Pol Pot-Ieng Sary trial archived there. Finally, the editors are grateful to Professor Bert Lockwood, editor of the series in which this book appears, for placing it in a list of books of distinction in the field of human rights.

Index

Khmer names are typically written with the surname first. Khmer names are indexed accordingly.

www.ingramcontent.com/pod-product-compliance
Lightning Source LLC
Chambersburg PA
CBHW071353220926
51613CB00012B/263
9780812235395